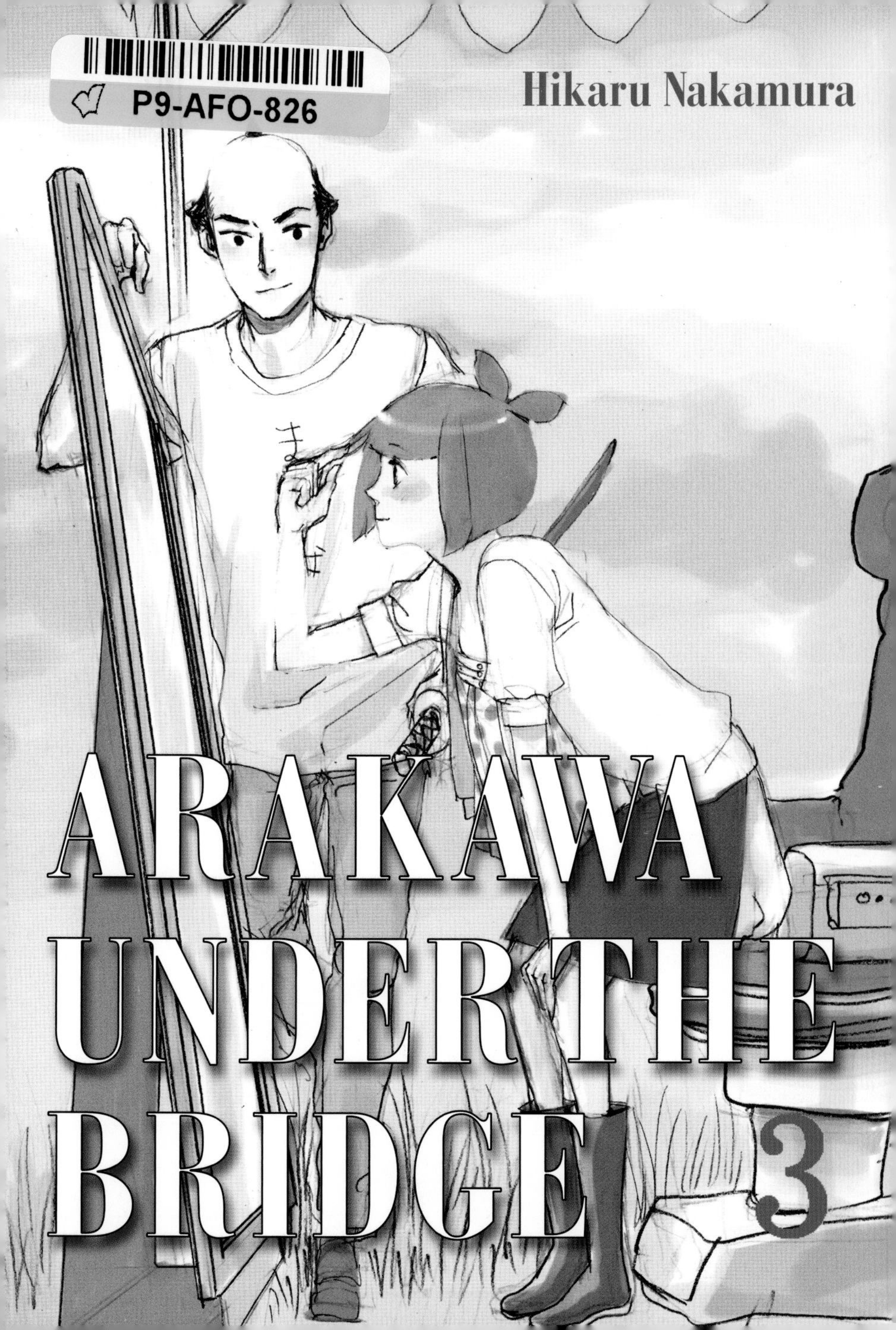
Hikaru Nakamura
ARAKAWA
UNDER THE
BRIDGE
3

C O N T E N T S

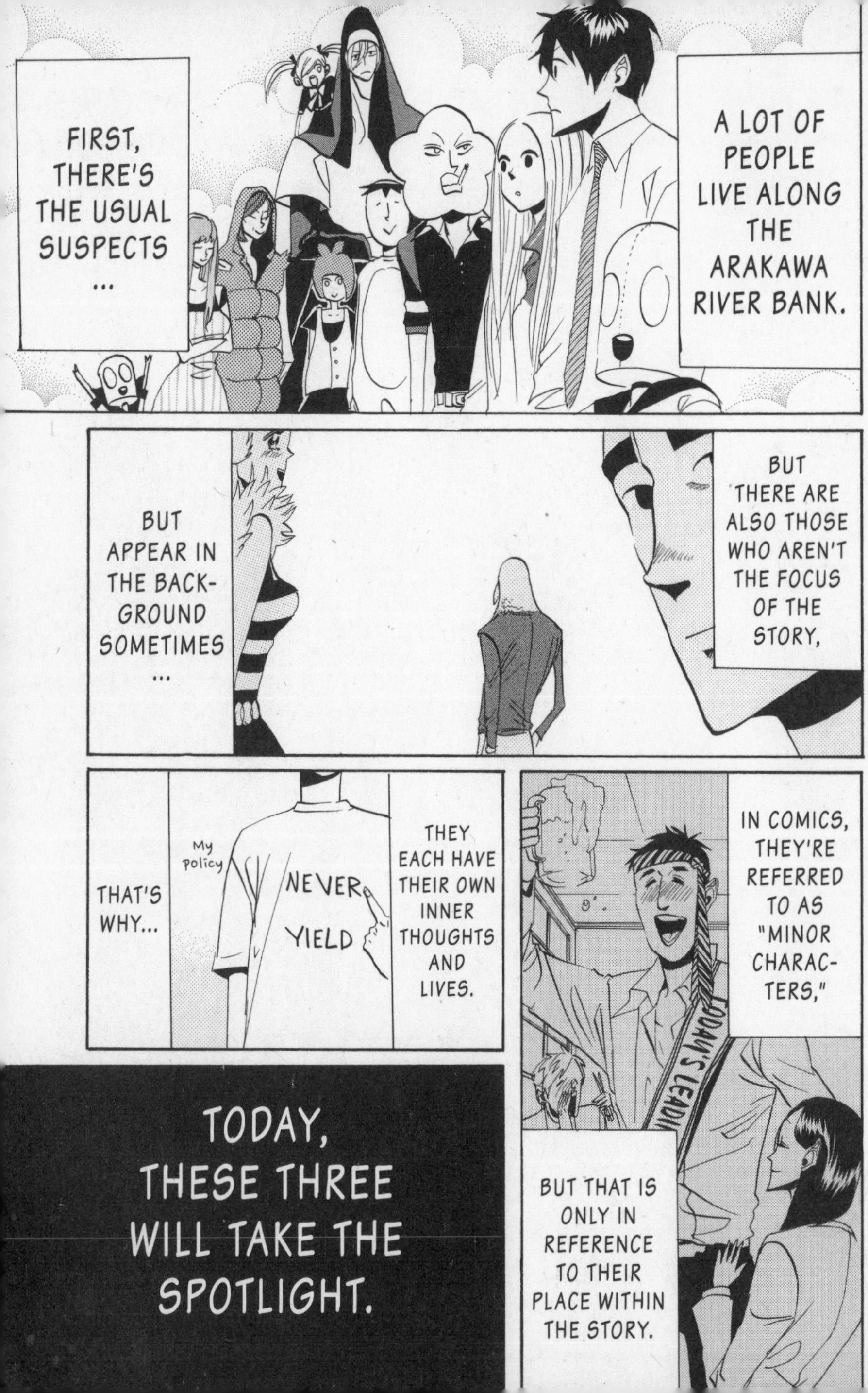
A LOT OF PEOPLE LIVE ALONG THE ARAKAWA RIVER BANK.
FIRST, THERE'S THE USUAL SUSPECTS ...
BUT THERE ARE ALSO THOSE WHO AREN'T THE FOCUS OF THE STORY,
BUT APPEAR IN THE BACK-GROUND SOMETIMES ...
IN COMICS, THEY'RE REFERRED TO AS "MINOR CHARAC-TERS,"
BUT THAT IS ONLY IN REFERENCE TO THEIR PLACE WITHIN THE STORY.
THEY EACH HAVE THEIR OWN INNER THOUGHTS AND LIVES.
My Policy
NEVER YIELD
THAT'S WHY...
TODAY, THESE THREE WILL TAKE THE SPOTLIGHT.

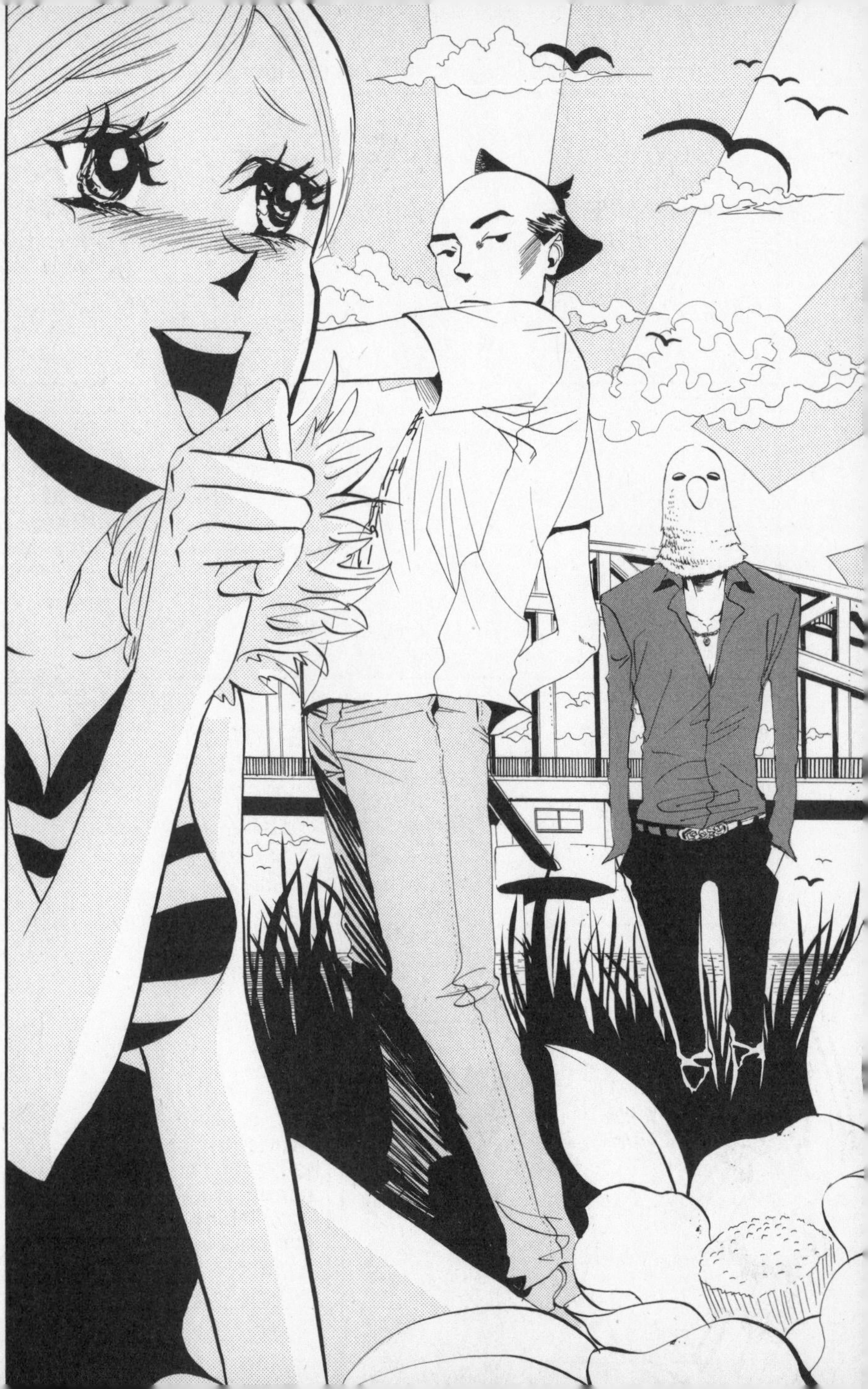

Chapter 108: Last Samurai

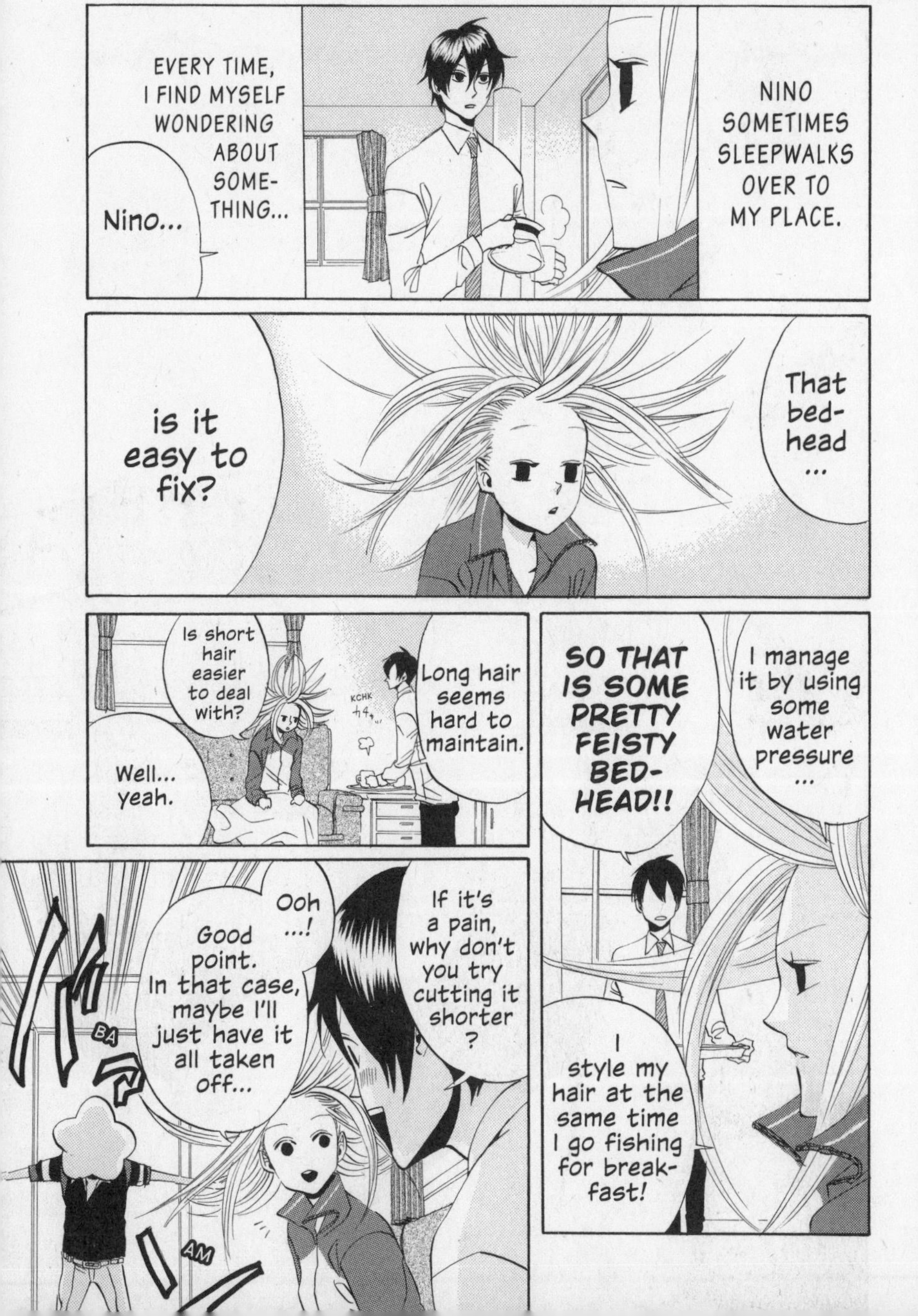
NINO SOMETIMES SLEEPWALKS OVER TO MY PLACE.
EVERY TIME, I FIND MYSELF WONDERING ABOUT SOME-THING...
Nino...
That bed-head ...
is it easy to fix?
I manage it by using some water pressure ...
SO THAT IS SOME PRETTY FEISTY BED-HEAD!!
I style my hair at the same time I go fishing for break-fast!
Long hair seems hard to maintain.
KCHK
Is short hair easier to deal with?
Well... yeah.
If it's a pain, why don't you try cutting it shorter ?
Ooh ...!
Good point. In that case, maybe I'll just have it all taken off...
BA
AM

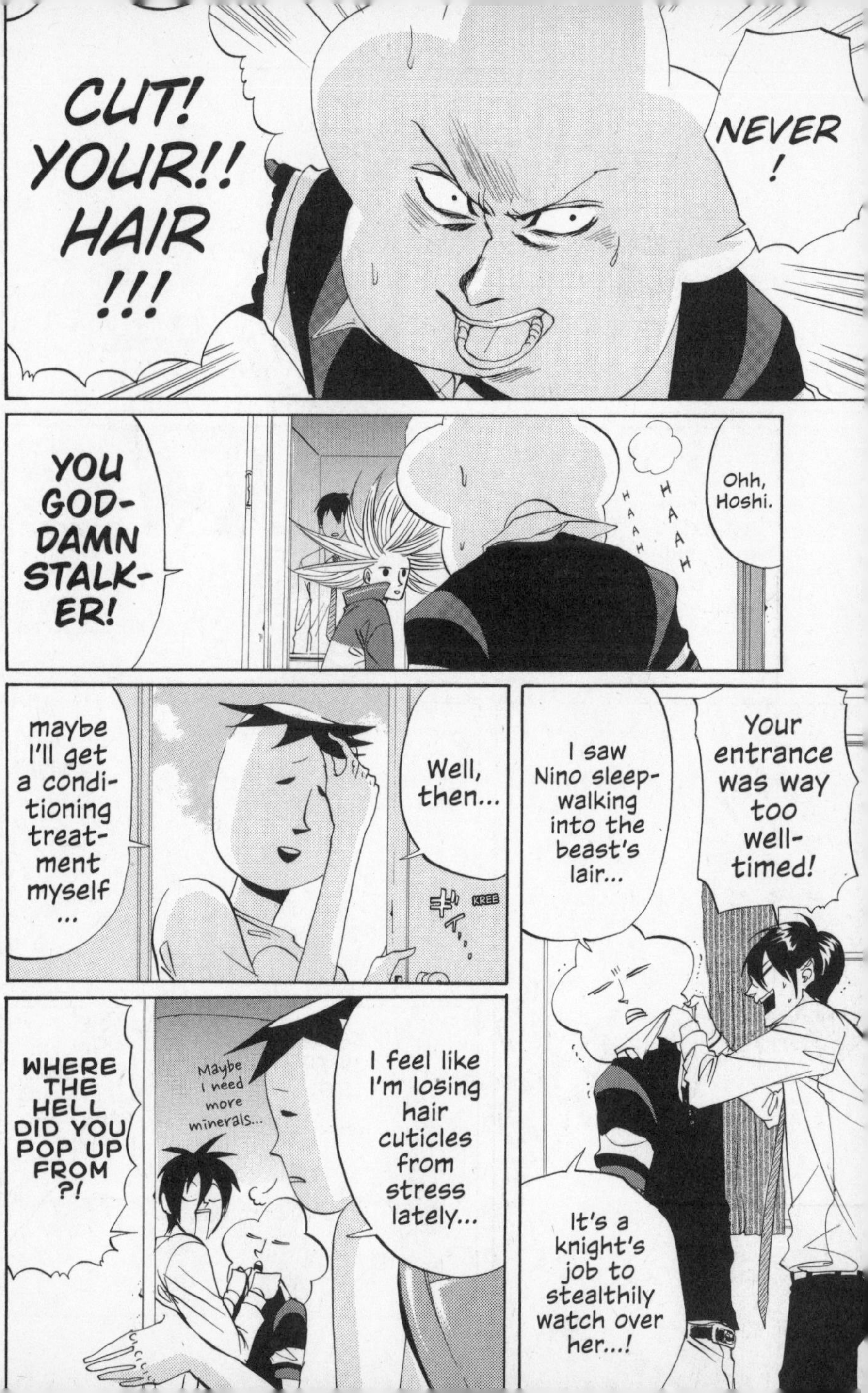
NEVER !
CUT! YOUR!! HAIR !!!
Ohh, Hoshi.
HAAHH HAAHH
YOU GOD-DAMN STALKER!
Your entrance was way too well-timed!
I saw Nino sleep-walking into the beast's lair...
It's a knight's job to stealthily watch over her...!
Well, then...
ギィ…
KREE
maybe I'll get a conditioning treatment myself ...
I feel like I'm losing hair cuticles from stress lately...
Maybe I need more minerals...
WHERE THE HELL DID YOU POP UP FROM ?!

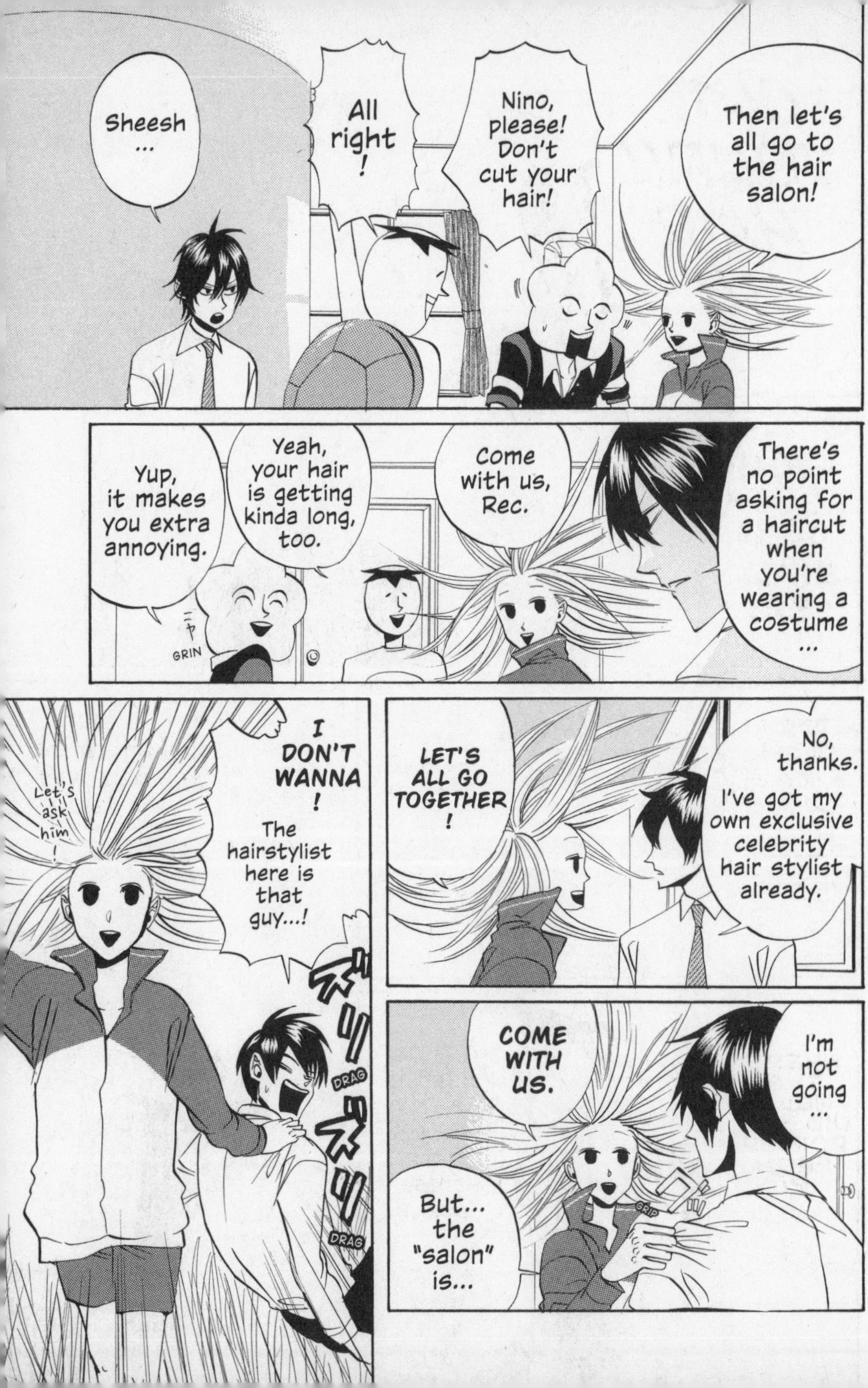
Then let's all go to the hair salon!
Nino, please! Don't cut your hair!
All right!
Sheesh...
There's no point asking for a haircut when you're wearing a costume...
Come with us, Rec.
Yeah, your hair is getting kinda long, too.
Yup, it makes you extra annoying.
ニヤ
GRIN
No, thanks.
I've got my own exclusive celebrity hair stylist already.
LET'S ALL GO TOGETHER!
I'm not going...
COME WITH US.
But... the "salon" is...
GRIP
I DON'T WANNA!
The hairstylist here is that guy...!
Let's ask him!
DRAG
DRAG

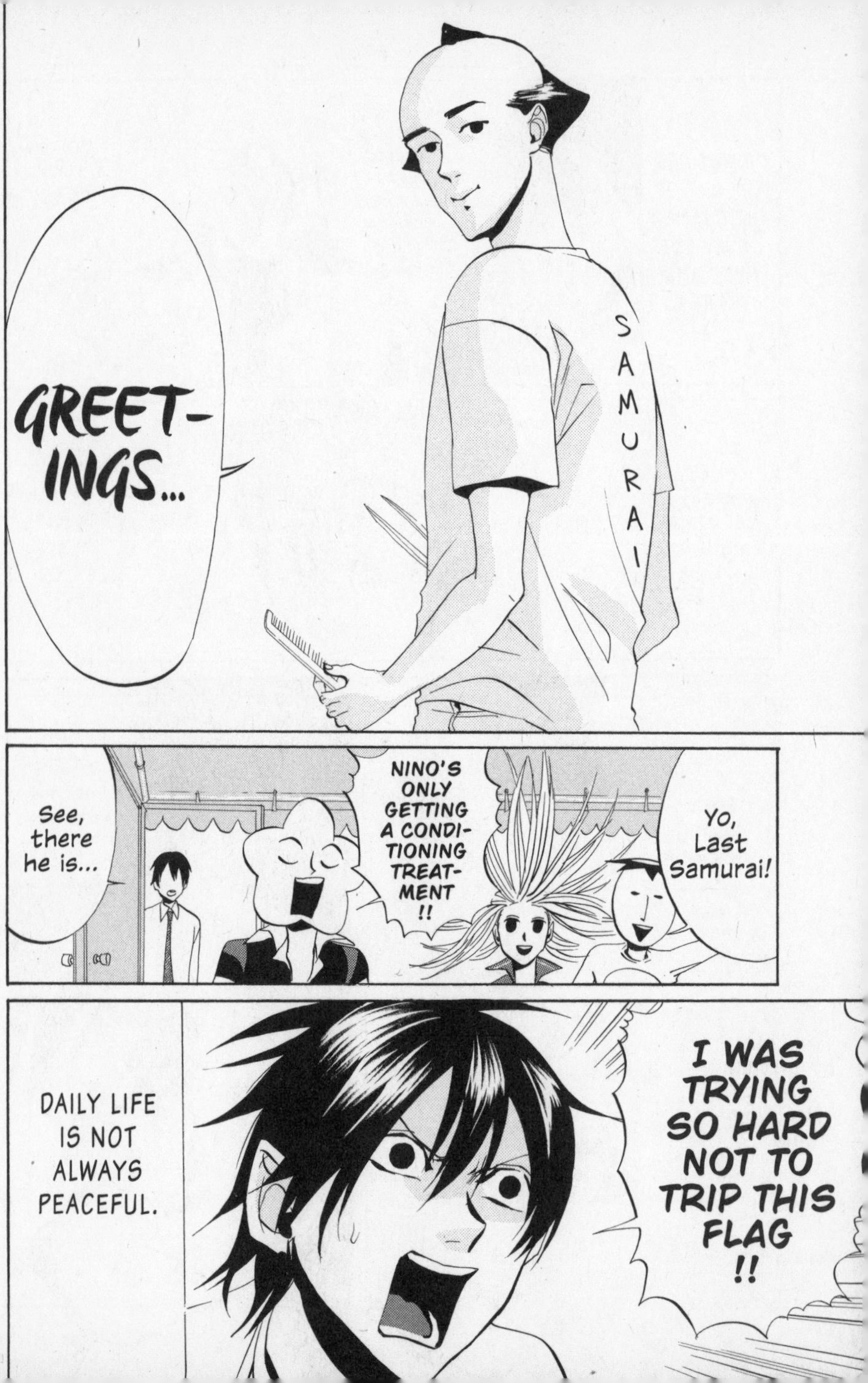
SAMURAI
GREET-INGS...
Yo, Last Samurai!
NINO'S ONLY GETTING A CONDITIONING TREATMENT !!
See, there he is...
I WAS TRYING SO HARD NOT TO TRIP THIS FLAG !!
DAILY LIFE IS NOT ALWAYS PEACEFUL.

Chapter 109: Haircut

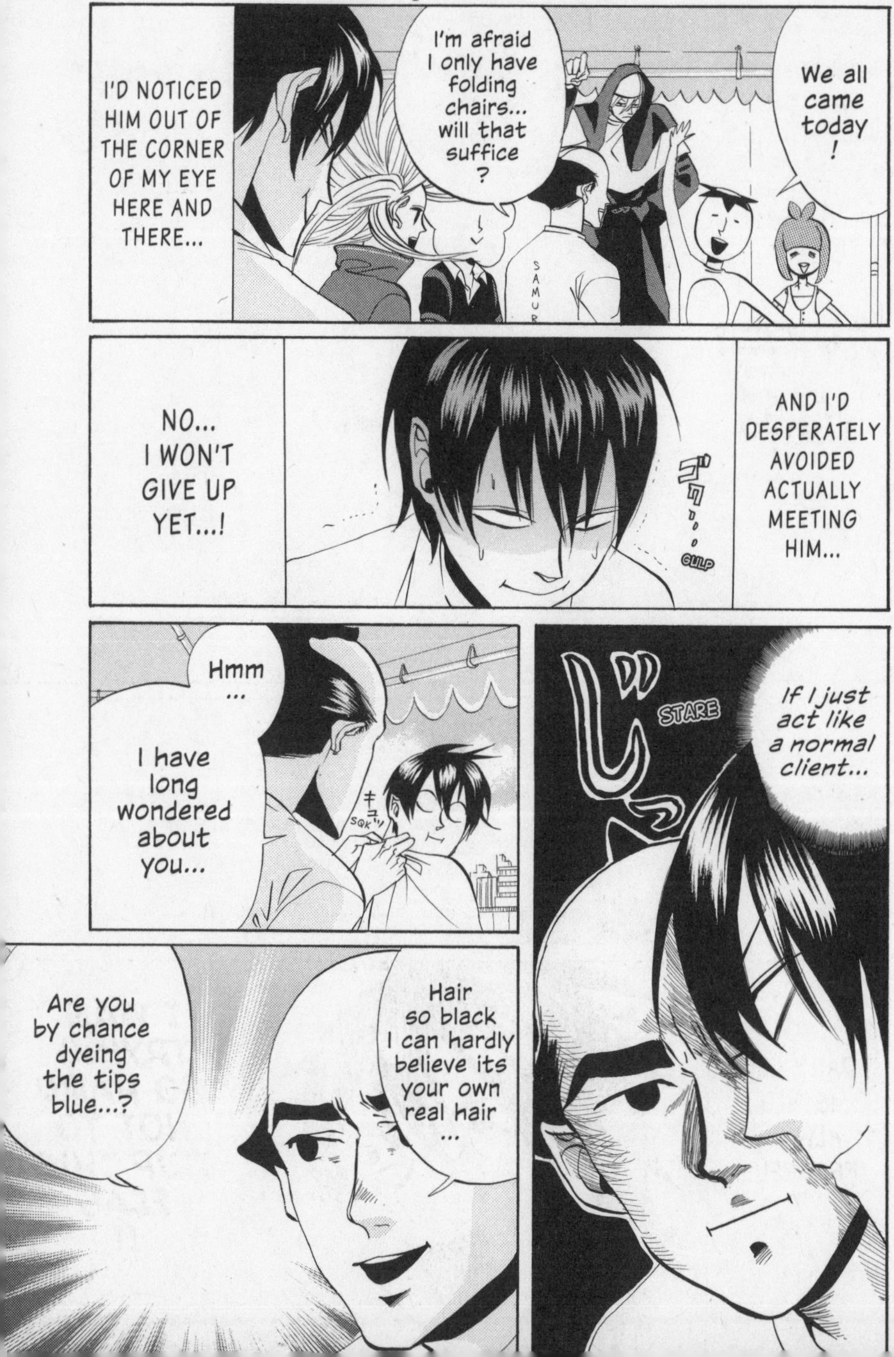
We all came today!
I'm afraid I only have folding chairs... will that suffice?
I'D NOTICED HIM OUT OF THE CORNER OF MY EYE HERE AND THERE...
AND I'D DESPERATELY AVOIDED ACTUALLY MEETING HIM...
GULP
NO... I WON'T GIVE UP YET...!
STARE
If I just act like a normal client...
Hmm...
I have long wondered about you...
SQK
Hair so black I can hardly believe its your own real hair...
Are you by chance dyeing the tips blue...?

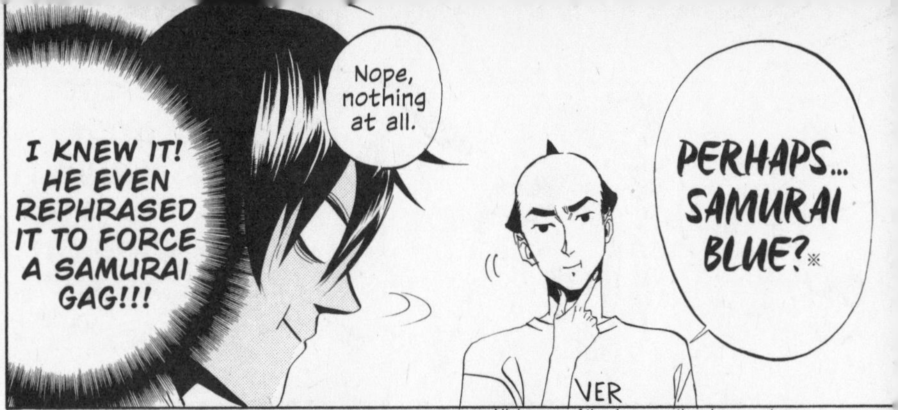
PERHAPS... SAMURAI BLUE?※
Nope, nothing at all.
I KNEW IT! HE EVEN REPHRASED IT TO FORCE A SAMURAI GAG!!!
VER

※ Nickname of the Japan national soccer team

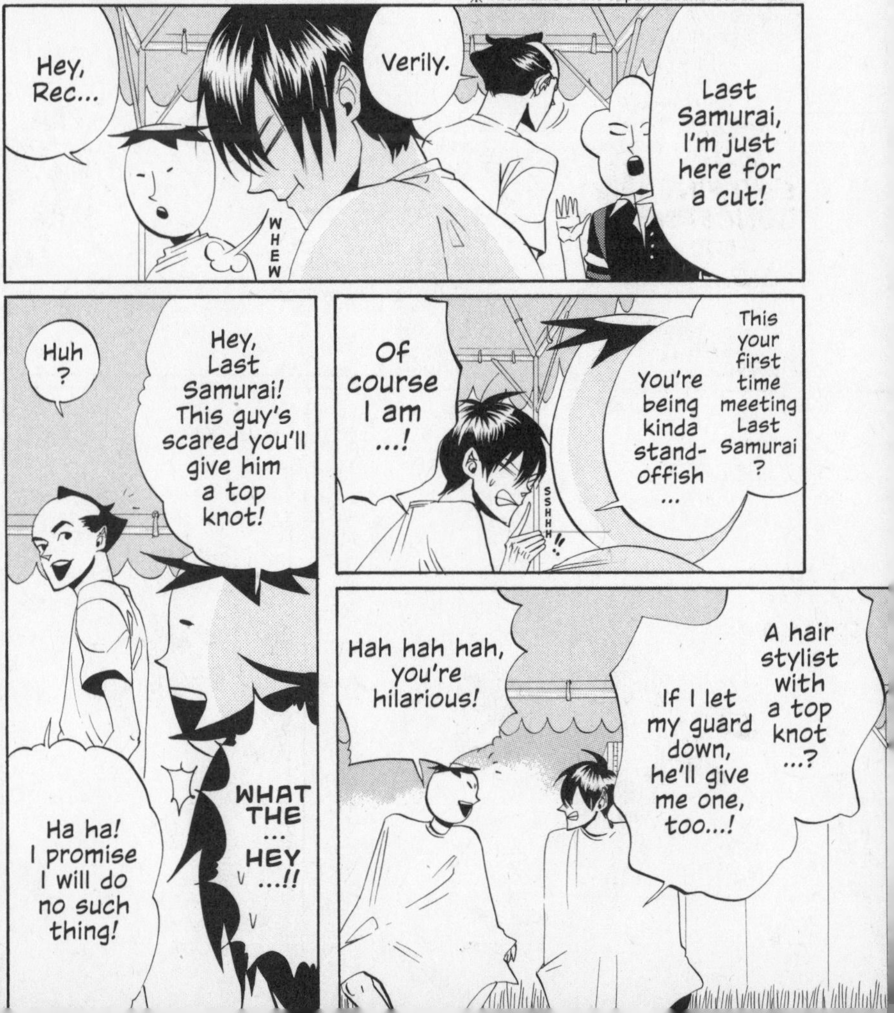
Last Samurai, I'm just here for a cut!
Verily.
Hey, Rec...
WHEW
This your first time meeting Last Samurai?
You're being kinda stand-offish ...
Of course I am ...!
SSHHH!!
A hair stylist with a top knot ...?
If I let my guard down, he'll give me one, too...!
Hah hah hah, you're hilarious!
Hey, Last Samurai! This guy's scared you'll give him a top knot!
Huh?
Ha ha! I promise I will do no such thing!
WHAT THE ... HEY ...!!

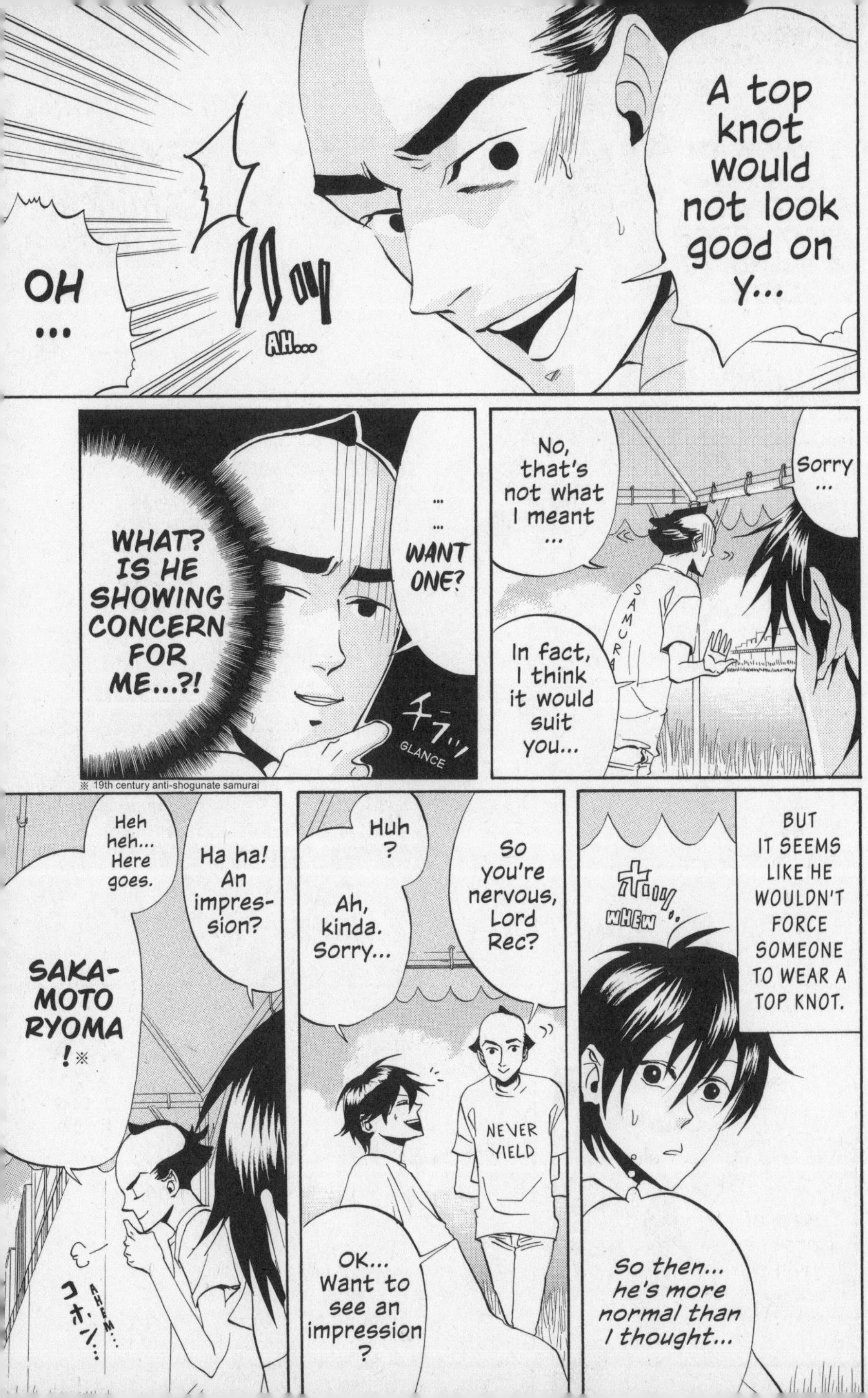
A top knot would not look good on y...
AH...
OH...
Sorry...
No, that's not what I meant...
In fact, I think it would suit you...
... ... WANT ONE?
GLANCE
WHAT? IS HE SHOWING CONCERN FOR ME...?!
BUT IT SEEMS LIKE HE WOULDN'T FORCE SOMEONE TO WEAR A TOP KNOT.
WHEW
So then... he's more normal than I thought...
So you're nervous, Lord Rec?
Huh?
Ah, kinda. Sorry...
OK... Want to see an impression?
Ha ha! An impression?
Heh heh... Here goes.
SAKAMOTO RYOMA!※
AHEM...
※ 19th century anti-shogunate samurai

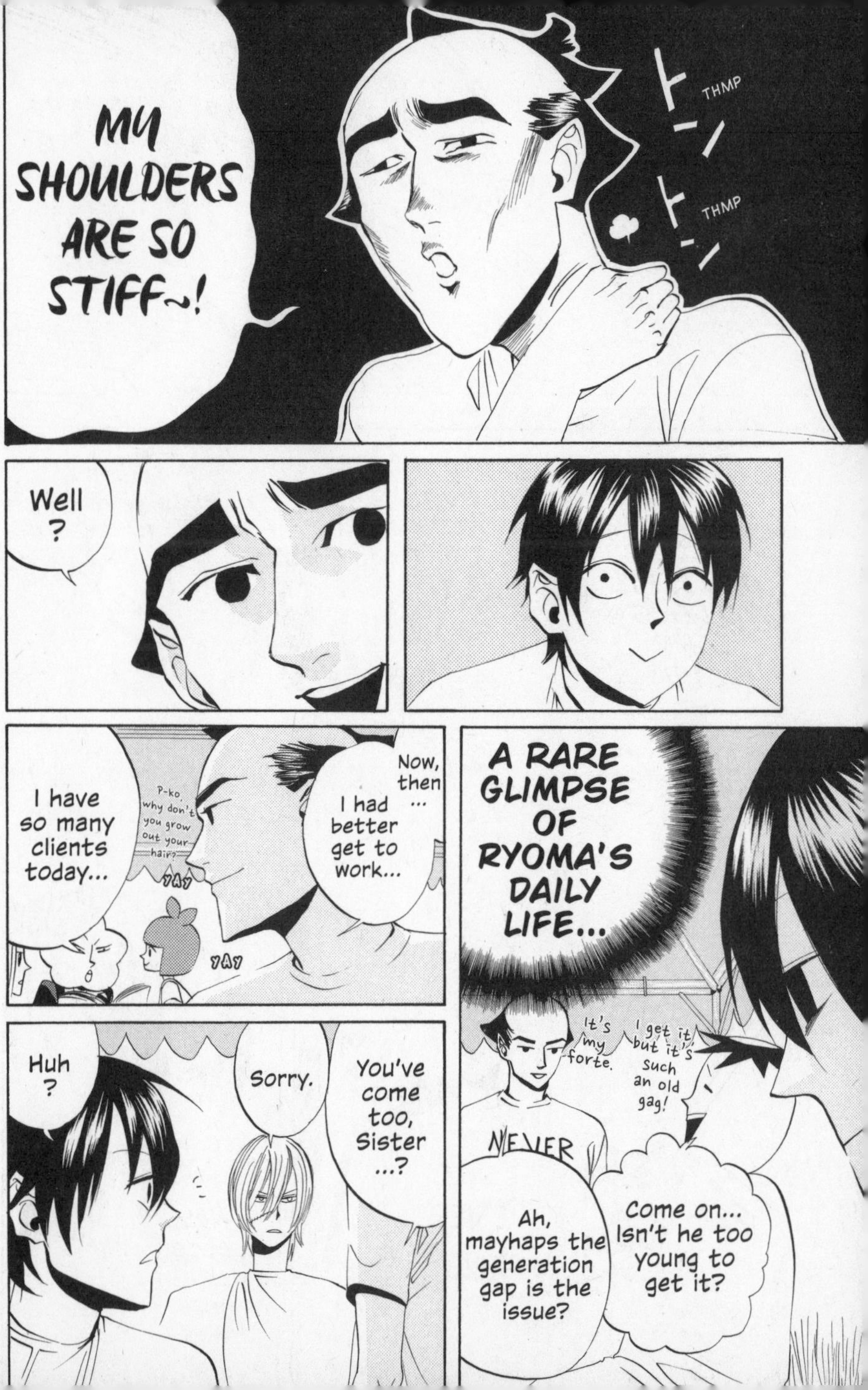
THMP
THMP
MY SHOULDERS ARE SO STIFF~!
Well?
A RARE GLIMPSE OF RYOMA'S DAILY LIFE...
I get it, but it's such an old gag!
It's my forte.
NEVER
Come on... Isn't he too young to get it?
Ah, mayhaps the generation gap is the issue?
Now, then...
I had better get to work...
P-ko, why don't you grow out your hair?
YAY
I have so many clients today...
YAY
You've come too, Sister...?
Sorry.
Huh?

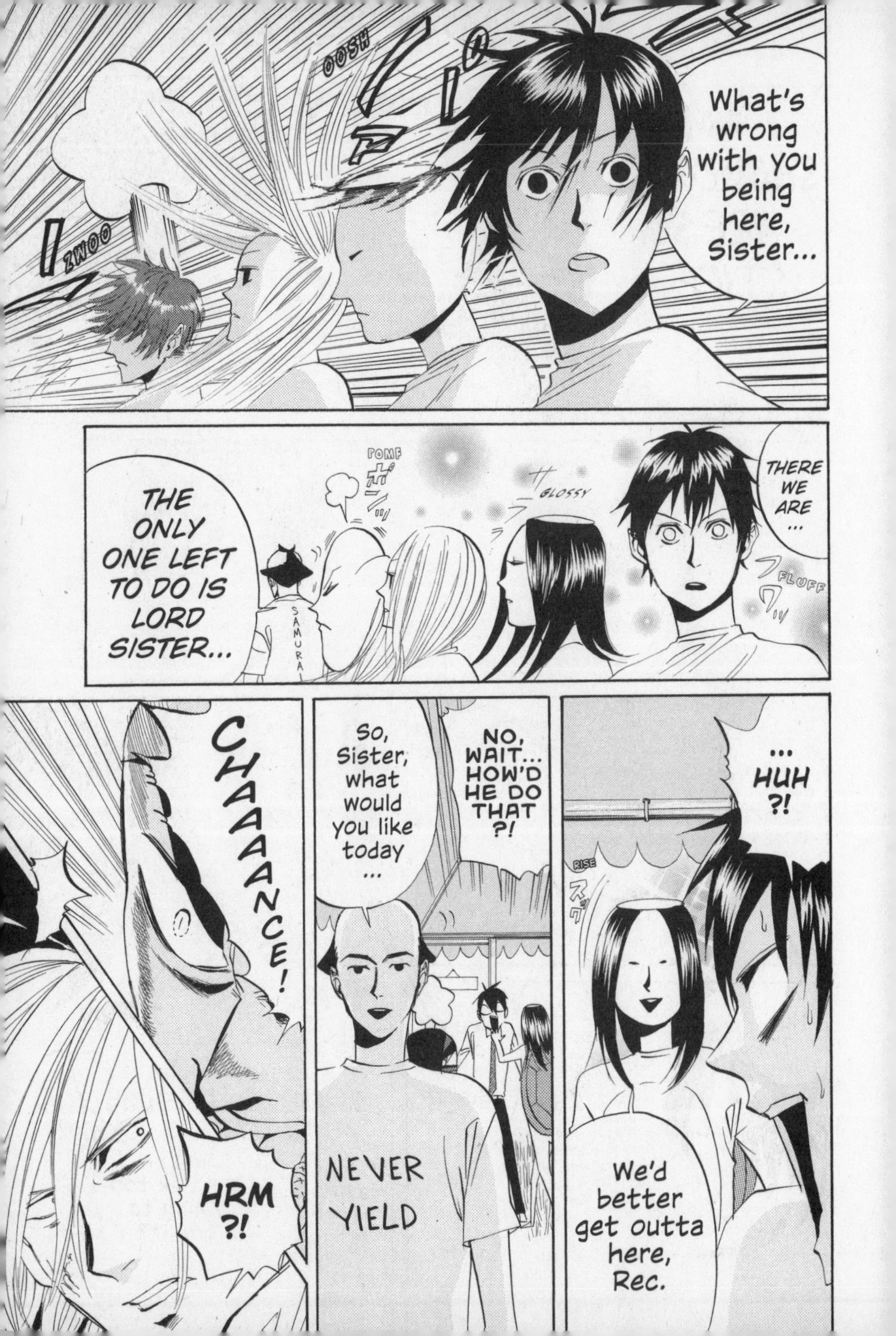
What's wrong with you being here, Sister...
OOSH
ZWOO
THERE WE ARE...
FLUFF
GLOSSY
POMF
SAMURAI
THE ONLY ONE LEFT TO DO IS LORD SISTER...
...HUH?!
RISE
We'd better get outta here, Rec.
NO, WAIT... HOW'D HE DO THAT?!
So, Sister, what would you like today...
NEVER YIELD
CHAAAAANCE!
HRM?!

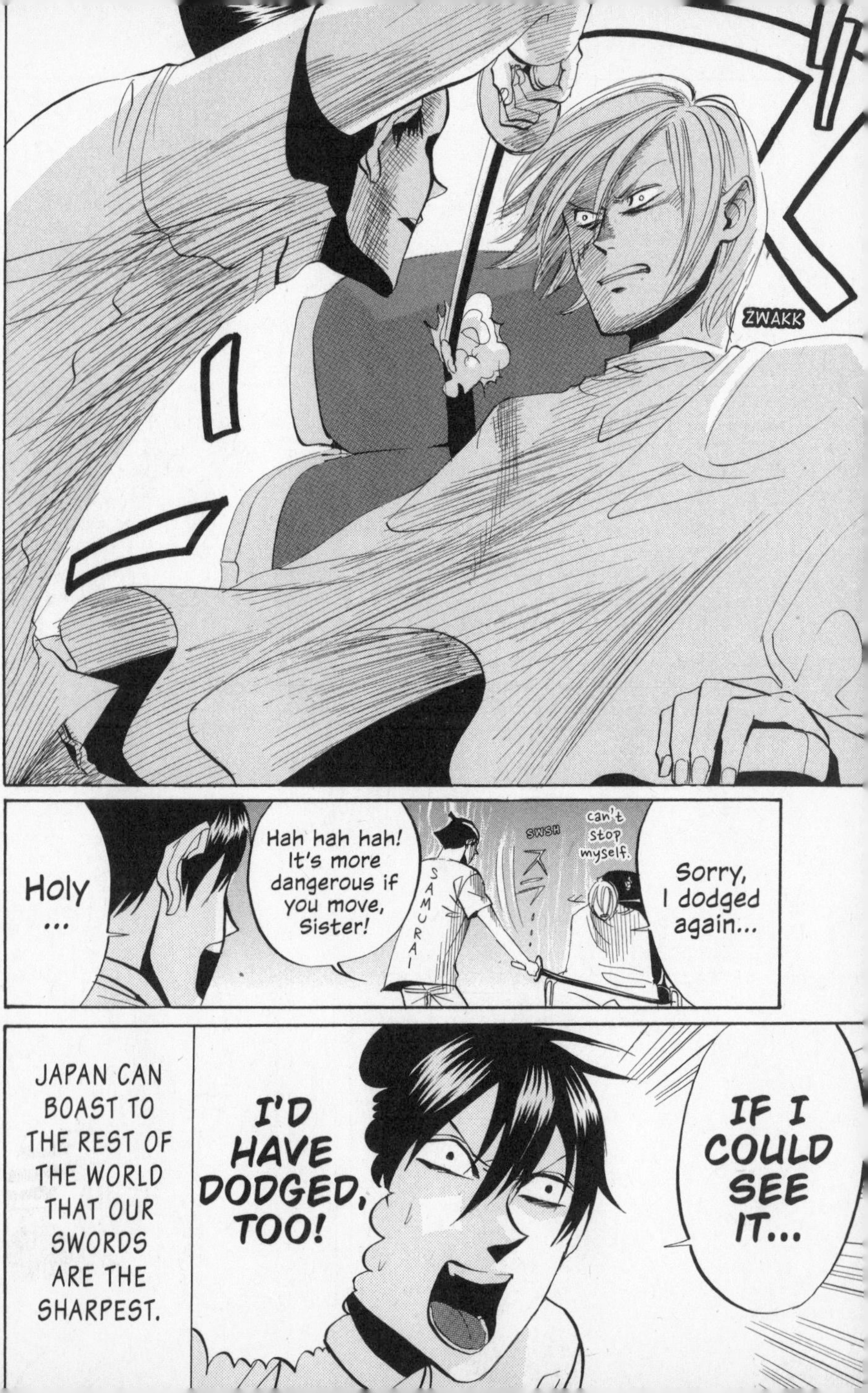
ZWAKK
Sorry, I dodged again...
can't stop myself.
SWSH
SAMURAI
Hah hah hah! It's more dangerous if you move, Sister!
Holy ...
IF I COULD SEE IT...
I'D HAVE DODGED, TOO!
JAPAN CAN BOAST TO THE REST OF THE WORLD THAT OUR SWORDS ARE THE SHARPEST.

Chapter 110: Billy and Jacqueline

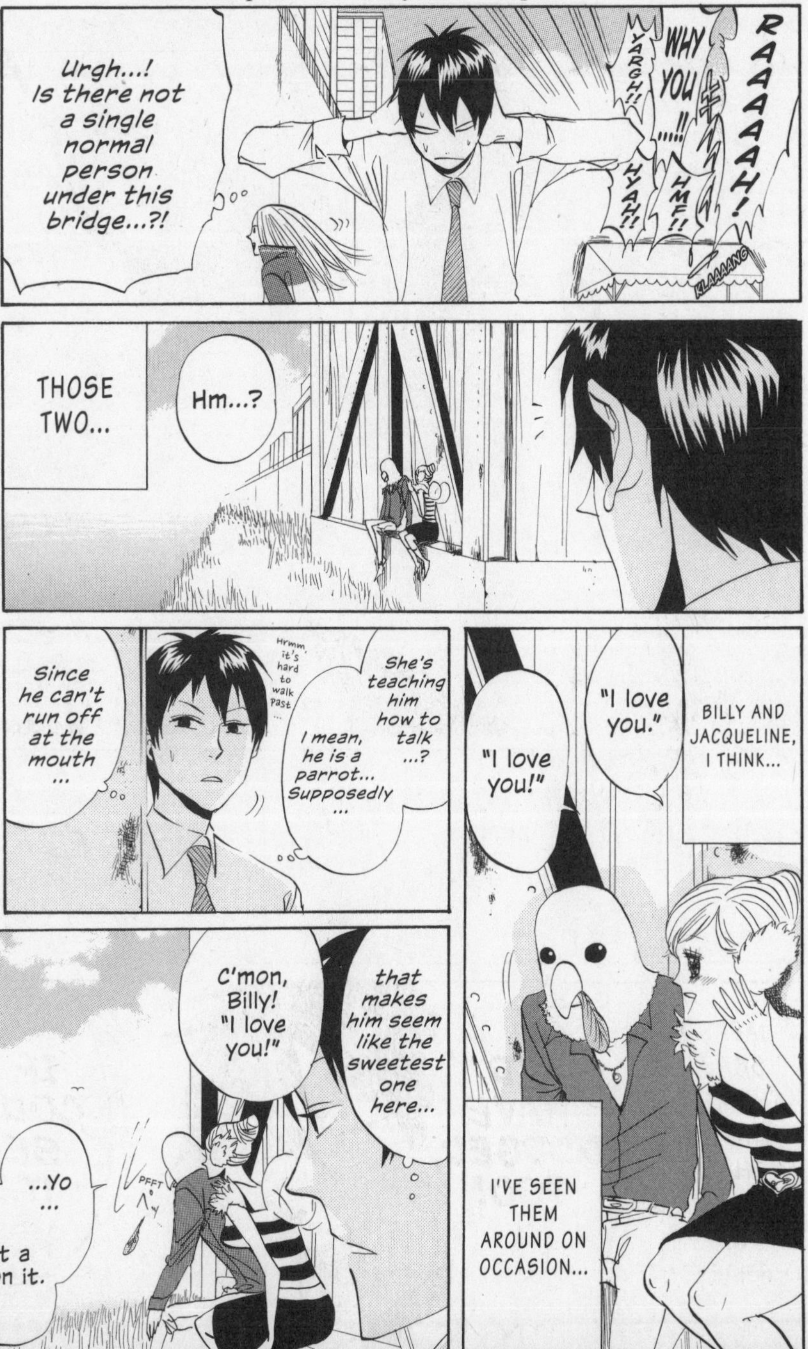
RAAAAAAH!
WHY YOU ...!!
YARGH!!
HMF!!
HYAH!!
KLAAAANG
Urgh...! Is there not a single normal person under this bridge...?!
Hm...?
THOSE TWO...
BILLY AND JACQUELINE, I THINK...
"I love you."
"I love you!"
I'VE SEEN THEM AROUND ON OCCASION...
She's teaching him how to talk ...?
Hrmm it's hard to walk past ...
I mean, he is a parrot... Supposedly ...
Since he can't run off at the mouth ...
that makes him seem like the sweetest one here...
C'mon, Billy! "I love you!"
PFFT
...Yo ... Put a lid on it.

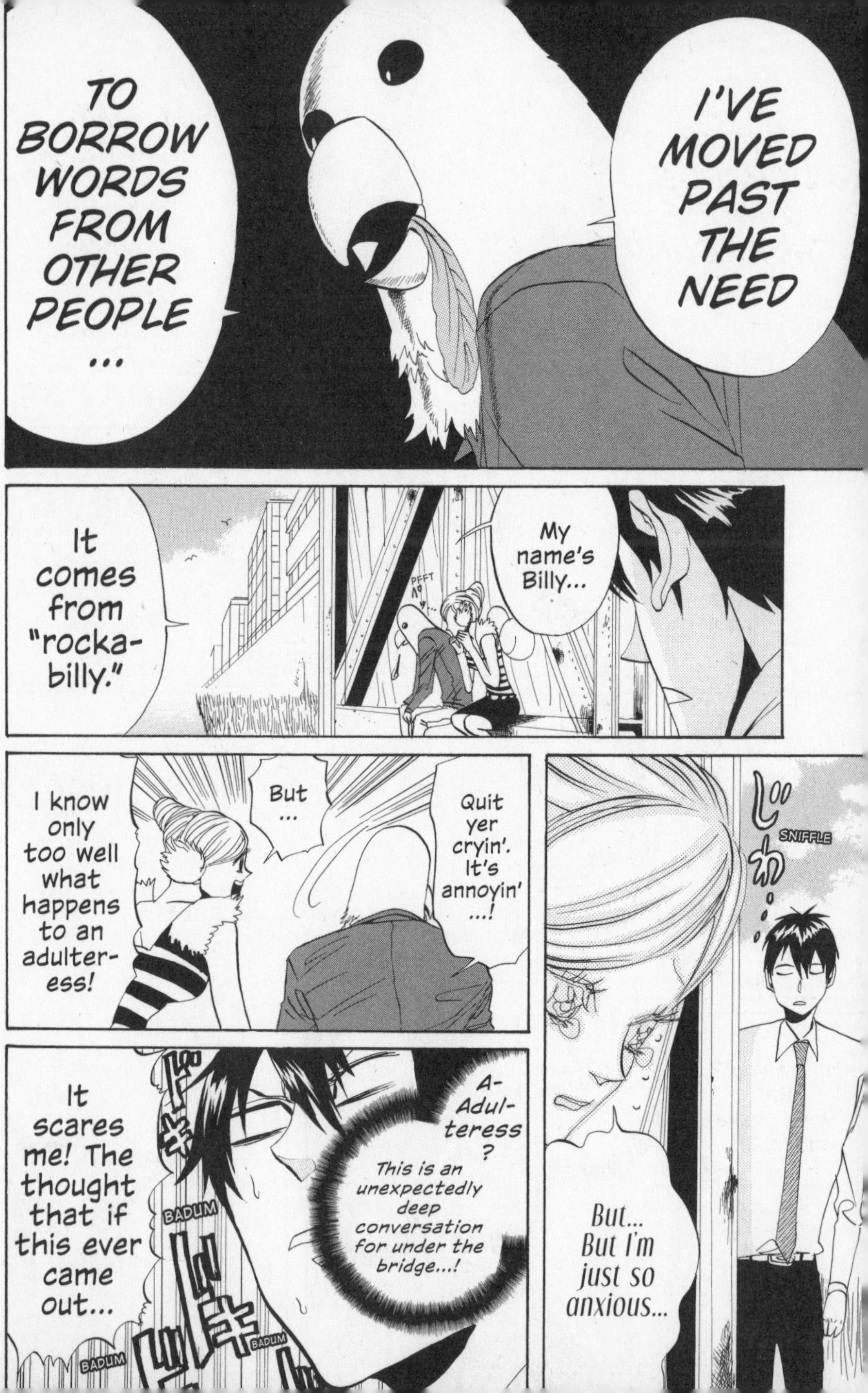
I'VE MOVED PAST THE NEED
TO BORROW WORDS FROM OTHER PEOPLE ...
My name's Billy...
PFFT
It comes from "rocka-billy."
SNIFFLE
Quit yer cryin'. It's annoyin' ...!
But ...
I know only too well what happens to an adulter-ess!
But... But I'm just so anxious...
A-Adul-teress?
This is an unexpectedly deep conversation for under the bridge...!
It scares me! The thought that if this ever came out...
BADUM
BADUM
BADUM

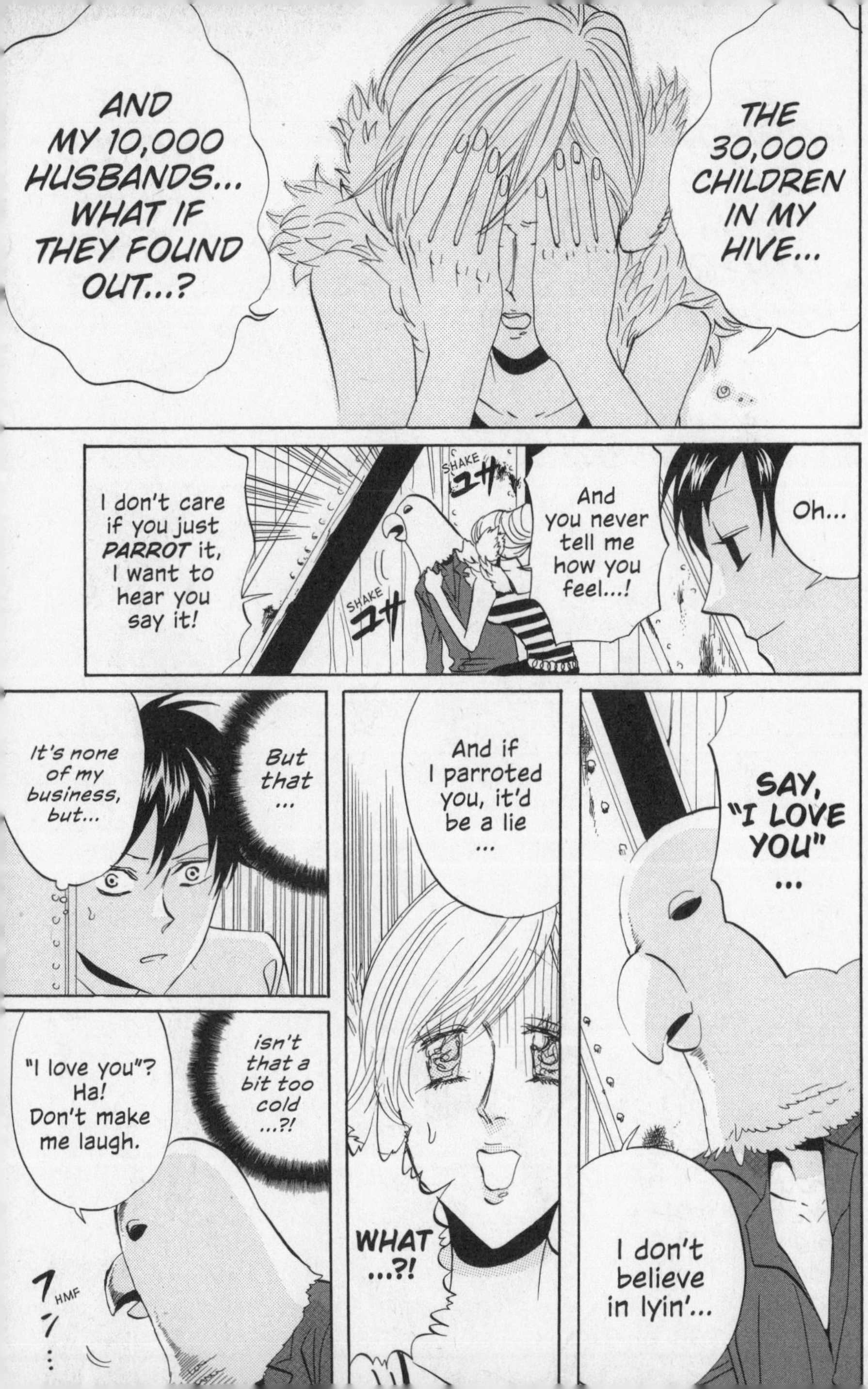
THE 30,000 CHILDREN IN MY HIVE...
AND MY 10,000 HUSBANDS... WHAT IF THEY FOUND OUT...?
Oh...
And you never tell me how you feel...!
SHAKE ユサ
SHAKE ユサ
I don't care if you just *PARROT* it, I want to hear you say it!
SAY, "I LOVE YOU" ...
I don't believe in lyin'...
And if I parroted you, it'd be a lie ...
WHAT ...?!
But that ...
It's none of my business, but...
isn't that a bit too cold ...?!
"I love you"? Ha! Don't make me laugh.
HMF

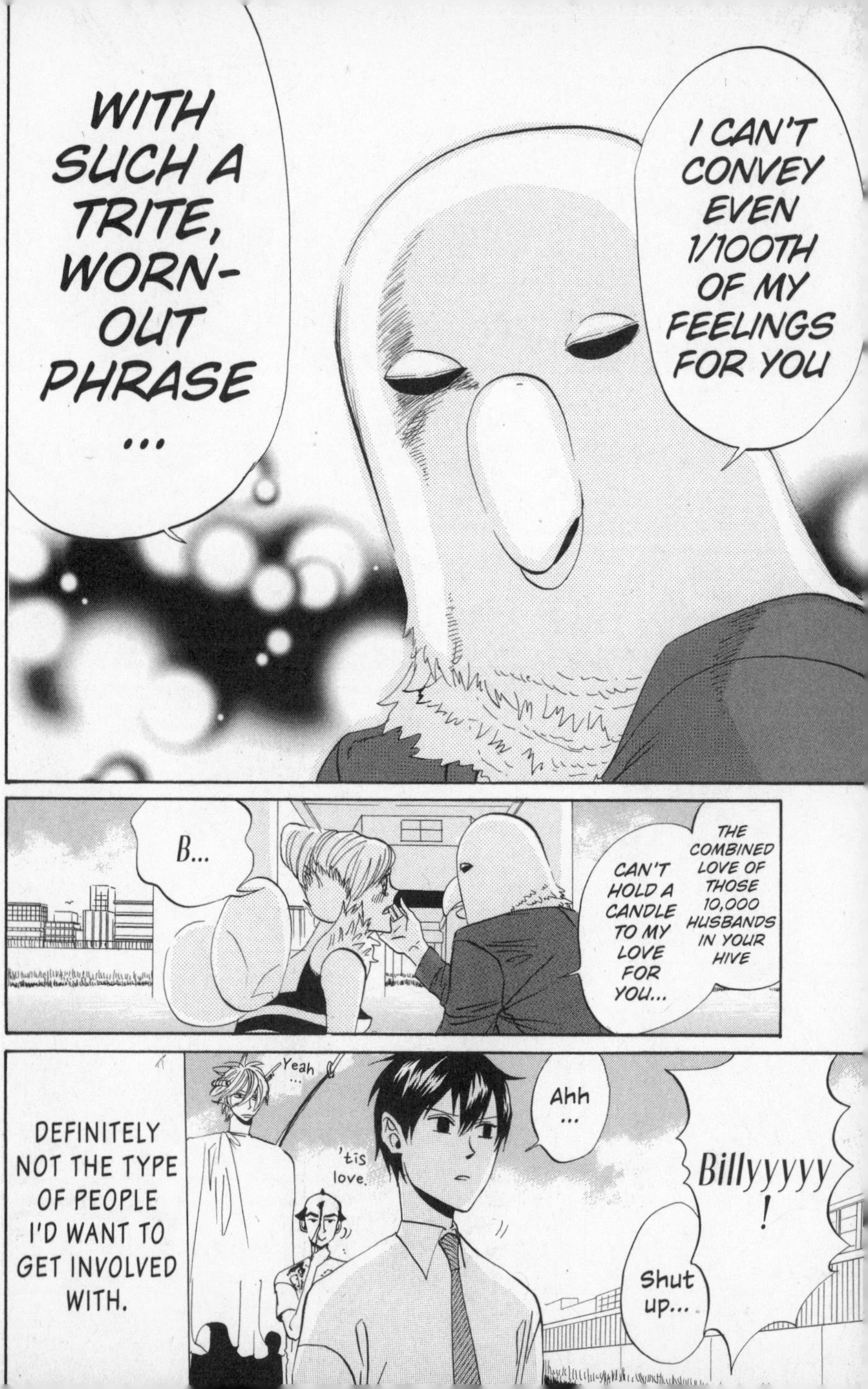
I CAN'T CONVEY EVEN 1/100TH OF MY FEELINGS FOR YOU
WITH SUCH A TRITE, WORN-OUT PHRASE ...
THE COMBINED LOVE OF THOSE 10,000 HUSBANDS IN YOUR HIVE
CAN'T HOLD A CANDLE TO MY LOVE FOR YOU...
B...
Billyyyyy!
Ahh ...
Shut up...
Yeah ...
'tis love.
DEFINITELY NOT THE TYPE OF PEOPLE I'D WANT TO GET INVOLVED WITH.

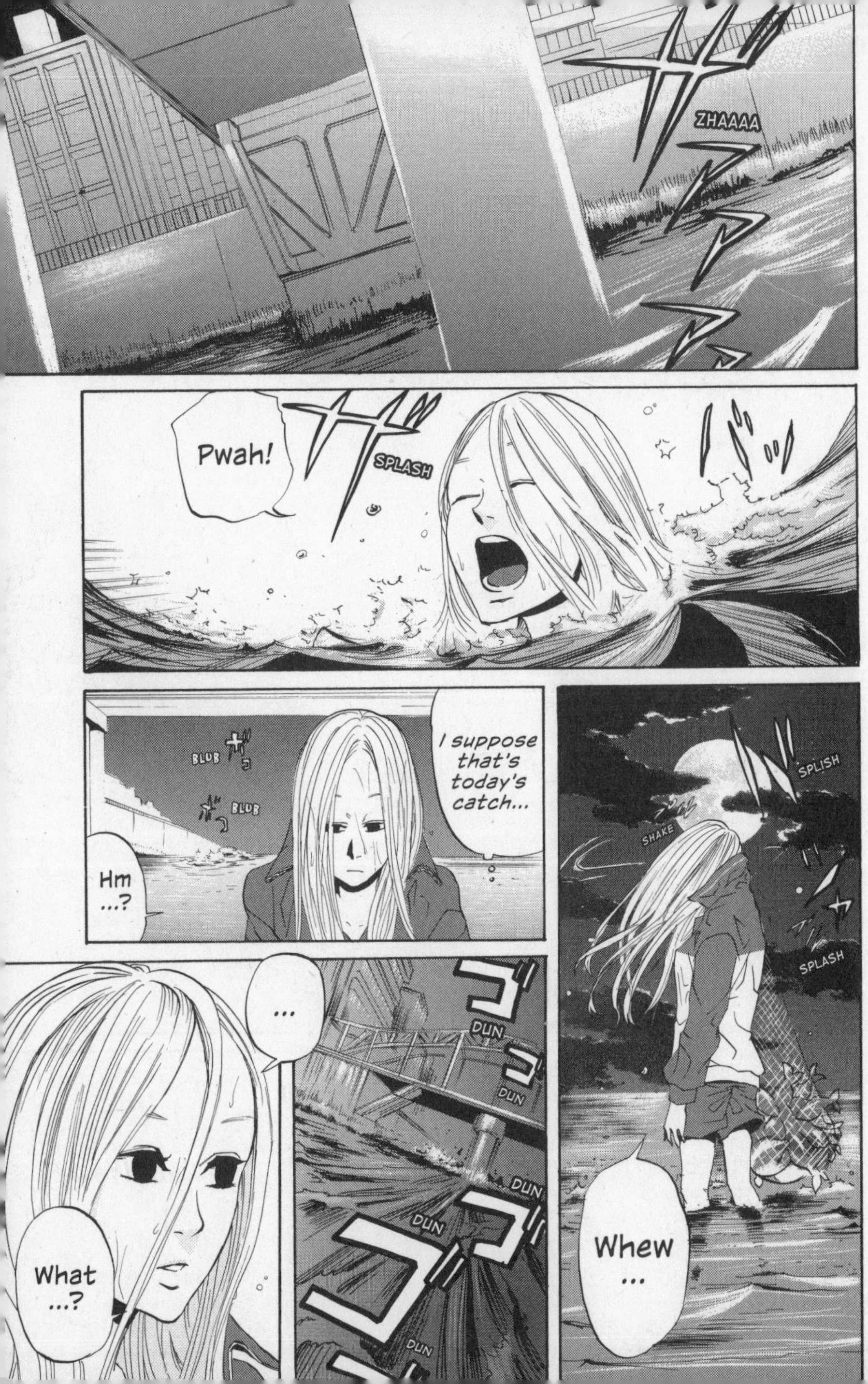

ZHAAAA
SPLASH
Pwah!
SPLISH
SHAKE
SPLASH
Whew ...
I suppose that's today's catch...
BLUB
BLUB
Hm ...?
DUN
DUN
DUN
DUN
DUN
...
What ...?

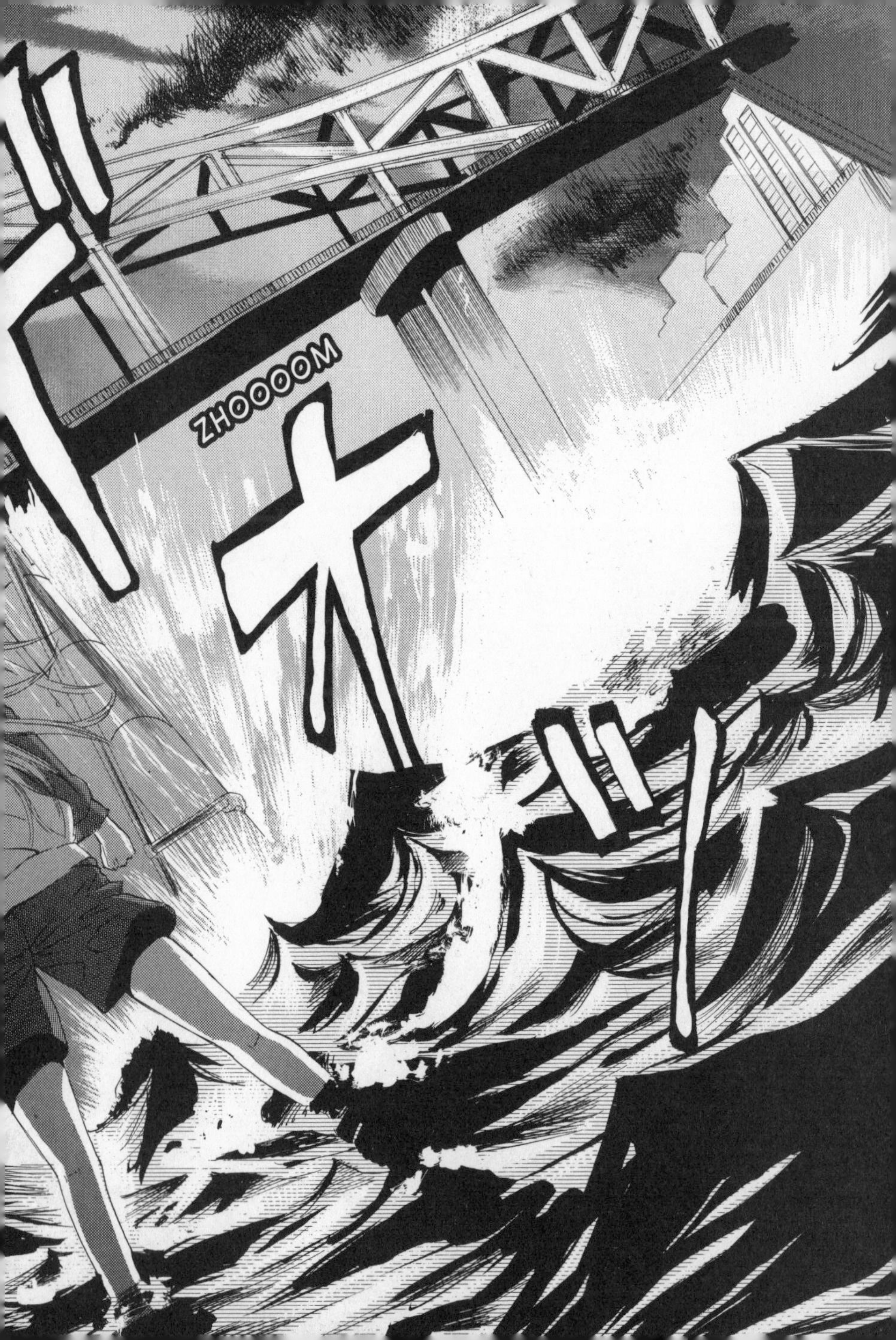
ZHOOOOM

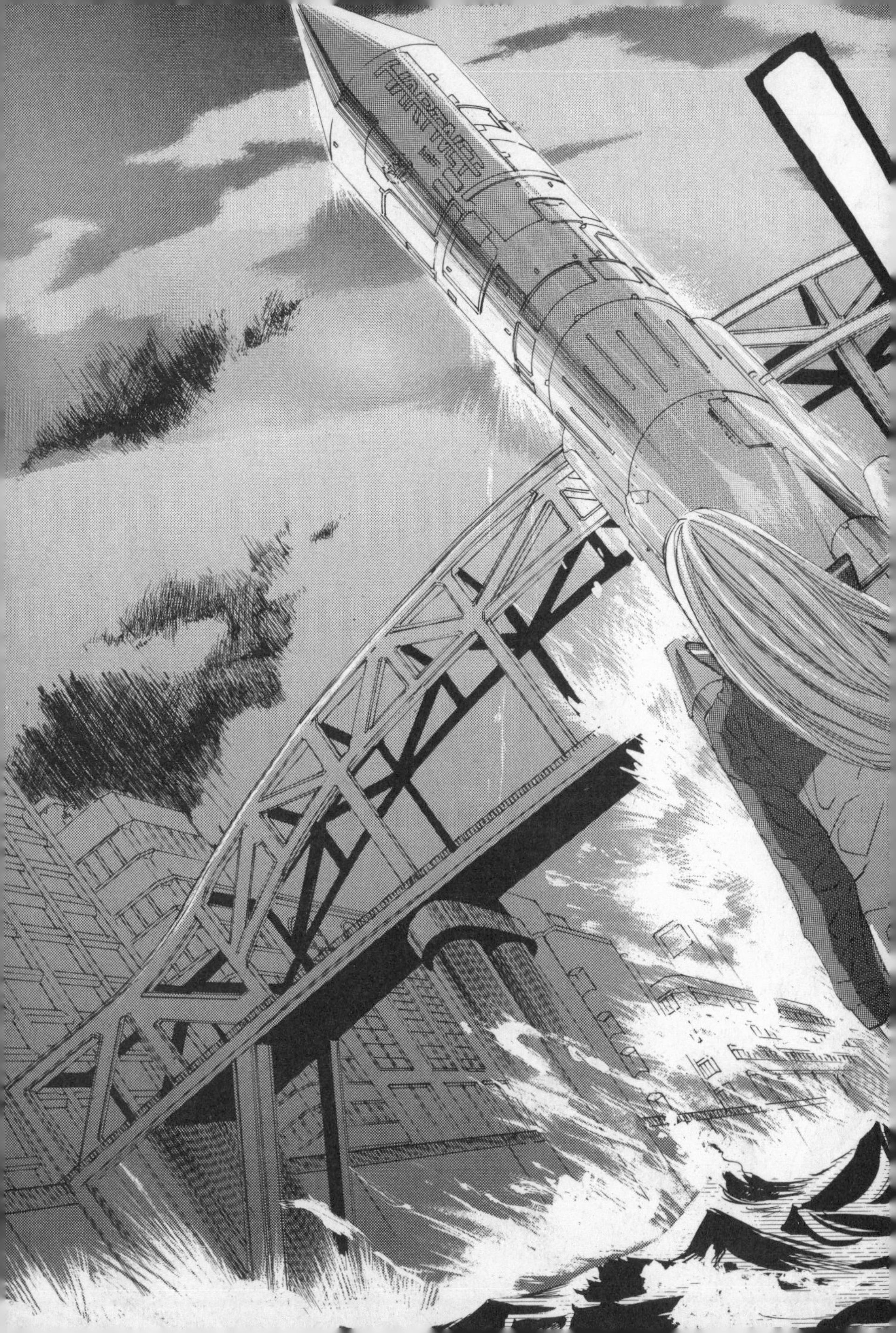

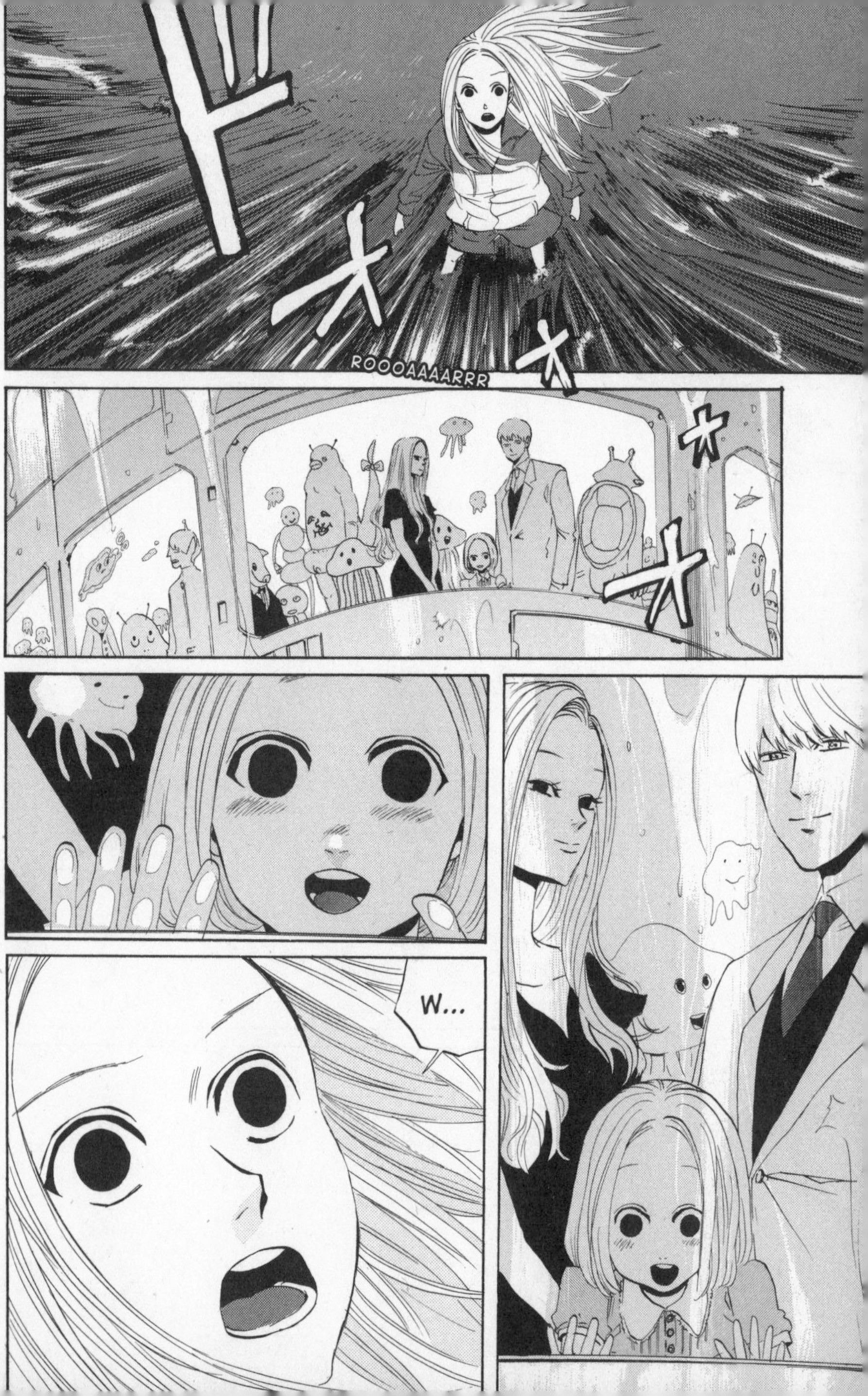
ROOOAAAARRR
W...

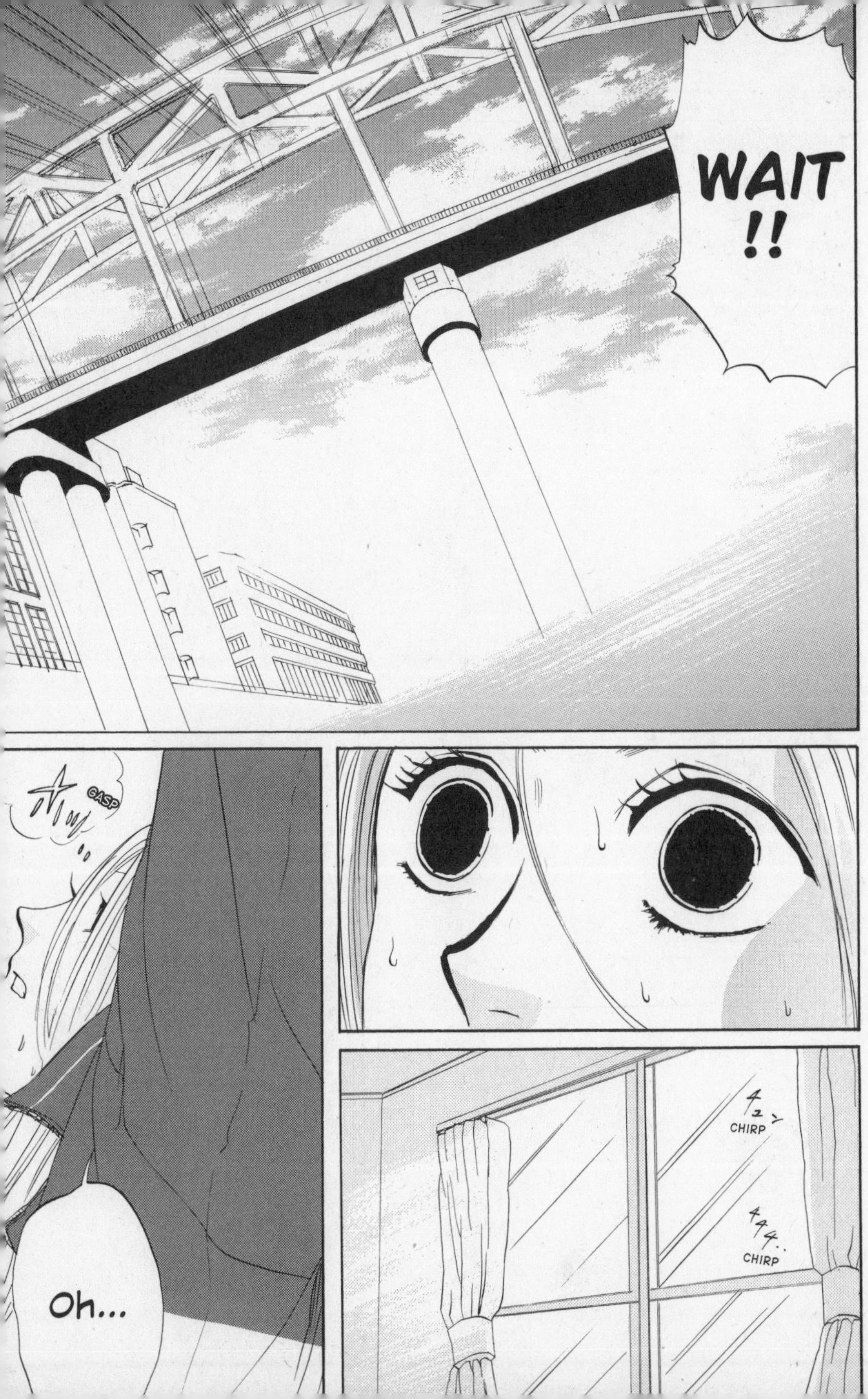
WAIT !!
CHIRP
CHIRP
GASP
Oh...

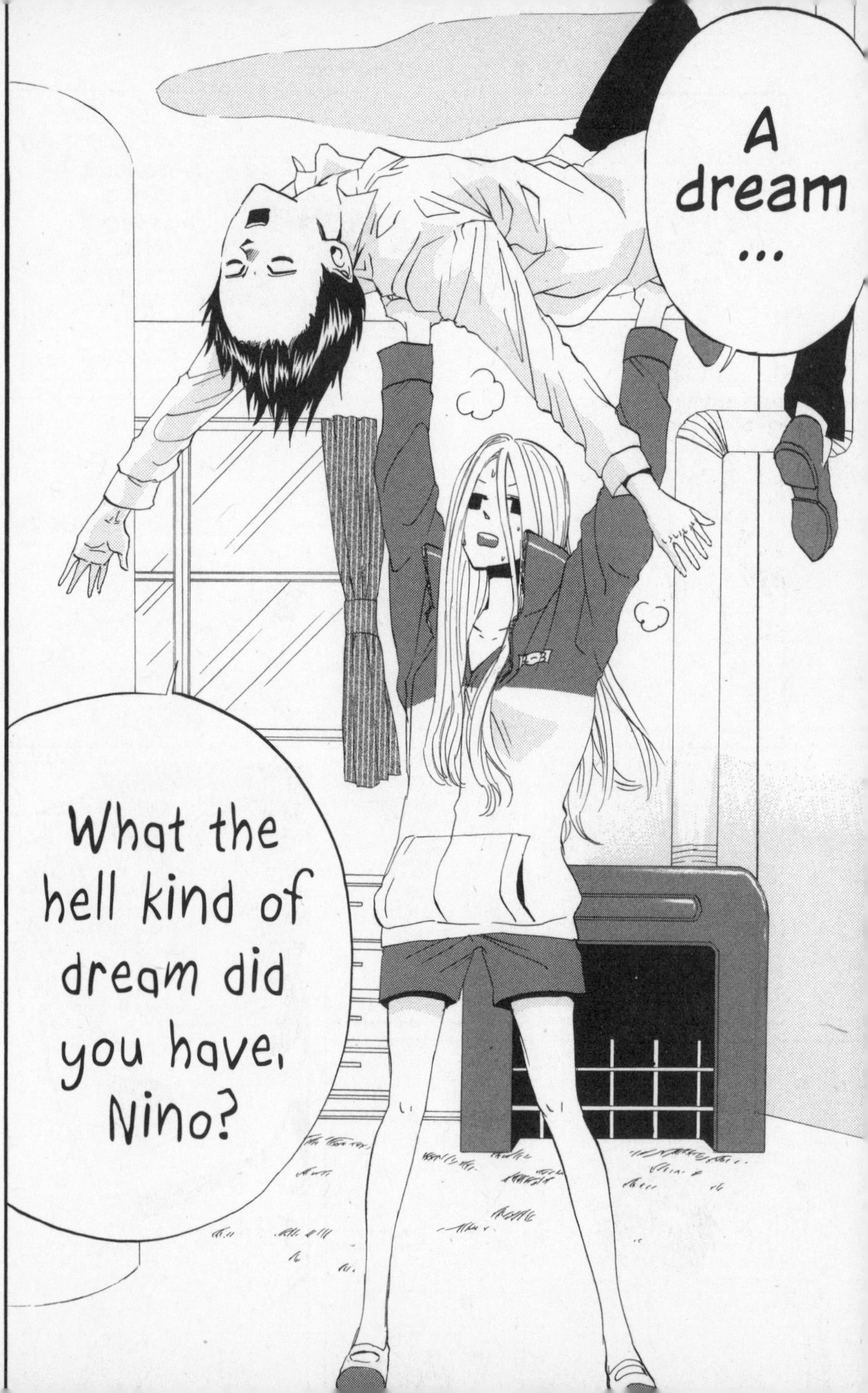
A dream ...
What the hell kind of dream did you have, Nino?

Chapter 111: Trade

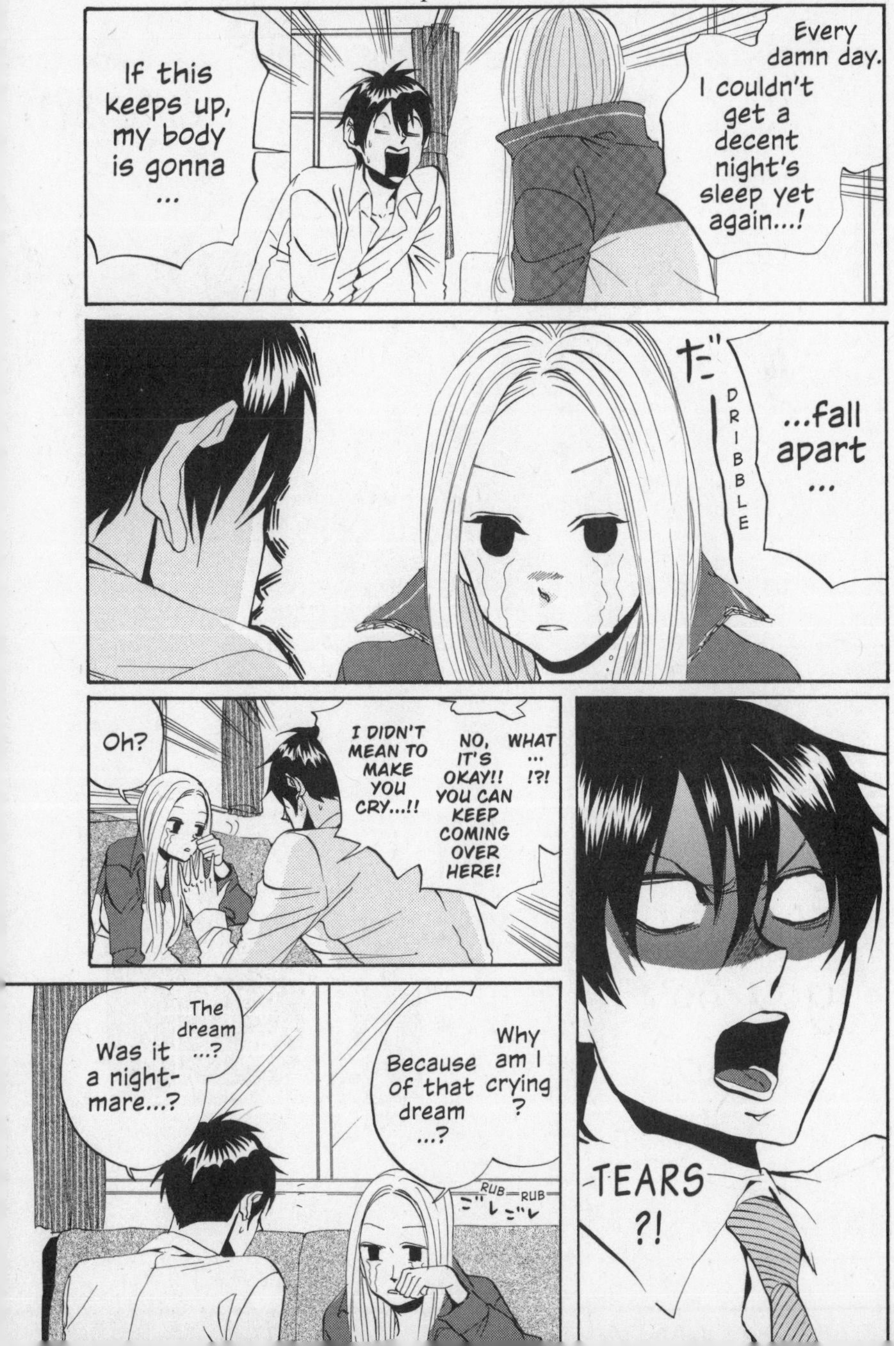
Every damn day. I couldn't get a decent night's sleep yet again...!
If this keeps up, my body is gonna ...
...fall apart ...
だー DRIBBLE
TEARS ?!
WHAT ... !?!
NO, IT'S OKAY!! YOU CAN KEEP COMING OVER HERE!
I DIDN'T MEAN TO MAKE YOU CRY...!!
Oh?
Why am I crying ?
Because of that dream ...?
The dream ...?
Was it a night-mare...?
ごしごし RUB RUB

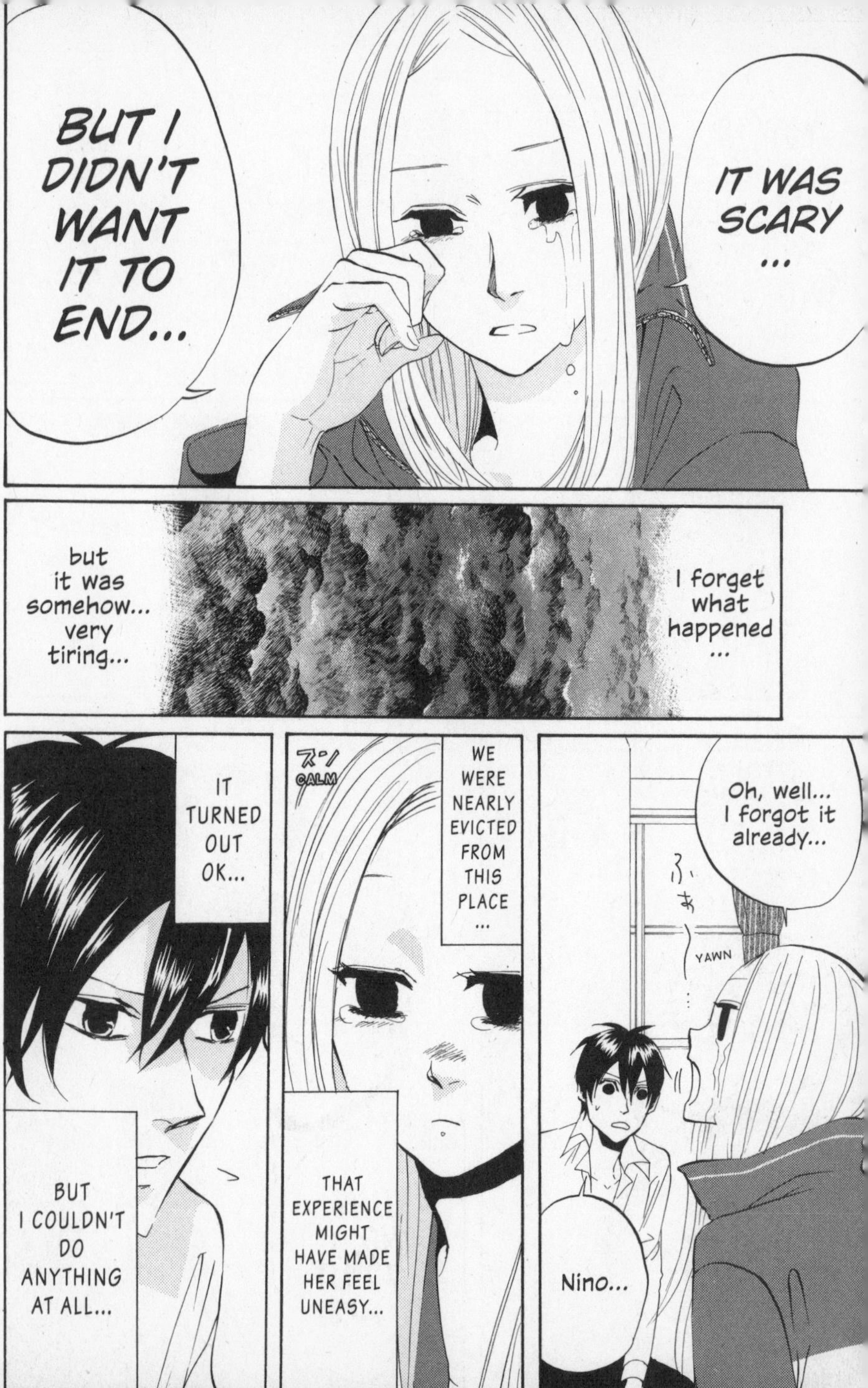
IT WAS SCARY ...
BUT I DIDN'T WANT IT TO END...
I forget what happened ...
but it was somehow... very tiring...
Oh, well... I forgot it already...
ふあ
YAWN
Nino...
スン
CALM
WE WERE NEARLY EVICTED FROM THIS PLACE ...
THAT EXPERIENCE MIGHT HAVE MADE HER FEEL UNEASY...
IT TURNED OUT OK...
BUT I COULDN'T DO ANYTHING AT ALL...

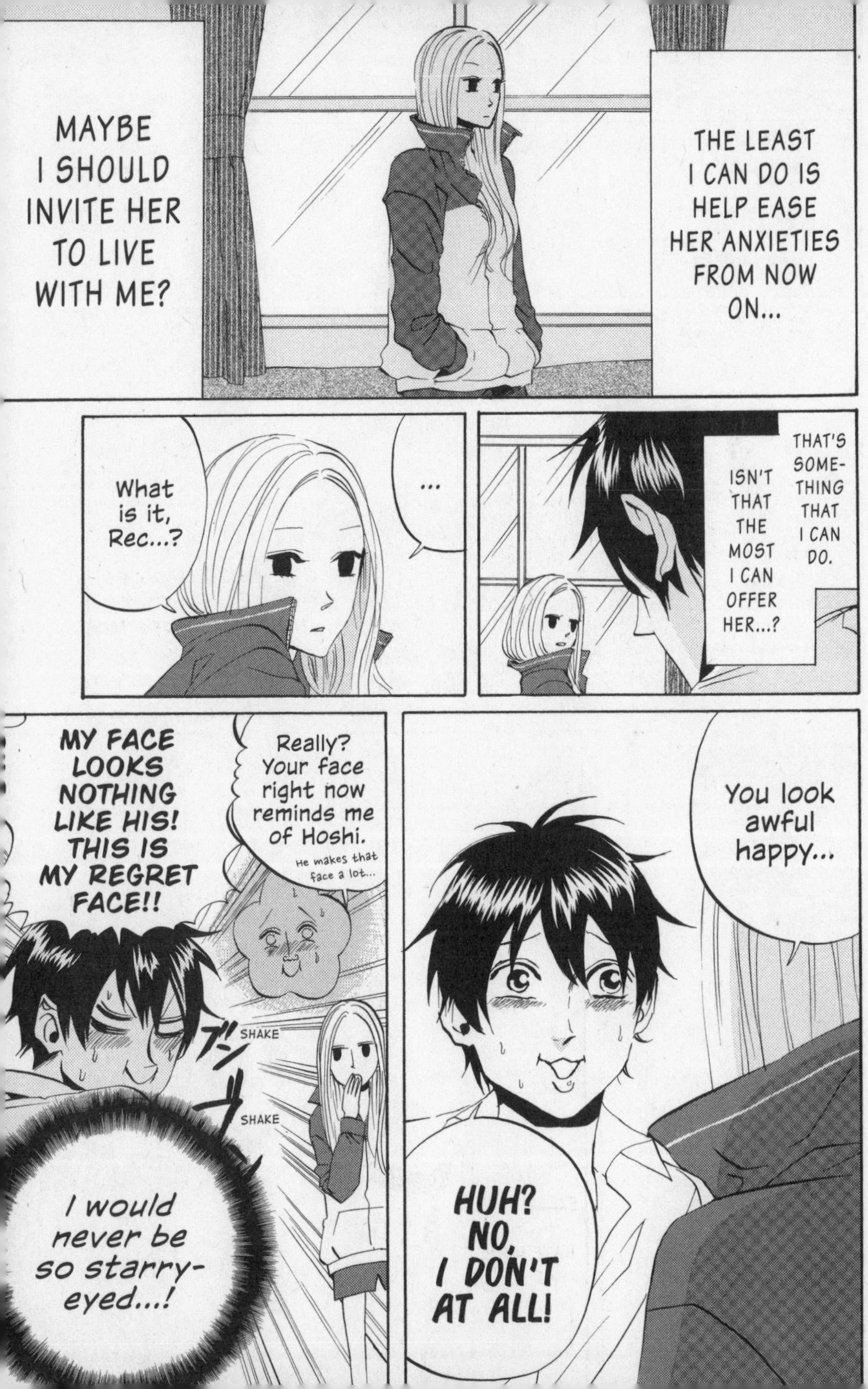
THE LEAST I CAN DO IS HELP EASE HER ANXIETIES FROM NOW ON...
MAYBE I SHOULD INVITE HER TO LIVE WITH ME?
THAT'S SOME-THING THAT I CAN DO.
ISN'T THAT THE MOST I CAN OFFER HER...?
...
What is it, Rec...?
You look awful happy...
HUH? NO, I DON'T AT ALL!
Really? Your face right now reminds me of Hoshi.
He makes that face a lot...
MY FACE LOOKS NOTHING LIKE HIS! THIS IS MY REGRET FACE!!
SHAKE
SHAKE
I would never be so starry-eyed...!

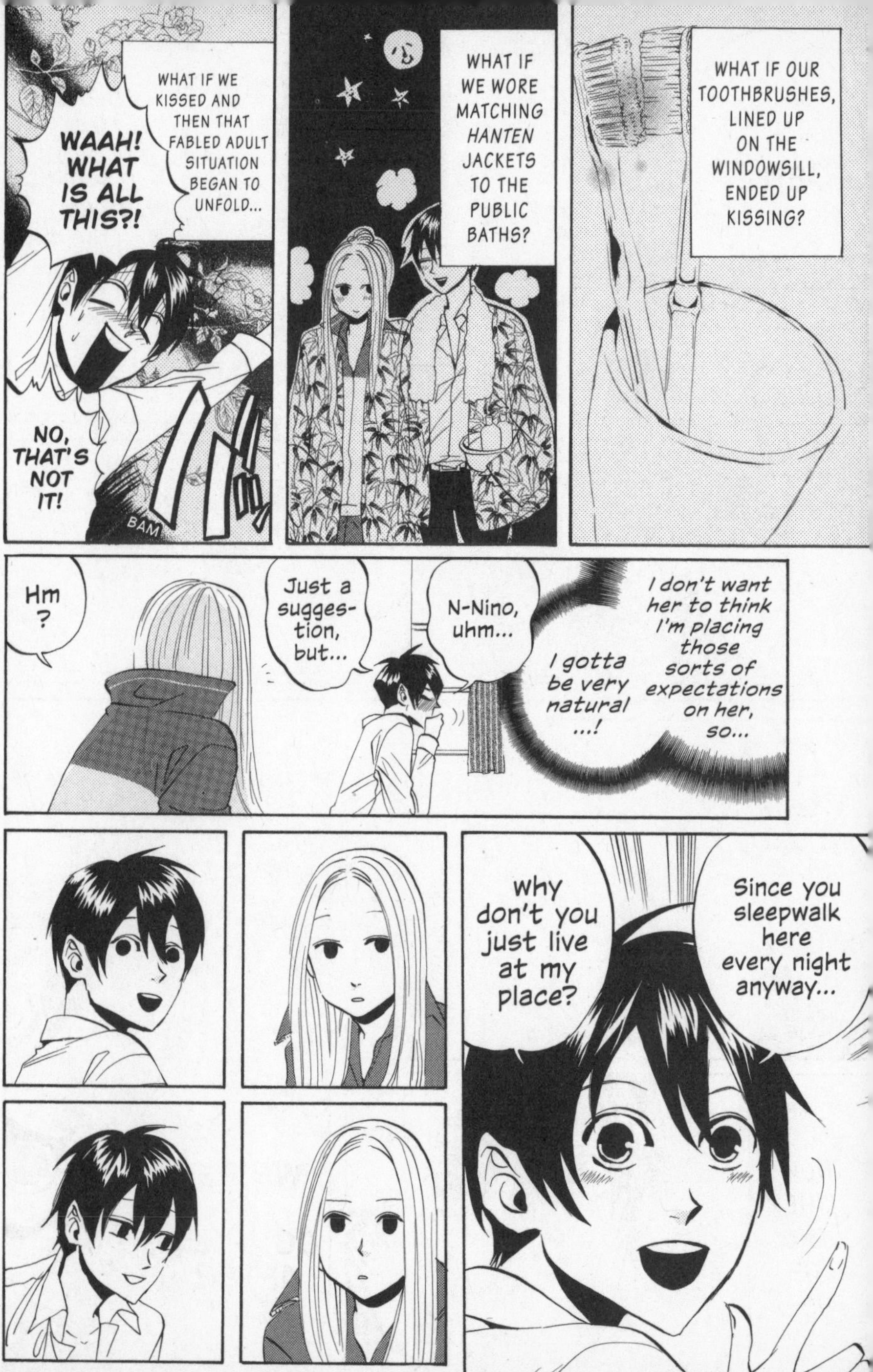
WHAT IF OUR TOOTHBRUSHES, LINED UP ON THE WINDOWSILL, ENDED UP KISSING?
WHAT IF WE WORE MATCHING *HANTEN* JACKETS TO THE PUBLIC BATHS?
WHAT IF WE KISSED AND THEN THAT FABLED ADULT SITUATION BEGAN TO UNFOLD...
WAAH! WHAT IS ALL THIS?!
NO, THAT'S NOT IT!
BAM
I don't want her to think I'm placing those sorts of expectations on her, so...
I gotta be very natural ...!
N-Nino, uhm...
Just a sugges-tion, but...
Hm?
Since you sleepwalk here every night anyway...
Why don't you just live at my place?

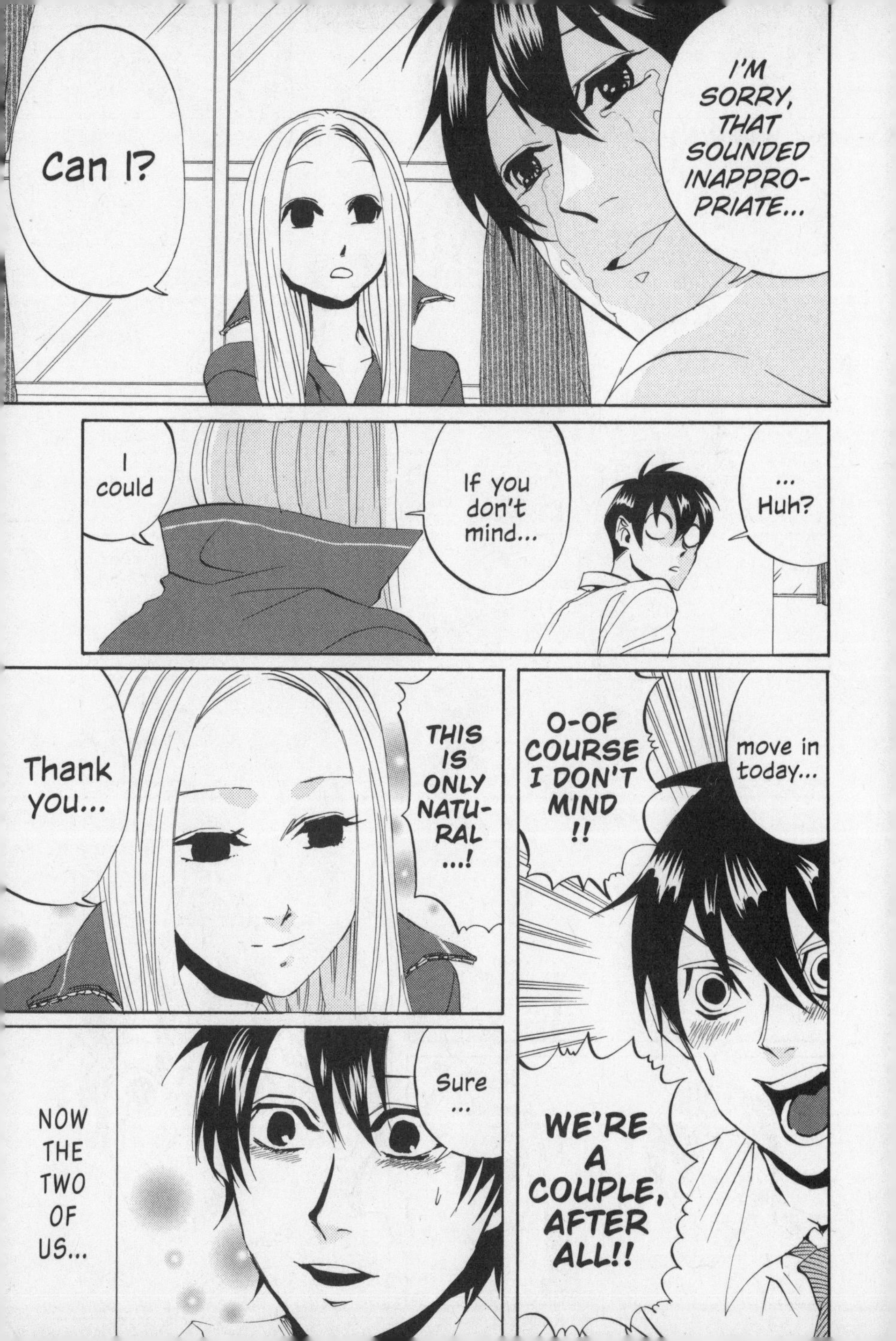
I'M SORRY, THAT SOUNDED INAPPROPRIATE...
Can I?
... Huh?
If you don't mind...
I could
move in today...
O-OF COURSE I DON'T MIND !!
WE'RE A COUPLE, AFTER ALL!!
THIS IS ONLY NATURAL...!
Thank you...
Sure ...
NOW THE TWO OF US...

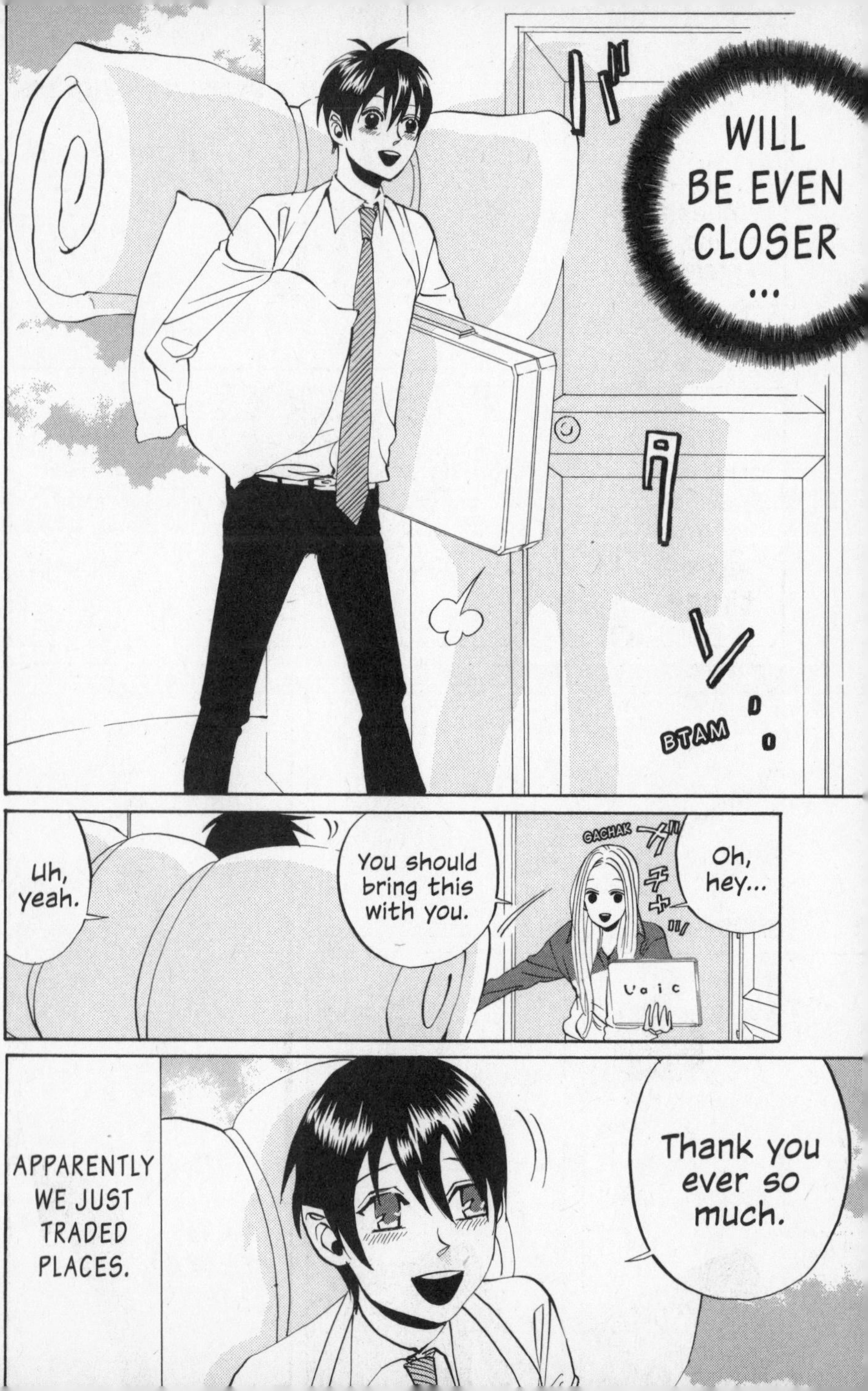
WILL BE EVEN CLOSER ...
BTAM
Oh, hey...
GACHAK
You should bring this with you.
Uh, yeah.
Thank you ever so much.
APPARENTLY WE JUST TRADED PLACES.

Chapter 112: Nino's House

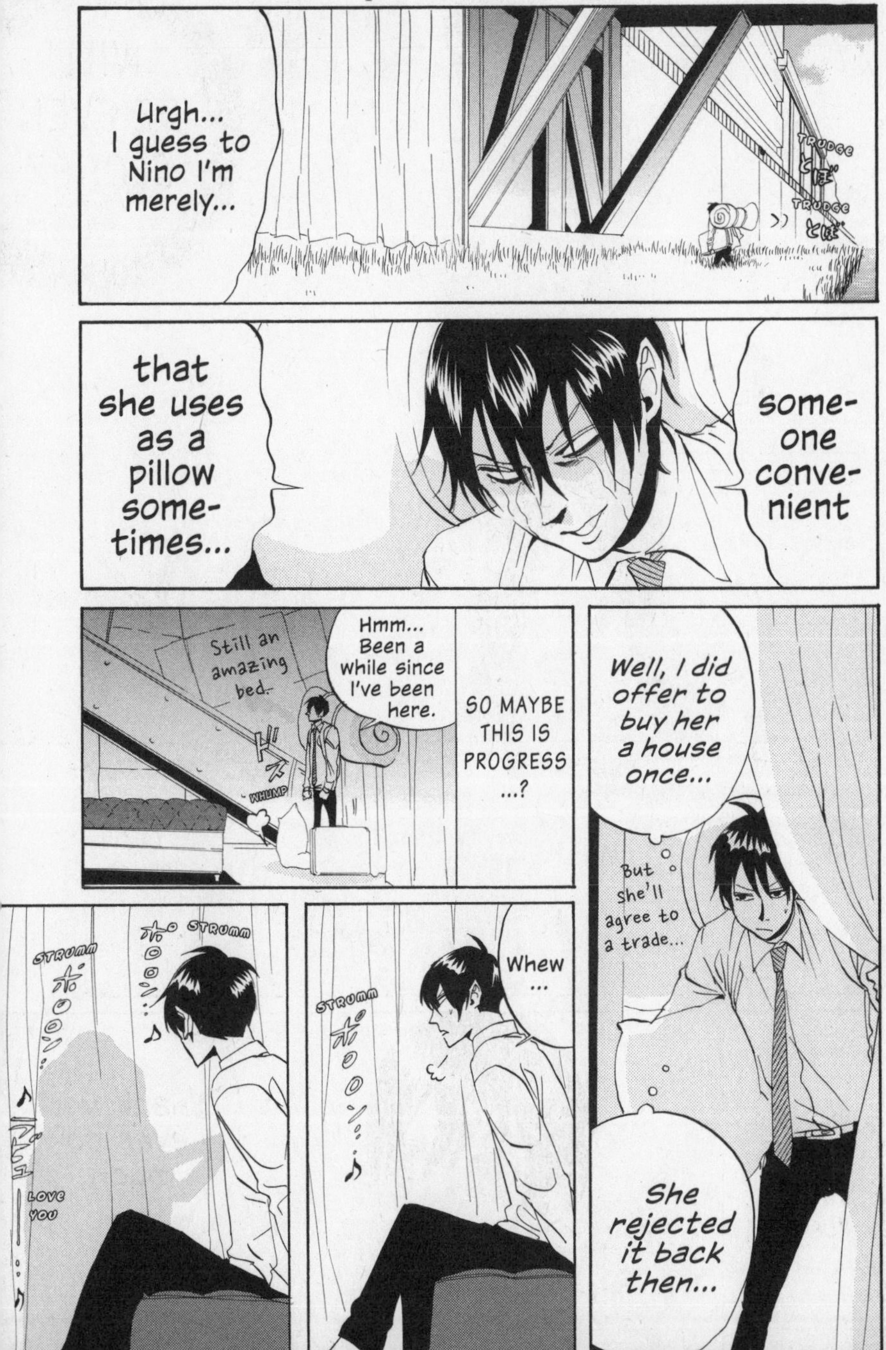
Urgh... I guess to Nino I'm merely...
TRUDGE とぼ
TRUDGE とぼ
someone convenient
that she uses as a pillow sometimes...
Well, I did offer to buy her a house once...
She rejected it back then...
But she'll agree to a trade...
SO MAYBE THIS IS PROGRESS ...?
Hmm... Been a while since I've been here.
Still an amazing bed.
WHUMP
Whew ...
STRUMM
STRUMM
STRUMM
LOVE YOU

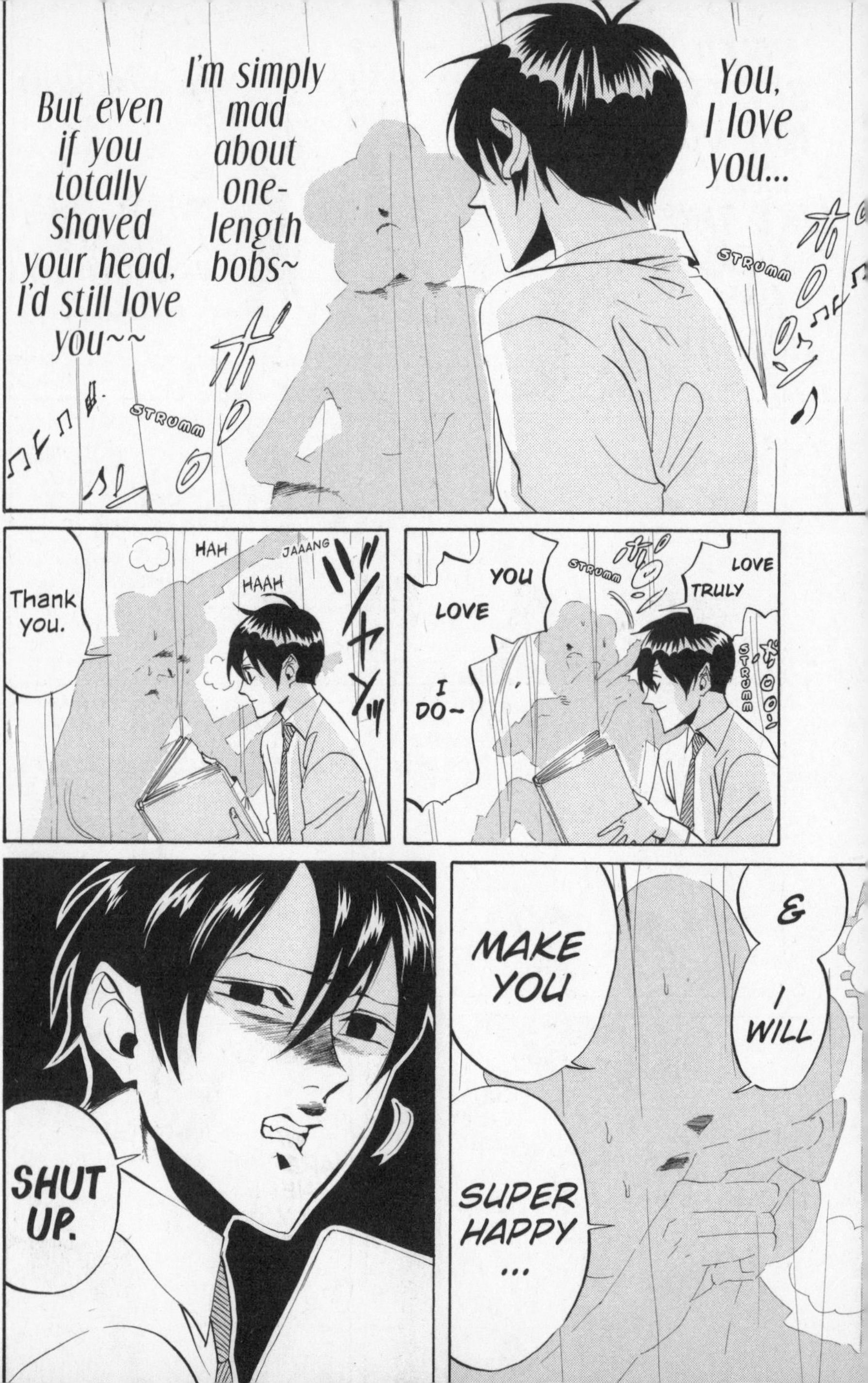
You, I love you...
STRUMM
I'm simply mad about one-length bobs~
But even if you totally shaved your head, I'd still love you~~
STRUMM
LOVE
TRULY
STRUMM
STRUMM
YOU
LOVE
I DO~
JAAANG
HAH
HAAH
Thank you.
&
I WILL
MAKE YOU
SUPER HAPPY ...
SHUT UP.

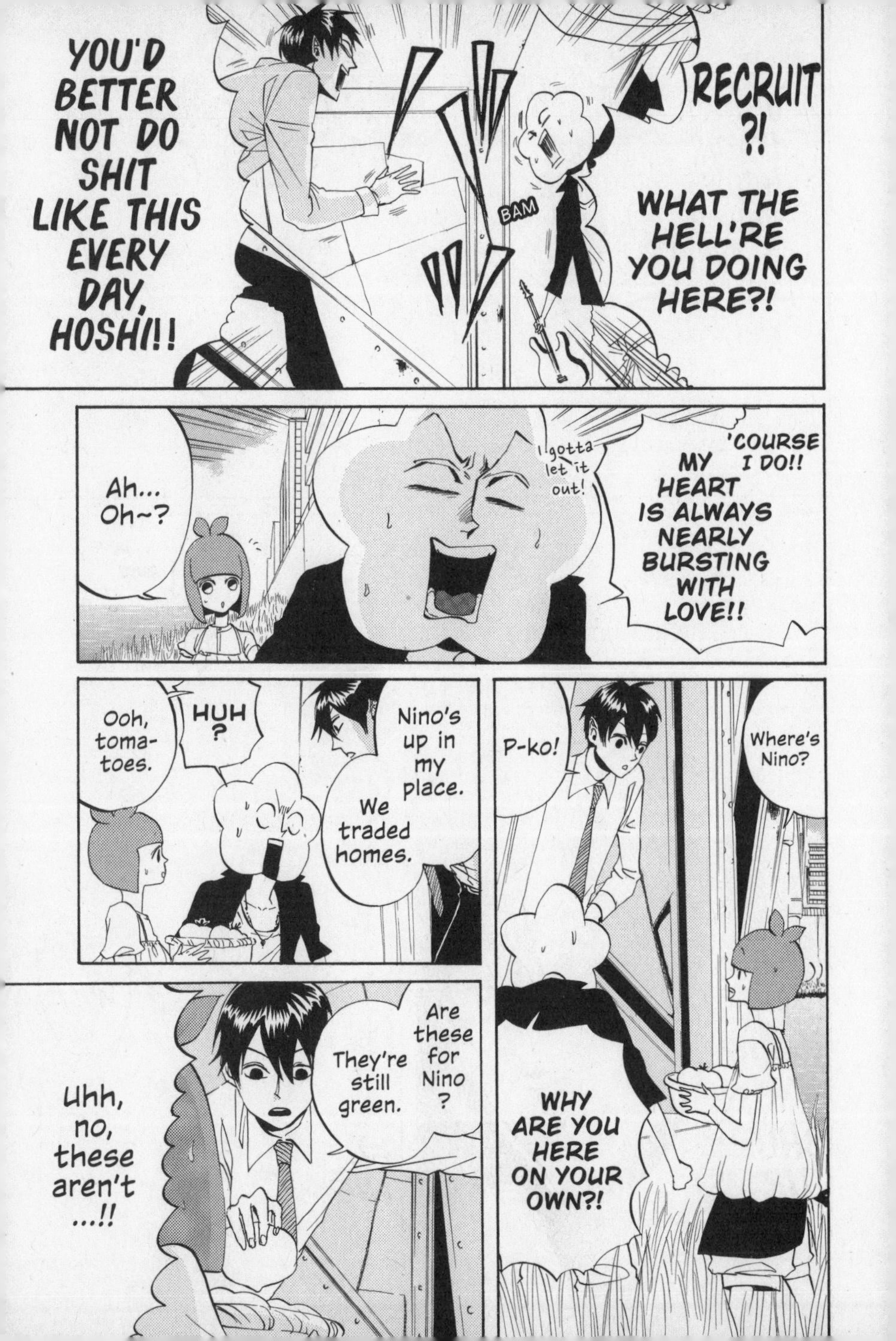
RECRUIT?!
WHAT THE HELL'RE YOU DOING HERE?!
BAM
YOU'D BETTER NOT DO SHIT LIKE THIS EVERY DAY, HOSHI!!
'COURSE I DO!! MY HEART IS ALWAYS NEARLY BURSTING WITH LOVE!!
I gotta let it out!
Ah... Oh~?
Where's Nino?
P-ko!
WHY ARE YOU HERE ON YOUR OWN?!
Nino's up in my place.
We traded homes.
HUH?
Ooh, toma-toes.
Are these for Nino?
They're still green.
Uhh, no, these aren't ...!!

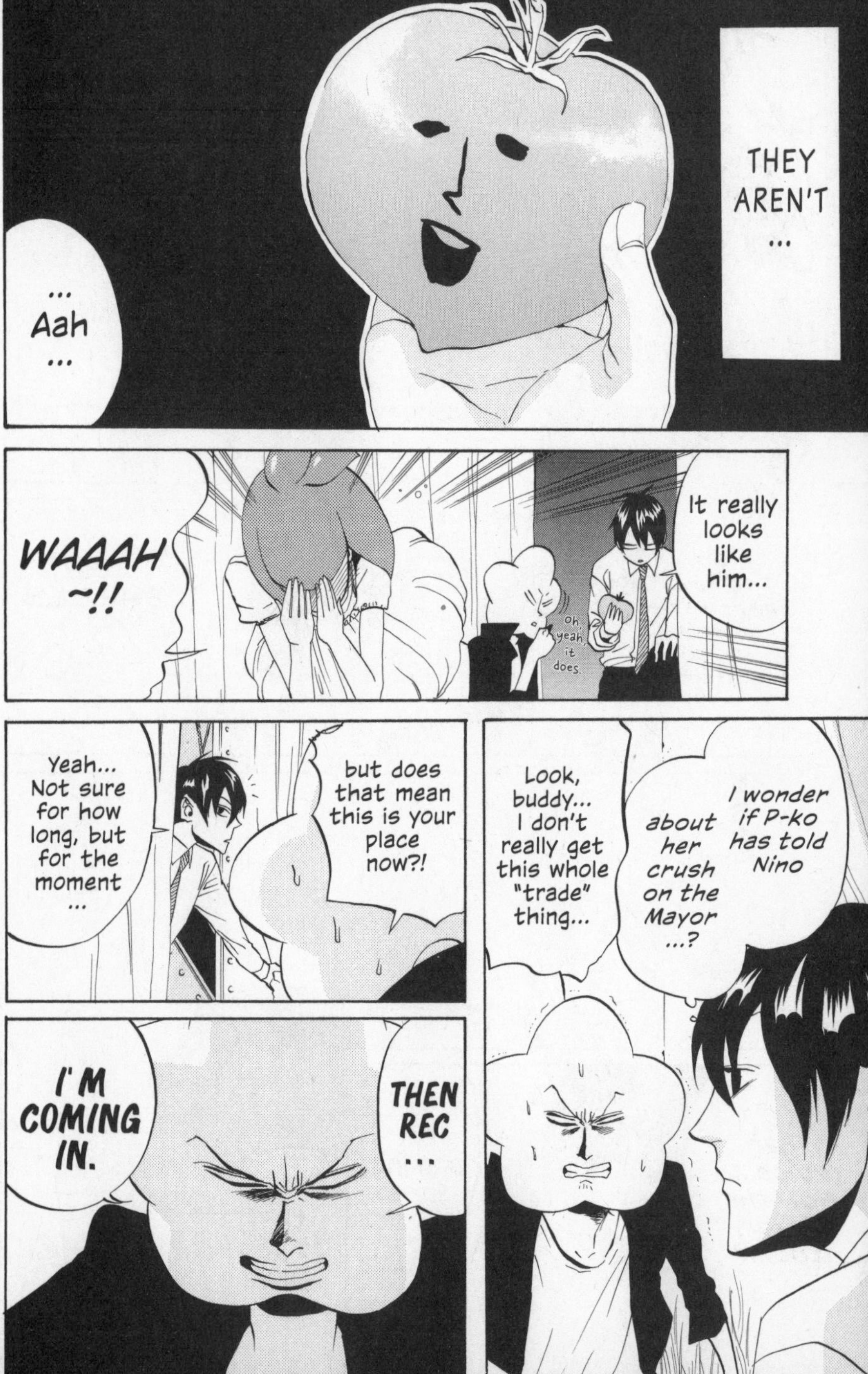
THEY AREN'T ...
... Aah ...
It really looks like him...
Oh, yeah, it does.
WAAAH ~!!
I wonder if P-ko has told Nino about her crush on the Mayor ...?
Look, buddy... I don't really get this whole "trade" thing...
but does that mean this is your place now?!
Yeah... Not sure for how long, but for the moment ...
THEN REC ...
I'M COMING IN.

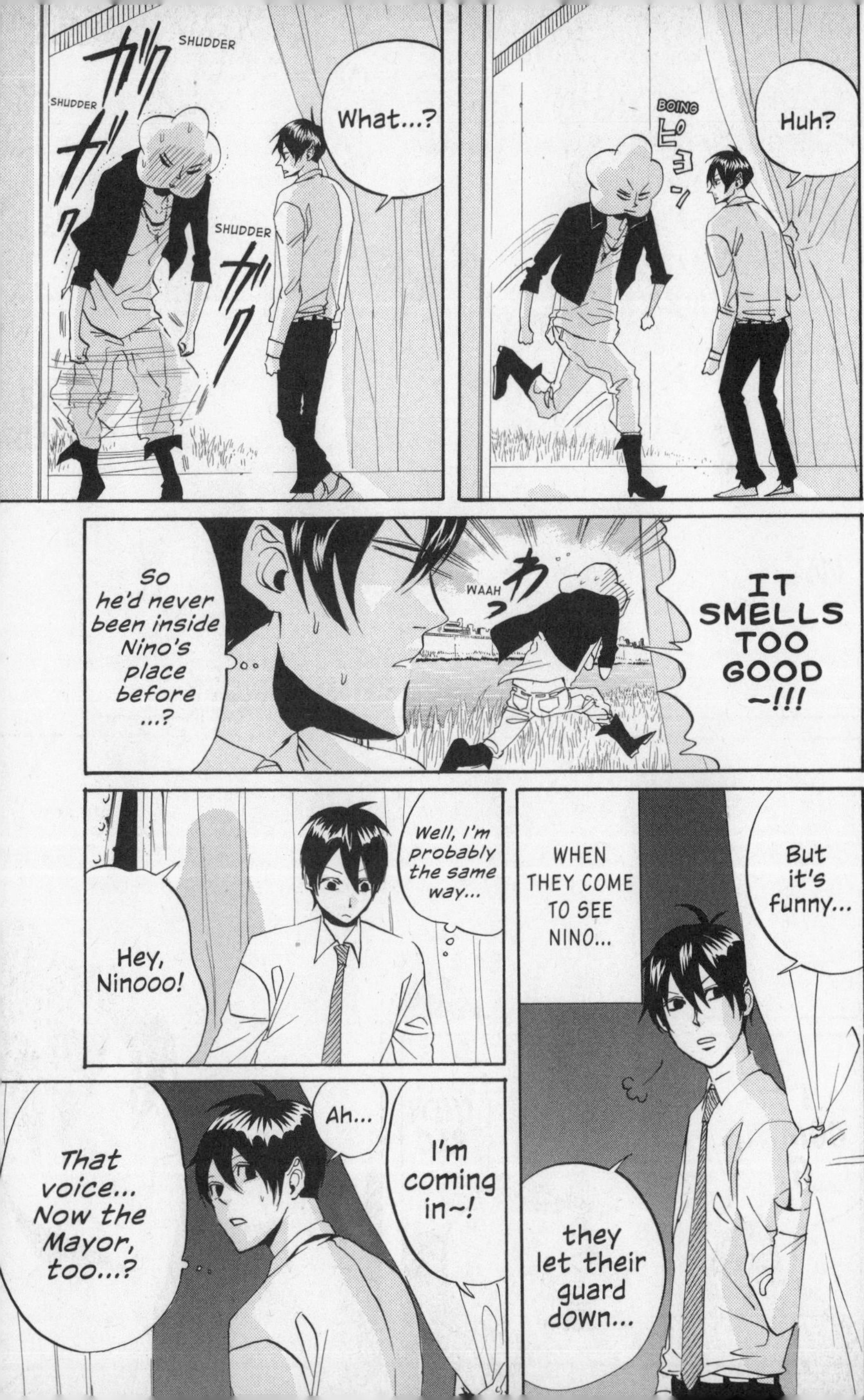

BOING
Huh?
SHUDDER
SHUDDER
SHUDDER
What...?
IT SMELLS TOO GOOD ~!!!
WAAH
So he'd never been inside Nino's place before ...?
But it's funny...
WHEN THEY COME TO SEE NINO...
they let their guard down...
Well, I'm probably the same way...
Hey, Ninooo!
I'm coming in~!
Ah...
That voice... Now the Mayor, too...?

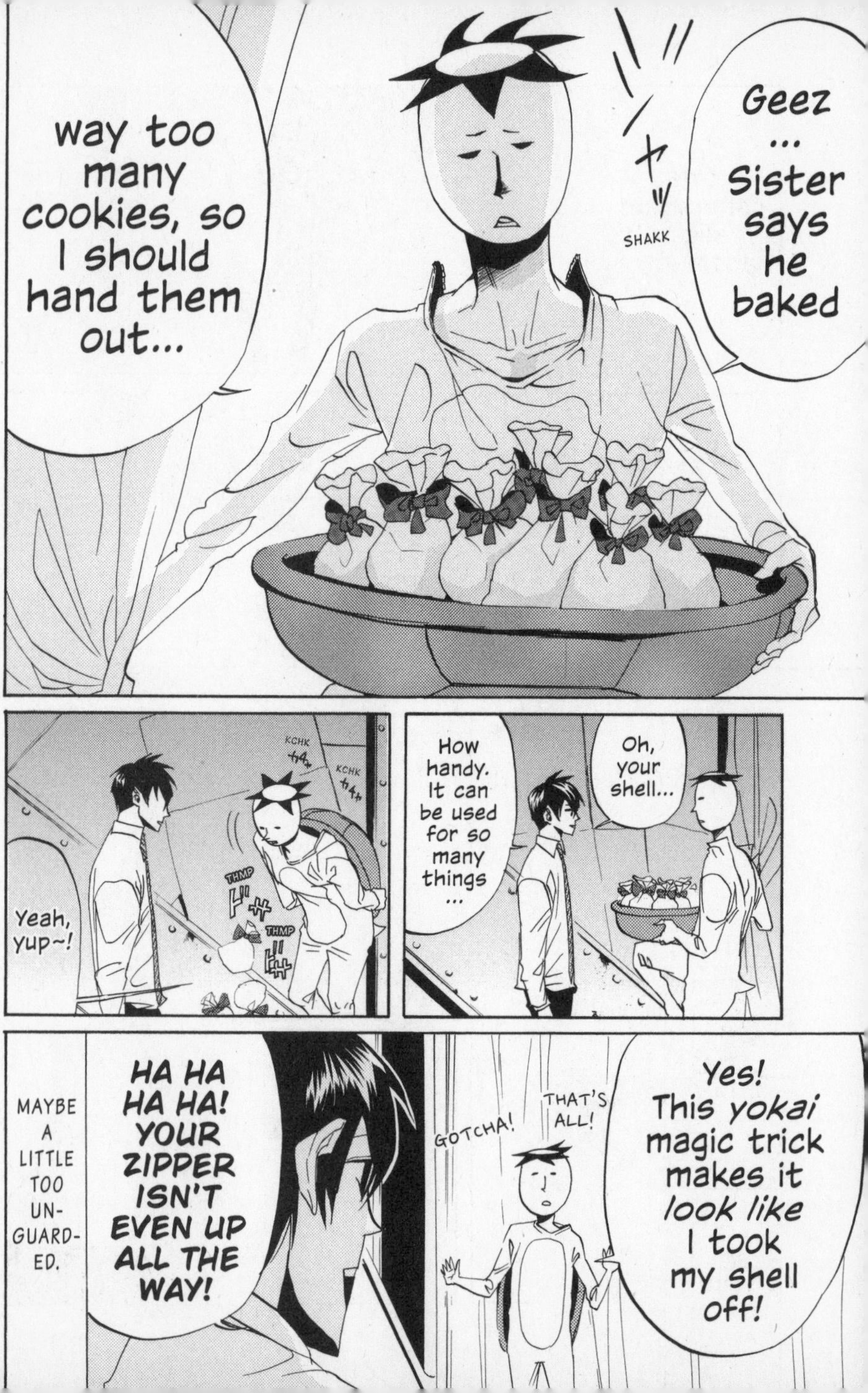
Geez ... Sister says he baked
way too many cookies, so I should hand them out...
SHAKK
Oh, your shell...
How handy. It can be used for so many things ...
KCHK
KCHK
THMP
THMP
Yeah, yup~!
Yes! This *yokai* magic trick makes it *look like* I took my shell off!
THAT'S ALL!
GOTCHA!
HA HA HA HA! YOUR ZIPPER ISN'T EVEN UP ALL THE WAY!
MAYBE A LITTLE TOO UN-GUARD-ED.

Chapter 113: Venusian

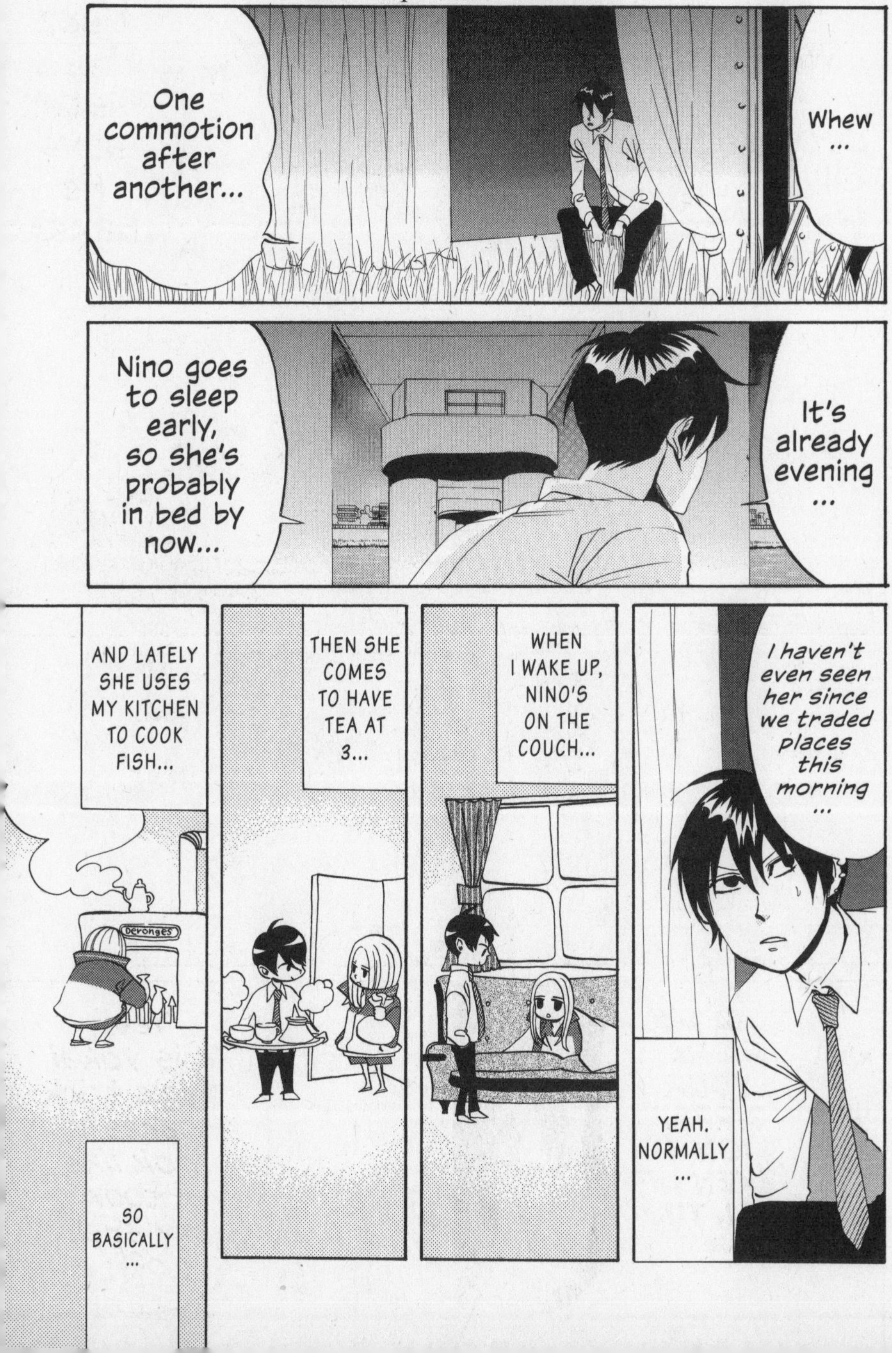
Whew ...
One commotion after another...
It's already evening ...
Nino goes to sleep early, so she's probably in bed by now...
I haven't even seen her since we traded places this morning ...
YEAH. NORMALLY ...
WHEN I WAKE UP, NINO'S ON THE COUCH...
THEN SHE COMES TO HAVE TEA AT 3...
AND LATELY SHE USES MY KITCHEN TO COOK FISH...
Devonges
SO BASICALLY ...

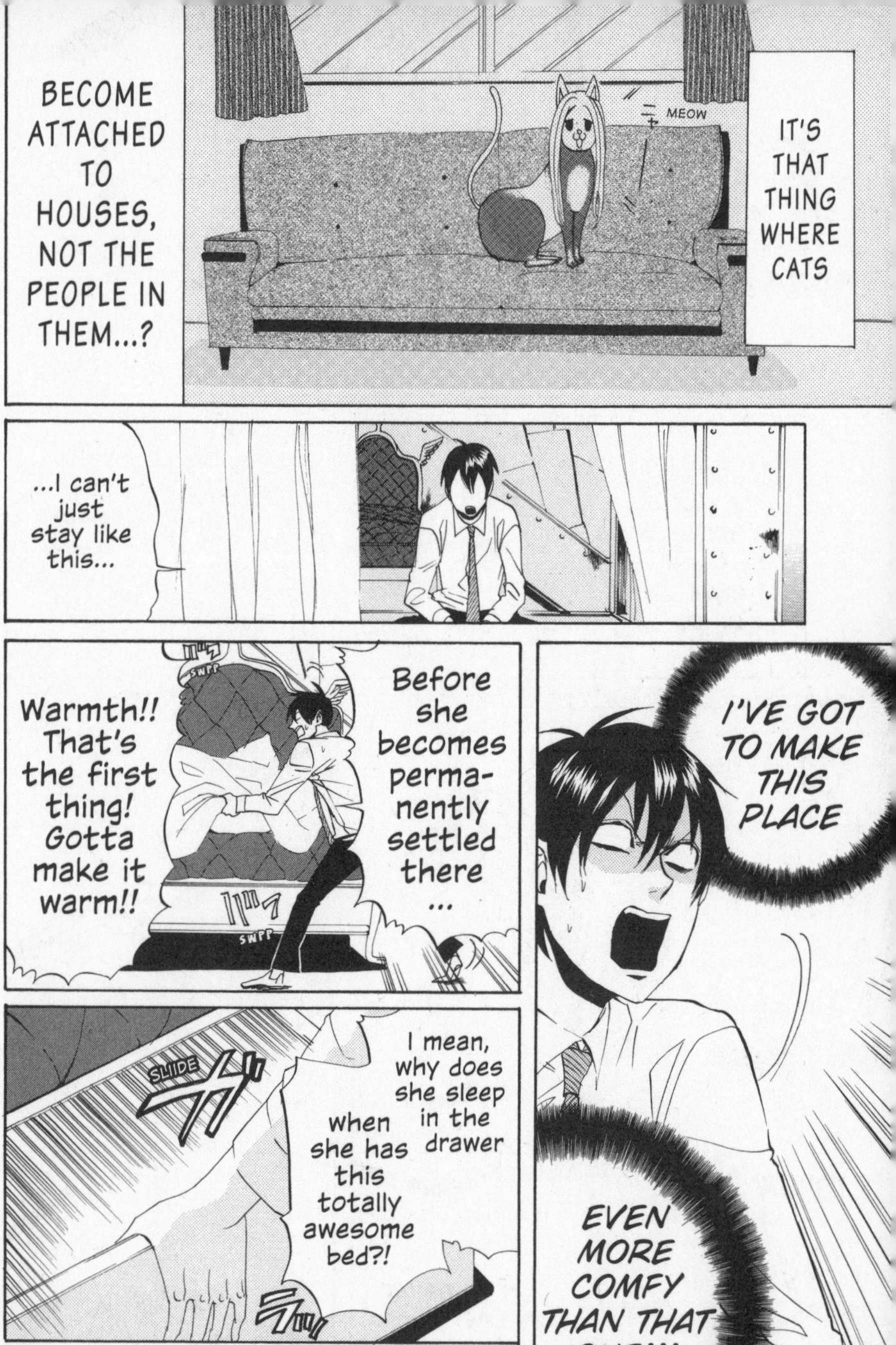
IT'S THAT THING WHERE CATS
MEOW
BECOME ATTACHED TO HOUSES, NOT THE PEOPLE IN THEM...?
...I can't just stay like this...
I'VE GOT TO MAKE THIS PLACE
EVEN MORE COMFY THAN THAT ONE!!!
Before she becomes perma-nently settled there ...
SWPP
Warmth!! That's the first thing! Gotta make it warm!!
SWPP
I mean, why does she sleep in the drawer when she has this totally awesome bed?!
SLIDE

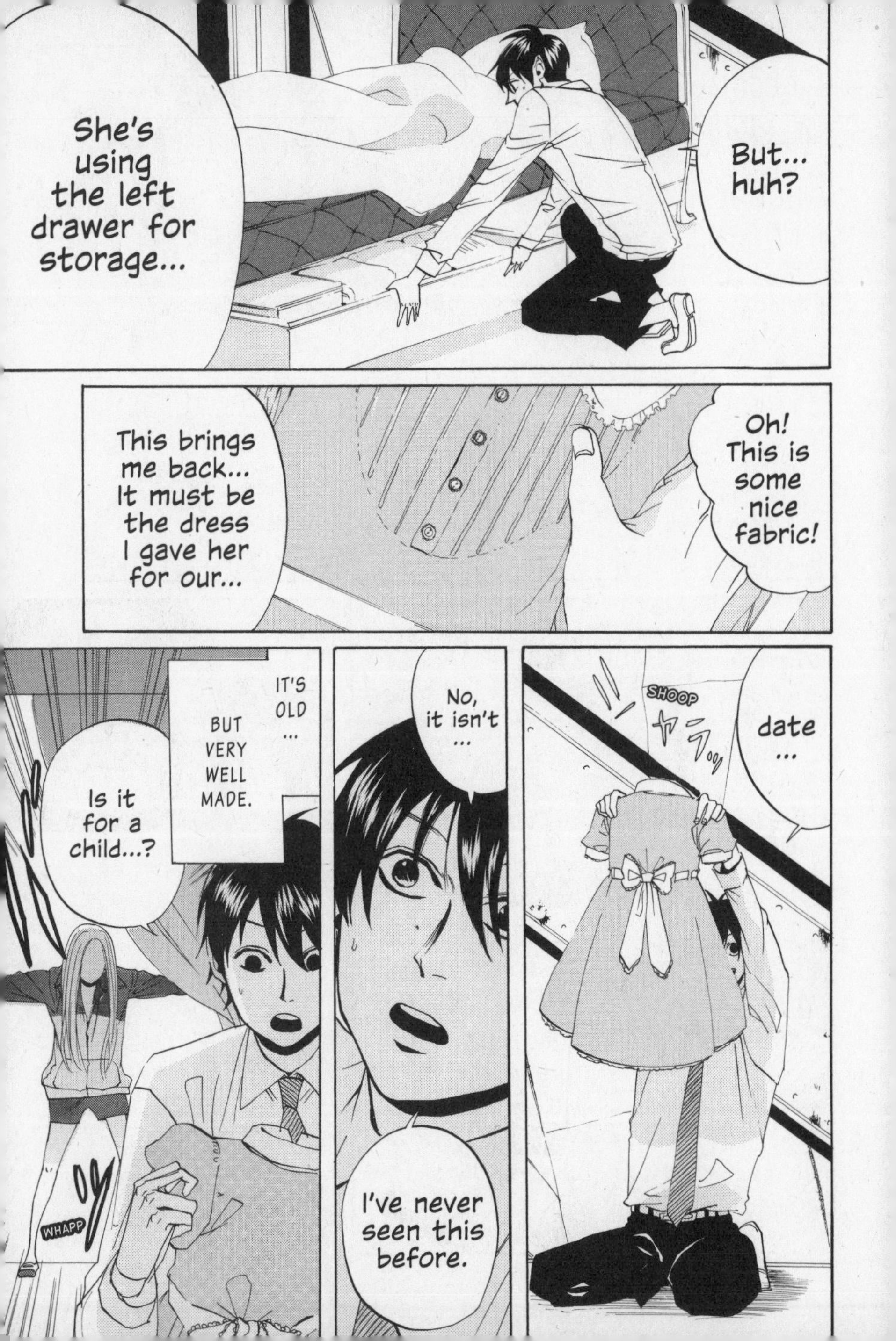
She's using the left drawer for storage...
But... huh?
Oh! This is some nice fabric!
This brings me back... It must be the dress I gave her for our...
date ...
SHOOP
No, it isn't ...
I've never seen this before.
IT'S OLD ...
BUT VERY WELL MADE.
Is it for a child...?
WHAPP

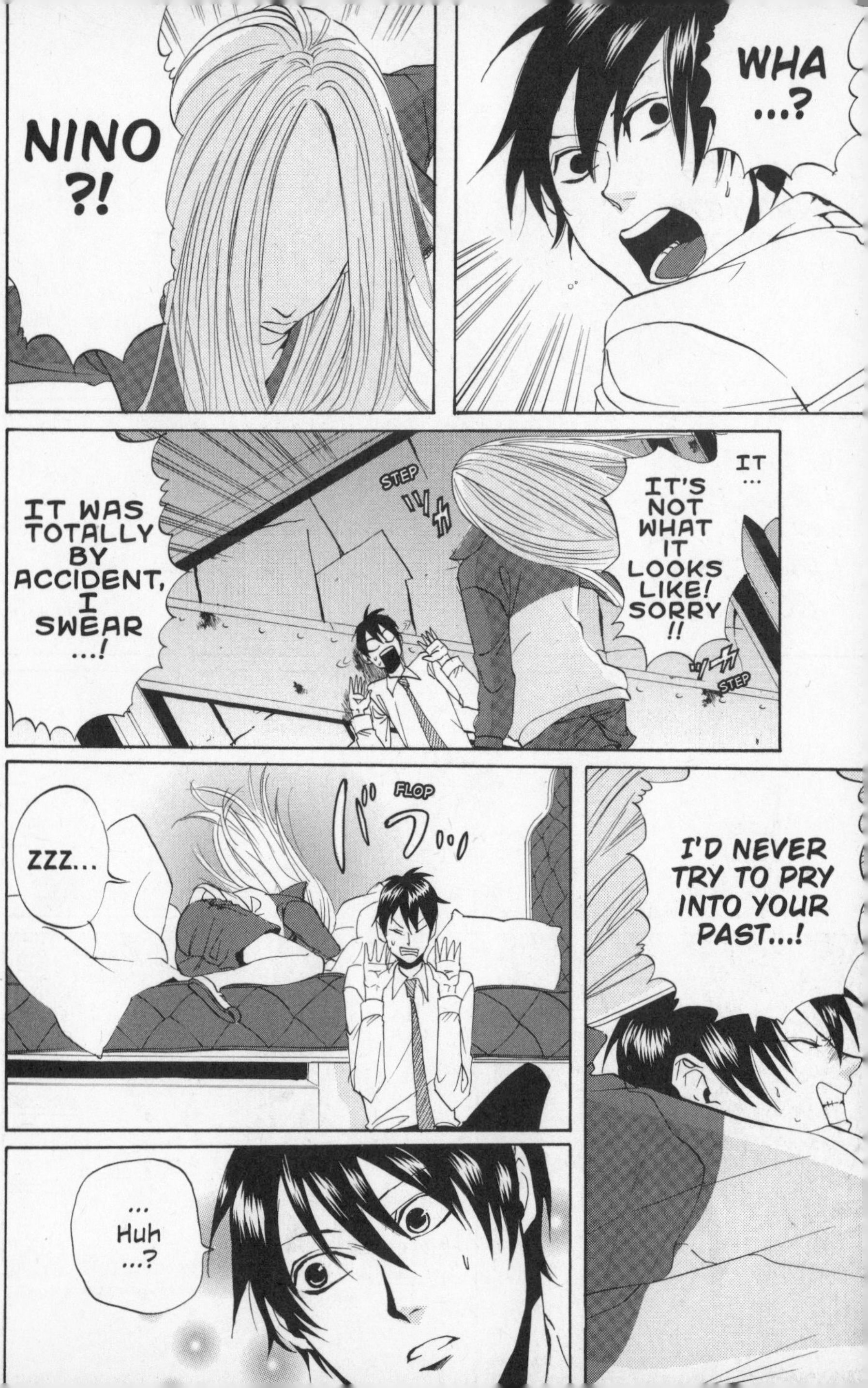
WHA ...?
NINO ?!
IT ...
IT'S NOT WHAT IT LOOKS LIKE! SORRY !!
STEP
STEP
IT WAS TOTALLY BY ACCIDENT, I SWEAR ...!
I'D NEVER TRY TO PRY INTO YOUR PAST...!
FLOP
ZZZ...
... Huh ...?

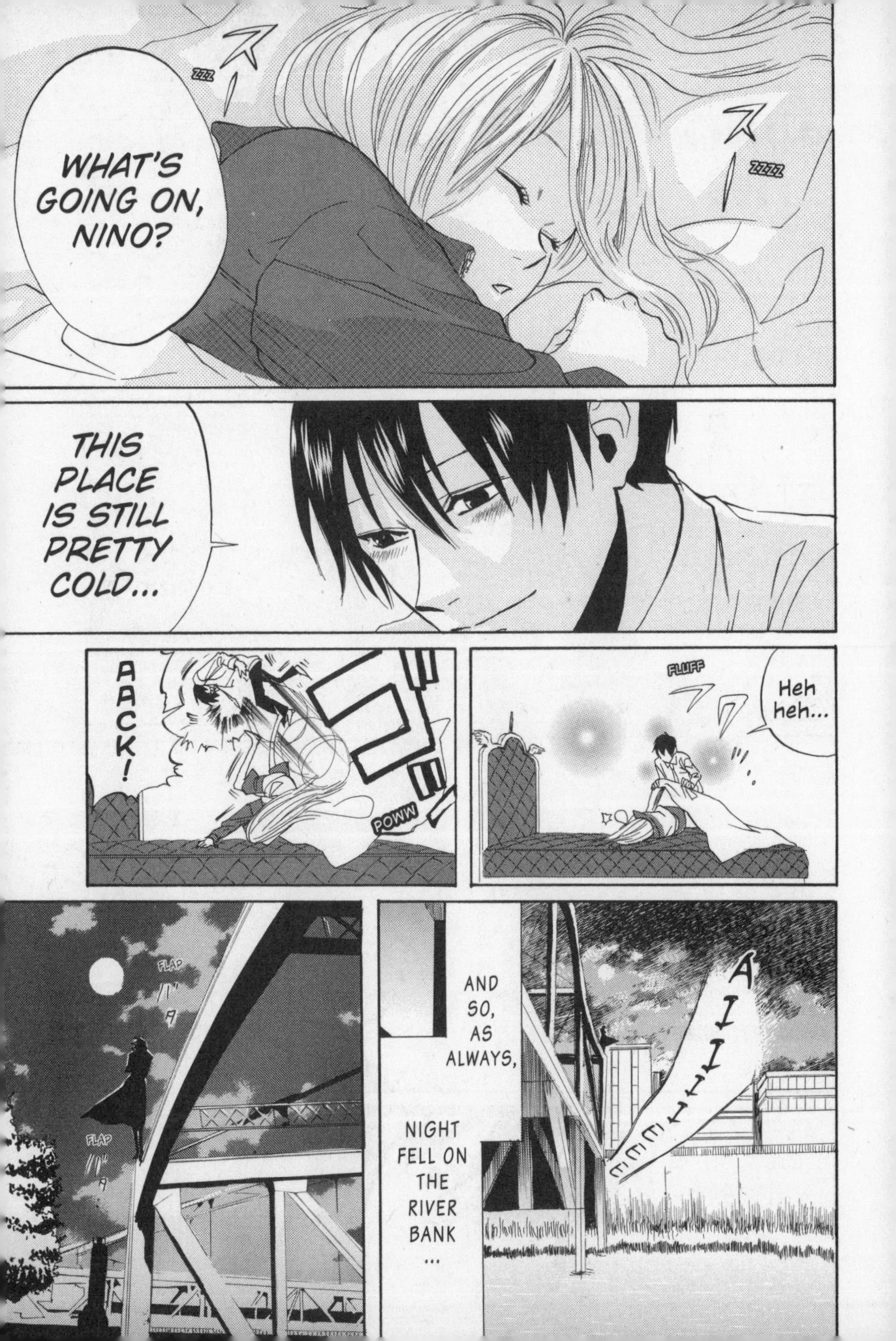
ZZZ
ZZZZ
WHAT'S GOING ON, NINO?
THIS PLACE IS STILL PRETTY COLD...
FLUFF
Heh heh...
AACK!
POWW
AND SO, AS ALWAYS,
NIGHT FELL ON THE RIVER BANK ...
AIIIIEEE
FLAP
FLAP

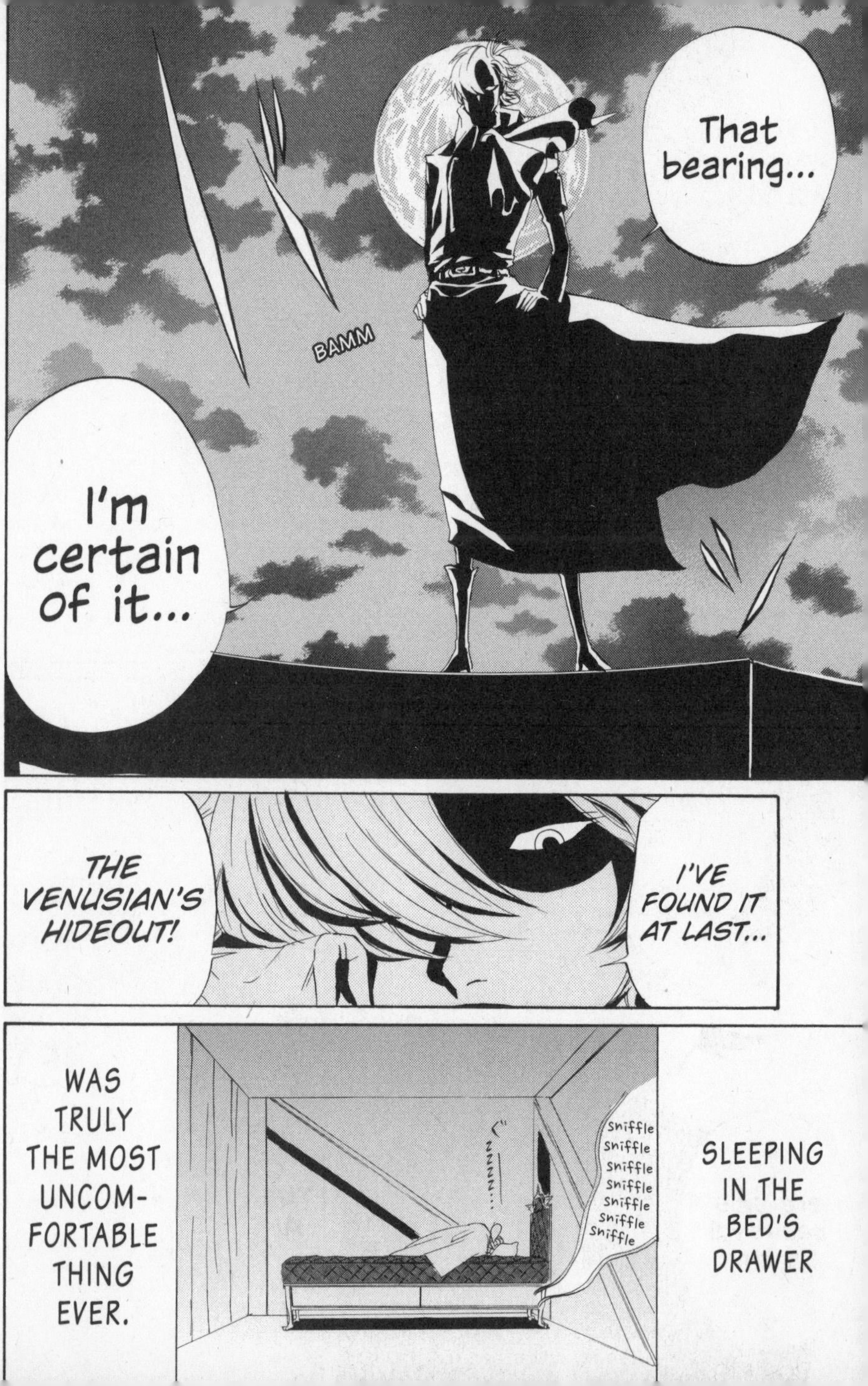
That bearing...
BAMM
I'm certain of it...
I'VE FOUND IT AT LAST...
THE VENUSIAN'S HIDEOUT!
SLEEPING IN THE BED'S DRAWER
sniffle sniffle sniffle sniffle sniffle sniffle sniffle
WAS TRULY THE MOST UNCOM-FORTABLE THING EVER.

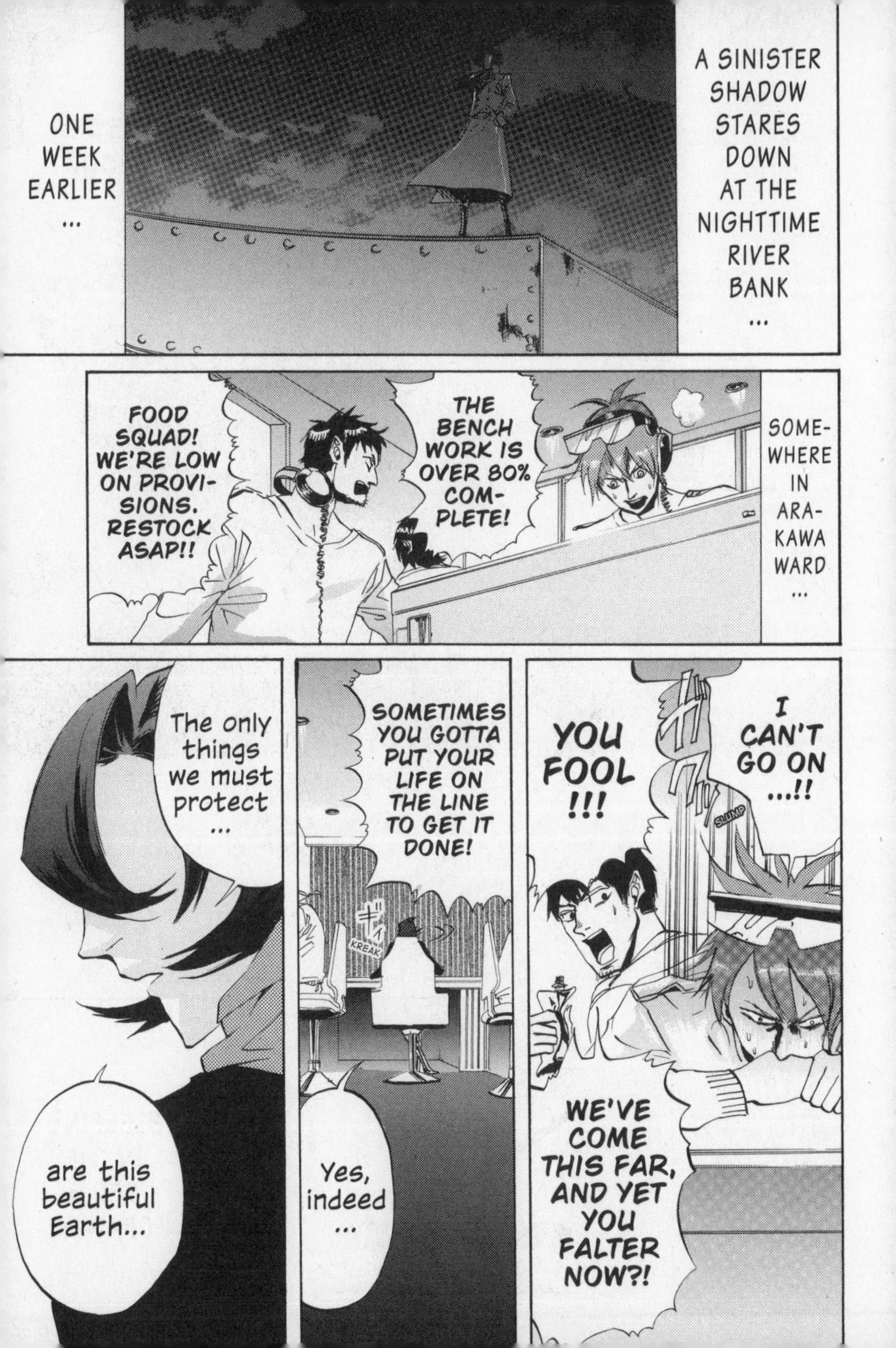

A SINISTER SHADOW STARES DOWN AT THE NIGHTTIME RIVER BANK ...
ONE WEEK EARLIER ...
SOMEWHERE IN ARAKAWA WARD ...
THE BENCH WORK IS OVER 80% COMPLETE!
FOOD SQUAD! WE'RE LOW ON PROVISIONS. RESTOCK ASAP!!
I CAN'T GO ON ...!!
SLUMP
YOU FOOL !!!
WE'VE COME THIS FAR, AND YET YOU FALTER NOW?!
SOMETIMES YOU GOTTA PUT YOUR LIFE ON THE LINE TO GET IT DONE!
KREAK
Yes, indeed ...
The only things we must protect ...
are this beautiful Earth...

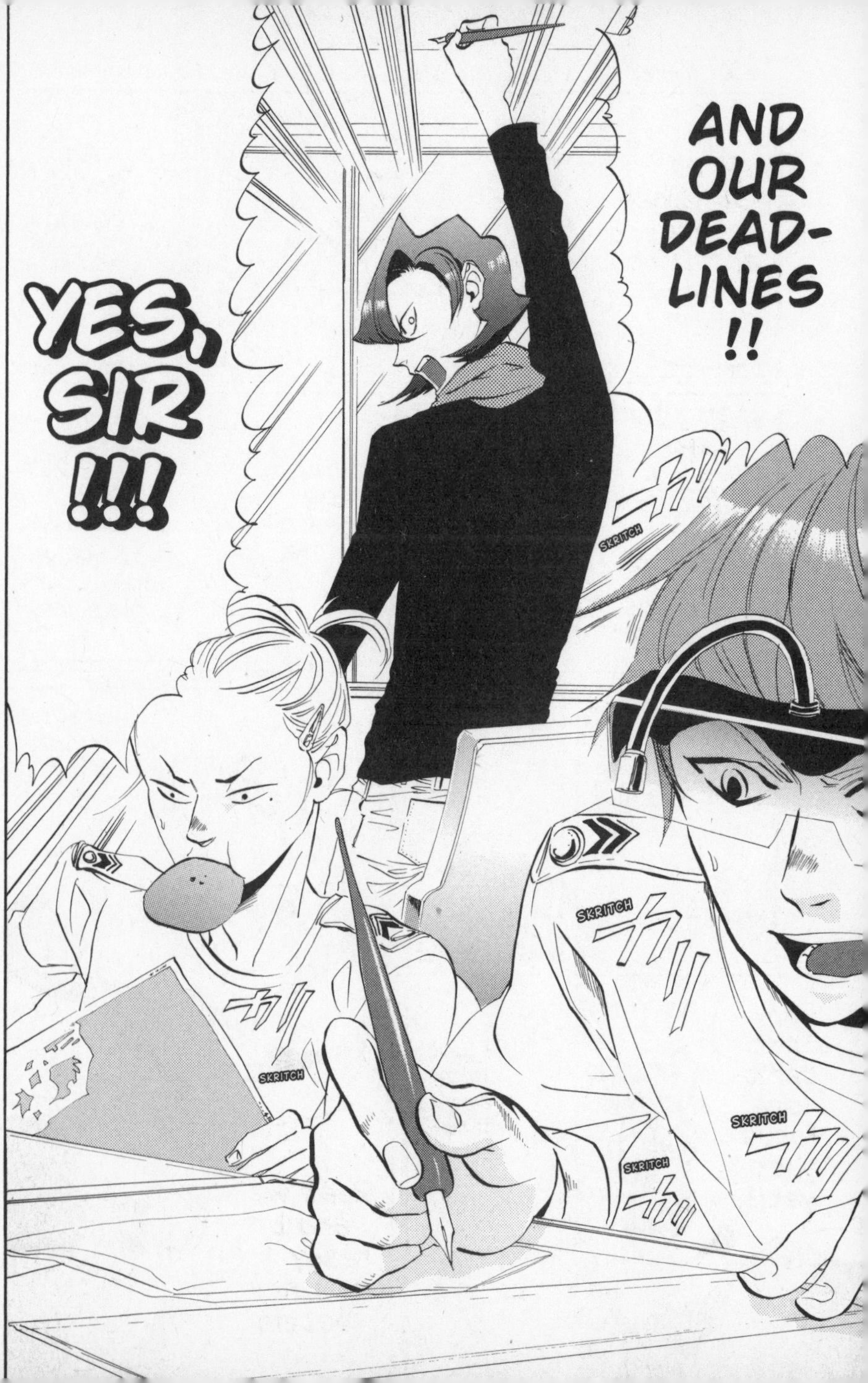
AND OUR DEAD-LINES !!
YES, SIR !!!!
SKRITCH
SKRITCH
SKRITCH
SKRITCH
SKRITCH

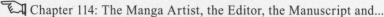

Chapter 114: The Manga Artist, the Editor, the Manuscript and...

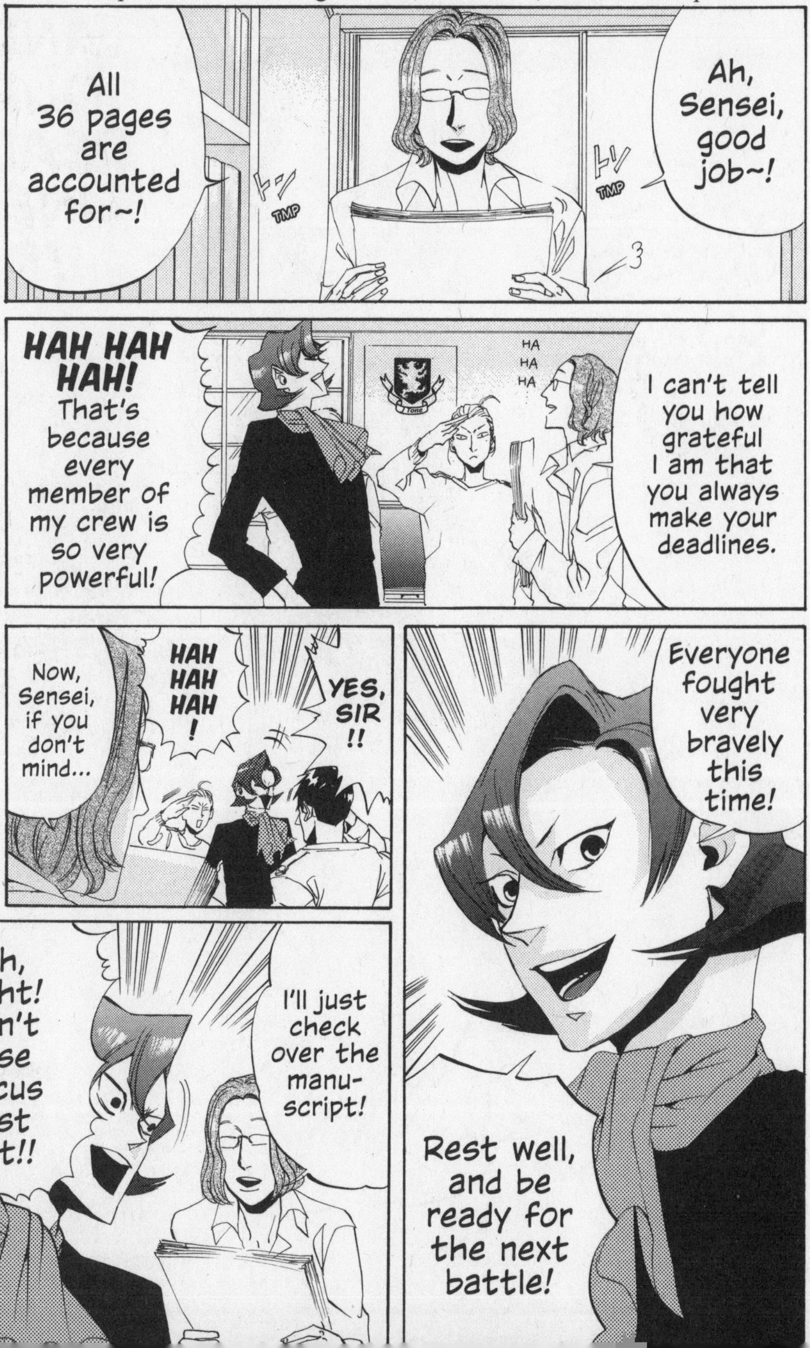
Ah, Sensei, good job~!
TMP
TMP
All 36 pages are accounted for~!
I can't tell you how grateful I am that you always make your deadlines.
HA HA HA
HAH HAH HAH! That's because every member of my crew is so very powerful!
Everyone fought very bravely this time!
Rest well, and be ready for the next battle!
YES, SIR!!
HAH HAH HAH!
Now, Sensei, if you don't mind...
I'll just check over the manu-script!
Oh, right! Can't lose focus just yet!!

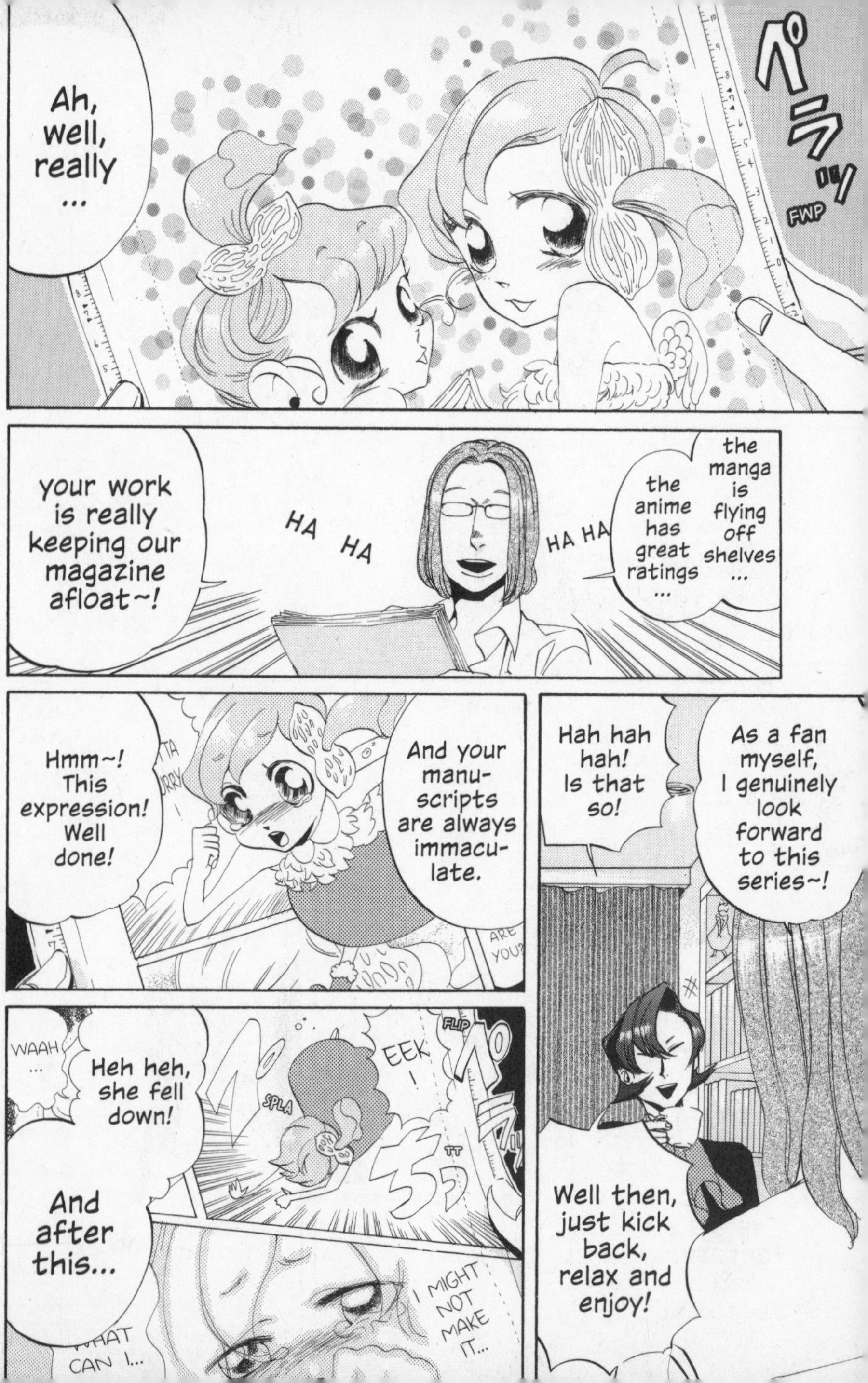
FWP
Ah, well, really ...
the manga is flying off shelves ...
the anime has great ratings ...
HA HA
HA HA
your work is really keeping our magazine afloat~!
As a fan myself, I genuinely look forward to this series~!
Hah hah hah! Is that so!
Well then, just kick back, relax and enjoy!
And your manu-scripts are always immacu-late.
Hmm~! This expression! Well done!
ARE YOU?
FLIP
EEK!
SPLA
Heh heh, she fell down!
WAAH ...
And after this...
I MIGHT NOT MAKE IT...
WHAT CAN I...

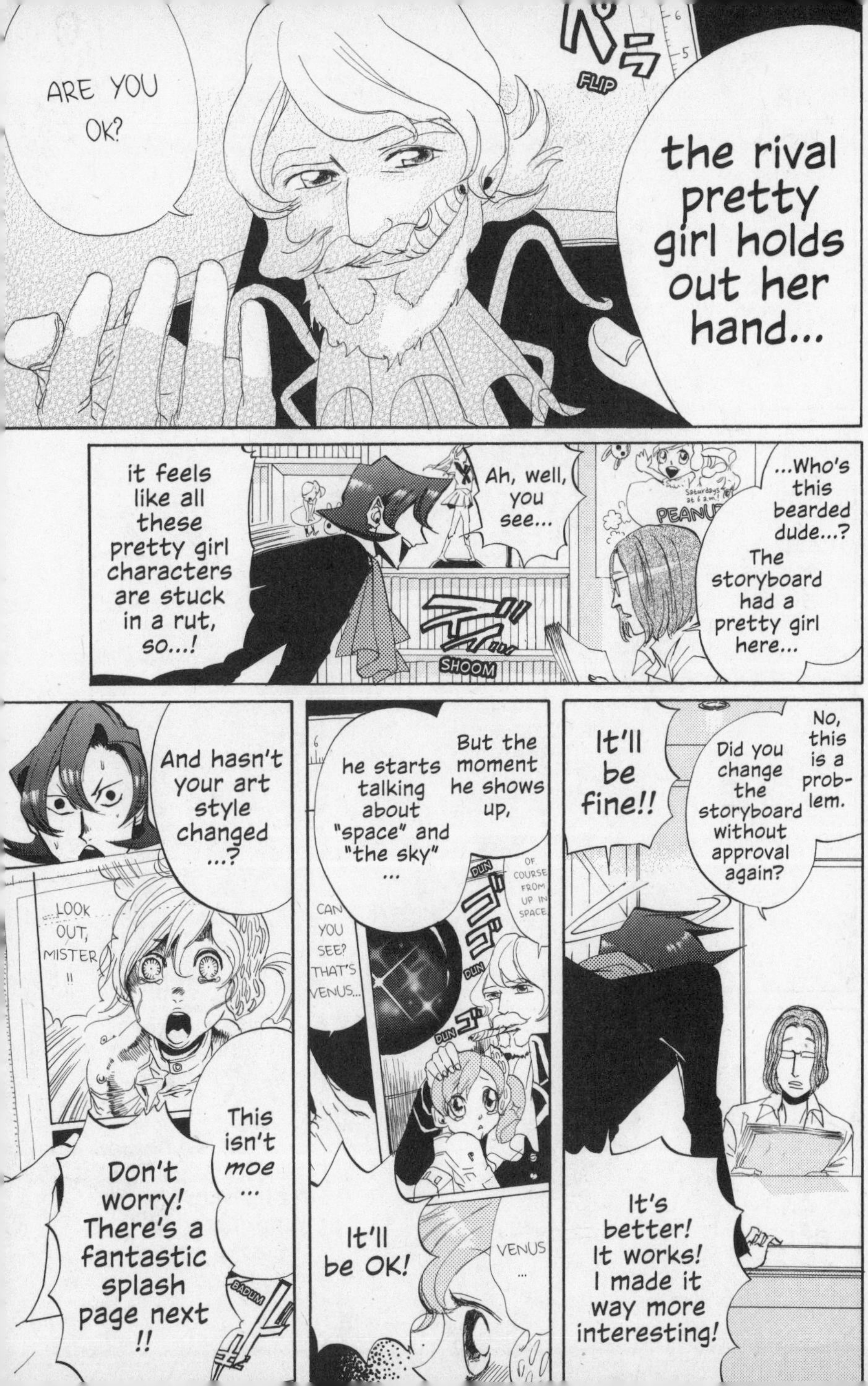
FLIP
the rival pretty girl holds out her hand...
ARE YOU OK?
...Who's this bearded dude...? The storyboard had a pretty girl here...
Saturdays at 6 a.m.!
Ah, well, you see...
SHOOM
it feels like all these pretty girl characters are stuck in a rut, so...!
No, this is a prob-lem.
Did you change the storyboard without approval again?
It'll be fine!!
It's better! It works! I made it way more interesting!
But the moment he shows up,
he starts talking about "space" and "the sky" ...
OF COURSE FROM UP IN SPACE
DUN
DUN
CAN YOU SEE? THAT'S VENUS...
DUN
It'll be OK!
VENUS ...
And hasn't your art style changed ...?
LOOK OUT, MISTER !!
This isn't *moe* ...
Don't worry! There's a fantastic splash page next !!
BADLIM

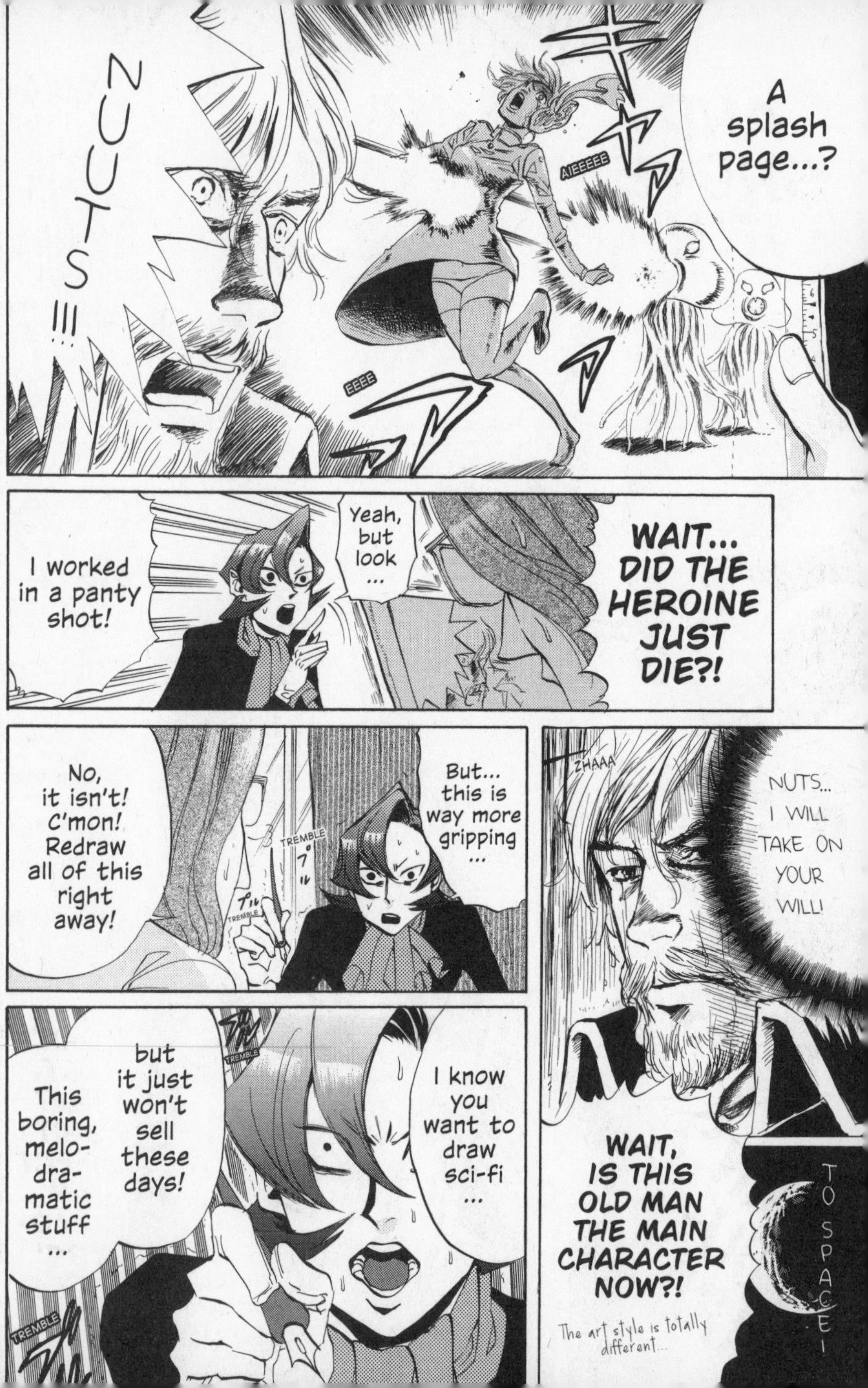
A splash page...?
AIEEEEE
NUUTS!!!
EEEE
WAIT... DID THE HEROINE JUST DIE?!
Yeah, but look ...
I worked in a panty shot!
ZHAAA
NUTS... I WILL TAKE ON YOUR WILL!
TO SPACE!
WAIT, IS THIS OLD MAN THE MAIN CHARACTER NOW?!
The art style is totally different...
But... this is way more gripping ...
TREMBLE
TREMBLE
No, it isn't! C'mon! Redraw all of this right away!
TREMBLE
I know you want to draw sci-fi ...
but it just won't sell these days!
This boring, melo-dramatic stuff ...
TREMBLE

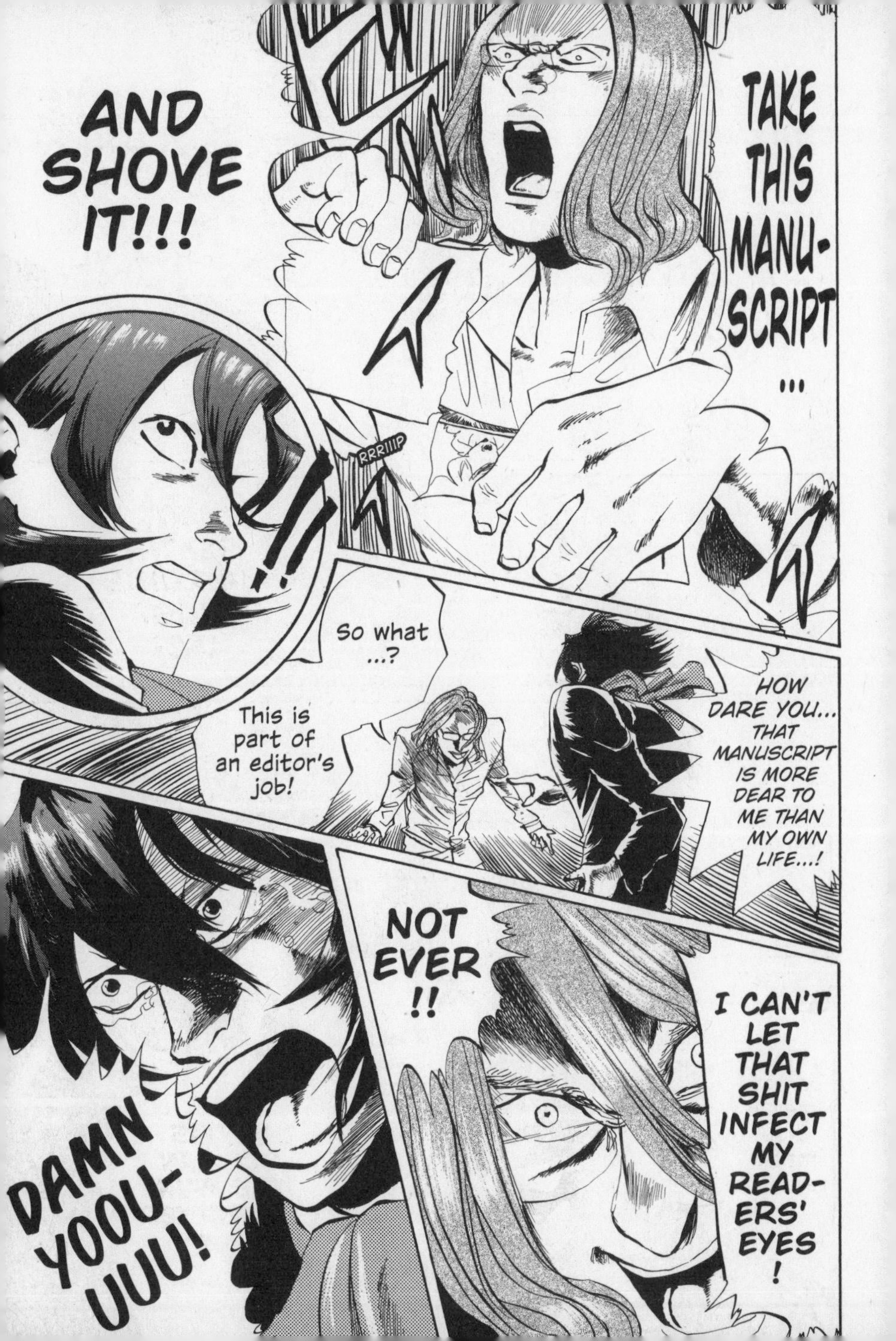
TAKE THIS MANU-SCRIPT ...
AND SHOVE IT!!!
RRRIIIP
!!
HOW DARE YOU... THAT MANUSCRIPT IS MORE DEAR TO ME THAN MY OWN LIFE...!
So what ...?
This is part of an editor's job!
I CAN'T LET THAT SHIT INFECT MY READ-ERS' EYES !
NOT EVER !!
DAMN YOOU-UUU!

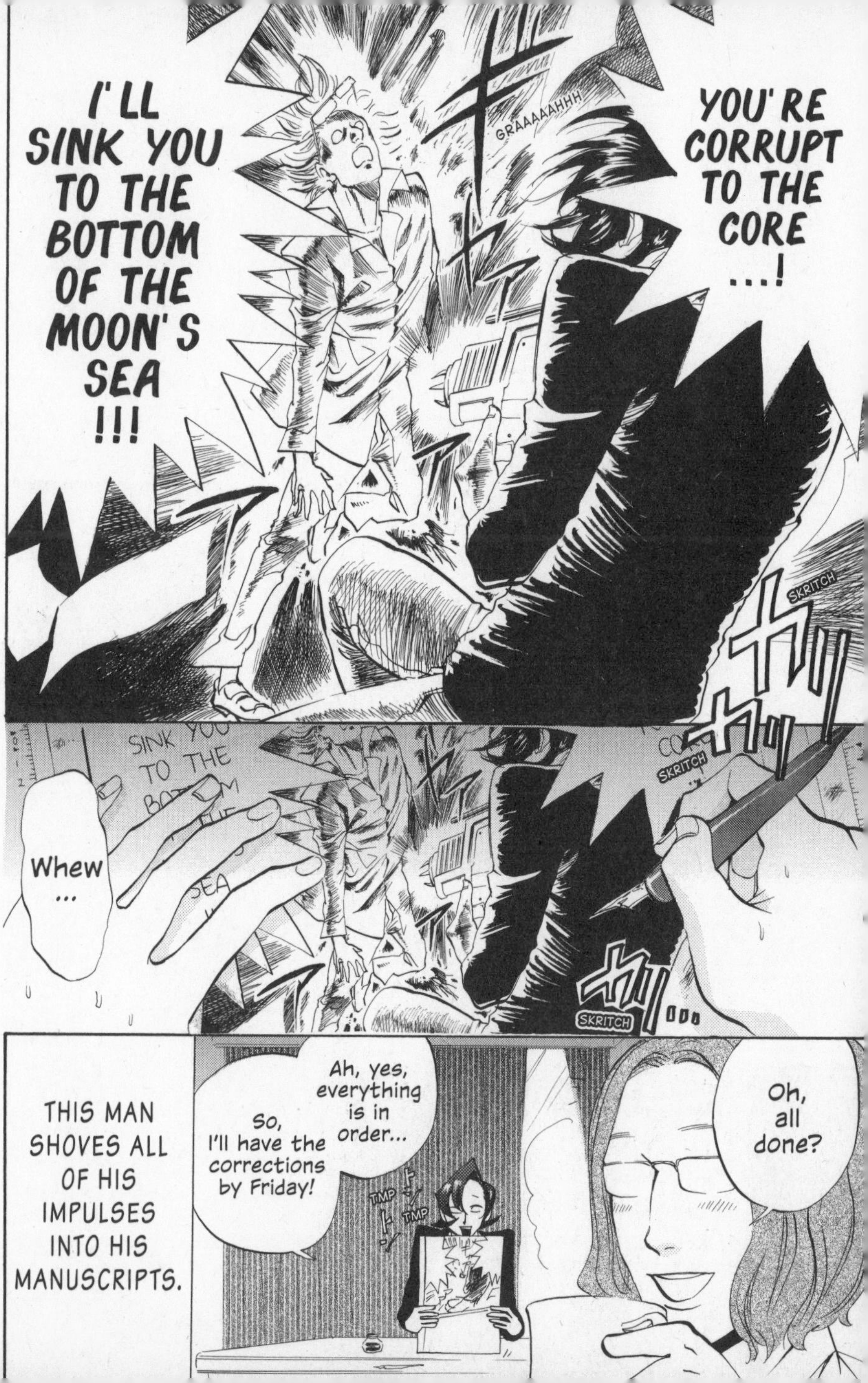
YOU'RE CORRUPT TO THE CORE ...!
I'LL SINK YOU TO THE BOTTOM OF THE MOON'S SEA !!!
GRAAAAAHHH
SKRITCH
SKRITCH
SINK YOU TO THE BOTTOM
SEA
CORE
Whew ...
SKRITCH
Oh, all done?
Ah, yes, everything is in order...
So, I'll have the corrections by Friday!
TMP
TMP
THIS MAN SHOVES ALL OF HIS IMPULSES INTO HIS MANUSCRIPTS.

Chapter 115: Illusion

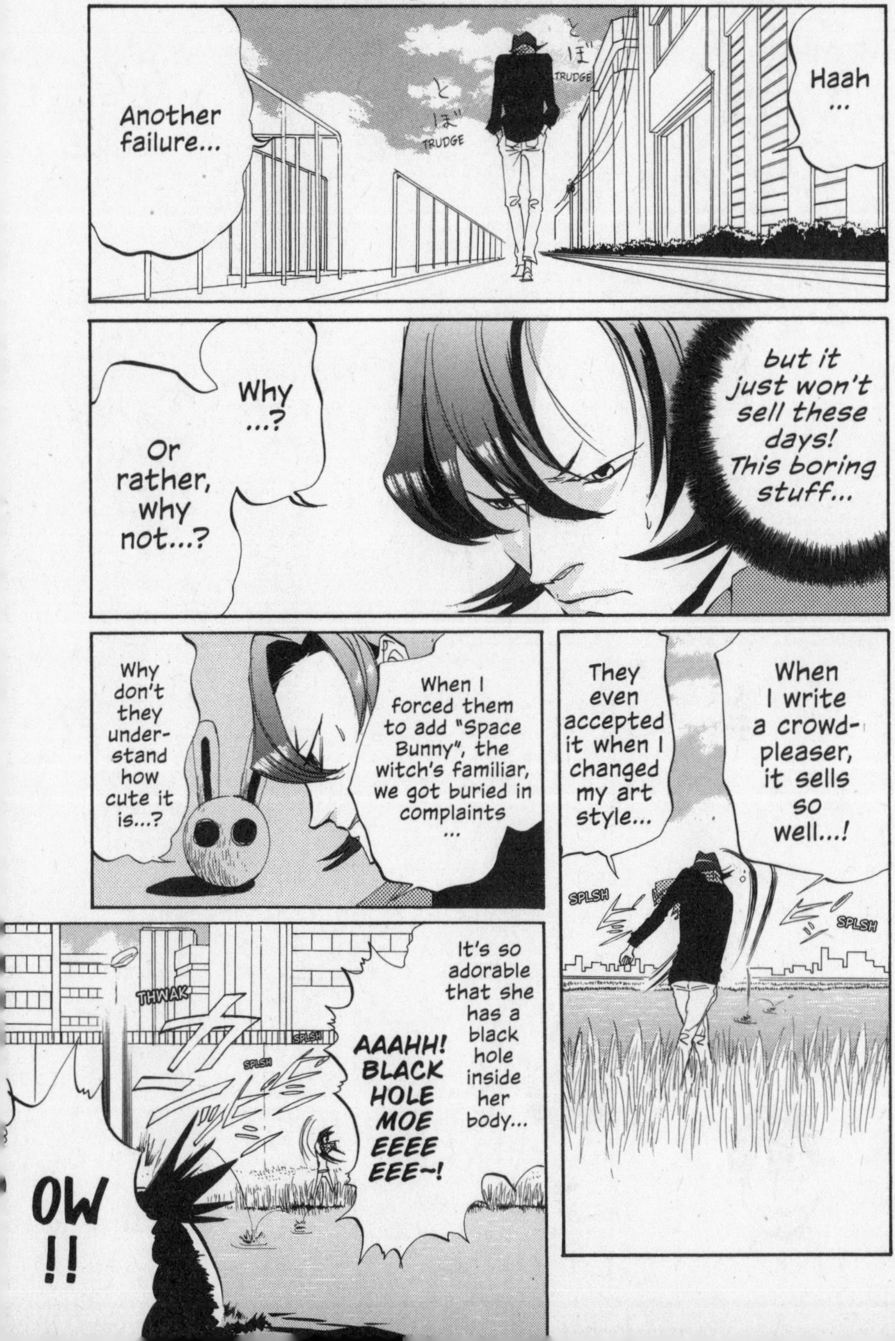

Haah ...
とぼ
TRUDGE
Another failure...
とぼ
TRUDGE
but it just won't sell these days! This boring stuff...
Why ...?
Or rather, why not...?
When I write a crowd-pleaser, it sells so well...!
They even accepted it when I changed my art style...
SPLSH
SPLSH
When I forced them to add "Space Bunny", the witch's familiar, we got buried in complaints ...
Why don't they understand how cute it is...?
It's so adorable that she has a black hole inside her body...
AAAHH! BLACK HOLE MOE EEEE EEE~!
THWAK
SPLSH
SPLSH
OW !!

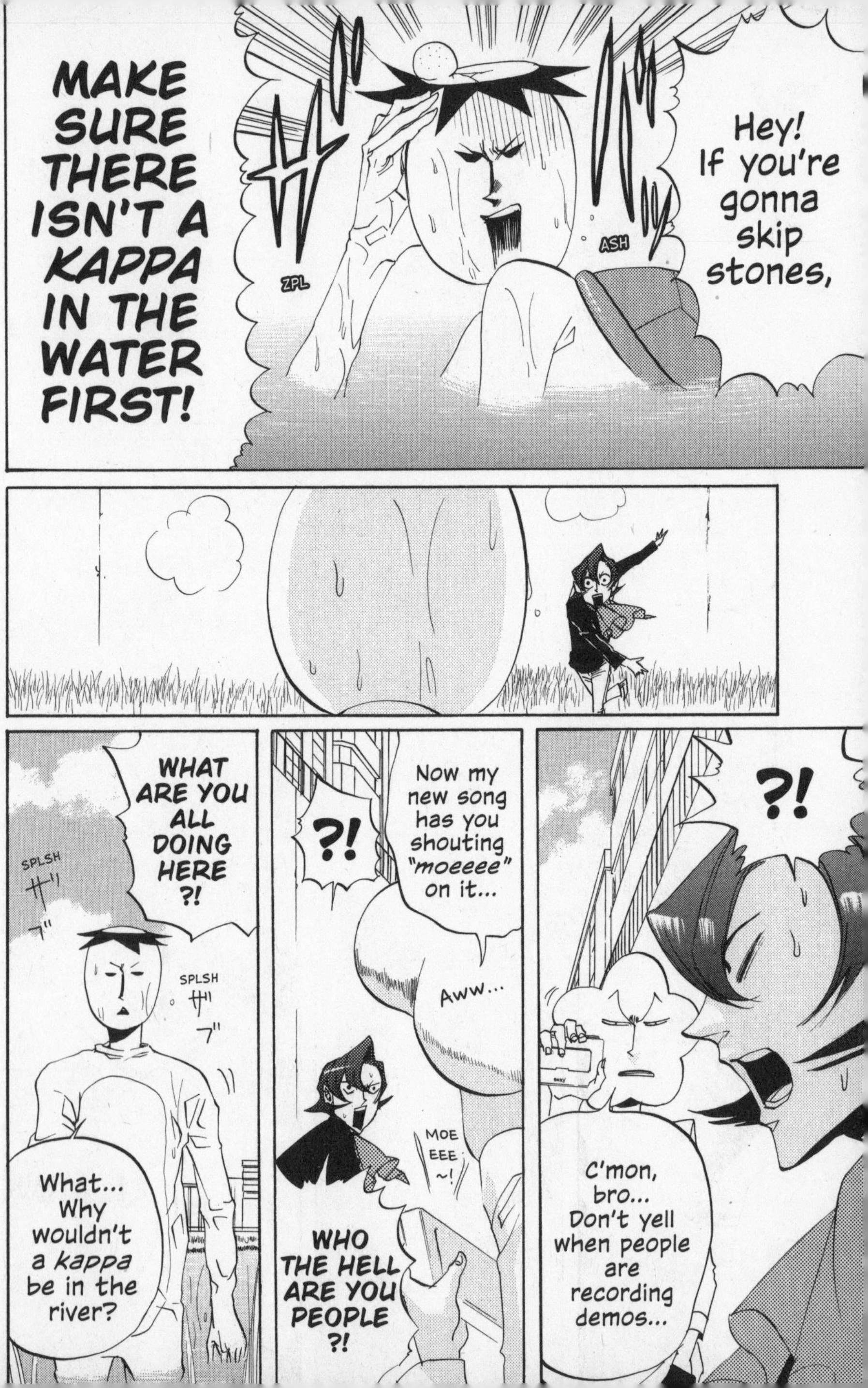
Hey! If you're gonna skip stones,
MAKE SURE THERE ISN'T A *KAPPA* IN THE WATER FIRST!
ASH
ZPL
?!
C'mon, bro... Don't yell when people are recording demos...
Now my new song has you shouting "*moeeee*" on it...
?!
Aww...
MOE EEE ~!
WHO THE HELL ARE YOU PEOPLE ?!
WHAT ARE YOU ALL DOING HERE ?!
SPLSH
SPLSH
What... Why wouldn't a *kappa* be in the river?

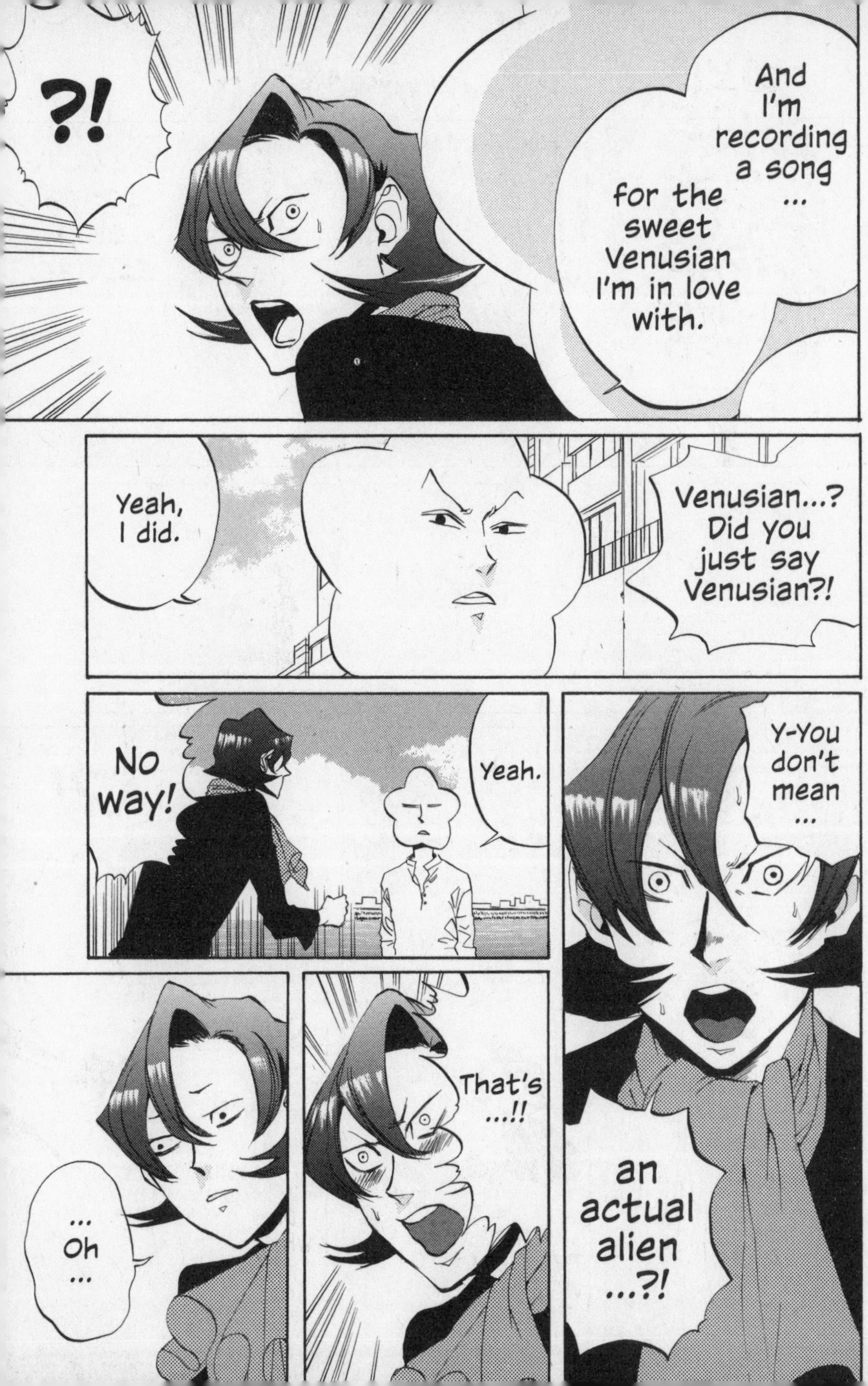
And I'm recording a song ... for the sweet Venusian I'm in love with.
?!
Venusian...? Did you just say Venusian?!
Yeah, I did.
Y-You don't mean ...
an actual alien ...?!
Yeah.
No way!
That's ...!!
... Oh ...

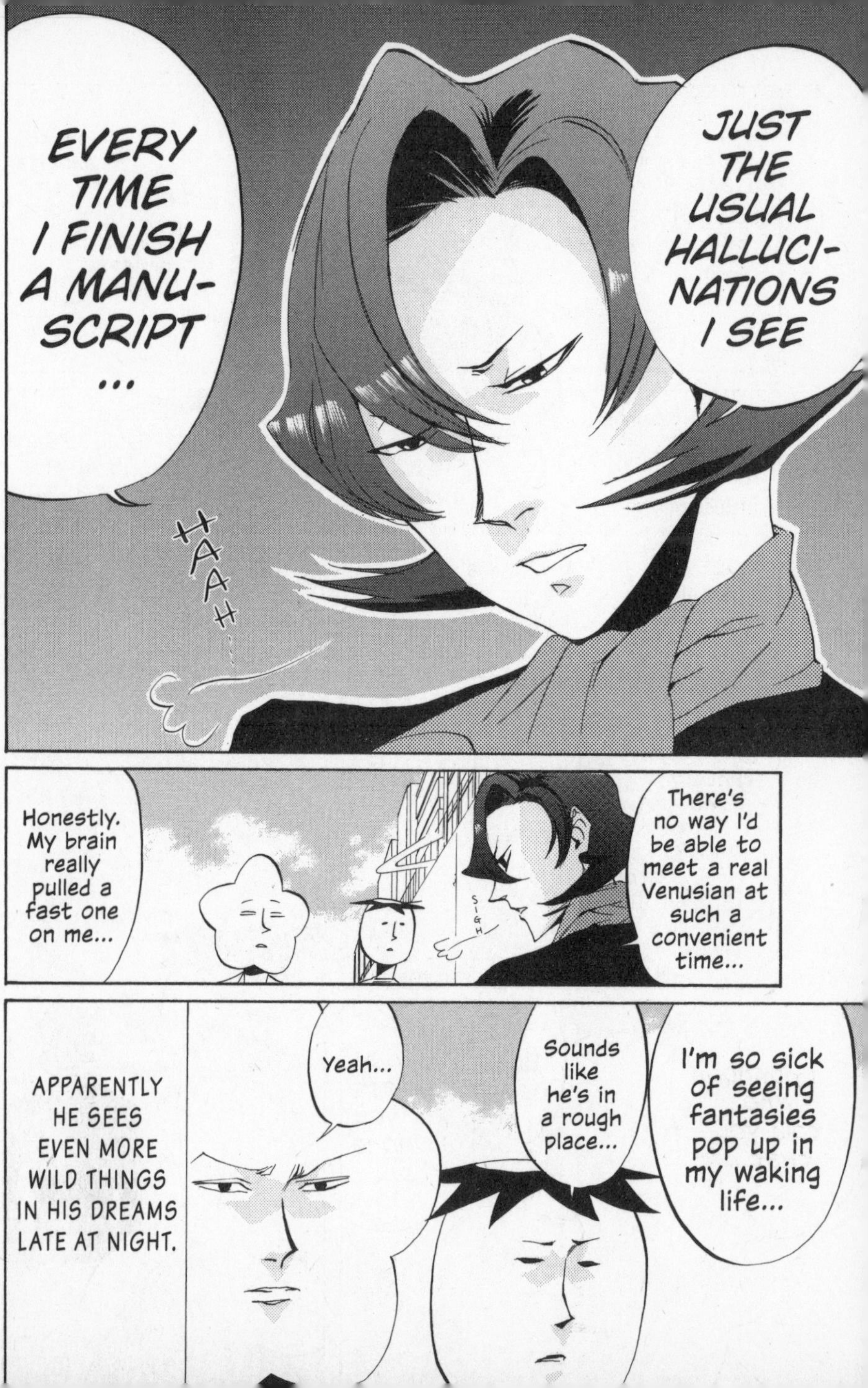
JUST THE USUAL HALLUCI-NATIONS I SEE
EVERY TIME I FINISH A MANU-SCRIPT ...
HAAAH...
There's no way I'd be able to meet a real Venusian at such a convenient time...
SIGH
Honestly. My brain really pulled a fast one on me...
I'm so sick of seeing fantasies pop up in my waking life...
Sounds like he's in a rough place...
Yeah...
APPARENTLY HE SEES EVEN MORE WILD THINGS IN HIS DREAMS LATE AT NIGHT.

Chapter 116: And On Top of the Bridge...

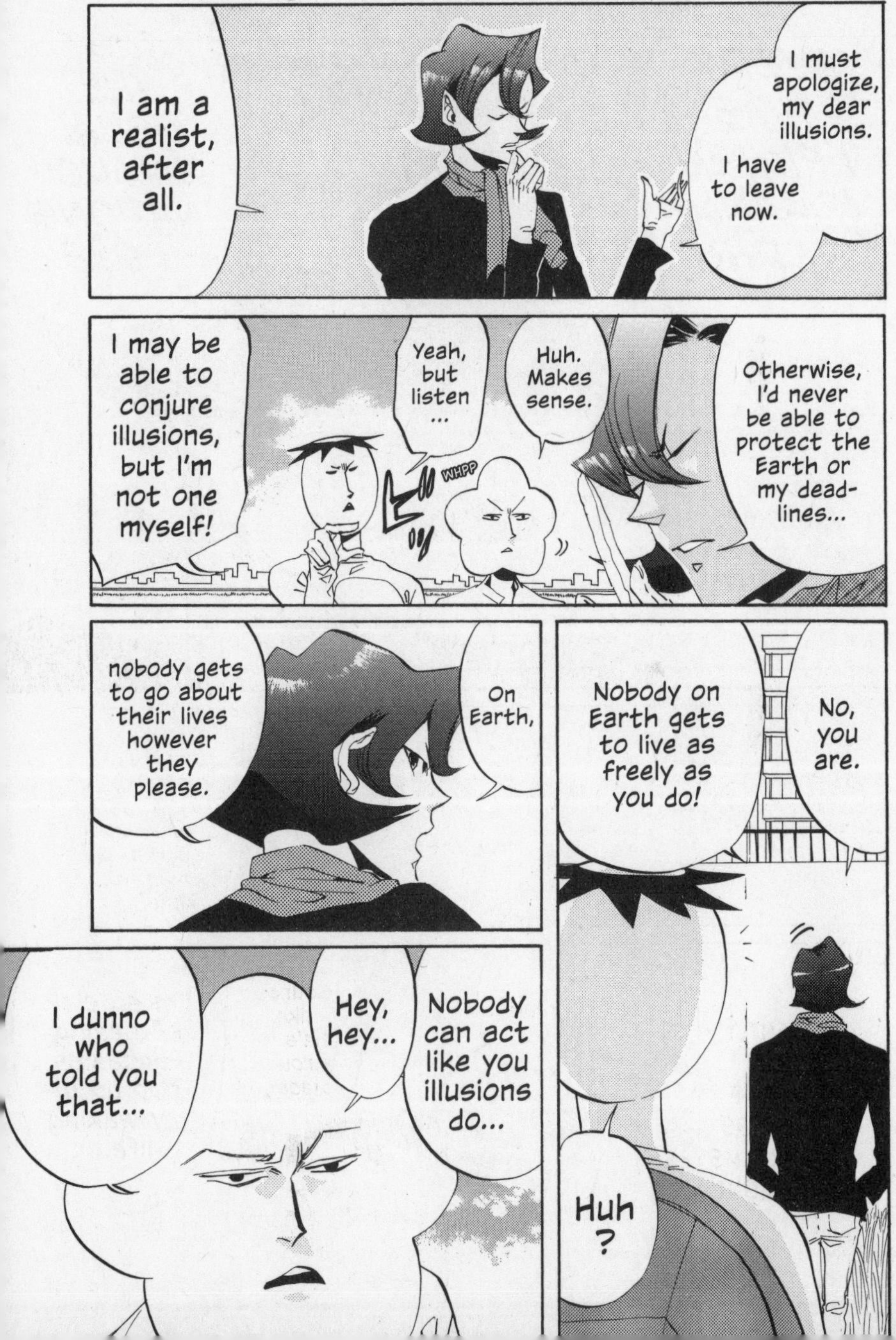
I must apologize, my dear illusions.
I have to leave now.
I am a realist, after all.
Otherwise, I'd never be able to protect the Earth or my deadlines...
Huh. Makes sense.
Yeah, but listen...
WHPP
I may be able to conjure illusions, but I'm not one myself!
No, you are.
Nobody on Earth gets to live as freely as you do!
Huh?
On Earth,
nobody gets to go about their lives however they please.
Nobody can act like you illusions do...
Hey, hey...
I dunno who told you that...

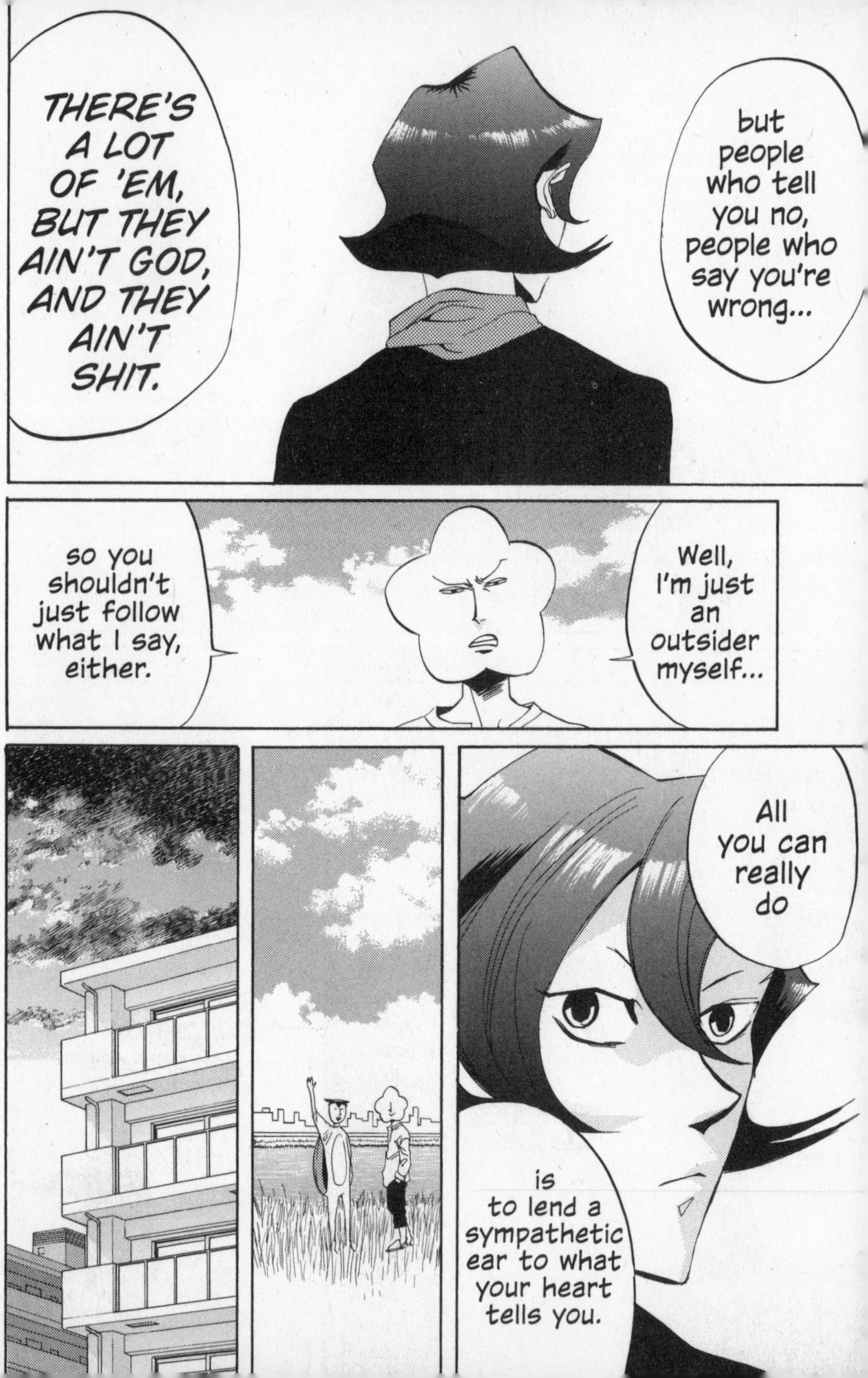
but people who tell you no, people who say you're wrong...
THERE'S A LOT OF 'EM, BUT THEY AIN'T GOD, AND THEY AIN'T SHIT.
Well, I'm just an outsider myself...
so you shouldn't just follow what I say, either.
All you can really do
is to lend a sympathetic ear to what your heart tells you.

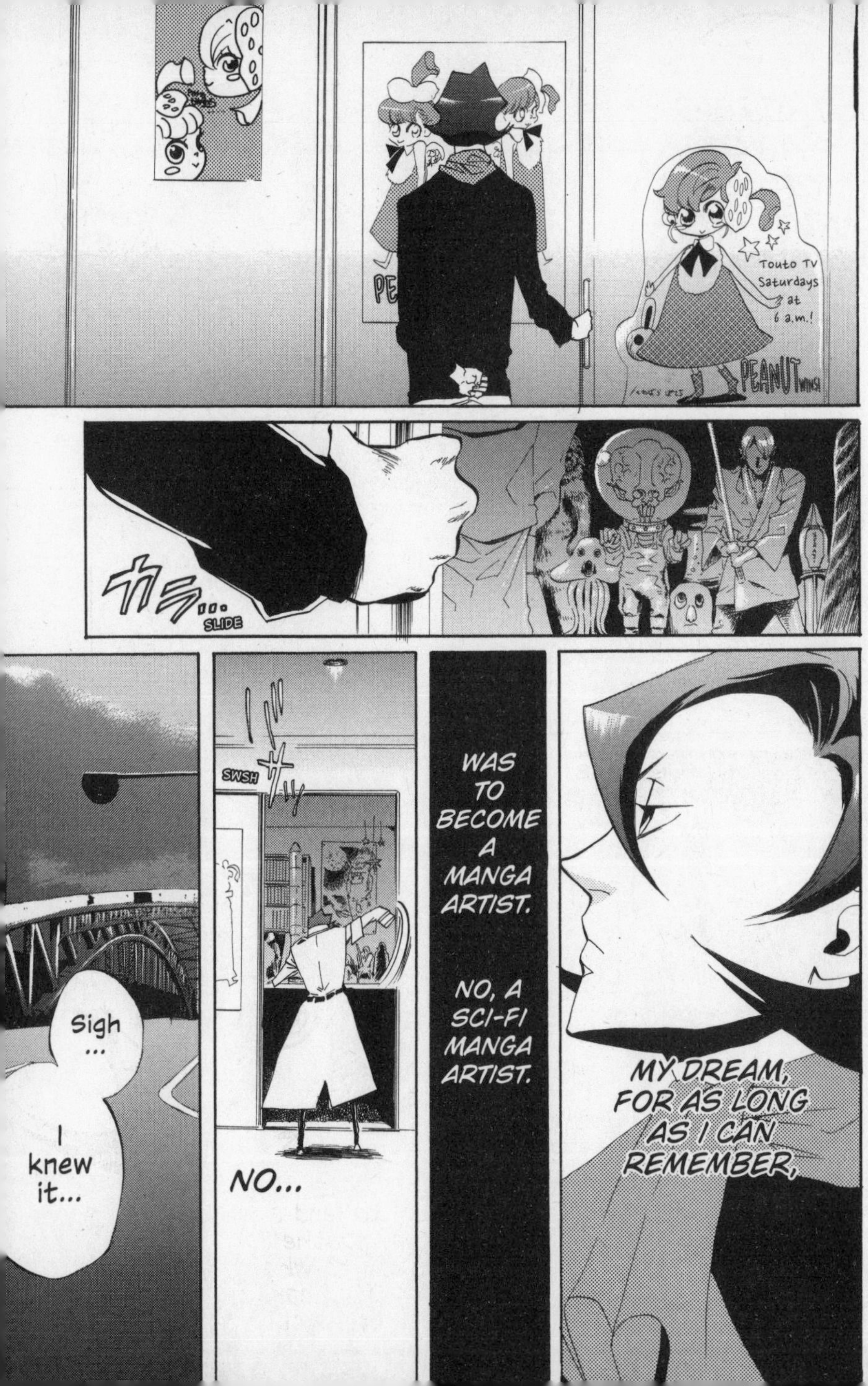
Touto TV Saturdays at 6 a.m.!
PEANUT
SLIDE
MY DREAM, FOR AS LONG AS I CAN REMEMBER,
WAS TO BECOME A MANGA ARTIST.
NO, A SCI-FI MANGA ARTIST.
SWSH
NO...
Sigh...
I knew it...

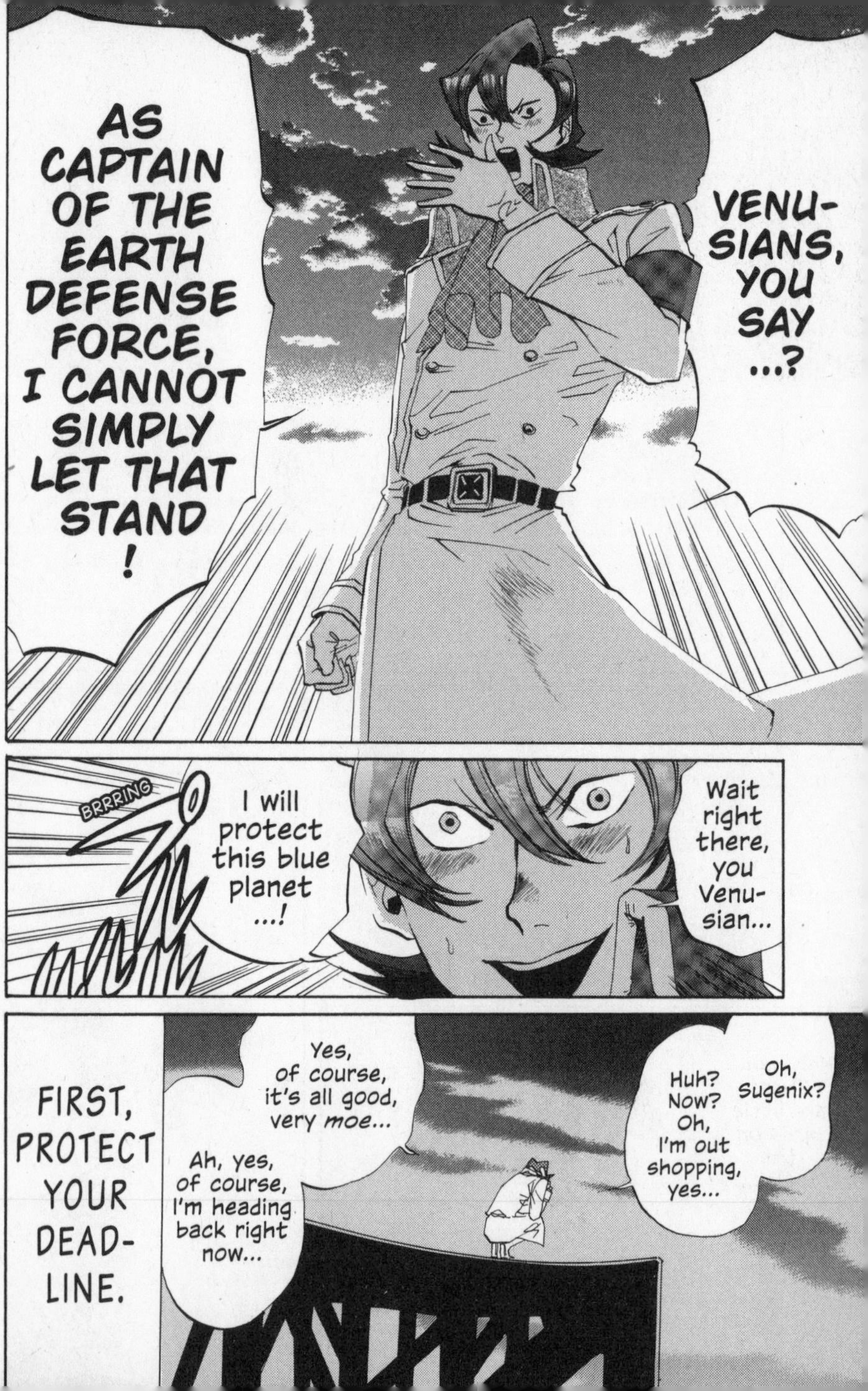
VENUSIANS, YOU SAY ...?
AS CAPTAIN OF THE EARTH DEFENSE FORCE, I CANNOT SIMPLY LET THAT STAND!
Wait right there, you Venusian...
I will protect this blue planet ...!
BRRRING
Oh, Sugenix?
Huh? Now? Oh, I'm out shopping, yes...
Yes, of course, it's all good, very *moe*...
Ah, yes, of course, I'm heading back right now...
FIRST, PROTECT YOUR DEADLINE.

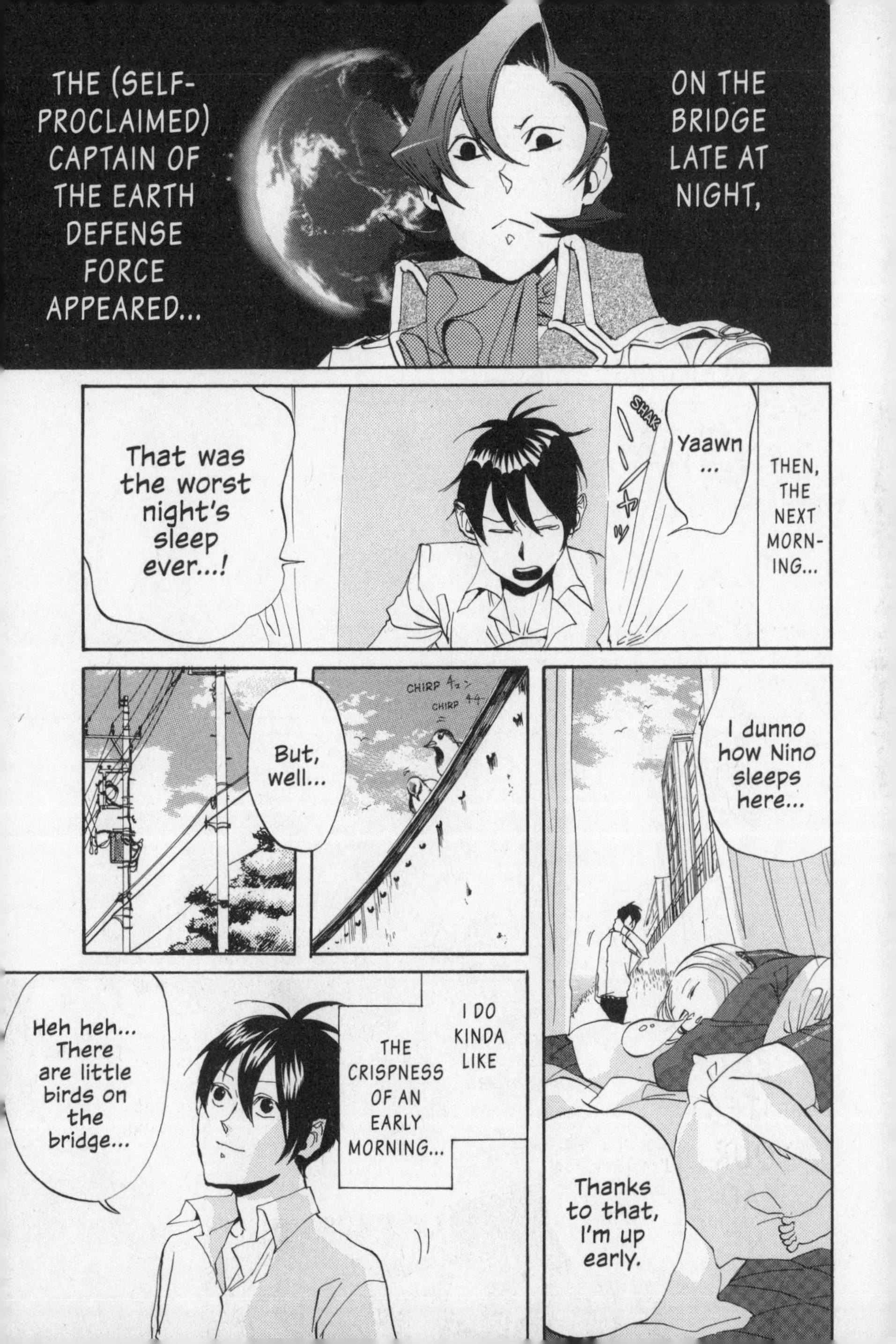
ON THE BRIDGE LATE AT NIGHT,
THE (SELF-PROCLAIMED) CAPTAIN OF THE EARTH DEFENSE FORCE APPEARED...
THEN, THE NEXT MORNING...
SHAK
Yaawn ...
That was the worst night's sleep ever...!
I dunno how Nino sleeps here...
Thanks to that, I'm up early.
CHIRP
CHIRP
But, well...
I DO KINDA LIKE
THE CRISPNESS OF AN EARLY MORNING...
Heh heh... There are little birds on the bridge...

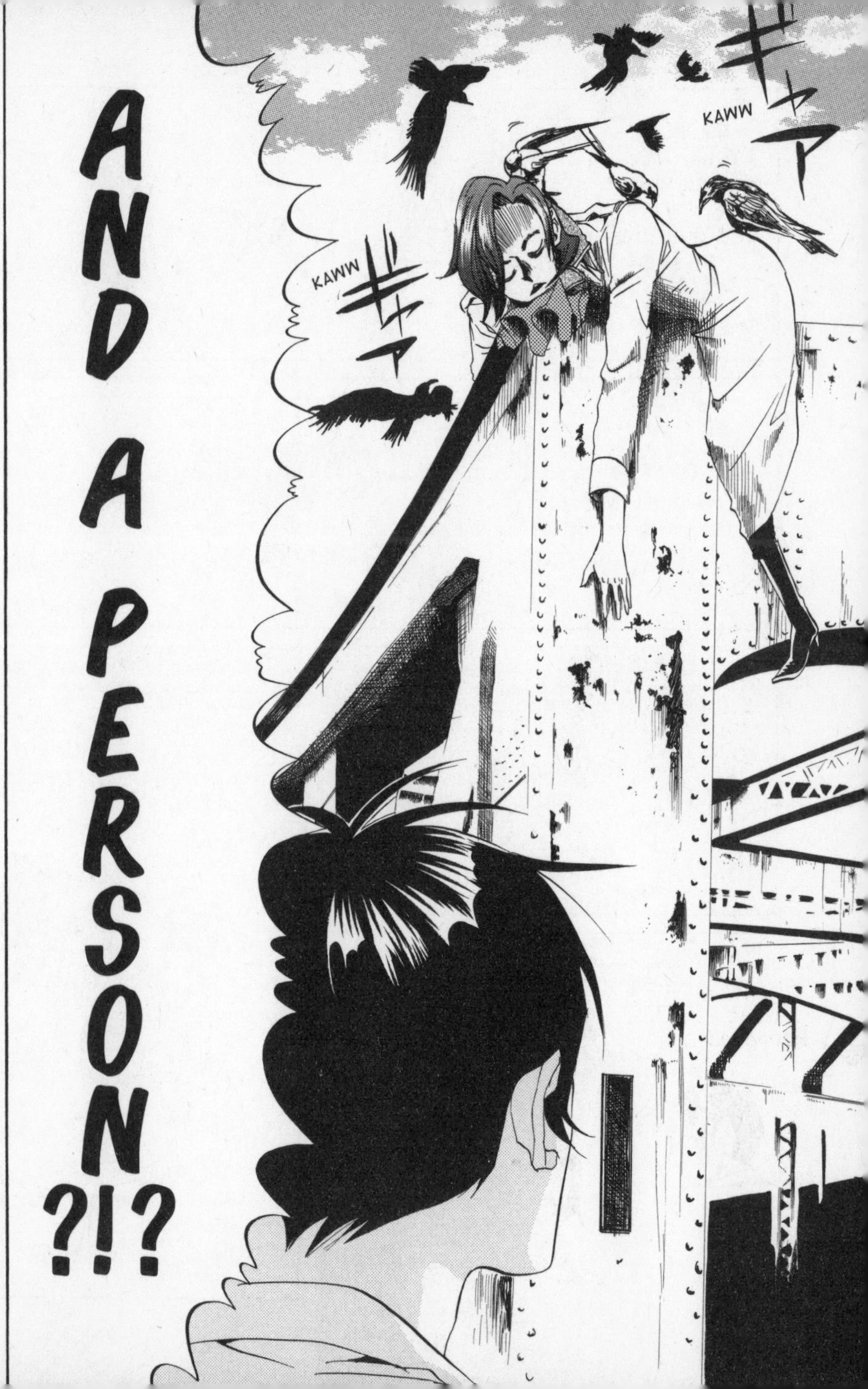
ギャア
KAWW
ギャア
KAWW
AND A PERSON?!?

Chapter 117: As the Will Commands

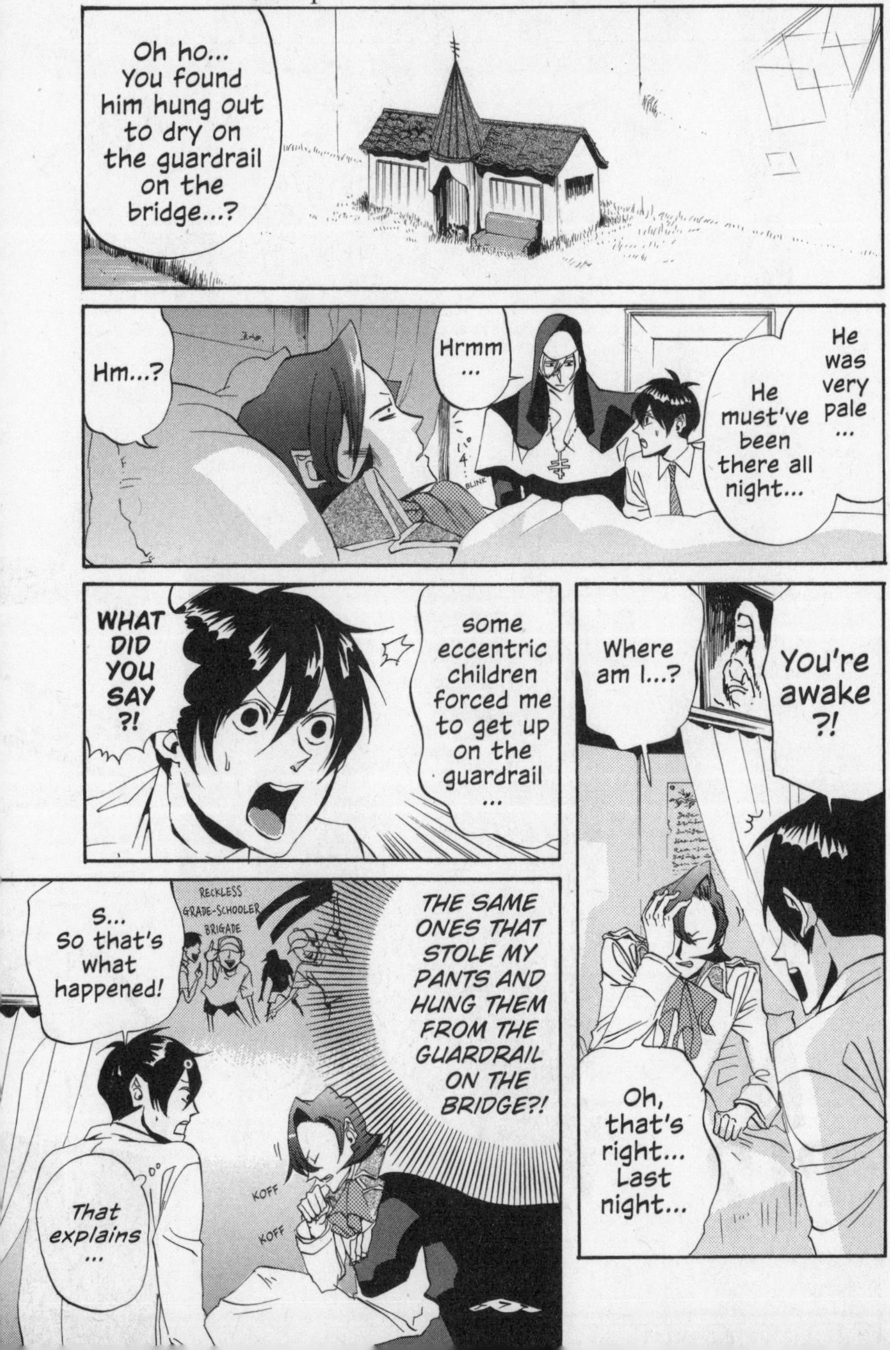
Oh ho... You found him hung out to dry on the guardrail on the bridge...?
He was very pale...
He must've been there all night...
Hrmm...
BLINK
Hm...?
You're awake?!
Where am I...?
Oh, that's right... Last night...
some eccentric children forced me to get up on the guardrail...
WHAT DID YOU SAY?!
THE SAME ONES THAT STOLE MY PANTS AND HUNG THEM FROM THE GUARDRAIL ON THE BRIDGE?!
RECKLESS GRADE-SCHOOLER BRIGADE
S... So that's what happened!
KOFF
KOFF
That explains...

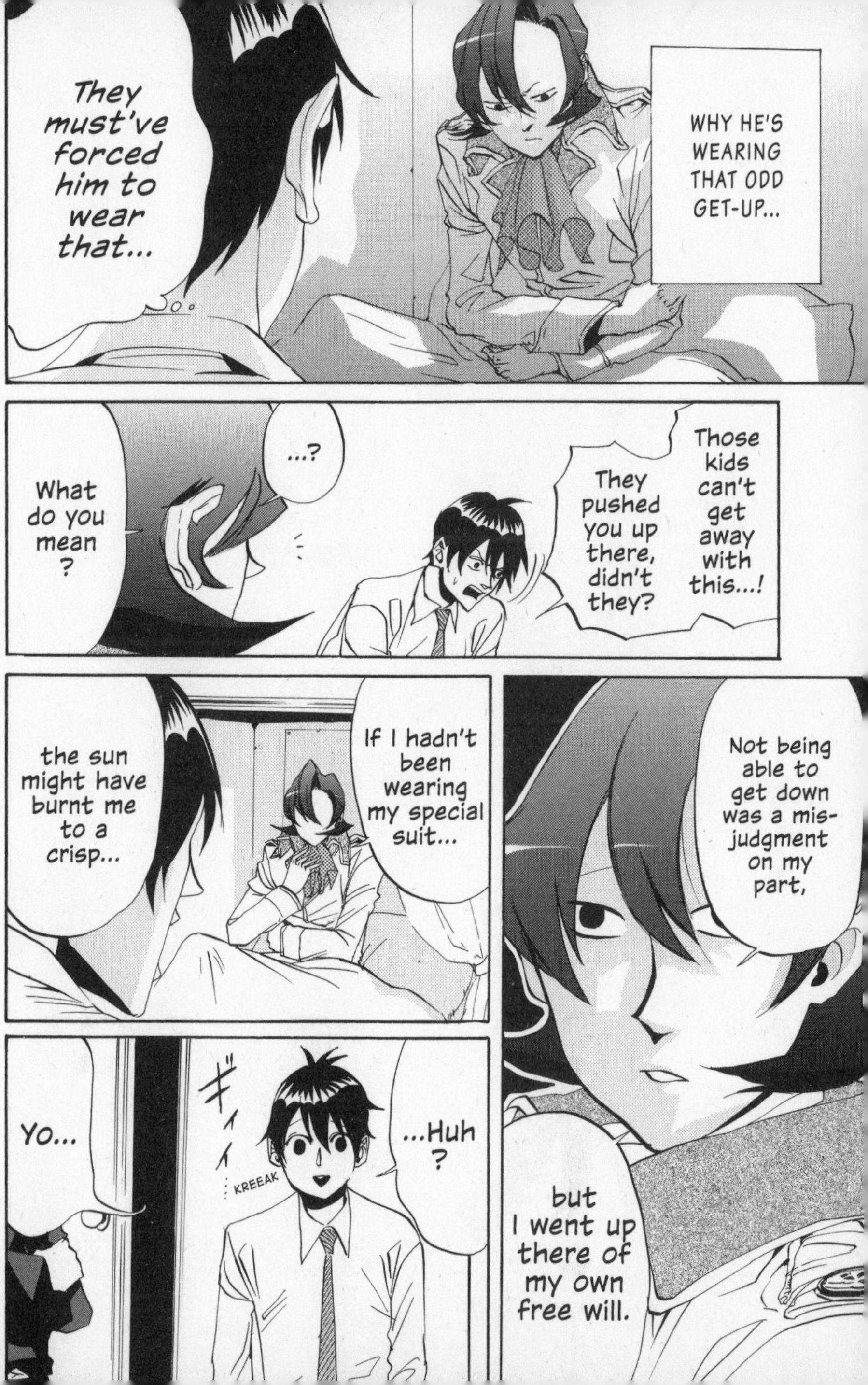
WHY HE'S WEARING THAT ODD GET-UP...
They must've forced him to wear that...
Those kids can't get away with this...!
They pushed you up there, didn't they?
...?
What do you mean?
Not being able to get down was a mis-judgment on my part,
but I went up there of my own free will.
If I hadn't been wearing my special suit...
the sun might have burnt me to a crisp...
...Huh?
ギィィ
KREEAK
Yo...

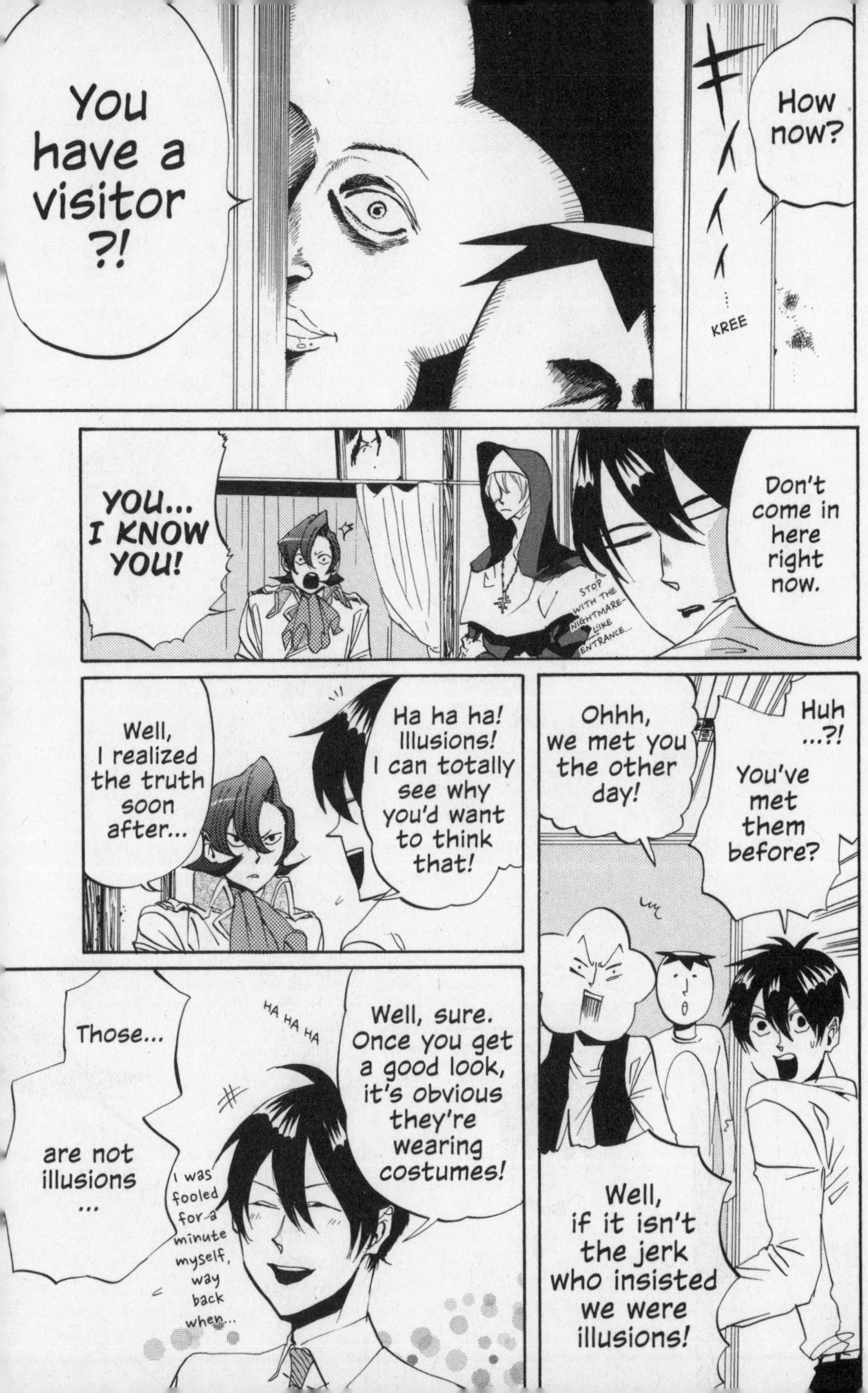
How now?
KREE
You have a visitor ?!
Don't come in here right now.
STOP WITH THE NIGHTMARE-LIKE ENTRANCE...
YOU... I KNOW YOU!
Huh ...?!
You've met them before?
Ohhh, we met you the other day!
Well, if it isn't the jerk who insisted we were illusions!
Ha ha ha! Illusions! I can totally see why you'd want to think that!
Well, I realized the truth soon after...
Well, sure. Once you get a good look, it's obvious they're wearing costumes!
HA HA HA
I was fooled for a minute myself, way back when...
Those...
are not illusions ...

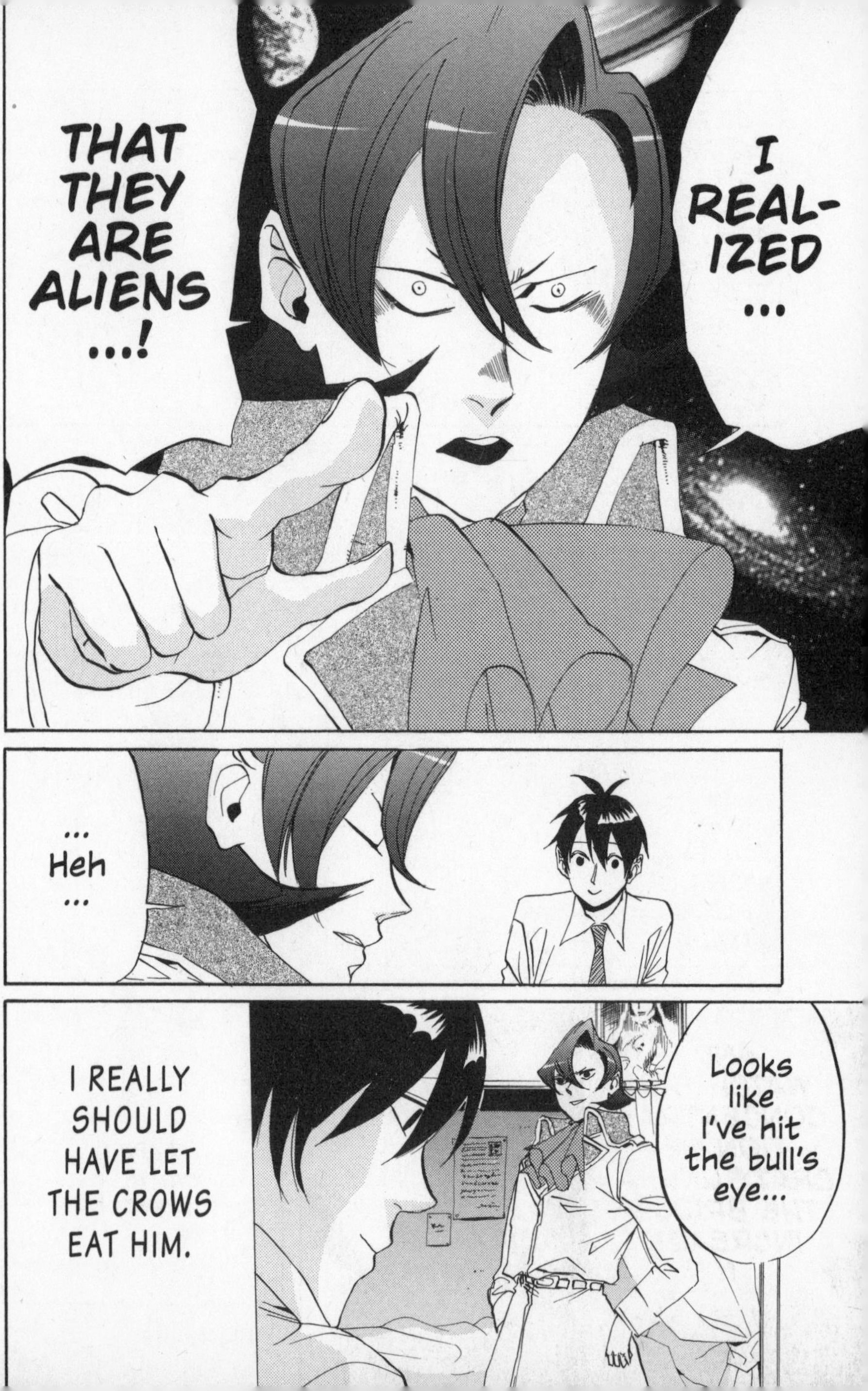
I REAL-IZED ...
THAT THEY ARE ALIENS ...!
... Heh ...
Looks like I've hit the bull's eye...
I REALLY SHOULD HAVE LET THE CROWS EAT HIM.

Chapter 118: Feeling

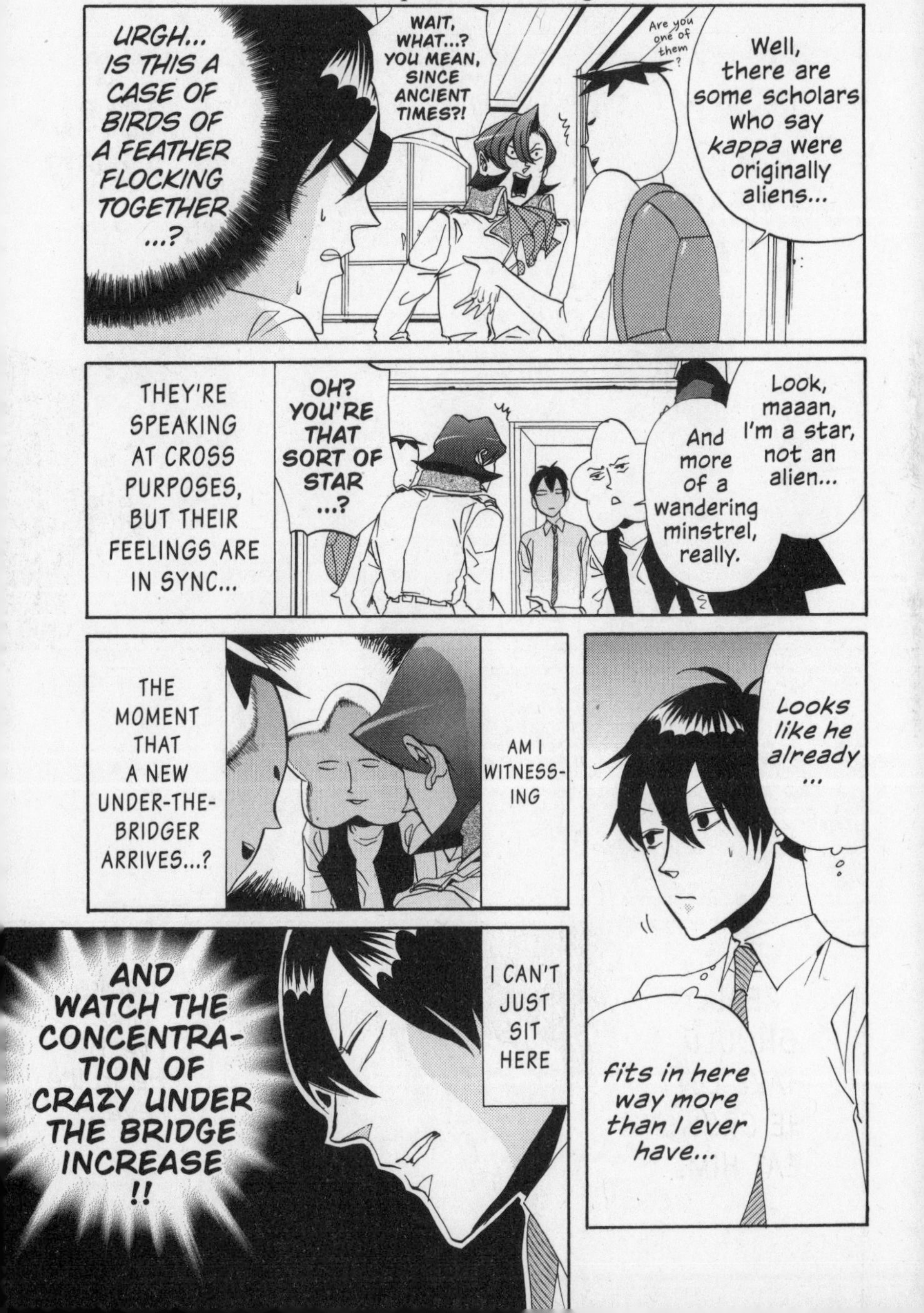
Well, there are some scholars who say *kappa* were originally aliens...
Are you one of them?
WAIT, WHAT...? YOU MEAN, SINCE ANCIENT TIMES?!
URGH... IS THIS A CASE OF BIRDS OF A FEATHER FLOCKING TOGETHER ...?
Look, maaan, I'm a star, not an alien...
And more of a wandering minstrel, really.
OH? YOU'RE THAT SORT OF STAR ...?
THEY'RE SPEAKING AT CROSS PURPOSES, BUT THEIR FEELINGS ARE IN SYNC...
Looks like he already ...
fits in here way more than I ever have...
AM I WITNESS-ING
THE MOMENT THAT A NEW UNDER-THE-BRIDGER ARRIVES...?
I CAN'T JUST SIT HERE
AND WATCH THE CONCENTRATION OF CRAZY UNDER THE BRIDGE INCREASE !!

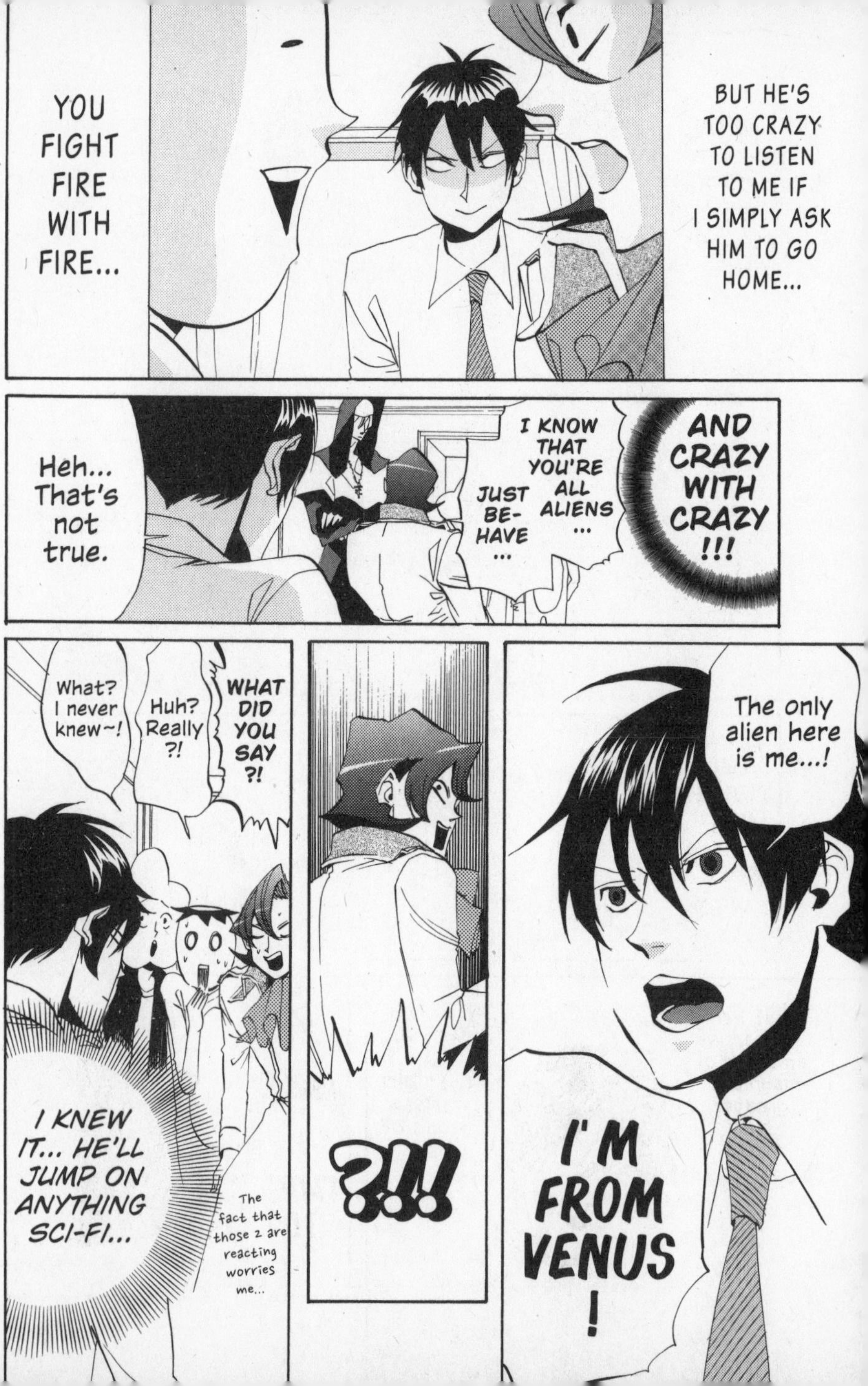
BUT HE'S TOO CRAZY TO LISTEN TO ME IF I SIMPLY ASK HIM TO GO HOME...
YOU FIGHT FIRE WITH FIRE...
AND CRAZY WITH CRAZY!!!
I KNOW THAT YOU'RE ALL ALIENS ...
JUST BE-HAVE ...
Heh... That's not true.
The only alien here is me...!
I'M FROM VENUS !
?!!
WHAT DID YOU SAY ?!
Huh? Really ?!
What? I never knew~!
I KNEW IT... HE'LL JUMP ON ANYTHING SCI-FI...
The fact that those 2 are reacting worries me...

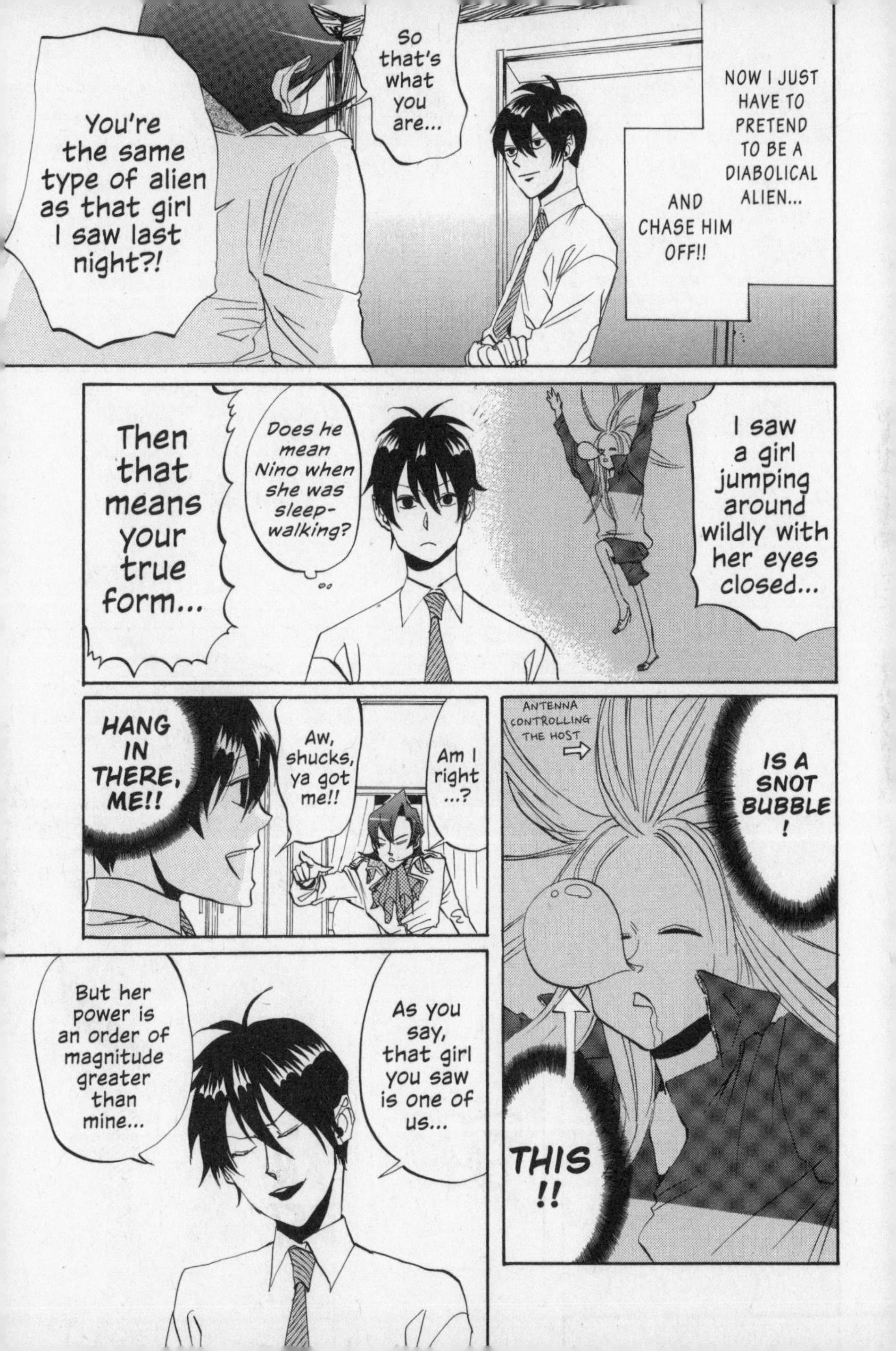
NOW I JUST HAVE TO PRETEND TO BE A DIABOLICAL ALIEN...
AND CHASE HIM OFF!!
So that's what you are...
You're the same type of alien as that girl I saw last night?!
I saw a girl jumping around wildly with her eyes closed...
Does he mean Nino when she was sleep-walking?
Then that means your true form...
IS A SNOT BUBBLE!
ANTENNA CONTROLLING THE HOST
THIS!!
Am I right...?
Aw, shucks, ya got me!!
HANG IN THERE, ME!!
As you say, that girl you saw is one of us...
But her power is an order of magnitude greater than mine...

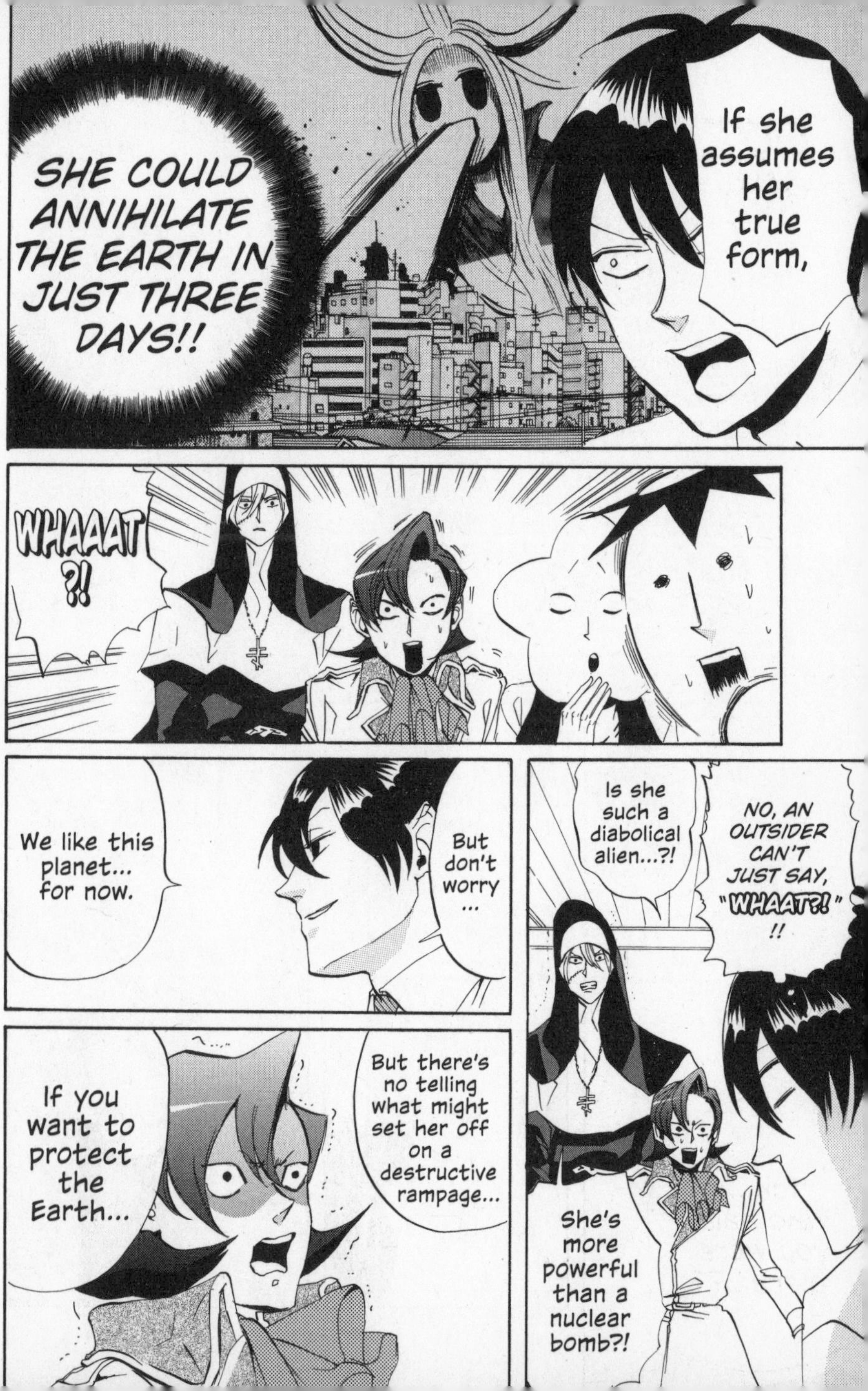
If she assumes her true form,
SHE COULD ANNIHILATE THE EARTH IN JUST THREE DAYS!!
WHAAAT?!
NO, AN OUTSIDER CAN'T JUST SAY, "WHAAAT?!" !!
Is she such a diabolical alien...?!
She's more powerful than a nuclear bomb?!
But don't worry...
We like this planet... for now.
But there's no telling what might set her off on a destructive rampage...
If you want to protect the Earth...

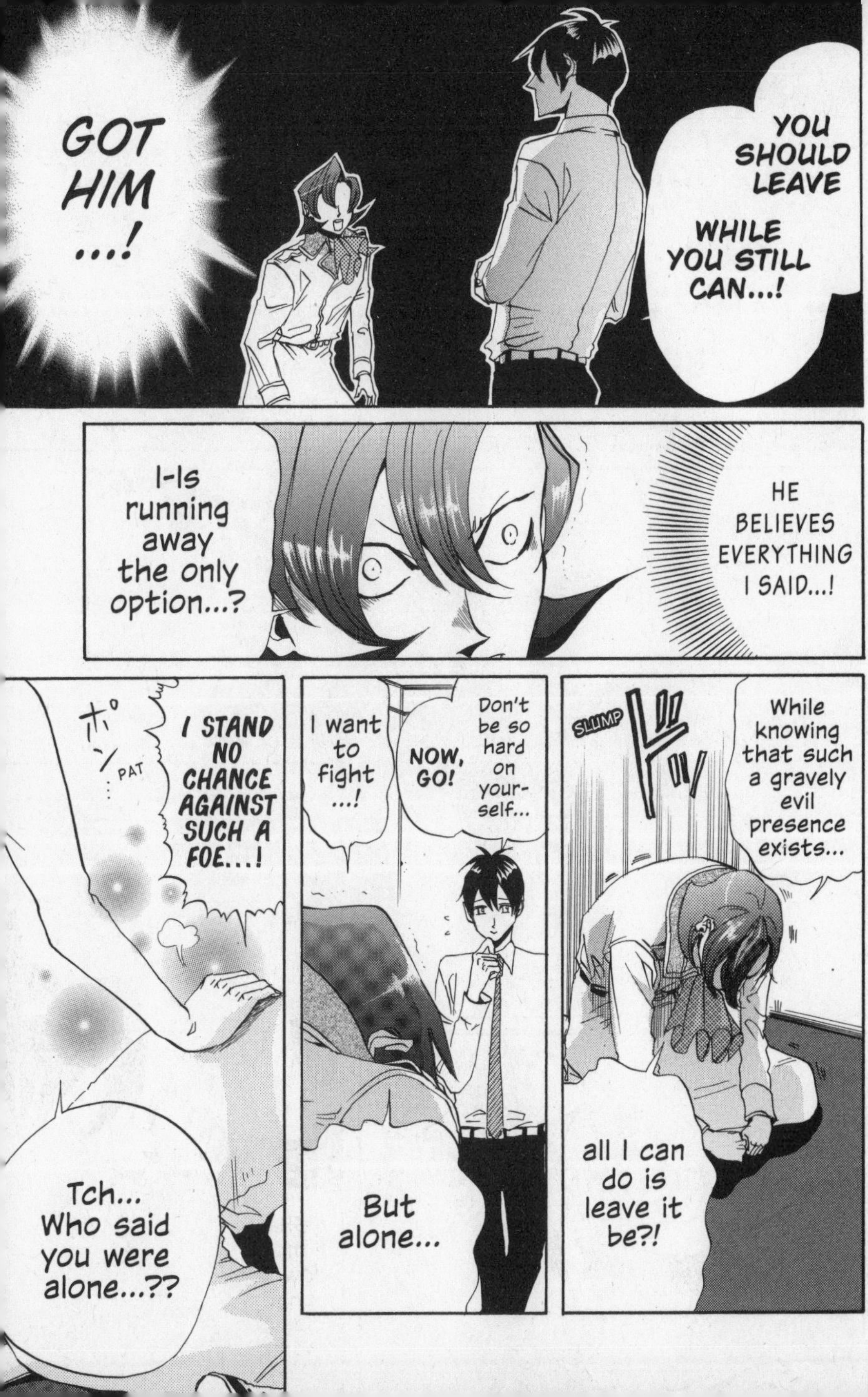

YOU SHOULD LEAVE
WHILE YOU STILL CAN...!
GOT HIM ...!
HE BELIEVES EVERYTHING I SAID...!
I-Is running away the only option...?
While knowing that such a gravely evil presence exists...
SLUMP
all I can do is leave it be?!
Don't be so hard on your-self...
NOW, GO!
I want to fight ...!
But alone...
I STAND NO CHANCE AGAINST SUCH A FOE...!
ポン
PAT
Tch... Who said you were alone...??

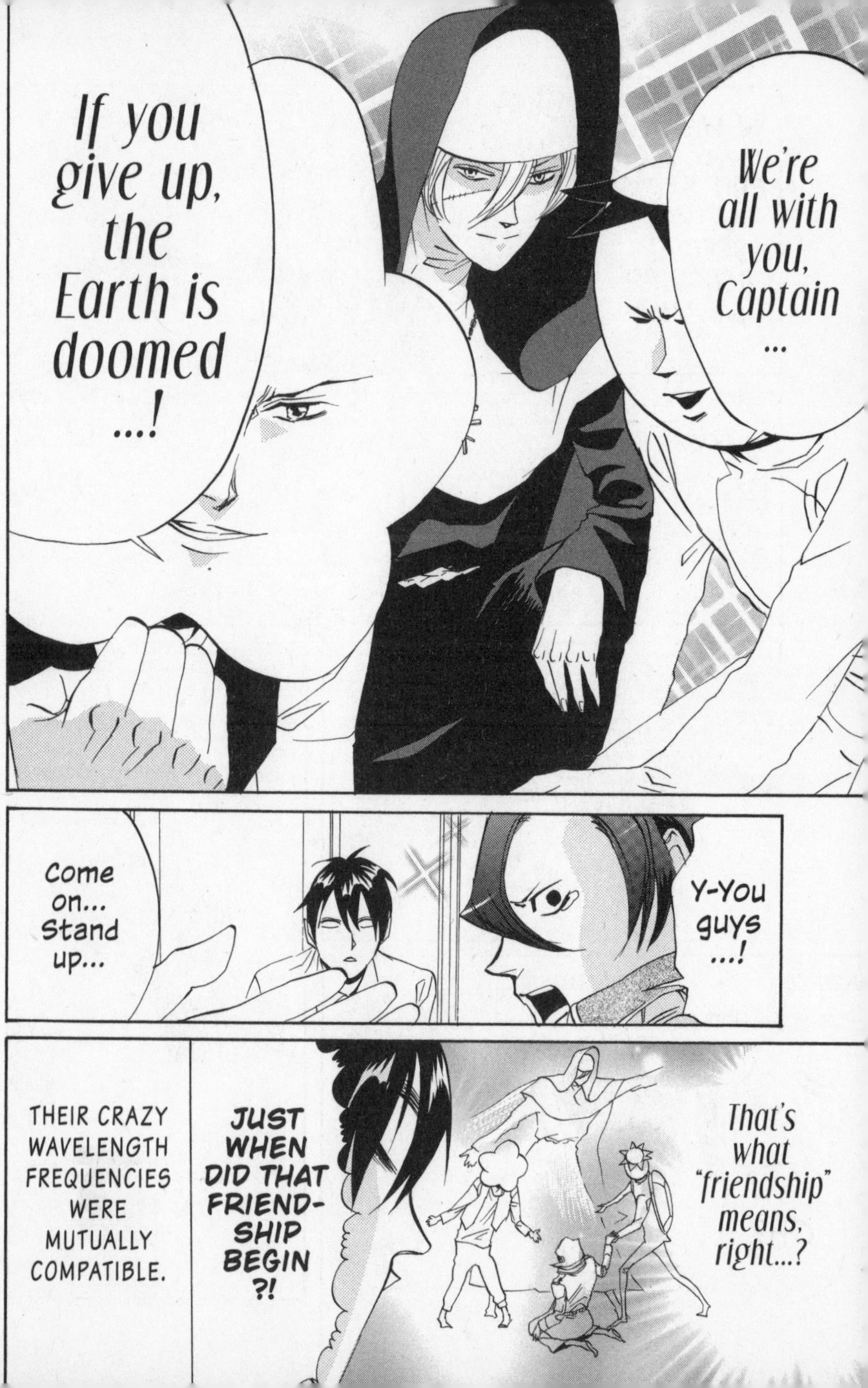
We're all with you, Captain ...
If you give up, the Earth is doomed ...!
Y-You guys ...!
Come on... Stand up...
That's what "friendship" means, right...?
JUST WHEN DID THAT FRIEND-SHIP BEGIN ?!
THEIR CRAZY WAVELENGTH FREQUENCIES WERE MUTUALLY COMPATIBLE.

Chapter 119: Venusian Queen

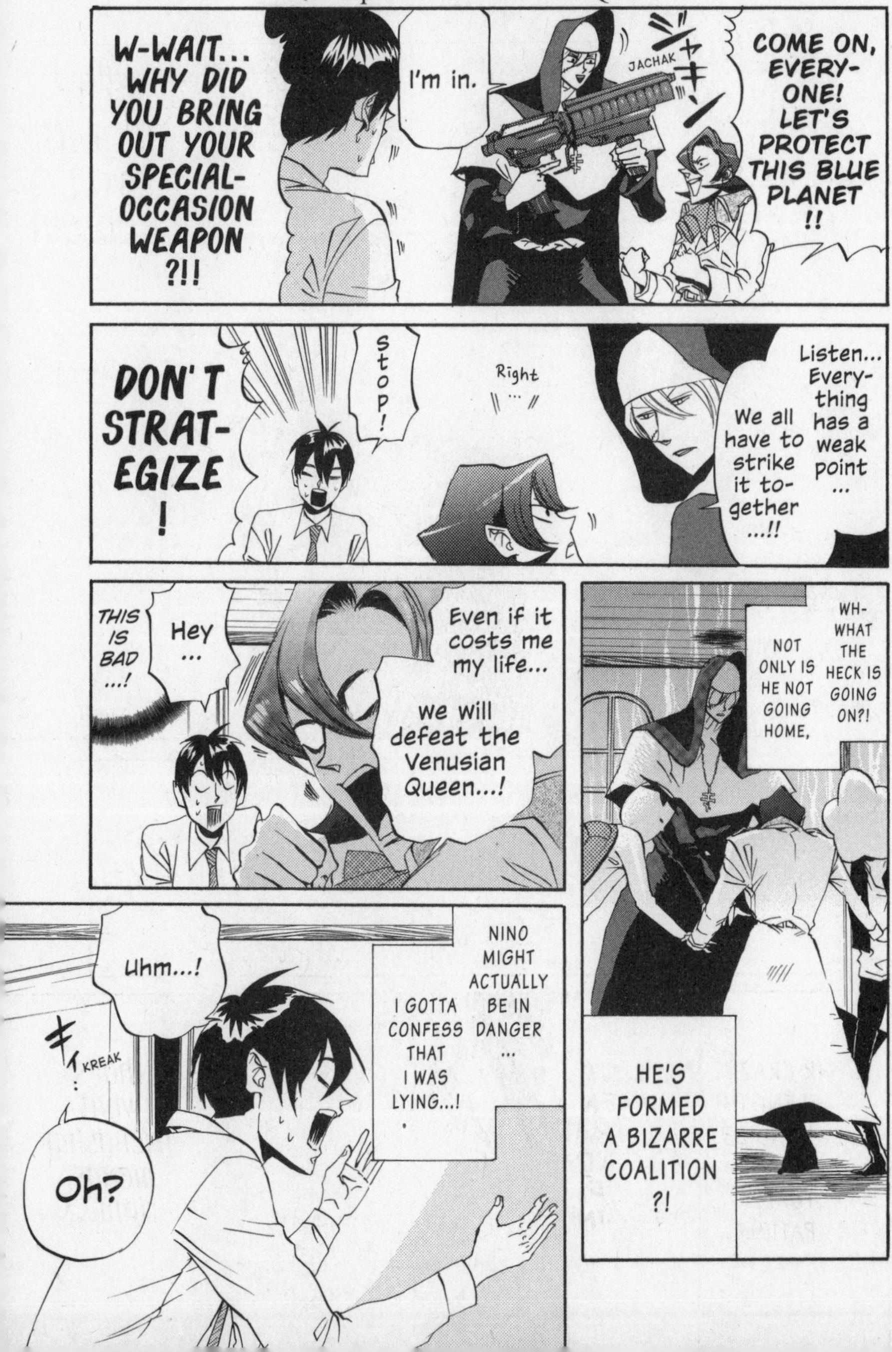
COME ON, EVERYONE! LET'S PROTECT THIS BLUE PLANET!!
JACHAK
I'm in.
W-WAIT... WHY DID YOU BRING OUT YOUR SPECIAL-OCCASION WEAPON?!!
Listen... Everything has a weak point...
We all have to strike it together...!!
Right...
STOP!
DON'T STRATEGIZE!
WH-WHAT THE HECK IS GOING ON?!
NOT ONLY IS HE NOT GOING HOME,
HE'S FORMED A BIZARRE COALITION?!
Even if it costs me my life...
we will defeat the Venusian Queen...!
Hey...
THIS IS BAD...!
NINO MIGHT ACTUALLY BE IN DANGER...
I GOTTA CONFESS THAT I WAS LYING...!
Uhm...!
KREAK
Oh?

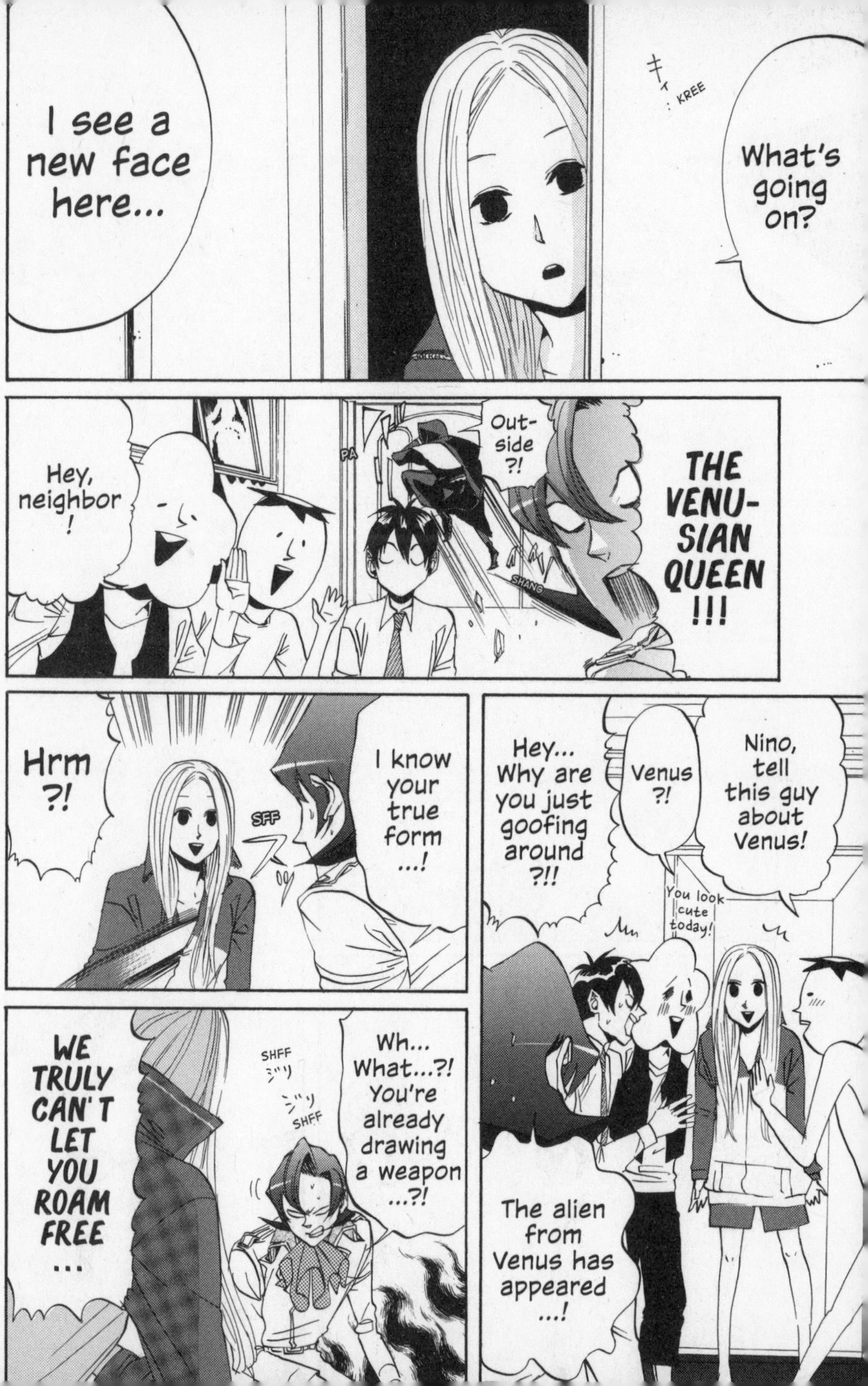

キィ
KREE
What's going on?
...
I see a new face here...
THE VENUSIAN QUEEN!!!
Out-side?!
SHANG
PA
Hey, neighbor!
Nino, tell this guy about Venus!
Venus?!
Hey... Why are you just goofing around?!!
You look cute today!
The alien from Venus has appeared...!
I know your true form...!
SFF
Hrm?!
Wh... What...?! You're already drawing a weapon...?!
SHFF
ジリ
ジリ
SHFF
WE TRULY CAN'T LET YOU ROAM FREE...

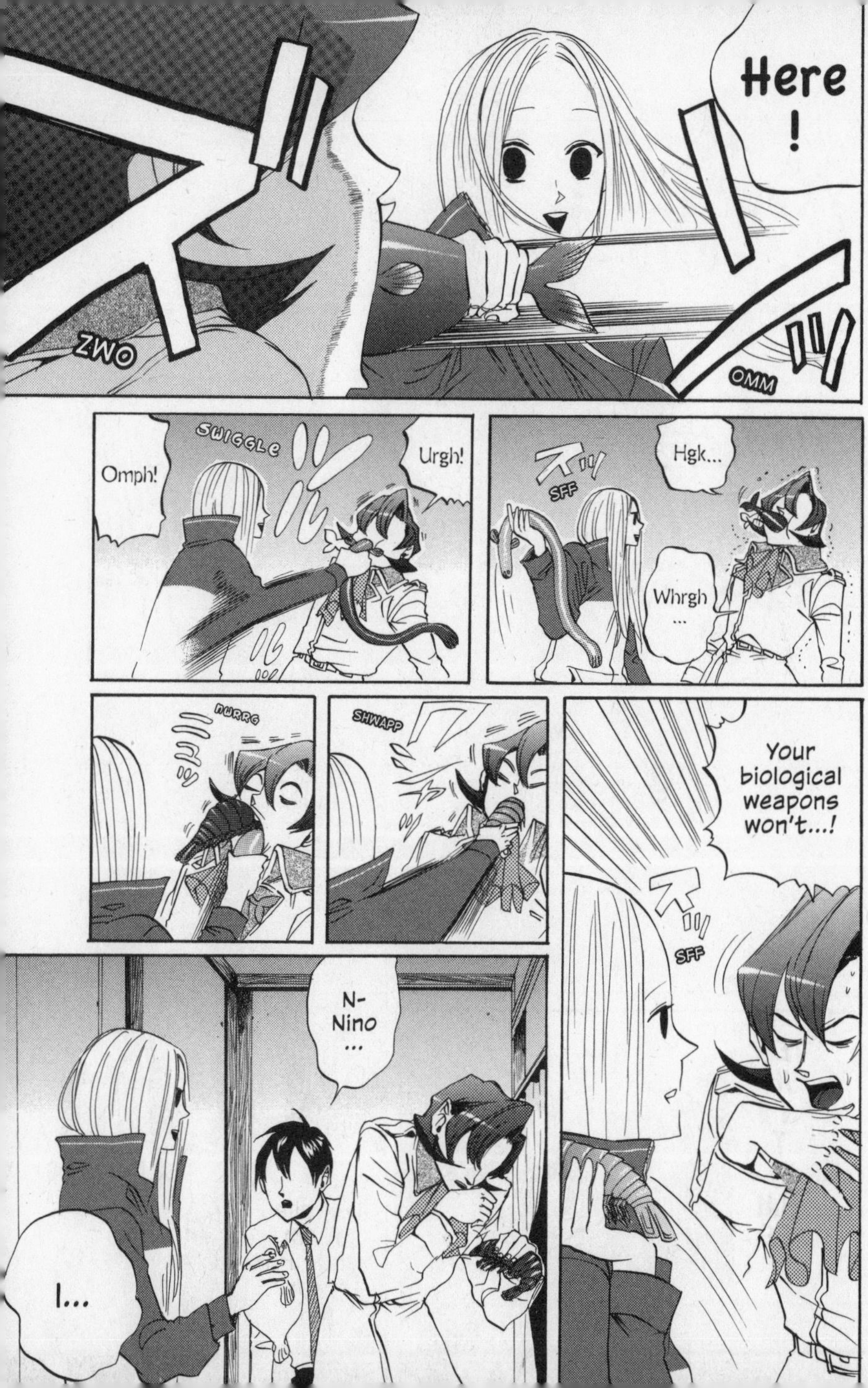
Here!
OMM
ZWO
Hgk...
SFF
Whrgh ...
Urgh!
SWIGGLE
Omph!
Your biological weapons won't...!
SFF
SHWAPP
NURRG
N-Nino ...
I...

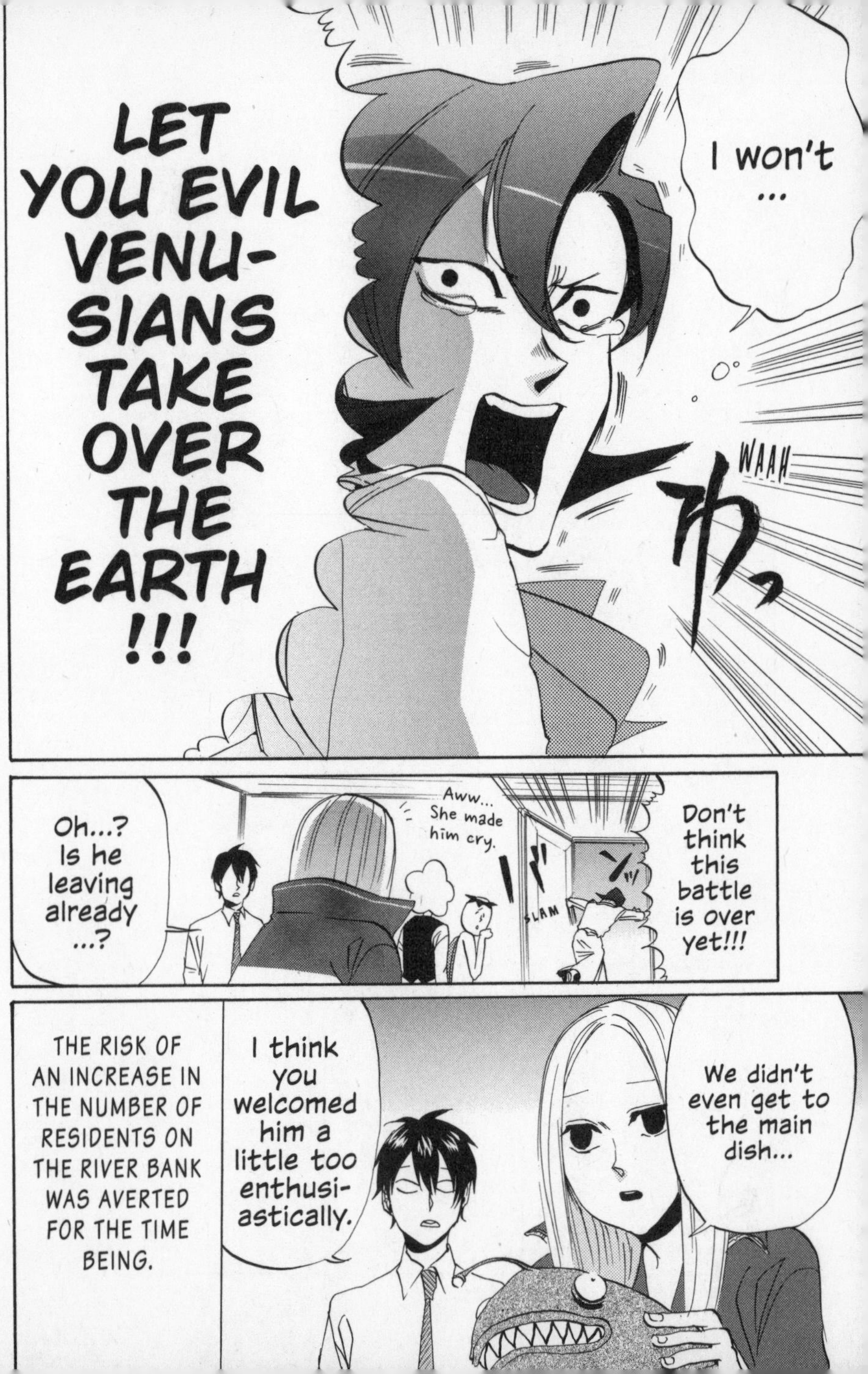
I won't ...
LET YOU EVIL VENUSIANS TAKE OVER THE EARTH!!!
WAAH
Don't think this battle is over yet!!!
SLAM
Aww... She made him cry.
Oh...? Is he leaving already...?
We didn't even get to the main dish...
I think you welcomed him a little too enthusiastically.
THE RISK OF AN INCREASE IN THE NUMBER OF RESIDENTS ON THE RIVER BANK WAS AVERTED FOR THE TIME BEING.

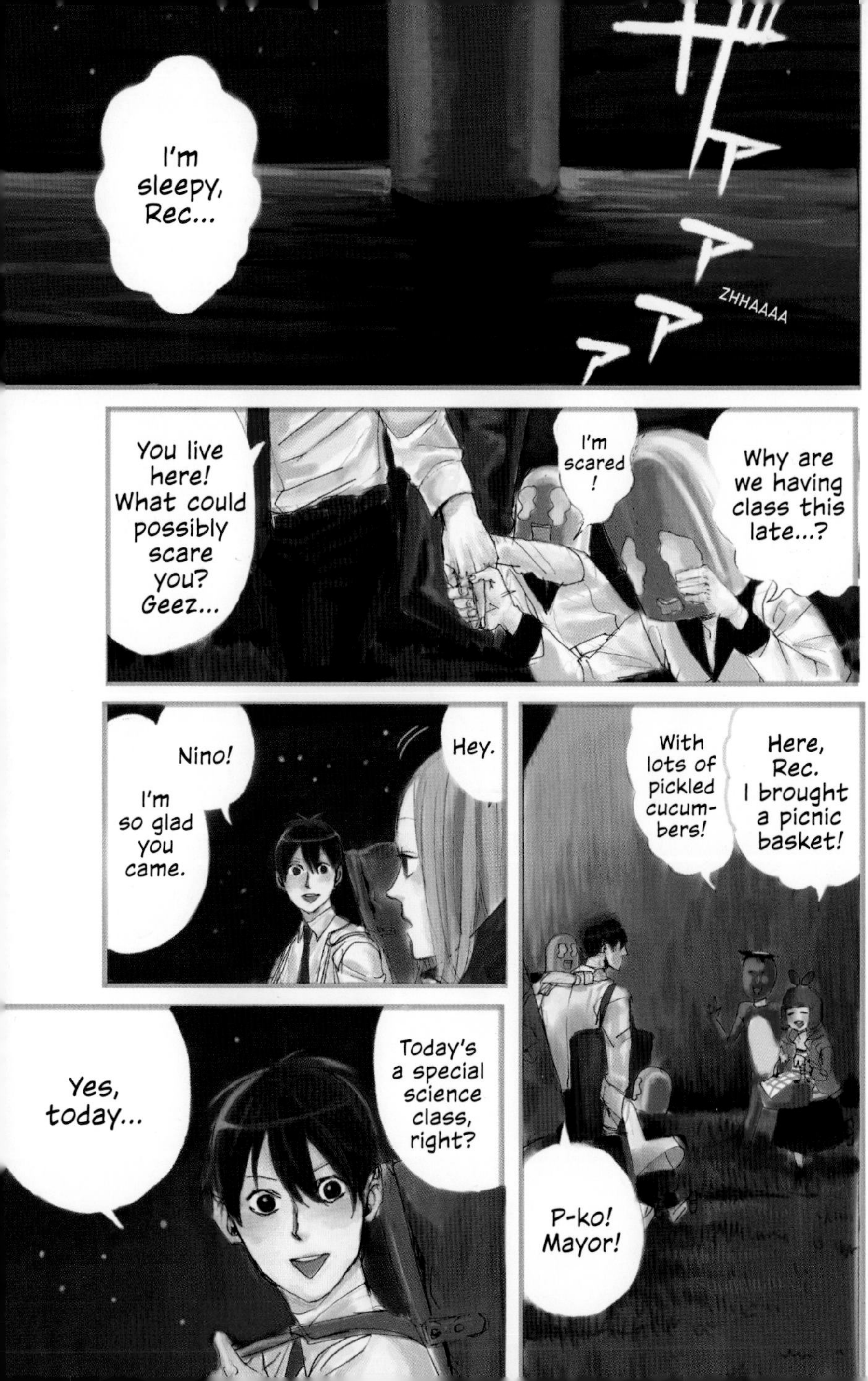
ZHHAAAA
I'm sleepy, Rec...
Why are we having class this late...?
I'm scared!
You live here! What could possibly scare you? Geez...
Here, Rec. I brought a picnic basket!
With lots of pickled cucumbers!
P-ko! Mayor!
Hey.
Nino!
I'm so glad you came.
Today's a special science class, right?
Yes, today...

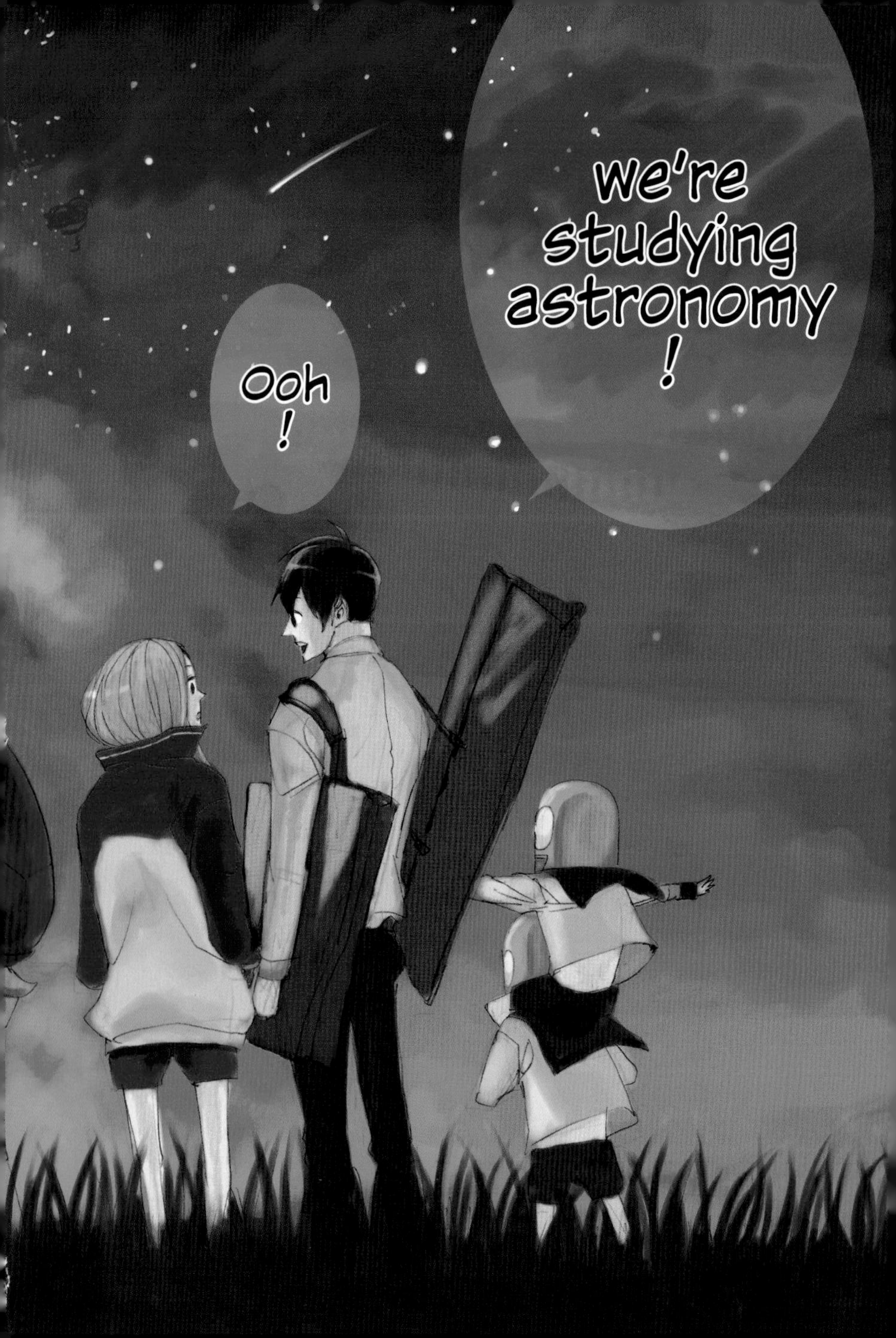
we're studying astronomy!
Ooh!

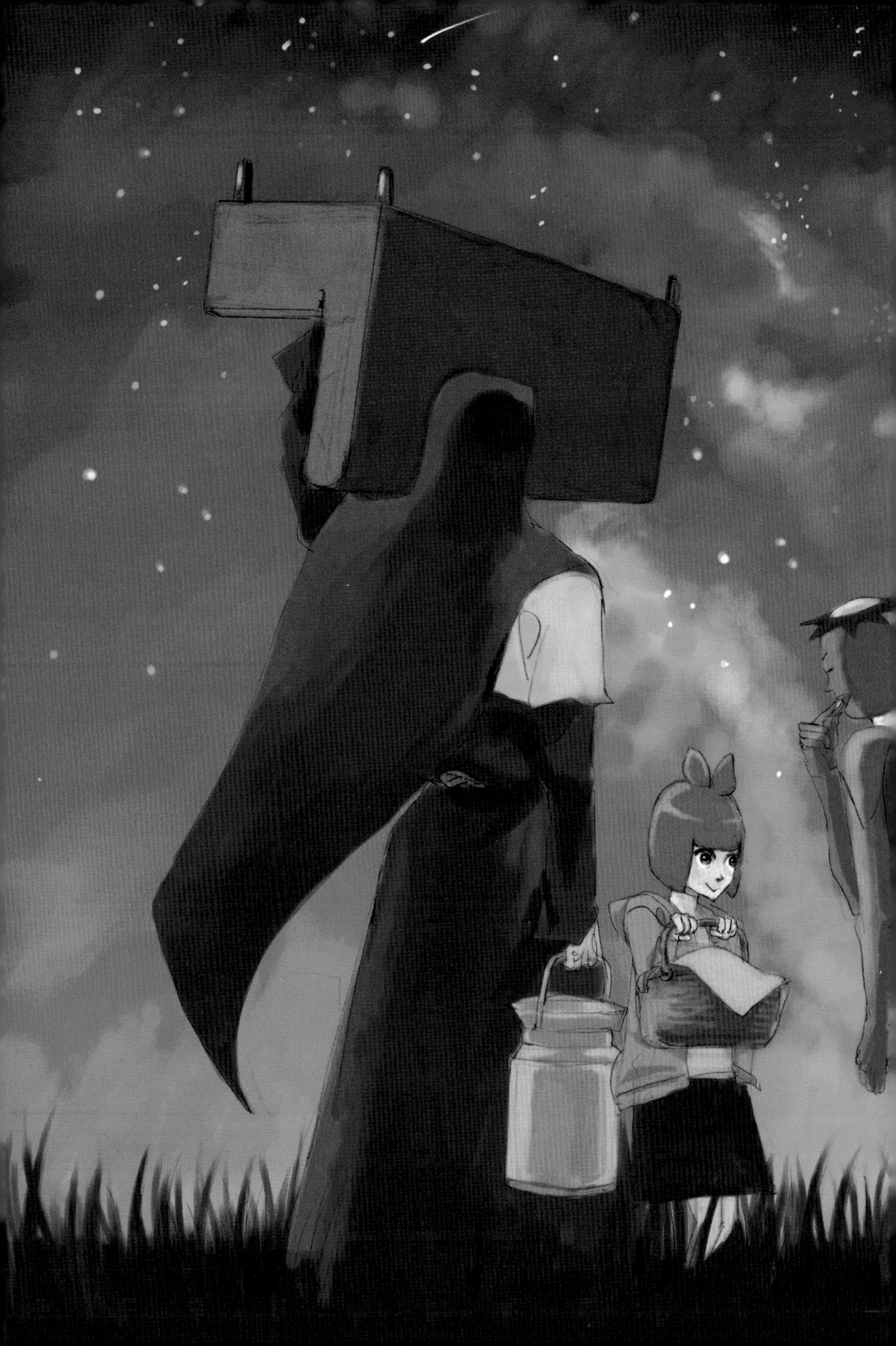

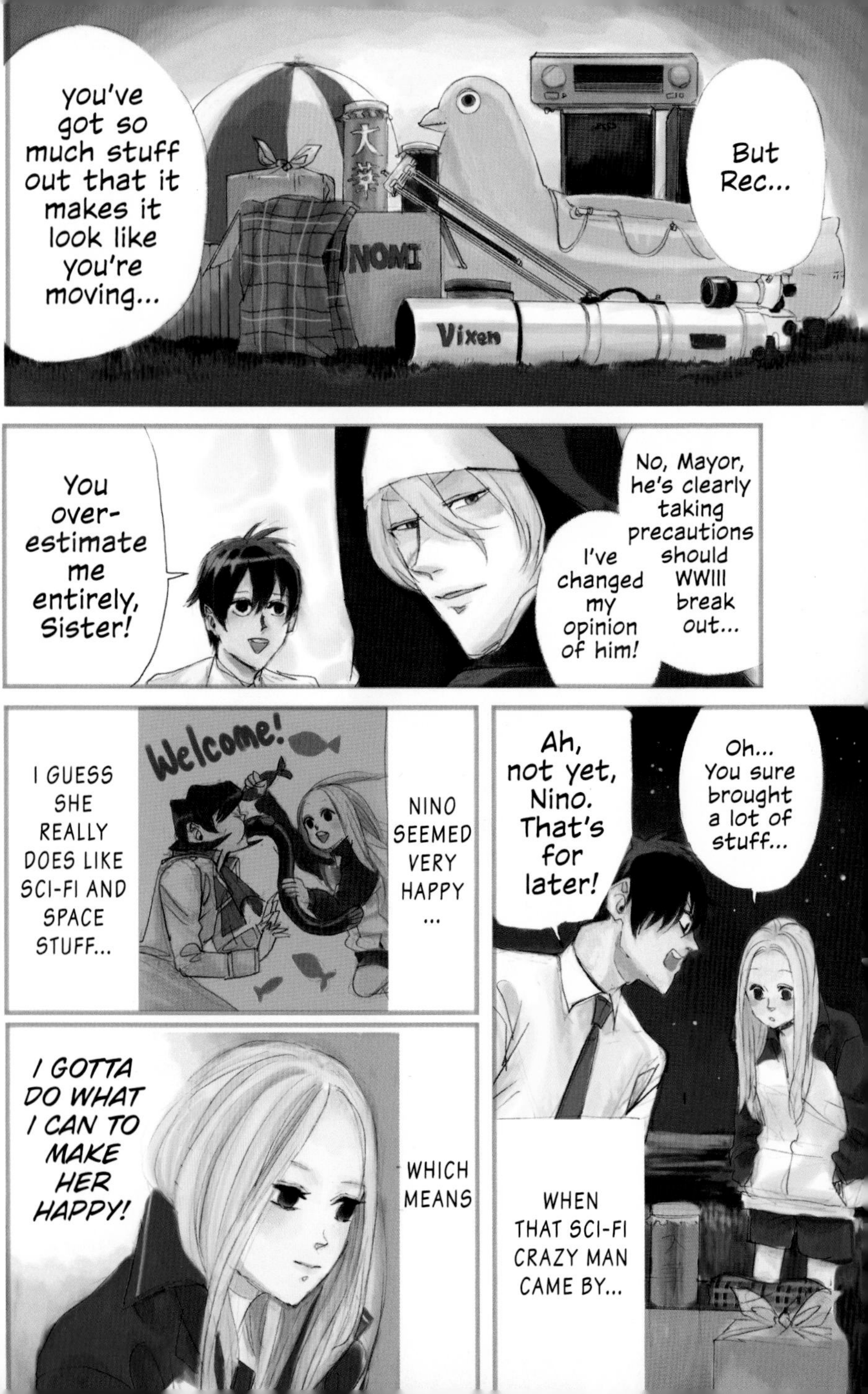
But Rec...
you've got so much stuff out that it makes it look like you're moving...
NOMI
Vixen
No, Mayor, he's clearly taking precautions should WWIII break out...
I've changed my opinion of him!
You over-estimate me entirely, Sister!
Oh... You sure brought a lot of stuff...
Ah, not yet, Nino. That's for later!
WHEN THAT SCI-FI CRAZY MAN CAME BY...
NINO SEEMED VERY HAPPY ...
Welcome!
I GUESS SHE REALLY DOES LIKE SCI-FI AND SPACE STUFF...
WHICH MEANS
I GOTTA DO WHAT I CAN TO MAKE HER HAPPY!

Chapter 120: Astronomy

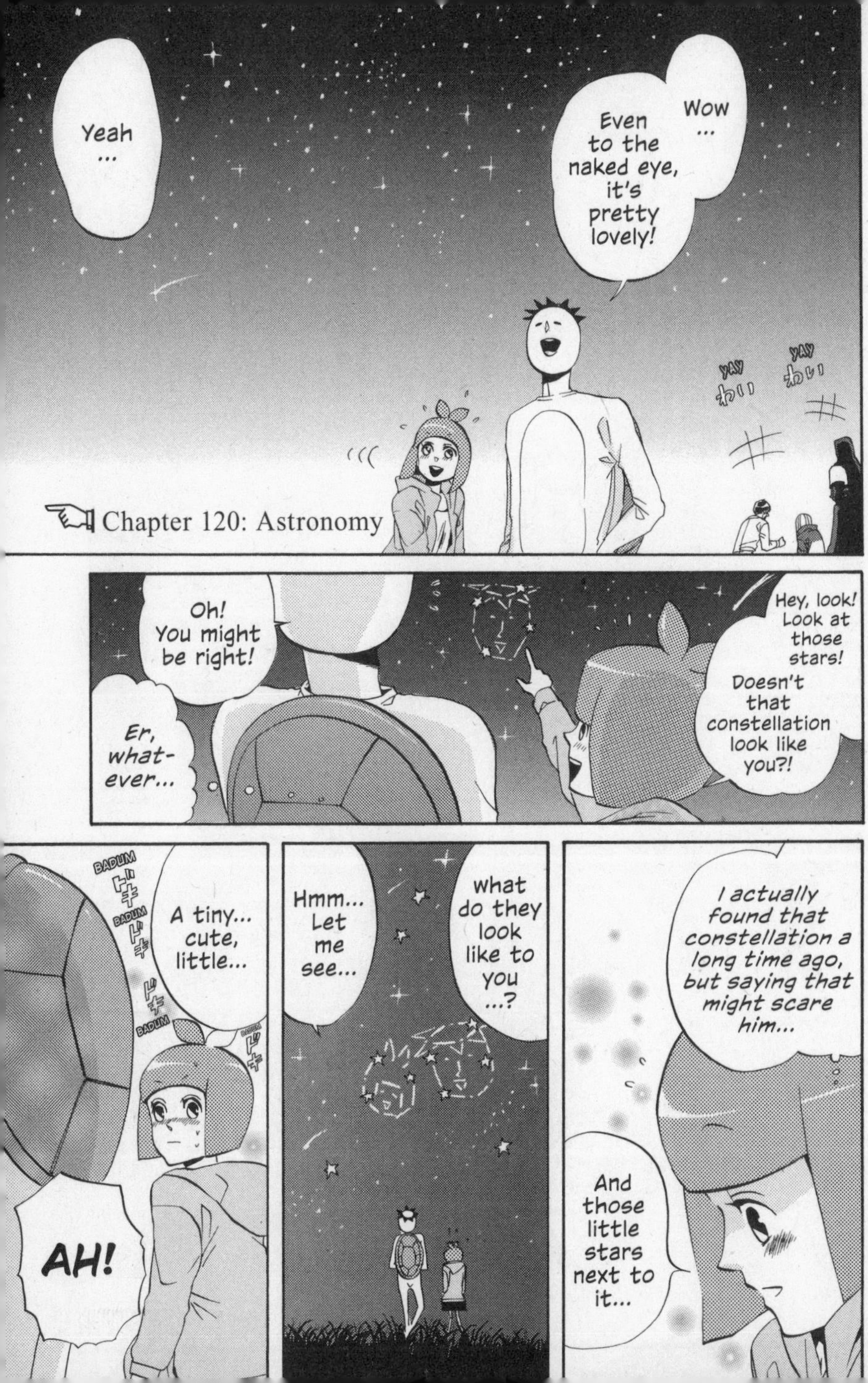
Wow ...
Even to the naked eye, it's pretty lovely!
YAY
YAY
Yeah ...
Chapter 120: Astronomy
Hey, look! Look at those stars!
Doesn't that constellation look like you?!
Oh! You might be right!
Er, whatever...
I actually found that constellation a long time ago, but saying that might scare him...
And those little stars next to it...
what do they look like to you ...?
Hmm... Let me see...
BADUM
BADUM
BADUM
BADUM
A tiny... cute, little...
AH!

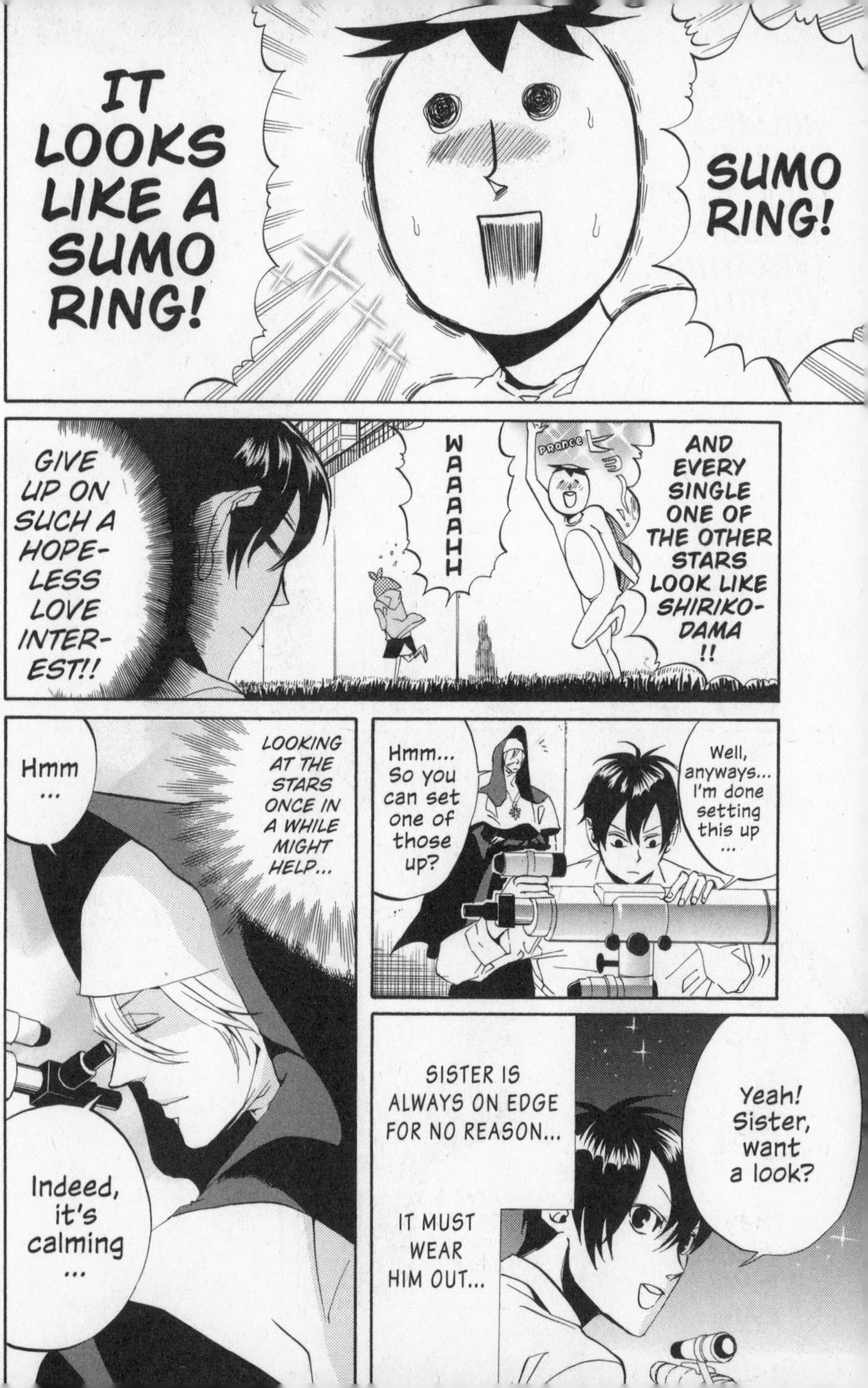
SUMO RING!
IT LOOKS LIKE A SUMO RING!
AND EVERY SINGLE ONE OF THE OTHER STARS LOOK LIKE SHIRIKO-DAMA!!
Prance
WAAAAAHH
GIVE UP ON SUCH A HOPE-LESS LOVE INTER-EST!!
Well, anyways... I'm done setting this up...
Hmm... So you can set one of those up?
Yeah! Sister, want a look?
SISTER IS ALWAYS ON EDGE FOR NO REASON...
IT MUST WEAR HIM OUT...
LOOKING AT THE STARS ONCE IN A WHILE MIGHT HELP...
Hmm...
Indeed, it's calming...

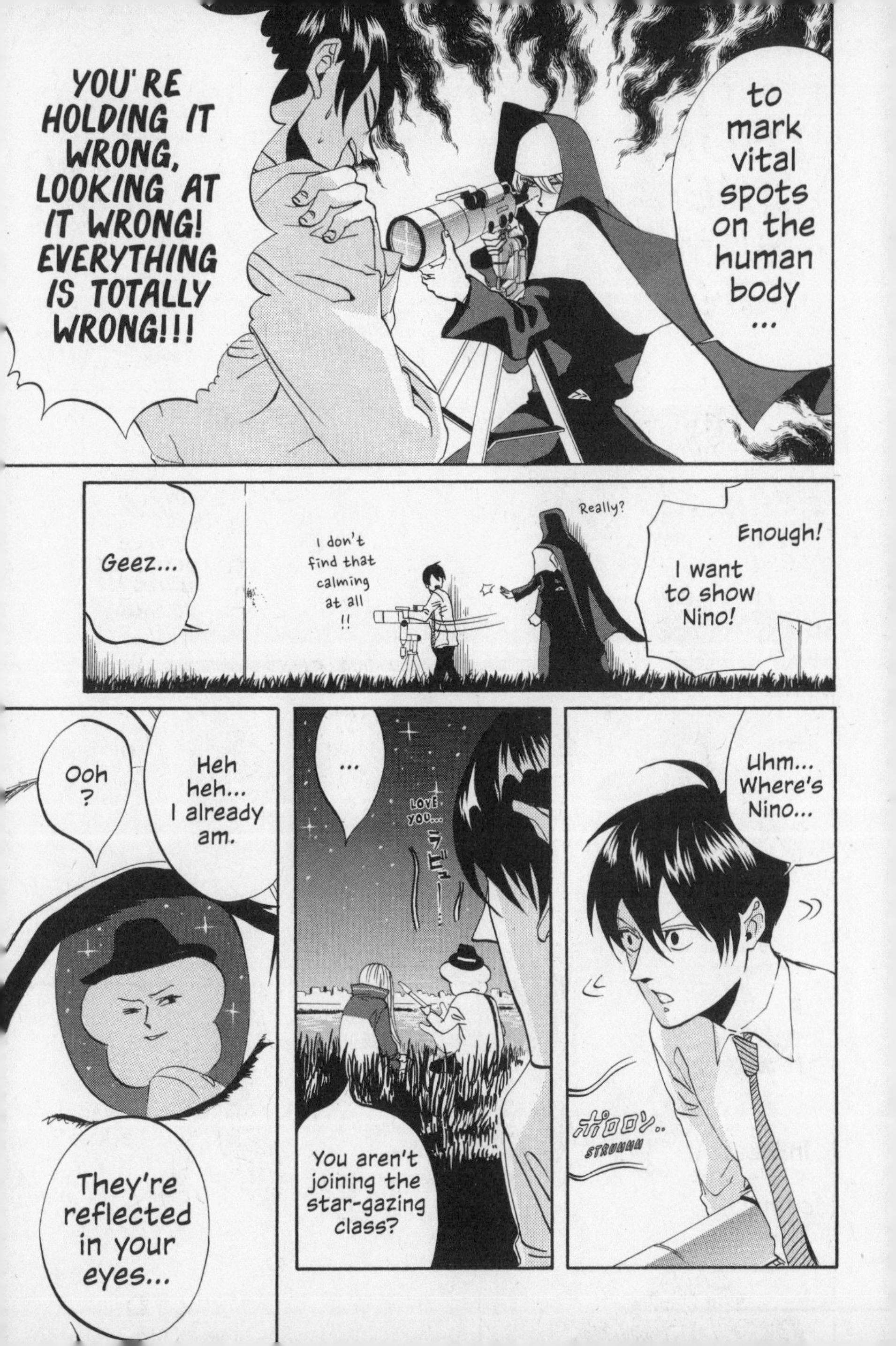
to mark vital spots on the human body ...
YOU'RE HOLDING IT WRONG, LOOKING AT IT WRONG! EVERYTHING IS TOTALLY WRONG!!!
Enough! I want to show Nino!
Really?
I don't find that calming at all !!
Geez...
Uhm... Where's Nino...
ポロロン。。
STRUMMM
...
LOVE YOU...
ラビュー!
You aren't joining the star-gazing class?
Heh heh... I already am.
Ooh ?
They're reflected in your eyes...

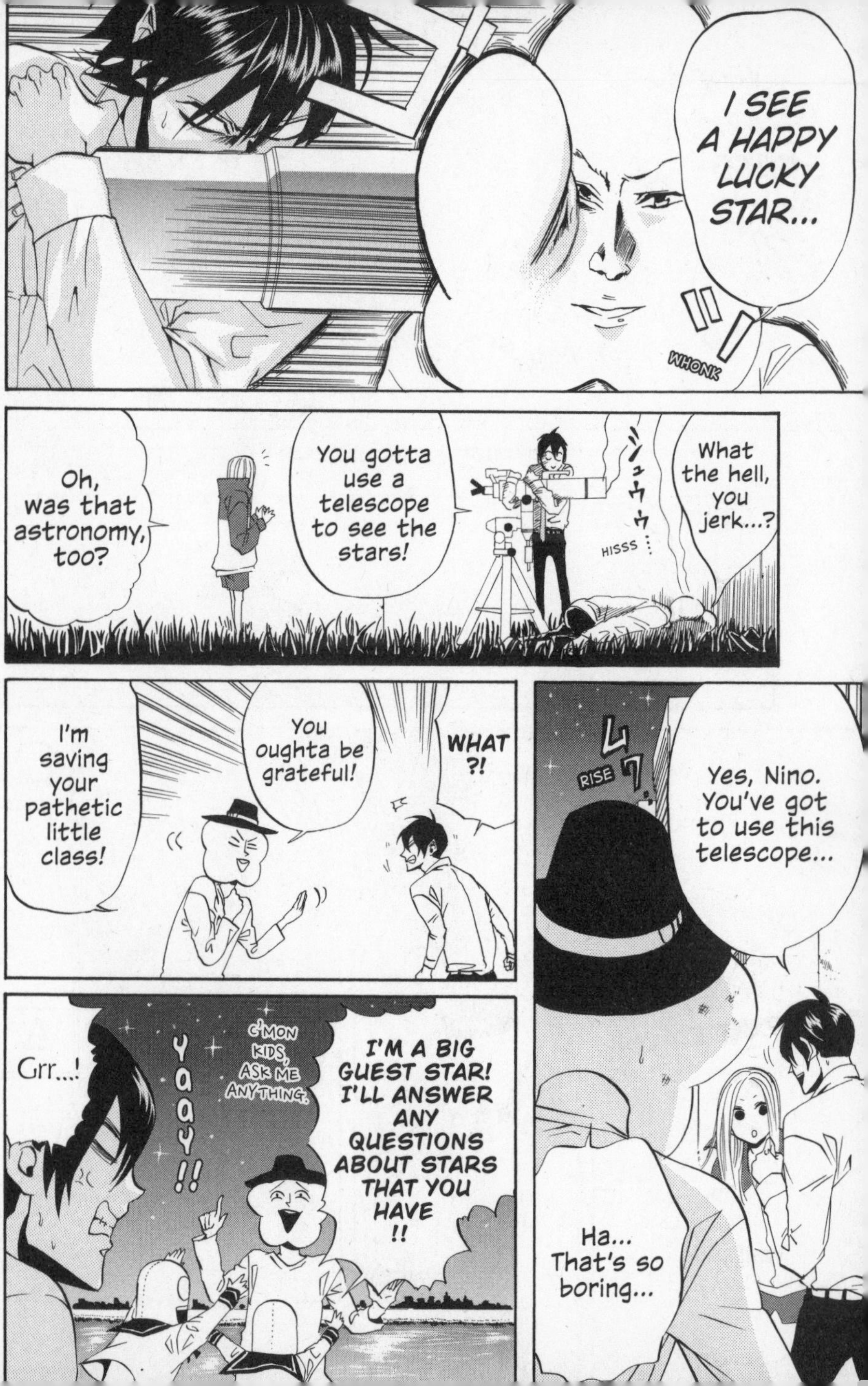
I SEE A HAPPY LUCKY STAR...
WHONK
What the hell, you jerk...?
シュウウ
HISSS...
You gotta use a telescope to see the stars!
Oh, was that astronomy, too?
ムク
RISE
Yes, Nino. You've got to use this telescope...
Ha... That's so boring...
WHAT?!
You oughta be grateful!
I'm saving your pathetic little class!
I'M A BIG GUEST STAR! I'LL ANSWER ANY QUESTIONS ABOUT STARS THAT YOU HAVE!!
C'MON KIDS, ASK ME ANYTHING.
Yaay!!
Grr...!

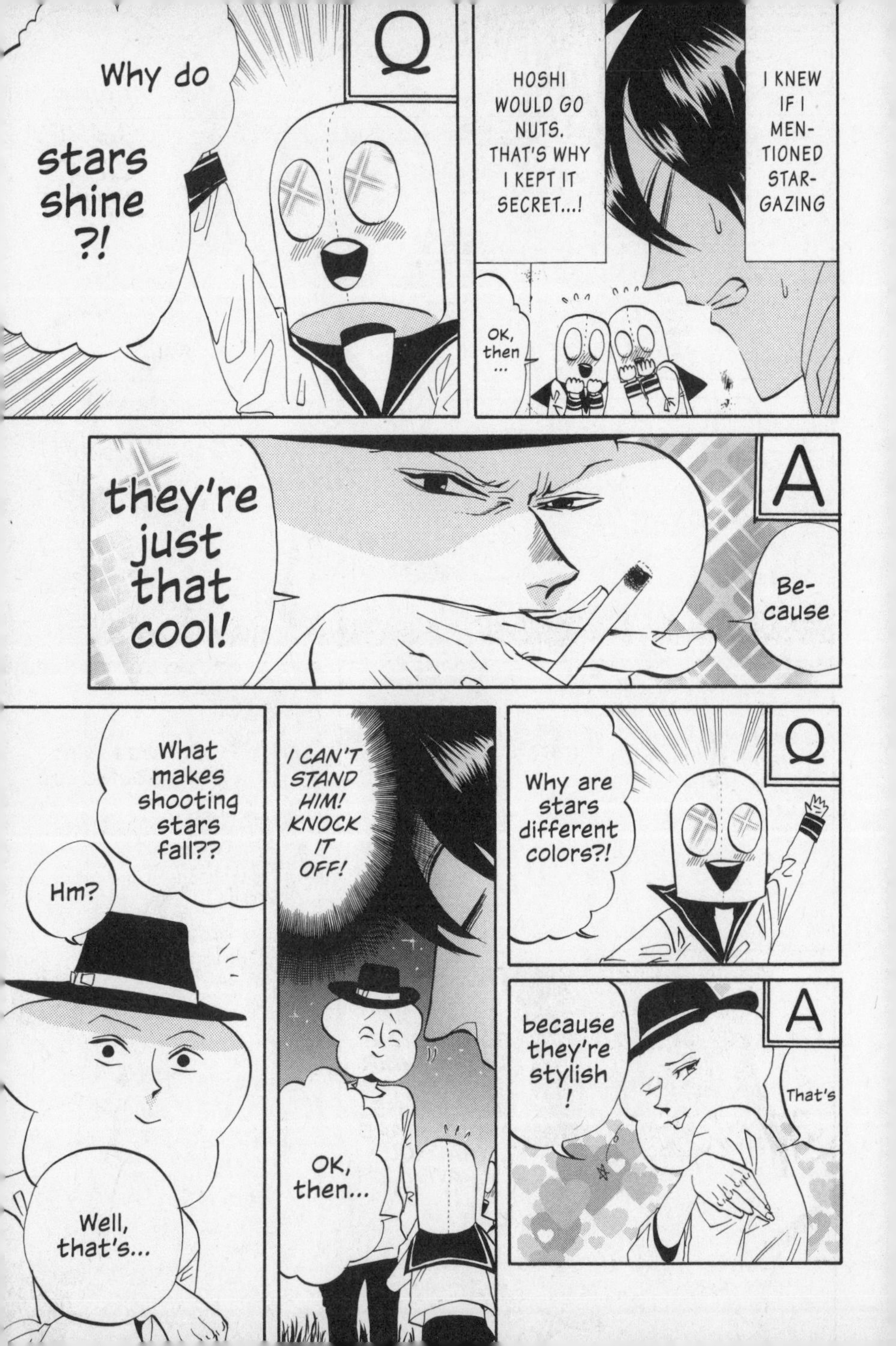
I KNEW IF I MENTIONED STARGAZING
HOSHI WOULD GO NUTS. THAT'S WHY I KEPT IT SECRET...!
OK, then...
Q
Why do stars shine?!
A
Because
they're just that cool!
Q
Why are stars different colors?!
A
That's
because they're stylish!
I CAN'T STAND HIM! KNOCK IT OFF!
OK, then...
What makes shooting stars fall??
Hm?
Well, that's...

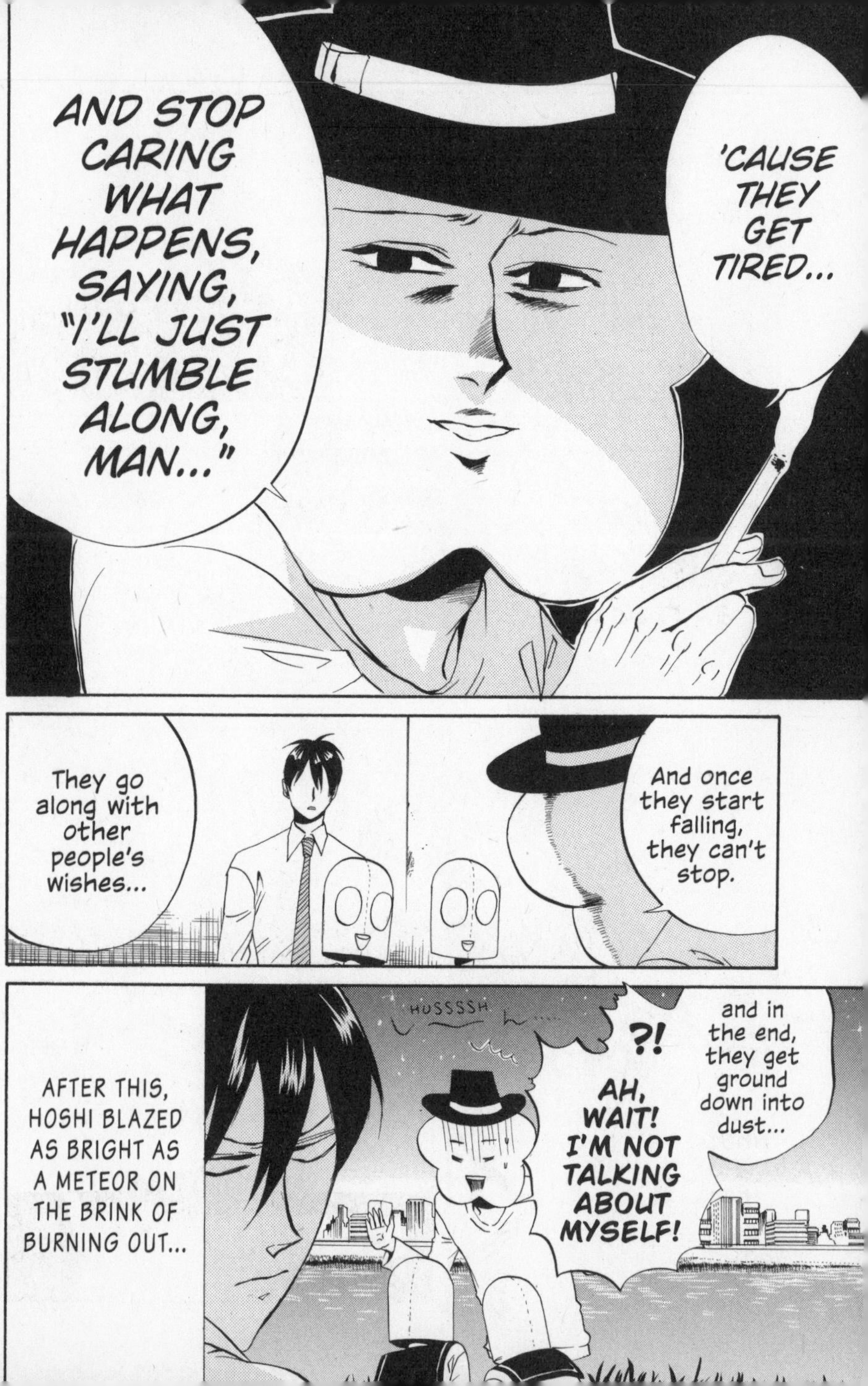
'CAUSE THEY GET TIRED...
AND STOP CARING WHAT HAPPENS, SAYING, "I'LL JUST STUMBLE ALONG, MAN..."
And once they start falling, they can't stop.
They go along with other people's wishes...
and in the end, they get ground down into dust...
HUSSSSH
?!
AH, WAIT! I'M NOT TALKING ABOUT MYSELF!
AFTER THIS, HOSHI BLAZED AS BRIGHT AS A METEOR ON THE BRINK OF BURNING OUT...

Chapter 121: Prepared for Anything

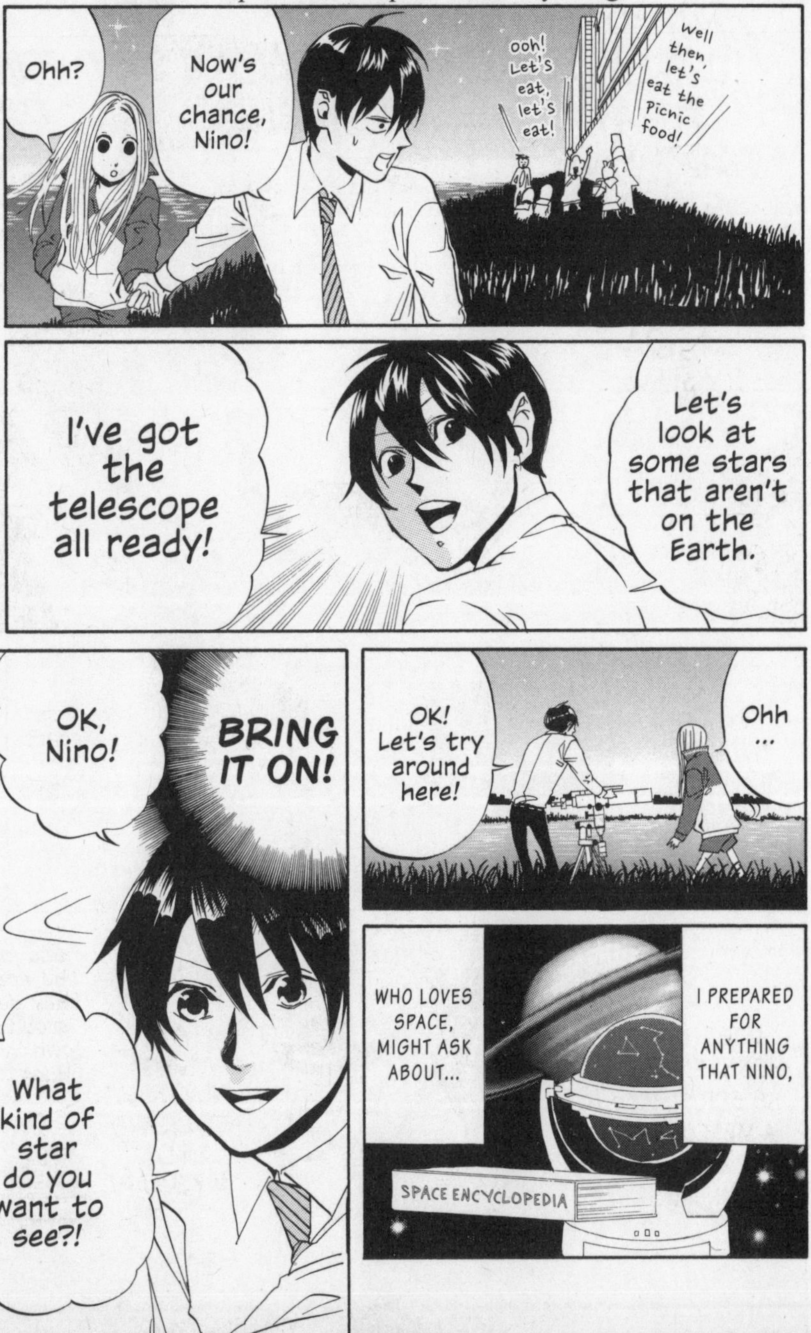
well then, let's eat the Picnic food!
ooh! Let's eat, let's eat!
Now's our chance, Nino!
Ohh?
Let's look at some stars that aren't on the Earth.
I've got the telescope all ready!
Ohh ...
OK! Let's try around here!
I PREPARED FOR ANYTHING THAT NINO,
WHO LOVES SPACE, MIGHT ASK ABOUT...
SPACE ENCYCLOPEDIA
BRING IT ON!
OK, Nino!
What kind of star do you want to see?!

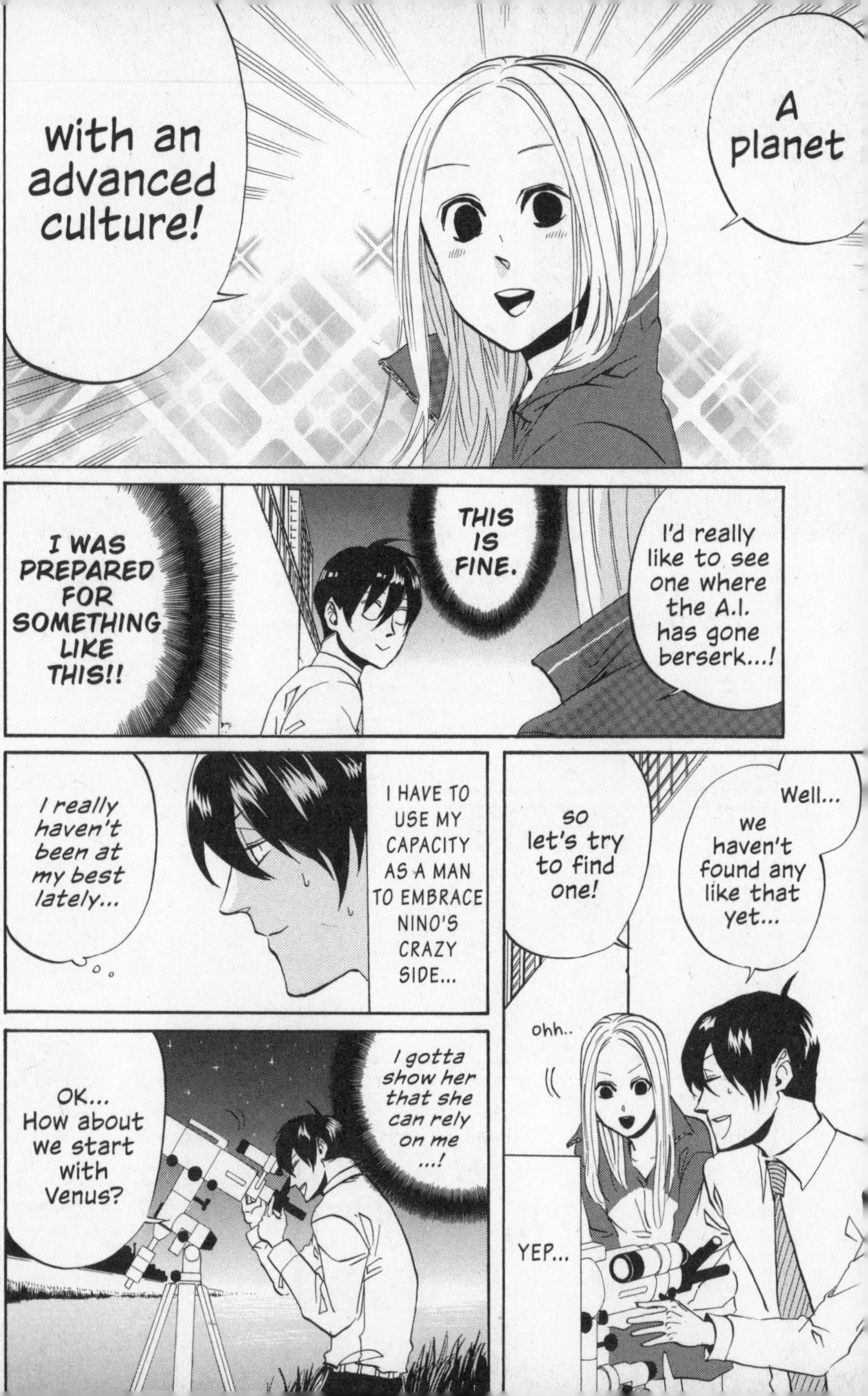
A planet
with an advanced culture!
I'd really like to see one where the A.I. has gone berserk...!
THIS IS FINE.
I WAS PREPARED FOR SOMETHING LIKE THIS!!
Well... we haven't found any like that yet...
so let's try to find one!
ohh..
YEP...
I HAVE TO USE MY CAPACITY AS A MAN TO EMBRACE NINO'S CRAZY SIDE...
I really haven't been at my best lately...
I gotta show her that she can rely on me ...!
OK... How about we start with Venus?

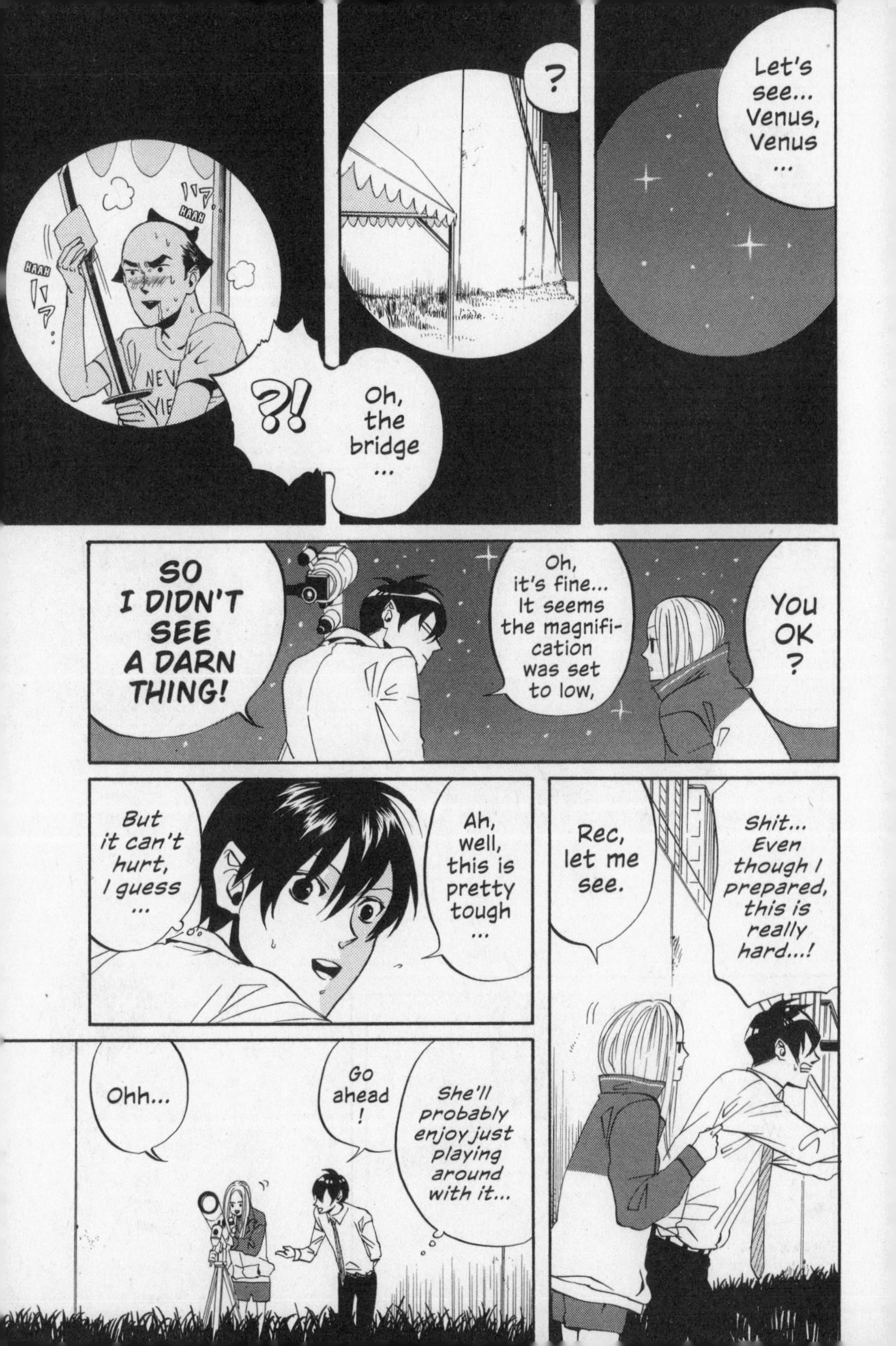
Let's see... Venus, Venus ...
?
Oh, the bridge ...
ハァ...
HAAH
HAAH
ハァ...
?!
You OK ?
Oh, it's fine... It seems the magnification was set to low,
SO I DIDN'T SEE A DARN THING!
Shit... Even though I prepared, this is really hard...!
Rec, let me see.
Ah, well, this is pretty tough ...
But it can't hurt, I guess ...
She'll probably enjoy just playing around with it...
Go ahead !
Ohh...

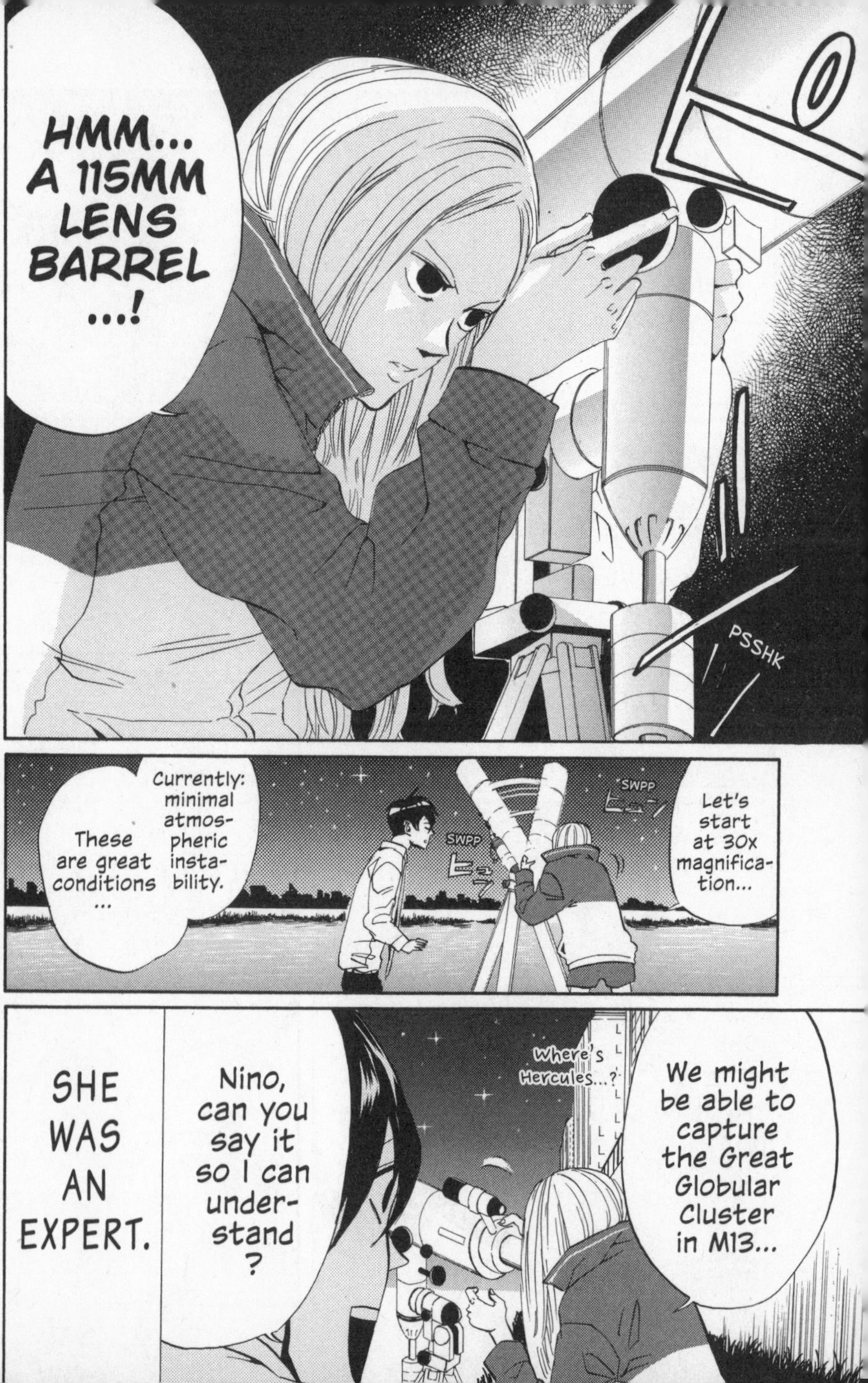
HMM... A 115MM LENS BARREL ...!
PSSHK
Let's start at 30x magnification...
SWPP
SWPP
Currently: minimal atmospheric instability.
These are great conditions ...
We might be able to capture the Great Globular Cluster in M13...
Where's Hercules...?
Nino, can you say it so I can understand?
SHE WAS AN EXPERT.

Chapter 122: The Fate of the Stars

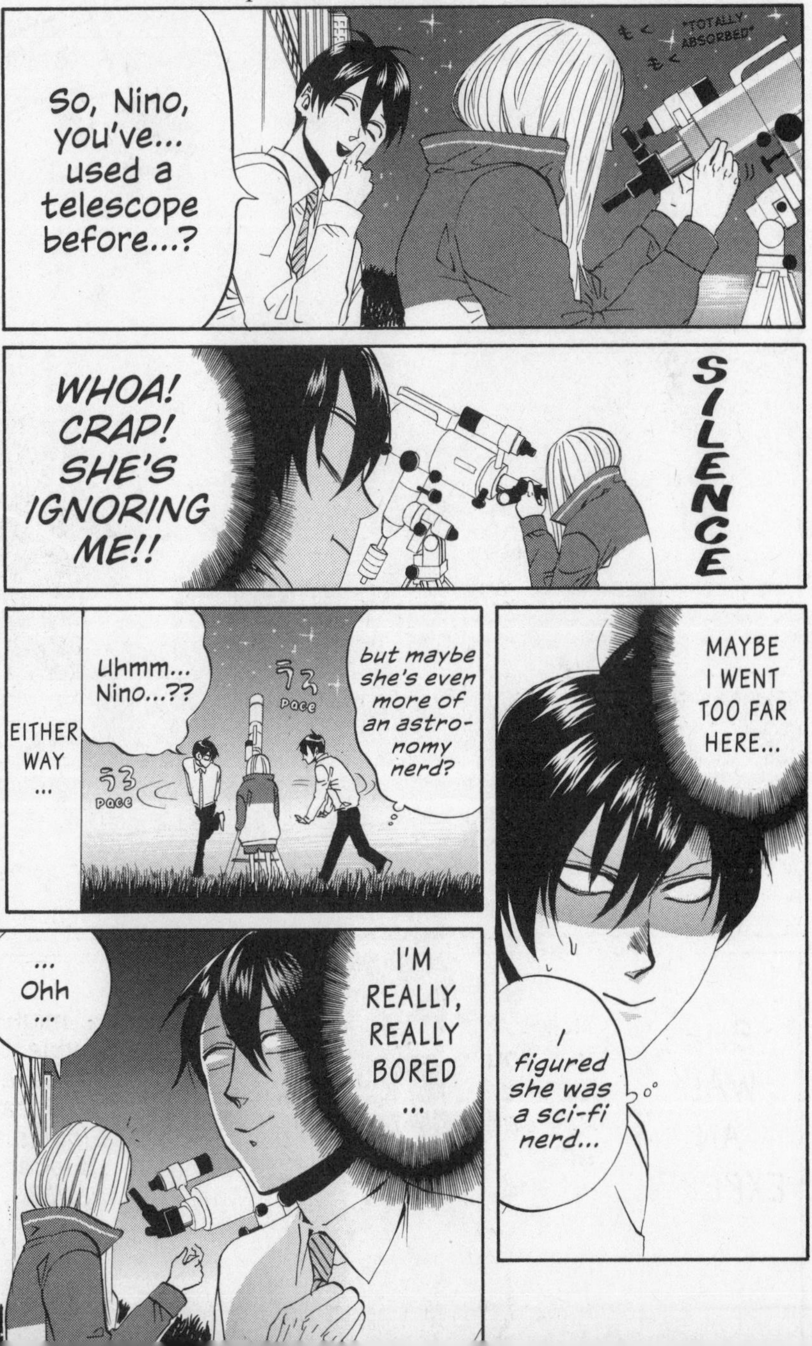
TOTALLY ABSORBED
もく もく
So, Nino, you've... used a telescope before...?
SILENCE
WHOA! CRAP! SHE'S IGNORING ME!!
MAYBE I WENT TOO FAR HERE...
I figured she was a sci-fi nerd...
but maybe she's even more of an astronomy nerd?
うろ pace
Uhmm... Nino...??
うろ pace
EITHER WAY ...
I'M REALLY, REALLY BORED ...
... Ohh ...

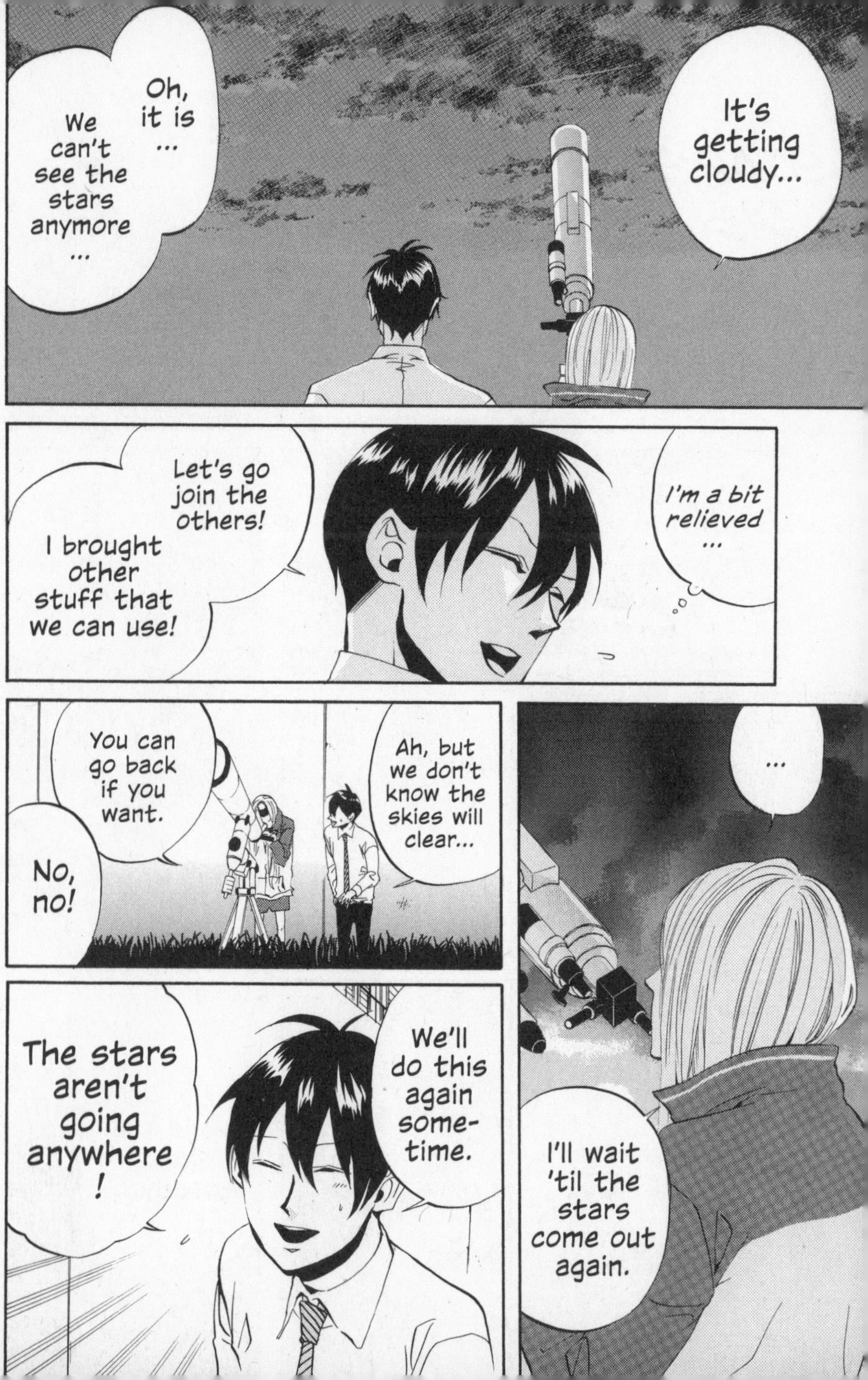
It's getting cloudy...
Oh, it is ...
We can't see the stars anymore ...
I'm a bit relieved ...
Let's go join the others!
I brought other stuff that we can use!
...
I'll wait 'til the stars come out again.
Ah, but we don't know the skies will clear...
You can go back if you want.
No, no!
We'll do this again some-time.
The stars aren't going anywhere!

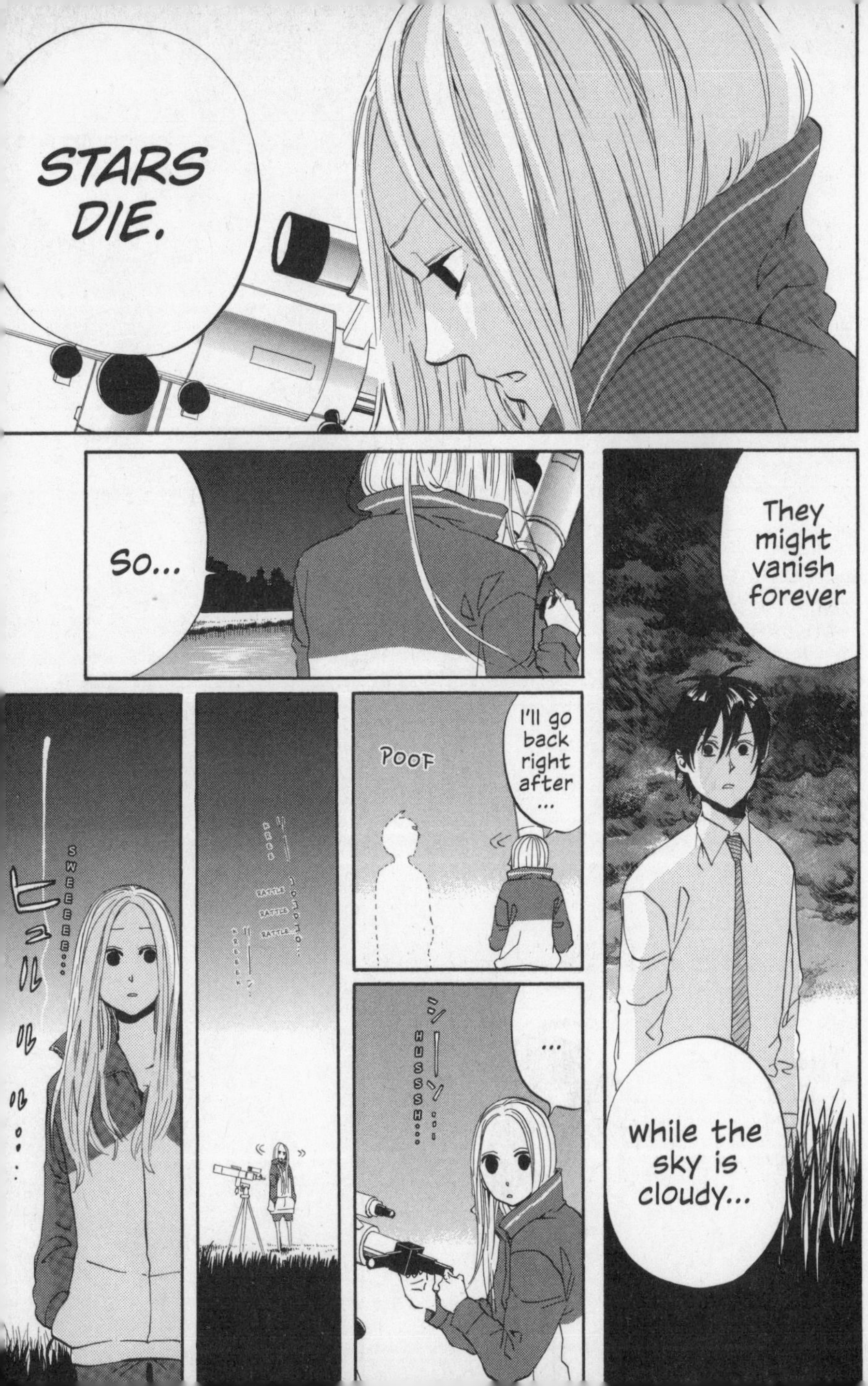
STARS DIE.
They might vanish forever
While the sky is cloudy...
So...
I'll go back right after...
POOF
...
HUSSSH...
KREEE
RATTLE RATTLE RATTLE...
KREEEK
SWEEEEE...

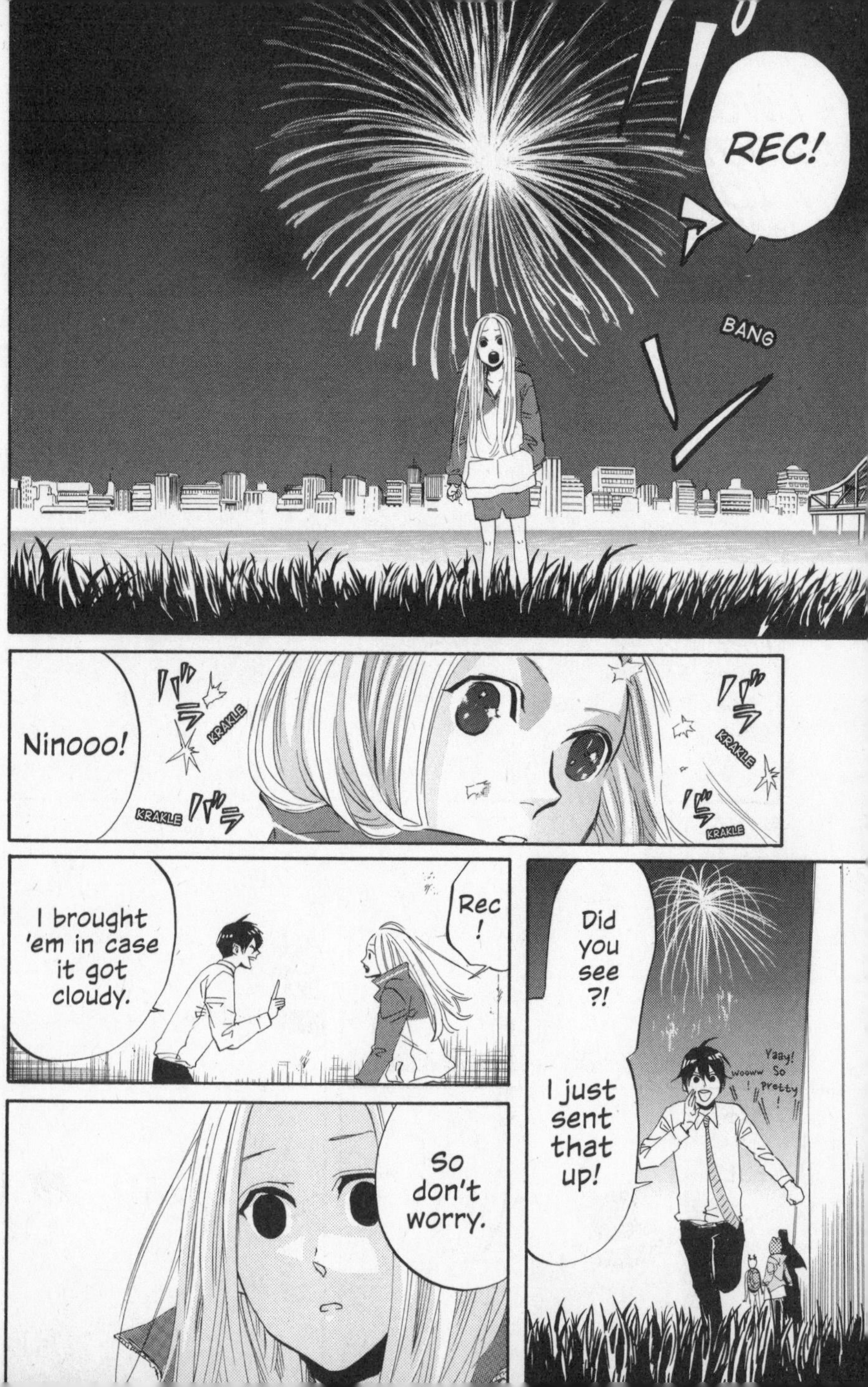
REC!
BANG
KRAKLE
KRAKLE
Ninooo!
KRAKLE
KRAKLE
Did you see?!
I just sent that up!
Yaay!
wooow!
So pretty!
Rec!
I brought 'em in case it got cloudy.
So don't worry.

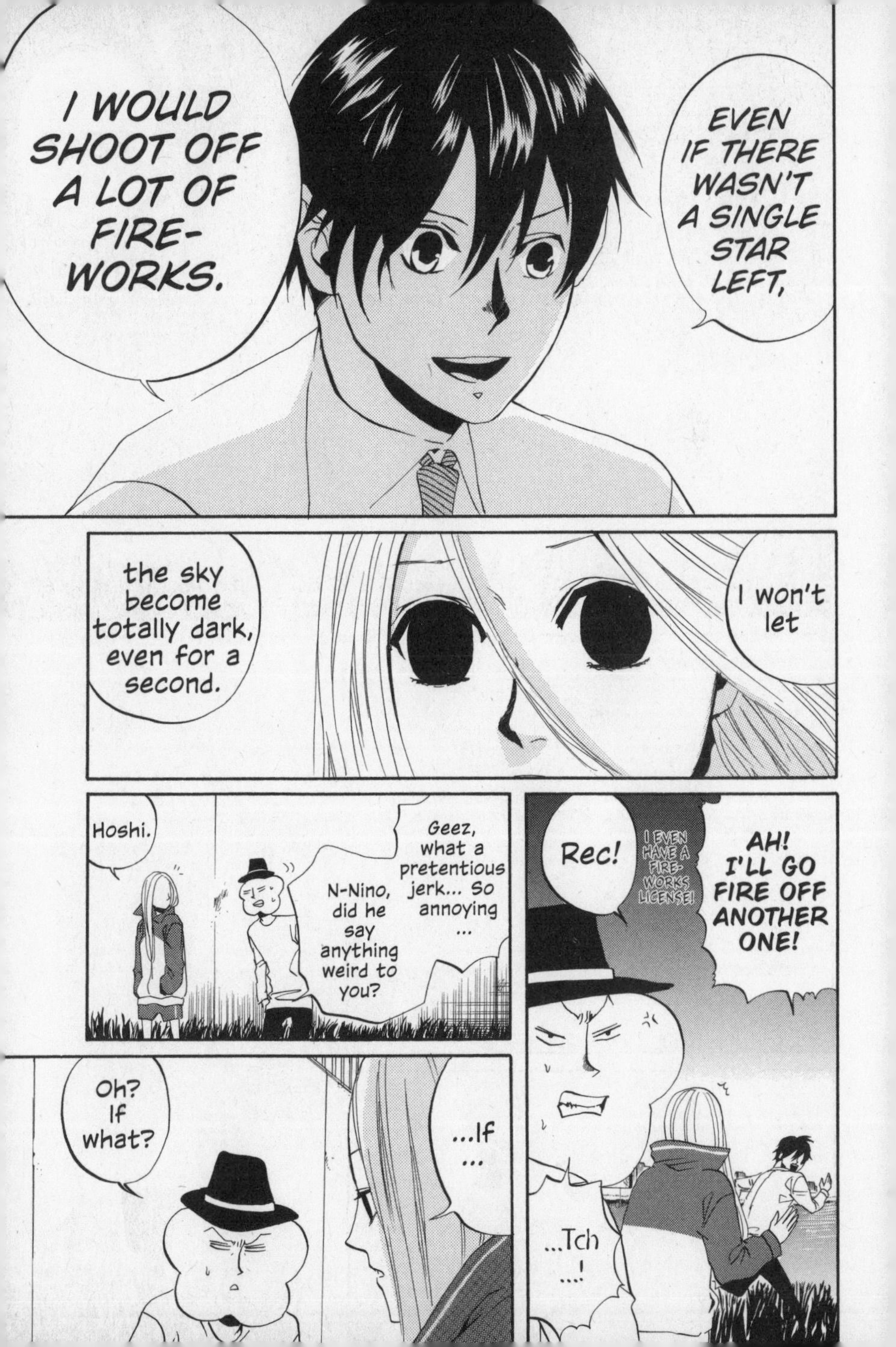

EVEN IF THERE WASN'T A SINGLE STAR LEFT,
I WOULD SHOOT OFF A LOT OF FIRE-WORKS.
I won't let
the sky become totally dark, even for a second.
AH! I'LL GO FIRE OFF ANOTHER ONE!
I EVEN HAVE A FIRE-WORKS LICENSE!
Rec!
...Tch ...!
Geez, what a pretentious jerk... So annoying ...
N-Nino, did he say anything weird to you?
Hoshi.
...If ...
Oh? If what?

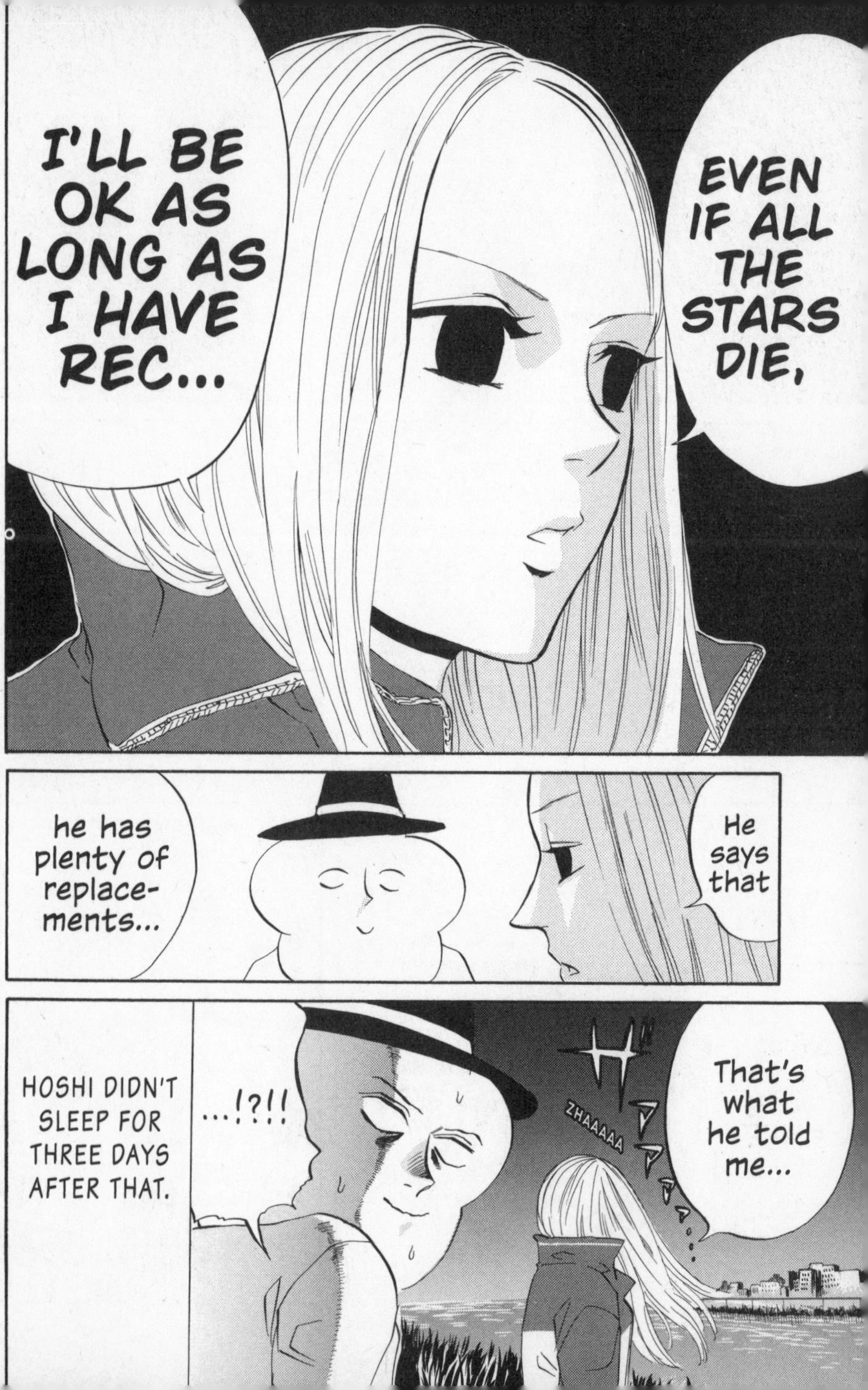
EVEN IF ALL THE STARS DIE,
I'LL BE OK AS LONG AS I HAVE REC...
He says that
he has plenty of replacements...
That's what he told me...
ZHAAAAA
...!?!!
HOSHI DIDN'T SLEEP FOR THREE DAYS AFTER THAT.

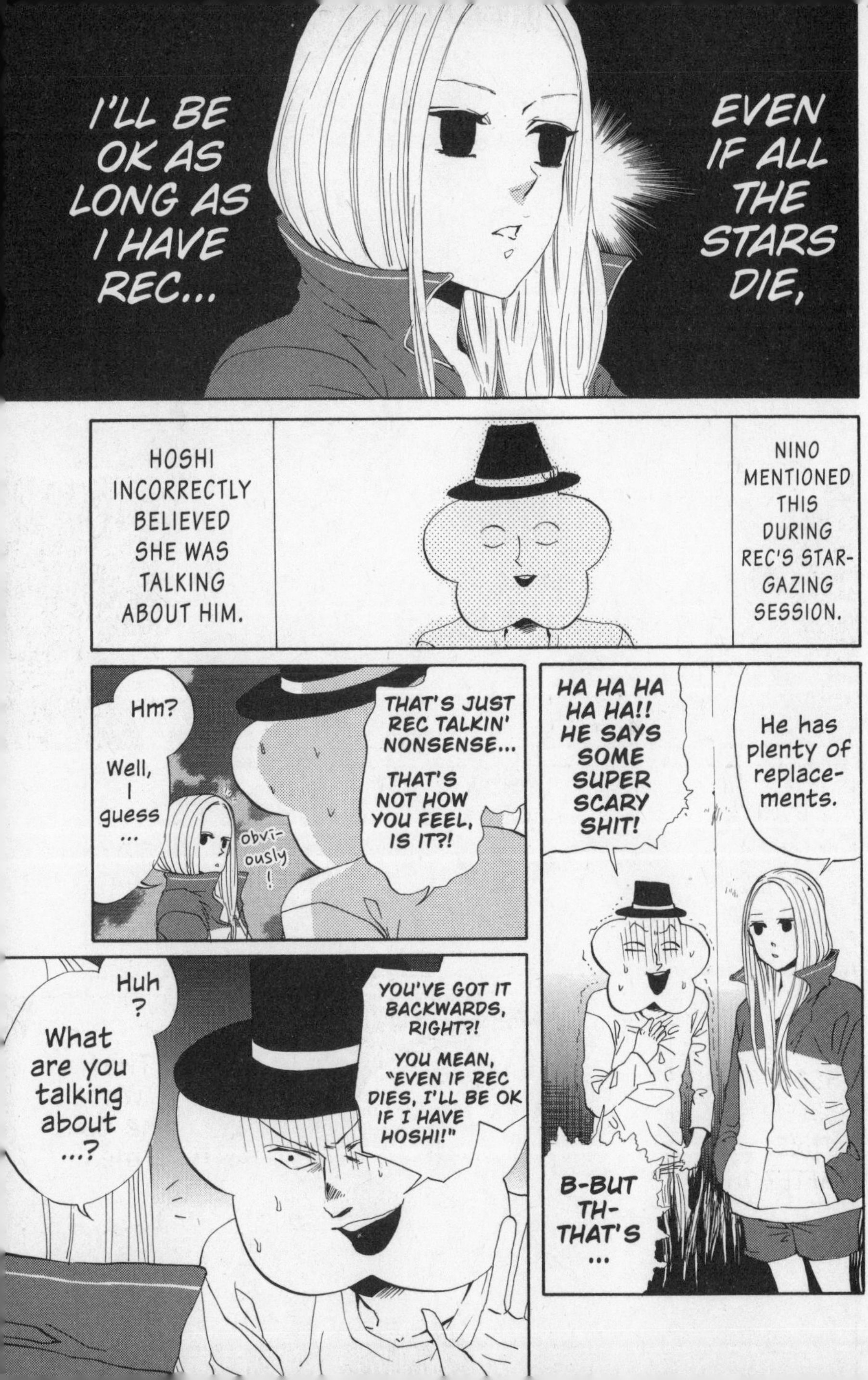
EVEN IF ALL THE STARS DIE,
I'LL BE OK AS LONG AS I HAVE REC...
NINO MENTIONED THIS DURING REC'S STAR-GAZING SESSION.
HOSHI INCORRECTLY BELIEVED SHE WAS TALKING ABOUT HIM.
He has plenty of replace-ments.
HA HA HA HA HA!! HE SAYS SOME SUPER SCARY SHIT!
B-BUT TH-THAT'S ...
THAT'S JUST REC TALKIN' NONSENSE... THAT'S NOT HOW YOU FEEL, IS IT?!
Hm? Well, I guess ...
obvi-ously!
YOU'VE GOT IT BACKWARDS, RIGHT?! YOU MEAN, "EVEN IF REC DIES, I'LL BE OK IF I HAVE HOSHI!"
Huh? What are you talking about ...?

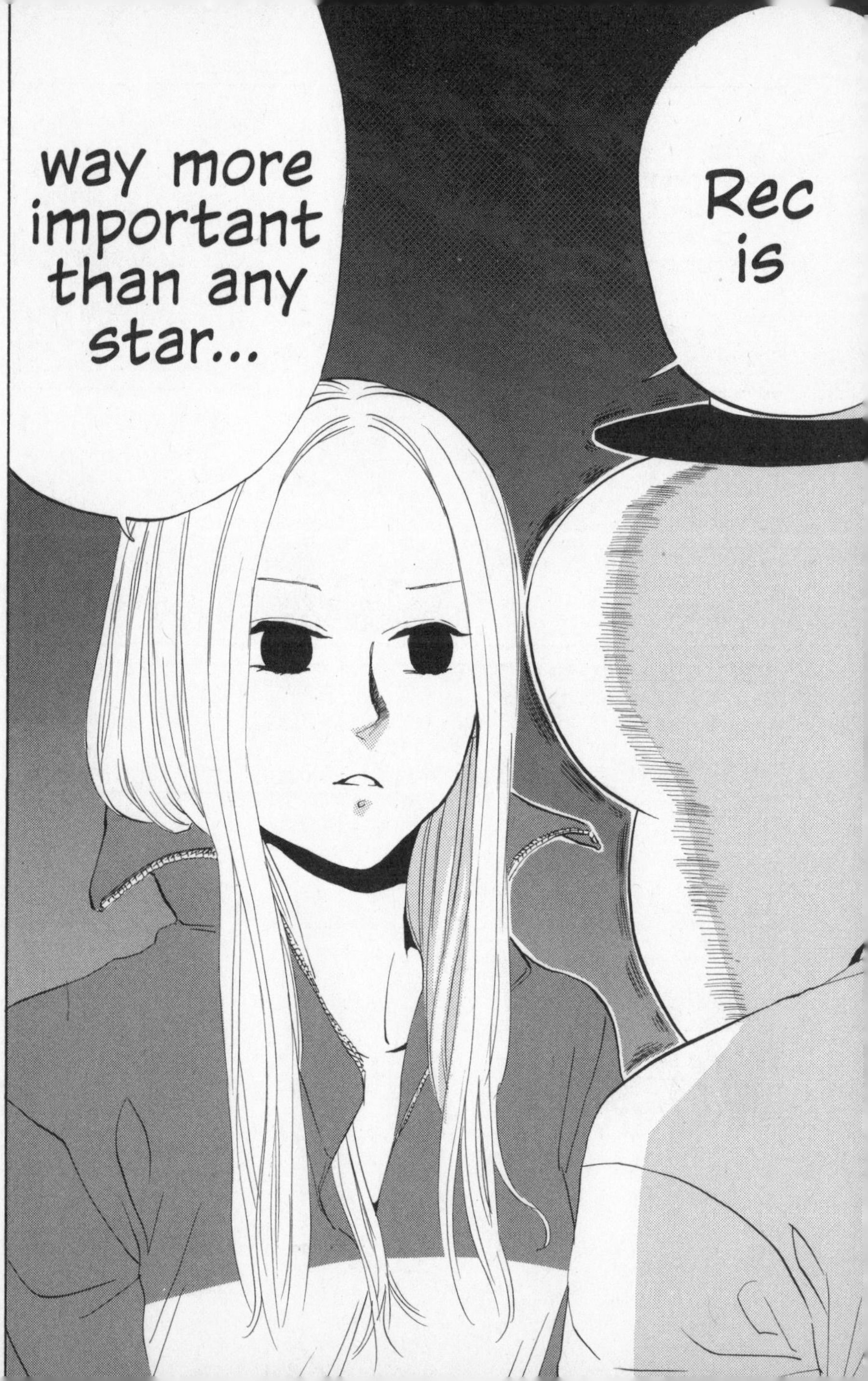
Rec is
way more important than any star...

Chapter 123: Hoshi's Misunderstanding

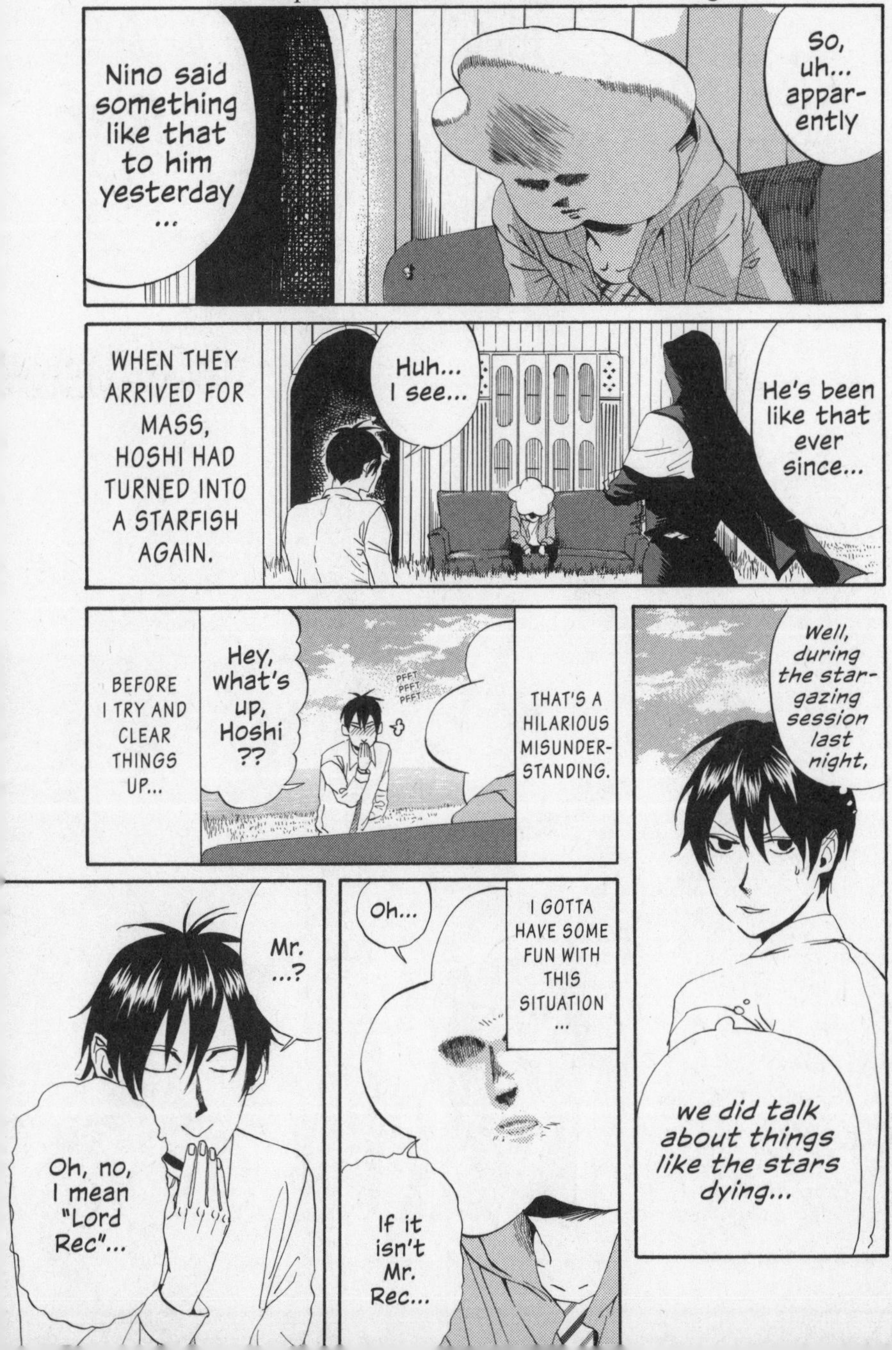
So, uh... apparently
Nino said something like that to him yesterday ...
He's been like that ever since...
Huh... I see...
WHEN THEY ARRIVED FOR MASS, HOSHI HAD TURNED INTO A STARFISH AGAIN.
Well, during the star-gazing session last night,
we did talk about things like the stars dying...
THAT'S A HILARIOUS MISUNDERSTANDING.
Hey, what's up, Hoshi??
PFFT PFFT PFFT
BEFORE I TRY AND CLEAR THINGS UP...
I GOTTA HAVE SOME FUN WITH THIS SITUATION ...
Oh...
If it isn't Mr. Rec...
Mr. ...?
Oh, no, I mean "Lord Rec"...

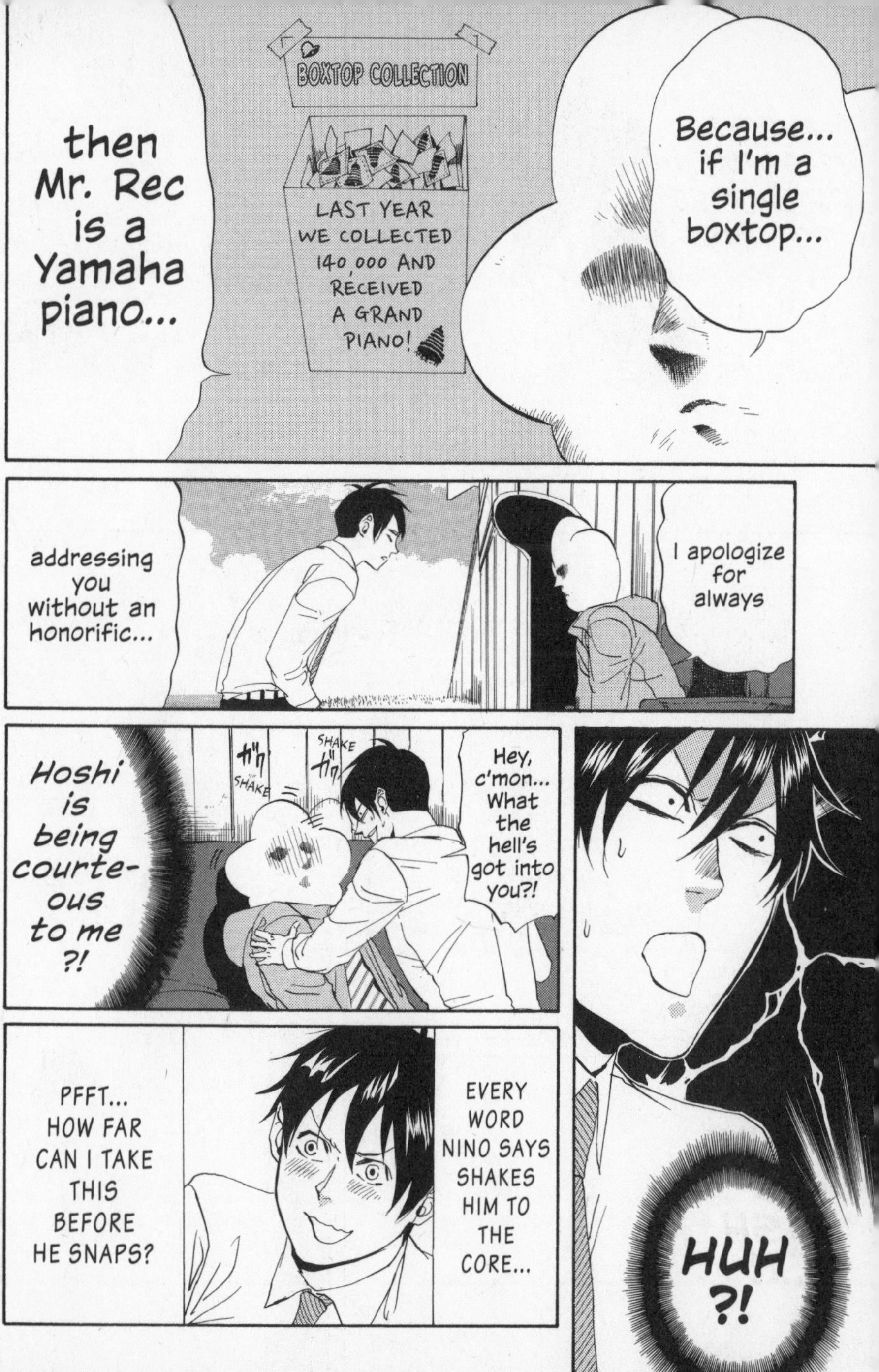
Because... if I'm a single boxtop...
BOXTOP COLLECTION
LAST YEAR WE COLLECTED 140,000 AND RECEIVED A GRAND PIANO!
then Mr. Rec is a Yamaha piano...
I apologize for always
addressing you without an honorific...
HUH ?!
SHAKE
SHAKE
Hey, c'mon... What the hell's got into you?!
Hoshi is being courte-ous to me ?!
EVERY WORD NINO SAYS SHAKES HIM TO THE CORE...
PFFT... HOW FAR CAN I TAKE THIS BEFORE HE SNAPS?

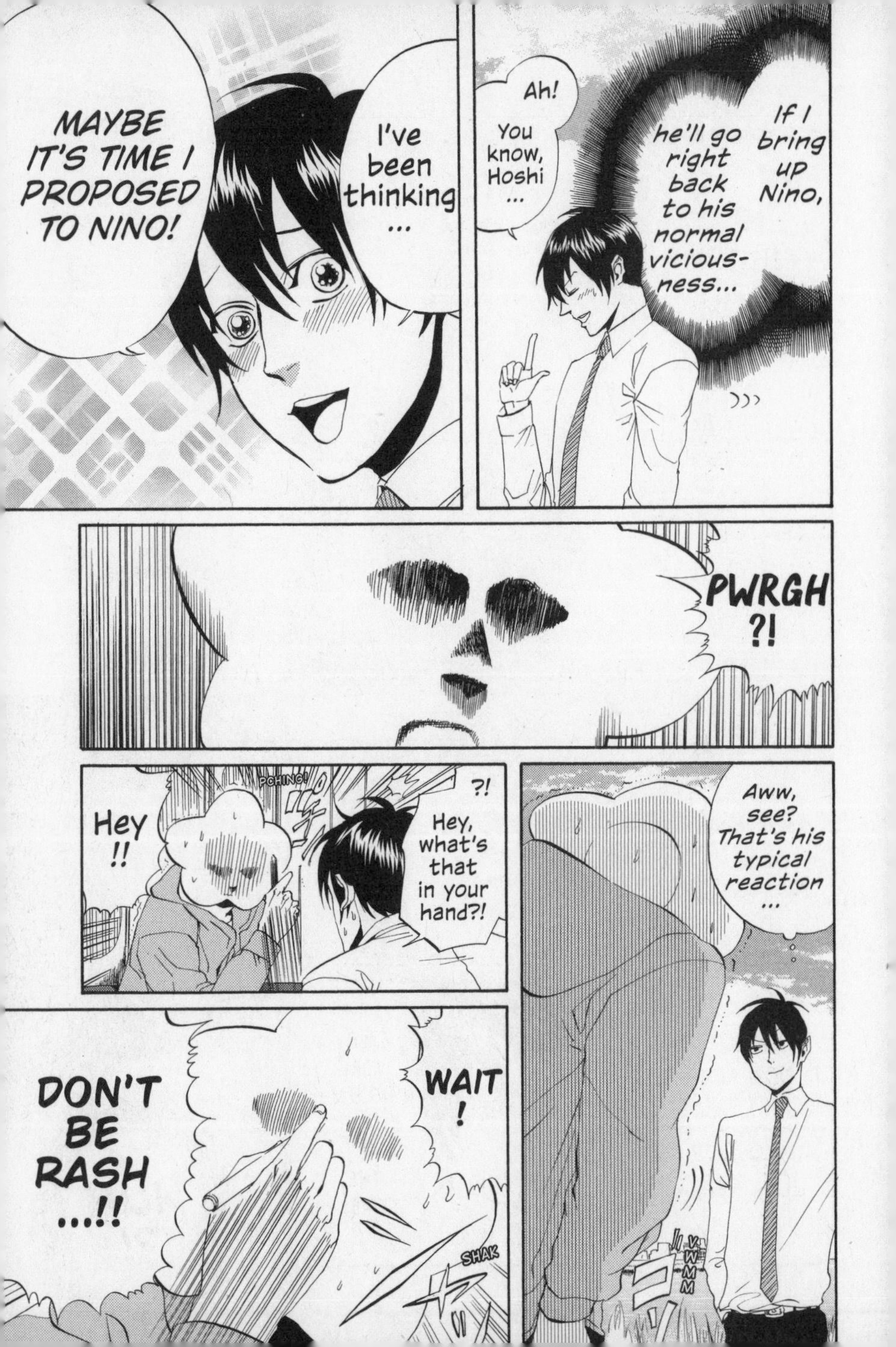
Ah!
You know, Hoshi ...
If I bring up Nino, he'll go right back to his normal vicious-ness...
I've been thinking ...
MAYBE IT'S TIME I PROPOSED TO NINO!
PWRGH ?!
Aww, see? That's his typical reaction ...
VWMM
?!
Hey, what's that in your hand?!
PCHING!
Hey !!
WAIT !
DON'T BE RASH ...!!
SHAK

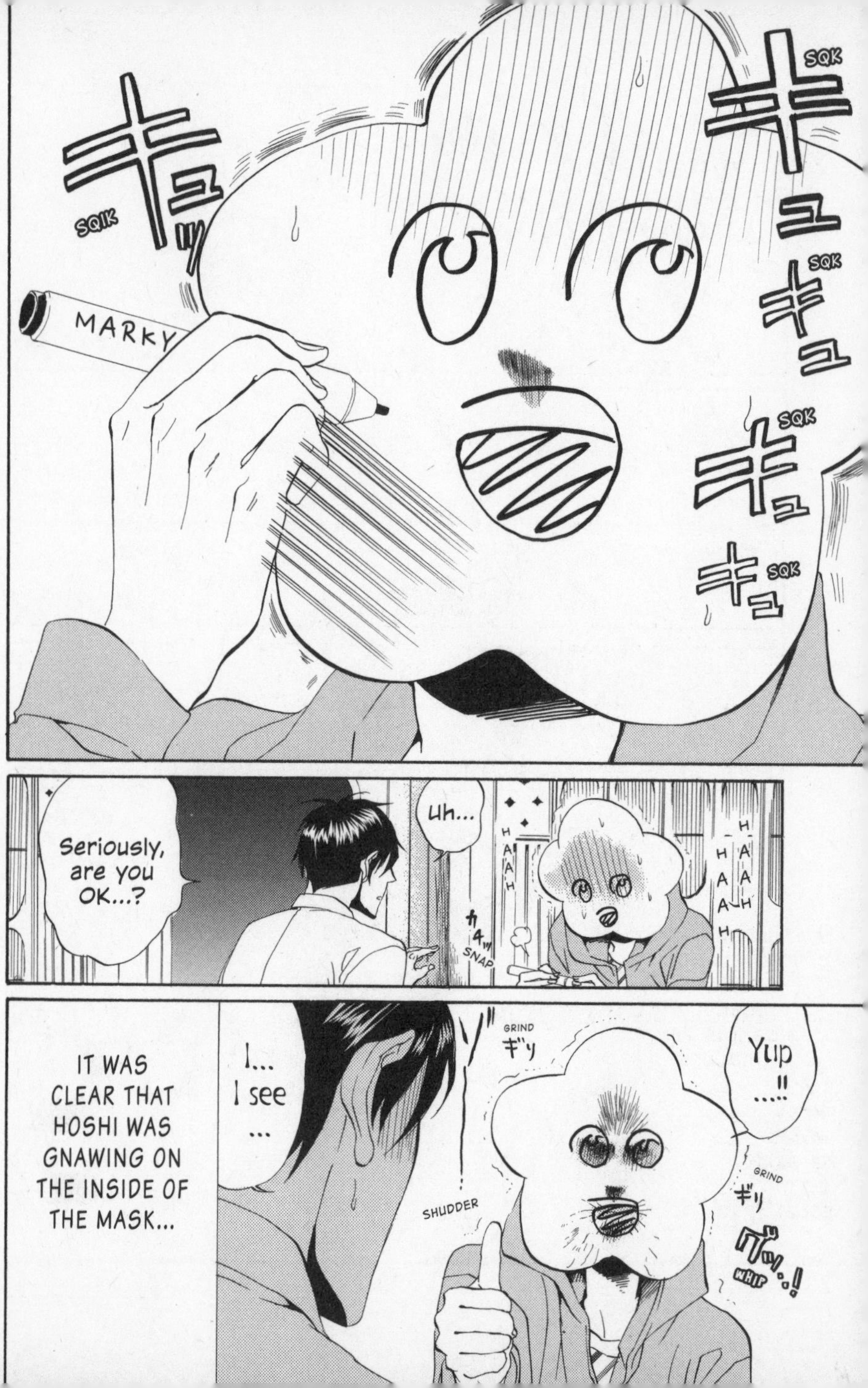
キュ
SQK
キュ
SQK
ギュ
SQK
キュ
SQK
キュッ
SQIK
MARKY
HAAAH
HAAAH
Uh...
SNAP
Seriously, are you OK...?
Yup...!!
GRIND
ギリ
GRIND
ギリ
WHIP
SHUDDER
I... I see...
IT WAS CLEAR THAT HOSHI WAS GNAWING ON THE INSIDE OF THE MASK...

Chapter 124: Friendship Party

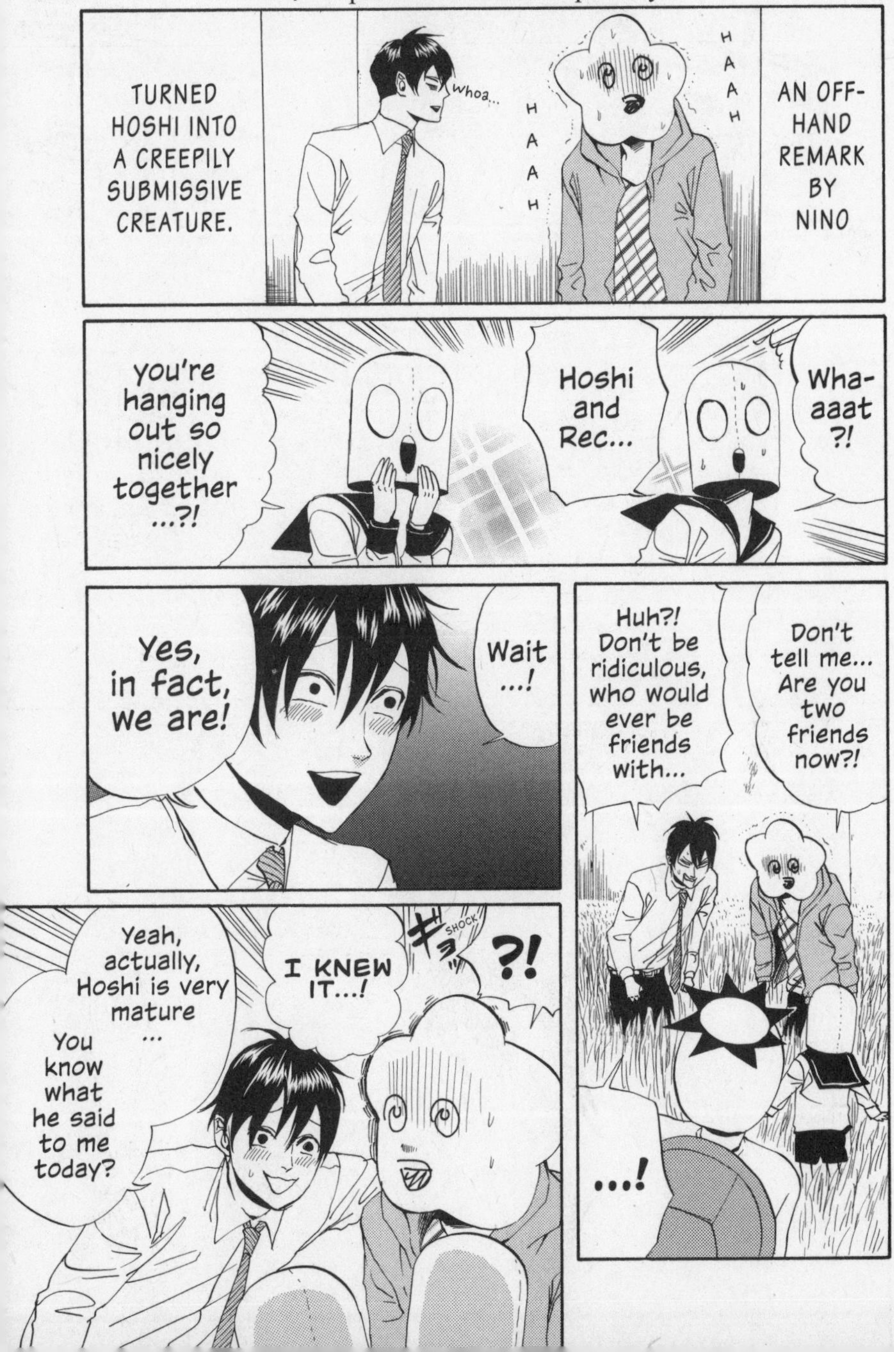

AN OFF-HAND REMARK BY NINO
HAAH
HAAH
whoa...
TURNED HOSHI INTO A CREEPILY SUBMISSIVE CREATURE.
Wha-aaat?!
Hoshi and Rec...
you're hanging out so nicely together...?!
Don't tell me... Are you two friends now?!
Huh?! Don't be ridiculous, who would ever be friends with...
...!
Wait...!
Yes, in fact, we are!
?!
SHOCK
I KNEW IT...!
Yeah, actually, Hoshi is very mature...
You know what he said to me today?

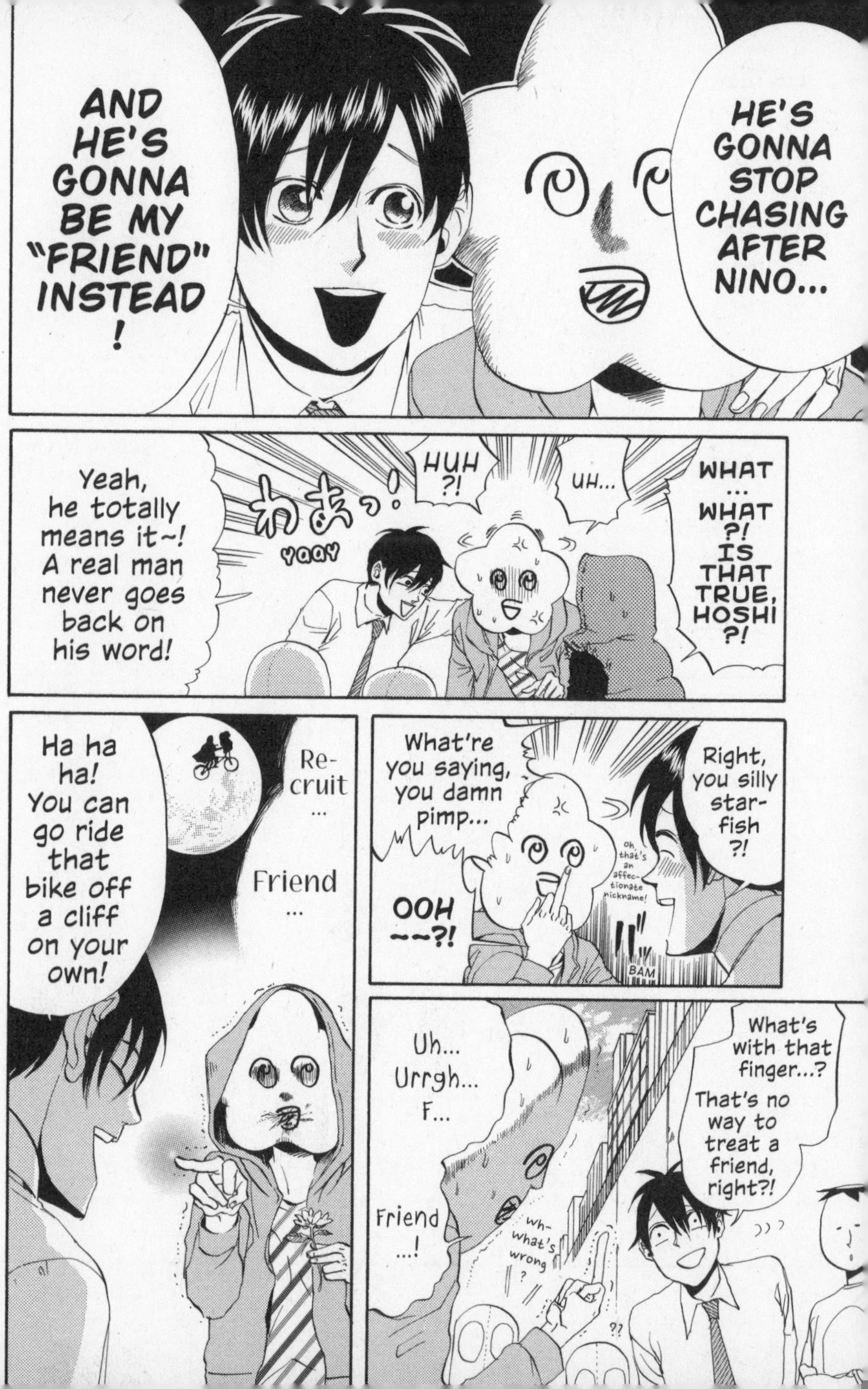
HE'S GONNA STOP CHASING AFTER NINO...
AND HE'S GONNA BE MY "FRIEND" INSTEAD!
WHAT... WHAT?! IS THAT TRUE, HOSHI?!
UH...
HUH?!
わぁっ!
YAAY
Yeah, he totally means it~! A real man never goes back on his word!
Right, you silly star-fish?!
oh, that's an affec-tionate nickname!
What're you saying, you damn pimp...
OOH~~?!
BAM
What's with that finger...?
That's no way to treat a friend, right?!
Uh... Urrgh... F...
Friend...!
wh-what's wrong?
??
Re-cruit...
Friend...
Ha ha ha! You can go ride that bike off a cliff on your own!

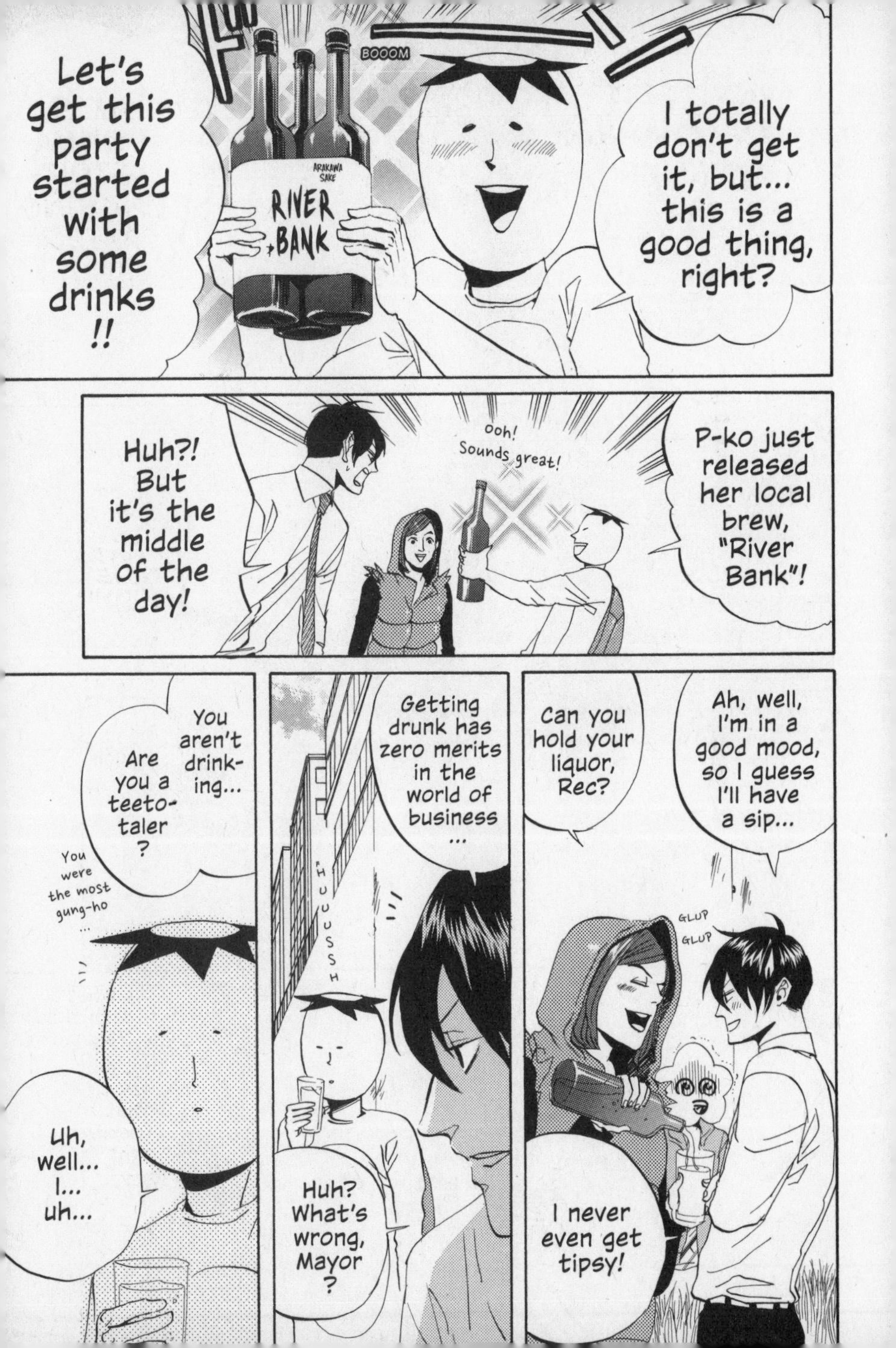
BOOOM
I totally don't get it, but... this is a good thing, right?
Let's get this party started with some drinks !!
ARAKAWA SAKE
RIVER BANK
P-ko just released her local brew, "River Bank"!
Ooh! Sounds great!
Huh?! But it's the middle of the day!
Ah, well, I'm in a good mood, so I guess I'll have a sip...
Can you hold your liquor, Rec?
GLUP GLUP
I never even get tipsy!
Getting drunk has zero merits in the world of business ...
HUUUSSH
Huh? What's wrong, Mayor ?
You aren't drink- ing...
Are you a teeto- taler ?
You were the most gung-ho ...
Uh, well... I... uh...

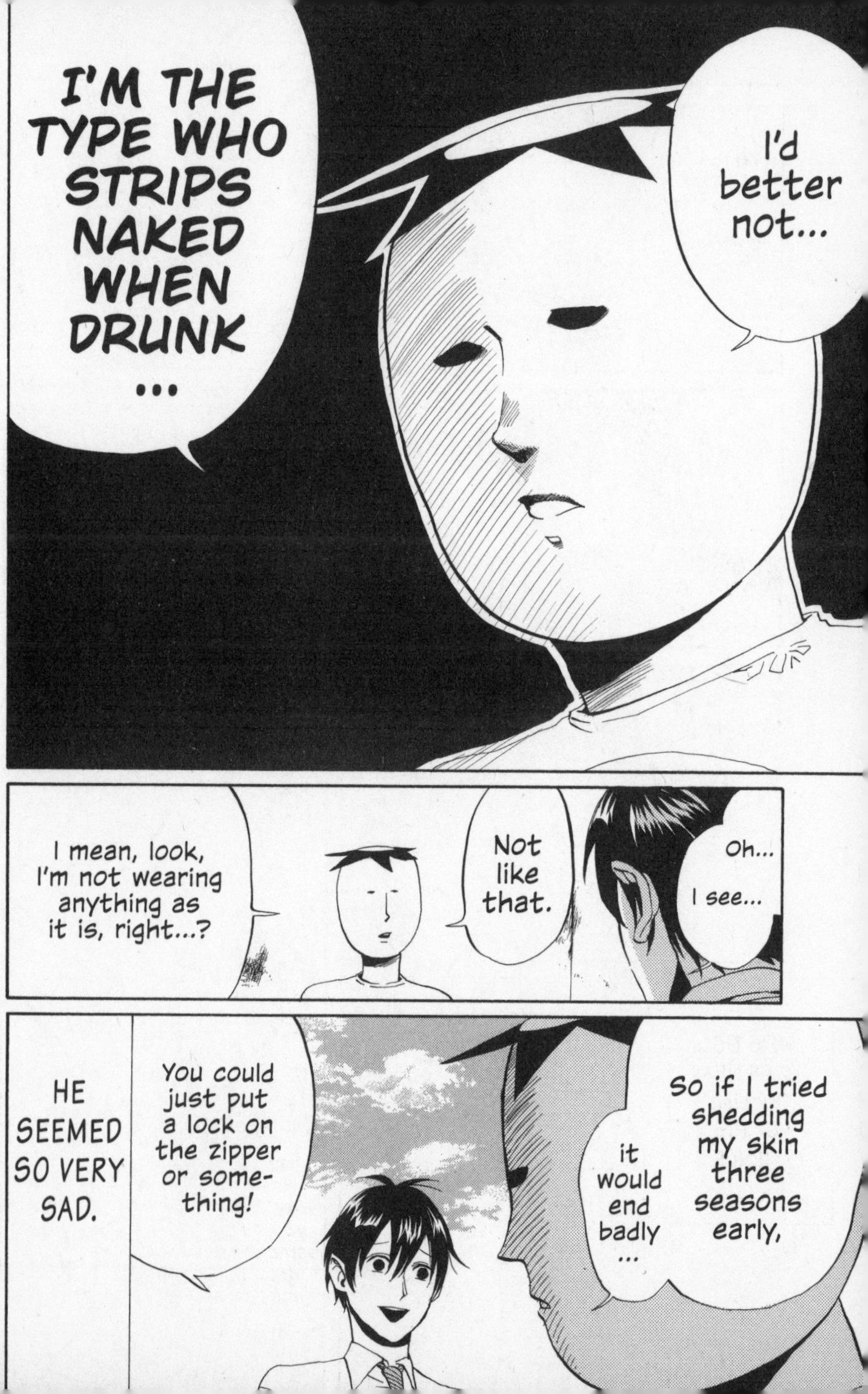
I'd better not...
I'M THE TYPE WHO STRIPS NAKED WHEN DRUNK ...
Oh... I see...
Not like that.
I mean, look, I'm not wearing anything as it is, right...?
So if I tried shedding my skin three seasons early,
it would end badly ...
You could just put a lock on the zipper or some-thing!
HE SEEMED SO VERY SAD.

Chapter 125: Booze, Music, Men, Women

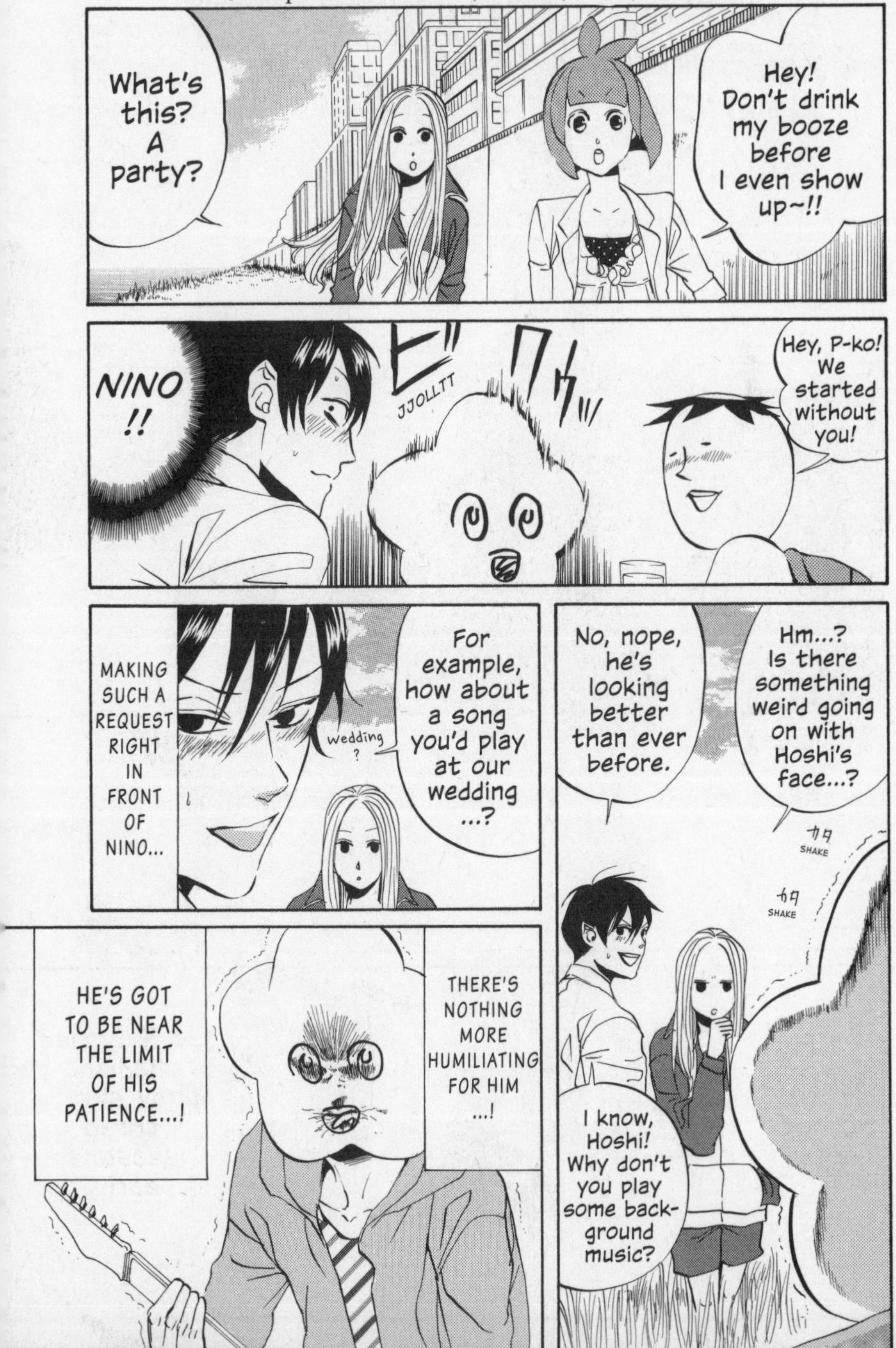
Hey! Don't drink my booze before I even show up~!!
What's this? A party?
Hey, P-ko! We started without you!
JJOLLTT
NINO!!
Hm...? Is there something weird going on with Hoshi's face...?
No, nope, he's looking better than ever before.
SHAKE
SHAKE
I know, Hoshi! Why don't you play some back-ground music?
For example, how about a song you'd play at our wedding...?
wedding?
MAKING SUCH A REQUEST RIGHT IN FRONT OF NINO...
THERE'S NOTHING MORE HUMILIATING FOR HIM...!
HE'S GOT TO BE NEAR THE LIMIT OF HIS PATIENCE...!

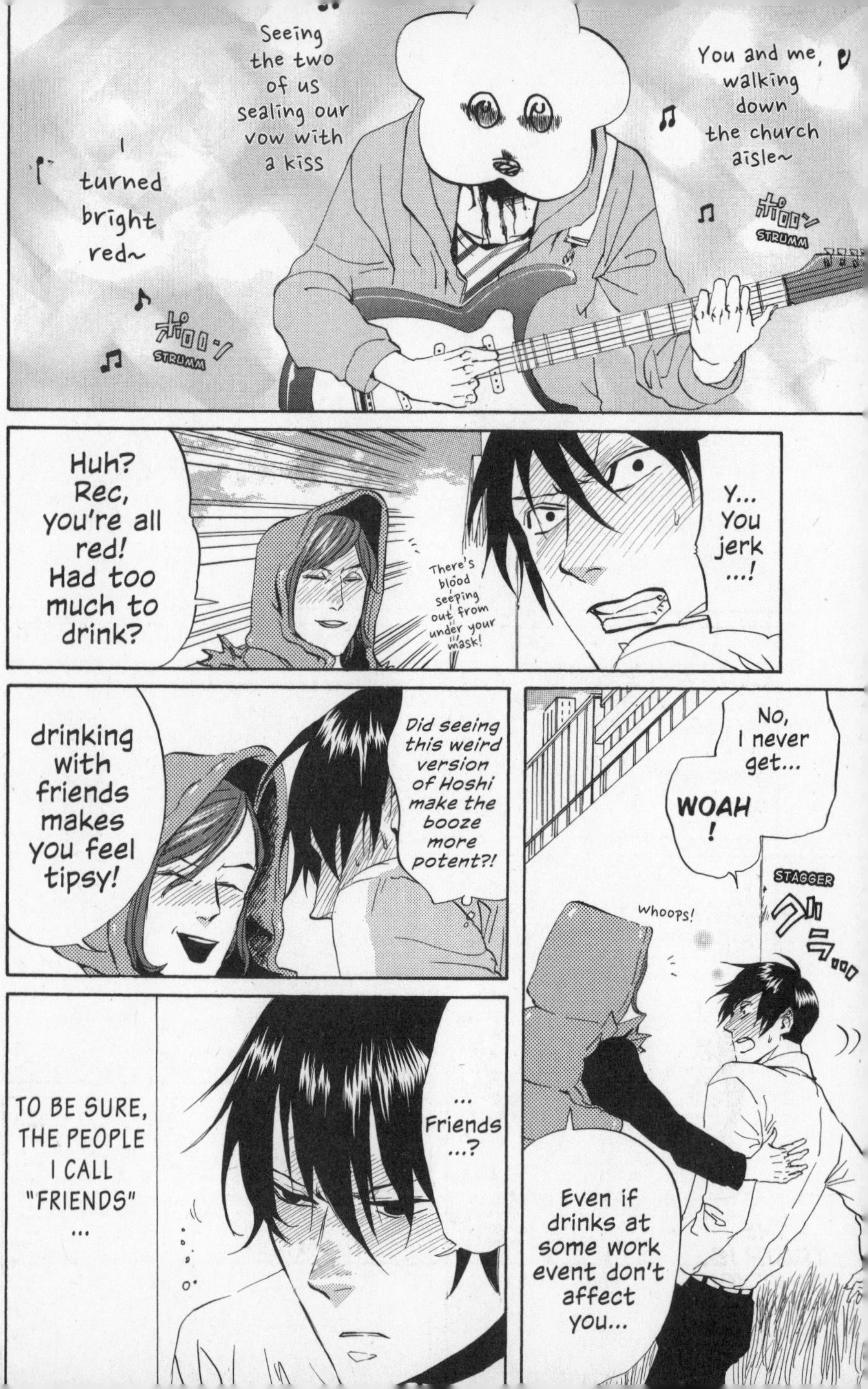
You and me, walking down the church aisle~
STRUMM
Seeing the two of us sealing our vow with a kiss
I turned bright red~
STRUMM
Y... You jerk ...!
There's blood seeping out from under your mask!
Huh? Rec, you're all red! Had too much to drink?
No, I never get... WOAH!
STAGGER
Whoops!
Even if drinks at some work event don't affect you...
Did seeing this weird version of Hoshi make the booze more potent?!
drinking with friends makes you feel tipsy!
... Friends ...?
TO BE SURE, THE PEOPLE I CALL "FRIENDS" ...

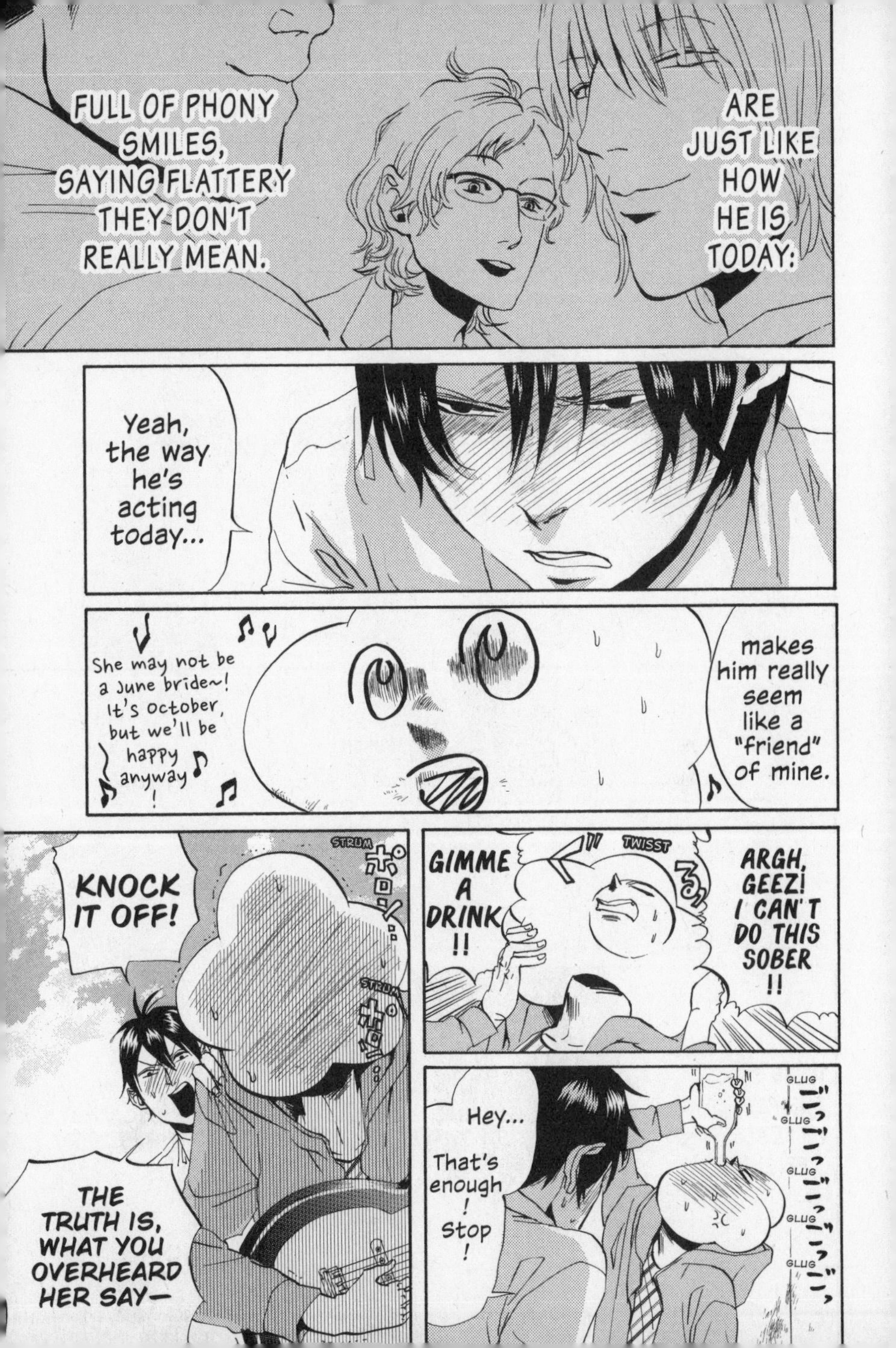
ARE JUST LIKE HOW HE IS TODAY:
FULL OF PHONY SMILES, SAYING FLATTERY THEY DON'T REALLY MEAN.
Yeah, the way he's acting today...
makes him really seem like a "friend" of mine.
She may not be a June bride~! It's October, but we'll be happy anyway!
ARGH, GEEZ! I CAN'T DO THIS SOBER!!
TWISST
GIMME A DRINK!!
GLUG GLUG GLUG GLUG GLUG
Hey... That's enough! Stop!
STRUM
KNOCK IT OFF!
STRUM
THE TRUTH IS, WHAT YOU OVERHEARD HER SAY—

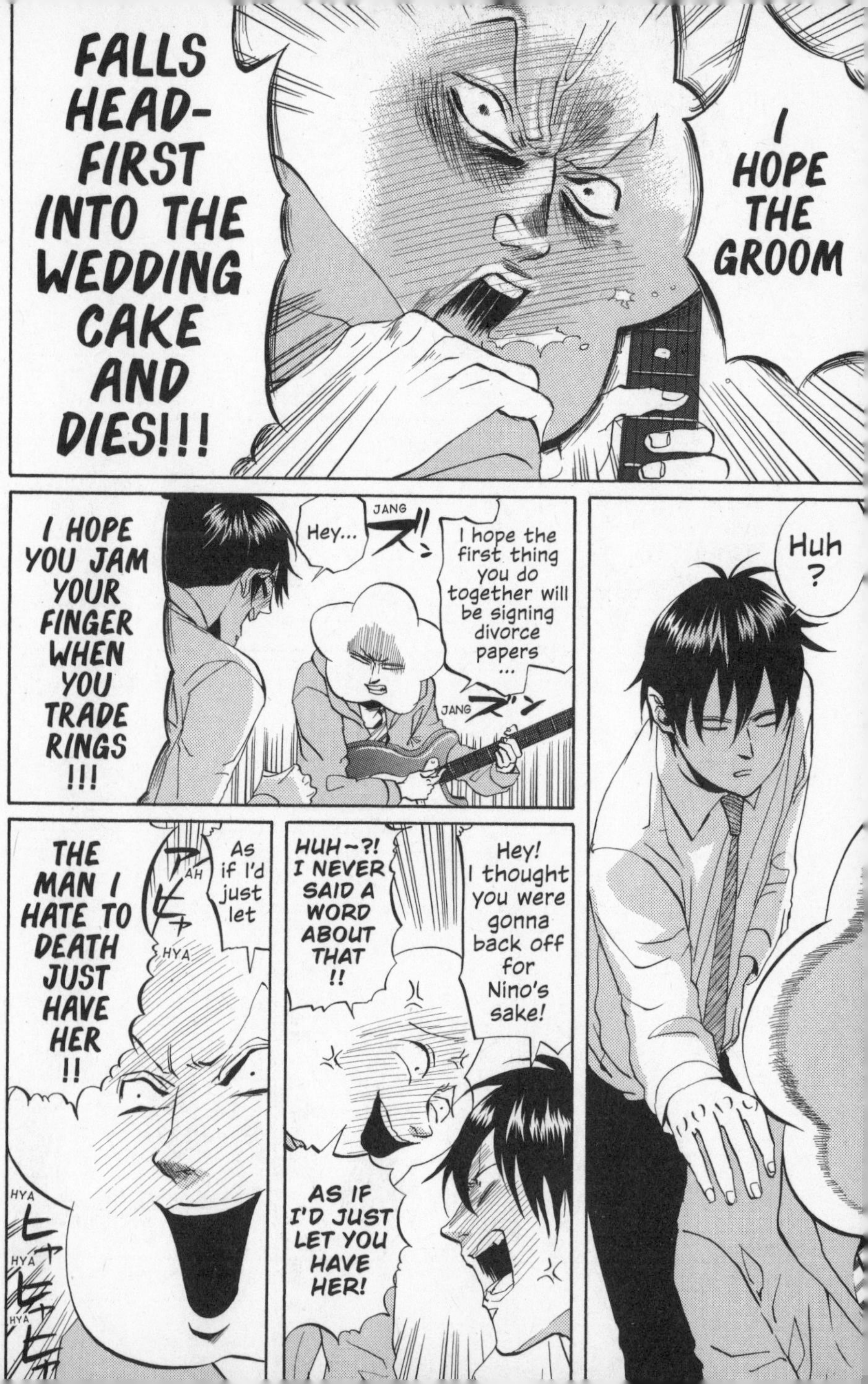
I HOPE THE GROOM
FALLS HEAD-FIRST INTO THE WEDDING CAKE AND DIES!!!
Huh?
Hey...
JANG
I hope the first thing you do together will be signing divorce papers ...
JANG
I HOPE YOU JAM YOUR FINGER WHEN YOU TRADE RINGS !!!
Hey! I thought you were gonna back off for Nino's sake!
HUH~?! I NEVER SAID A WORD ABOUT THAT !!
AS IF I'D JUST LET YOU HAVE HER!
As if I'd just let
AH
HYA
THE MAN I HATE TO DEATH JUST HAVE HER !!
HYA
HYA
HYA

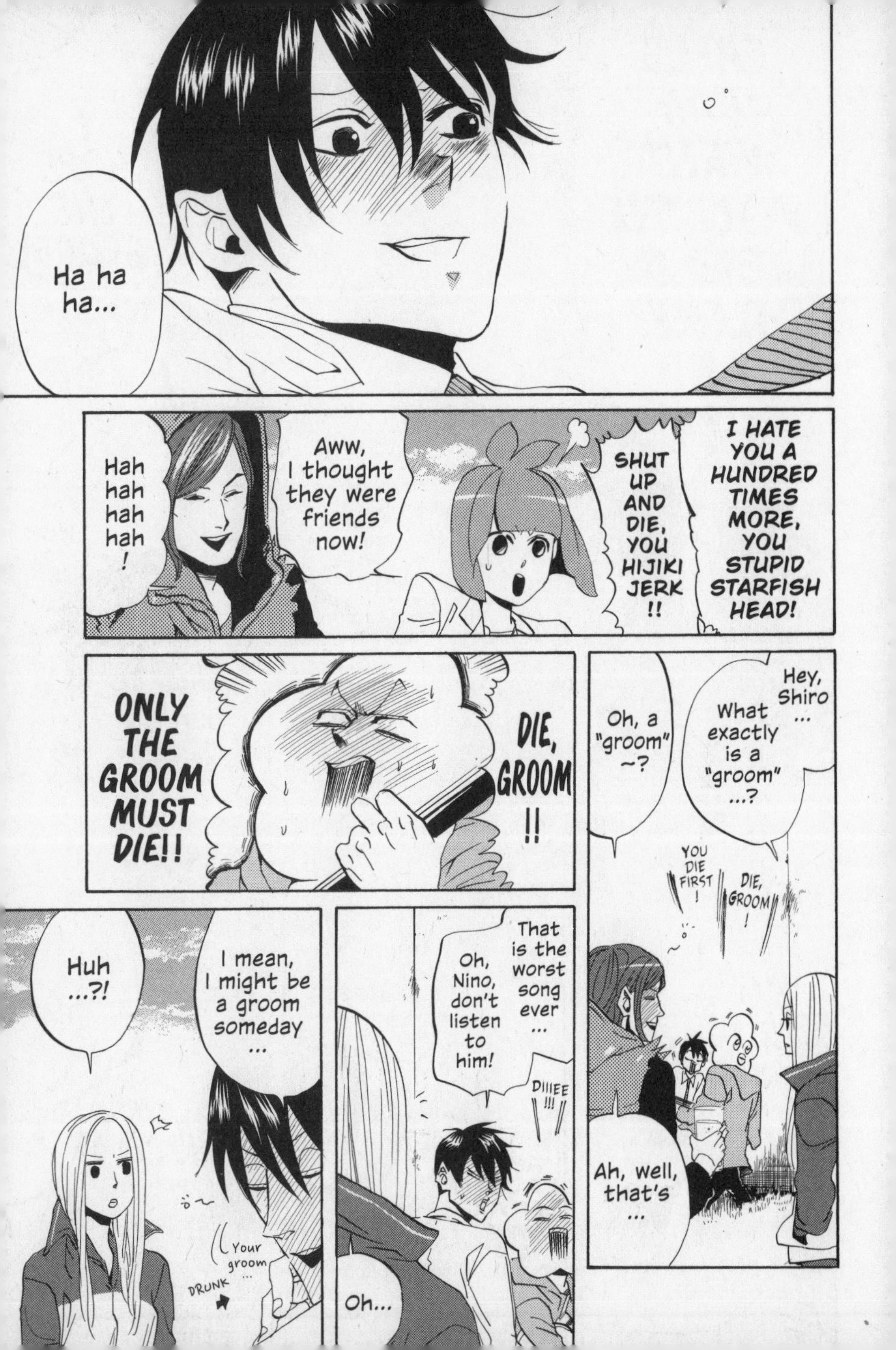

Ha ha ha...
I HATE YOU A HUNDRED TIMES MORE, YOU STUPID STARFISH HEAD!
SHUT UP AND DIE, YOU HIJIKI JERK!!
Aww, I thought they were friends now!
Hah hah hah hah!
Hey, Shiro... What exactly is a "groom"...?
Oh, a "groom" ~?
DIE, GROOM!
YOU DIE FIRST!
Ah, well, that's...
DIE, GROOM!!
ONLY THE GROOM MUST DIE!!
That is the worst song ever...
Oh, Nino, don't listen to him!
DIIIEE!!!
Oh...
I mean, I might be a groom someday...
Huh...?!
Your groom...
DRUNK

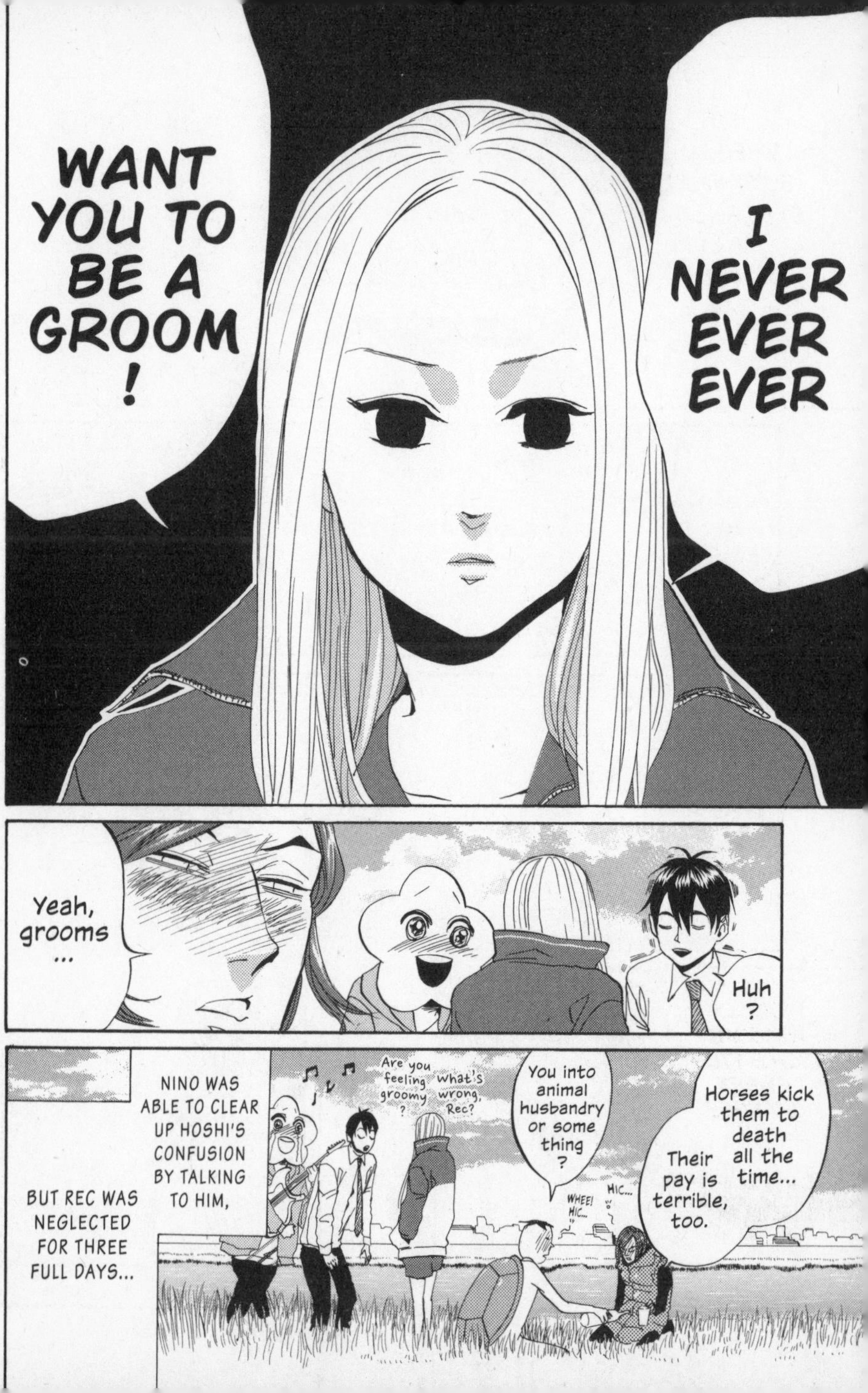
I NEVER EVER EVER
WANT YOU TO BE A GROOM!
Huh?
Yeah, grooms...
Horses kick them to death all the time...
Their pay is terrible, too.
HIC...
WHEE! HIC...
You into animal husbandry or some thing?
What's wrong, Rec?
Are you feeling groomy?
NINO WAS ABLE TO CLEAR UP HOSHI'S CONFUSION BY TALKING TO HIM,
BUT REC WAS NEGLECTED FOR THREE FULL DAYS...

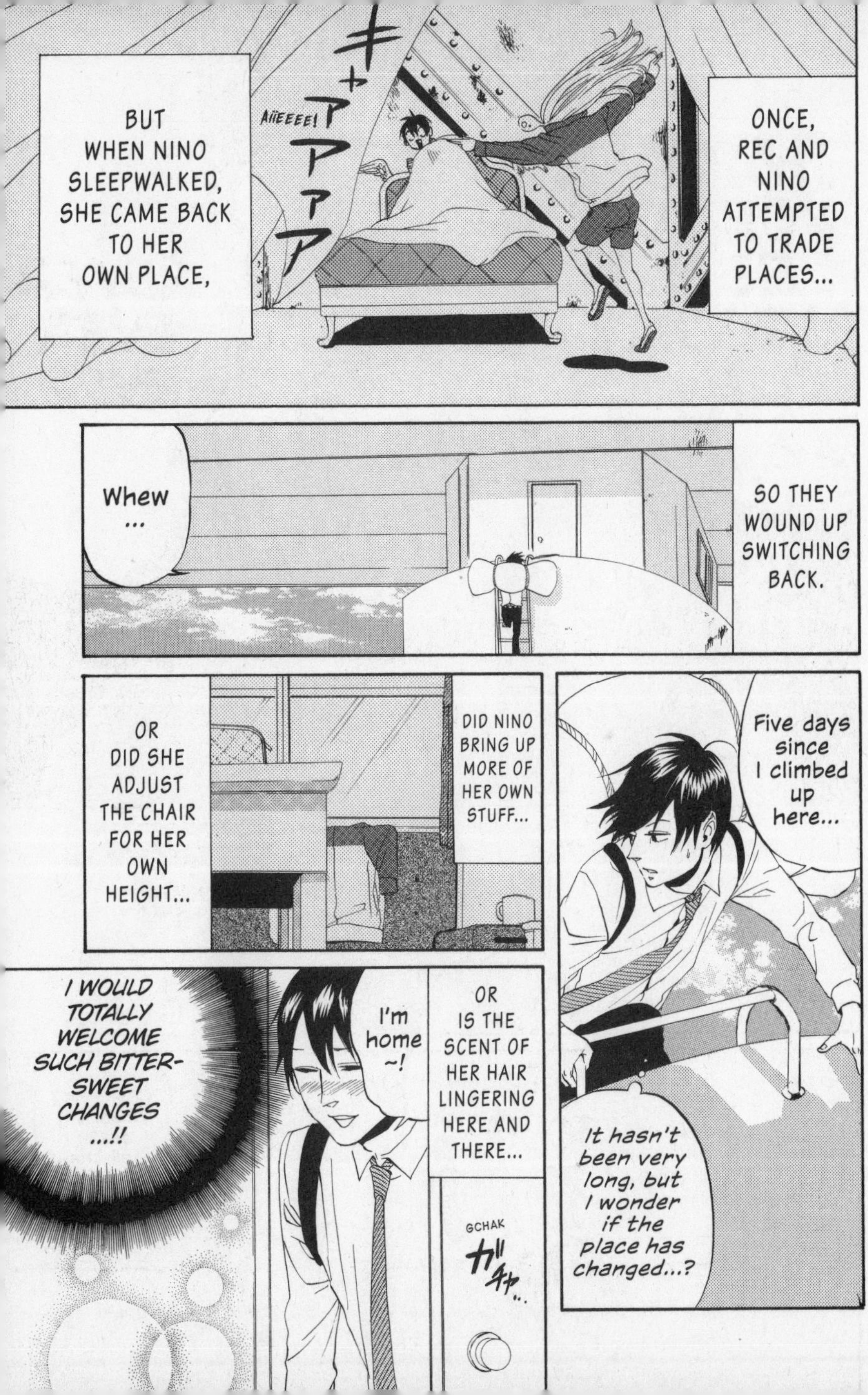
ONCE, REC AND NINO ATTEMPTED TO TRADE PLACES...
キャアアア
AIIEEEE!
BUT WHEN NINO SLEEPWALKED, SHE CAME BACK TO HER OWN PLACE,
SO THEY WOUND UP SWITCHING BACK.
Whew ...
Five days since I climbed up here...
It hasn't been very long, but I wonder if the place has changed...?
DID NINO BRING UP MORE OF HER OWN STUFF...
OR DID SHE ADJUST THE CHAIR FOR HER OWN HEIGHT...
OR IS THE SCENT OF HER HAIR LINGERING HERE AND THERE...
GCHAK
ガチャ..
I'm home ~!
I WOULD TOTALLY WELCOME SUCH BITTER-SWEET CHANGES ...!!

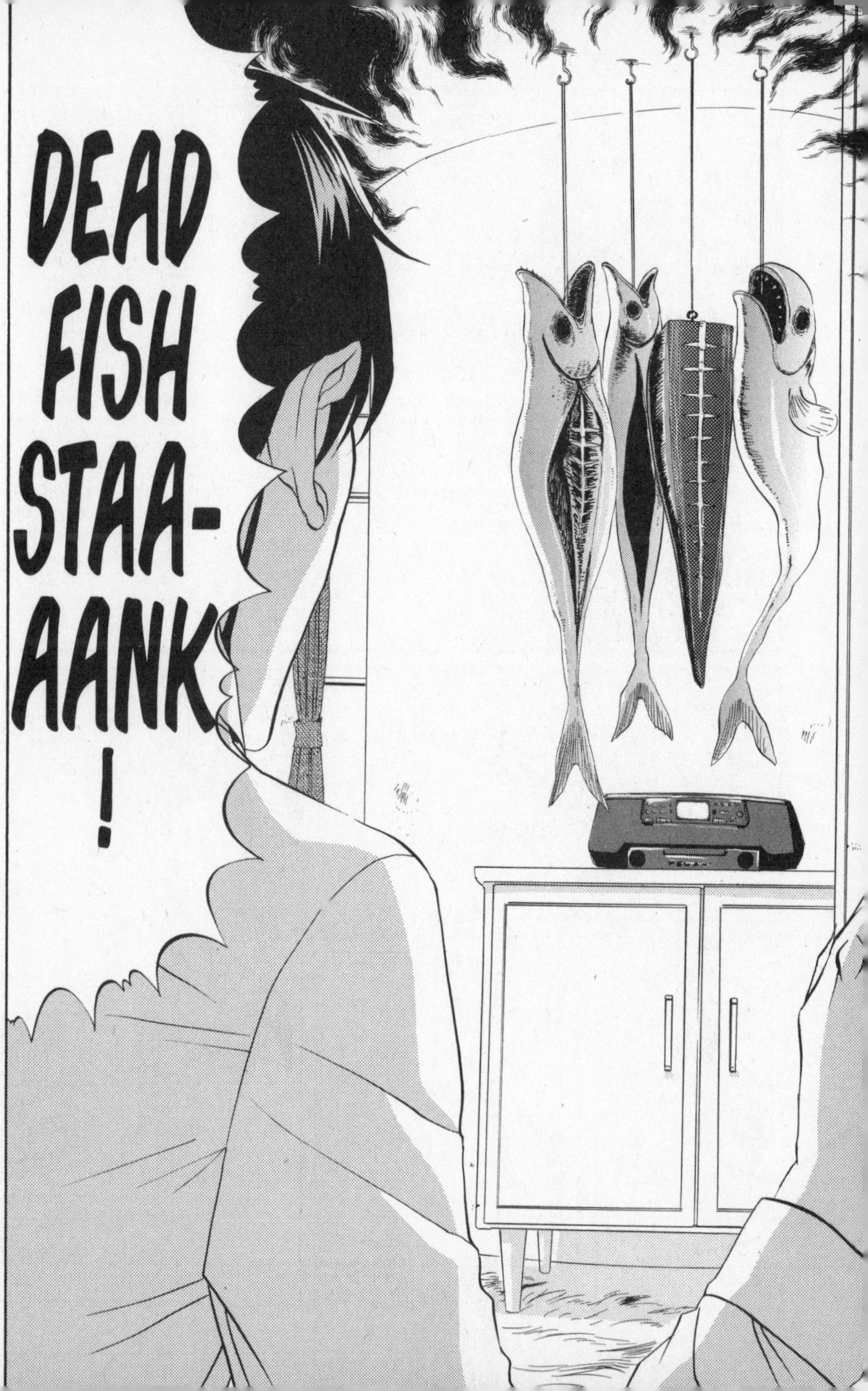
DEAD FISH STAA-AANK!

Chapter 126: Inside the Can

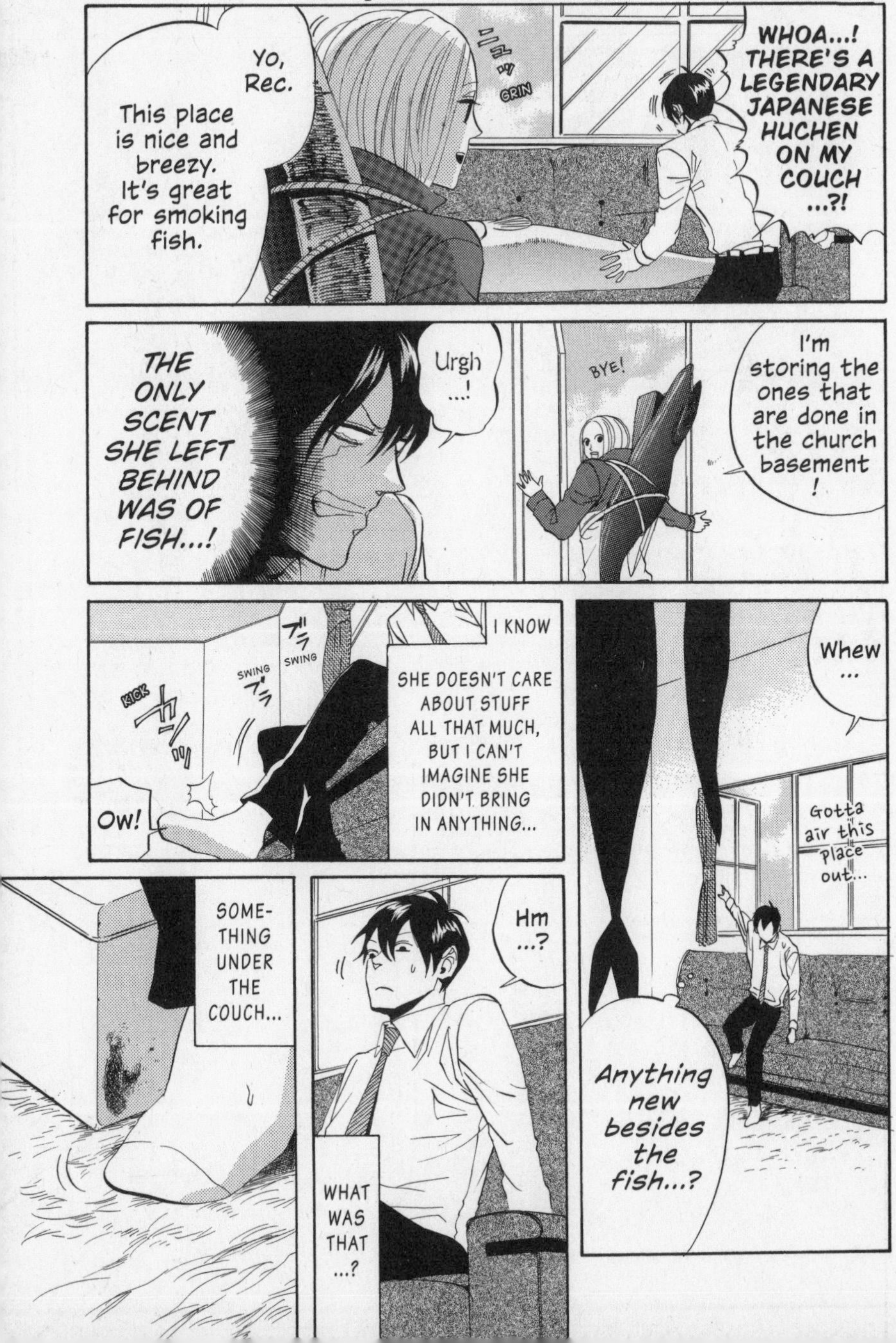
WHOA...! THERE'S A LEGENDARY JAPANESE HUCHEN ON MY COUCH ...?!
GRIN
Yo, Rec.
This place is nice and breezy. It's great for smoking fish.
I'm storing the ones that are done in the church basement!
BYE!
Urgh ...!
THE ONLY SCENT SHE LEFT BEHIND WAS OF FISH...!
Whew ...
Gotta air this place out...
Anything new besides the fish...?
I KNOW
SHE DOESN'T CARE ABOUT STUFF ALL THAT MUCH, BUT I CAN'T IMAGINE SHE DIDN'T BRING IN ANYTHING...
SWING
SWING
KICK
Ow!
Hm ...?
WHAT WAS THAT ...?
SOME-THING UNDER THE COUCH...

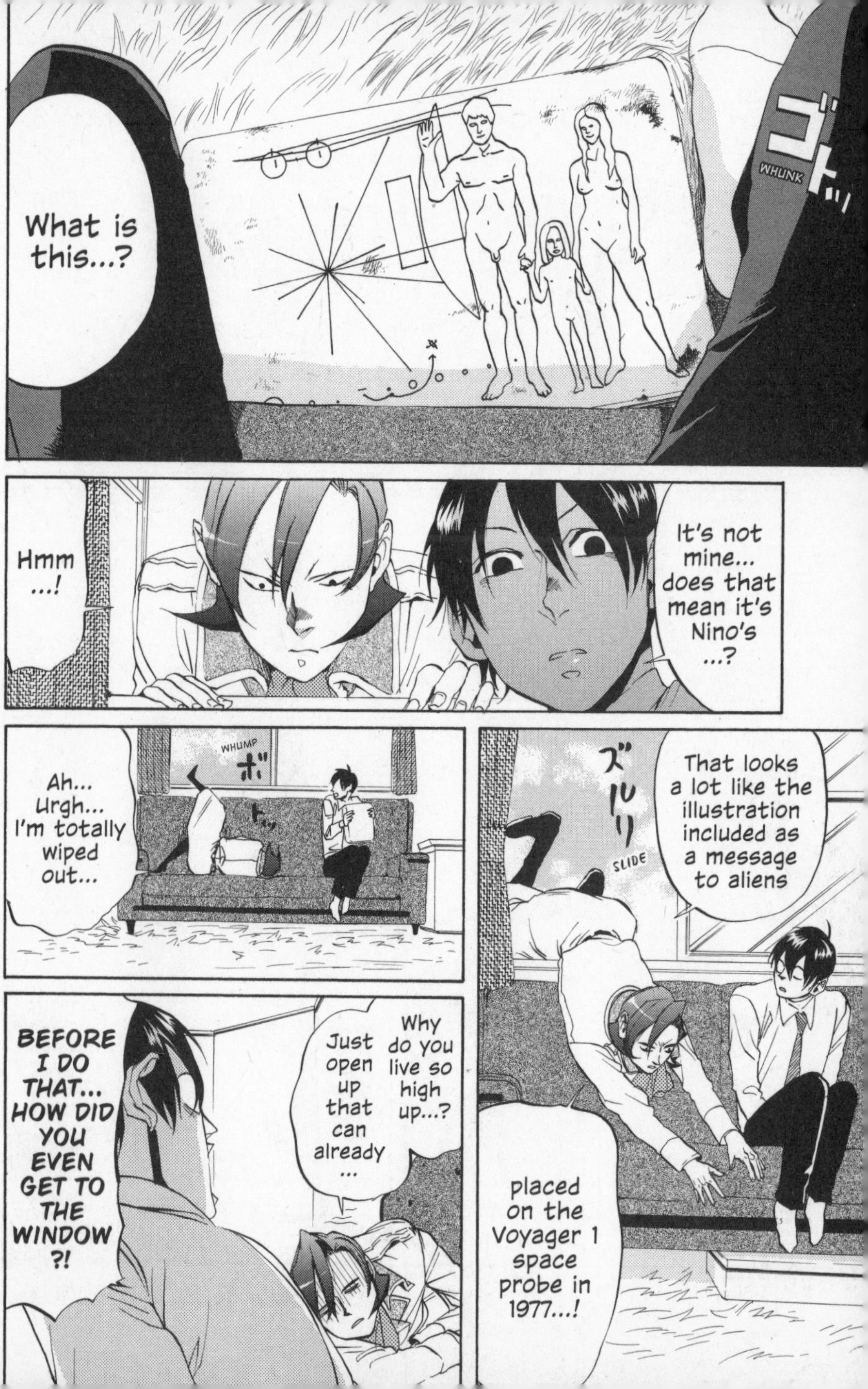

ゴトッ
WHUNK
What is this...?
It's not mine... does that mean it's Nino's ...?
Hmm ...!
ズルリ
SLIDE
That looks a lot like the illustration included as a message to aliens
placed on the Voyager 1 space probe in 1977...!
WHUMP
ボトッ
Ah... Urgh... I'm totally wiped out...
Why do you live so high up...?
Just open up that can already ...
BEFORE I DO THAT... HOW DID YOU EVEN GET TO THE WINDOW ?!

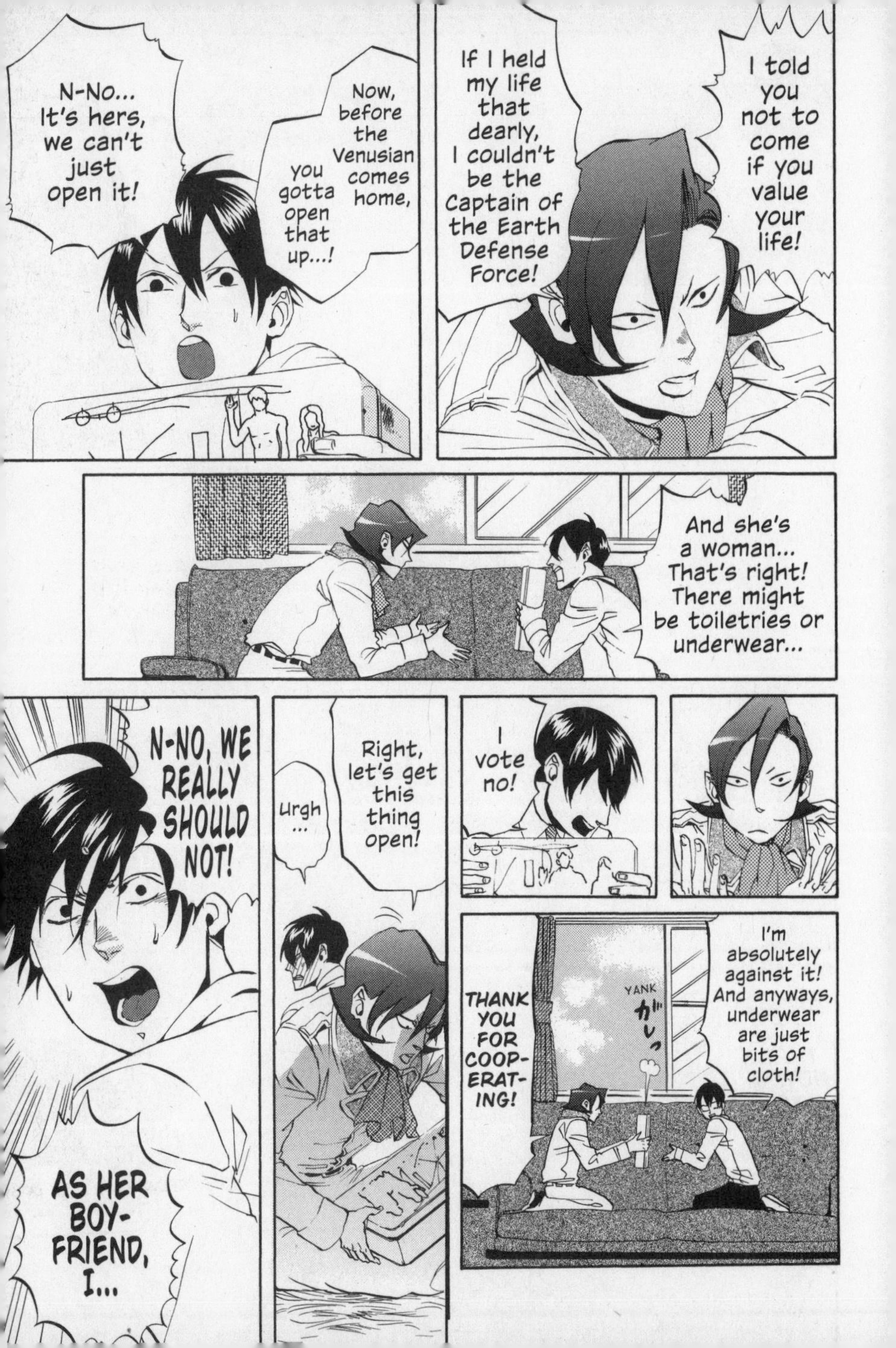
I told you not to come if you value your life!
If I held my life that dearly, I couldn't be the Captain of the Earth Defense Force!
Now, before the Venusian comes home,
you gotta open that up...!
N-No... It's hers, we can't just open it!
And she's a woman... That's right! There might be toiletries or underwear...
I vote no!
I'm absolutely against it! And anyways, underwear are just bits of cloth!
YANK
ガレっ
THANK YOU FOR COOPERATING!
Right, let's get this thing open!
Urgh...
N-NO, WE REALLY SHOULD NOT!
AS HER BOYFRIEND, I...

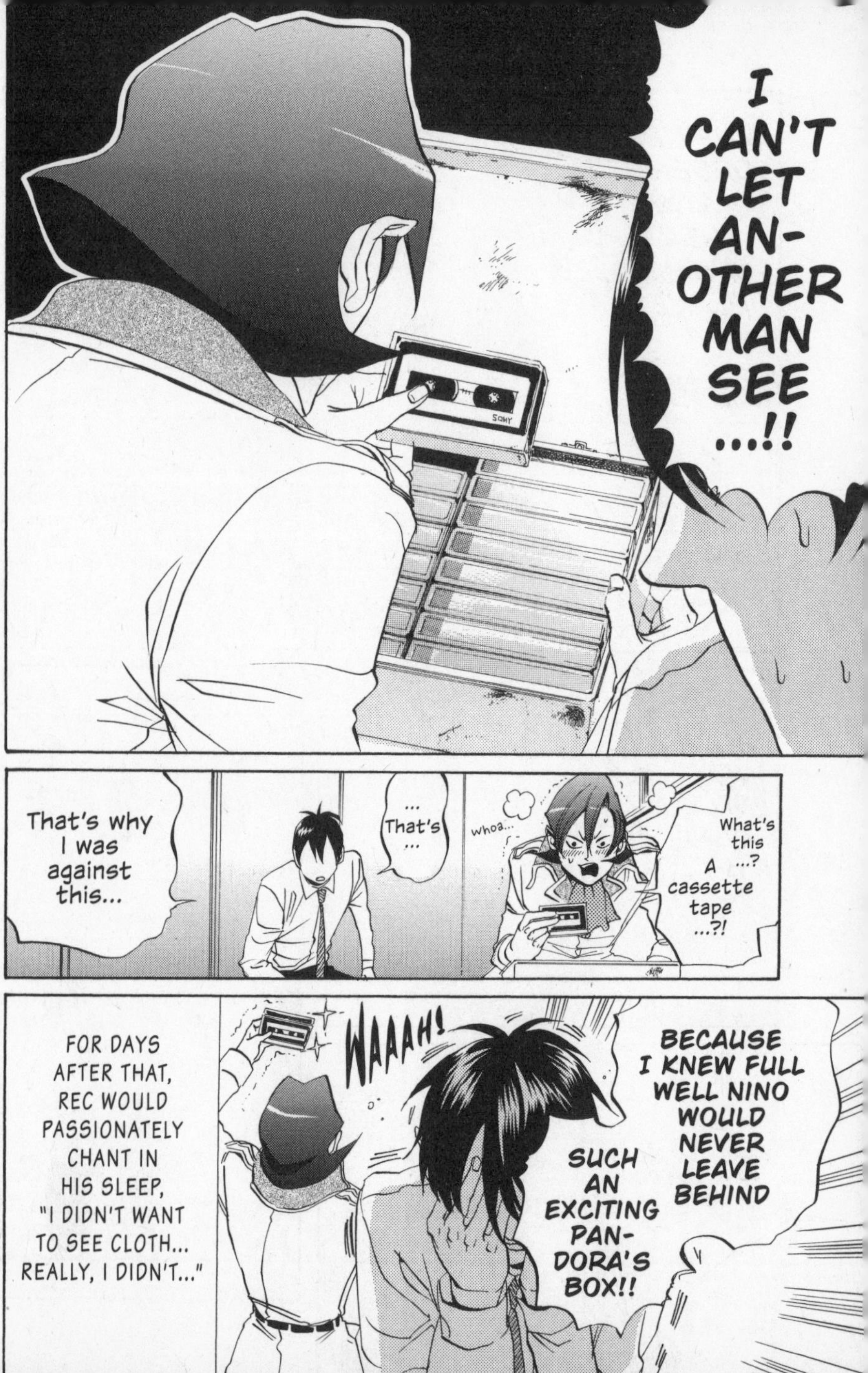
I CAN'T LET AN-OTHER MAN SEE ...!!
What's this ...? A cassette tape ...?!
whoa...
... That's ...
That's why I was against this...
BECAUSE I KNEW FULL WELL NINO WOULD NEVER LEAVE BEHIND
SUCH AN EXCITING PAN-DORA'S BOX!!
WAAAH!
FOR DAYS AFTER THAT, REC WOULD PASSIONATELY CHANT IN HIS SLEEP, "I DIDN'T WANT TO SEE CLOTH... REALLY, I DIDN'T..."

Chapter 127: Cassette Tape

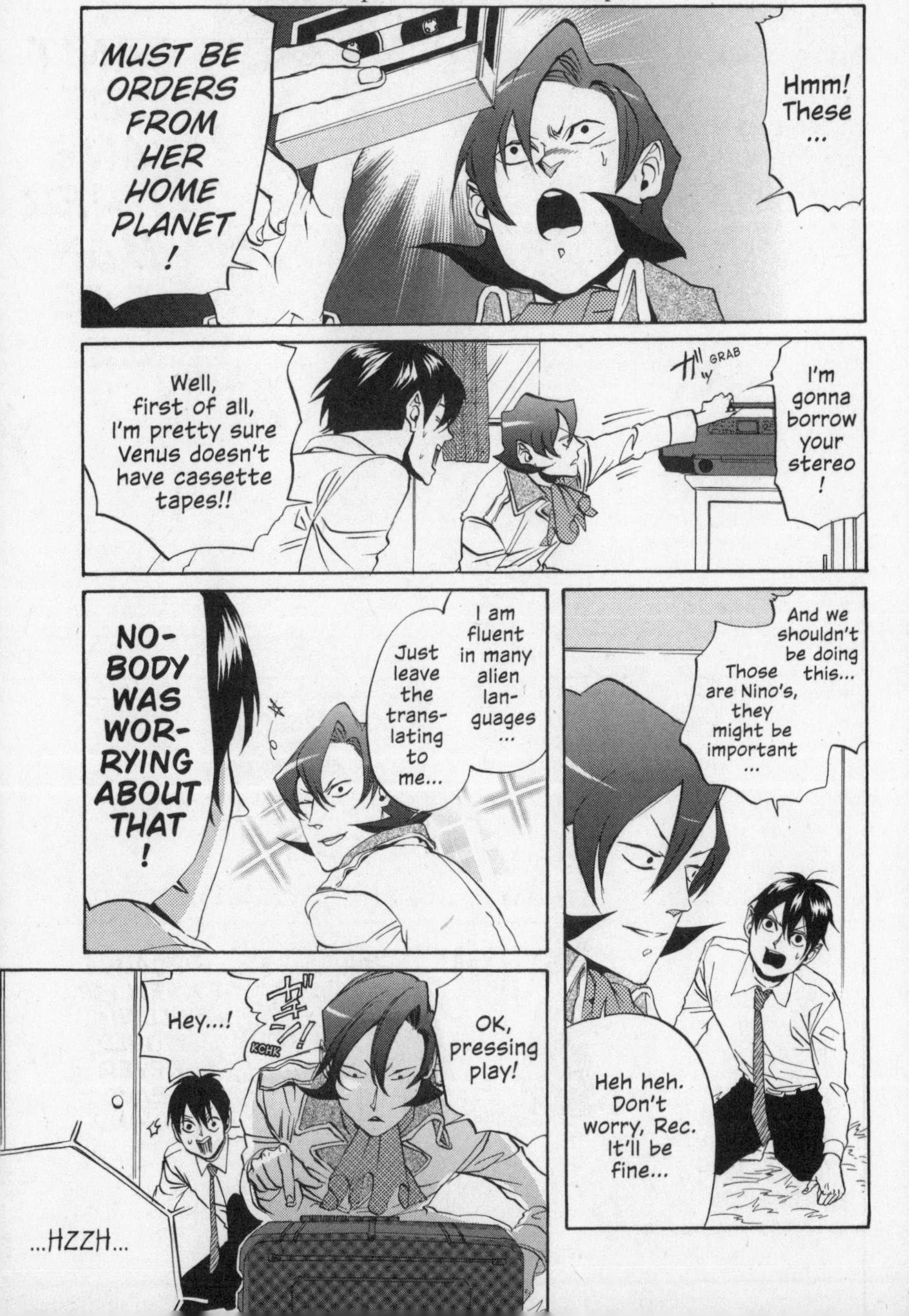

Hmm! These ...
MUST BE ORDERS FROM HER HOME PLANET !
GRAB
I'm gonna borrow your stereo !
Well, first of all, I'm pretty sure Venus doesn't have cassette tapes!!
And we shouldn't be doing this...
Those are Nino's, they might be important ...
Heh heh. Don't worry, Rec. It'll be fine...
I am fluent in many alien lan-guages ...
Just leave the trans-lating to me...
NO-BODY WAS WOR-RYING ABOUT THAT !
OK, pressing play!
KCHK
Hey...!
...HZZH...

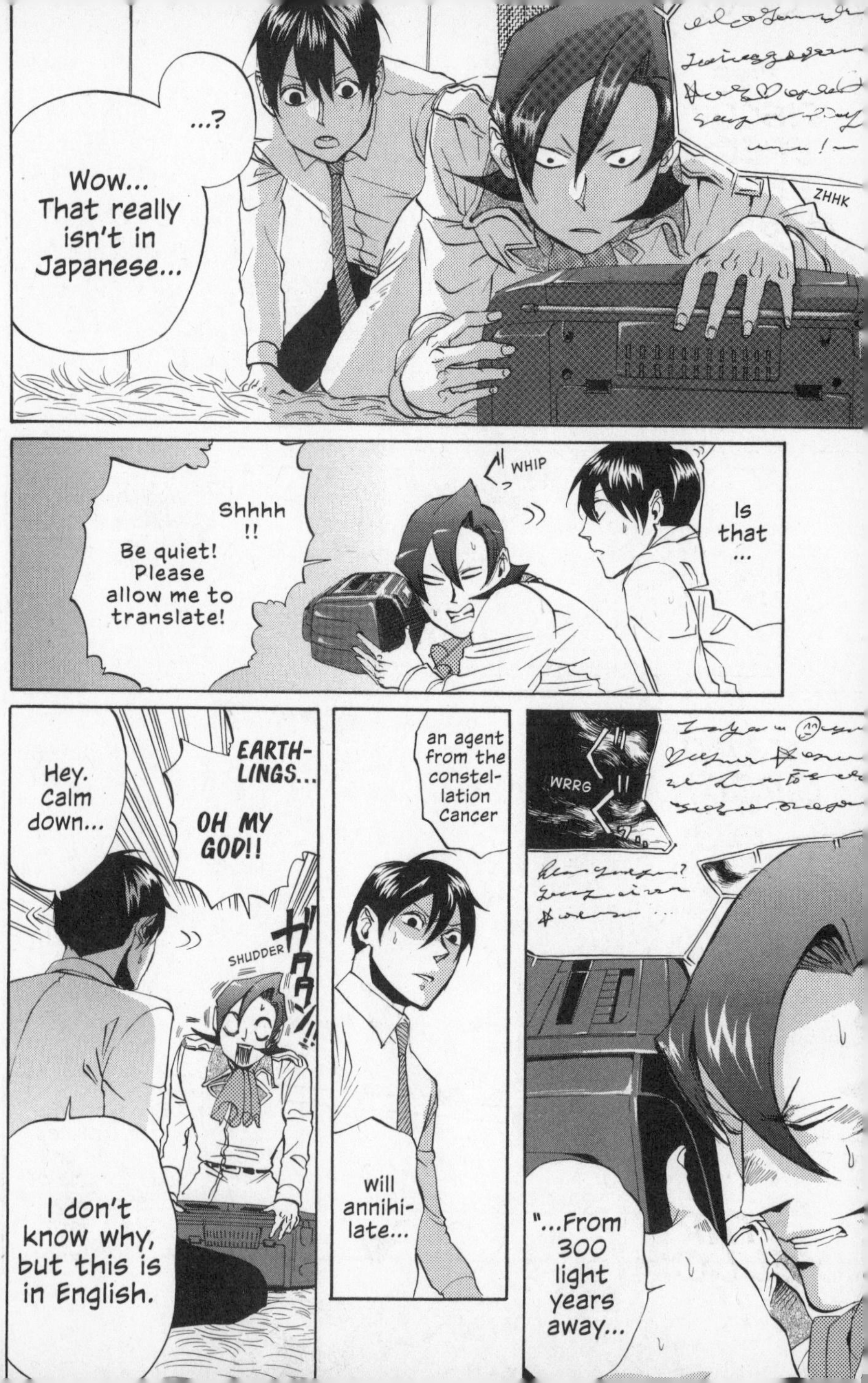
ZHHK
...?
Wow... That really isn't in Japanese...
Is that ...
WHIP
Shhhh !!
Be quiet! Please allow me to translate!
WRRG
"...From 300 light years away...
an agent from the constellation Cancer
will annihilate...
EARTH-LINGS...
OH MY GOD!!
Hey. Calm down...
SHUDDER
I don't know why, but this is in English.

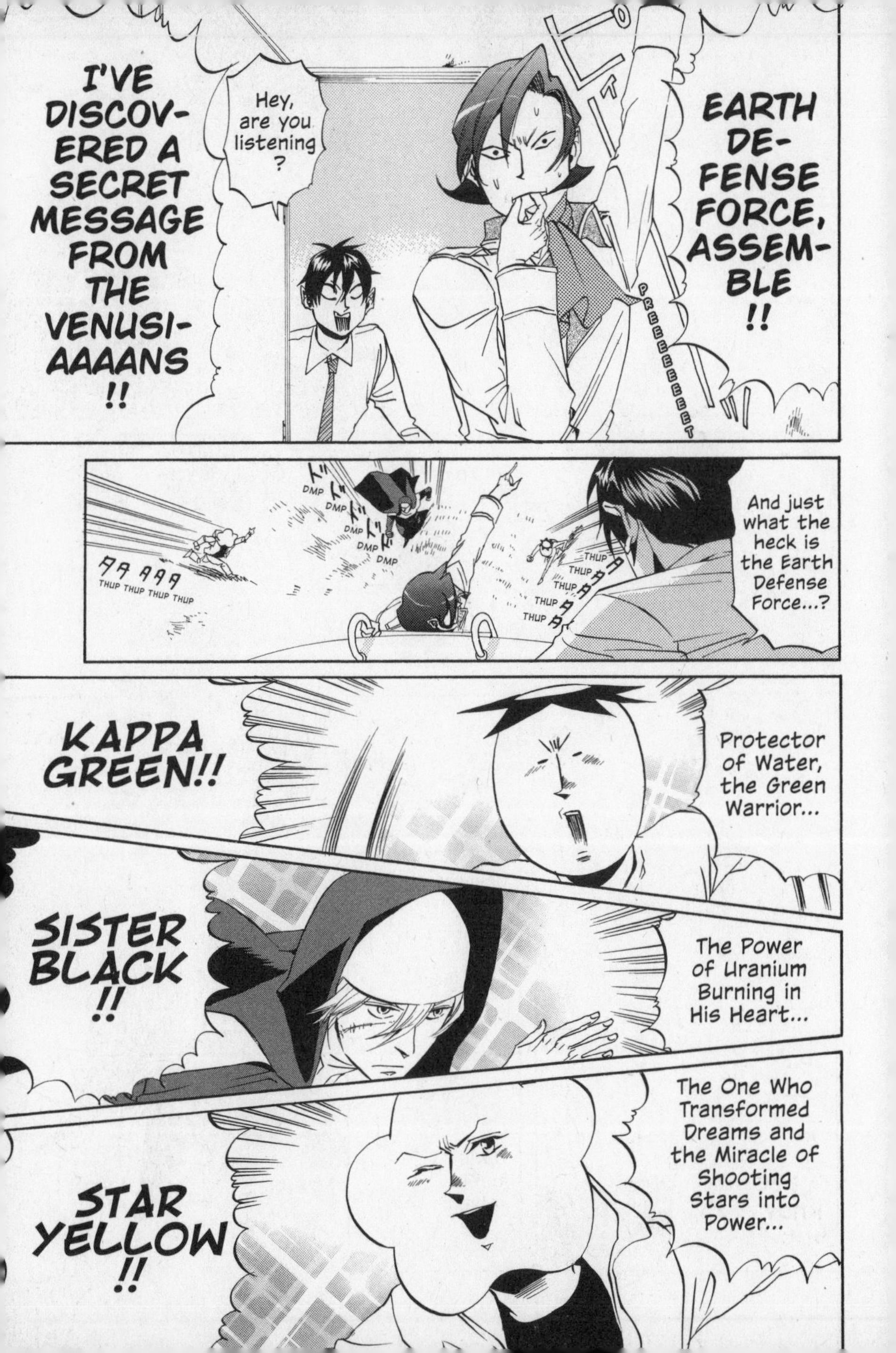
EARTH DE-FENSE FORCE, ASSEM-BLE!!
PREEEEEEEEET
Hey, are you listening?
I'VE DISCOV-ERED A SECRET MESSAGE FROM THE VENUSI-AAAANS!!
And just what the heck is the Earth Defense Force...?
THUP THUP THUP THUP THUP
DMP DMP DMP DMP DMP
THUP THUP THUP THUP
Protector of Water, the Green Warrior...
KAPPA GREEN!!
The Power of Uranium Burning in His Heart...
SISTER BLACK!!
The One Who Transformed Dreams and the Miracle of Shooting Stars into Power...
STAR YELLOW!!

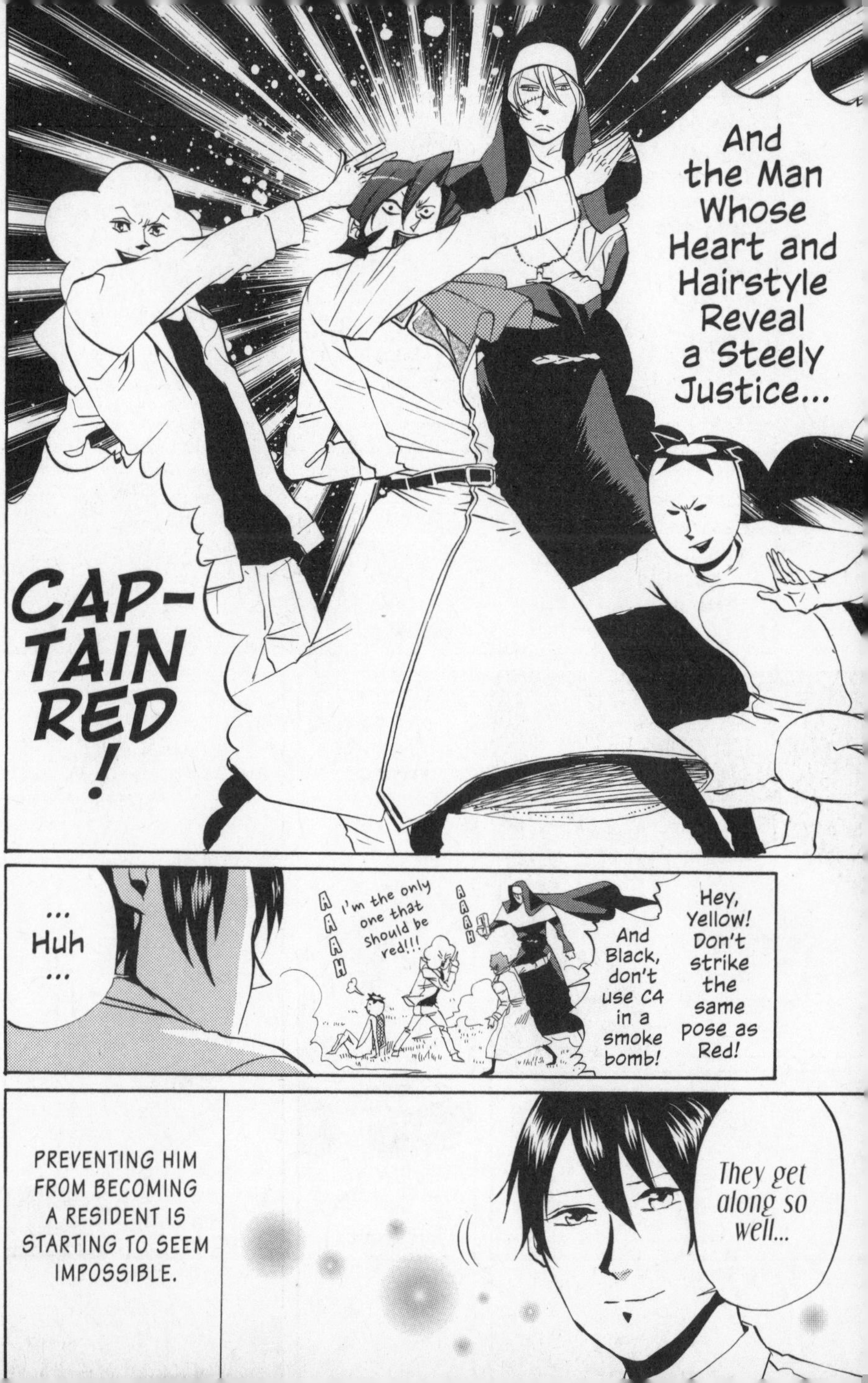
And the Man Whose Heart and Hairstyle Reveal a Steely Justice...
CAP-TAIN RED!
Hey, Yellow! Don't strike the same pose as Red!
And Black, don't use C4 in a smoke bomb!
AAAH
I'm the only one that should be red!!!
AAAAH
... Huh ...
They get along so well...
PREVENTING HIM FROM BECOMING A RESIDENT IS STARTING TO SEEM IMPOSSIBLE.

Chapter 128: Message from Venus

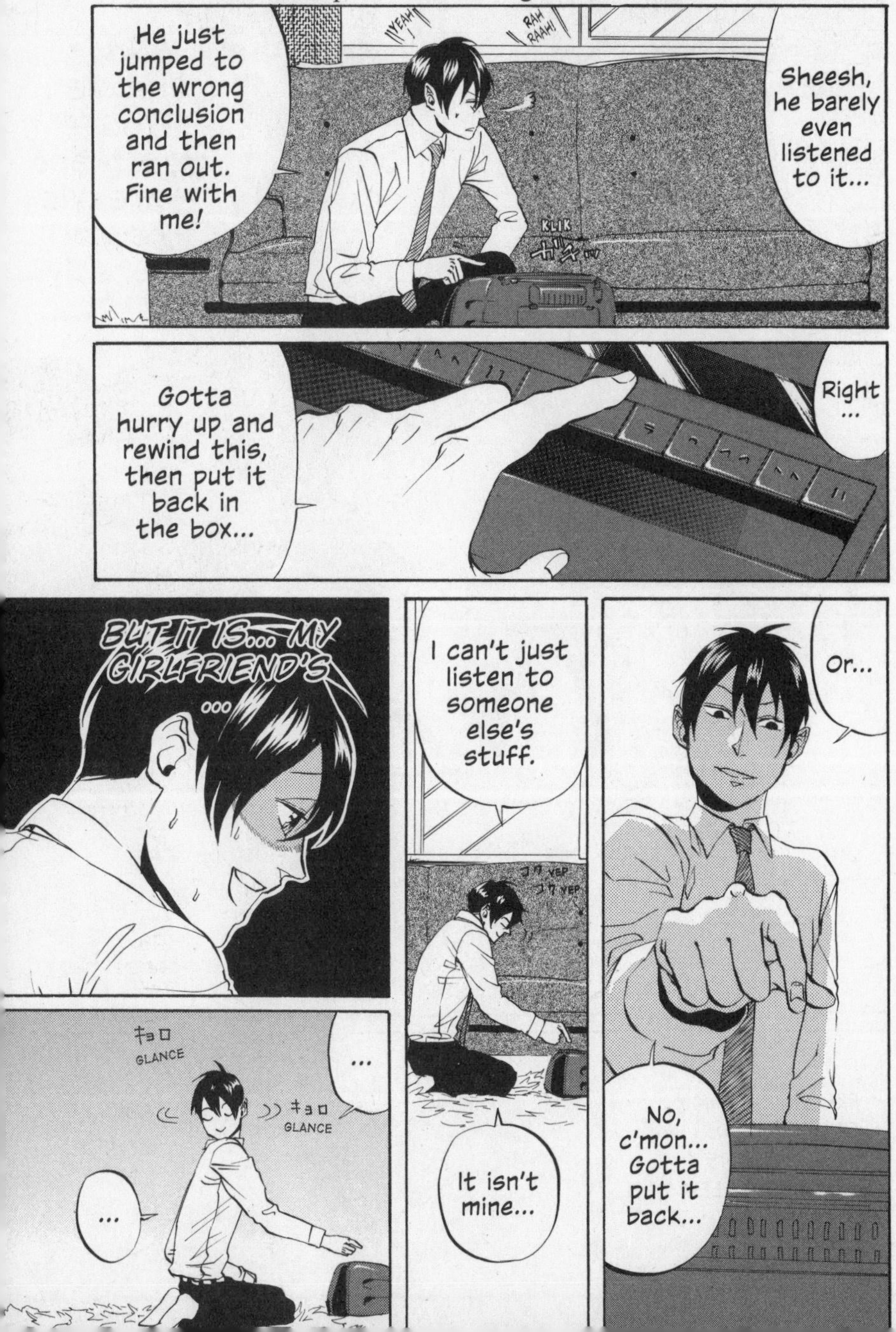
Sheesh, he barely even listened to it...
RAAH RAAH!
YEAH!
He just jumped to the wrong conclusion and then ran out. Fine with me!
KLIK
Right...
Gotta hurry up and rewind this, then put it back in the box...
Or...
No, c'mon... Gotta put it back...
I can't just listen to someone else's stuff.
YEP YEP
It isn't mine...
BUT IT IS... MY GIRLFRIEND'S...
...
キョロ GLANCE
キョロ GLANCE
...

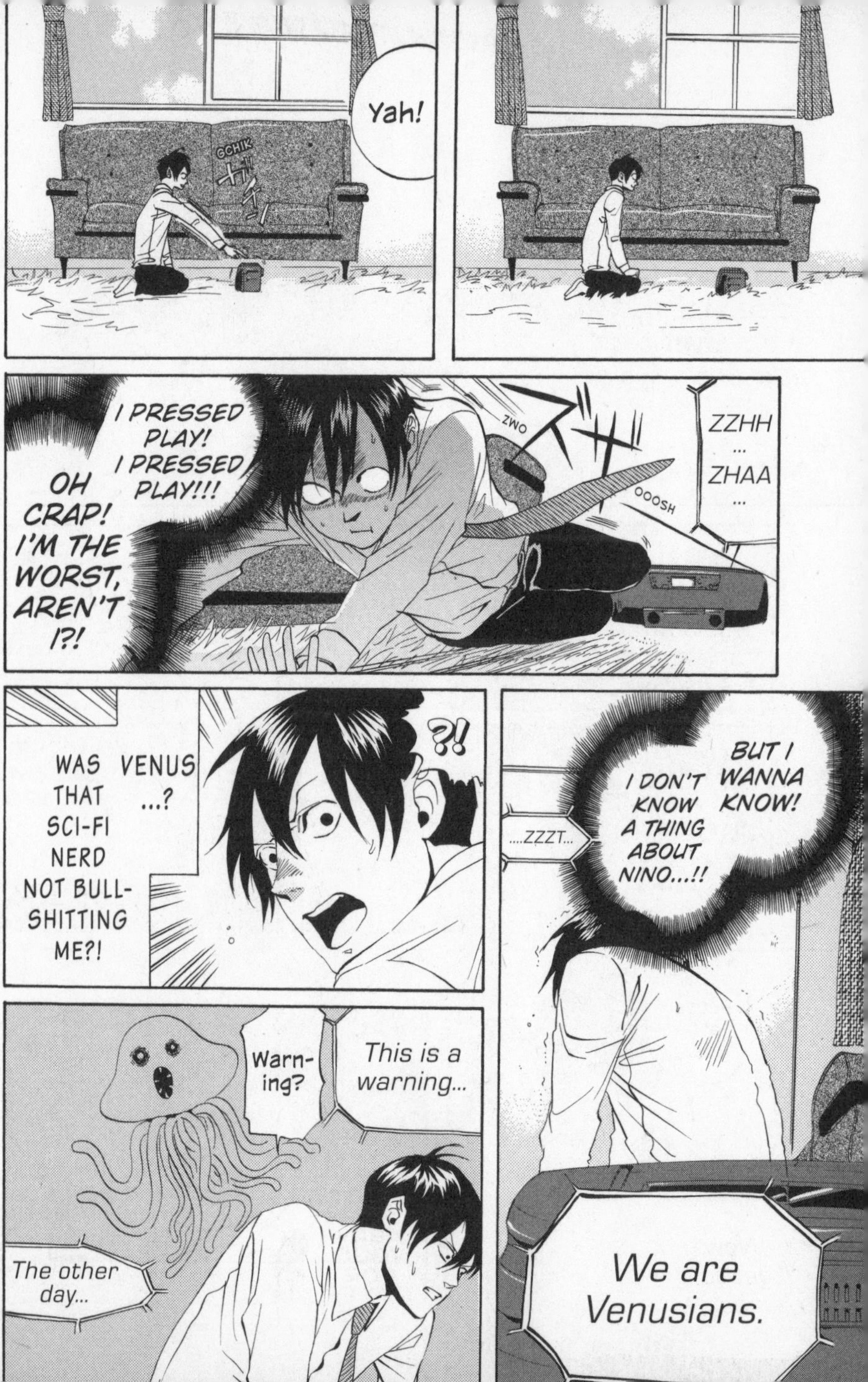
Yah!
GCHIK
ZZHH ... ZHAA ...
ZWO
OOOSH
I PRESSED PLAY! I PRESSED PLAY!!!
OH CRAP! I'M THE WORST, AREN'T I?!
BUT I WANNA KNOW!
I DON'T KNOW A THING ABOUT NINO...!!
....ZZZT...
We are Venusians.
?!
VENUS ...?
WAS THAT SCI-FI NERD NOT BULLSHITTING ME?!
This is a warning...
Warning?
The other day...

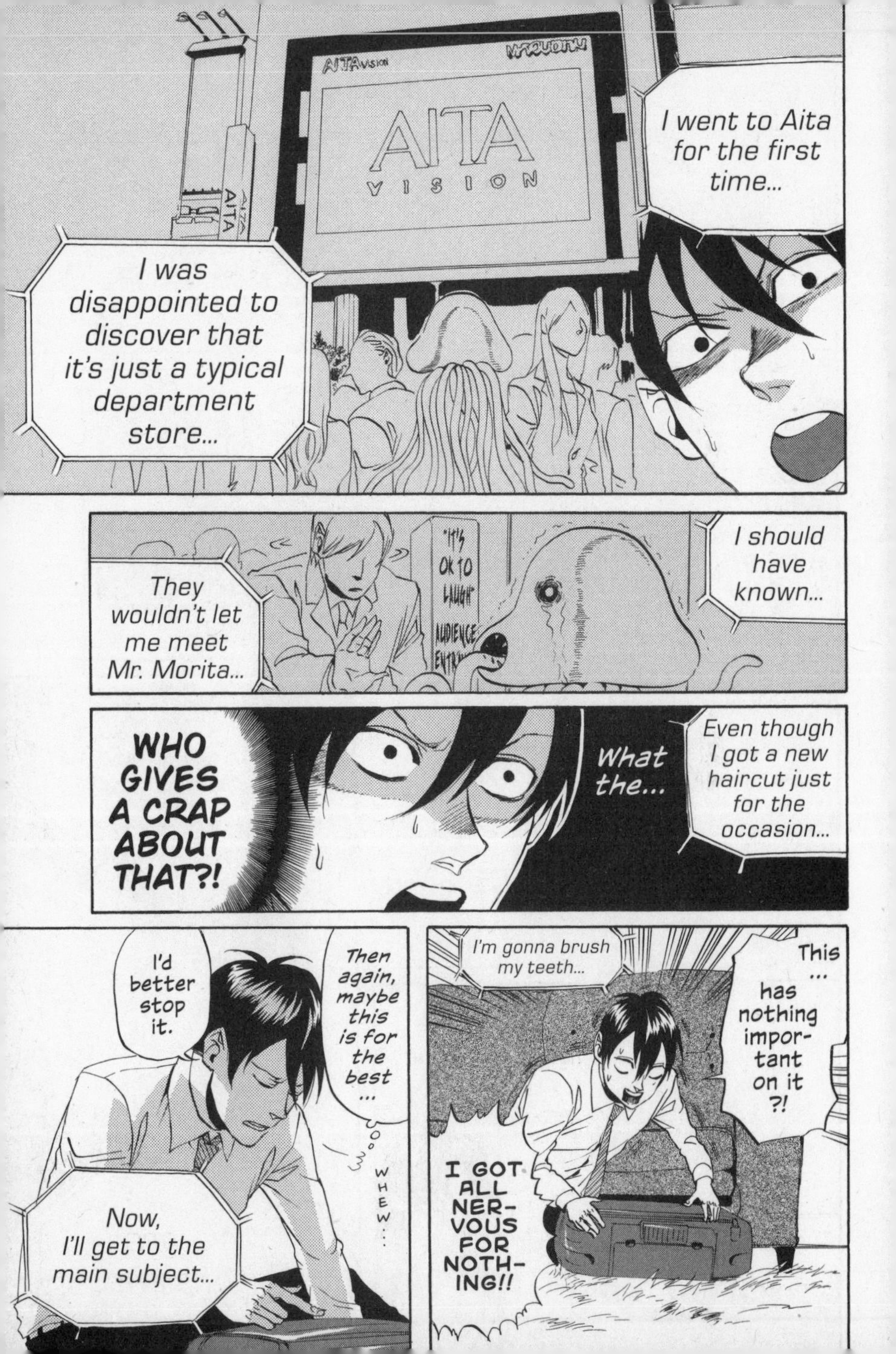
AITA VISION
I went to Aita for the first time...
I was disappointed to discover that it's just a typical department store...
I should have known...
"IT'S OK TO LAUGH"
They wouldn't let me meet Mr. Morita...
Even though I got a new haircut just for the occasion...
What the...
WHO GIVES A CRAP ABOUT THAT?!
This ... has nothing impor-tant on it?!
I'm gonna brush my teeth...
I GOT ALL NER-VOUS FOR NOTH-ING!!
Then again, maybe this is for the best...
WHEW...
I'd better stop it.
Now, I'll get to the main subject...

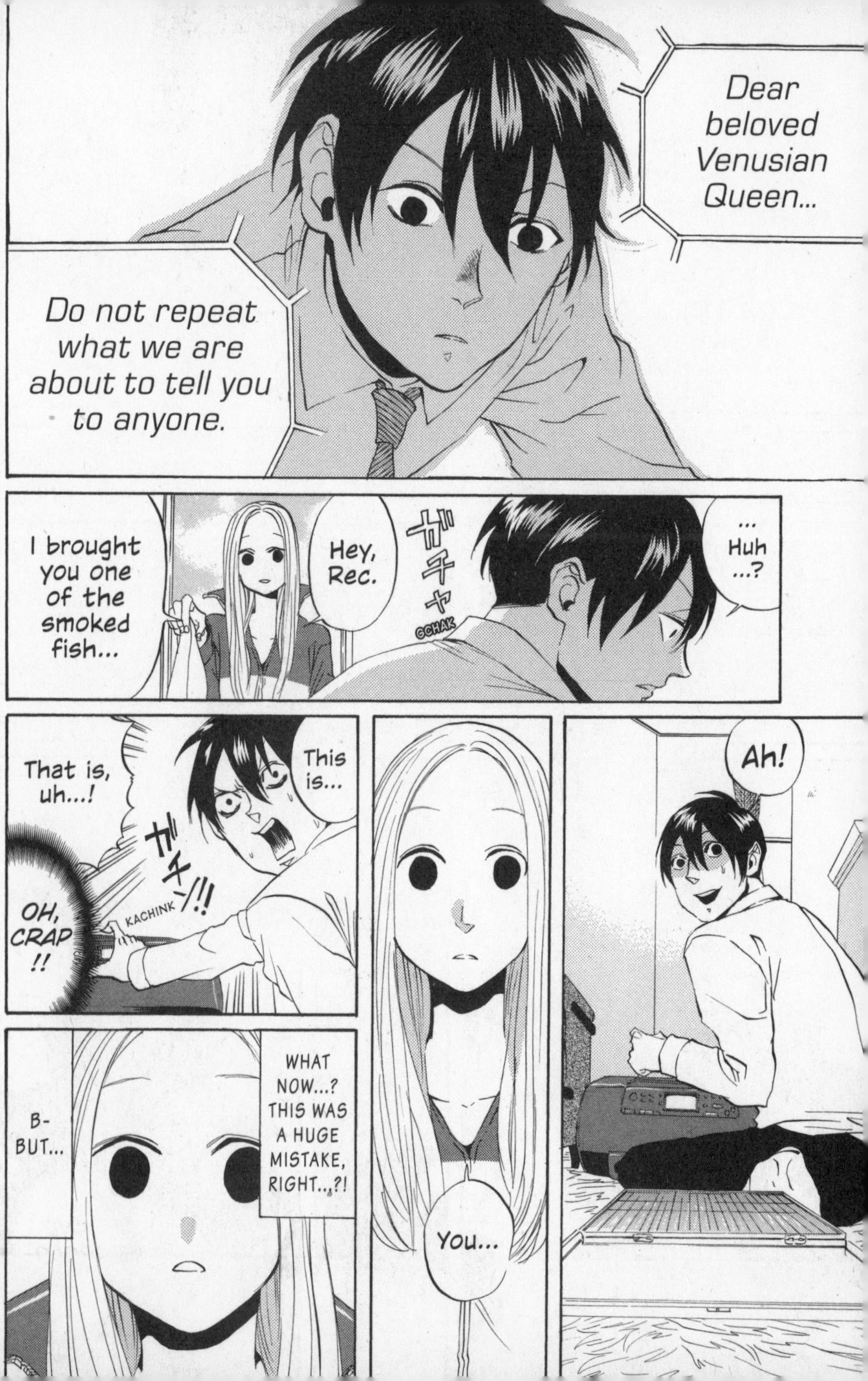
Dear beloved Venusian Queen...
Do not repeat what we are about to tell you to anyone.
... Huh ...?
ガチャ
GCHAK
Hey, Rec.
I brought you one of the smoked fish...
Ah!
You...
This is...
That is, uh...!
ガチーン!!
KACHINK
OH, CRAP !!
WHAT NOW...? THIS WAS A HUGE MISTAKE, RIGHT...?!
B- BUT...

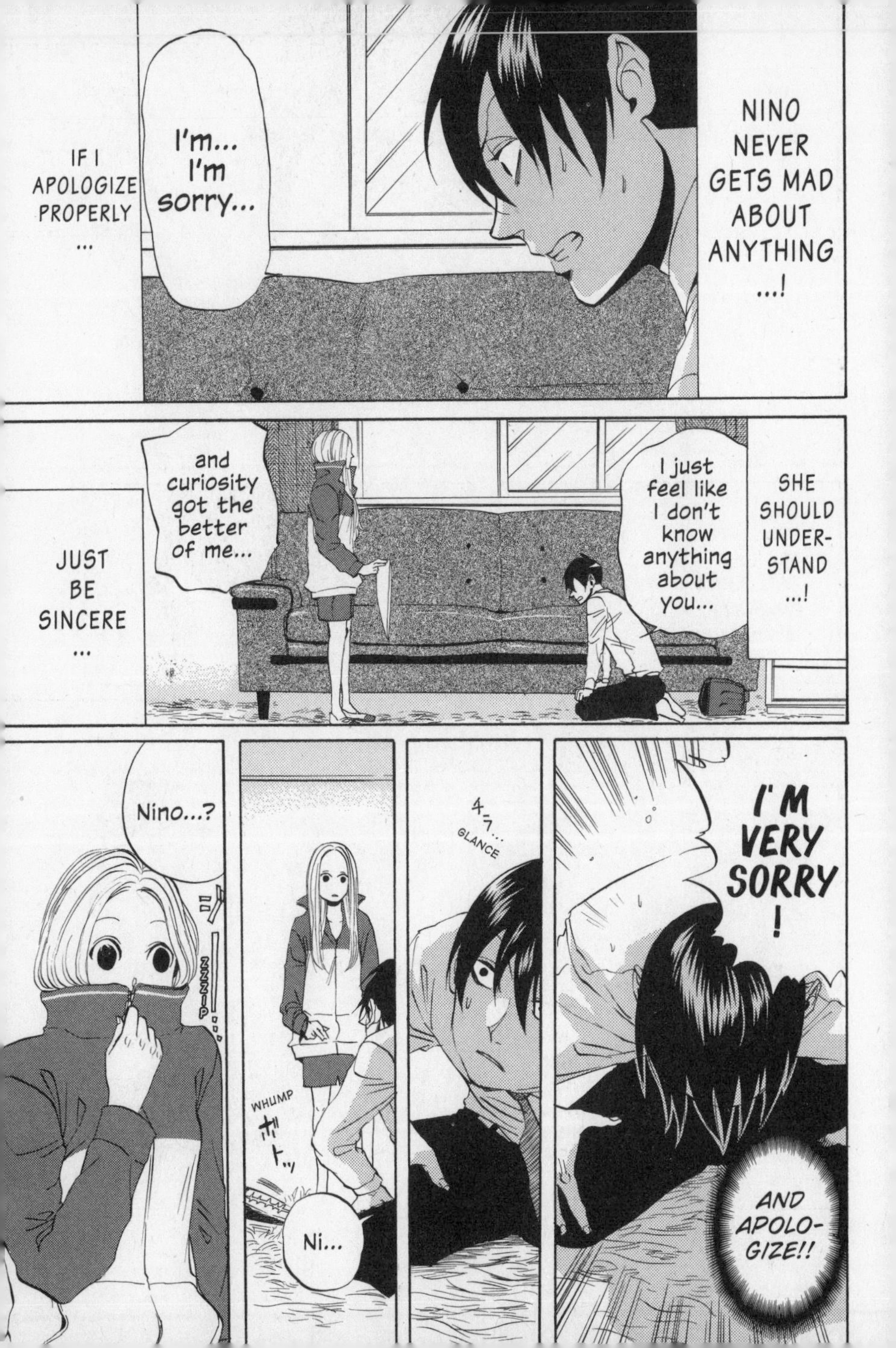
NINO NEVER GETS MAD ABOUT ANYTHING ...!
I'm... I'm sorry...
IF I APOLOGIZE PROPERLY ...
SHE SHOULD UNDER-STAND ...!
I just feel like I don't know anything about you...
and curiosity got the better of me...
JUST BE SINCERE ...
I'M VERY SORRY !
AND APOLO-GIZE!!
GLANCE
WHUMP
Ni...
Nino...?
ZZZIP

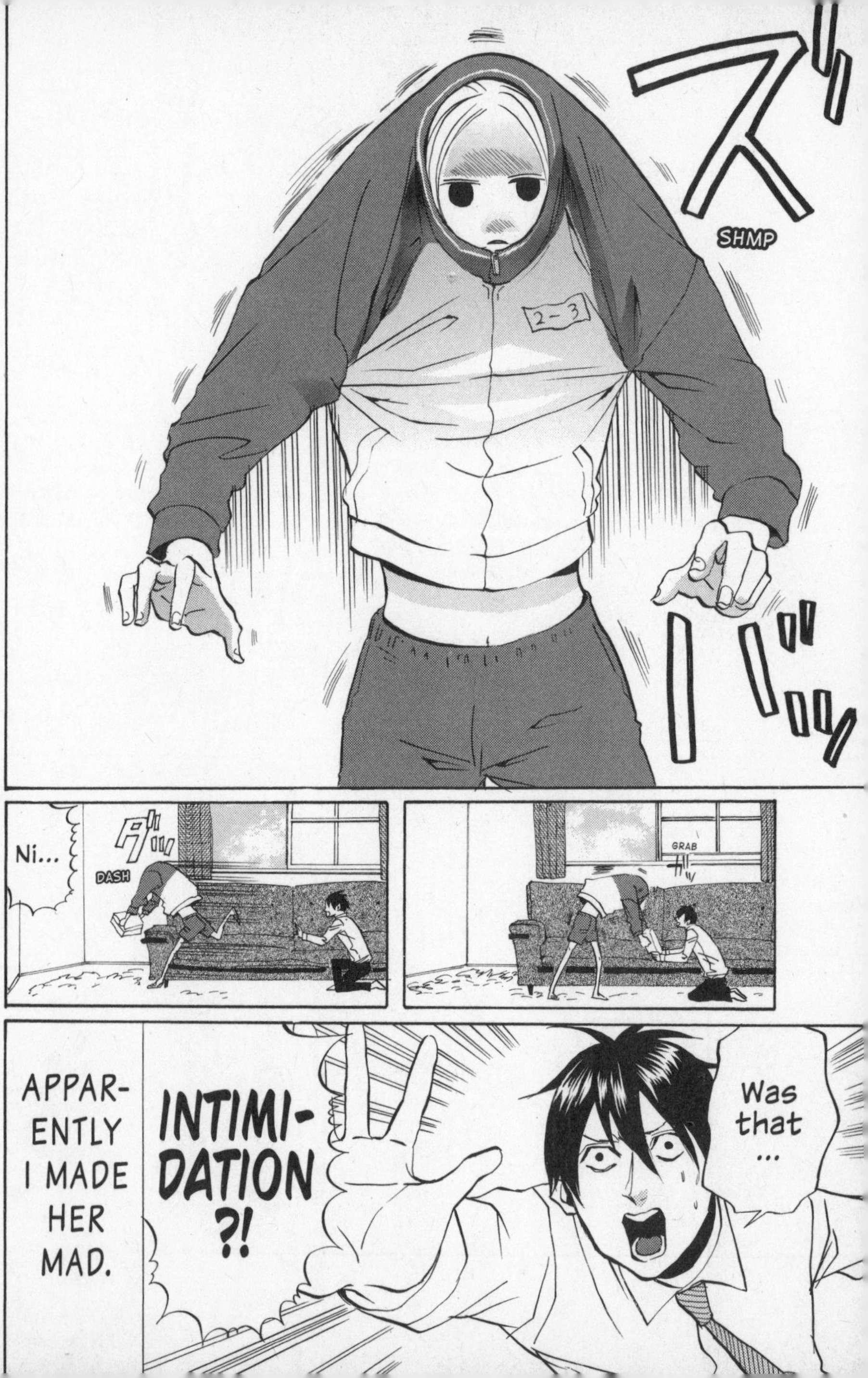
SHMP
2-3
GRAB
Ni...
DASH
Was that ...
INTIMI-DATION ?!
APPAR-ENTLY I MADE HER MAD.

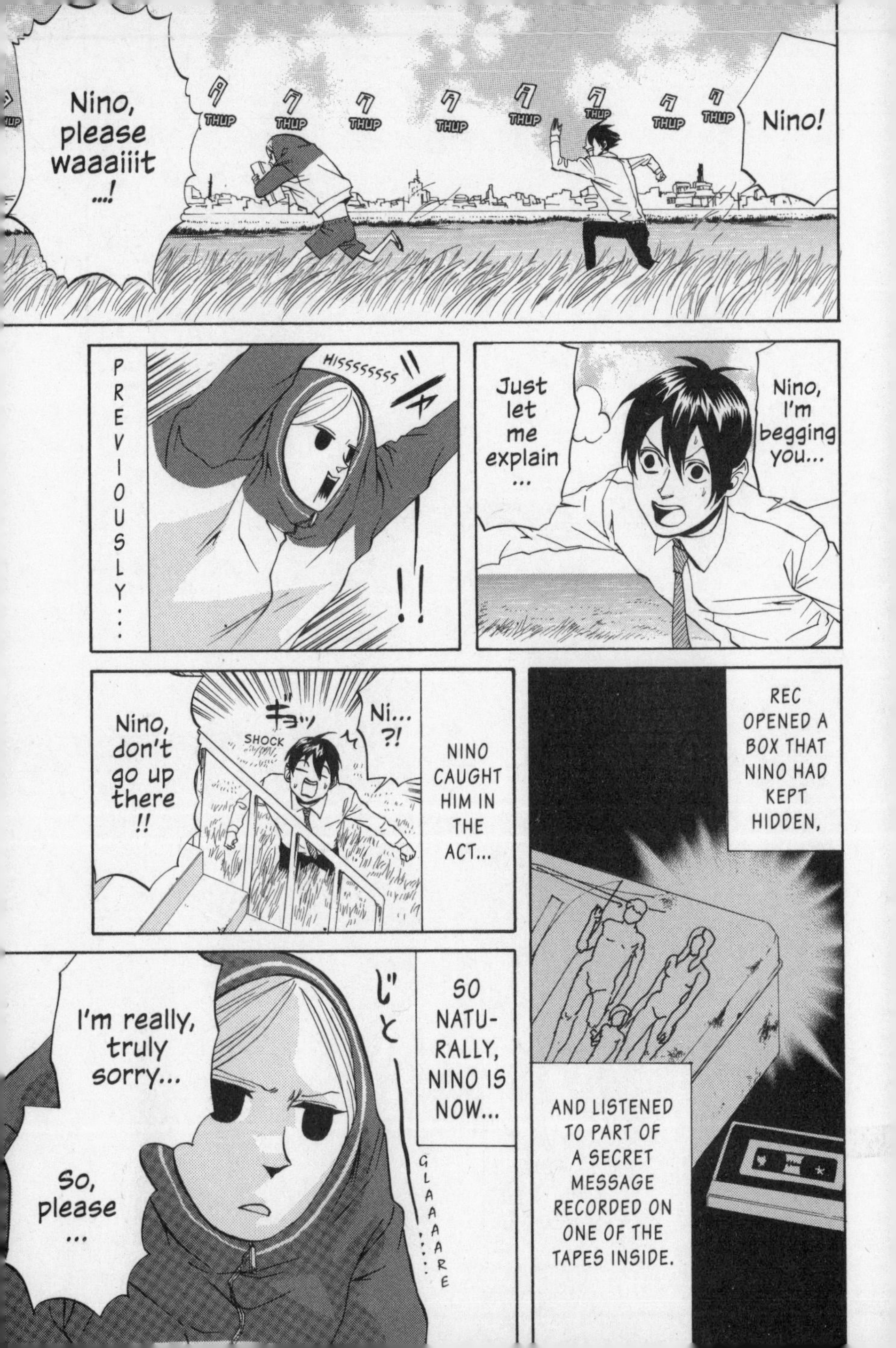

Nino!
THUP THUP THUP THUP THUP THUP THUP THUP THUP
Nino, please waaaiiit ...!
Nino, I'm begging you...
Just let me explain ...
HISSSSSSSS
!!
PREVIOUSLY...
REC OPENED A BOX THAT NINO HAD KEPT HIDDEN,
AND LISTENED TO PART OF A SECRET MESSAGE RECORDED ON ONE OF THE TAPES INSIDE.
NINO CAUGHT HIM IN THE ACT...
Ni... ?!
SHOCK
Nino, don't go up there !!
SO NATU-RALLY, NINO IS NOW...
GLAAAAARE
I'm really, truly sorry...
So, please ...

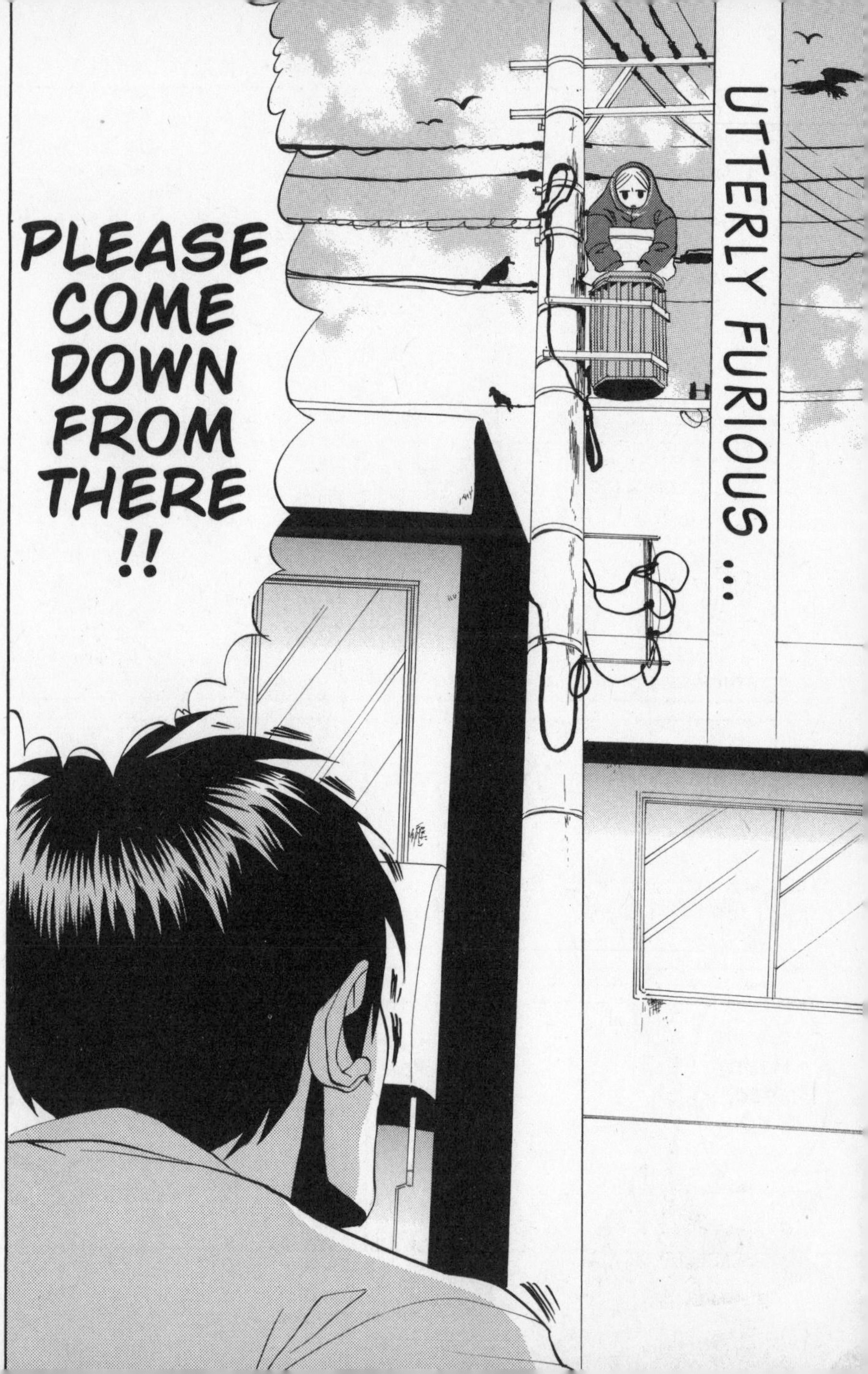
UTTERLY FURIOUS ...
PLEASE COME DOWN FROM THERE !!

Chapter 129: Atop a Telephone Pole

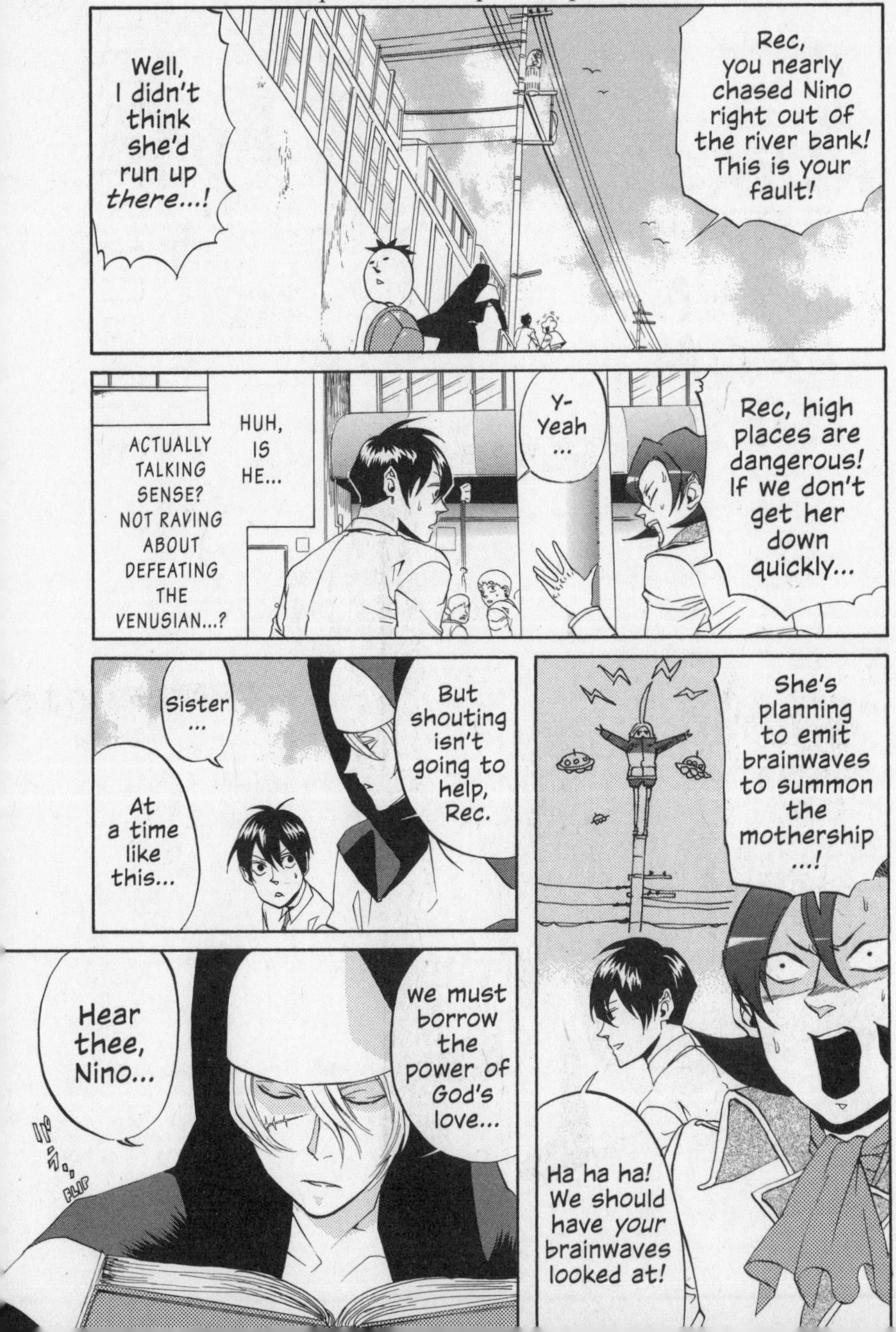
Rec, you nearly chased Nino right out of the river bank! This is your fault!
Well, I didn't think she'd run up *there*...!
Rec, high places are dangerous! If we don't get her down quickly...
Y-Yeah...
HUH, IS HE...
ACTUALLY TALKING SENSE? NOT RAVING ABOUT DEFEATING THE VENUSIAN...?
She's planning to emit brainwaves to summon the mothership...!
Ha ha ha! We should have *your* brainwaves looked at!
But shouting isn't going to help, Rec.
Sister...
At a time like this...
we must borrow the power of God's love...
Hear thee, Nino...
FLIP

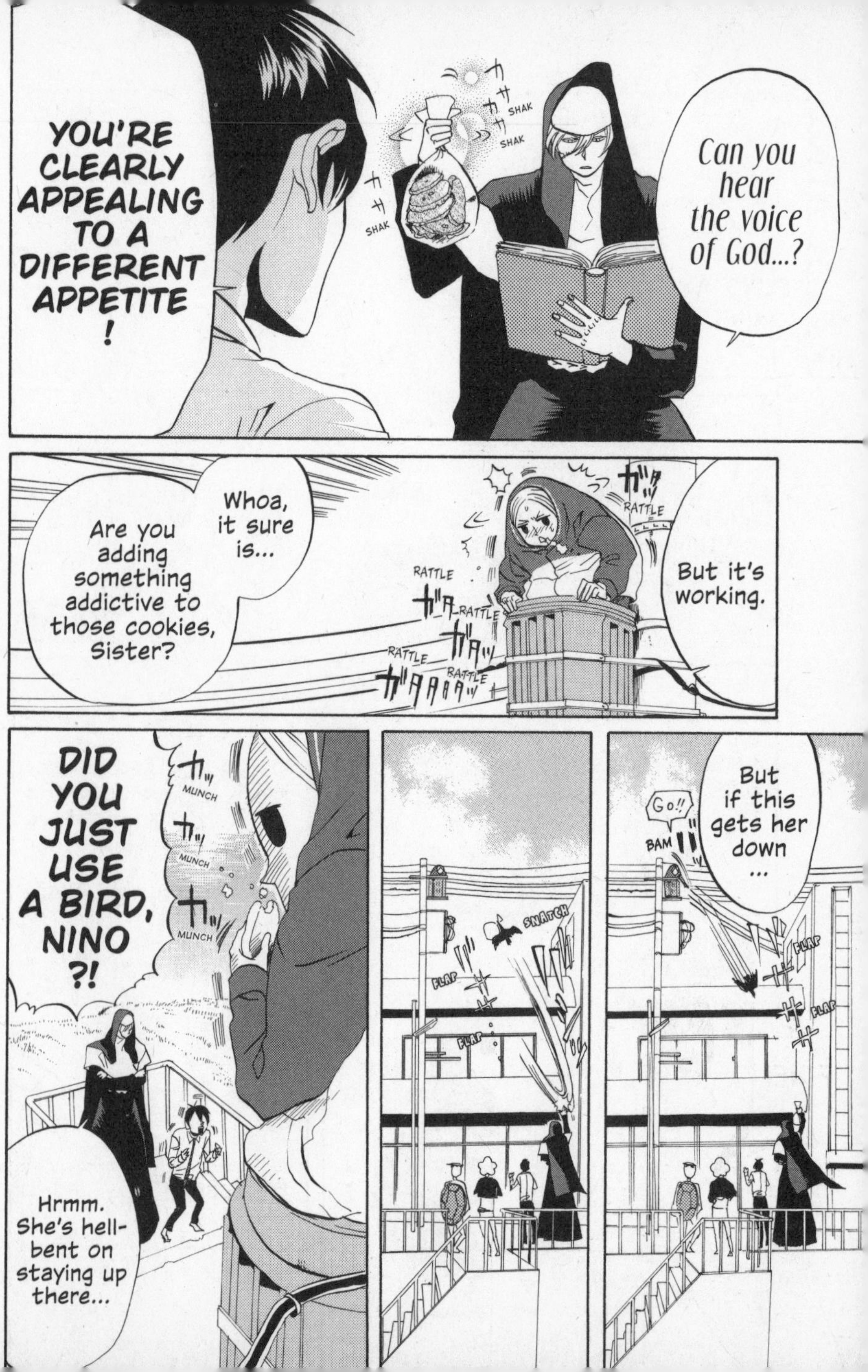
Can you hear the voice of God...?
SHAK
SHAK
SHAK
YOU'RE CLEARLY APPEALING TO A DIFFERENT APPETITE!
But it's working.
RATTLE
RATTLE
RATTLE
RATTLE
RATTLE
Whoa, it sure is...
Are you adding something addictive to those cookies, Sister?
But if this gets her down...
Go!!
BAM
FLAP
FLAP
SNATCH
FLAP
FLAP
DID YOU JUST USE A BIRD, NINO?!
MUNCH
MUNCH
MUNCH
Hrmm. She's hell-bent on staying up there...

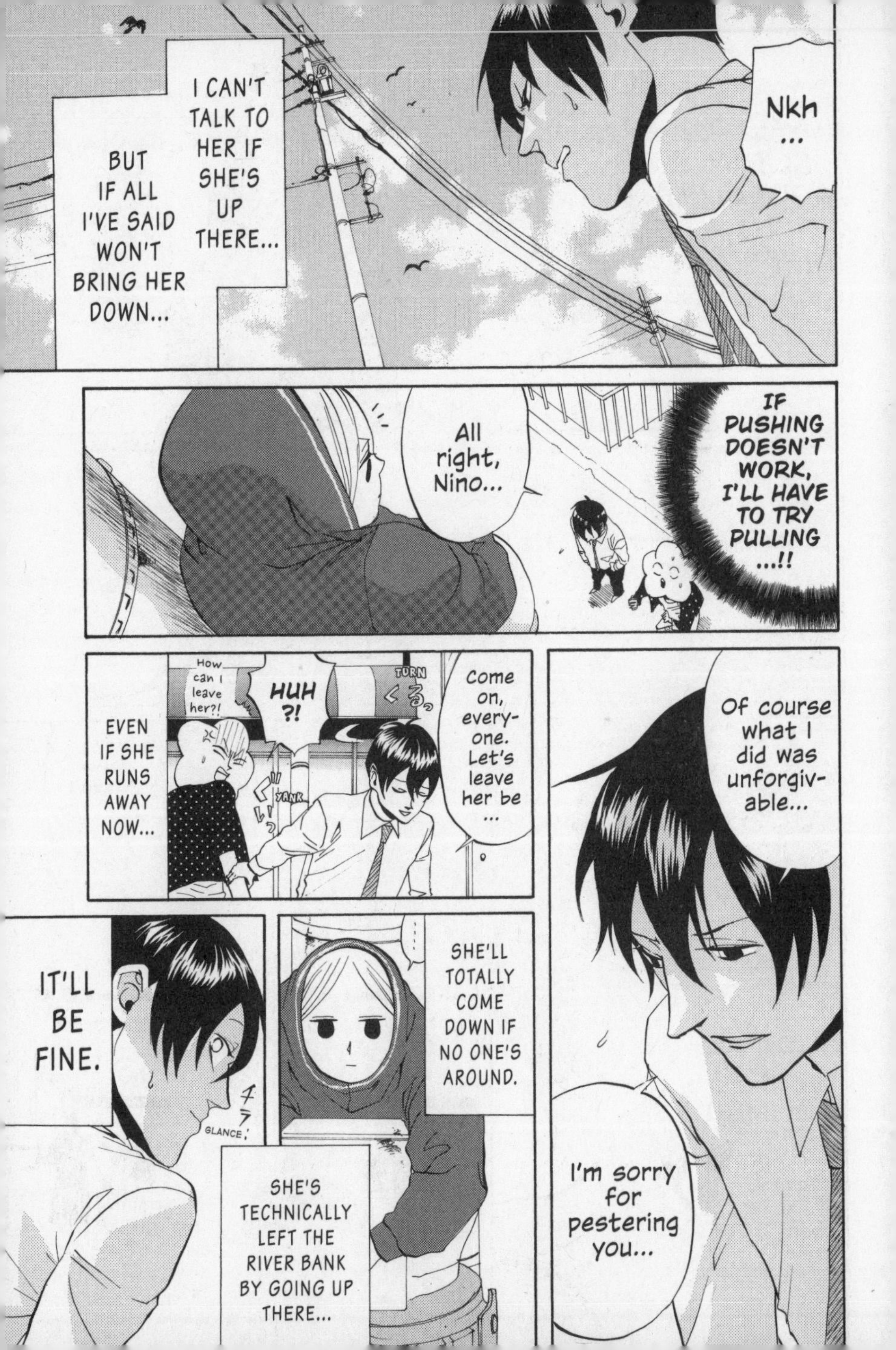
Nkh...
I CAN'T TALK TO HER IF SHE'S UP THERE...
BUT IF ALL I'VE SAID WON'T BRING HER DOWN...
IF PUSHING DOESN'T WORK, I'LL HAVE TO TRY PULLING...!!
All right, Nino...
Of course what I did was unforgivable...
I'm sorry for pestering you...
Come on, everyone. Let's leave her be...
TURN
HUH?!
How can I leave her?!
YANK
EVEN IF SHE RUNS AWAY NOW...
SHE'LL TOTALLY COME DOWN IF NO ONE'S AROUND.
SHE'S TECHNICALLY LEFT THE RIVER BANK BY GOING UP THERE...
IT'LL BE FINE.
GLANCE

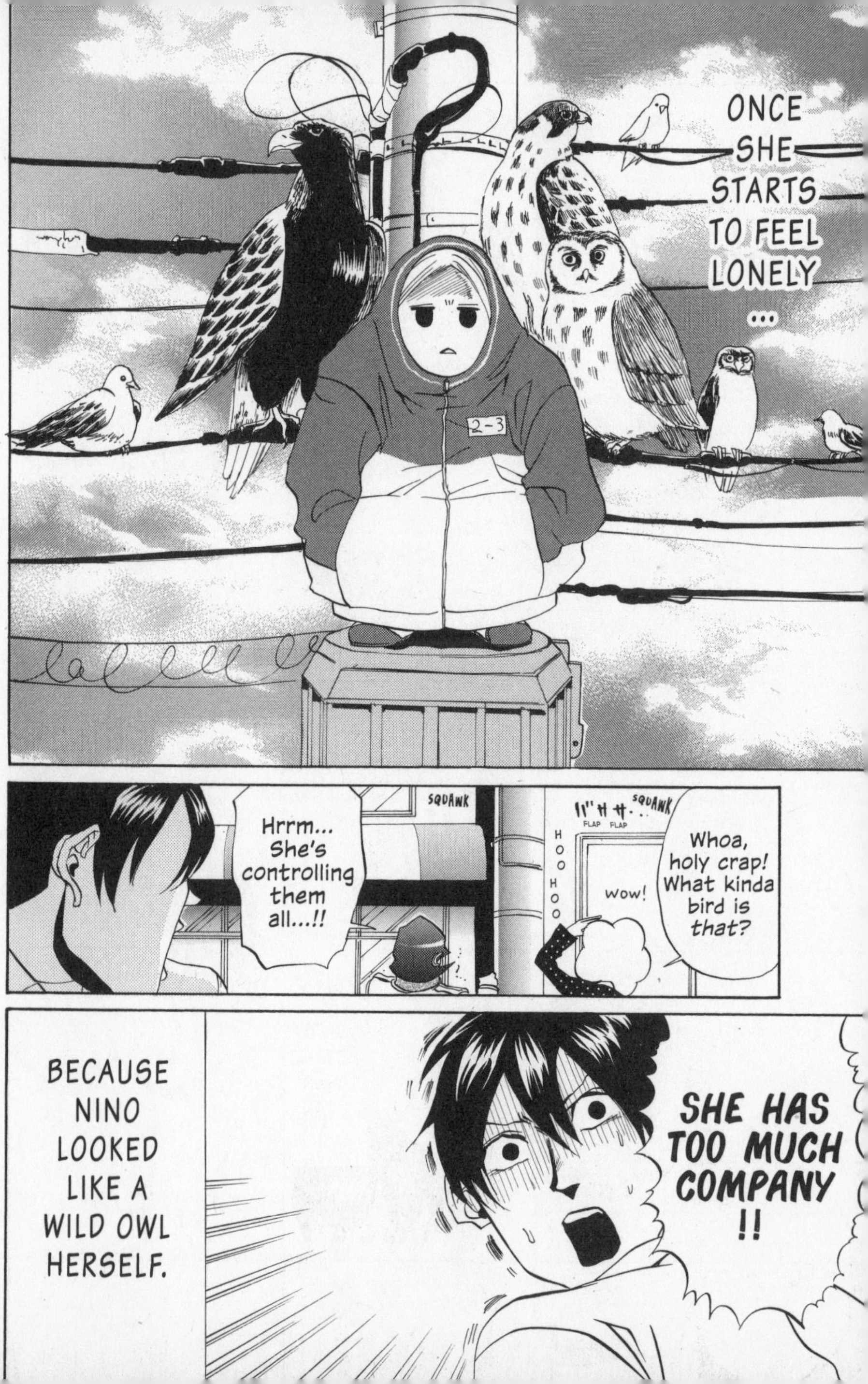
ONCE SHE STARTS TO FEEL LONELY ...
SQUAWK
FLAP FLAP
HOO HOO
Whoa, holy crap! What kinda bird is *that*?
wow!
SQUAWK
Hrrm... She's controlling them all...!!
SHE HAS TOO MUCH COMPANY !!
BECAUSE NINO LOOKED LIKE A WILD OWL HERSELF.

Chapter 130: Messages

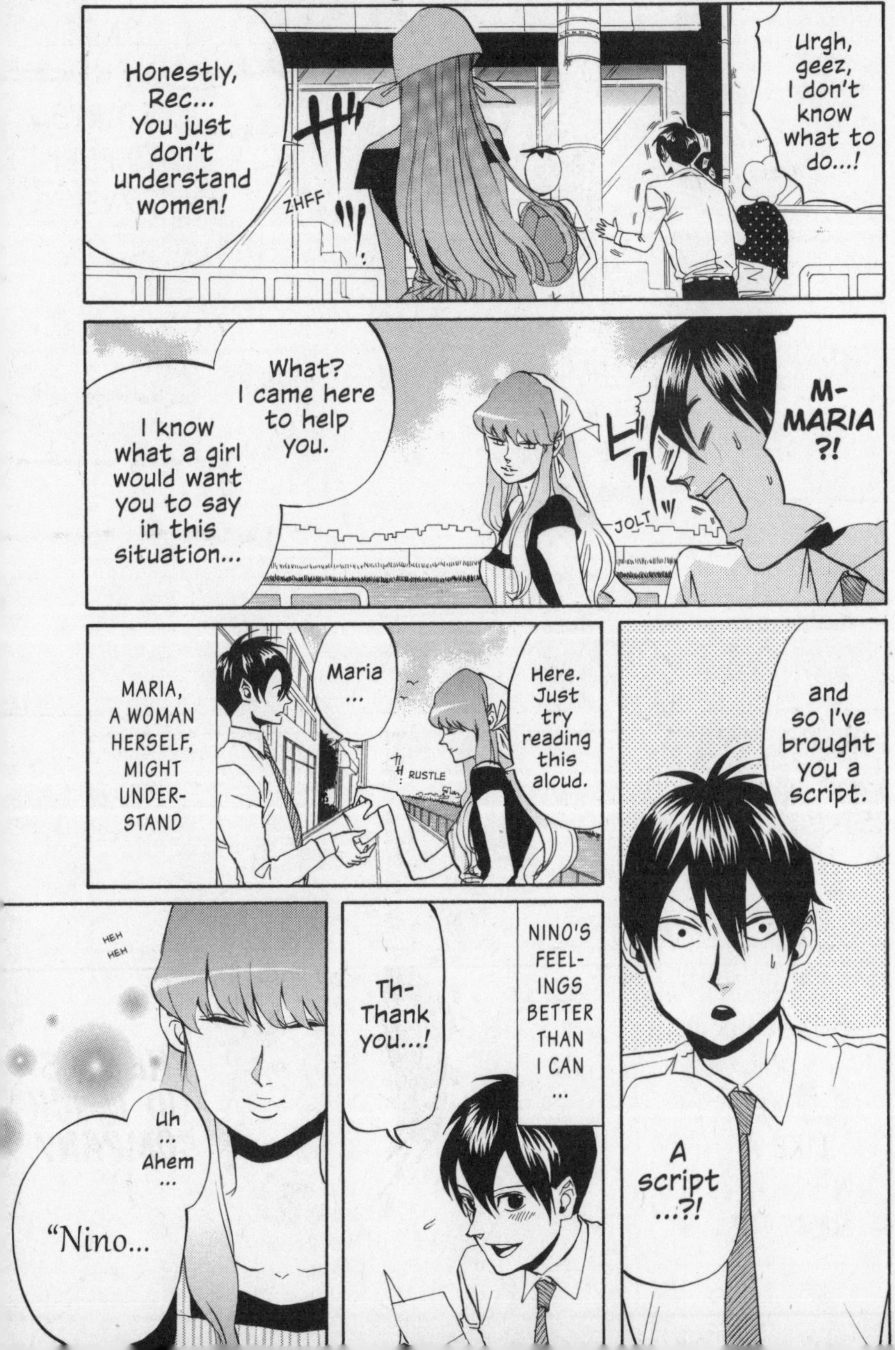

Urgh, geez, I don't know what to do...!
Honestly, Rec... You just don't understand women!
ZHFF
M-MARIA?!
JOLT
What? I came here to help you.
I know what a girl would want you to say in this situation...
and so I've brought you a script.
A script...?!
Here. Just try reading this aloud.
Maria...
RUSTLE
MARIA, A WOMAN HERSELF, MIGHT UNDERSTAND
NINO'S FEELINGS BETTER THAN I CAN...
Th-Thank you...!
HEH HEH
Uh... Ahem...
"Nino...

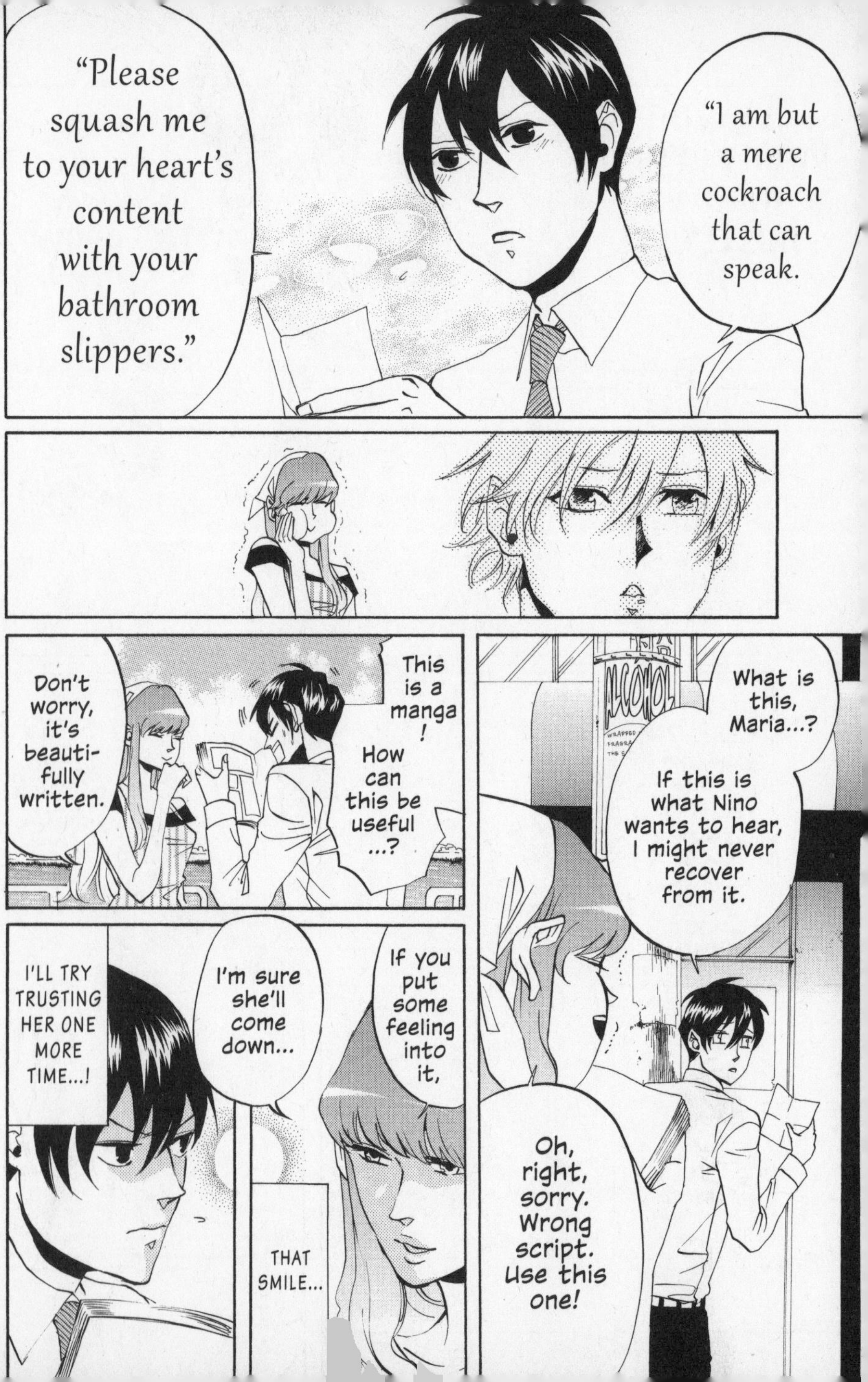
"I am but a mere cockroach that can speak.
"Please squash me to your heart's content with your bathroom slippers."
ALCOHOL
What is this, Maria...?
If this is what Nino wants to hear, I might never recover from it.
Oh, right, sorry. Wrong script. Use this one!
This is a manga! How can this be useful ...?
Don't worry, it's beautifully written.
If you put some feeling into it,
I'm sure she'll come down...
THAT SMILE...
I'LL TRY TRUSTING HER ONE MORE TIME...!

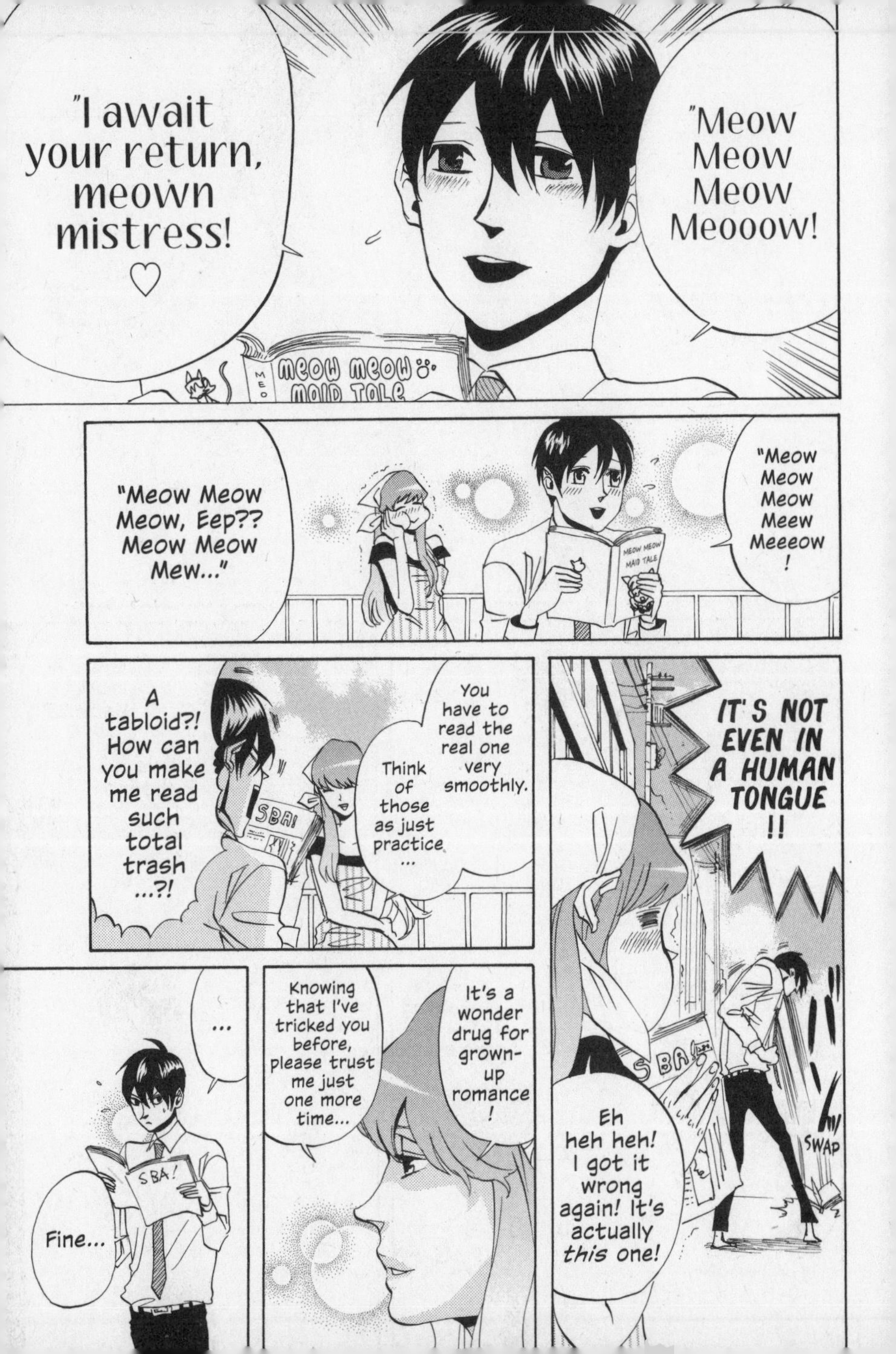
"Meow Meow Meow Meooow!
"I await your return, meown mistress! ♡
MEOW MEOW MAID TALE
"Meow Meow Meow Meew Meeeow!
"Meow Meow Meow, Eep?? Meow Meow Mew..."
MEOW MEOW MAID TALE
IT'S NOT EVEN IN A HUMAN TONGUE!!
SBA!
Eh heh heh! I got it wrong again! It's actually *this* one!
SWAP
You have to read the real one very smoothly.
Think of those as just practice...
A tabloid?! How can you make me read such total trash...?!
SBA!
It's a wonder drug for grown-up romance!
Knowing that I've tricked you before, please trust me just one more time...
...
SBA!
Fine...

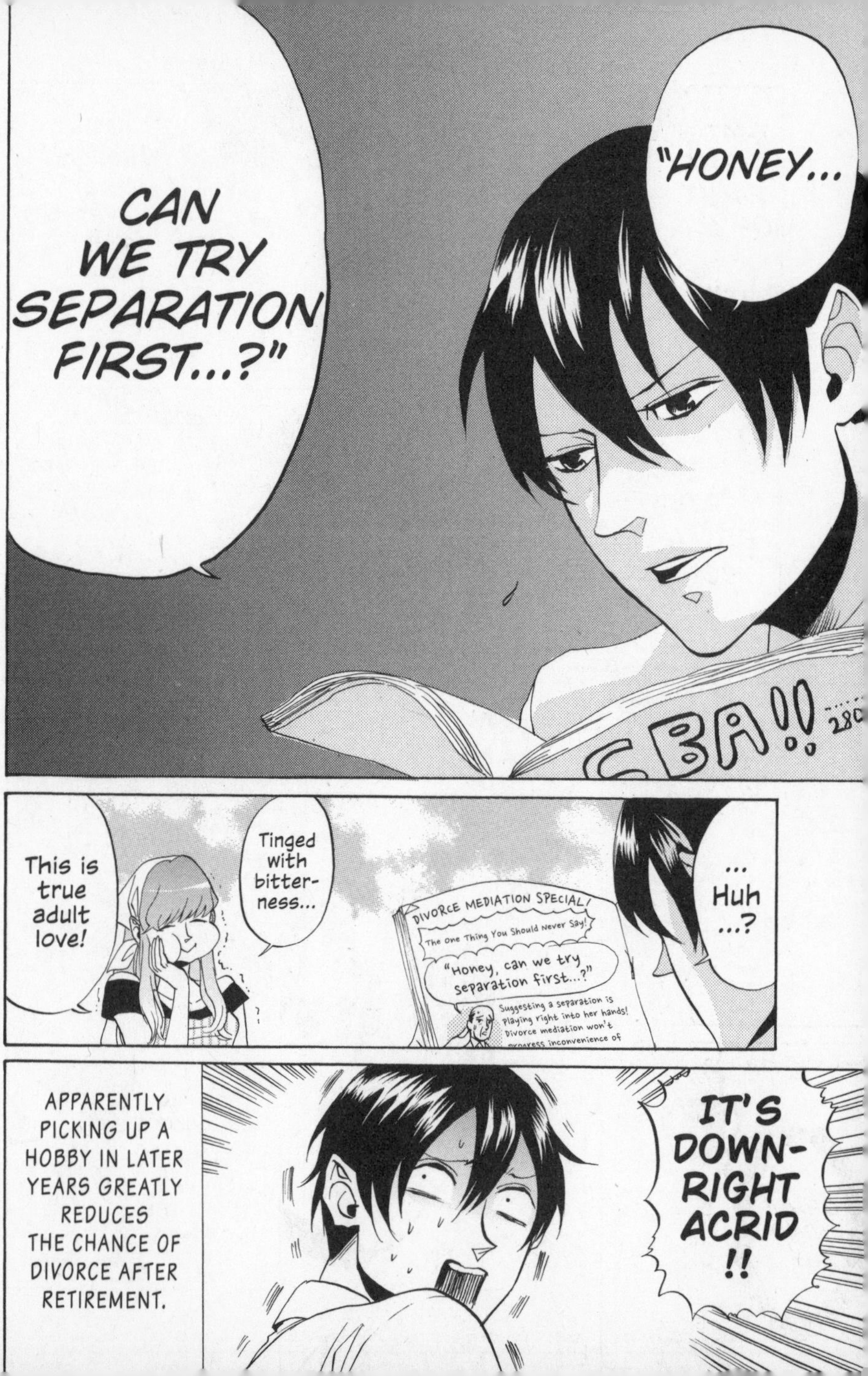
"HONEY...
CAN WE TRY SEPARATION FIRST...?"
... Huh ...?
DIVORCE MEDIATION SPECIAL!
The One Thing You Should Never Say!
"Honey, can we try separation first...?"
Suggesting a separation is playing right into her hands! Divorce mediation won't
Tinged with bitterness...
This is true adult love!
IT'S DOWNRIGHT ACRID!!
APPARENTLY PICKING UP A HOBBY IN LATER YEARS GREATLY REDUCES THE CHANCE OF DIVORCE AFTER RETIREMENT.

Chapter 131: Weightier Than Words

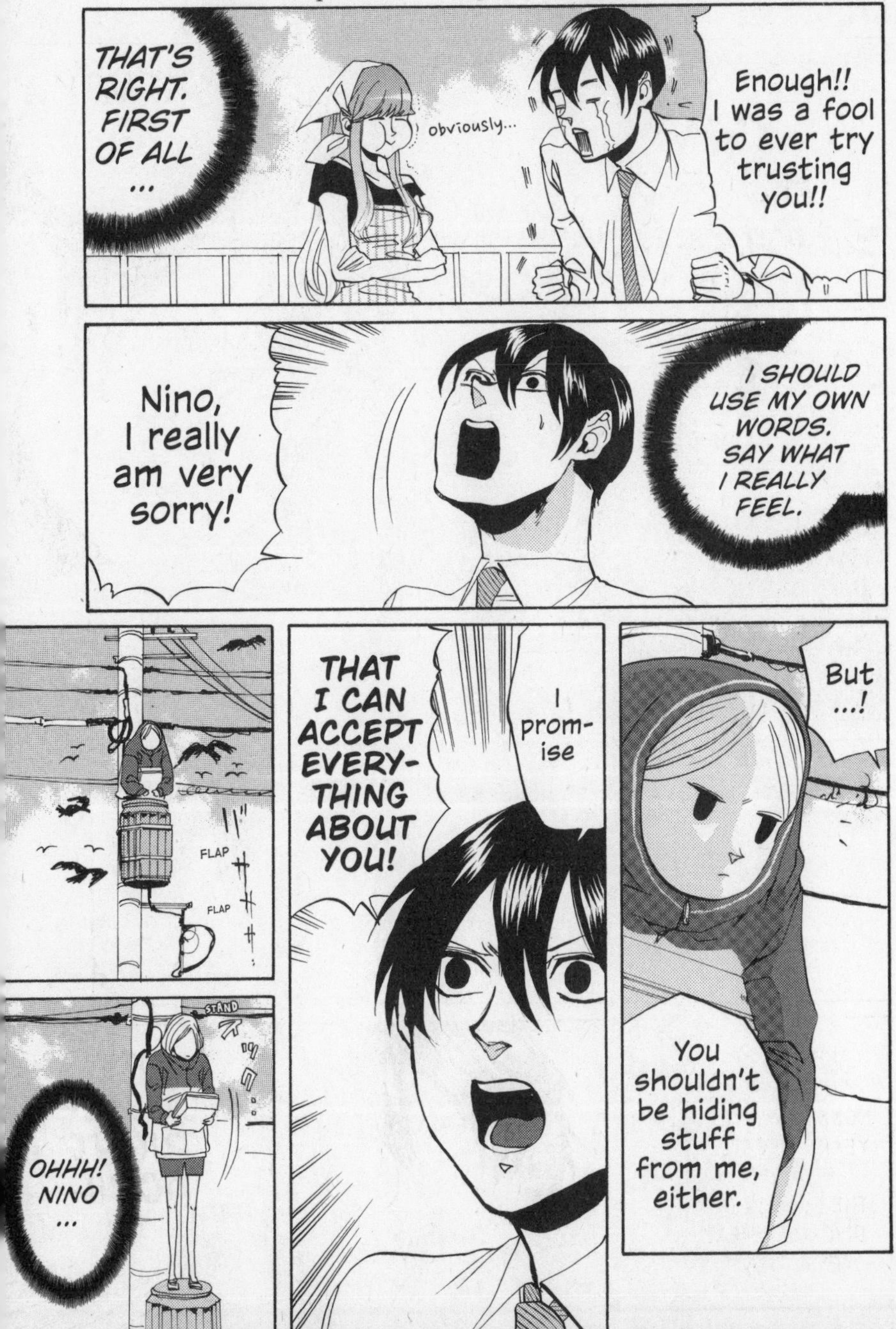
Enough!! I was a fool to ever try trusting you!!
obviously...
THAT'S RIGHT. FIRST OF ALL ...
I SHOULD USE MY OWN WORDS. SAY WHAT I REALLY FEEL.
Nino, I really am very sorry!
But ...!
You shouldn't be hiding stuff from me, either.
I promise
THAT I CAN ACCEPT EVERYTHING ABOUT YOU!
FLAP
FLAP
STAND
OHHH! NINO ...

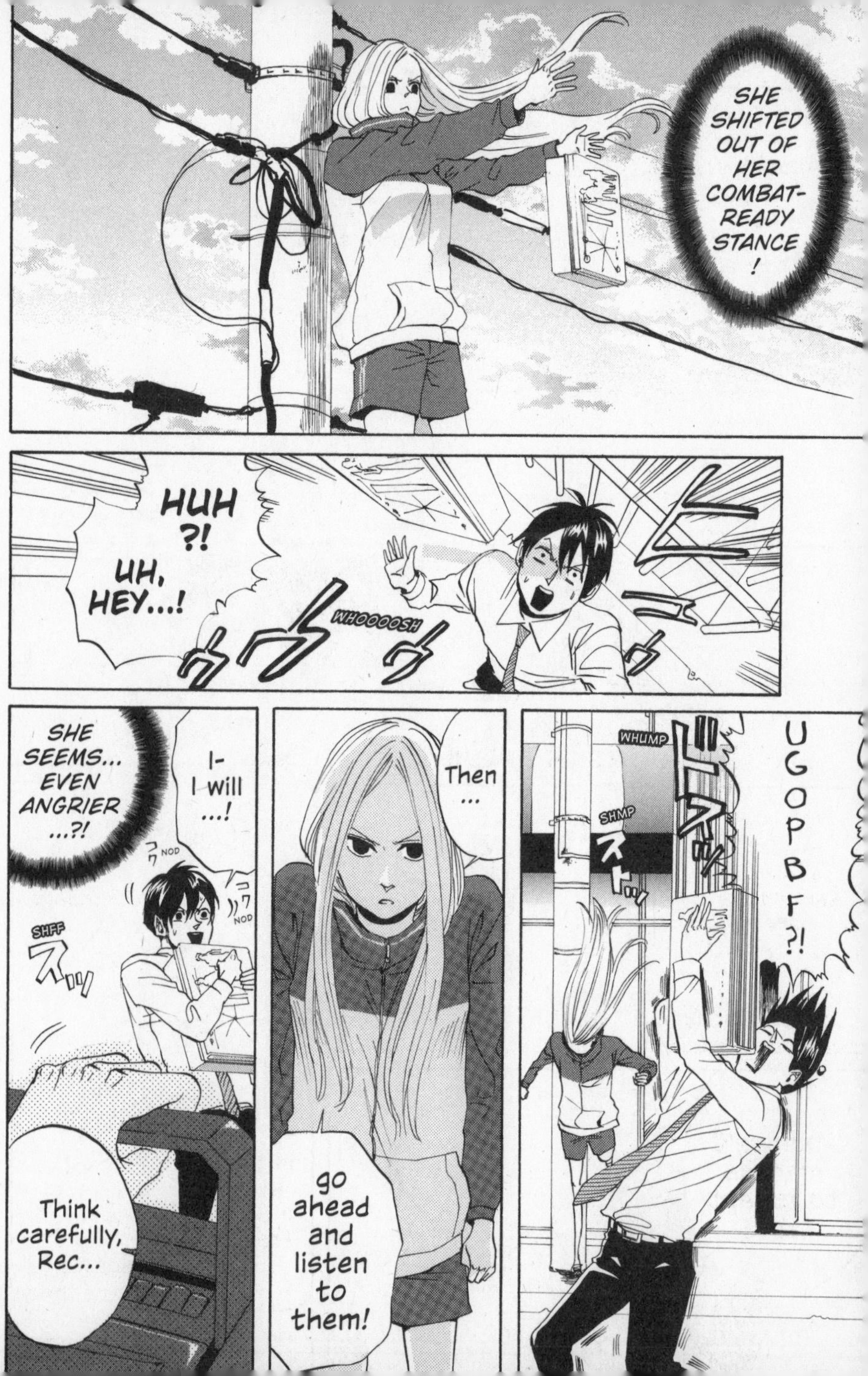
SHE SHIFTED OUT OF HER COMBAT-READY STANCE!
HUH?!
UH, HEY...!
WHOOOOSH
WHUMP
SHMP
UGOPBF?!
Then...
go ahead and listen to them!
SHE SEEMS... EVEN ANGRIER...?!
I- I will...!
NOD
NOD
SHFF
Think carefully, Rec...

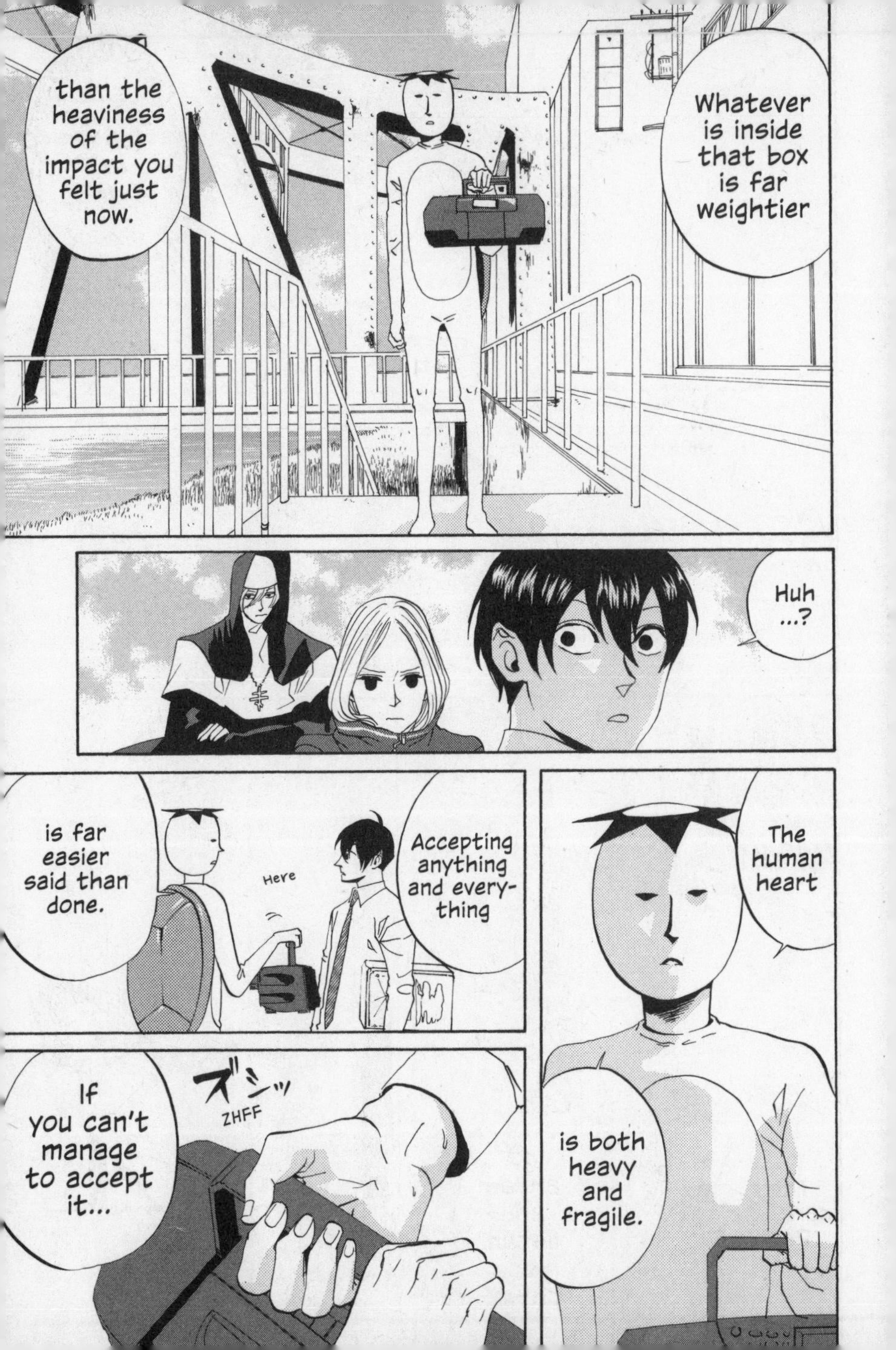
Whatever is inside that box is far weightier
than the heaviness of the impact you felt just now.
Huh ...?
The human heart
is both heavy and fragile.
Accepting anything and every-thing
Here
is far easier said than done.
ズシッ
ZHFF
If you can't manage to accept it...

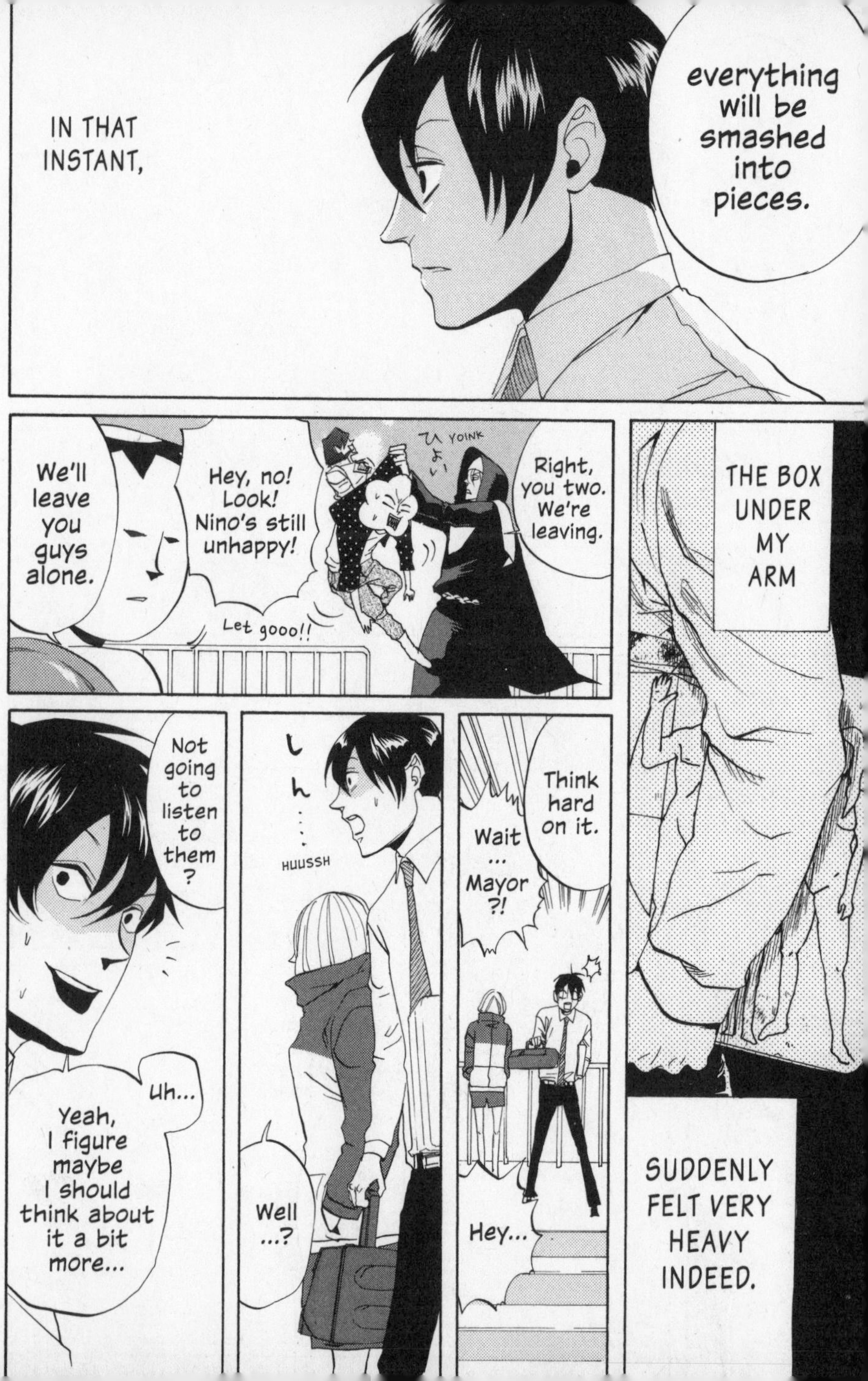

everything will be smashed into pieces.
IN THAT INSTANT,
THE BOX UNDER MY ARM
SUDDENLY FELT VERY HEAVY INDEED.
Right, you two. We're leaving.
ひょい YOINK
Hey, no! Look! Nino's still unhappy!
Let gooo!!
We'll leave you guys alone.
Think hard on it.
Wait ... Mayor ?!
Hey...
しん... HUUSSH
Well ...?
Not going to listen to them ?
Uh... Yeah, I figure maybe I should think about it a bit more...

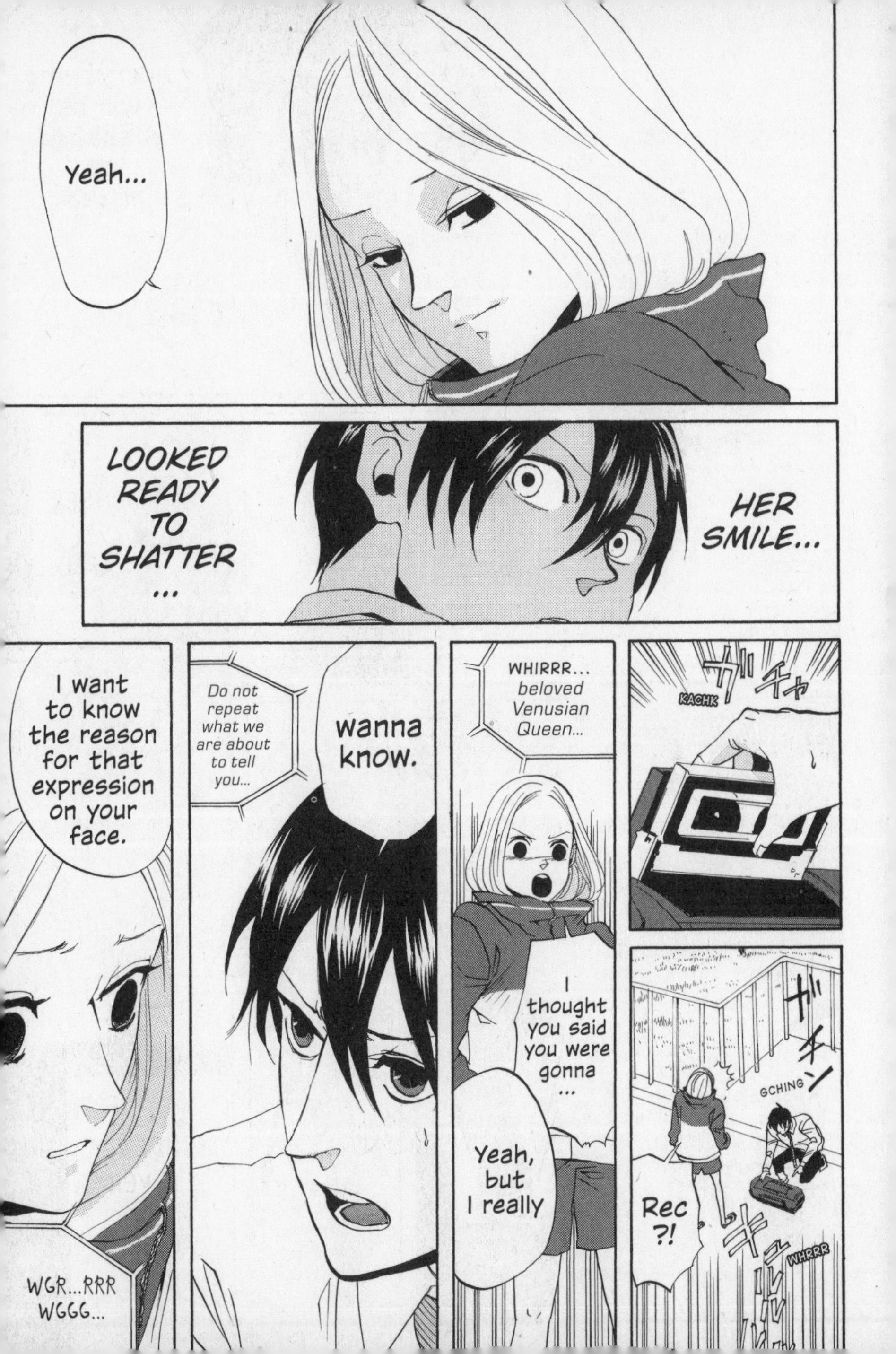
Yeah...
HER SMILE...
LOOKED READY TO SHATTER ...
ガチャ
KACHK
ガチン
GCHING
Rec ?!
WHRRR
WHIRRR... beloved Venusian Queen...
I thought you said you were gonna ...
Yeah, but I really
wanna know.
Do not repeat what we are about to tell you...
I want to know the reason for that expression on your face.
WGR...RRR WGGG...

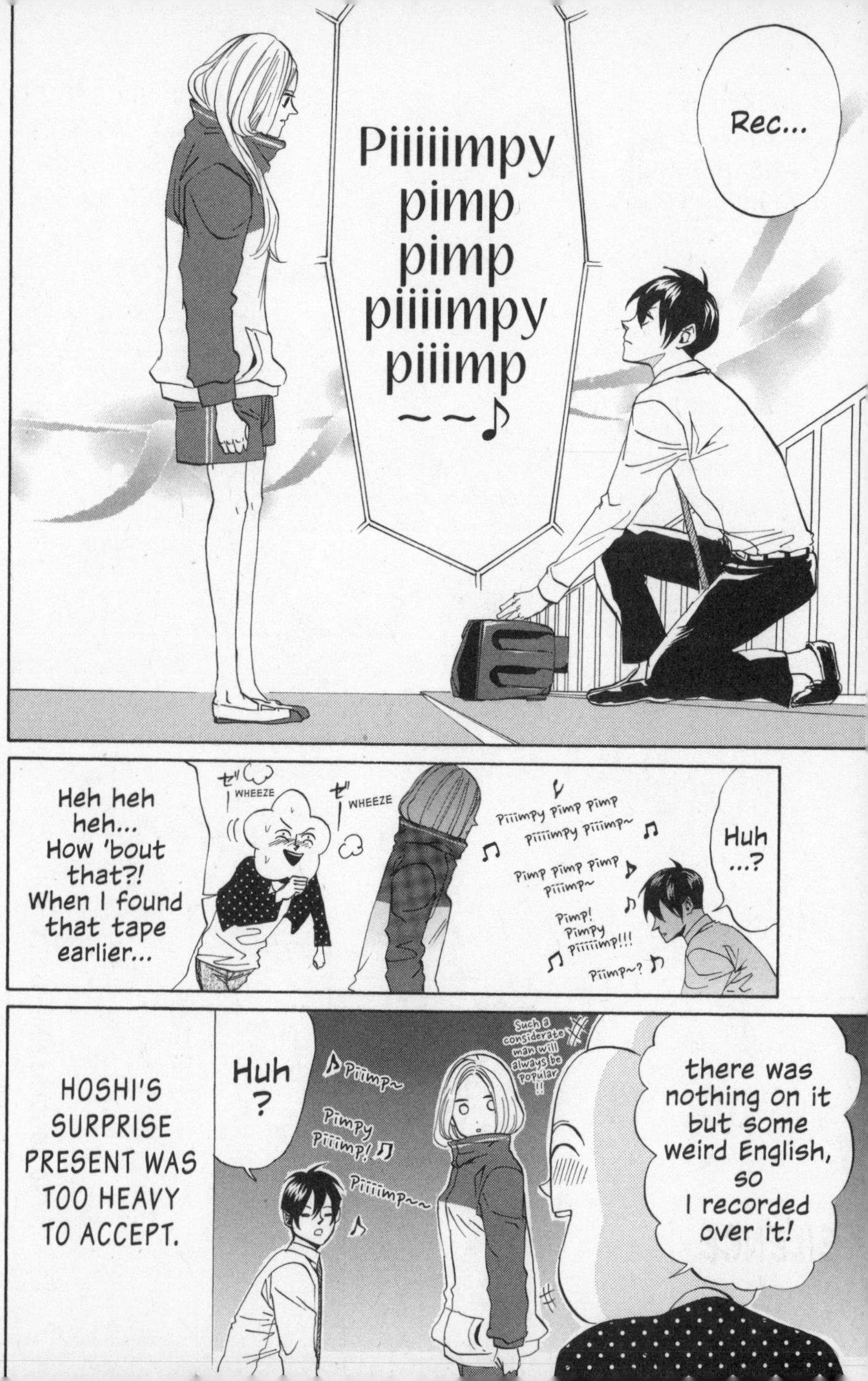
Rec...
Piiiiimpy pimp pimp piiiimpy piiimp ~~♪
Huh ...?
Piiimpy Pimp Pimp
Piiiimpy Piiimp~
Pimp Pimp Pimp
Piiimp~
Pimp! Pimpy Piiiiimp!!!
Piimp~?
WHEEZE
WHEEZE
Heh heh heh... How 'bout that?! When I found that tape earlier...
there was nothing on it but some weird English, so I recorded over it!
Such a considerate man will always be popular!!
Piiimp~
Pimpy Piiimp!
Piiiimp~~
Huh ?
HOSHI'S SURPRISE PRESENT WAS TOO HEAVY TO ACCEPT.

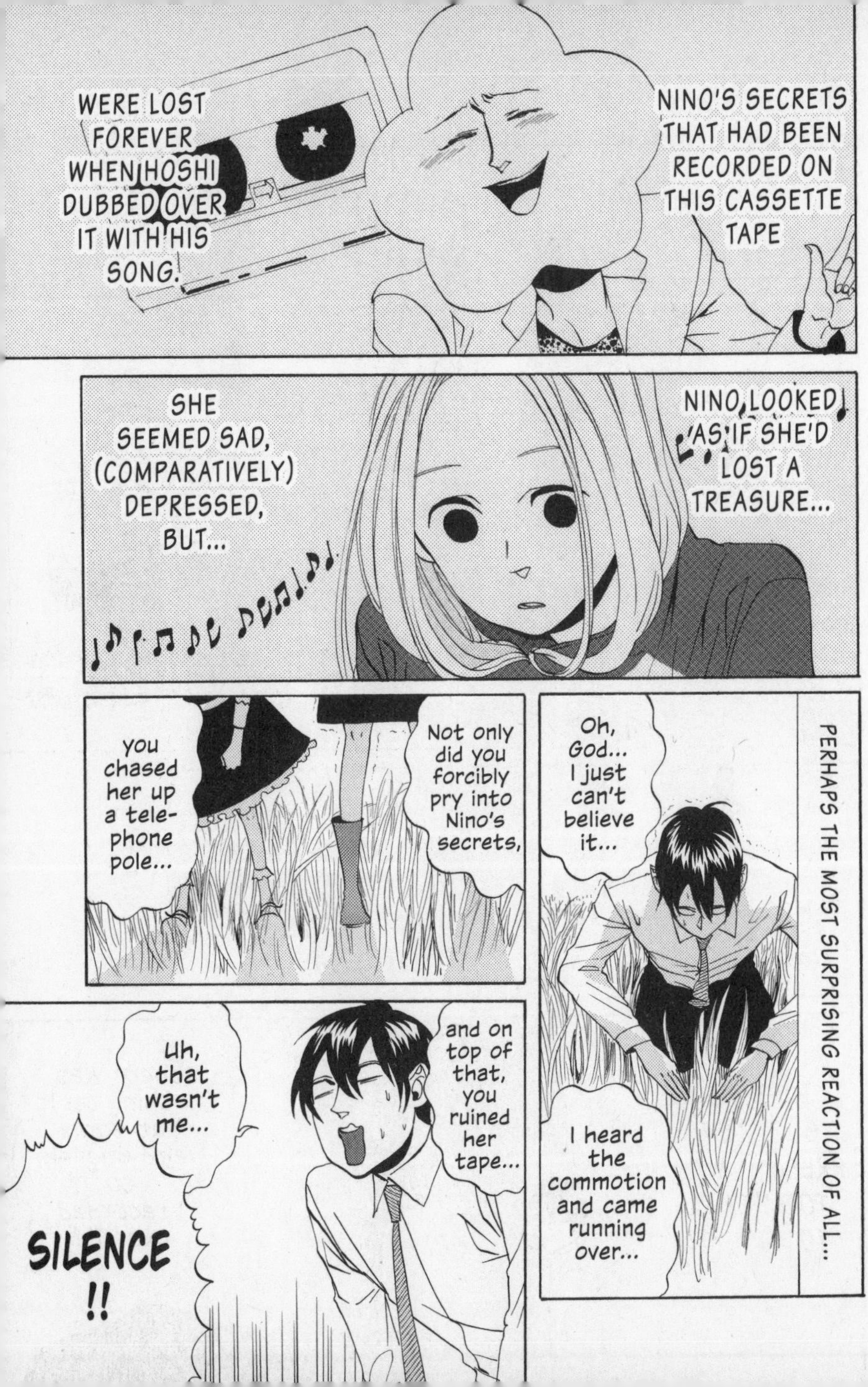
NINO'S SECRETS THAT HAD BEEN RECORDED ON THIS CASSETTE TAPE
WERE LOST FOREVER WHEN HOSHI DUBBED OVER IT WITH HIS SONG.
NINO LOOKED AS IF SHE'D LOST A TREASURE...
SHE SEEMED SAD, (COMPARATIVELY) DEPRESSED, BUT...
PERHAPS THE MOST SURPRISING REACTION OF ALL...
Oh, God... I just can't believe it...
I heard the commotion and came running over...
Not only did you forcibly pry into Nino's secrets,
you chased her up a tele-phone pole...
and on top of that, you ruined her tape...
Uh, that wasn't me...
SILENCE !!

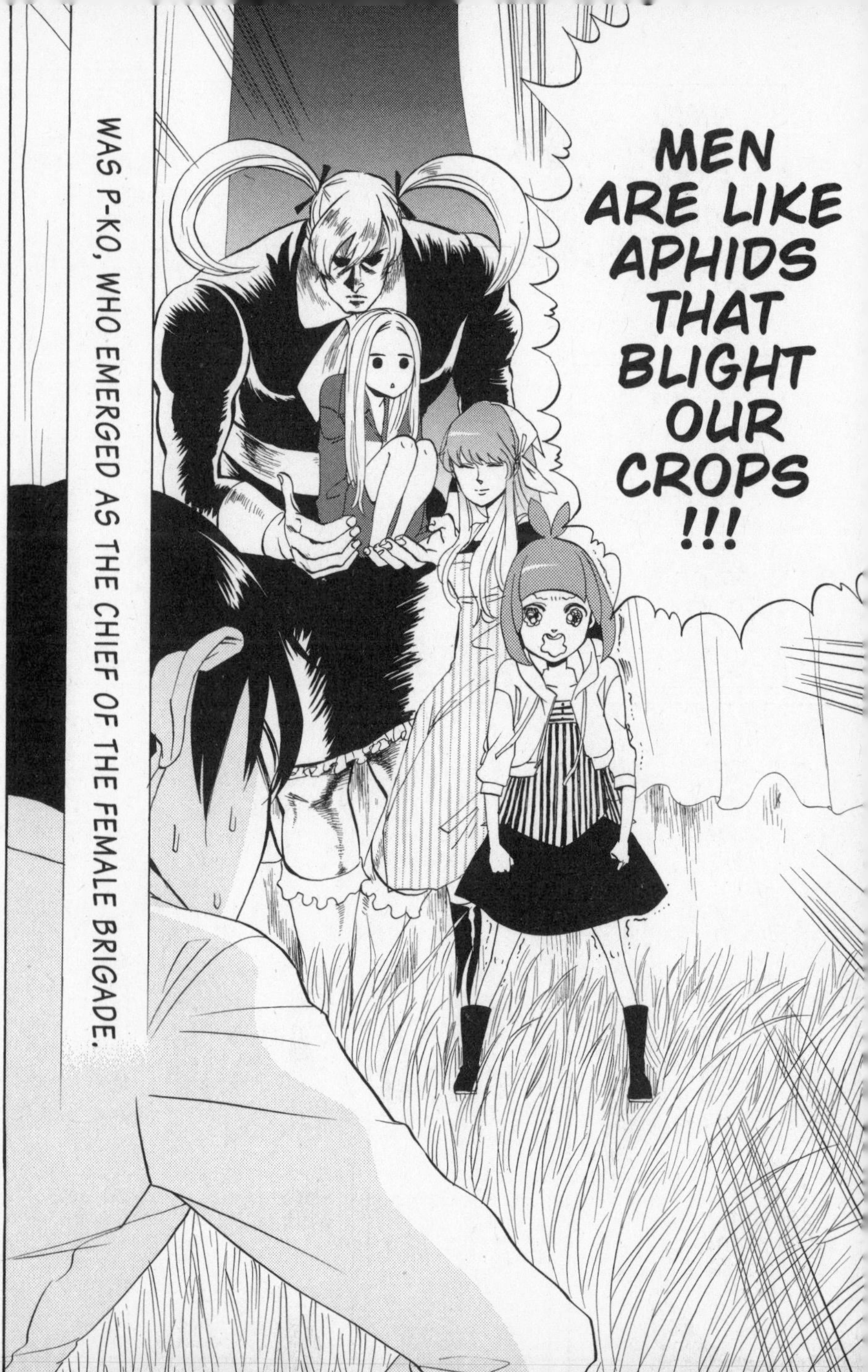
MEN ARE LIKE APHIDS THAT BLIGHT OUR CROPS!!!
WAS P-KO, WHO EMERGED AS THE CHIEF OF THE FEMALE BRIGADE.

Chapter 132: Pajama Party

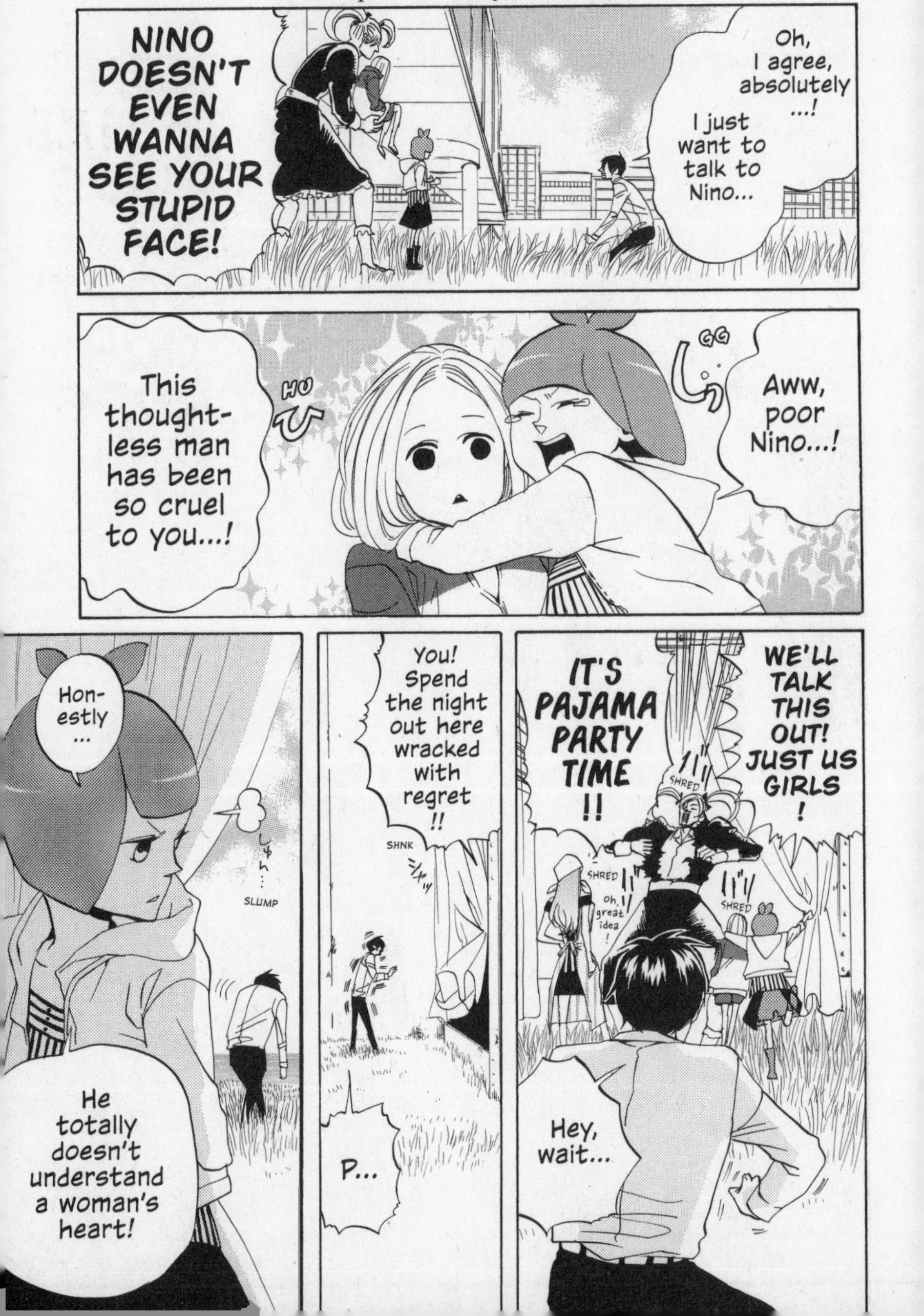
Oh, I agree, absolutely ...!
I just want to talk to Nino...
NINO DOESN'T EVEN WANNA SEE YOUR STUPID FACE!
GG
Aww, poor Nino...!
HU
This thoughtless man has been so cruel to you...!
WE'LL TALK THIS OUT! JUST US GIRLS!
IT'S PAJAMA PARTY TIME!!
SHRED
SHRED
Oh, great idea!
SHRED
Hey, wait...
You! Spend the night out here wracked with regret!!
SHNK
P...
Hon-estly...
SLUMP
He totally doesn't understand a woman's heart!

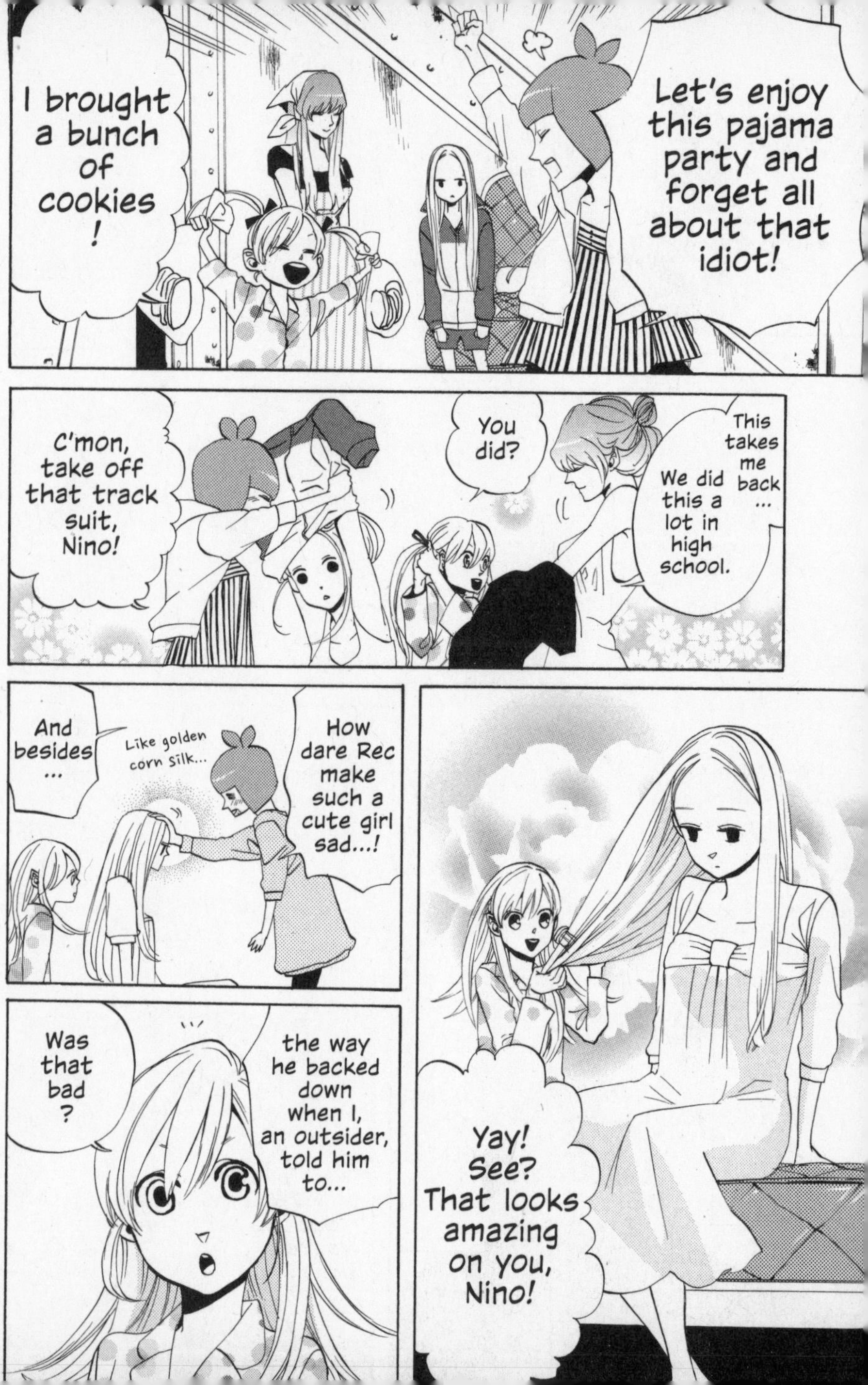
Let's enjoy this pajama party and forget all about that idiot!
I brought a bunch of cookies!
This takes me back...
We did this a lot in high school.
You did?
C'mon, take off that track suit, Nino!
Yay! See? That looks amazing on you, Nino!
How dare Rec make such a cute girl sad...!
Like golden corn silk...
And besides...
the way he backed down when I, an outsider, told him to...
Was that bad?

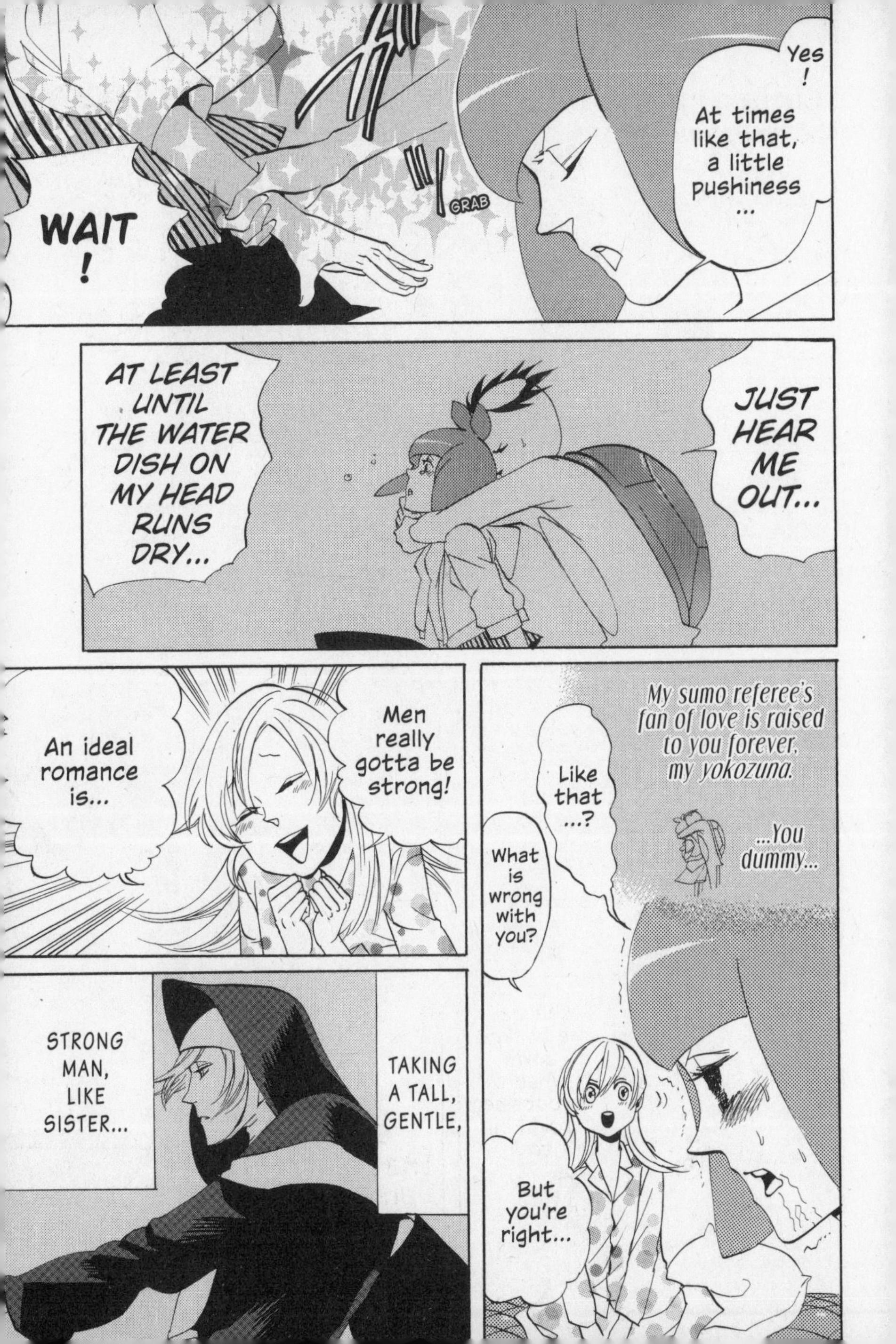
Yes! At times like that, a little pushiness...
GRAB
WAIT!
JUST HEAR ME OUT...
AT LEAST UNTIL THE WATER DISH ON MY HEAD RUNS DRY...
My sumo referee's fan of love is raised to you forever, my yokozuna.
...You dummy...
Like that...?
What is wrong with you?
But you're right...
Men really gotta be strong!
An ideal romance is...
TAKING A TALL, GENTLE,
STRONG MAN, LIKE SISTER...

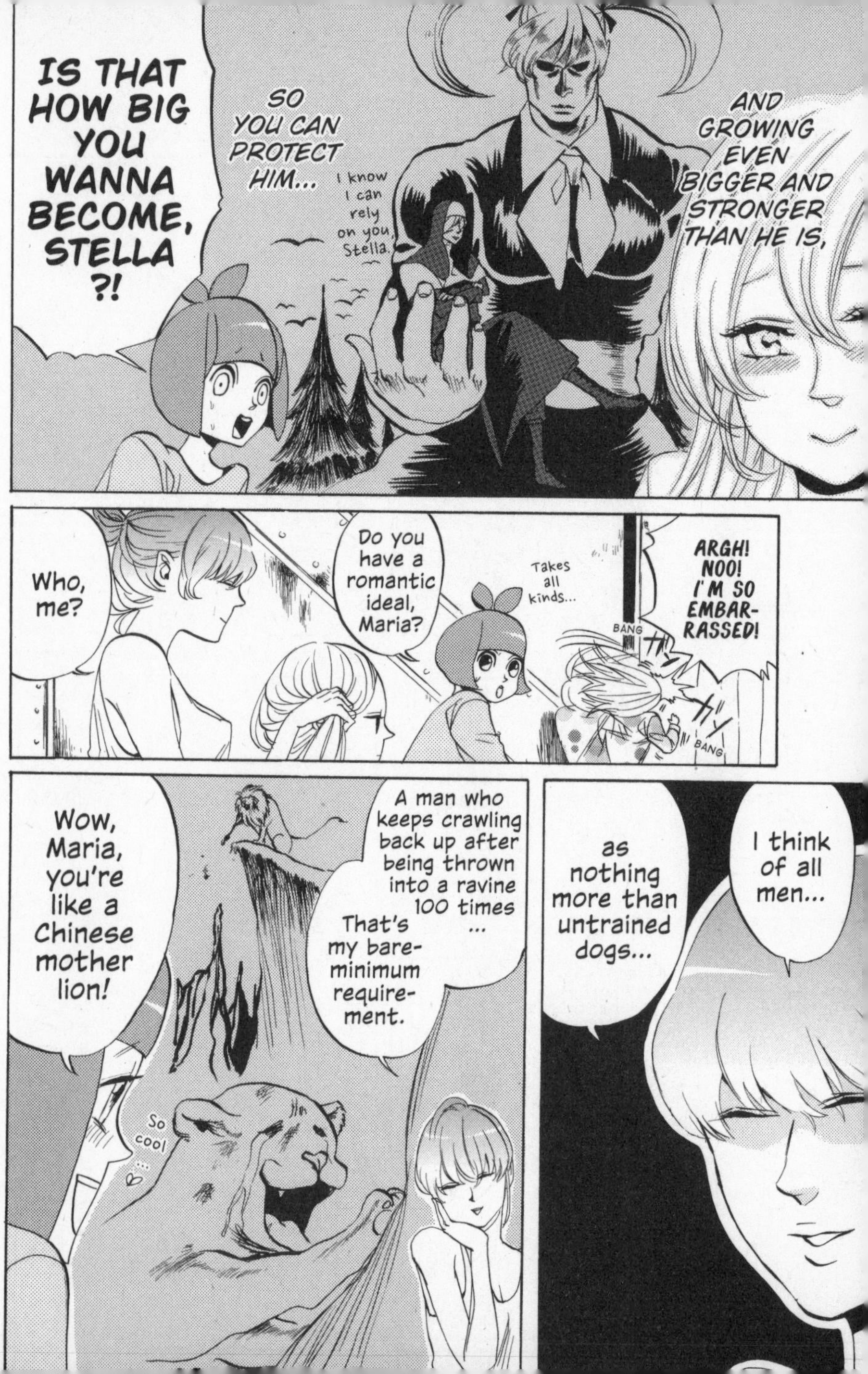
AND GROWING EVEN BIGGER AND STRONGER THAN HE IS,
I know I can rely on you, Stella.
SO YOU CAN PROTECT HIM...
IS THAT HOW BIG YOU WANNA BECOME, STELLA ?!
ARGH! NOO! I'M SO EMBARRASSED!
BANG
BANG
Takes all kinds...
Do you have a romantic ideal, Maria?
Who, me?
I think of all men...
as nothing more than untrained dogs...
A man who keeps crawling back up after being thrown into a ravine 100 times ...
That's my bare-minimum requirement.
Wow, Maria, you're like a Chinese mother lion!
So cool...

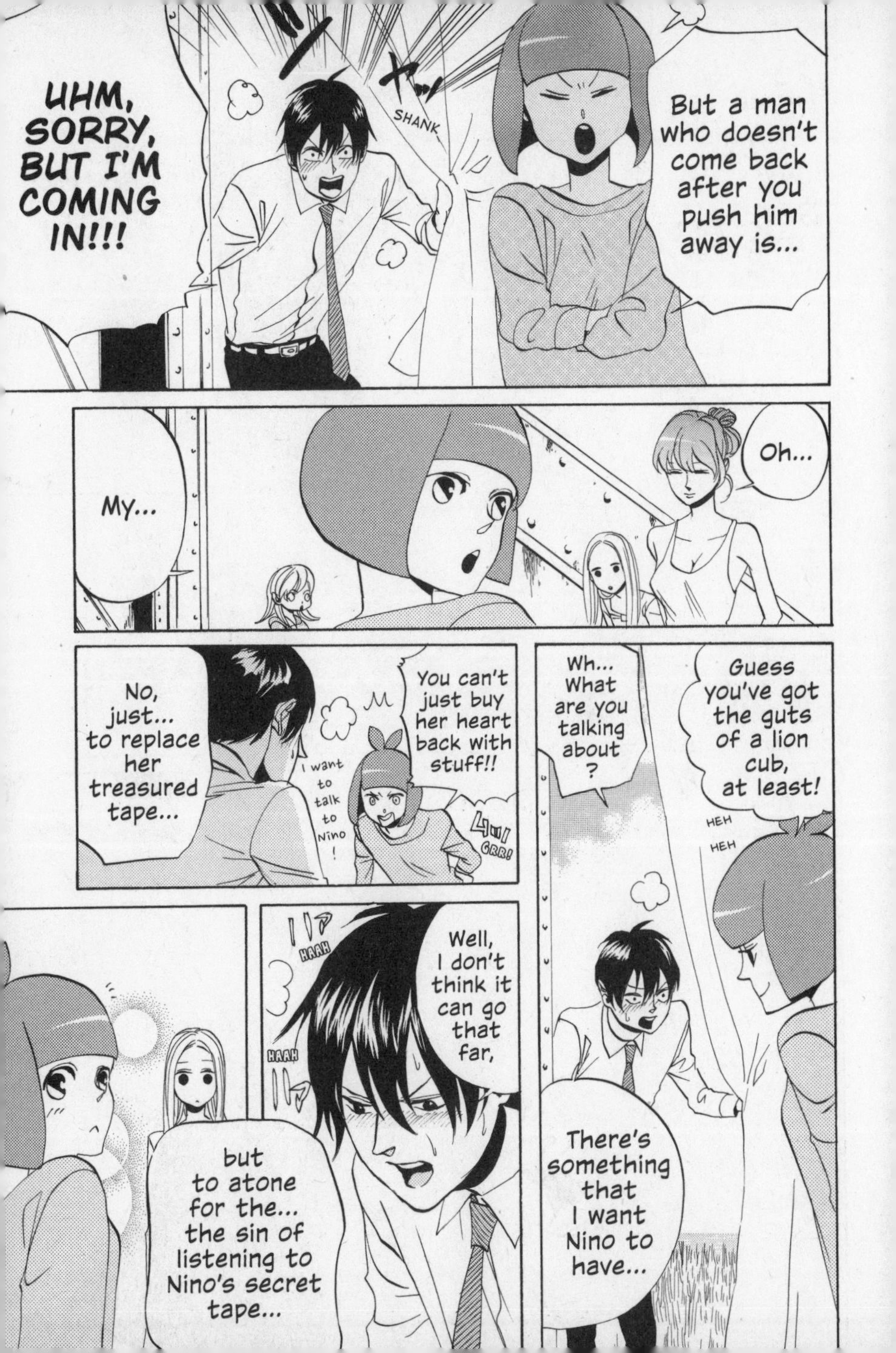
But a man who doesn't come back after you push him away is...
SHANK
UHM, SORRY, BUT I'M COMING IN!!!
Oh...
My...
Guess you've got the guts of a lion cub, at least!
HEH HEH
Wh... What are you talking about?
You can't just buy her heart back with stuff!!
I want to talk to Nino!
GRR!
No, just... to replace her treasured tape...
There's something that I want Nino to have...
Well, I don't think it can go that far,
HAAH
HAAH
but to atone for the... the sin of listening to Nino's secret tape...

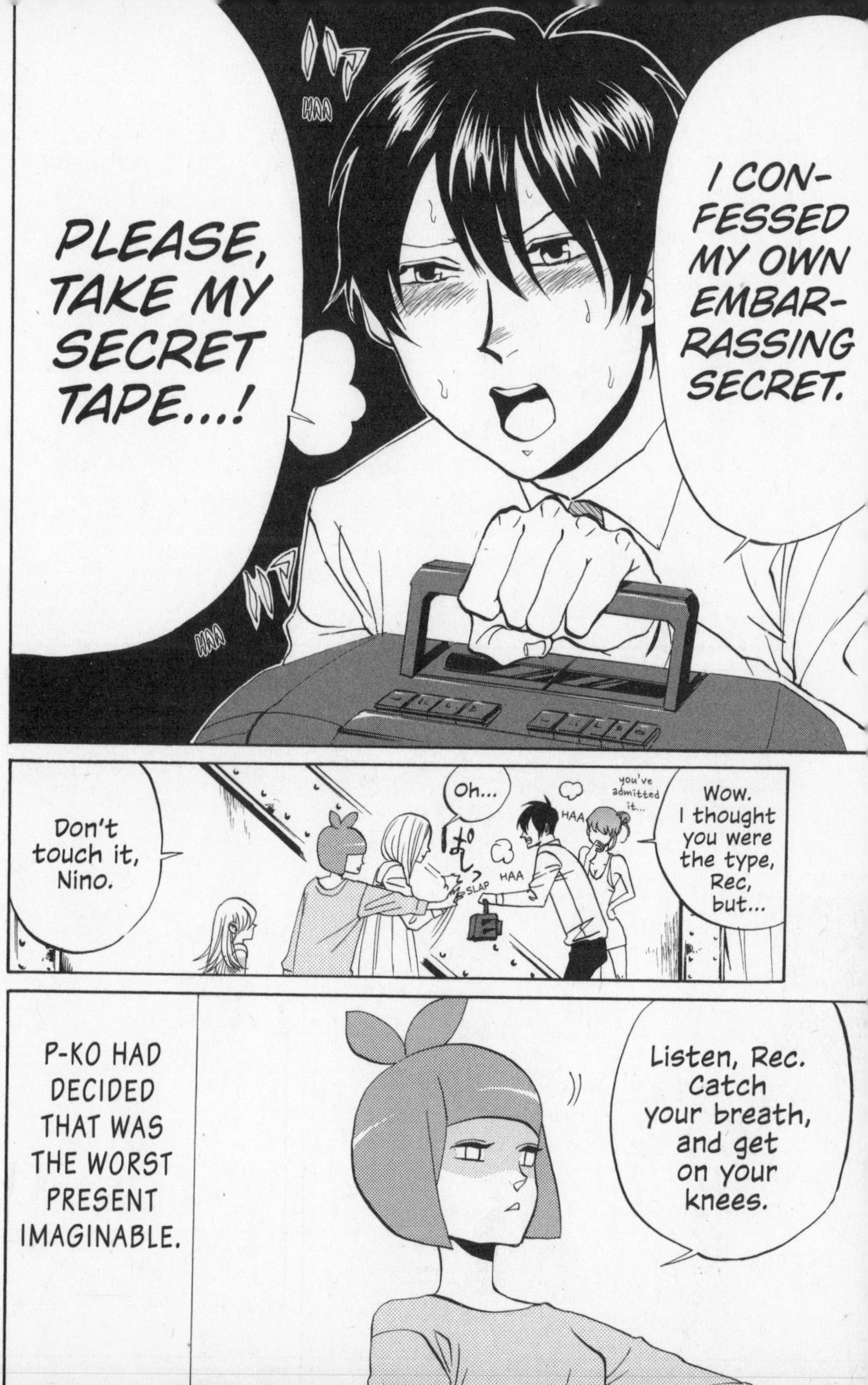
I CON-
FESSED
MY OWN
EMBAR-
RASSING
SECRET.
PLEASE,
TAKE MY
SECRET
TAPE...!
HAA
HAA
Wow.
I thought
you were
the type,
Rec,
but...
you've admitted it...
HAA
Oh...
ぱしっ
SLAP
HAA
Don't
touch it,
Nino.
Listen, Rec.
Catch
your breath,
and get
on your
knees.
P-KO HAD
DECIDED
THAT WAS
THE WORST
PRESENT
IMAGINABLE.

Chapter 133: Rec's Secret Tape

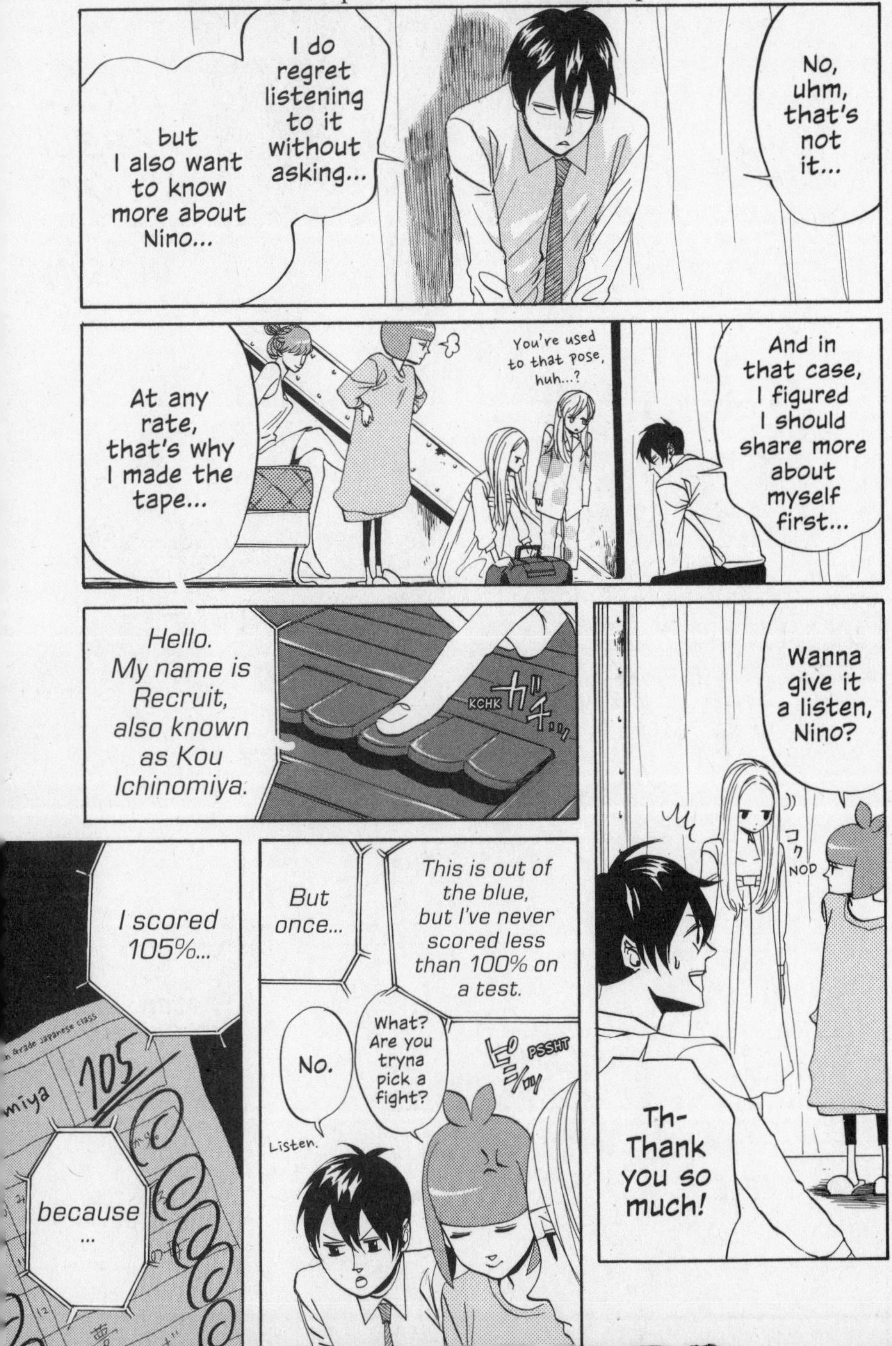

No, uhm, that's not it...
I do regret listening to it without asking...
but I also want to know more about Nino...
And in that case, I figured I should share more about myself first...
You're used to that pose, huh...?
At any rate, that's why I made the tape...
Wanna give it a listen, Nino?
NOD
Th- Thank you so much!
Hello. My name is Recruit, also known as Kou Ichinomiya.
KCHK
This is out of the blue, but I've never scored less than 100% on a test.
But once...
What? Are you tryna pick a fight?
PSSHT
No.
Listen.
I scored 105%...
105
because ...

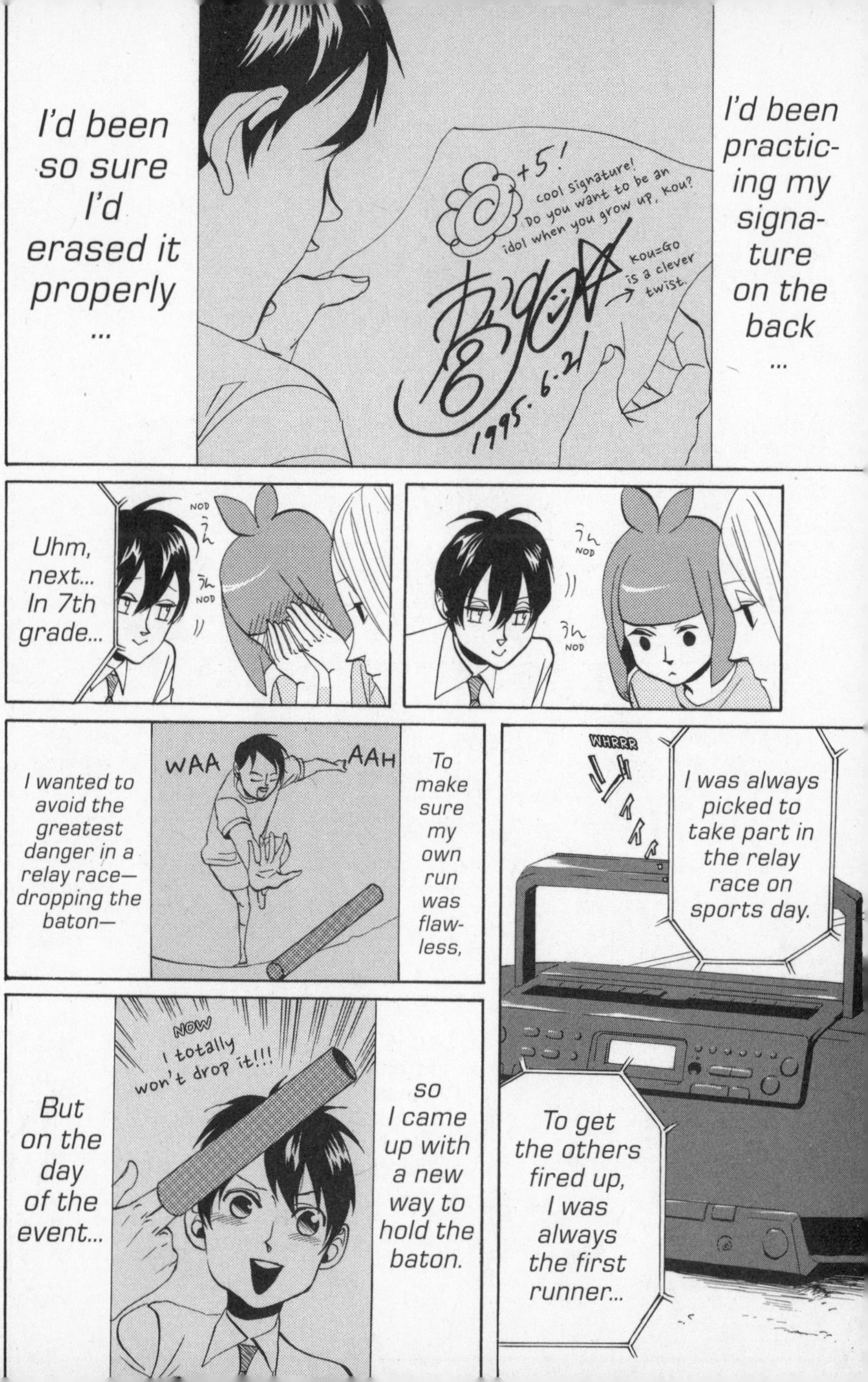
I'd been practicing my signature on the back ...
+5!
cool signature! Do you want to be an idol when you grow up, Kou?
Kou=Go is a clever twist.
1995.6.21
I'd been so sure I'd erased it properly ...
うん
NOD
うん
NOD
Uhm, next... In 7th grade...
NOD
うん
うん
NOD
WHRRR
I was always picked to take part in the relay race on sports day.
To get the others fired up, I was always the first runner...
To make sure my own run was flawless,
WAA
AAH
I wanted to avoid the greatest danger in a relay race—dropping the baton—
so I came up with a new way to hold the baton.
NOW I totally won't drop it!!!
But on the day of the event...

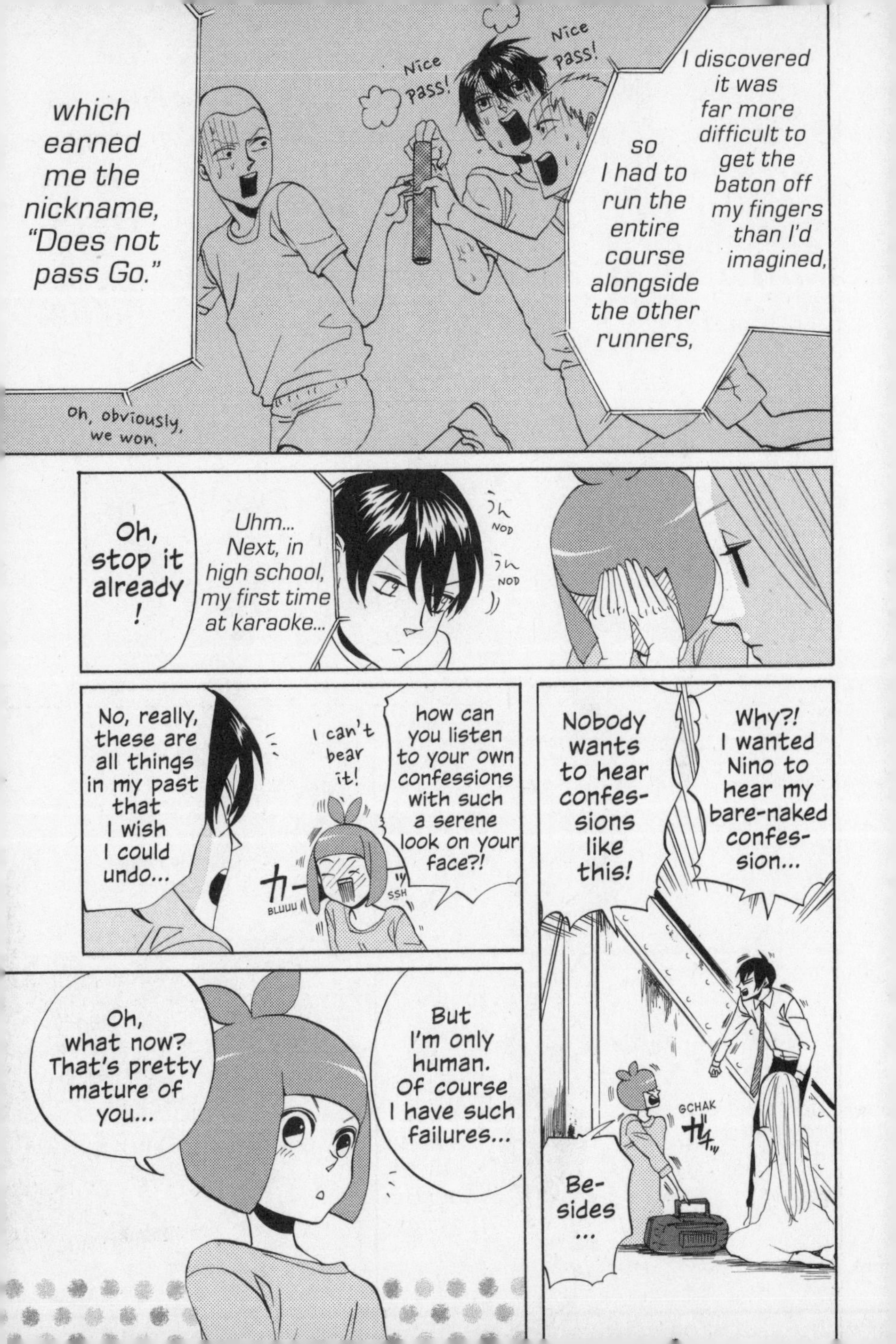

I discovered it was far more difficult to get the baton off my fingers than I'd imagined,
so I had to run the entire course alongside the other runners,
Nice pass!
Nice pass!
which earned me the nickname, "Does not pass Go."
Oh, obviously, we won.
うん
NOD
うん
NOD
Uhm... Next, in high school, my first time at karaoke...
Oh, stop it already!
Why?! I wanted Nino to hear my bare-naked confession...
Nobody wants to hear confessions like this!
GCHAK
Be-sides...
how can you listen to your own confessions with such a serene look on your face?!
I can't bear it!
SSH
カー
BLUUU
No, really, these are all things in my past that I wish I could undo...
But I'm only human. Of course I have such failures...
Oh, what now? That's pretty mature of you...

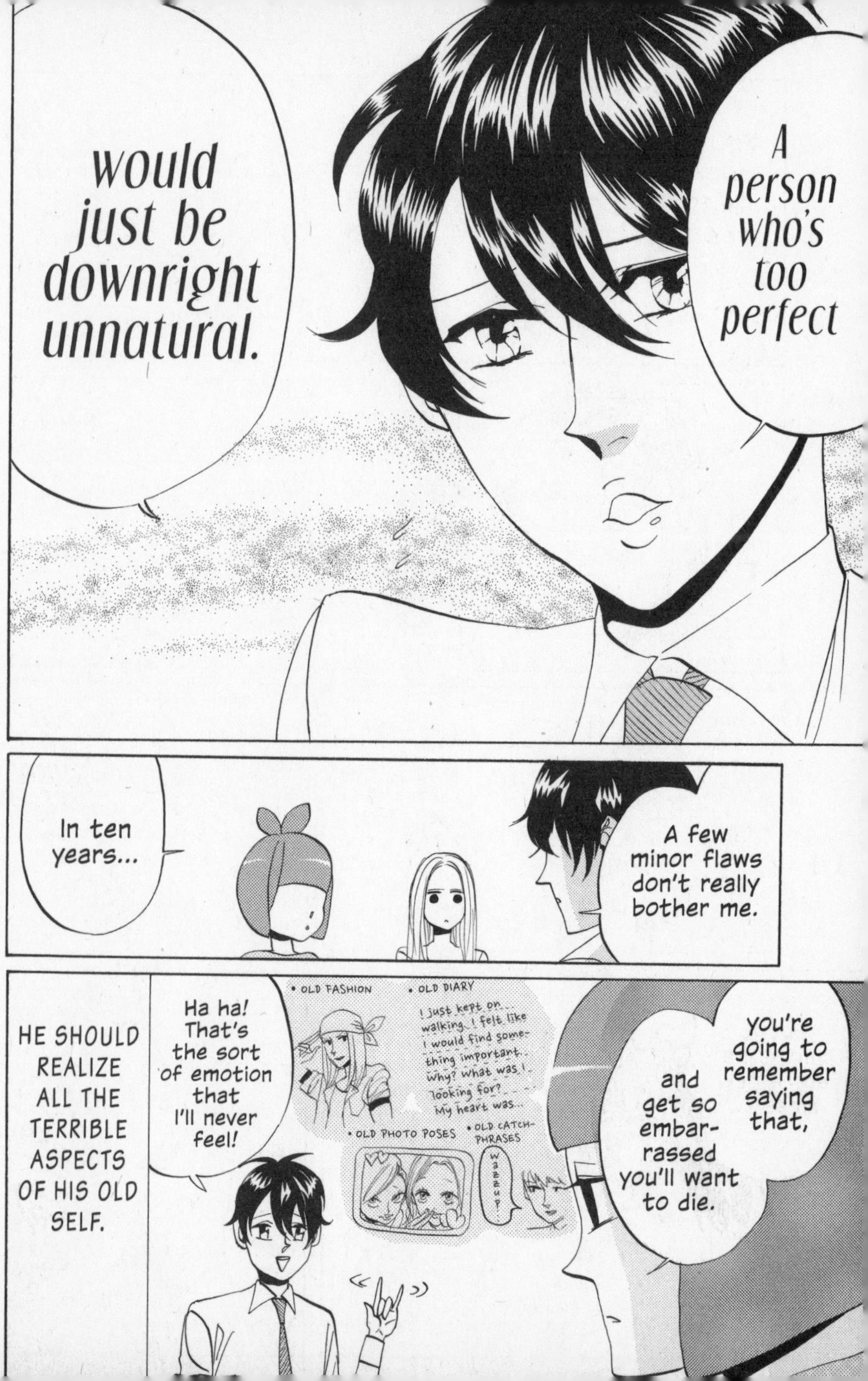
A person who's too perfect
would just be downright unnatural.
A few minor flaws don't really bother me.
In ten years...
you're going to remember saying that, and get so embarrassed you'll want to die.
• OLD DIARY
I just kept on walking. I felt like I would find something important. Why? What was I looking for? My heart was...
• OLD FASHION
Ha ha! That's the sort of emotion that I'll never feel!
• OLD CATCH-PHRASES
Wazzup!
• OLD PHOTO POSES
HE SHOULD REALIZE ALL THE TERRIBLE ASPECTS OF HIS OLD SELF.

Chapter 134: Put Your Heart into It

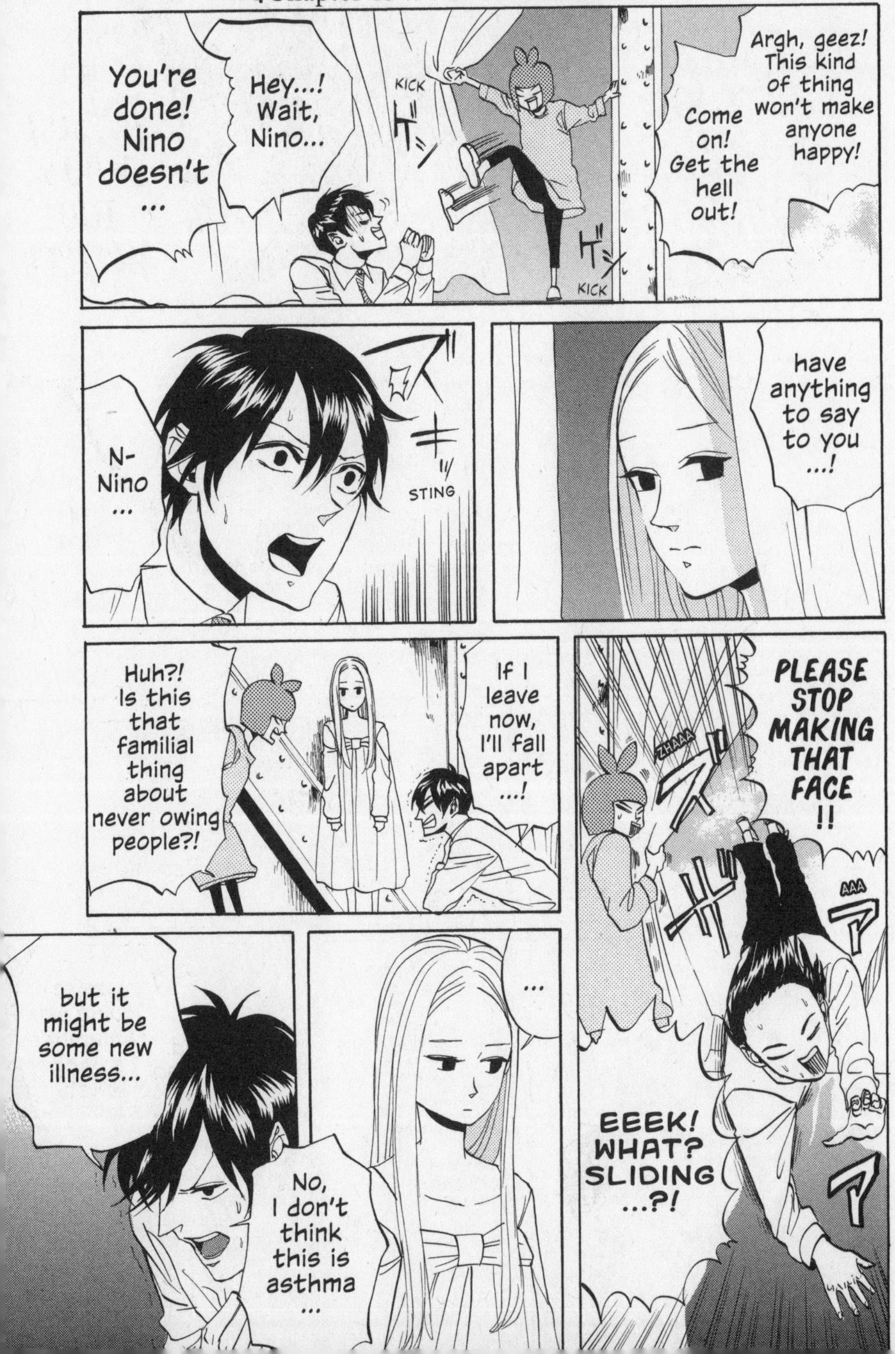
Argh, geez! This kind of thing won't make anyone happy!
Come on! Get the hell out!
KICK
KICK
Hey...! Wait, Nino...
You're done! Nino doesn't ...
have anything to say to you ...!
STING
N- Nino ...
PLEASE STOP MAKING THAT FACE !!
ZHAAA
AAA
EEEK! WHAT? SLIDING ...?!
If I leave now, I'll fall apart ...!
Huh?! Is this that familial thing about never owing people?!
...
No, I don't think this is asthma ...
but it might be some new illness...

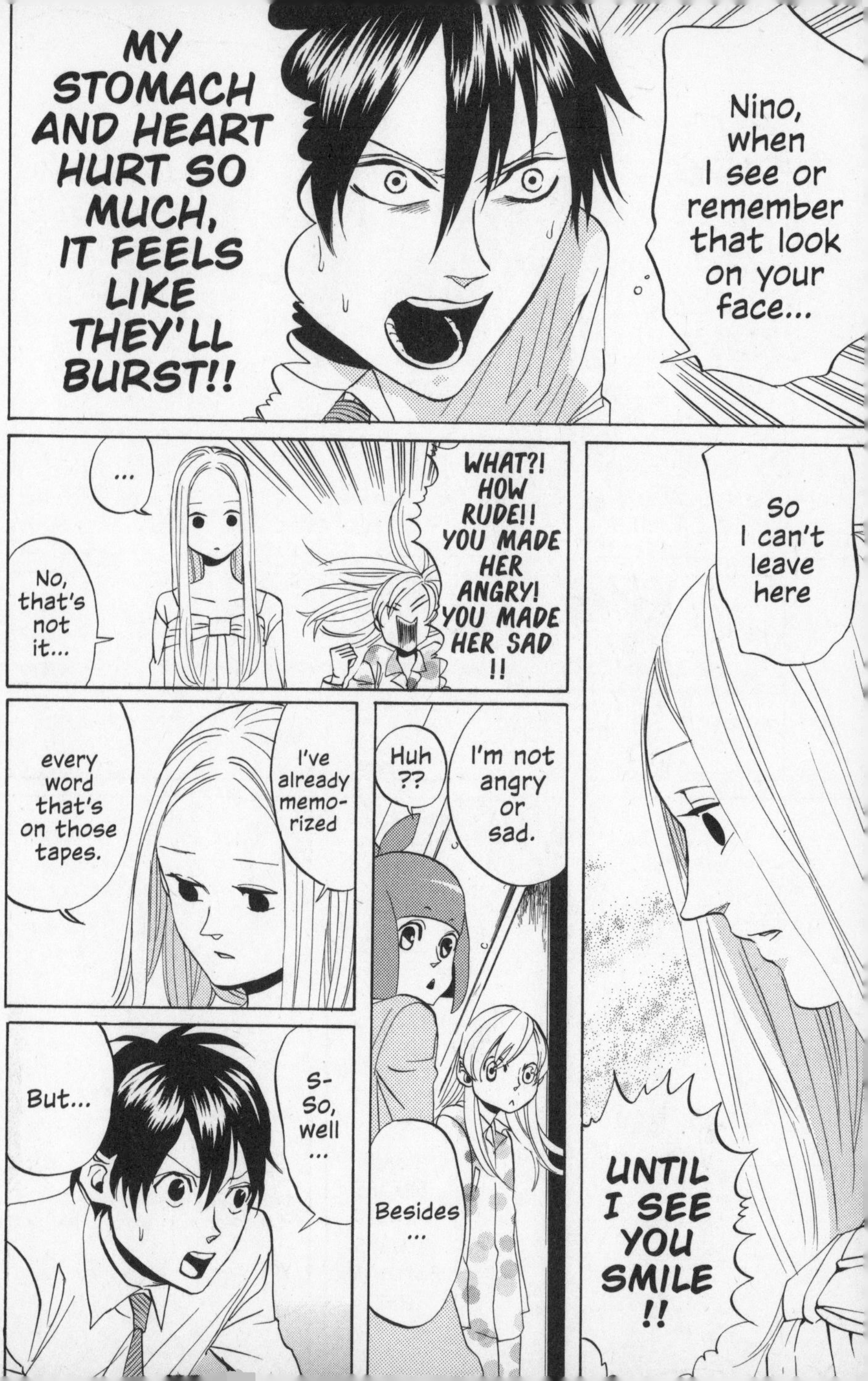
Nino, when I see or remember that look on your face...
MY STOMACH AND HEART HURT SO MUCH, IT FEELS LIKE THEY'LL BURST!!
So I can't leave here
UNTIL I SEE YOU SMILE!!
WHAT?! HOW RUDE!! YOU MADE HER ANGRY! YOU MADE HER SAD!!
...
No, that's not it...
I'm not angry or sad.
Huh??
Besides...
I've already memorized
every word that's on those tapes.
S-So, well...
But...

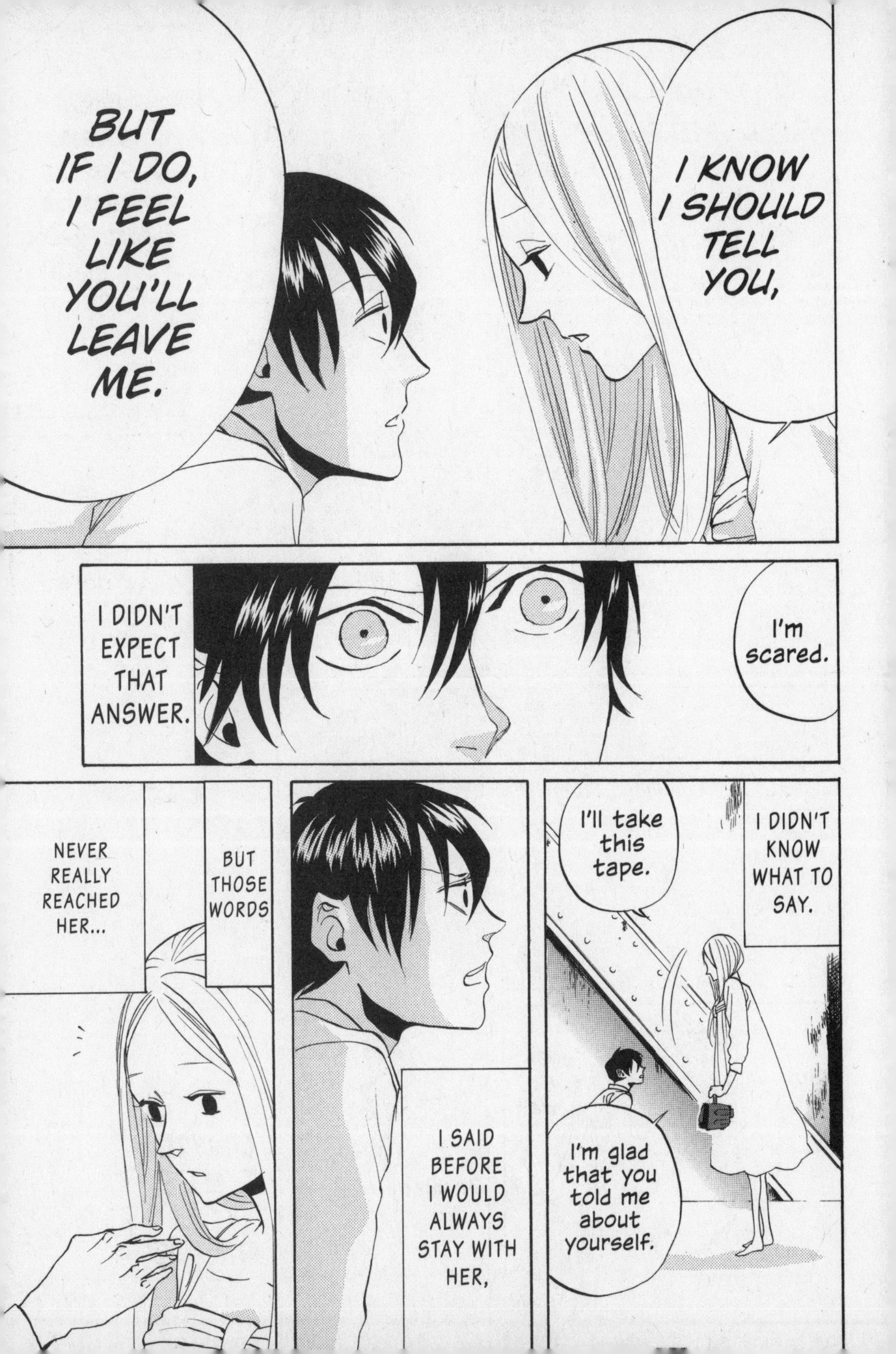
I KNOW I SHOULD TELL YOU,
BUT IF I DO, I FEEL LIKE YOU'LL LEAVE ME.
I'm scared.
I DIDN'T EXPECT THAT ANSWER.
I DIDN'T KNOW WHAT TO SAY.
I'll take this tape.
I'm glad that you told me about yourself.
I SAID BEFORE I WOULD ALWAYS STAY WITH HER,
BUT THOSE WORDS
NEVER REALLY REACHED HER...

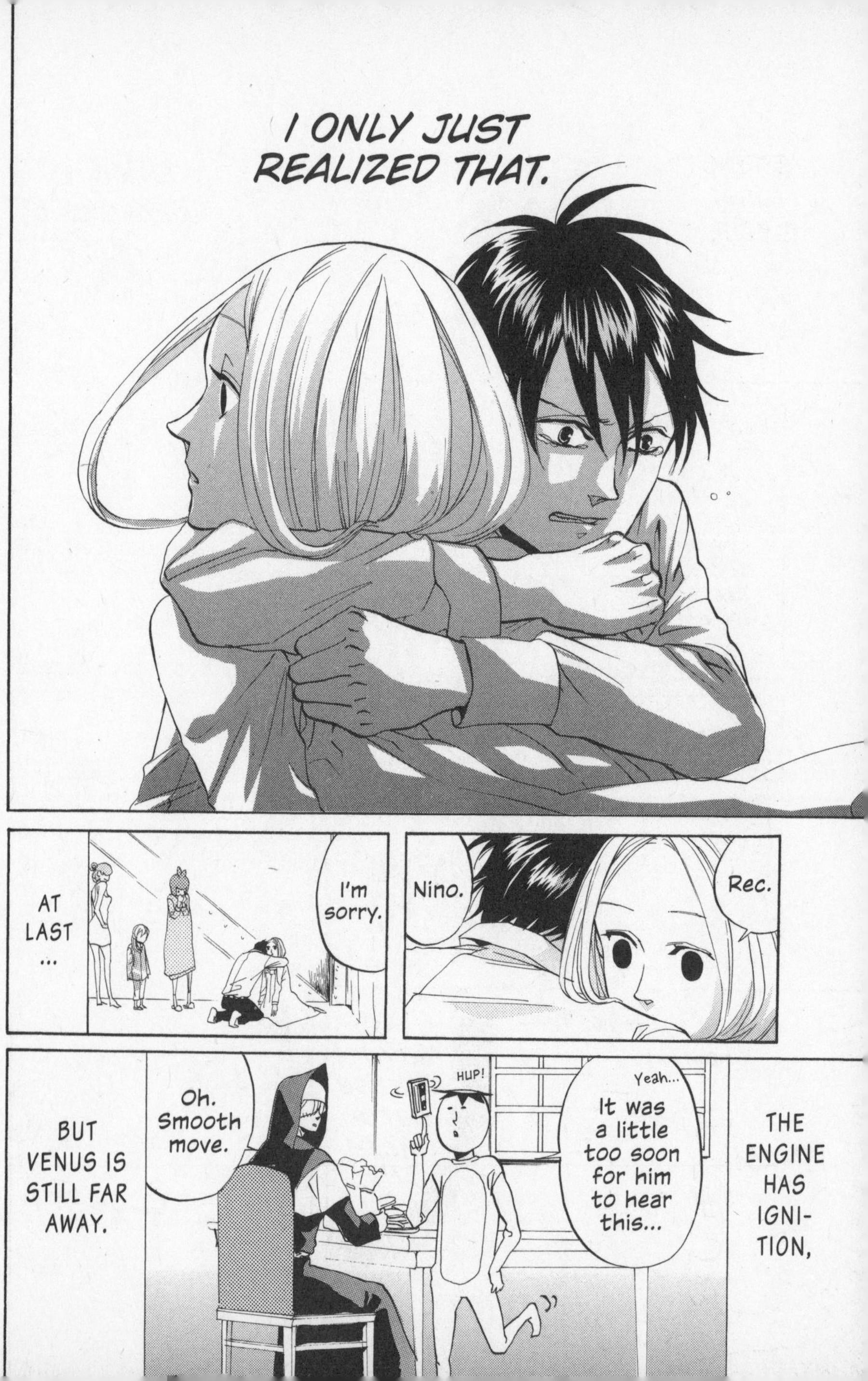
I ONLY JUST REALIZED THAT.
Rec.
Nino.
I'm sorry.
AT LAST ...
THE ENGINE HAS IGNITION,
Yeah...
It was a little too soon for him to hear this...
HUP!
Oh. Smooth move.
BUT VENUS IS STILL FAR AWAY.

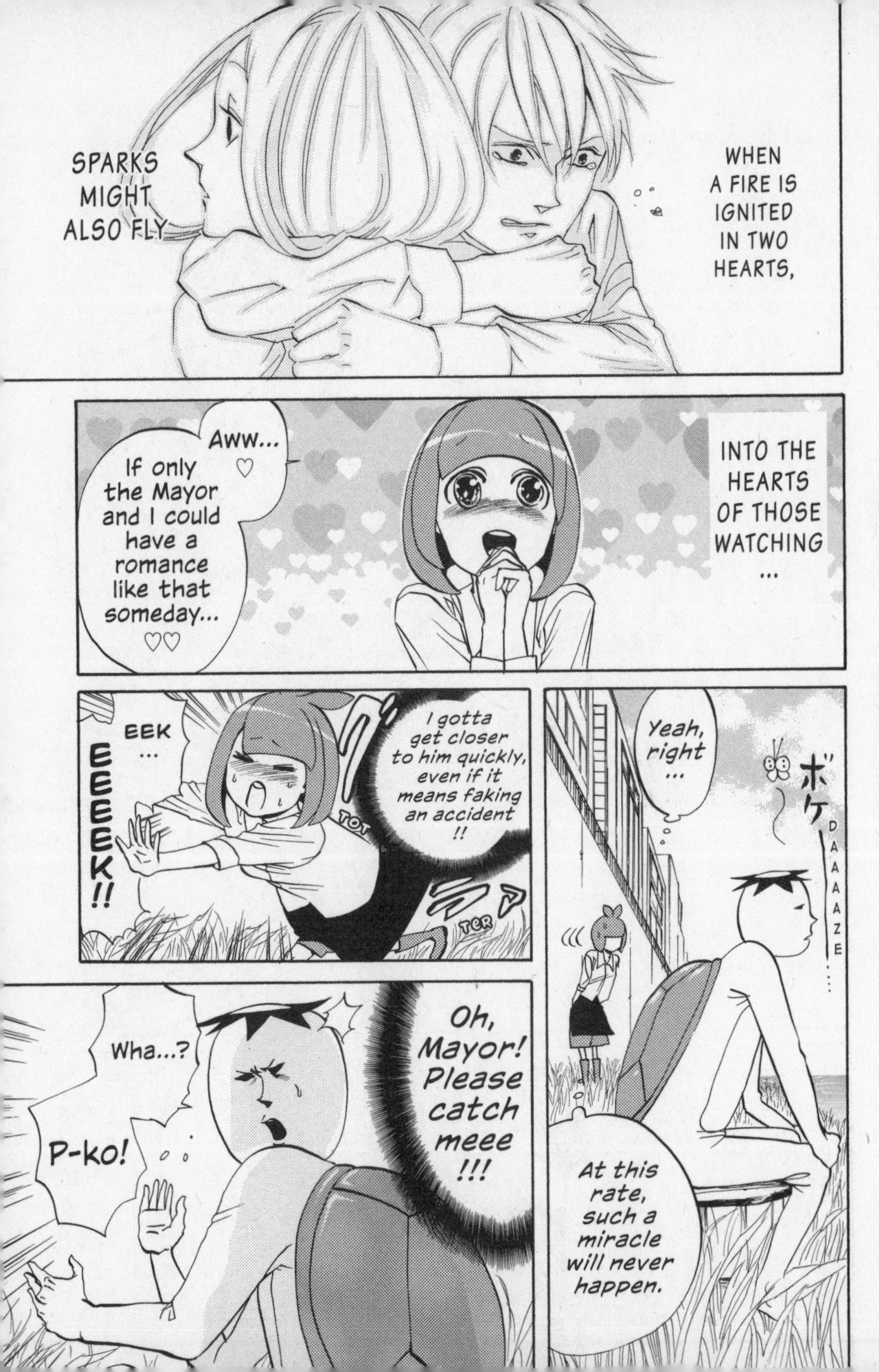
WHEN A FIRE IS IGNITED IN TWO HEARTS,
SPARKS MIGHT ALSO FLY
INTO THE HEARTS OF THOSE WATCHING ...
Aww...
If only the Mayor and I could have a romance like that someday... ♡♡
Yeah, right ...
ボケ
DAAAAZE ...
At this rate, such a miracle will never happen.
I gotta get closer to him quickly, even if it means faking an accident !!
TOT
EEK ...
EEEEEK!!
TER
Oh, Mayor! Please catch meee !!!
Wha...?
P-ko!

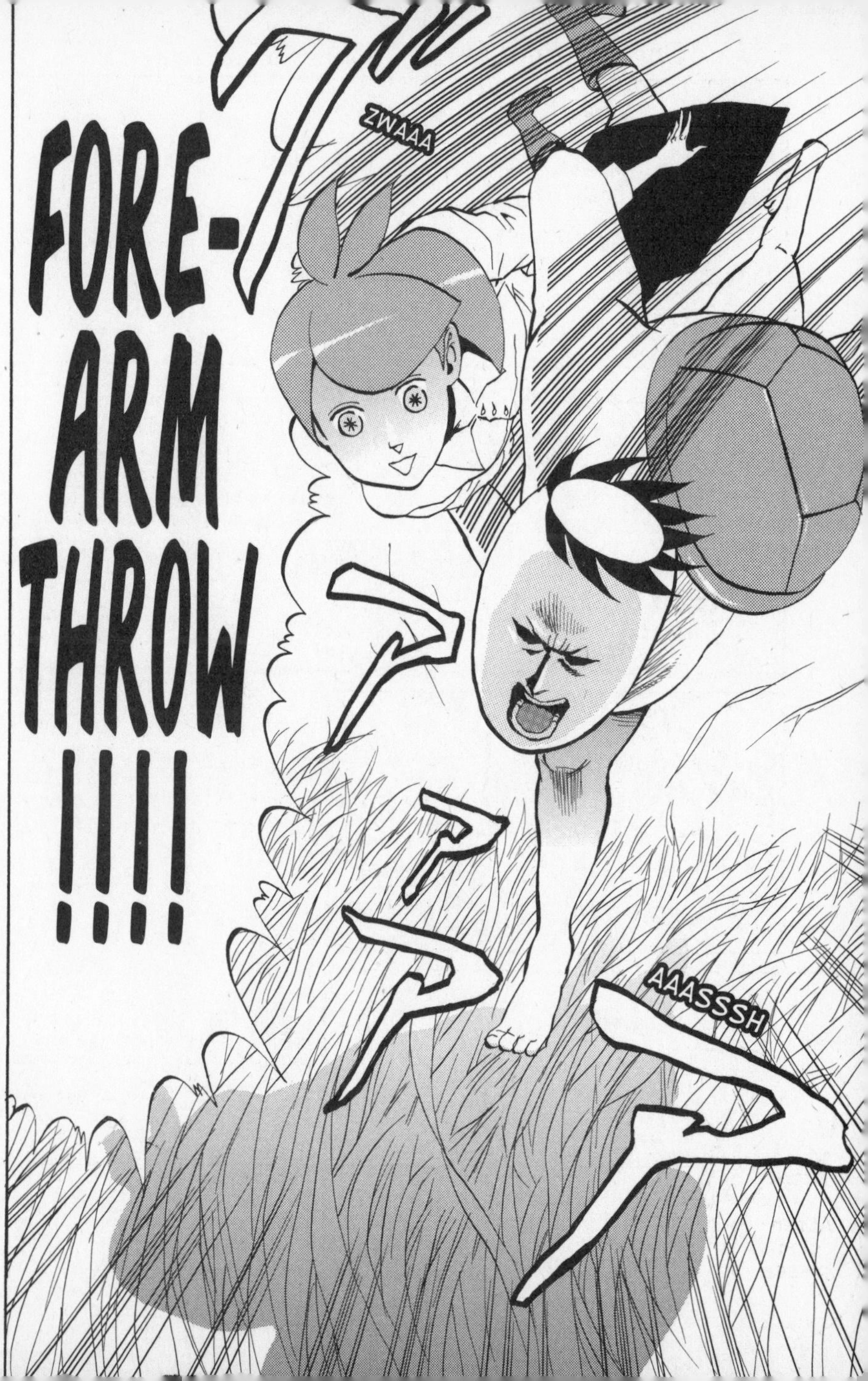
ZWAAA
FORE-ARM THROW!!!!
AAASSSH

Chapter 135: Arakawa Spring Sumo Event

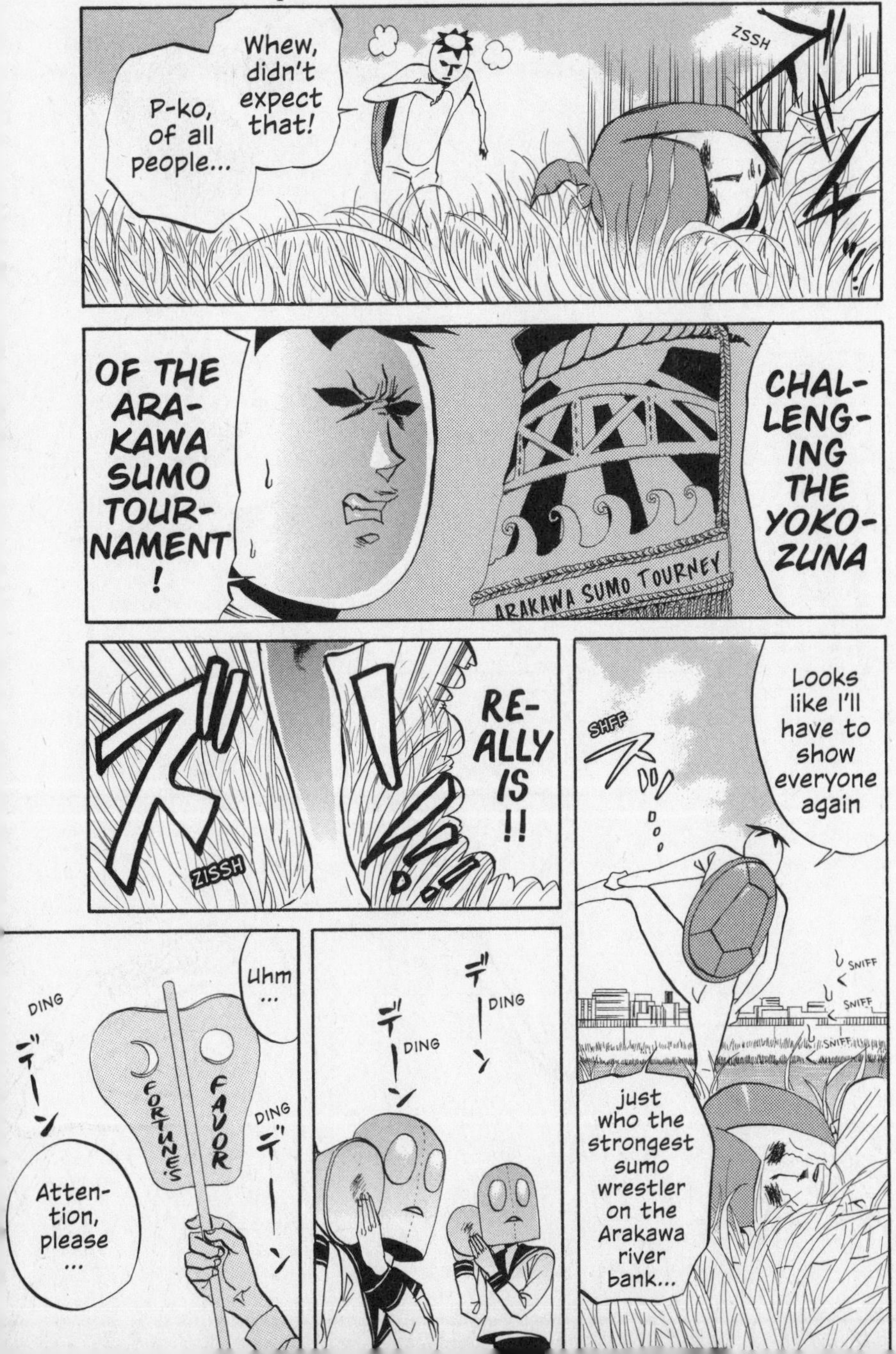
ZSSH
Whew, didn't expect that!
P-ko, of all people...
CHAL-LENG-ING THE YOKO-ZUNA
ARAKAWA SUMO TOURNEY
OF THE ARA-KAWA SUMO TOUR-NAMENT!
Looks like I'll have to show everyone again
SHFF
SNIFF
SNIFF
SNIFF
just who the strongest sumo wrestler on the Arakawa river bank...
RE-ALLY IS!!
ZISSH
DING
DING
Uhm...
DING
DING
FORTUNE'S FAVOR
Attention, please...

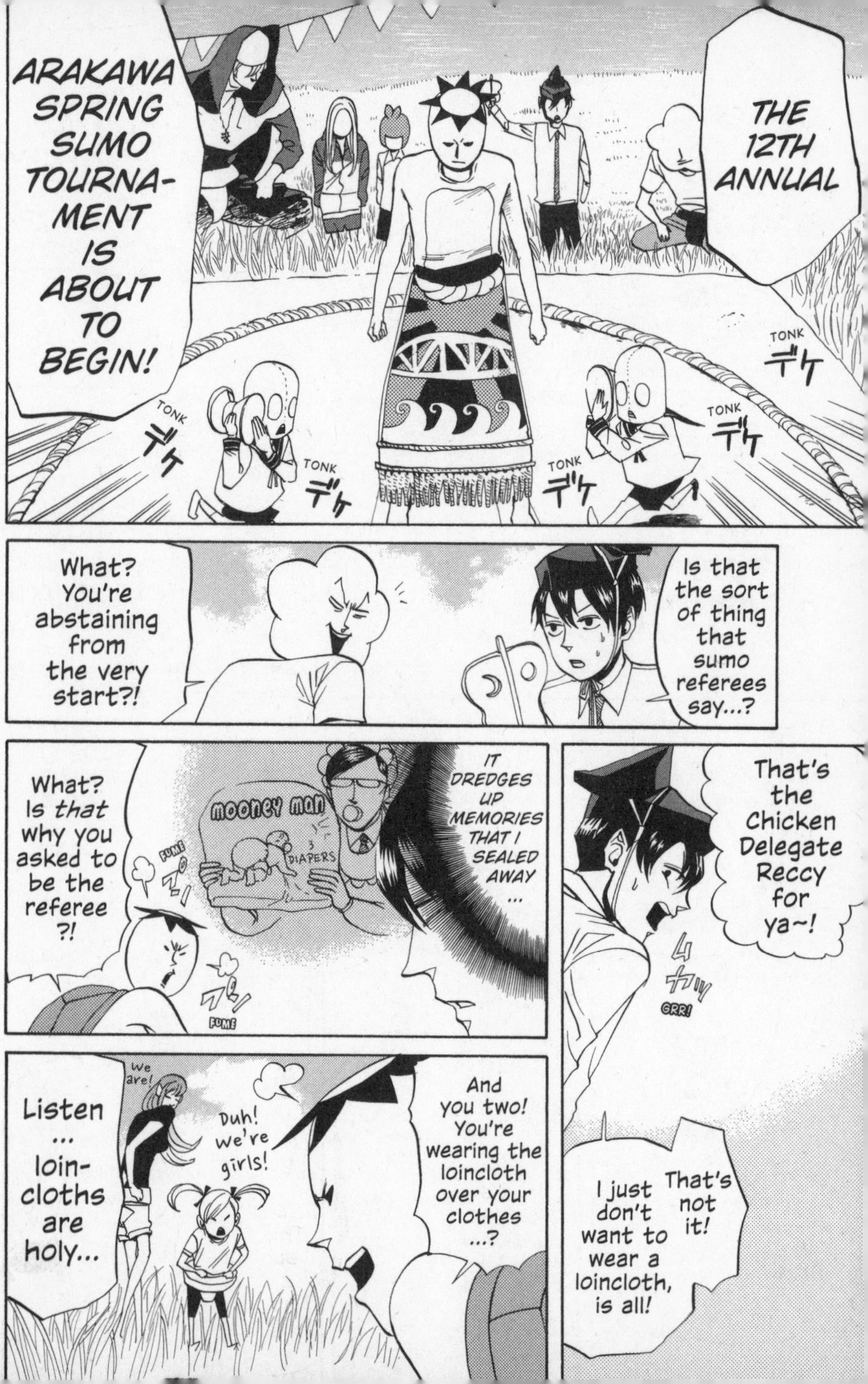
THE 12TH ANNUAL
ARAKAWA SPRING SUMO TOURNAMENT IS ABOUT TO BEGIN!
TONK デケ
TONK デケ
TONK デケ
TONK デケ
TONK デケ
Is that the sort of thing that sumo referees say...?
What? You're abstaining from the very start?!
That's the Chicken Delegate Reccy for ya~!
ムカッ GRR!
IT DREDGES UP MEMORIES THAT I SEALED AWAY ...
mooney man
3 DIAPERS
What? Is *that* why you asked to be the referee?!
FUME フン!
FUME フン!
That's not it!
I just don't want to wear a loincloth, is all!
And you two! You're wearing the loincloth over your clothes ...?
We are!
Duh! We're girls!
Listen ... loin-cloths are holy...

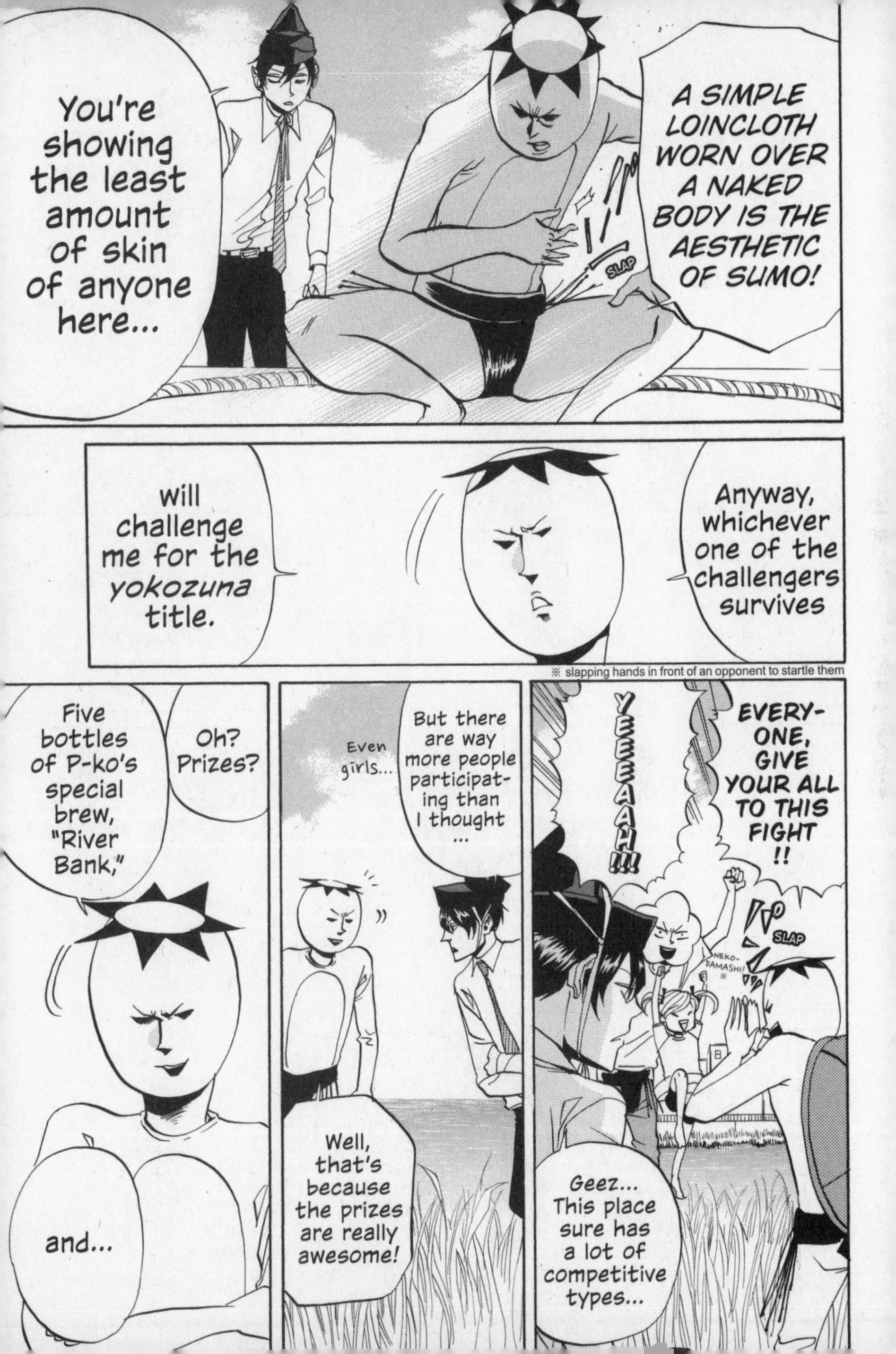
A SIMPLE LOINCLOTH WORN OVER A NAKED BODY IS THE AESTHETIC OF SUMO!
SLAP
You're showing the least amount of skin of anyone here...
Anyway, whichever one of the challengers survives
will challenge me for the *yokozuna* title.
EVERY-ONE, GIVE YOUR ALL TO THIS FIGHT !!
YEEEAAH!!!
SLAP
NEKO-DAMASHI!※
Geez... This place sure has a lot of competitive types...
But there are way more people participating than I thought ...
Even girls...
Well, that's because the prizes are really awesome!
Oh? Prizes?
Five bottles of P-ko's special brew, "River Bank,"
and...

※ slapping hands in front of an opponent to startle them

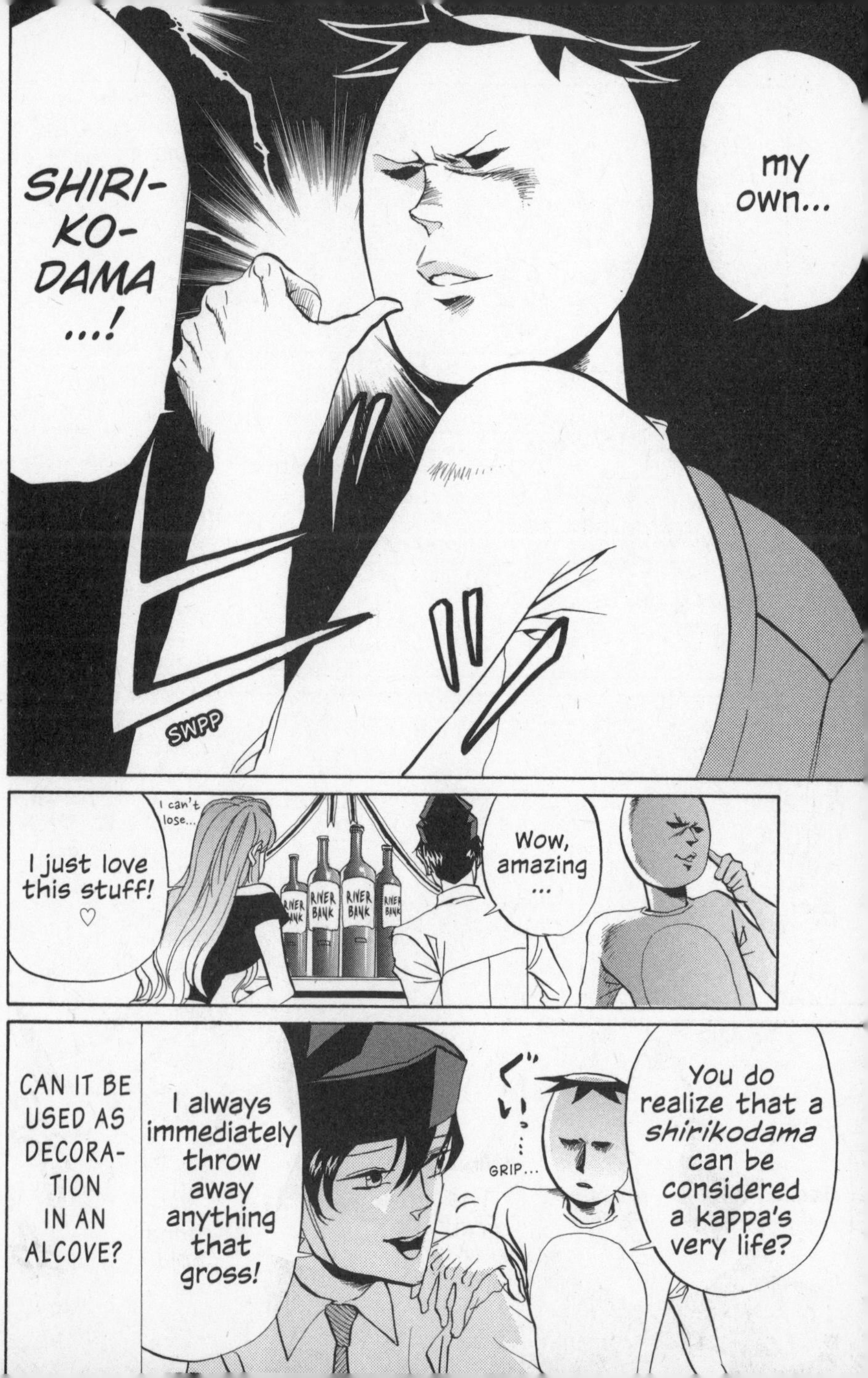
my own...
SHIRI-KO-DAMA...!
SWPP
Wow, amazing...
I can't lose...
I just love this stuff! ♡
You do realize that a *shirikodama* can be considered a kappa's very life?
GRIP...
I always immediately throw away anything that gross!
CAN IT BE USED AS DECORATION IN AN ALCOVE?

Chapter 136: The Path to Victory

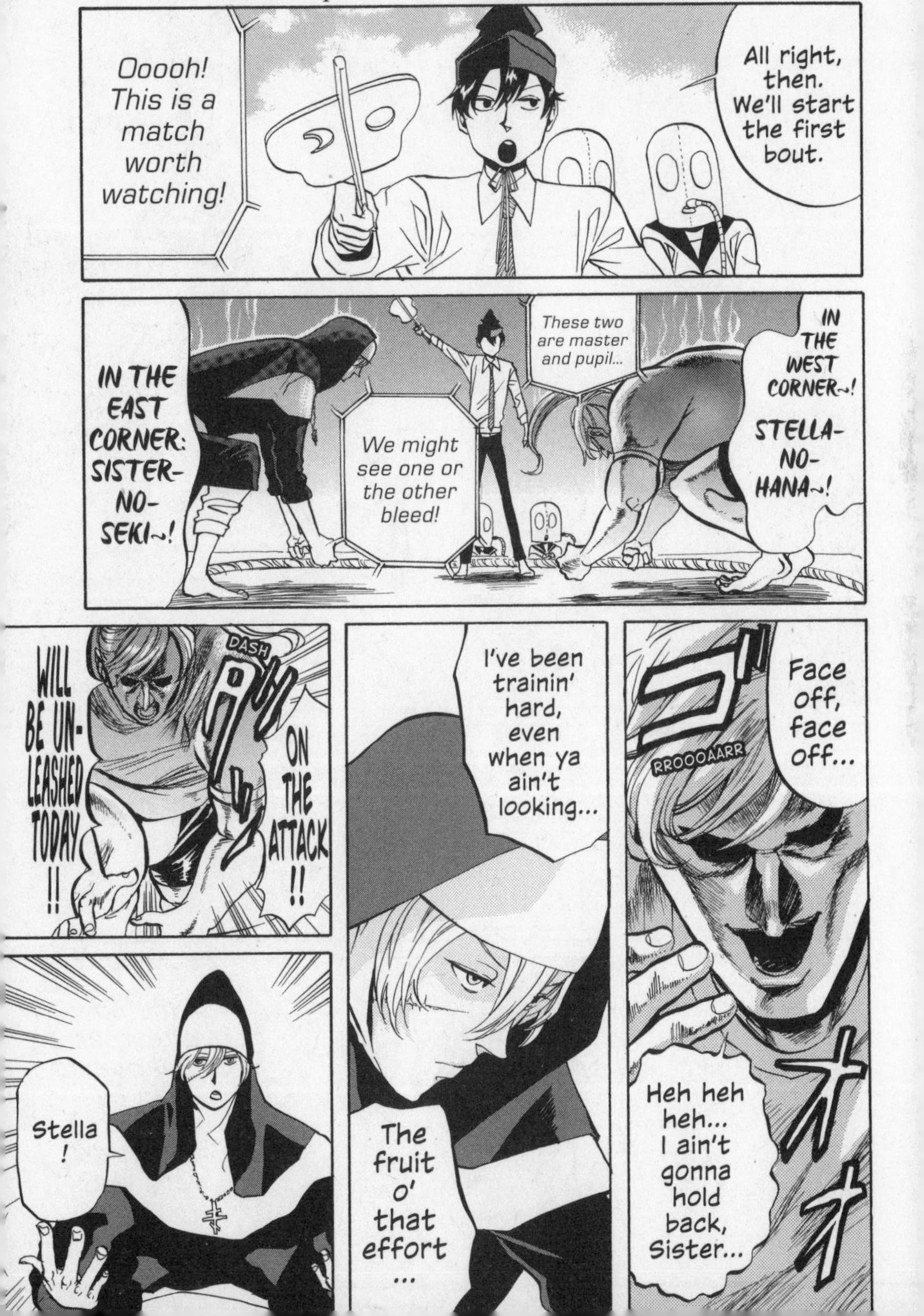
All right, then. We'll start the first bout.
Ooooh! This is a match worth watching!
IN THE WEST CORNER~! STELLA-NO-HANA~!
These two are master and pupil...
We might see one or the other bleed!
IN THE EAST CORNER: SISTER-NO-SEKI~!
Face off, face off...
RRROOOAARR
Heh heh heh... I ain't gonna hold back, Sister...
I've been trainin' hard, even when ya ain't looking...
The fruit o' that effort ...
DASH
ON THE ATTACK!!
WILL BE UN-LEASHED TODAY!!
Stella!

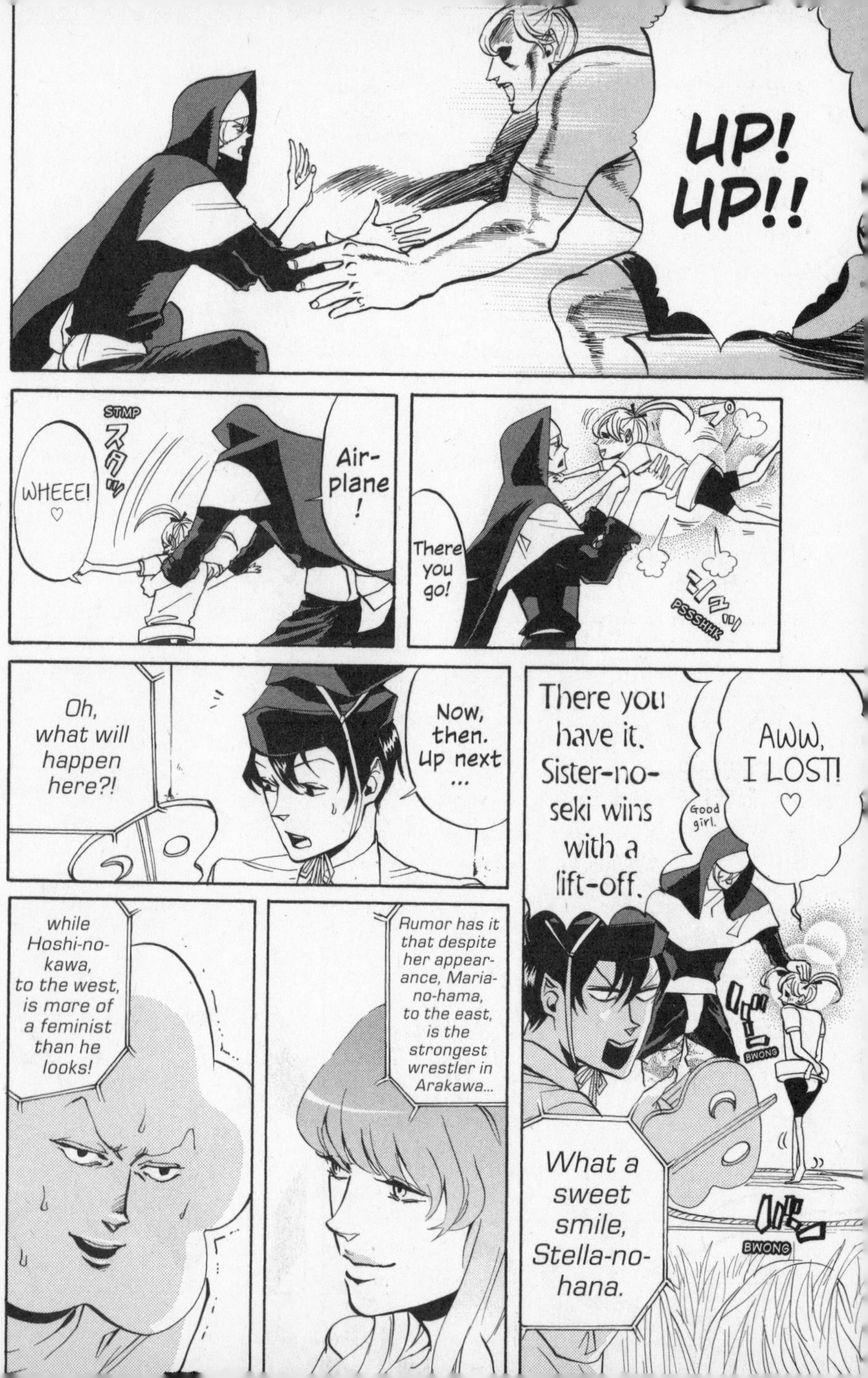
UP! UP!!
There you go!
PSSSHHK
Airplane!
STMP
WHEEE! ♡
AWW, I LOST! ♡
There you have it. Sister-no-seki wins with a lift-off.
Good girl.
BWONG
What a sweet smile, Stella-no-hana.
BWONG
Now, then. Up next ...
Oh, what will happen here?!
Rumor has it that despite her appearance, Maria-no-hama, to the east, is the strongest wrestler in Arakawa...
while Hoshi-no-kawa, to the west, is more of a feminist than he looks!

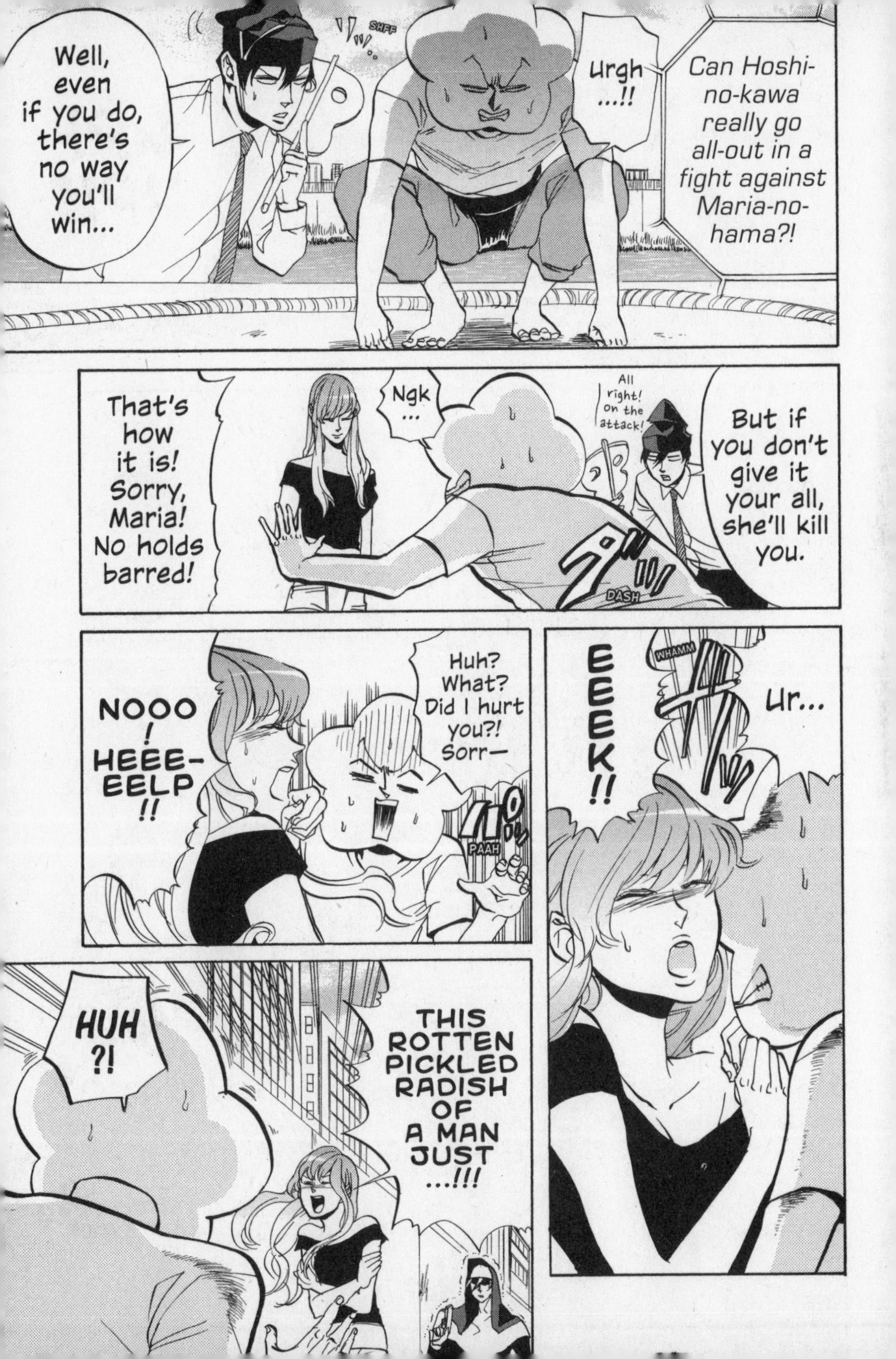
Can Hoshi-no-kawa really go all-out in a fight against Maria-no-hama?!
Urgh ...!!
SHFF
Well, even if you do, there's no way you'll win...
But if you don't give it your all, she'll kill you.
All right! On the attack!
Ngk ...
DASH
That's how it is! Sorry, Maria! No holds barred!
Ur...
WHAMM
EEEK!!
Huh? What? Did I hurt you?! Sorr—
NOOO! HEEEEELP!!
PAAH
THIS ROTTEN PICKLED RADISH OF A MAN JUST ...!!!
HUH ?!

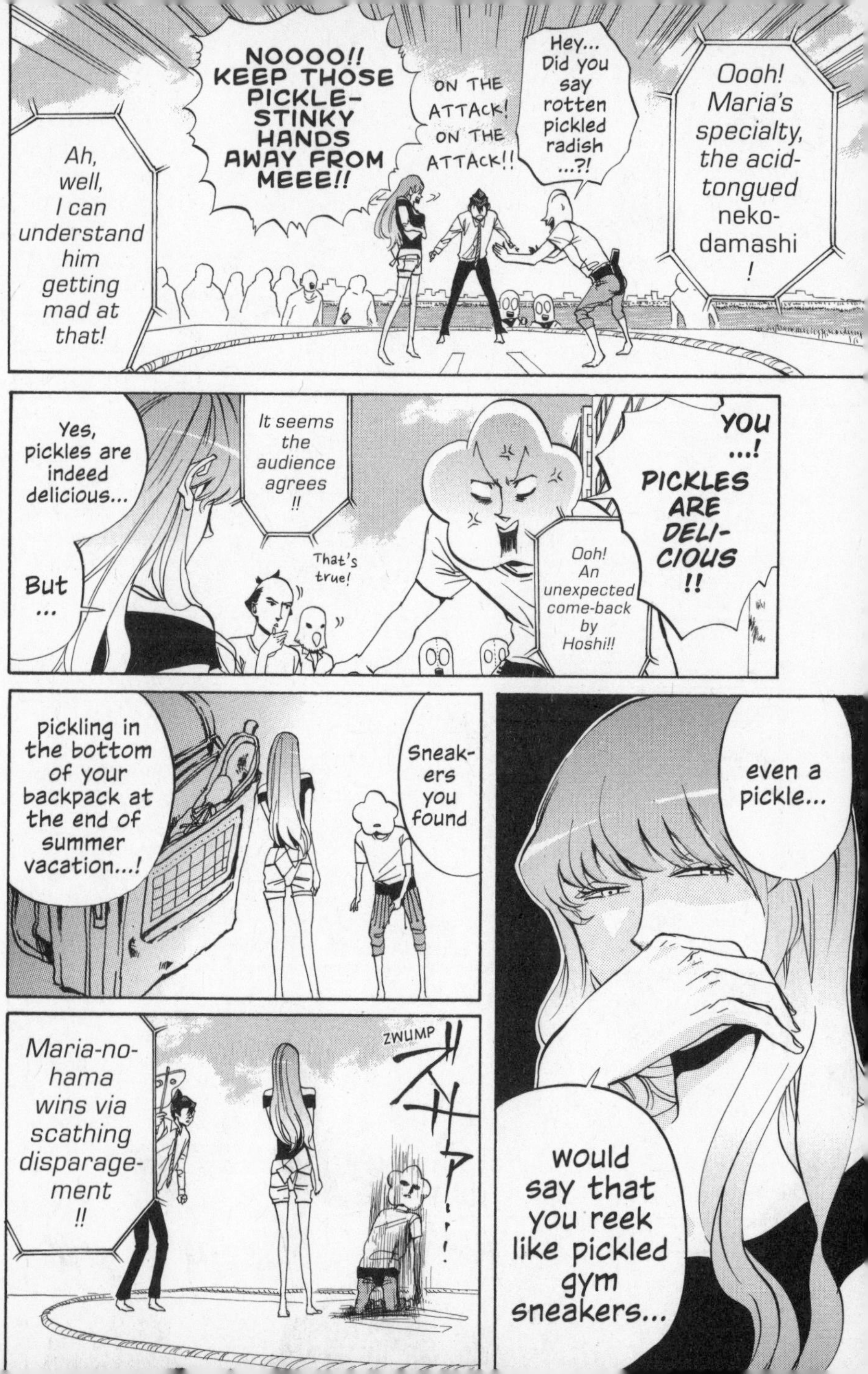
Oooh! Maria's specialty, the acid-tongued neko-damashi!
Hey... Did you say rotten pickled radish ...?!
ON THE ATTACK! ON THE ATTACK!!
NOOOO!! KEEP THOSE PICKLE-STINKY HANDS AWAY FROM MEEE!!
Ah, well, I can understand him getting mad at that!
YOU ...! PICKLES ARE DELI-CIOUS !!
Ooh! An unexpected come-back by Hoshi!!
It seems the audience agrees !!
That's true!
Yes, pickles are indeed delicious...
But ...
even a pickle...
would say that you reek like pickled gym sneakers...
Sneak-ers you found
pickling in the bottom of your backpack at the end of summer vacation...!
ZWUMP
Maria-no-hama wins via scathing disparage-ment !!

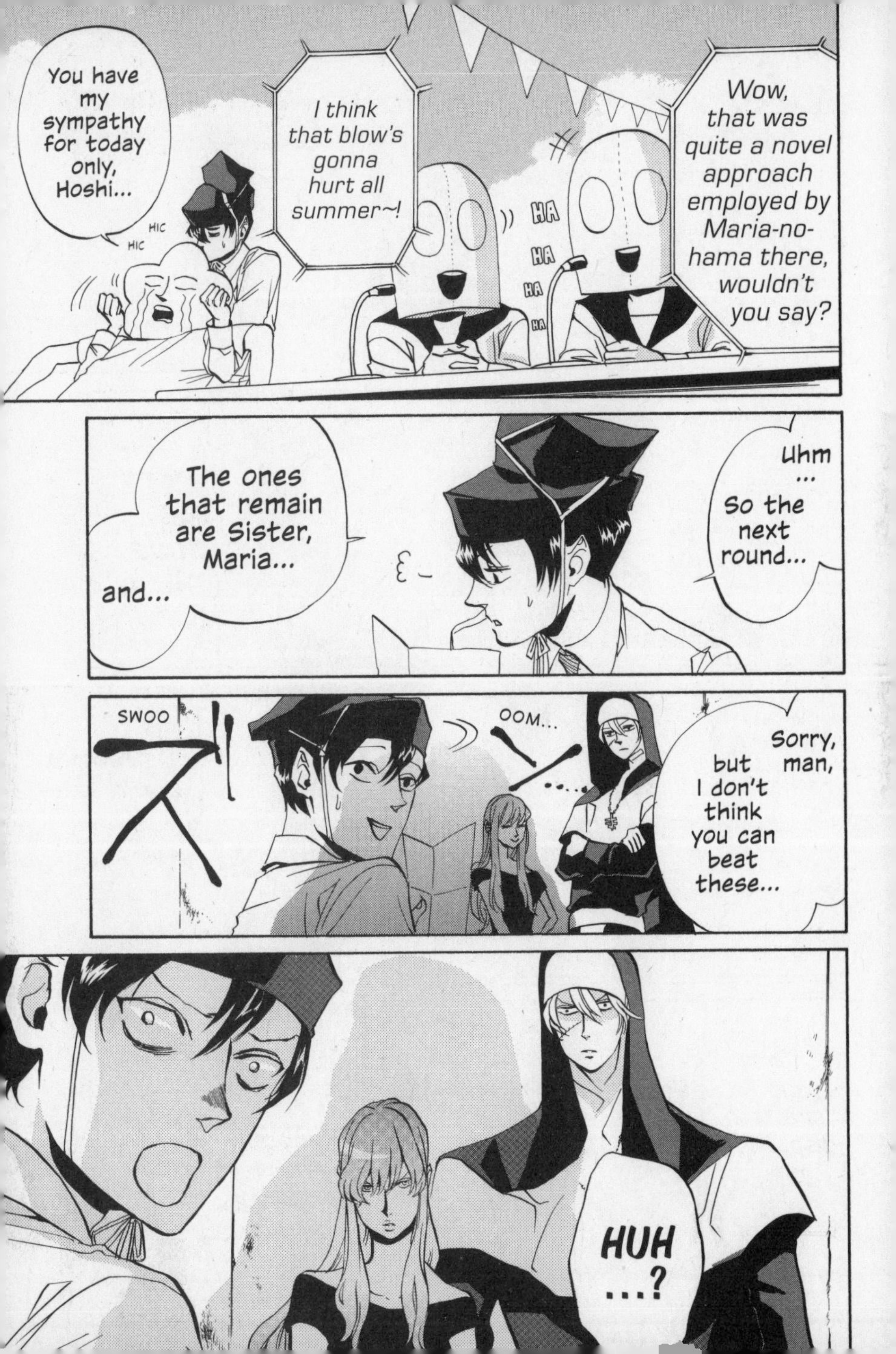
Wow, that was quite a novel approach employed by Maria-no-hama there, wouldn't you say?
HA HA HA HA
I think that blow's gonna hurt all summer~!
HIC HIC
You have my sympathy for today only, Hoshi...
Uhm ... So the next round...
The ones that remain are Sister, Maria... and...
Sorry, but man, I don't think you can beat these...
SWOO
OOM...
HUH ...?

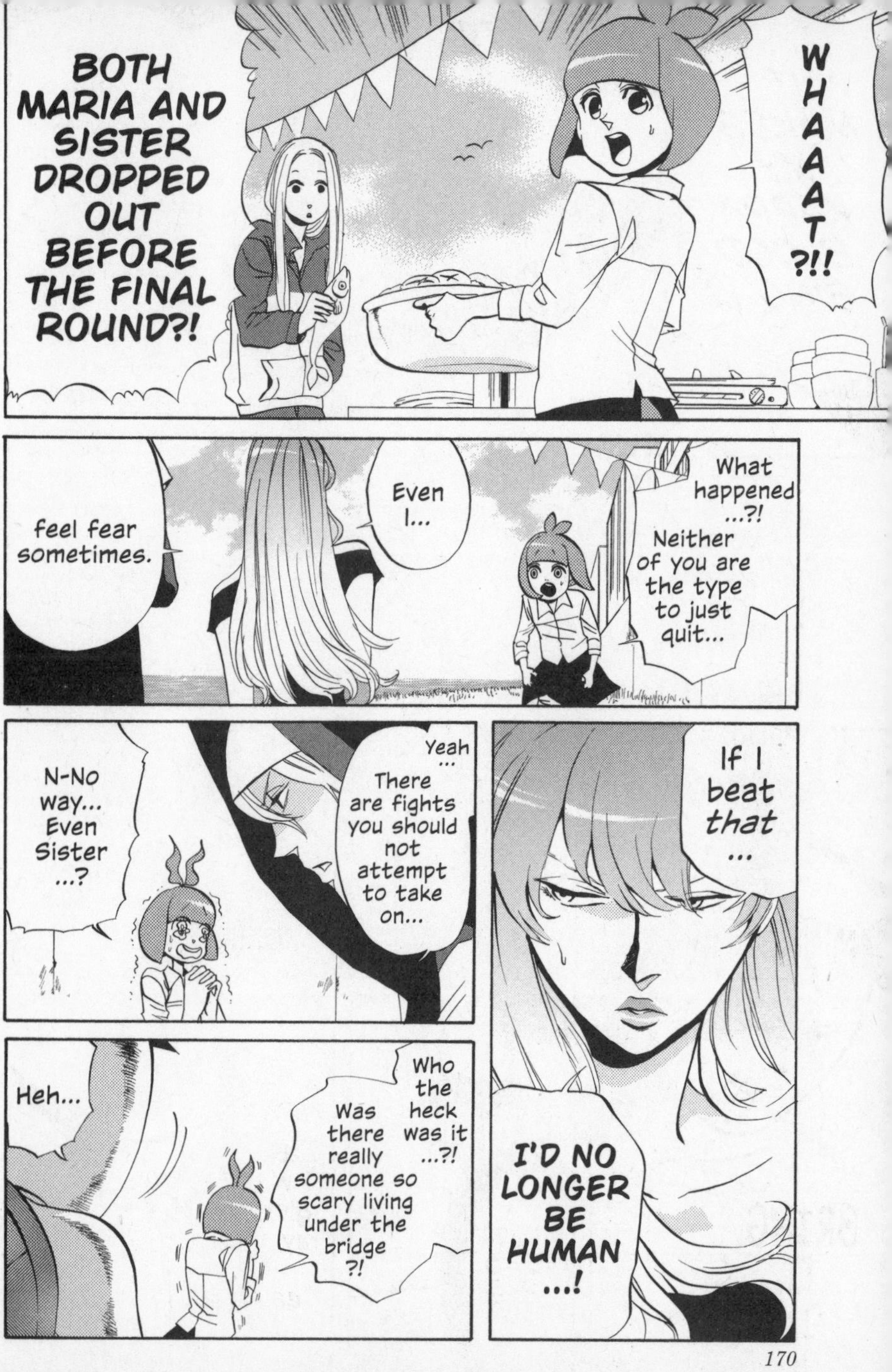

WHAAAT?!!
BOTH MARIA AND SISTER DROPPED OUT BEFORE THE FINAL ROUND?!
What happened...?!
Neither of you are the type to just quit...
Even I...
feel fear sometimes.
If I beat *that*...
I'D NO LONGER BE HUMAN...!
Yeah... There are fights you should not attempt to take on...
N-No way... Even Sister...?
Who the heck was it...?!
Was there really someone so scary living under the bridge?!
Heh...

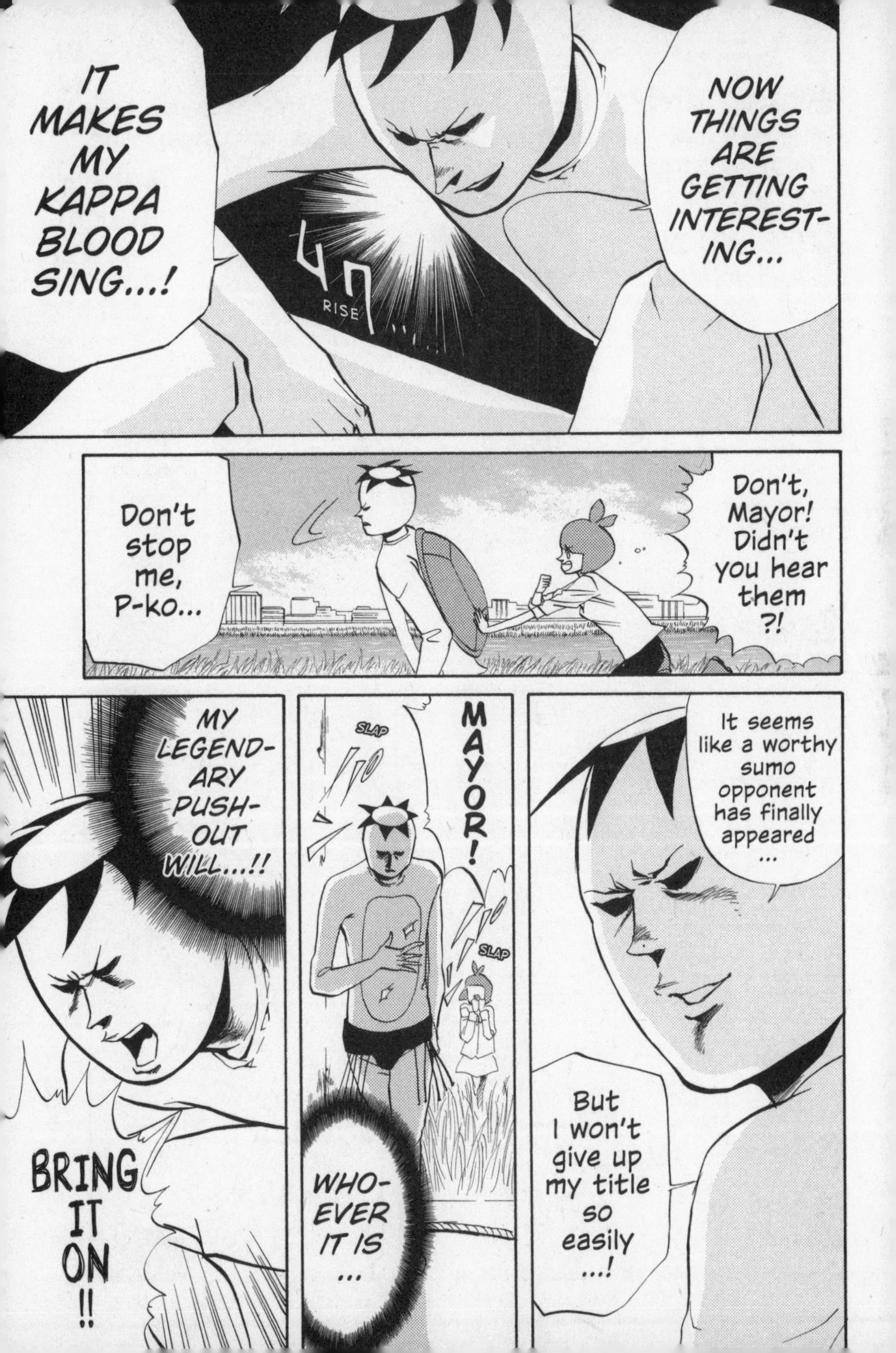
NOW THINGS ARE GETTING INTEREST-ING...
IT MAKES MY KAPPA BLOOD SING...!
RISE
Don't, Mayor! Didn't you hear them?!
Don't stop me, P-ko...
It seems like a worthy sumo opponent has finally appeared...
But I won't give up my title so easily...!
MAYOR!
SLAP
SLAP
WHO-EVER IT IS...
MY LEGEND-ARY PUSH-OUT WILL...!!
BRING IT ON!!

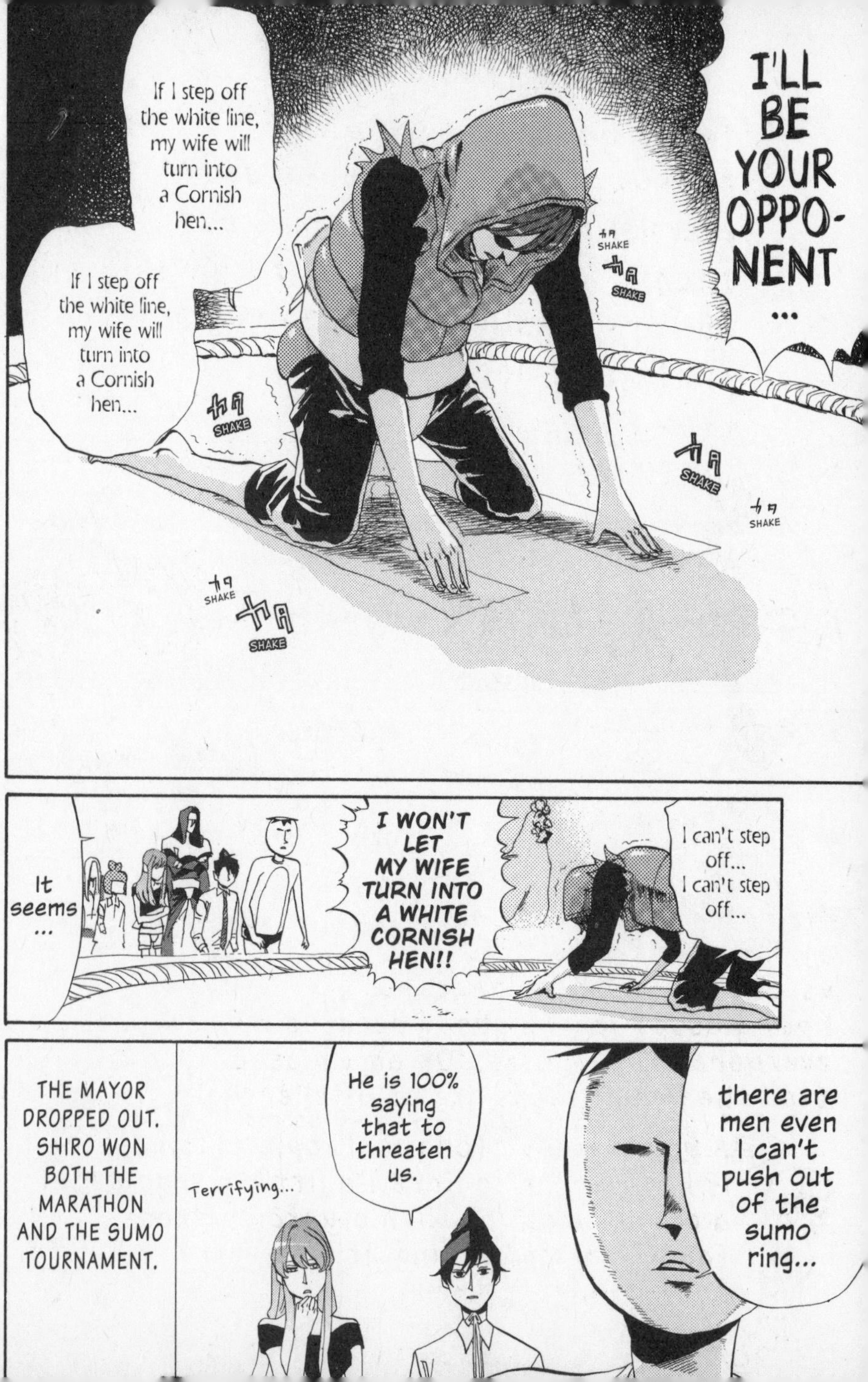
I'LL BE YOUR OPPONENT...
カタ SHAKE
カタ SHAKE
カタ SHAKE
カタ SHAKE
If I step off the white line, my wife will turn into a Cornish hen...
If I step off the white line, my wife will turn into a Cornish hen...
カタ SHAKE
カタ SHAKE
カタ SHAKE
I can't step off... I can't step off...
I WON'T LET MY WIFE TURN INTO A WHITE CORNISH HEN!!
It seems...
there are men even I can't push out of the sumo ring...
He is 100% saying that to threaten us.
Terrifying...
THE MAYOR DROPPED OUT. SHIRO WON BOTH THE MARATHON AND THE SUMO TOURNAMENT.

Afterword

Thank you for picking up this volume of Arakawa! Wowww... I'm so deeply moved every time a volume comes out. This is my thanks to all of you for reading it, my editors, and my friends and family. I'm so grateful. I hope you keep following the story of Rec and the others!

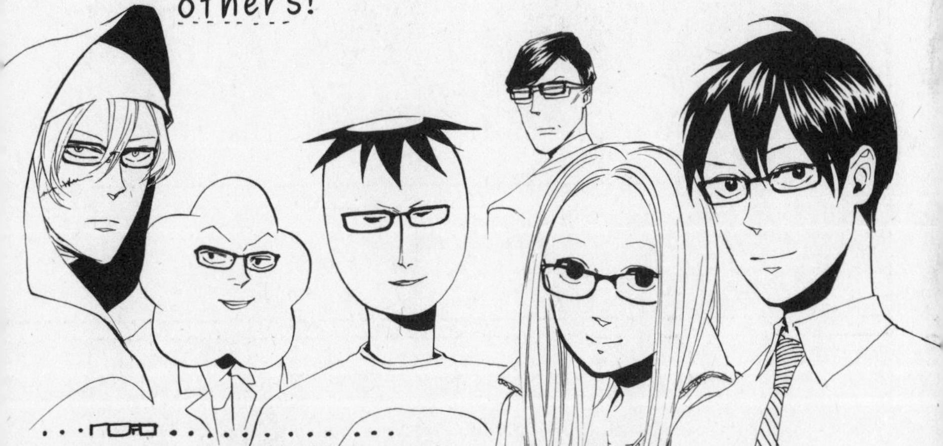

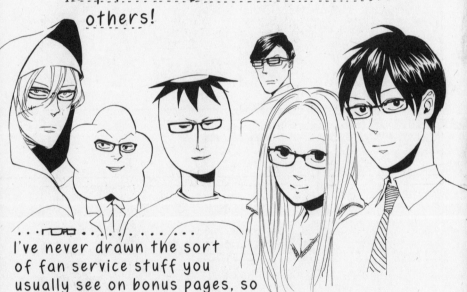

I've never drawn the sort of fan service stuff you usually see on bonus pages, so I put glasses on everybody because it seems like everyone likes glasses. (Or am I biased?) Even the Mayor looks like an intellectual.

A bonus manga follows. People often ask me if I like *yokai*, so I drew a little manga about a chance meeting with a *yokai*?? ghost?? fairy?? or something. It's neither horror nor a comedy...

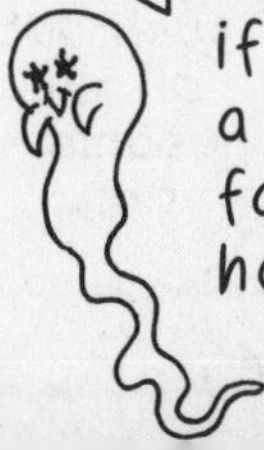

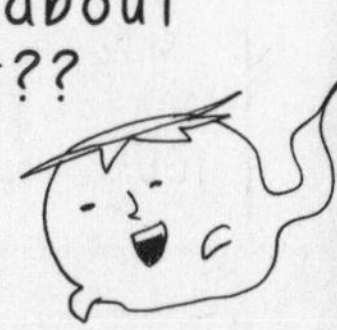

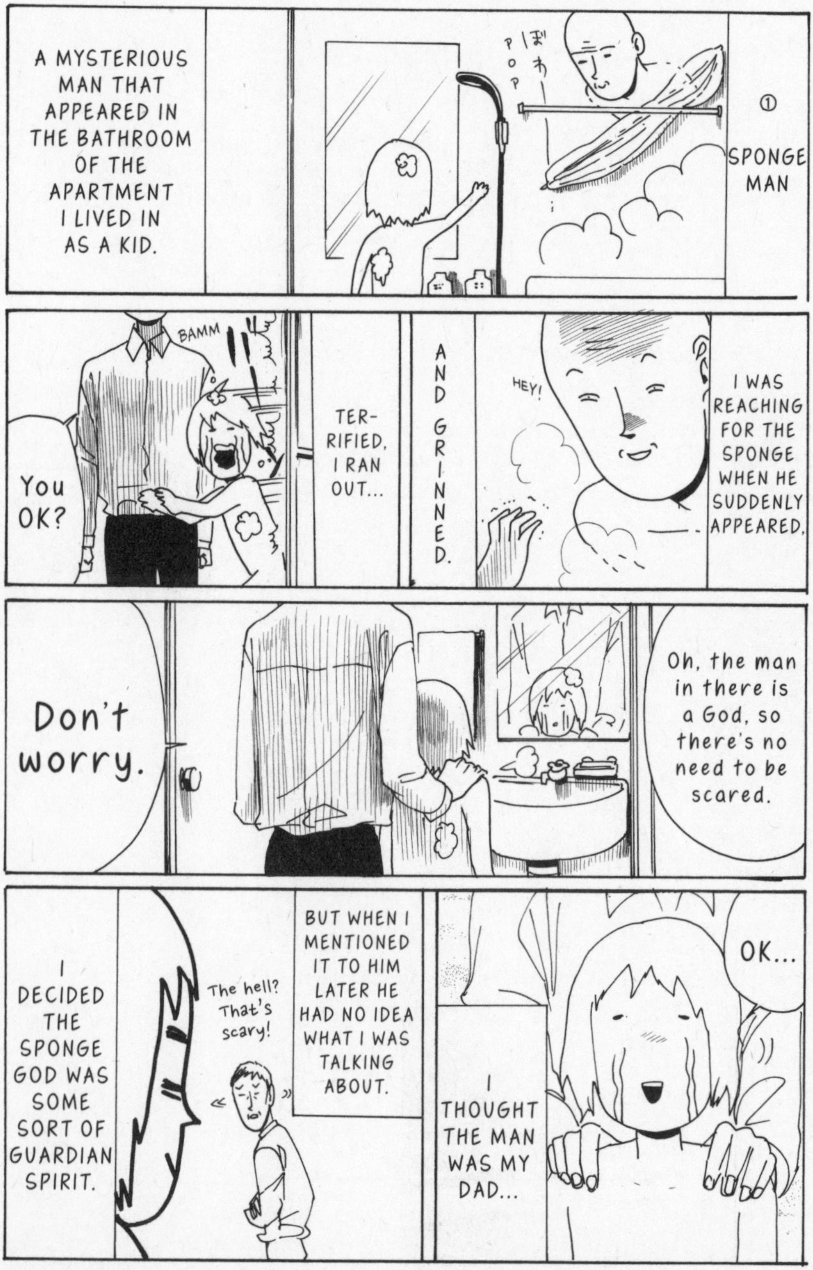
①
SPONGE MAN
ぽわ
POP
A MYSTERIOUS MAN THAT APPEARED IN THE BATHROOM OF THE APARTMENT I LIVED IN AS A KID.
I WAS REACHING FOR THE SPONGE WHEN HE SUDDENLY APPEARED,
HEY!
AND GRINNED.
TER-RIFIED, I RAN OUT...
BAMM
You OK?
Oh, the man in there is a God, so there's no need to be scared.
Don't worry.
OK...
I THOUGHT THE MAN WAS MY DAD...
BUT WHEN I MENTIONED IT TO HIM LATER HE HAD NO IDEA WHAT I WAS TALKING ABOUT.
The hell? That's scary!
I DECIDED THE SPONGE GOD WAS SOME SORT OF GUARDIAN SPIRIT.

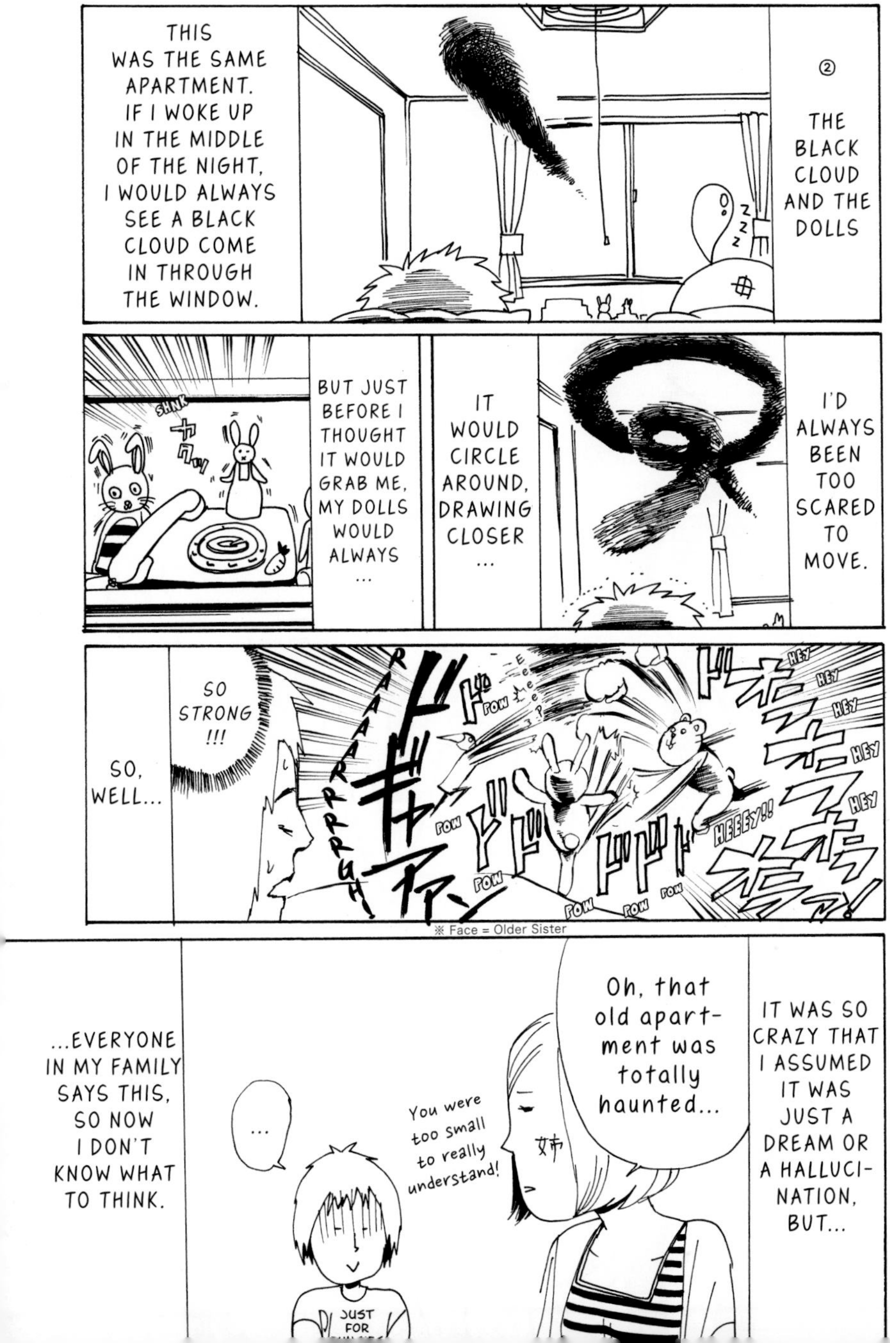
②
THE BLACK CLOUD AND THE DOLLS
THIS WAS THE SAME APARTMENT. IF I WOKE UP IN THE MIDDLE OF THE NIGHT, I WOULD ALWAYS SEE A BLACK CLOUD COME IN THROUGH THE WINDOW.
I'D ALWAYS BEEN TOO SCARED TO MOVE.
IT WOULD CIRCLE AROUND, DRAWING CLOSER ...
BUT JUST BEFORE I THOUGHT IT WOULD GRAB ME, MY DOLLS WOULD ALWAYS ...
SHNK
HEY
HEY
HEY
HEY
HEY
HEEEY!!
POW
EEEP
POW
POW
POW
POW
POW
POW
RAAAARRRUGH!
SO STRONG !!!
SO, WELL...
※ Face = Older Sister
IT WAS SO CRAZY THAT I ASSUMED IT WAS JUST A DREAM OR A HALLUCINATION, BUT...
Oh, that old apartment was totally haunted...
You were too small to really understand!
...
...EVERYONE IN MY FAMILY SAYS THIS, SO NOW I DON'T KNOW WHAT TO THINK.
JUST FOR

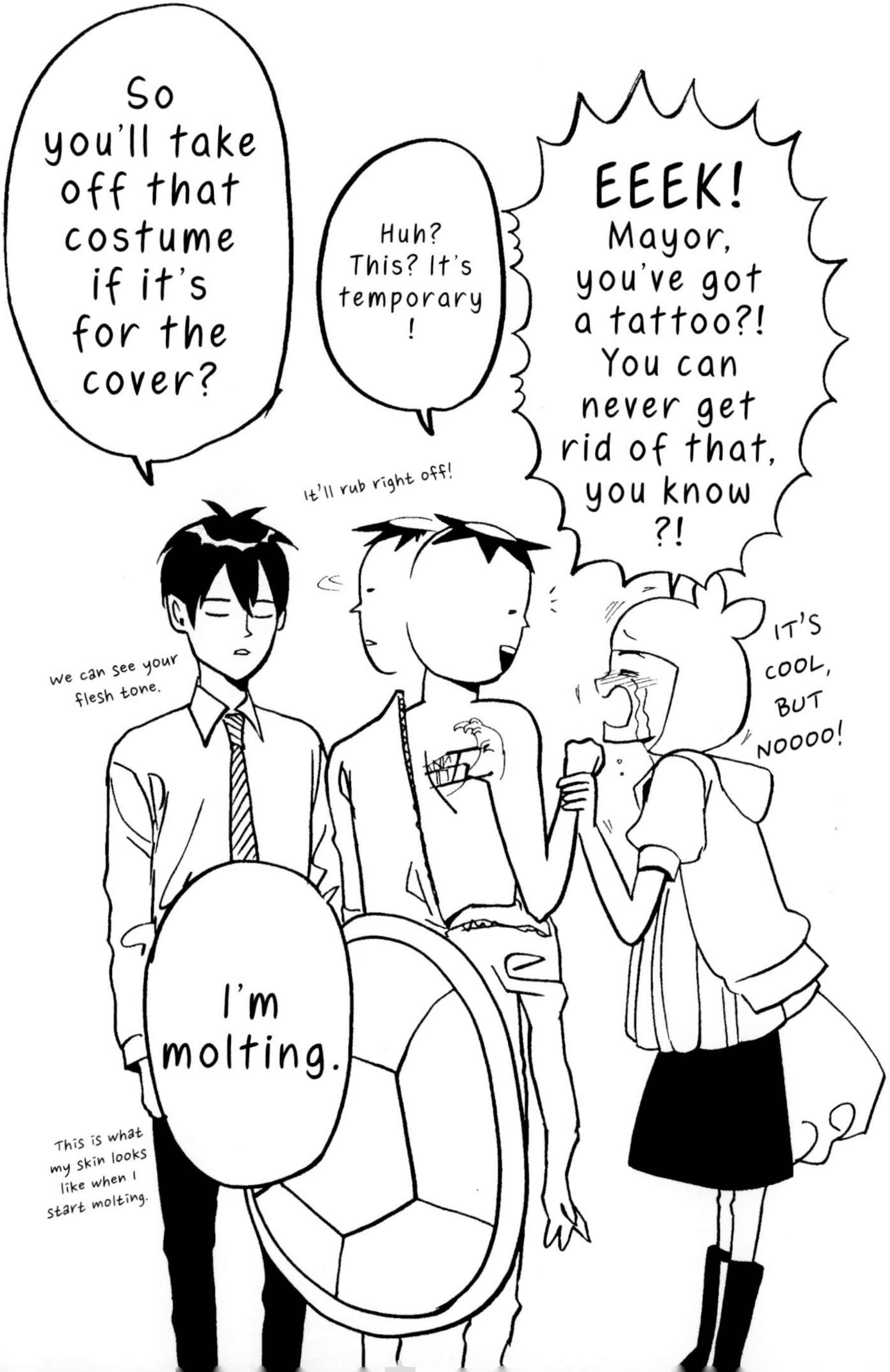
EEEK! Mayor, you've got a tattoo?! You can never get rid of that, you know?!
IT'S COOL, BUT NOOOO!
Huh? This? It's temporary!
It'll rub right off!
So you'll take off that costume if it's for the cover?
We can see your flesh tone.
I'm molting.
This is what my skin looks like when I start molting.

I NEVER MEANT TO HIDE IT,
BUT I HAVEN'T PUBLICLY ANNOUNCED
THE METAL BROTHERS' NAMES.

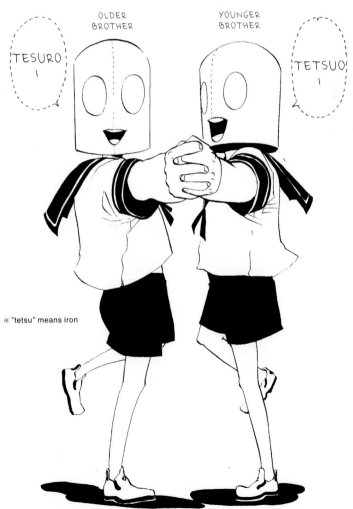

TETSUO!
YOUNGER BROTHER
OLDER BROTHER
TESURO!

※ "tetsu" means iron

EVEN I, THE ARTIST, CAN'T TELL THEM APART.

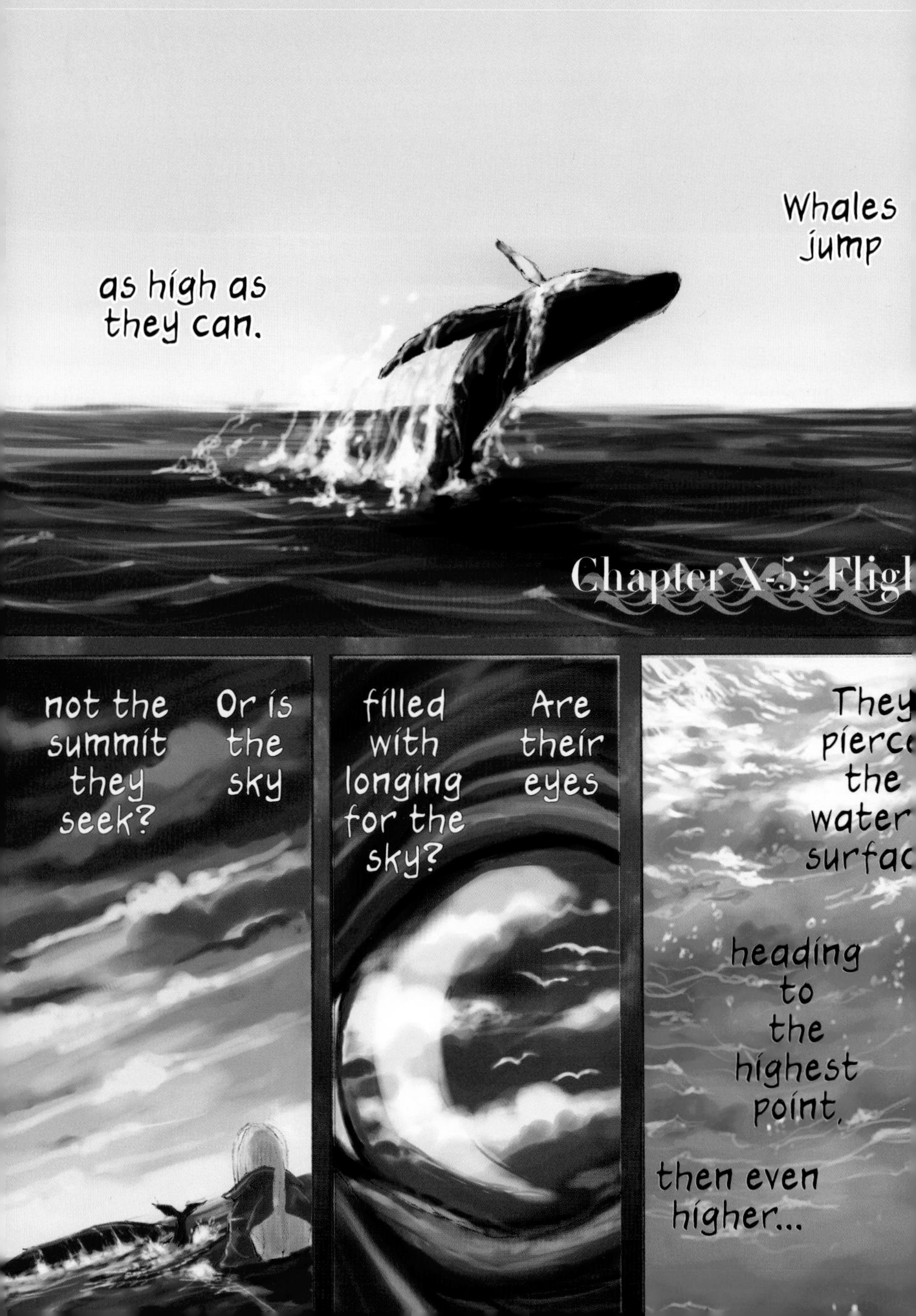
Whales jump
as high as they can.
Chapter X-5: Fligh
They pierc the water surfac
heading to the highest point,
then even higher...
Are their eyes
filled with longing for the sky?
Or is the sky
not the summit they seek?

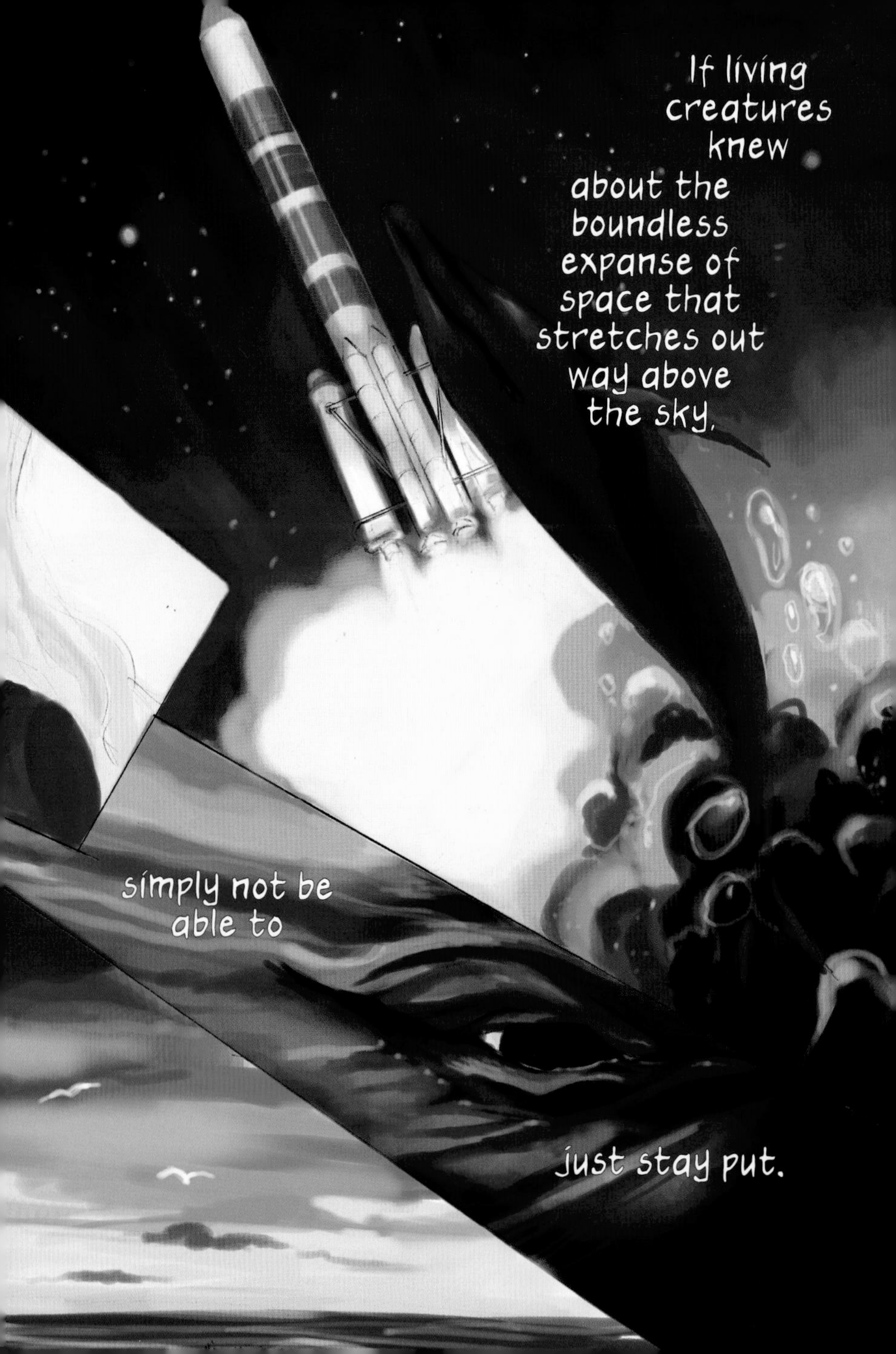
If living creatures knew about the boundless expanse of space that stretches out way above the sky,
simply not be able to
just stay put.

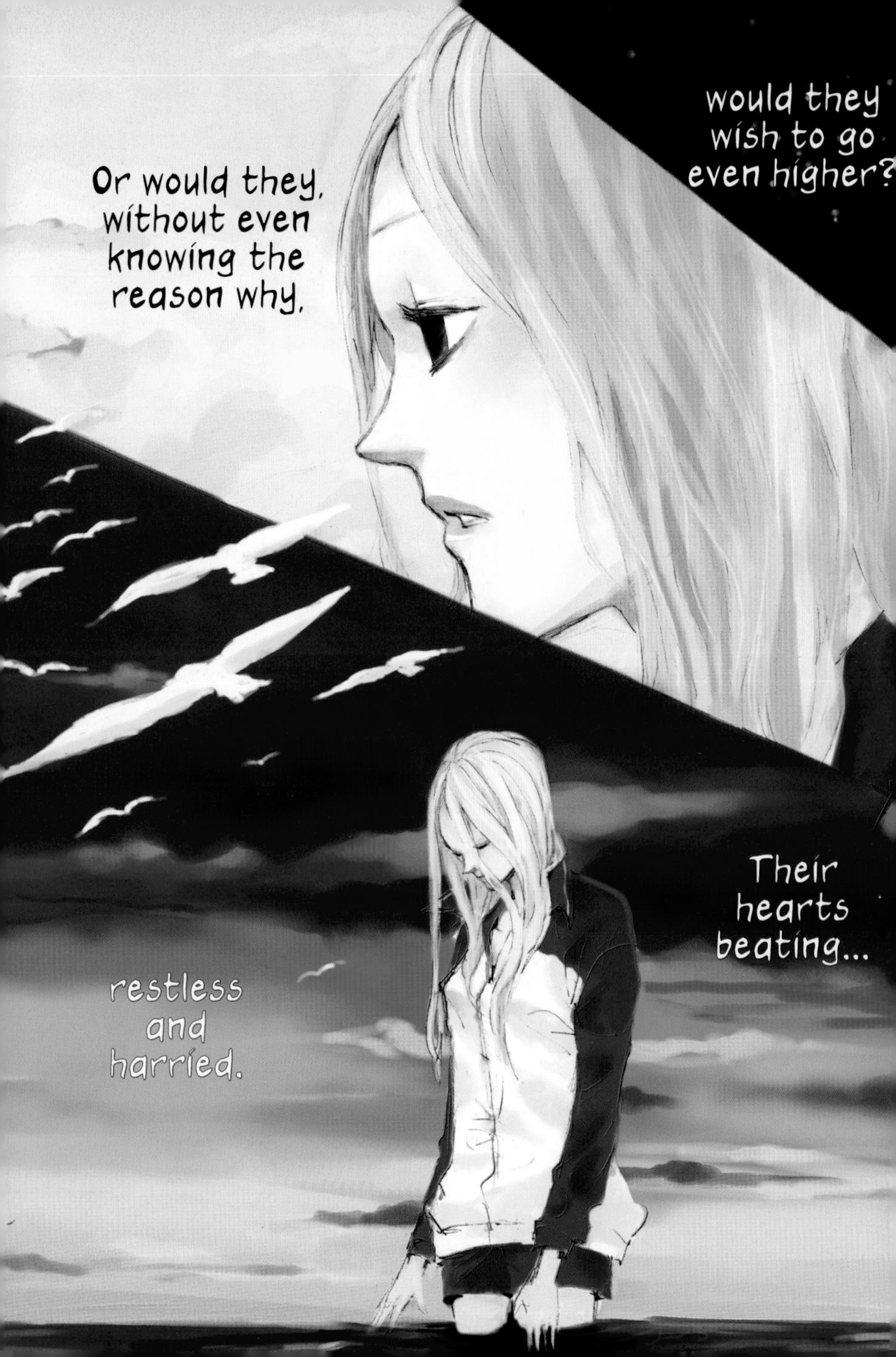
would they wish to go even higher?
Or would they, without even knowing the reason why,
Their hearts beating...
restless and harried.

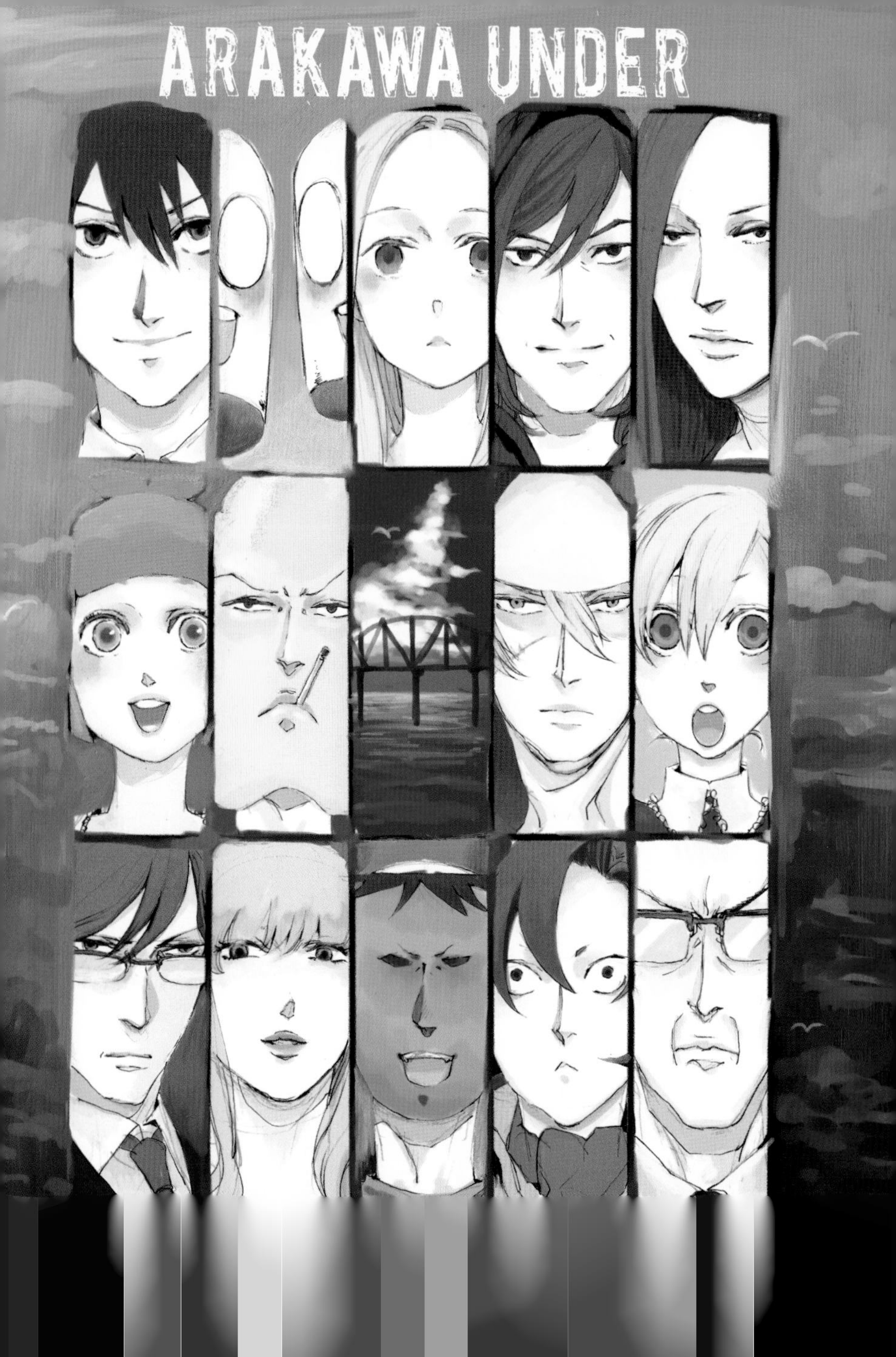
ARAKAWA UNDER

Polaroid cameras are fun, so I often use them. There's a film type called SX-70 that has colors that turn all sepia-toned and steeped in nostalgia as soon as it's used. It's a strange feeling, like events that happened moments ago suddenly becoming distant memories. This picture is my family's dog, Ryutaro. He loves to be petted. If I stop petting him, he starts tugging at me with a front paw like he's trying to train me. It's a funny feeling.

—Hikaru Nakamura

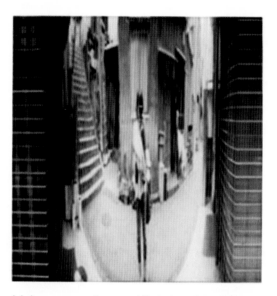

Living somewhere with lots of buildings, I long for something green, and buy lots of potted plants. I can't put anything too big in my tiny apartment, but I'd love to have a tree that scraped the ceiling. I used to climb trees every day as a kid. There was an easy tree to climb in my kindergarten playground. I think it was even more popular than the other things on the playground.

—Hikaru Nakamura

arakawa under the bridge

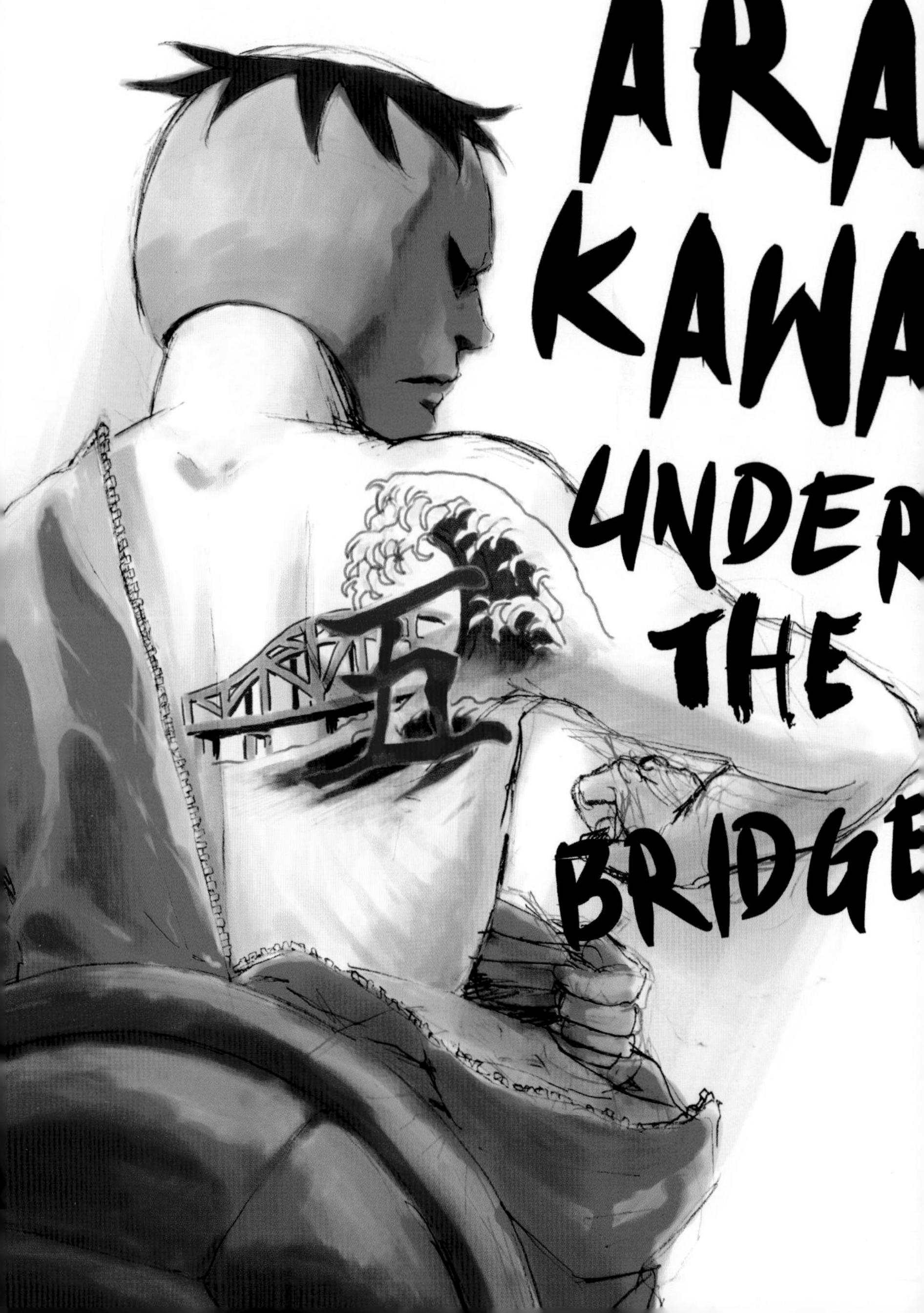
ARA
KAWA
UNDER
THE
BRIDGE

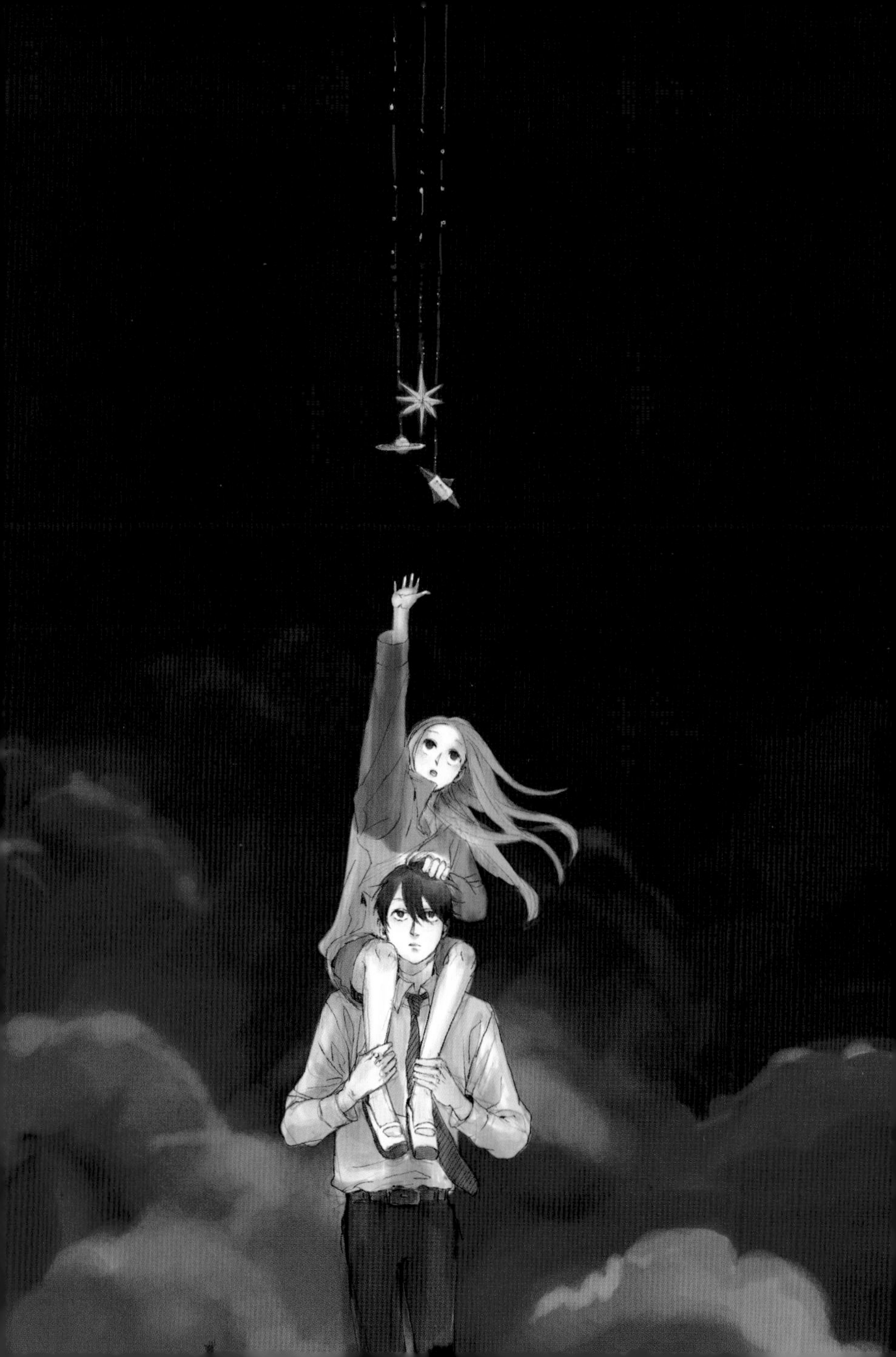

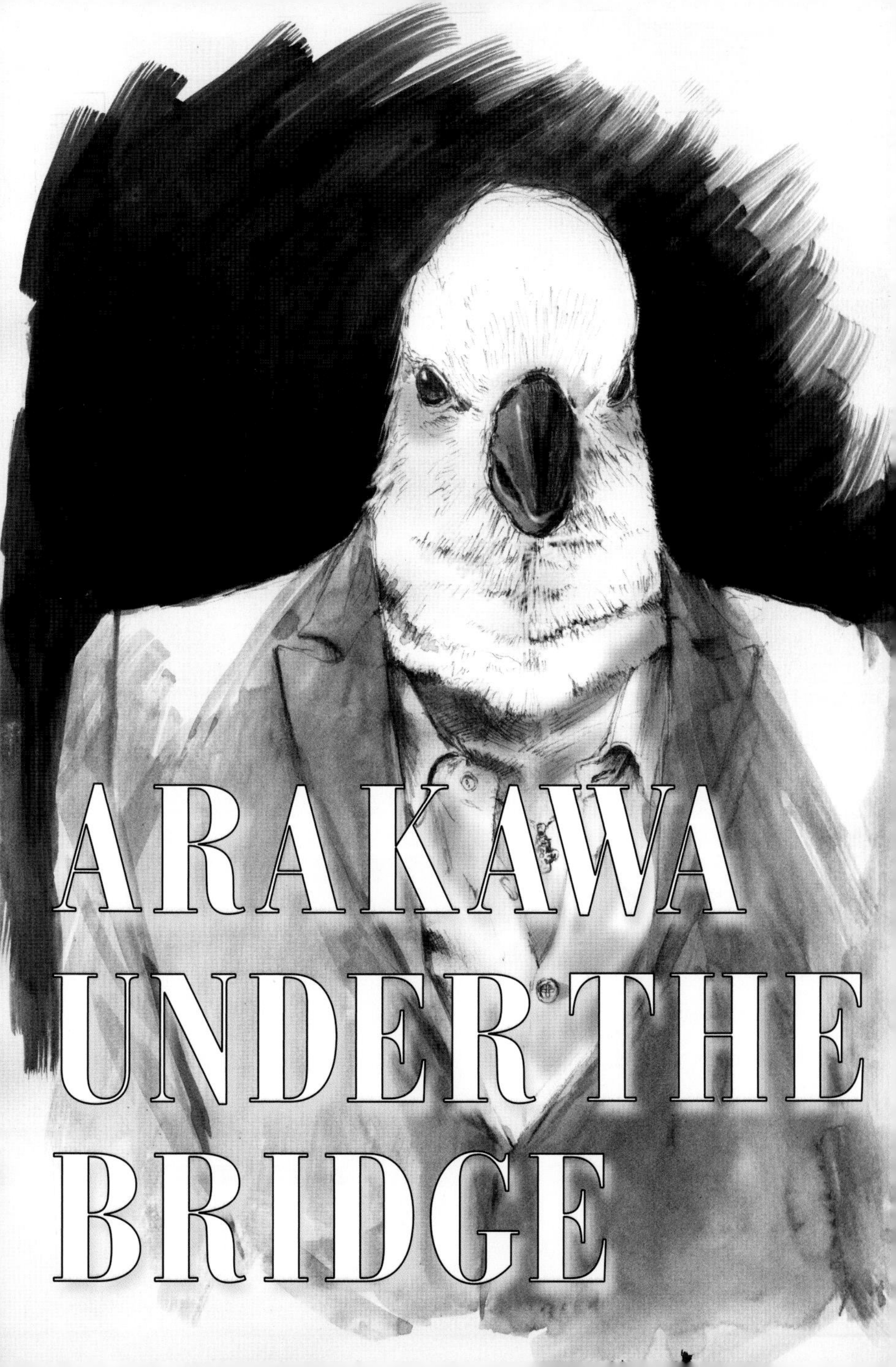
ARAKAWA
UNDER THE
BRIDGE

C O N T E N T S

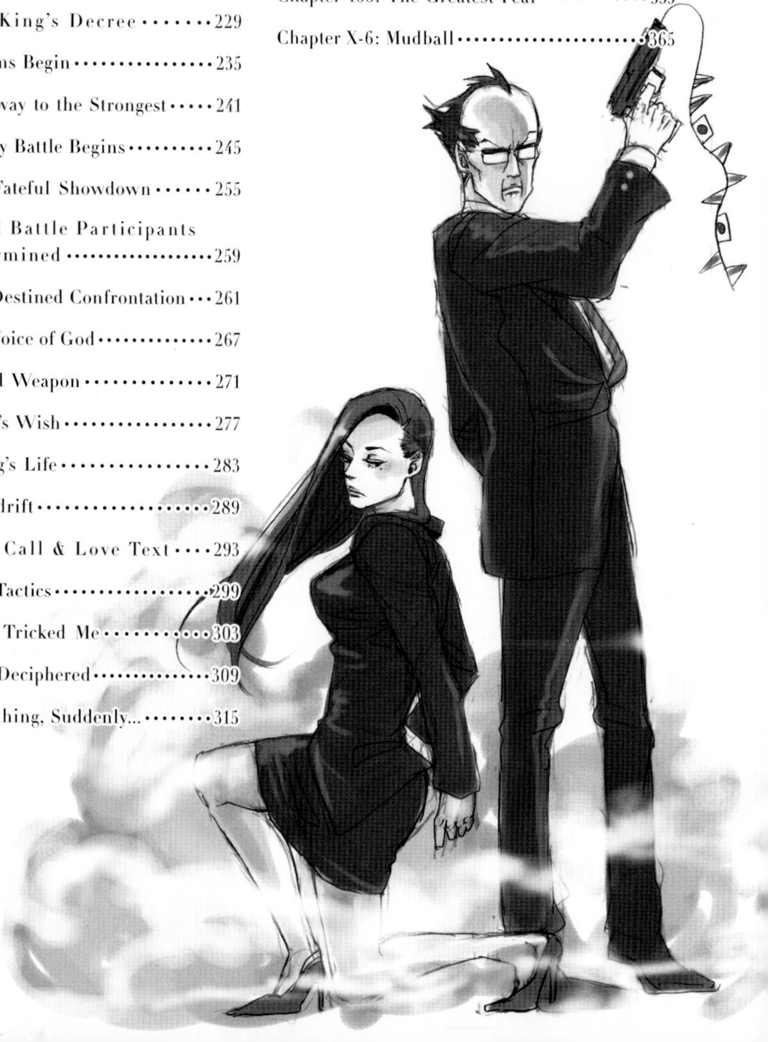

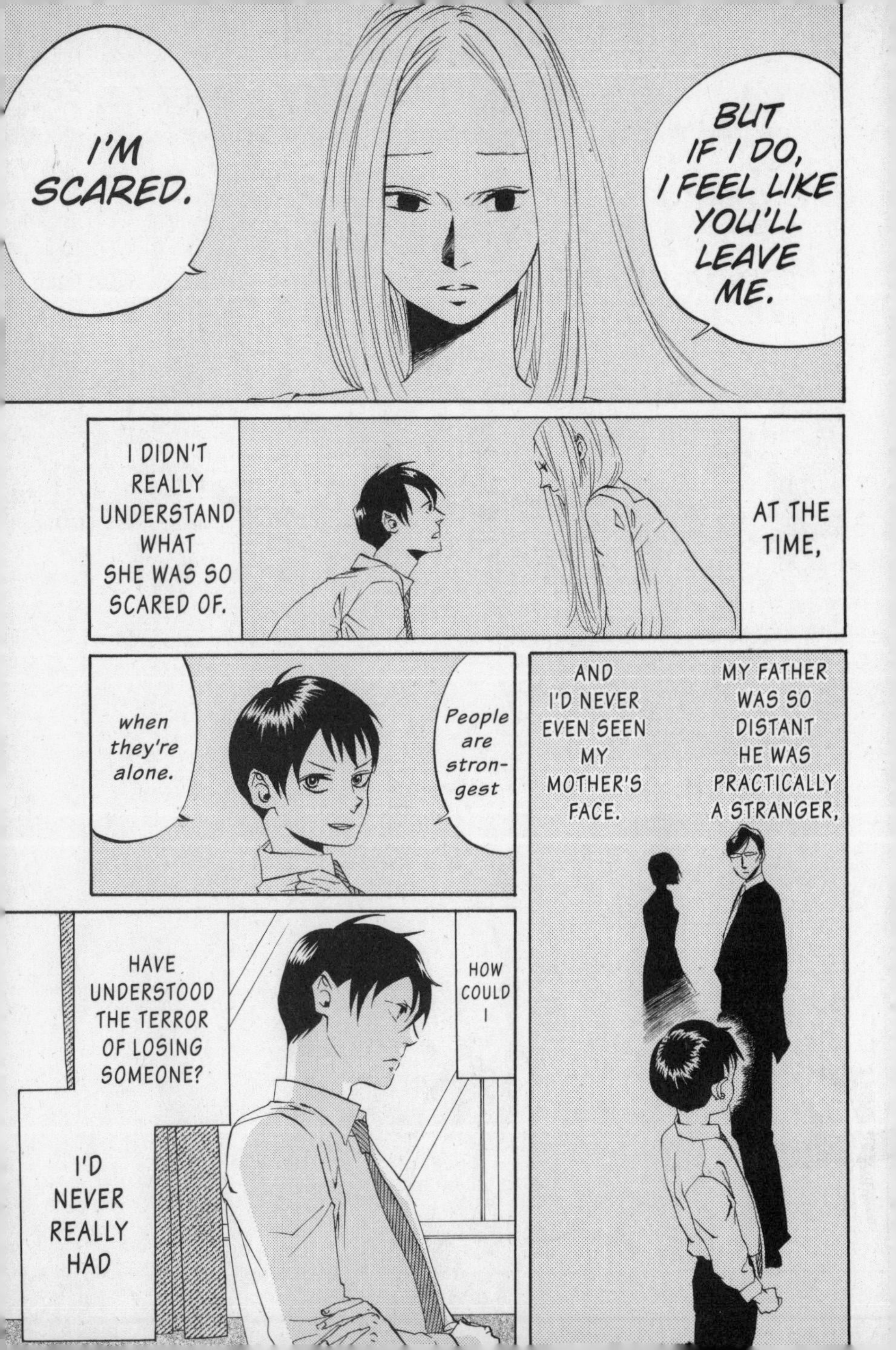
BUT IF I DO, I FEEL LIKE YOU'LL LEAVE ME.
I'M SCARED.
AT THE TIME,
I DIDN'T REALLY UNDERSTAND WHAT SHE WAS SO SCARED OF.
MY FATHER WAS SO DISTANT HE WAS PRACTICALLY A STRANGER,
AND I'D NEVER EVEN SEEN MY MOTHER'S FACE.
People are strongest
when they're alone.
HOW COULD I
HAVE UNDERSTOOD THE TERROR OF LOSING SOMEONE?
I'D NEVER REALLY HAD

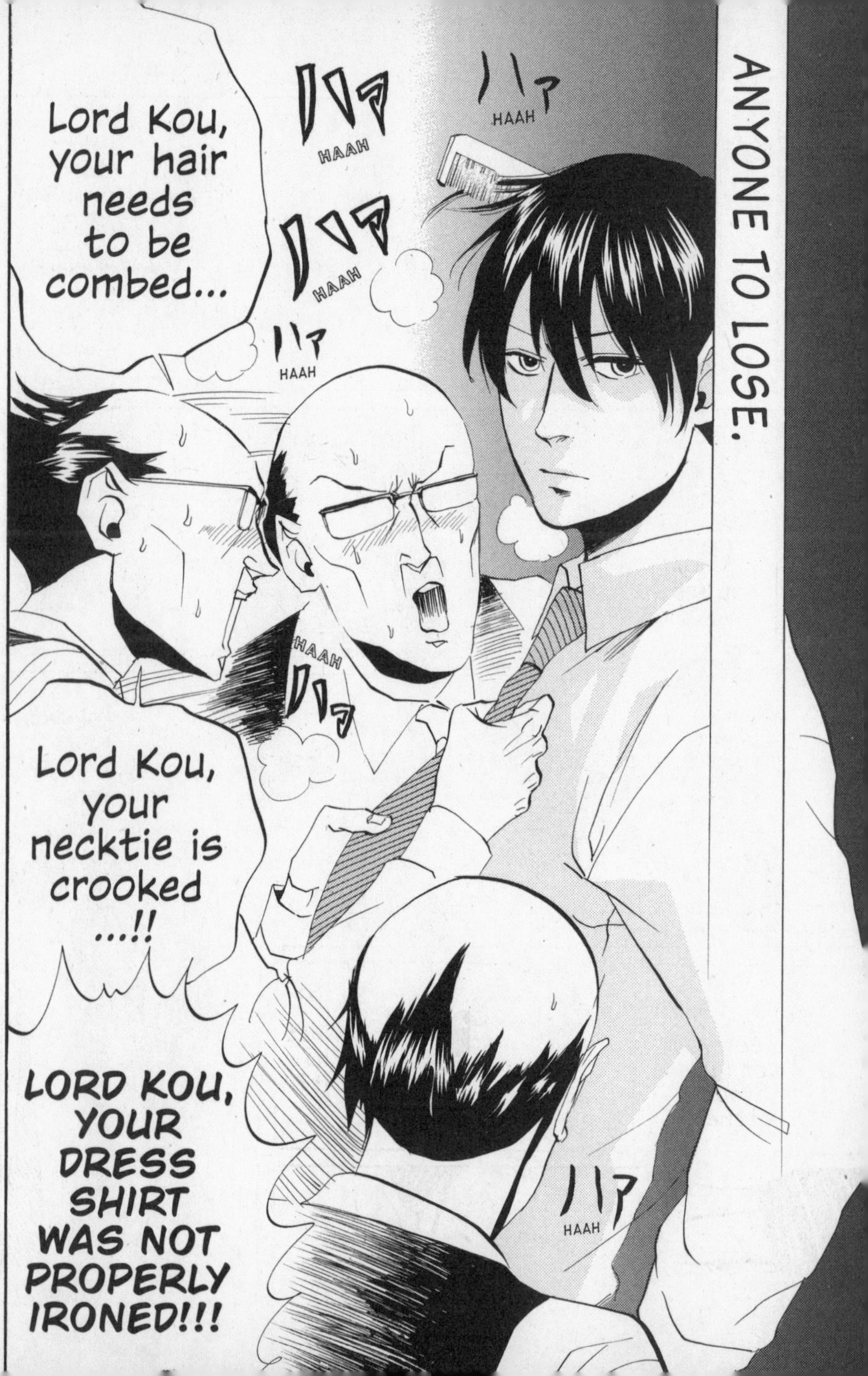
ANYONE TO LOSE.
ハア HAAH
ハア HAAH
ハア HAAH
Lord Kou, your hair needs to be combed...
ハア HAAH
ハア HAAH
Lord Kou, your necktie is crooked ...!!
ハア HAAH
LORD KOU, YOUR DRESS SHIRT WAS NOT PROPERLY IRONED!!!

Chapter 137: Business Meeting Under the Bridge

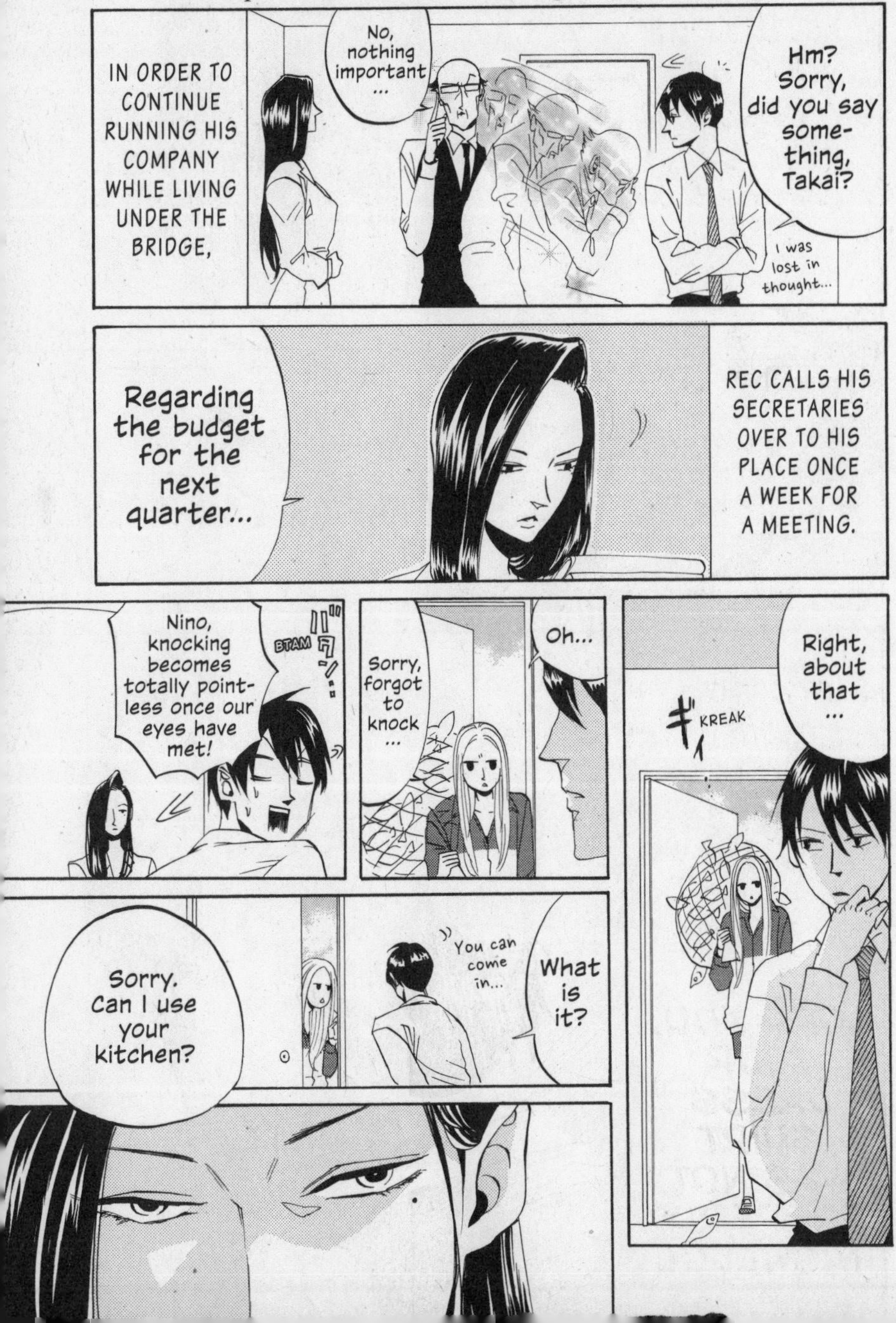

Hm? Sorry, did you say some-thing, Takai?
I was lost in thought...
No, nothing important ...
IN ORDER TO CONTINUE RUNNING HIS COMPANY WHILE LIVING UNDER THE BRIDGE,
REC CALLS HIS SECRETARIES OVER TO HIS PLACE ONCE A WEEK FOR A MEETING.
Regarding the budget for the next quarter...
Right, about that ...
KREAK
Oh...
Sorry, forgot to knock ...
BTAM
Nino, knocking becomes totally point-less once our eyes have met!
What is it?
You can come in...
Sorry. Can I use your kitchen?

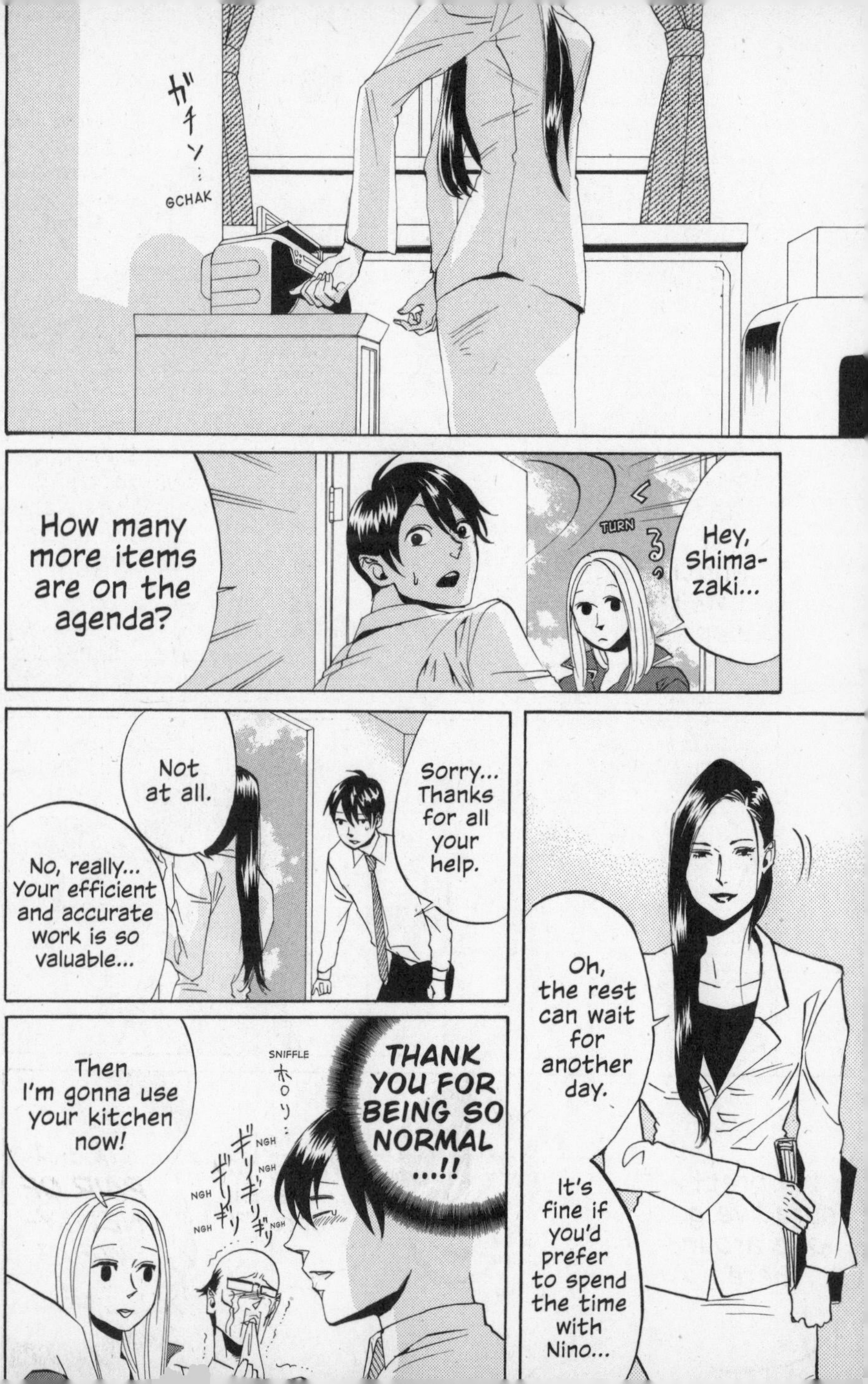
ガチン…
GCHAK
Hey, Shimazaki...
くるっ
TURN
How many more items are on the agenda?
Oh, the rest can wait for another day.
It's fine if you'd prefer to spend the time with Nino...
Sorry... Thanks for all your help.
Not at all.
No, really... Your efficient and accurate work is so valuable...
THANK YOU FOR BEING SO NORMAL ...!!
SNIFFLE
ホロリ…
ギリギリギリギリ
NGH
NGH
NGH
NGH
NGH
Then I'm gonna use your kitchen now!

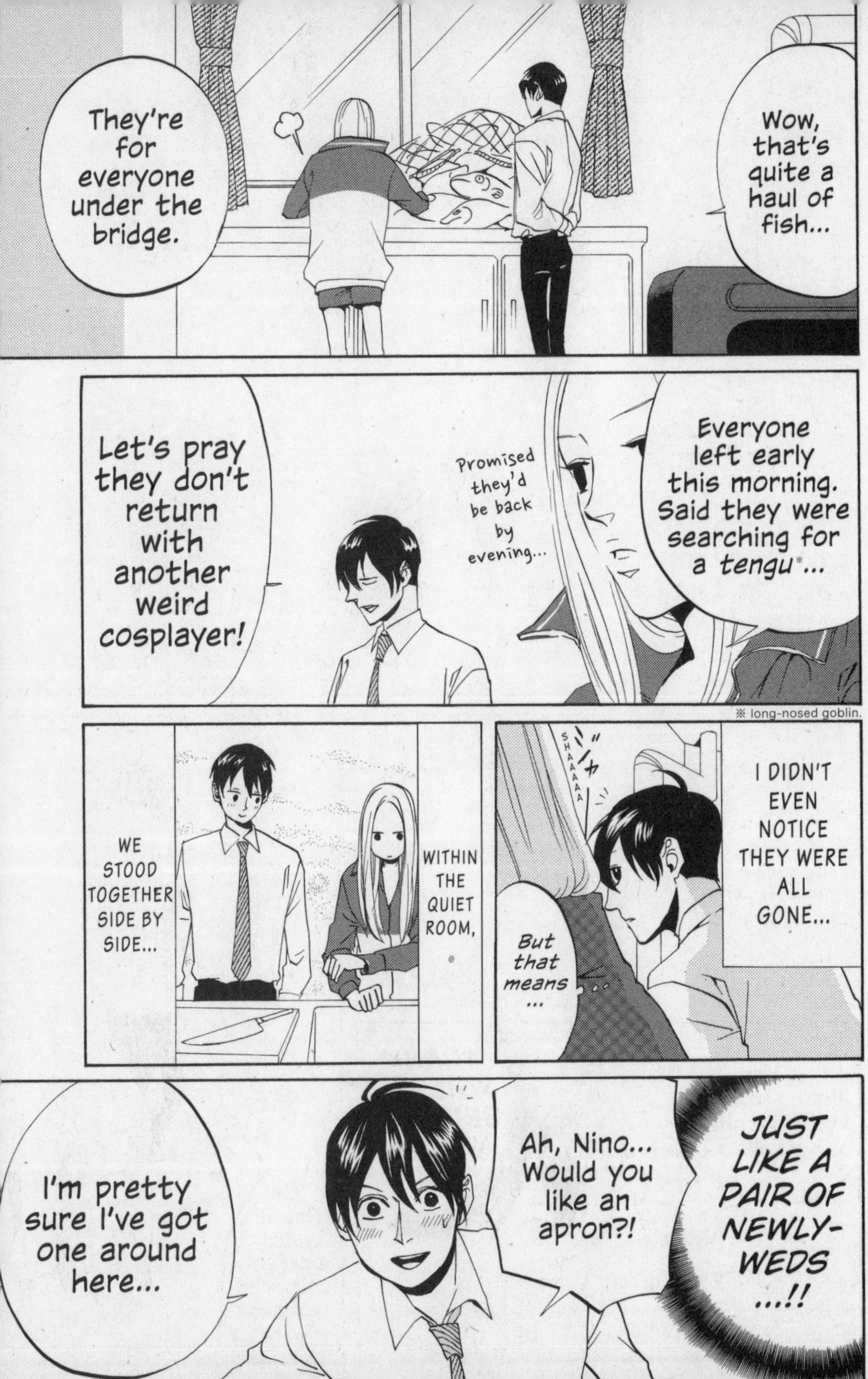
Wow, that's quite a haul of fish...
They're for everyone under the bridge.
Everyone left early this morning. Said they were searching for a *tengu*※...
Promised they'd be back by evening...
Let's pray they don't return with another weird cosplayer!
SHAAAAA
I DIDN'T EVEN NOTICE THEY WERE ALL GONE...
But that means ...
WITHIN THE QUIET ROOM,
WE STOOD TOGETHER SIDE BY SIDE...
JUST LIKE A PAIR OF NEWLY-WEDS ...!!
Ah, Nino... Would you like an apron?!
I'm pretty sure I've got one around here...
※ long-nosed goblin.

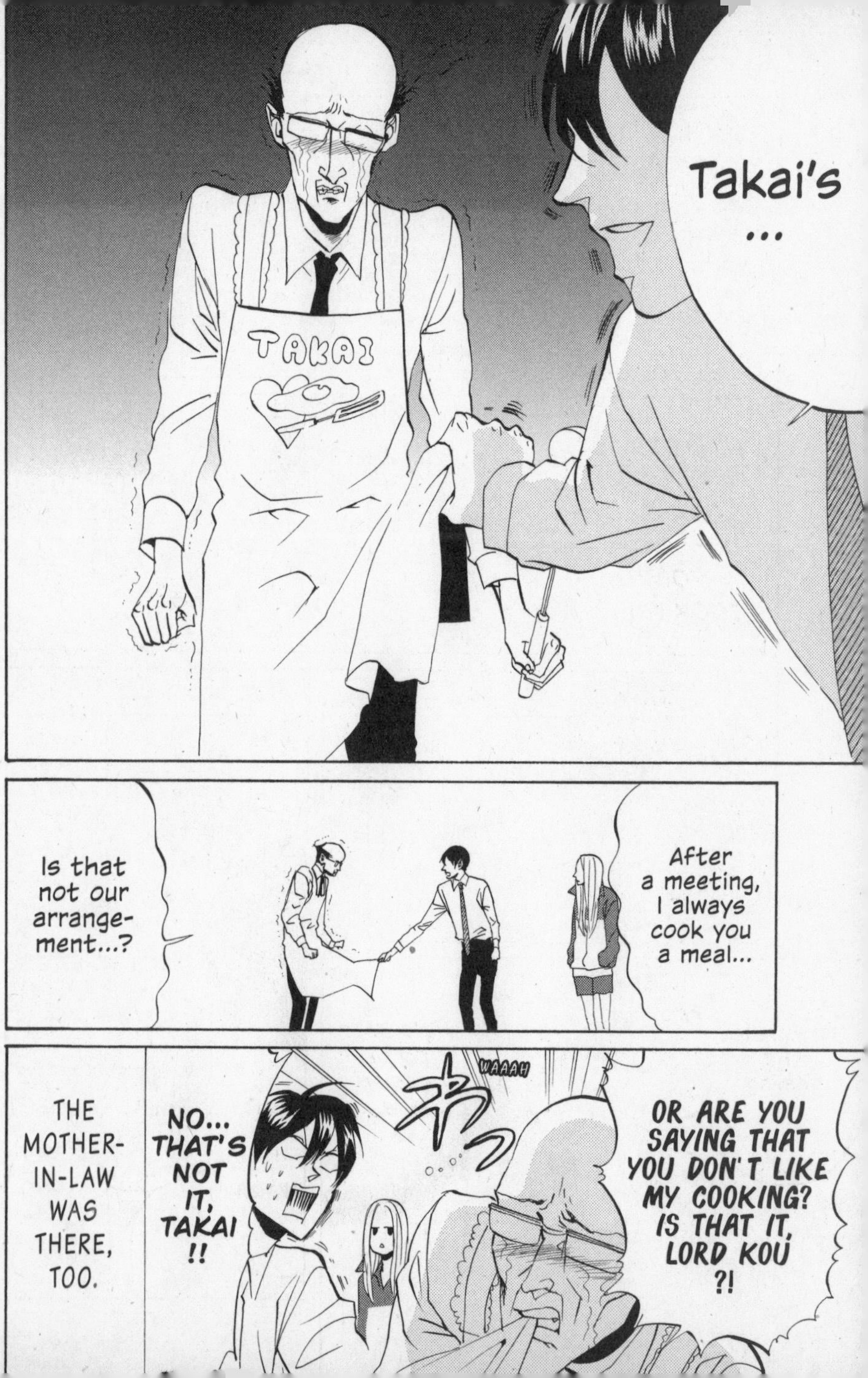
Takai's ...
TAKAI
After a meeting, I always cook you a meal...
Is that not our arrangement...?
OR ARE YOU SAYING THAT YOU DON'T LIKE MY COOKING? IS THAT IT, LORD KOU ?!
WAAAH
NO... THAT'S NOT IT, TAKAI !!
THE MOTHER-IN-LAW WAS THERE, TOO.

Chapter 138: War of the Wife and Her MIL

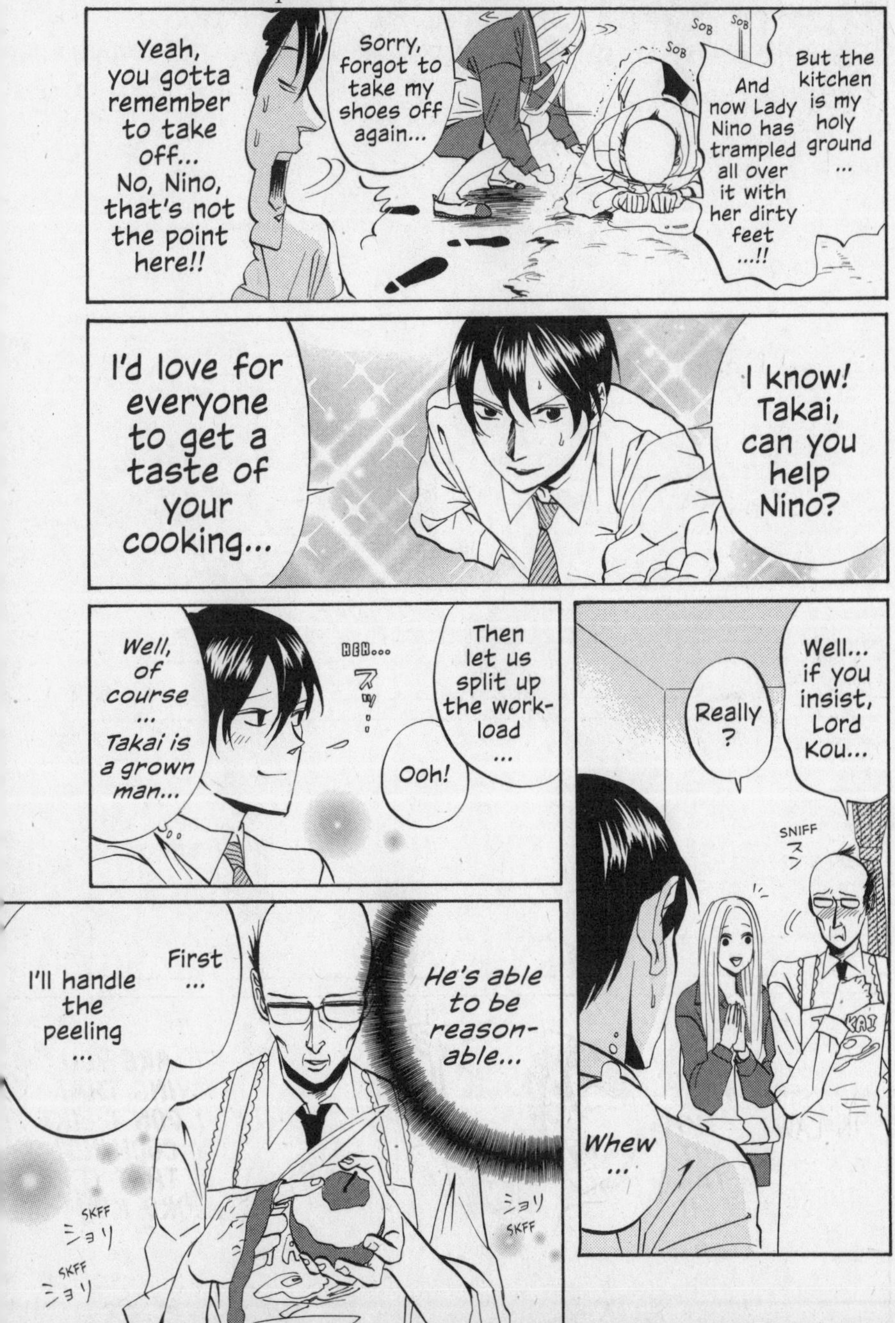
But the kitchen is my holy ground ...
And now Lady Nino has trampled all over it with her dirty feet ...!!
SOB SOB SOB
Sorry, forgot to take my shoes off again...
Yeah, you gotta remember to take off... No, Nino, that's not the point here!!
I know! Takai, can you help Nino?
I'd love for everyone to get a taste of your cooking...
Well... if you insist, Lord Kou...
Really?
SNIFF
Whew ...
Then let us split up the work-load ...
Ooh!
HEH...
Well, of course ... Takai is a grown man...
First ...
I'll handle the peeling ...
He's able to be reason-able...
SKFF
SKFF
SKFF

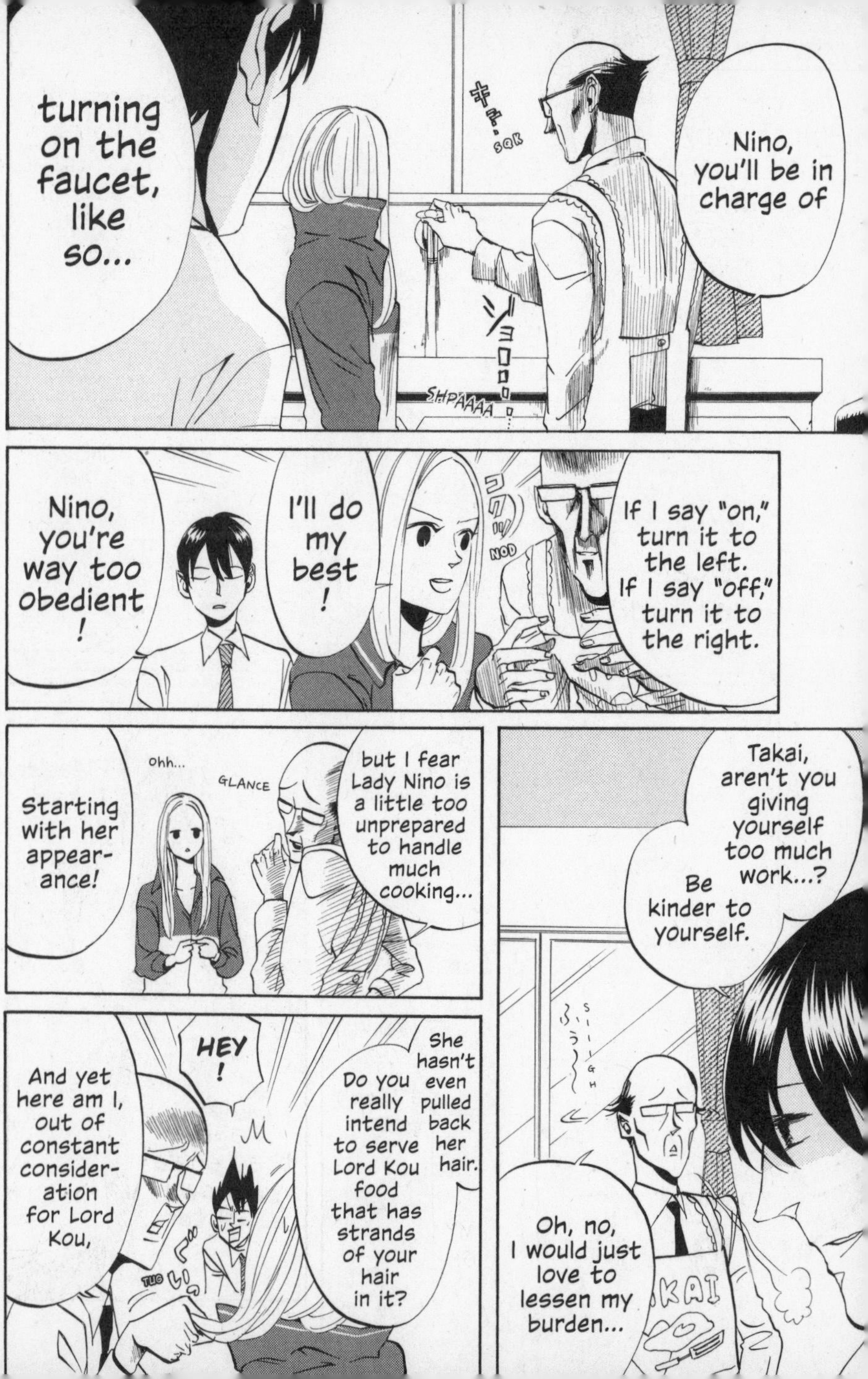
Nino, you'll be in charge of
SQK
turning on the faucet, like so...
SHPAAAA
If I say "on," turn it to the left. If I say "off," turn it to the right.
NOD
I'll do my best!
Nino, you're way too obedient!
Takai, aren't you giving yourself too much work...?
Be kinder to yourself.
SIIIGH
Oh, no, I would just love to lessen my burden...
but I fear Lady Nino is a little too unprepared to handle much cooking...
GLANCE
Ohh...
Starting with her appearance!
She hasn't even pulled back her hair.
Do you really intend to serve Lord Kou food that has strands of your hair in it?
HEY!
TUG
And yet here am I, out of constant consider-ation for Lord Kou,

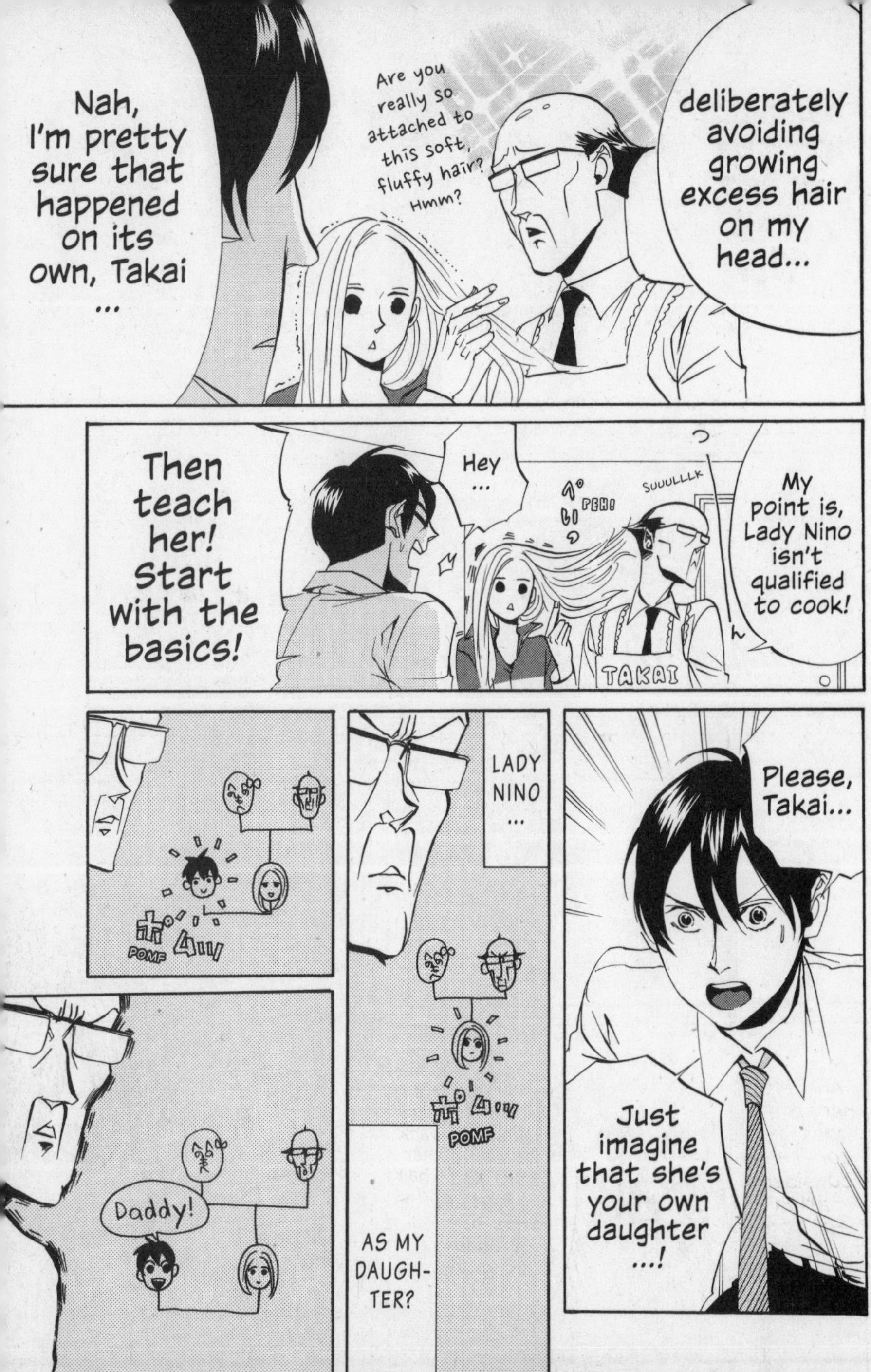

deliberately avoiding growing excess hair on my head...
Are you really so attached to this soft, fluffy hair? Hmm?
Nah, I'm pretty sure that happened on its own, Takai ...
My point is, Lady Nino isn't qualified to cook!
SUUULLLK
PEH!
TAKAI
Hey ...
Then teach her! Start with the basics!
Please, Takai...
Just imagine that she's your own daughter ...!
LADY NINO ...
POMF
AS MY DAUGH-TER?
POMF
Daddy!

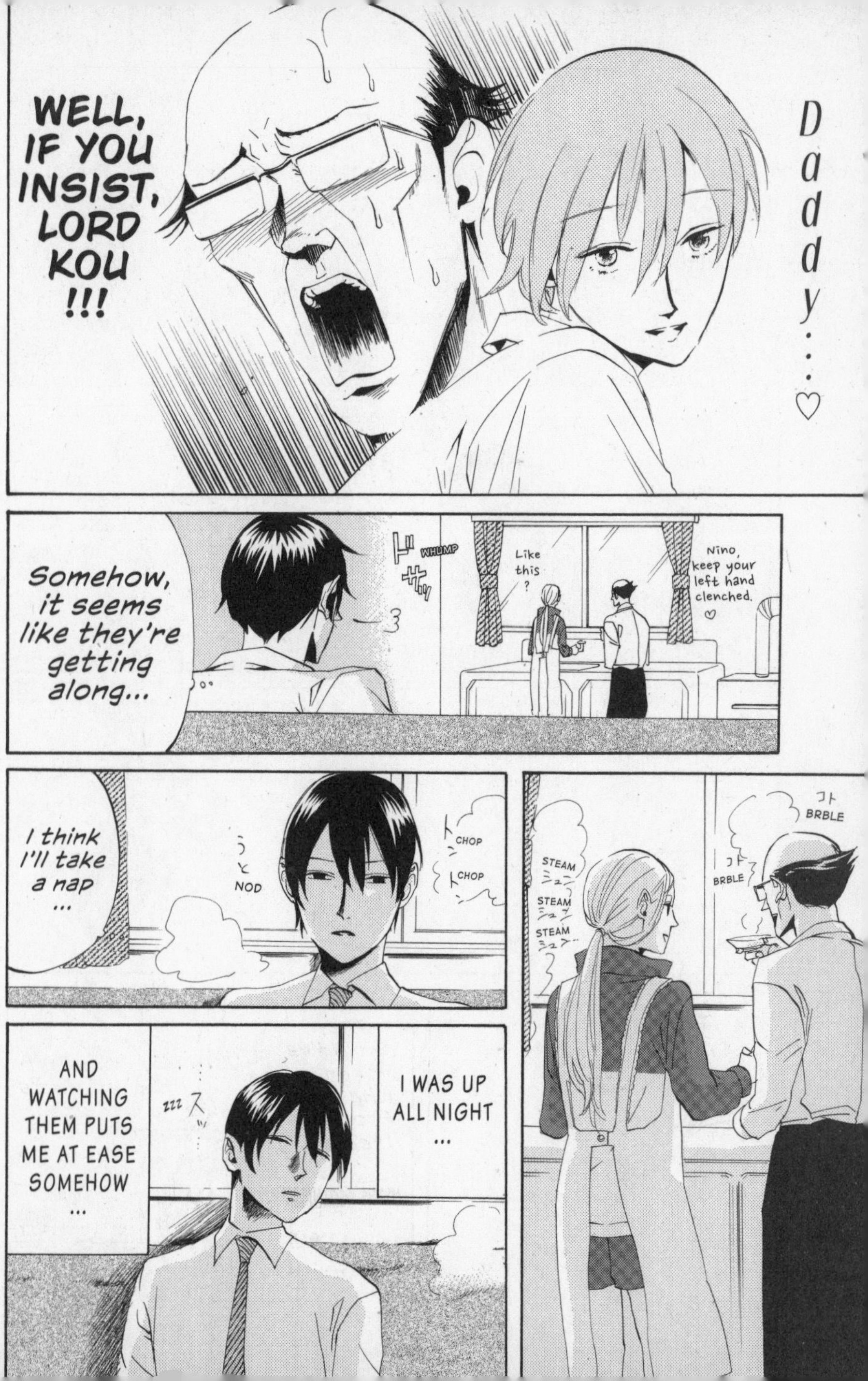

Daddy...♡
WELL, IF YOU INSIST, LORD KOU!!!
Nino, keep your left hand clenched. ♡
Like this?
WHUMP
Somehow, it seems like they're getting along...
BRBLE
BRBLE
STEAM
STEAM
STEAM
CHOP
CHOP
NOD
I think I'll take a nap...
I WAS UP ALL NIGHT...
zzz
AND WATCHING THEM PUTS ME AT EASE SOMEHOW...

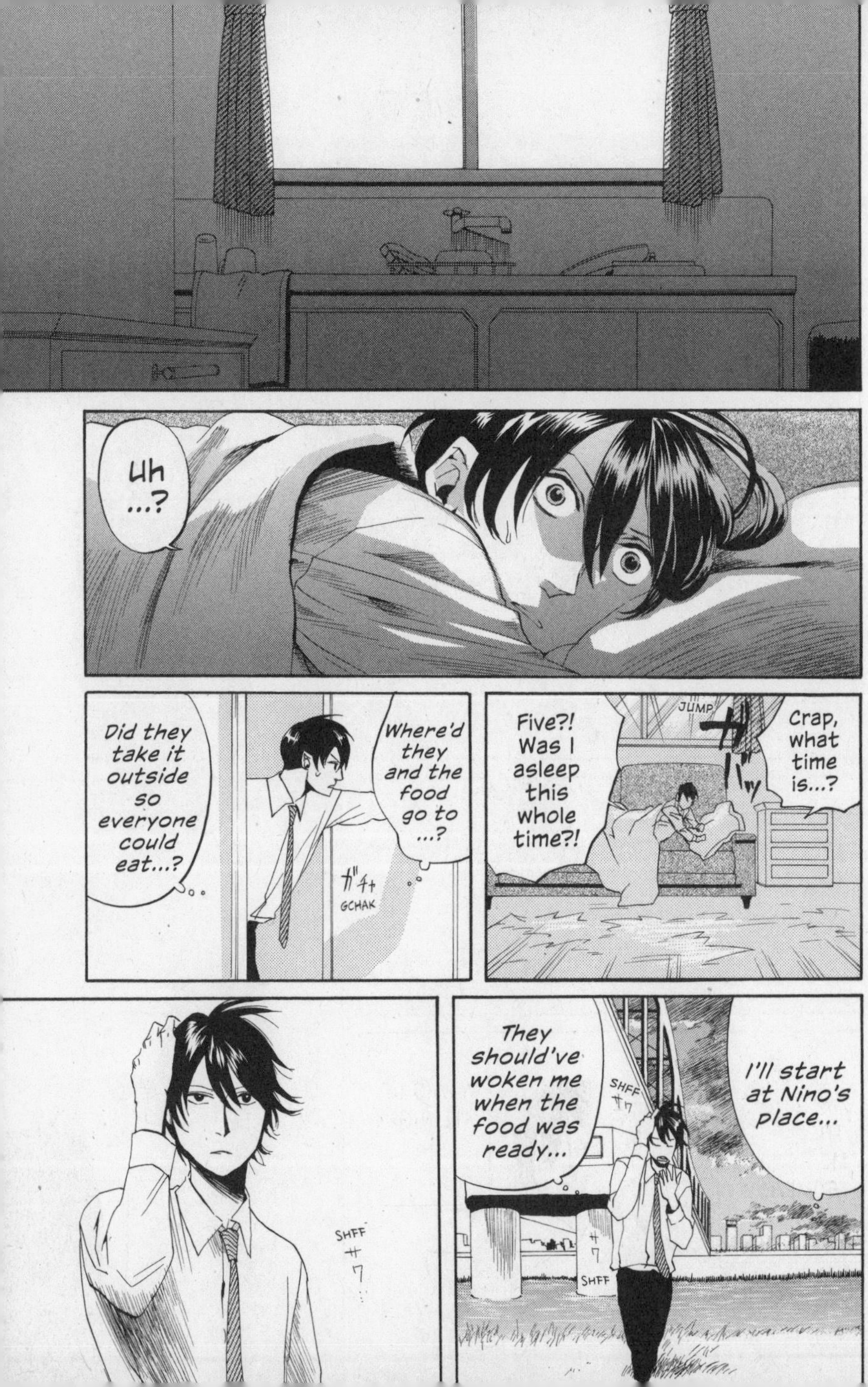
Uh ...?
Crap, what time is...?
JUMP
Five?! Was I asleep this whole time?!
Where'd they and the food go to ...?
GCHAK
Did they take it outside so everyone could eat...?
I'll start at Nino's place...
They should've woken me when the food was ready...
SHFF
SHFF
SHFF

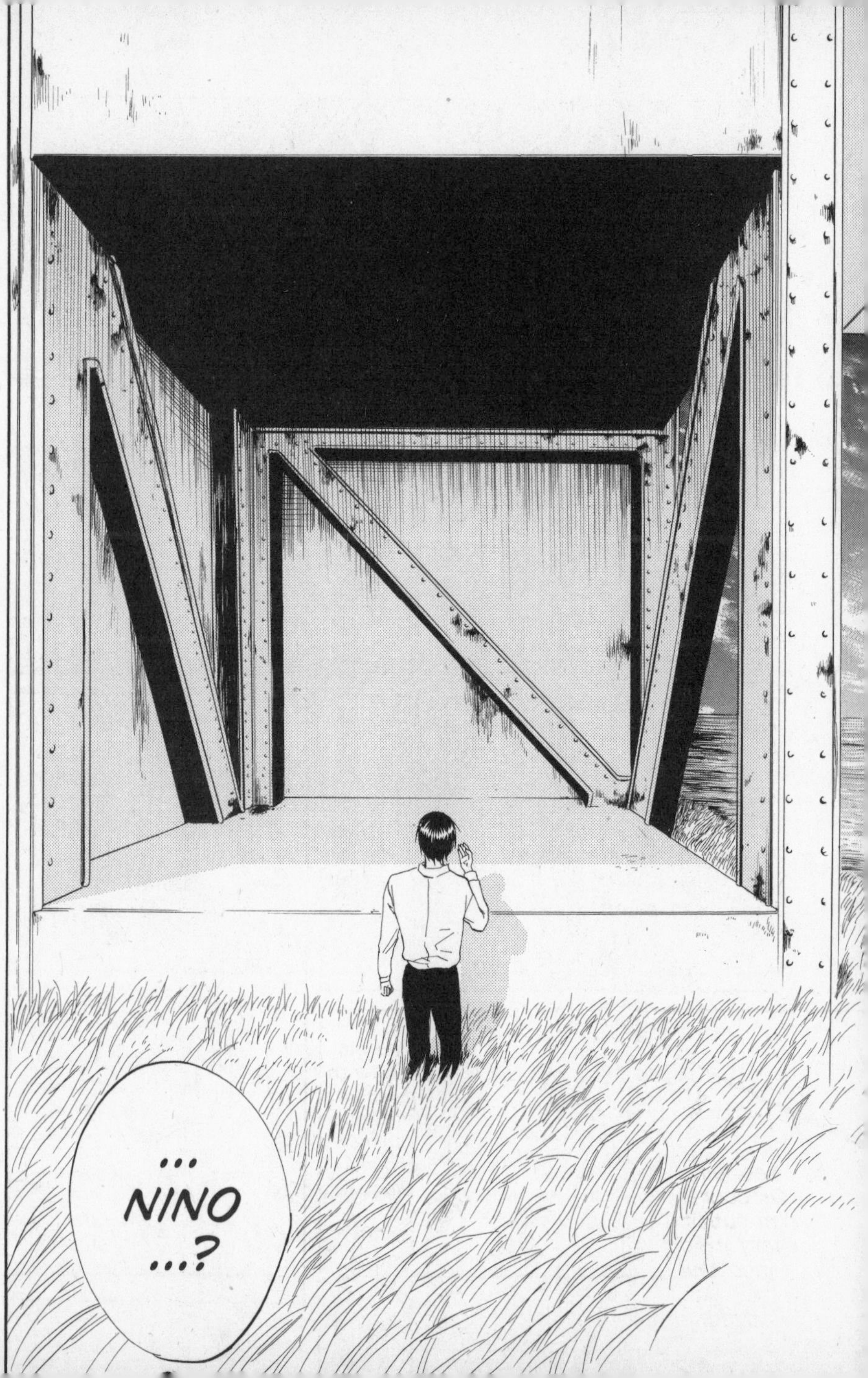
... NINO ...?

Chapter 139: Shriek

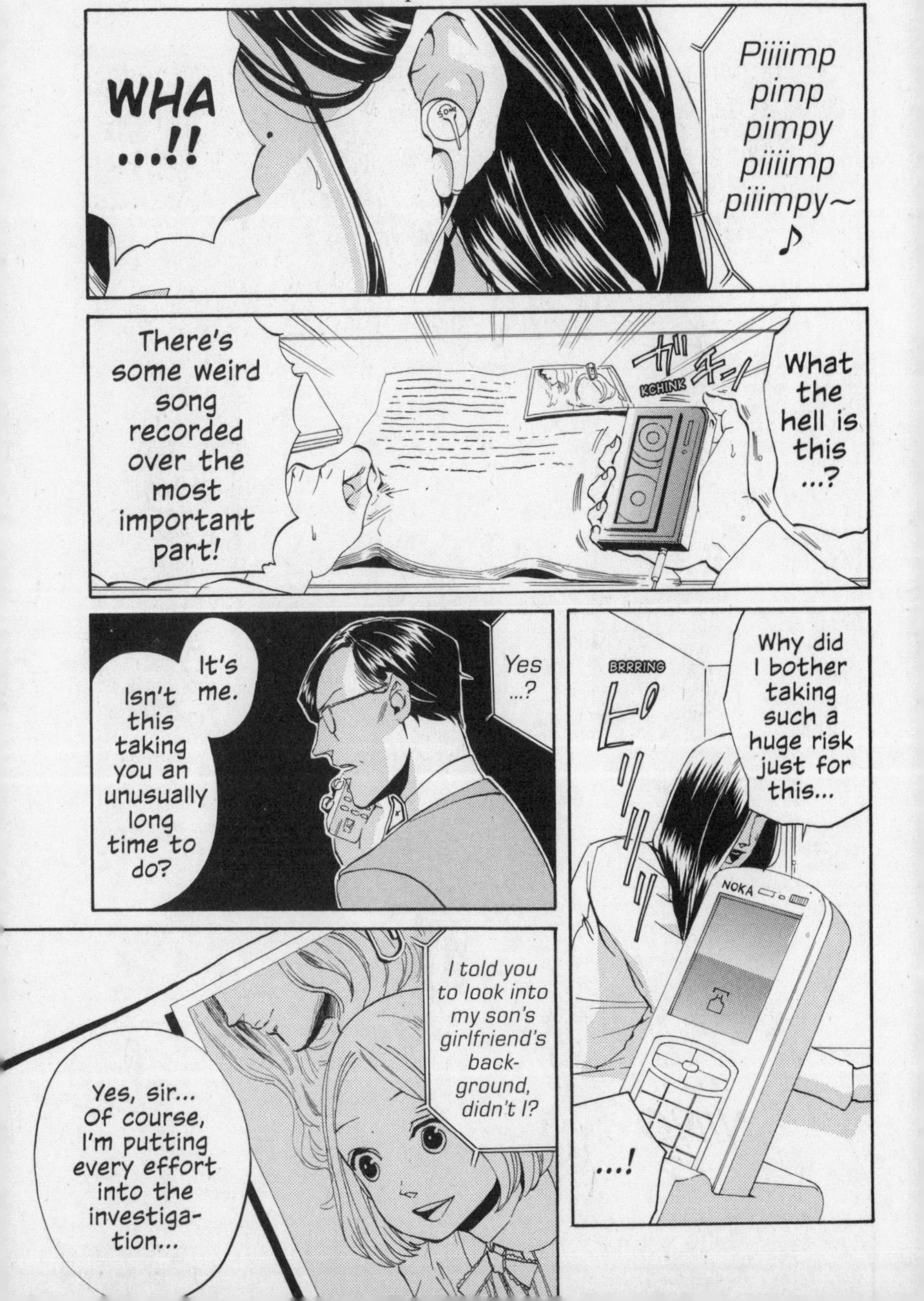
Piiiimp pimp pimpy piiiimp piiimpy~ ♪
WHA ...!!
What the hell is this ...?
KCHINK
There's some weird song recorded over the most important part!
Why did I bother taking such a huge risk just for this...
BRRRING
...!
NOKA
Yes ...?
It's me.
Isn't this taking you an unusually long time to do?
I told you to look into my son's girlfriend's background, didn't I?
Yes, sir... Of course, I'm putting every effort into the investigation...

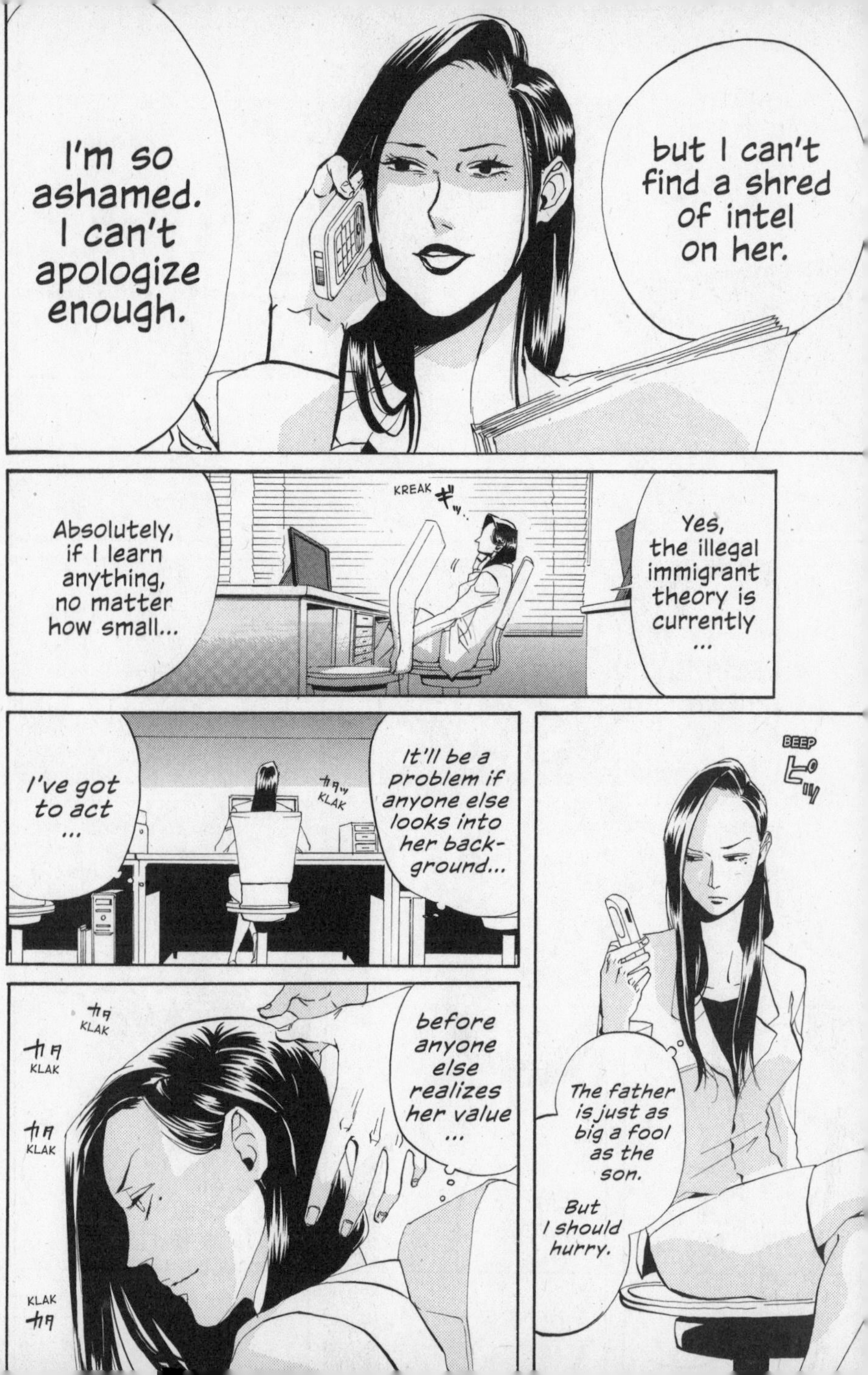
but I can't find a shred of intel on her.
I'm so ashamed. I can't apologize enough.
Yes, the illegal immigrant theory is currently ...
KREAK
ギッ..
Absolutely, if I learn anything, no matter how small...
BEEP
ピッ
The father is just as big a fool as the son.
But I should hurry.
It'll be a problem if anyone else looks into her back-ground...
カタッ
KLAK
I've got to act ...
before anyone else realizes her value ...
カタ
KLAK
カタ
KLAK
カタ
KLAK
KLAK
カタ

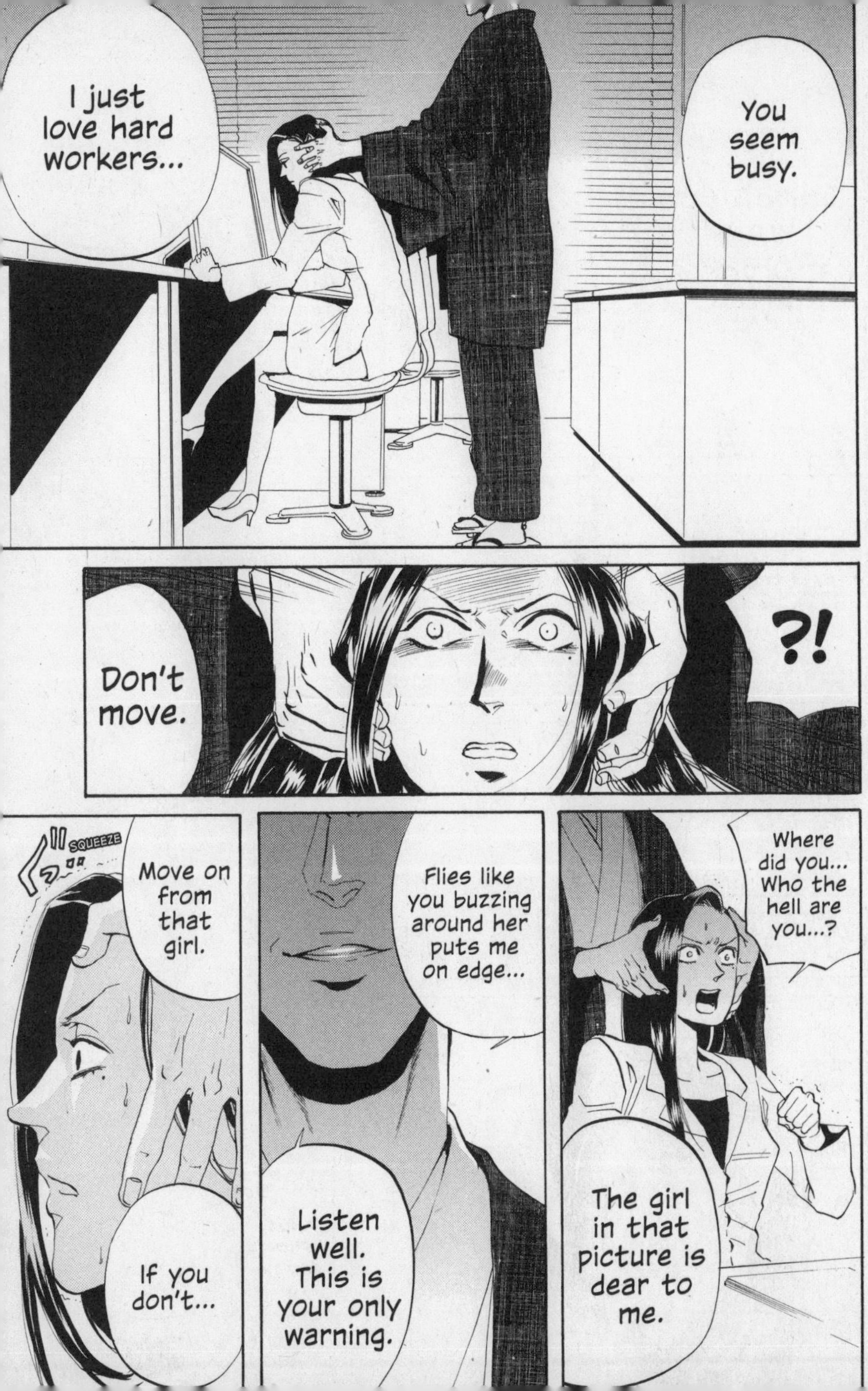
You seem busy.
I just love hard workers...
?!
Don't move.
Where did you... Who the hell are you...?
The girl in that picture is dear to me.
Flies like you buzzing around her puts me on edge...
Listen well. This is your only warning.
SQUEEZE
Move on from that girl.
If you don't...

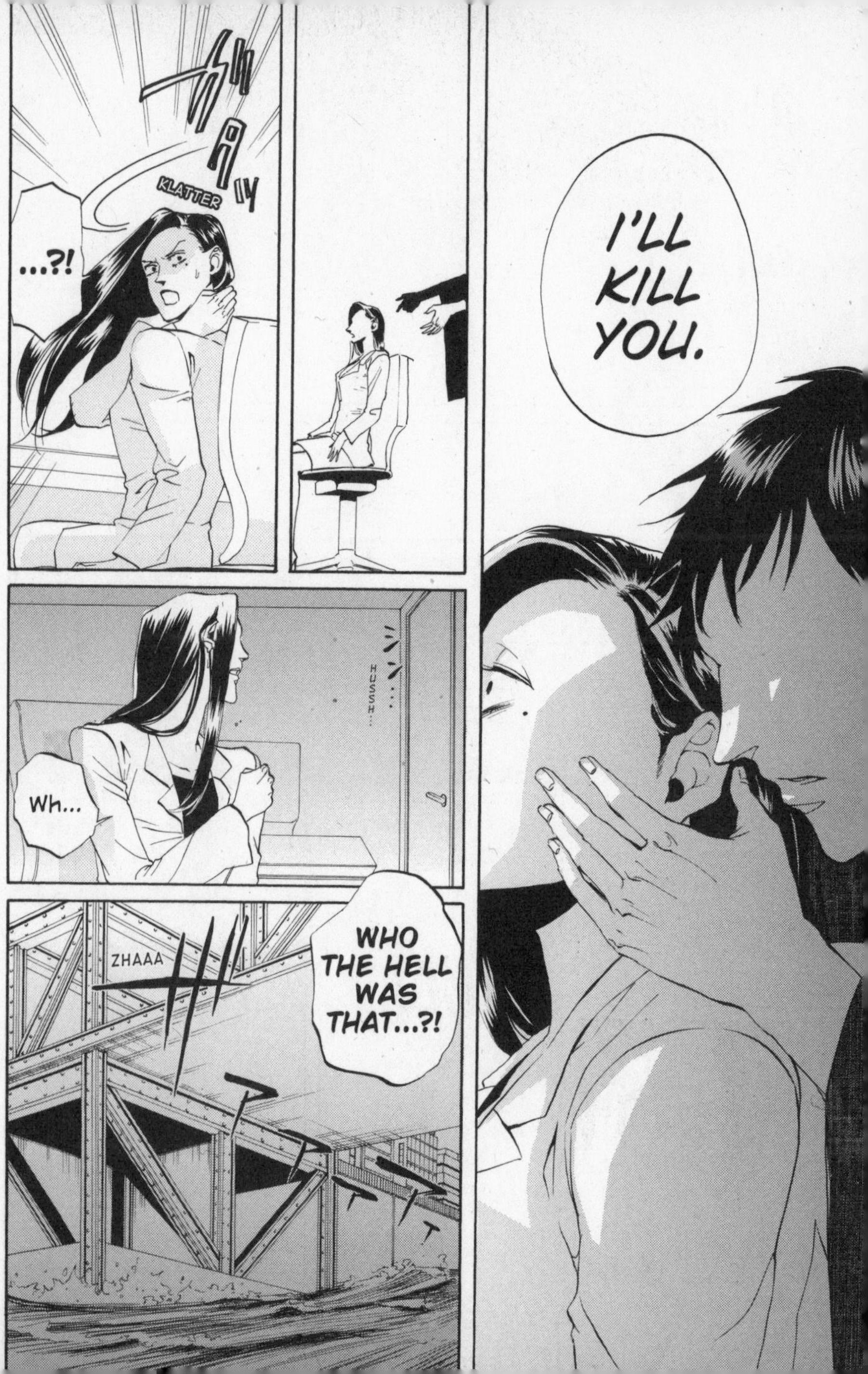
I'LL KILL YOU.
KLATTER
...?!
HUSSH...
Wh...
WHO THE HELL WAS THAT...?!
ZHAAA

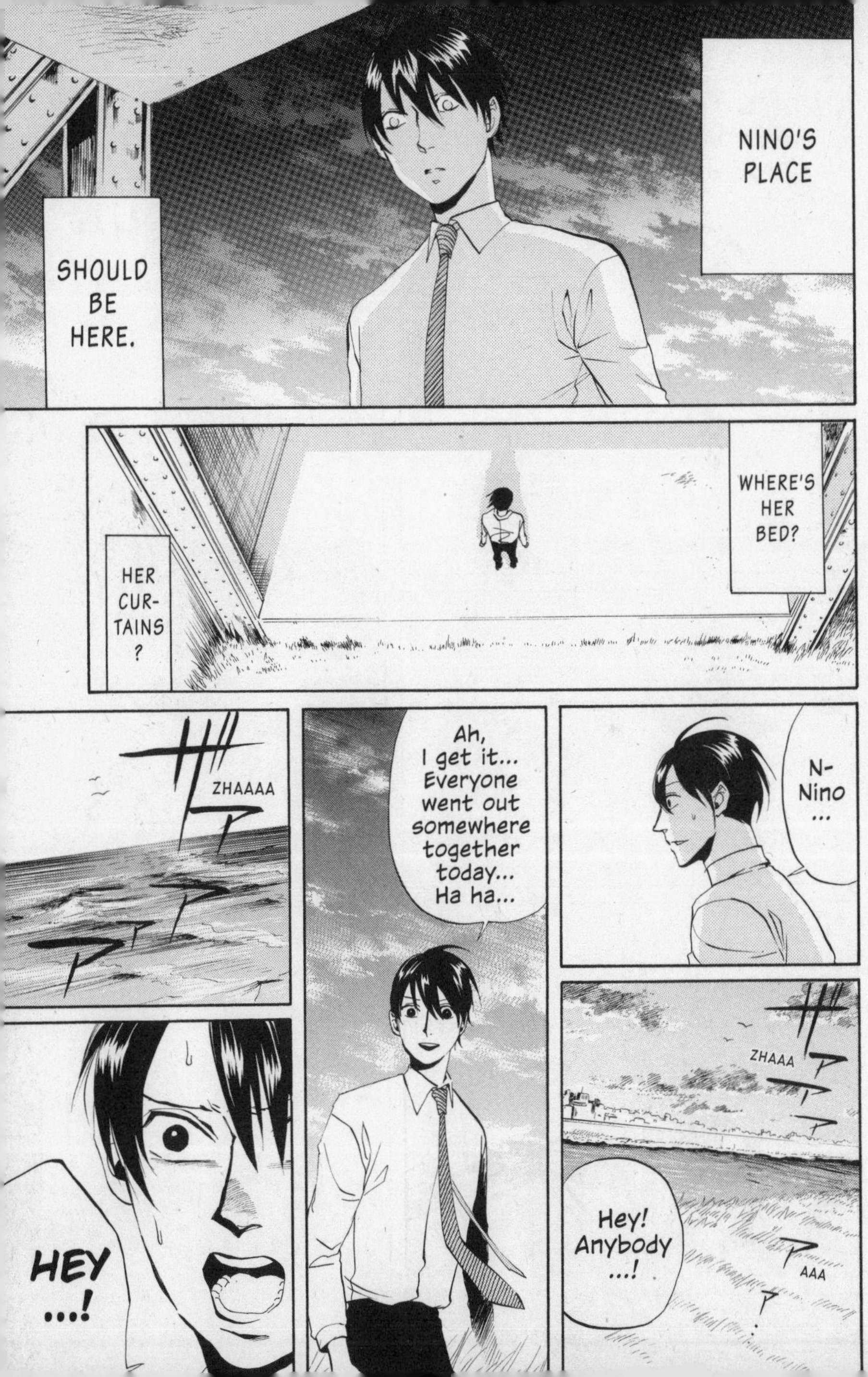
NINO'S PLACE
SHOULD BE HERE.
WHERE'S HER BED?
HER CURTAINS?
N-Nino...
ZHAAA
Hey! Anybody...!
AAA
Ah, I get it... Everyone went out somewhere together today... Ha ha...
ZHAAAA
HEY...!

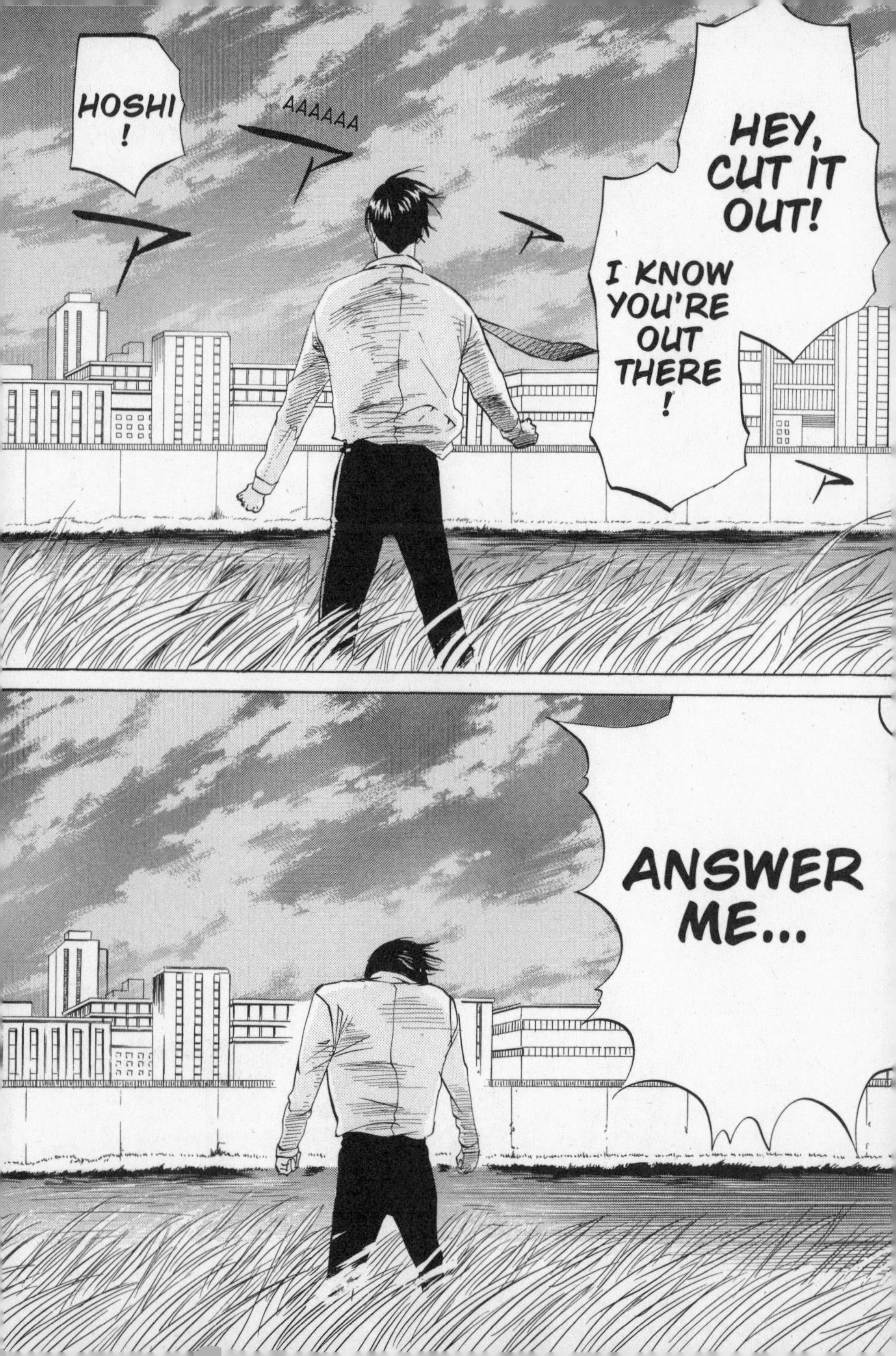
HEY, CUT IT OUT!
I KNOW YOU'RE OUT THERE!
AAAAAA
HOSHI!
ANSWER ME...

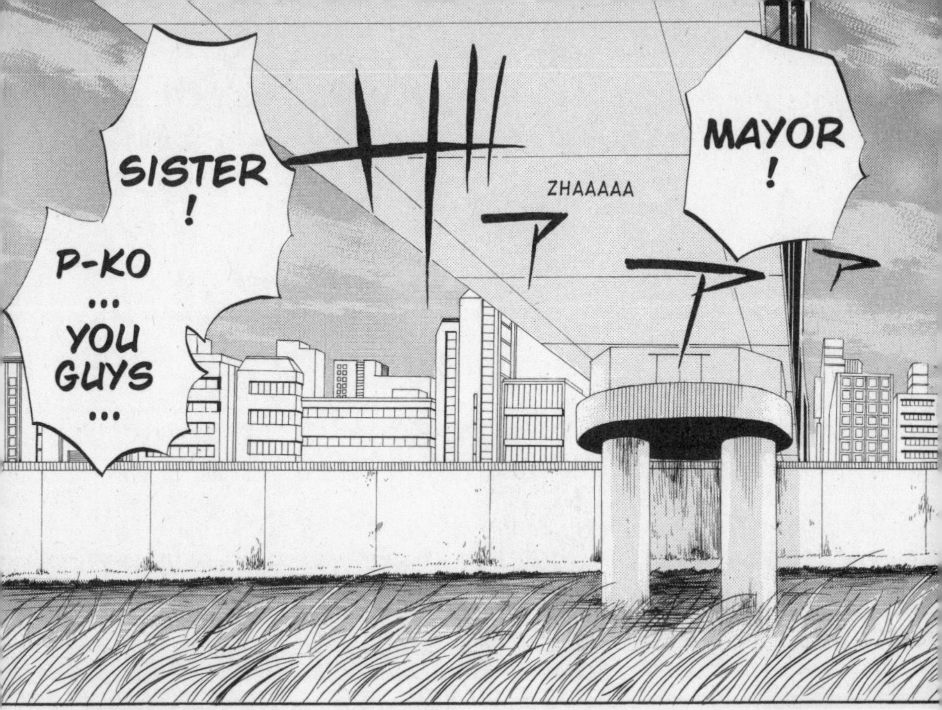
MAYOR
!
ザァァァ
ZHAAAAA
SISTER
!
P-KO
...
YOU
GUYS
...
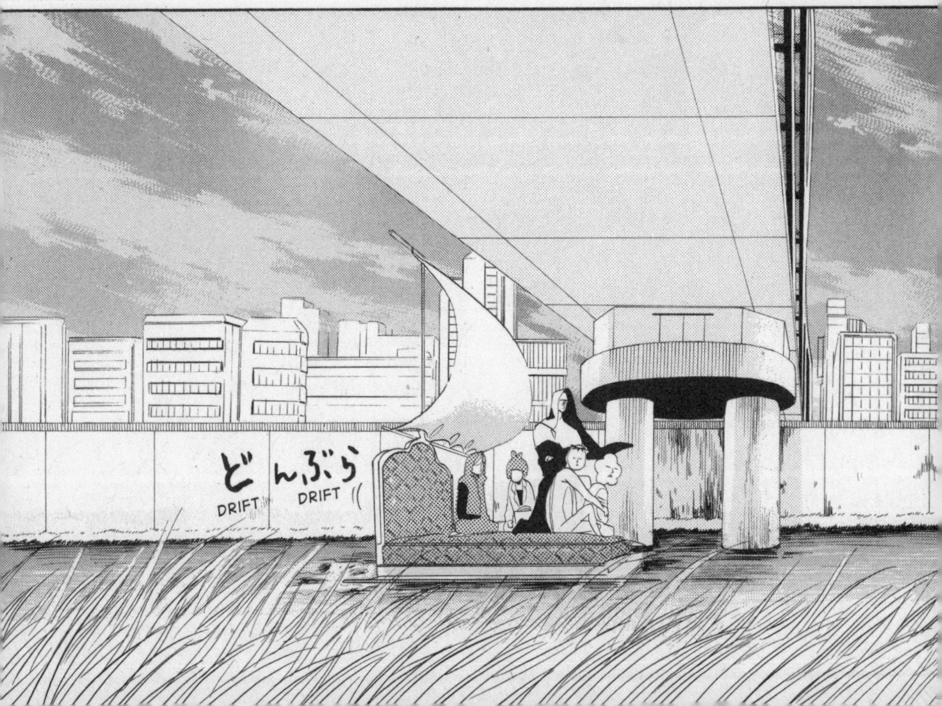
どんぶら
DRIFT
DRIFT

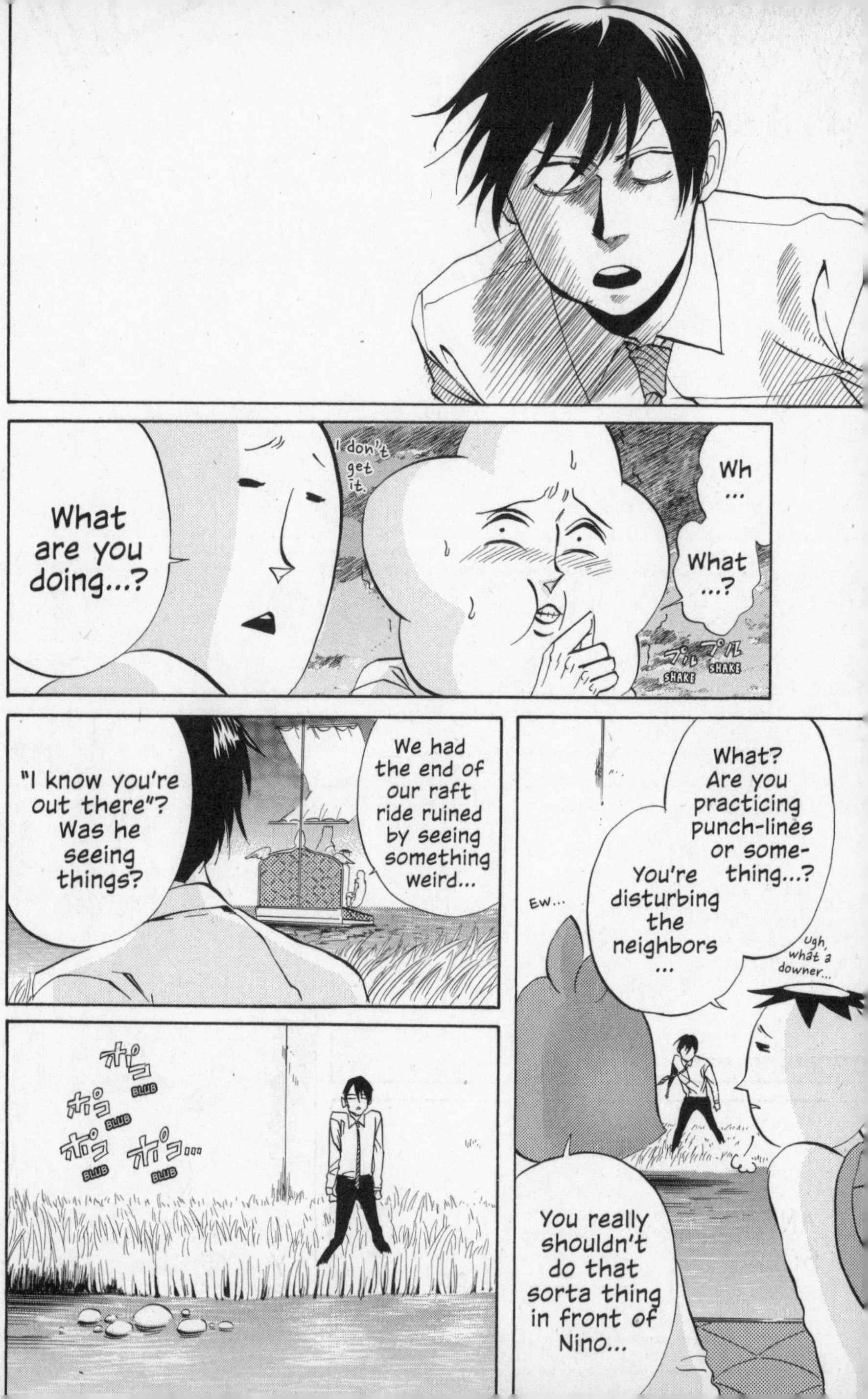
Wh ... What ...?
I don't get it.
SHAKE SHAKE
What are you doing...?
What? Are you practicing punch-lines or some-thing...?
Ugh, what a downer...
You're disturbing the neighbors ...
Ew...
You really shouldn't do that sorta thing in front of Nino...
We had the end of our raft ride ruined by seeing something weird...
"I know you're out there"? Was he seeing things?
BLUB BLUB BLUB BLUB

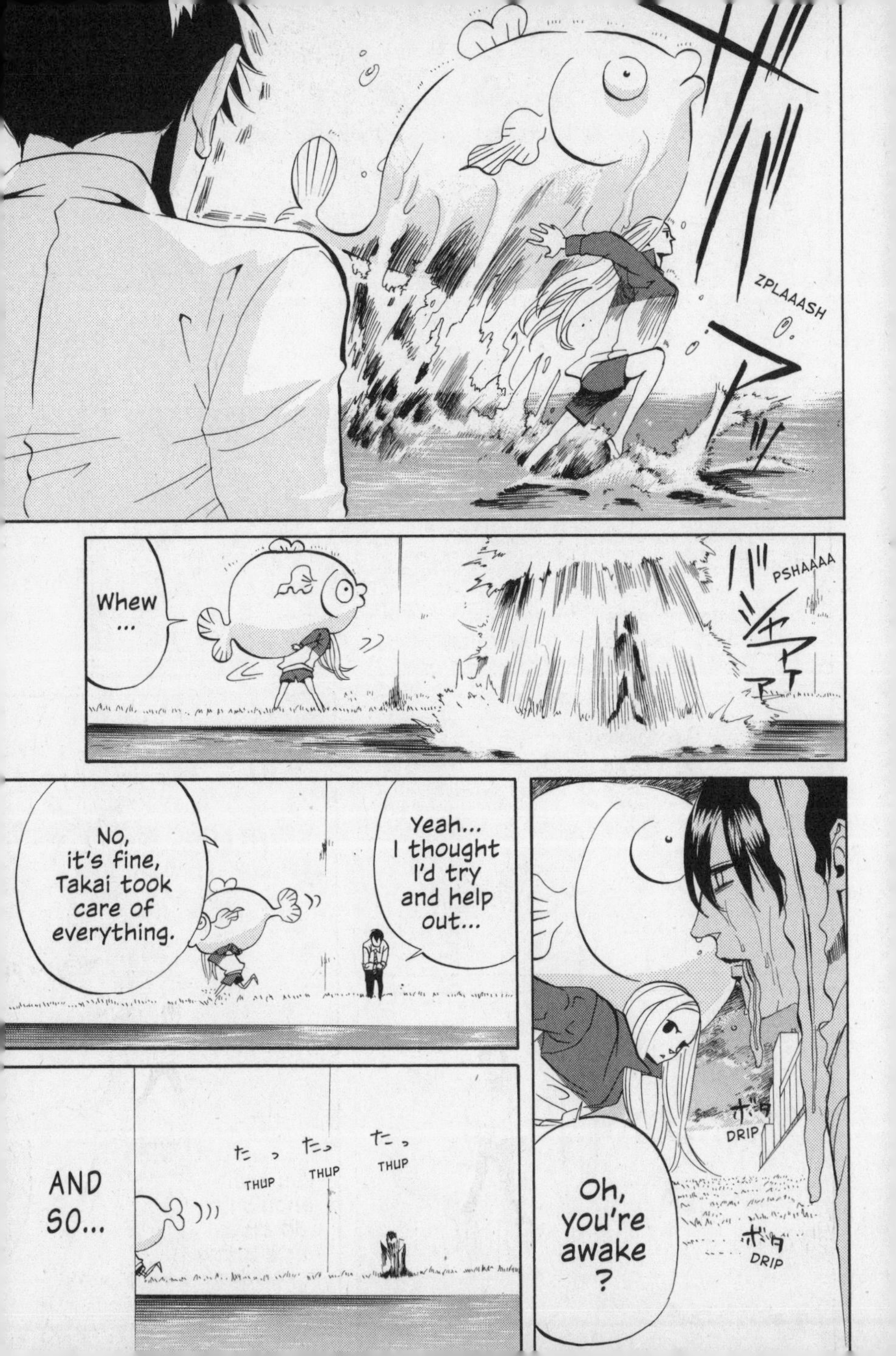
ZPLAAASH
PSHAAAA
Whew ...
ボタ
DRIP
ボタ
DRIP
Oh, you're awake ?
Yeah... I thought I'd try and help out...
No, it's fine, Takai took care of everything.
たっ たっ たっ
THUP THUP THUP
AND SO...

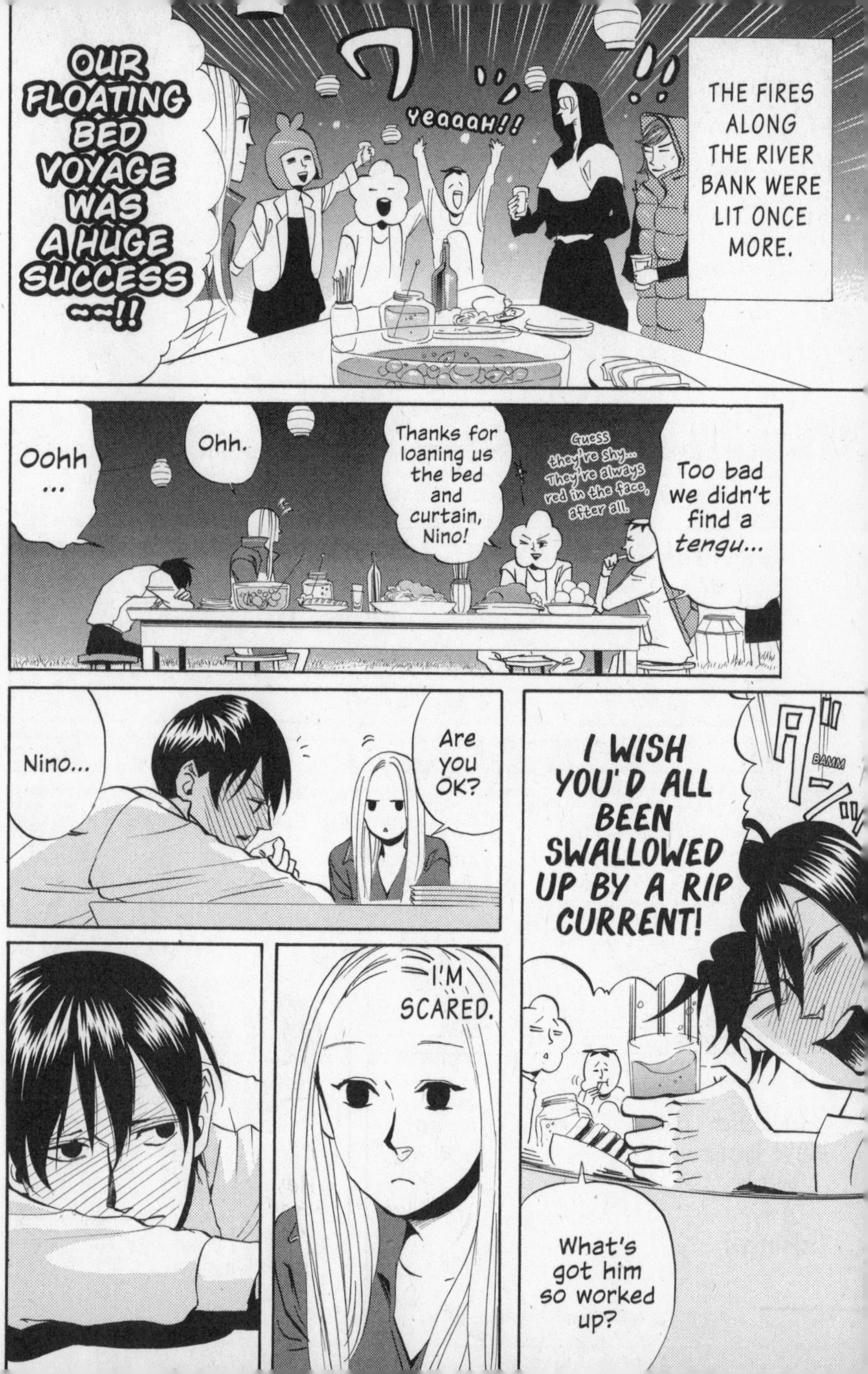
THE FIRES ALONG THE RIVER BANK WERE LIT ONCE MORE.
Yeaaah!!
OUR FLOATING BED VOYAGE WAS A HUGE SUCCESS~~!!
Too bad we didn't find a *tengu*...
Guess they're shy... They're always red in the face, after all.
Thanks for loaning us the bed and curtain, Nino!
Ohh.
Oohh...
BAMM
I WISH YOU'D ALL BEEN SWALLOWED UP BY A RIP CURRENT!
Are you OK?
Nino...
What's got him so worked up?
I'M SCARED.

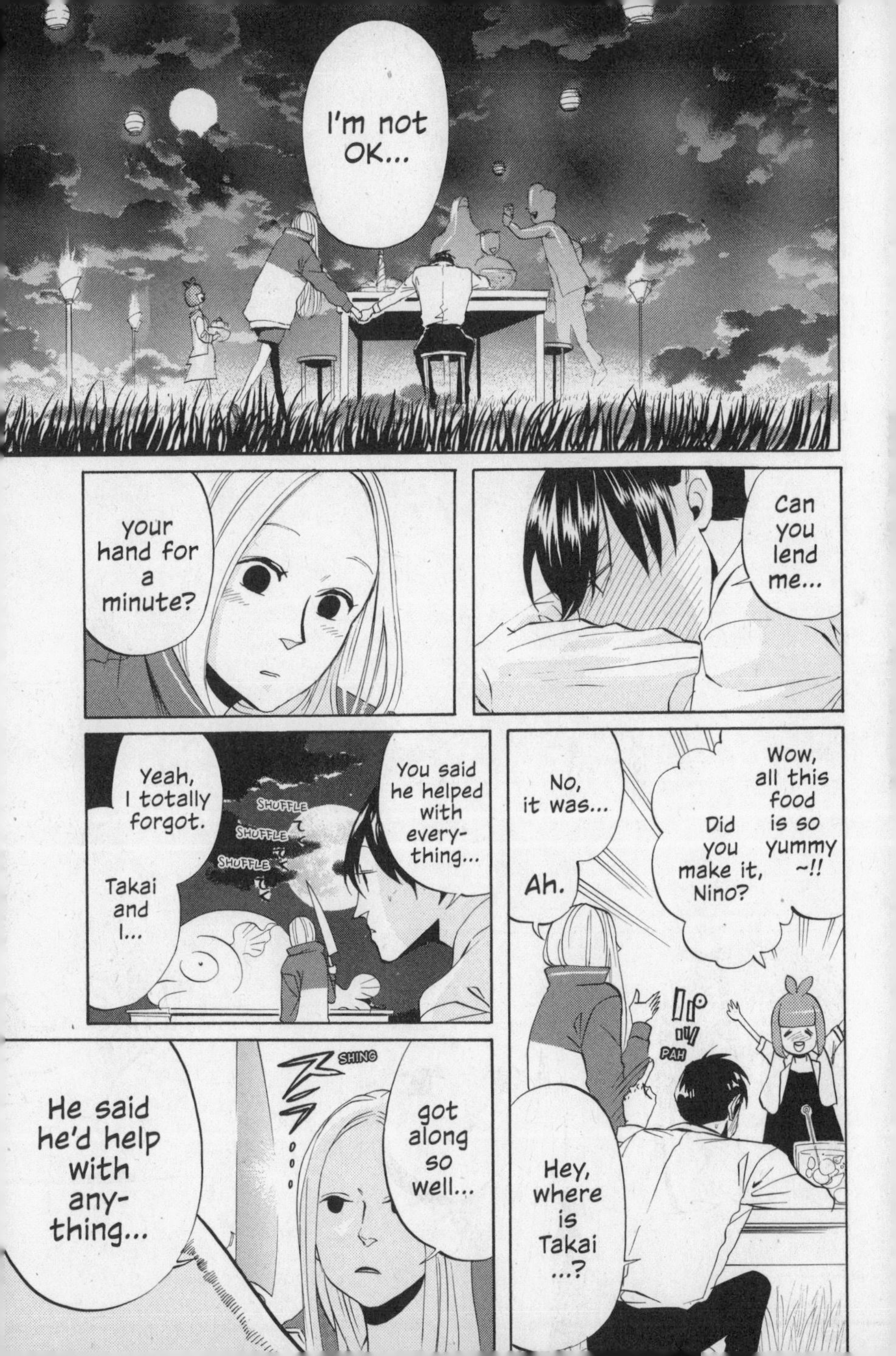
I'm not OK...
Can you lend me...
your hand for a minute?
Wow, all this food is so yummy~!!
Did you make it, Nino?
No, it was...
Ah.
PAH
Hey, where is Takai...?
You said he helped with every-thing...
Yeah, I totally forgot.
SHUFFLE
SHUFFLE
SHUFFLE
Takai and I...
got along so well...
SHING
He said he'd help with any-thing...

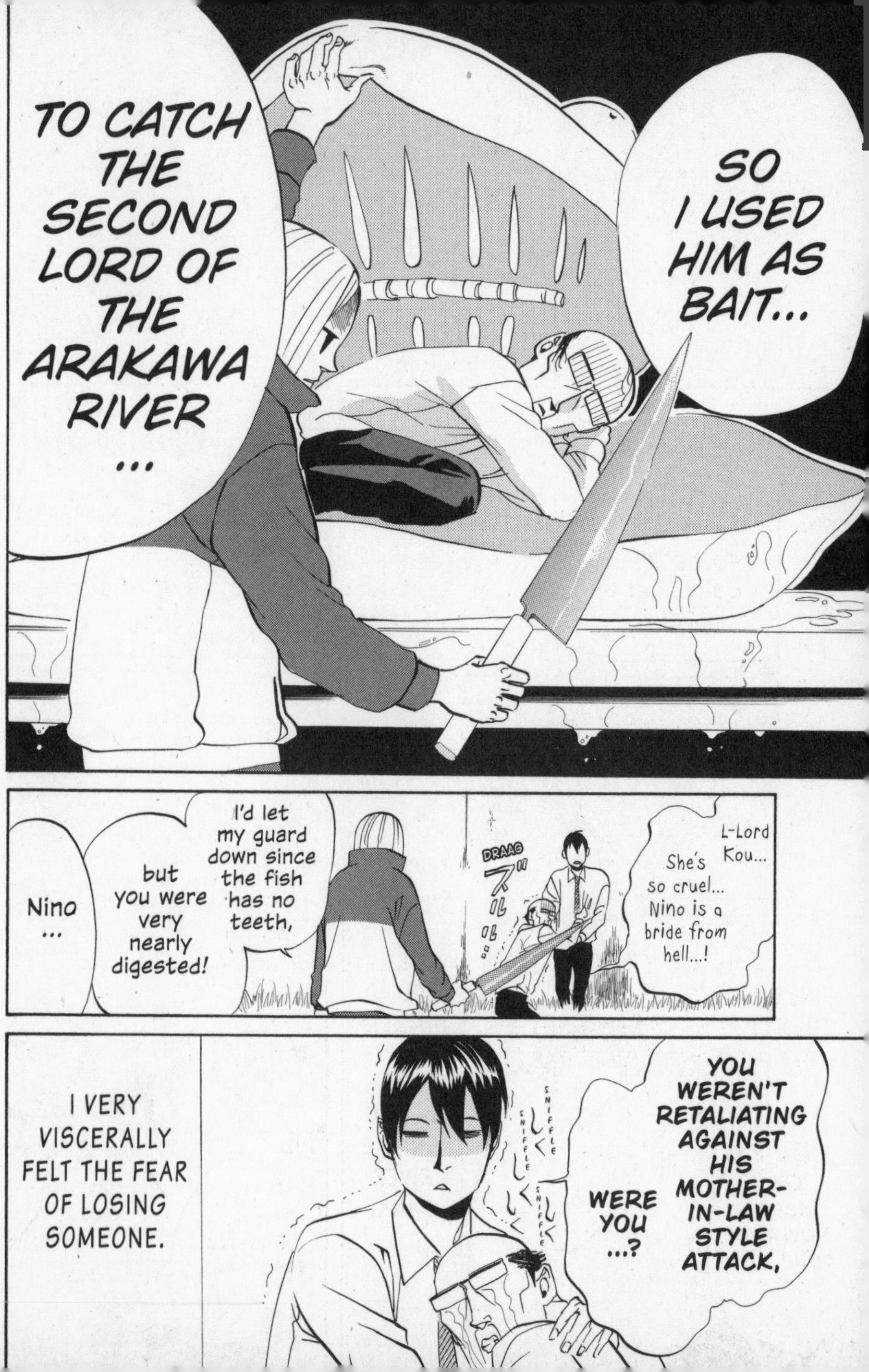
SO I USED HIM AS BAIT...
TO CATCH THE SECOND LORD OF THE ARAKAWA RIVER ...
L-Lord Kou...
She's so cruel... Nino is a bride from hell...!
DRAAG
I'd let my guard down since the fish has no teeth,
but you were very nearly digested!
Nino ...
YOU WEREN'T RETALIATING AGAINST HIS MOTHER-IN-LAW STYLE ATTACK,
WERE YOU ...?
SNIFFLE
SNIFFLE
I VERY VISCERALLY FELT THE FEAR OF LOSING SOMEONE.

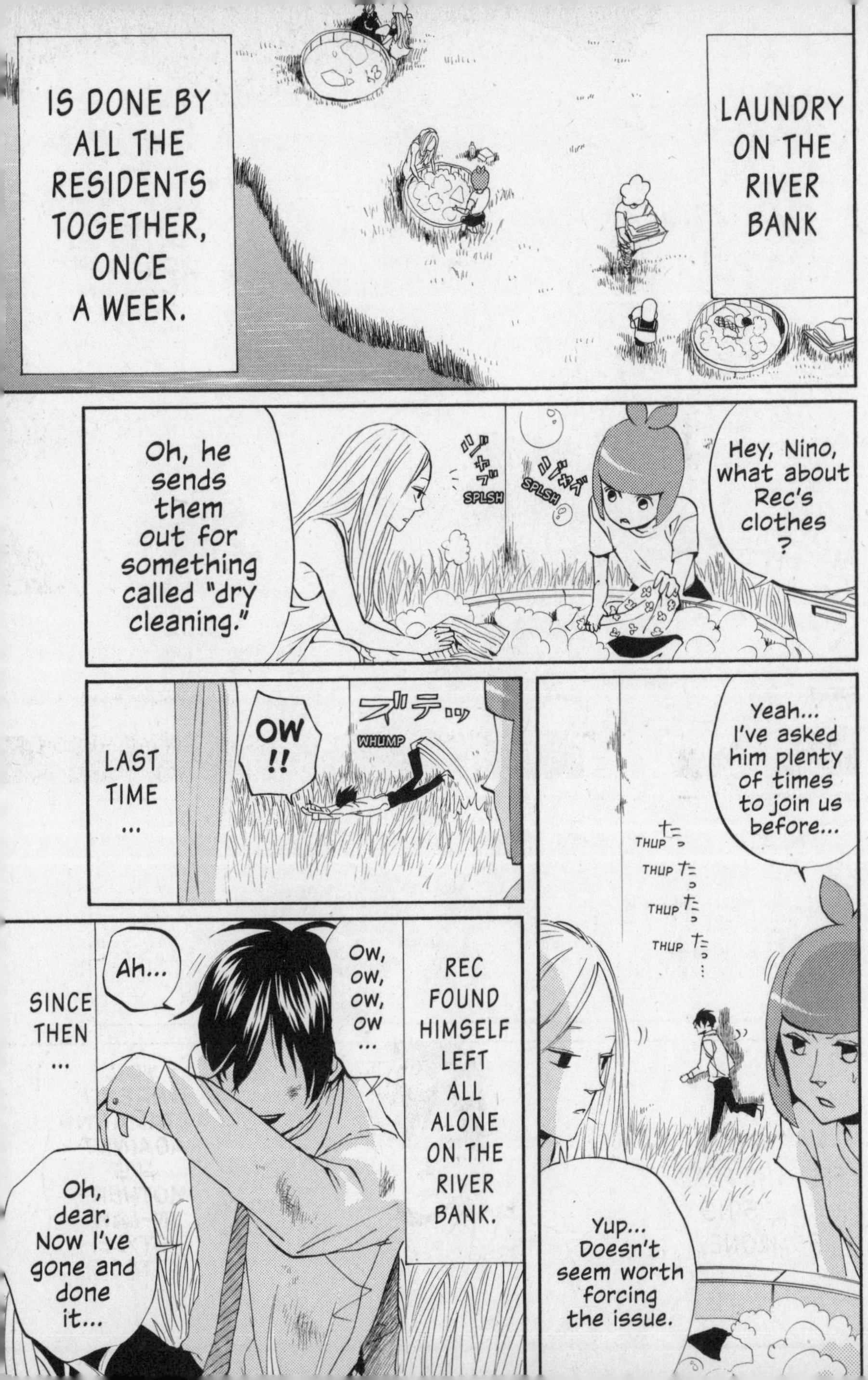
LAUNDRY ON THE RIVER BANK
IS DONE BY ALL THE RESIDENTS TOGETHER, ONCE A WEEK.
Hey, Nino, what about Rec's clothes?
SPLSH
SPLSH
Oh, he sends them out for something called "dry cleaning."
Yeah... I've asked him plenty of times to join us before...
THUP
THUP
THUP
THUP
Yup... Doesn't seem worth forcing the issue.
LAST TIME...
WHUMP
OW!!
REC FOUND HIMSELF LEFT ALL ALONE ON THE RIVER BANK.
Ow, ow, ow, ow...
Ah...
SINCE THEN...
Oh, dear. Now I've gone and done it...

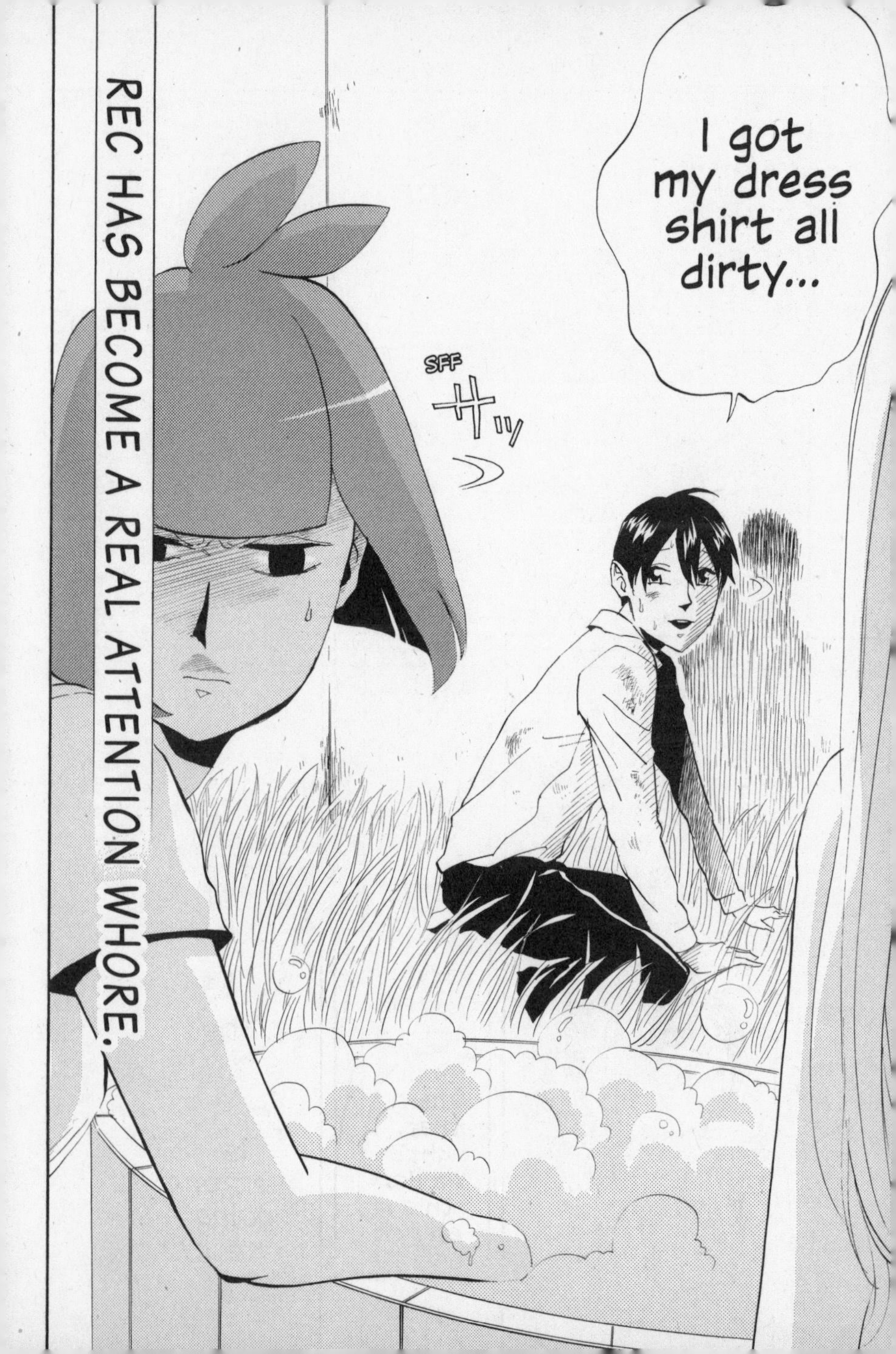
I got my dress shirt all dirty...
SFF
サッ
REC HAS BECOME A REAL ATTENTION WHORE.

Chapter 140: Laundry

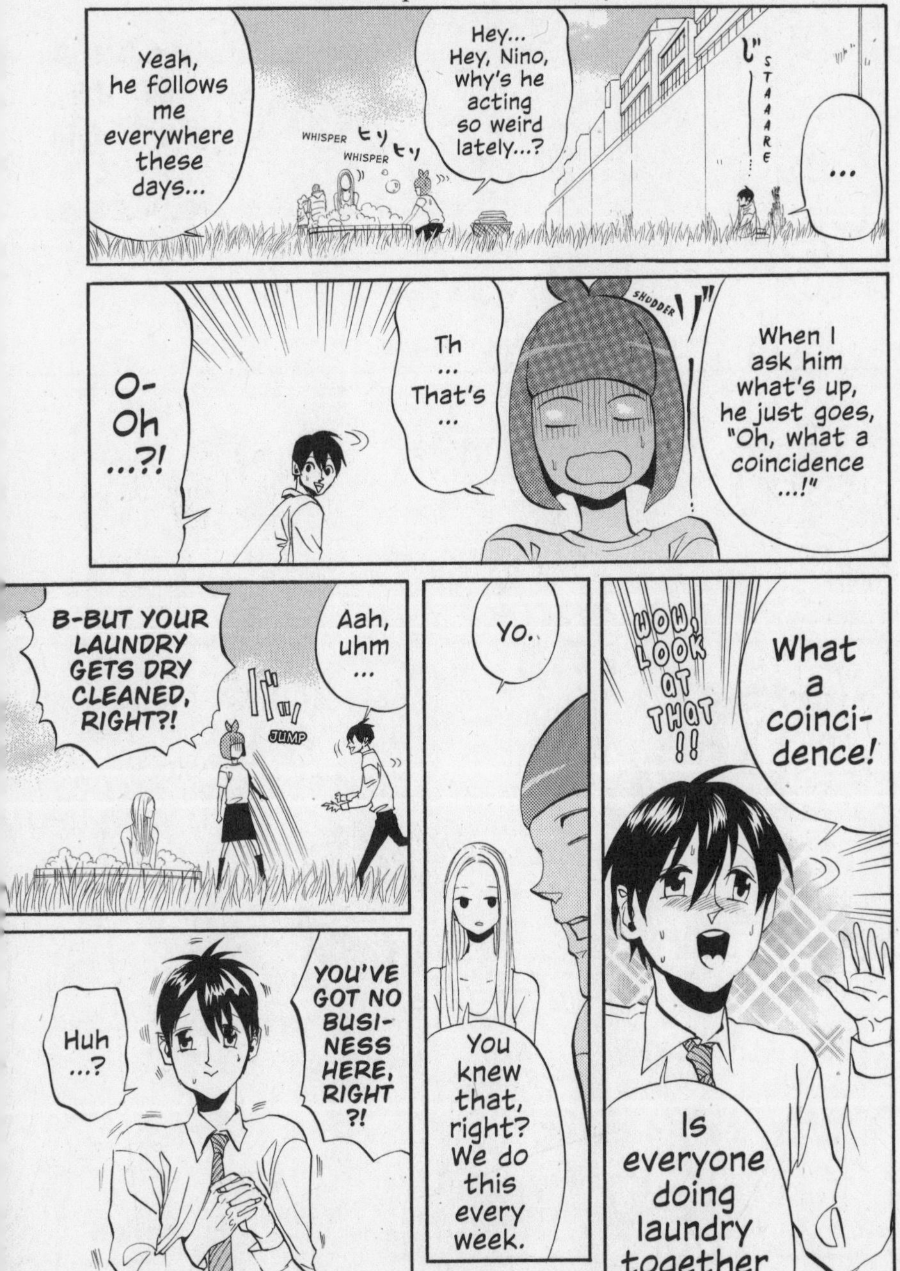
...
STAAARE
Hey... Hey, Nino, why's he acting so weird lately...?
WHISPER
WHISPER
Yeah, he follows me everywhere these days...
When I ask him what's up, he just goes, "Oh, what a coincidence ...!"
SHUDDER
Th ... That's ...
O-Oh ...?!
What a coincidence!
WOW, LOOK AT THAT!!
Is everyone doing laundry together?
Yo.
You knew that, right? We do this every week.
Aah, uhm ...
JUMP
B-BUT YOUR LAUNDRY GETS DRY CLEANED, RIGHT?!
YOU'VE GOT NO BUSINESS HERE, RIGHT?!
Huh ...?

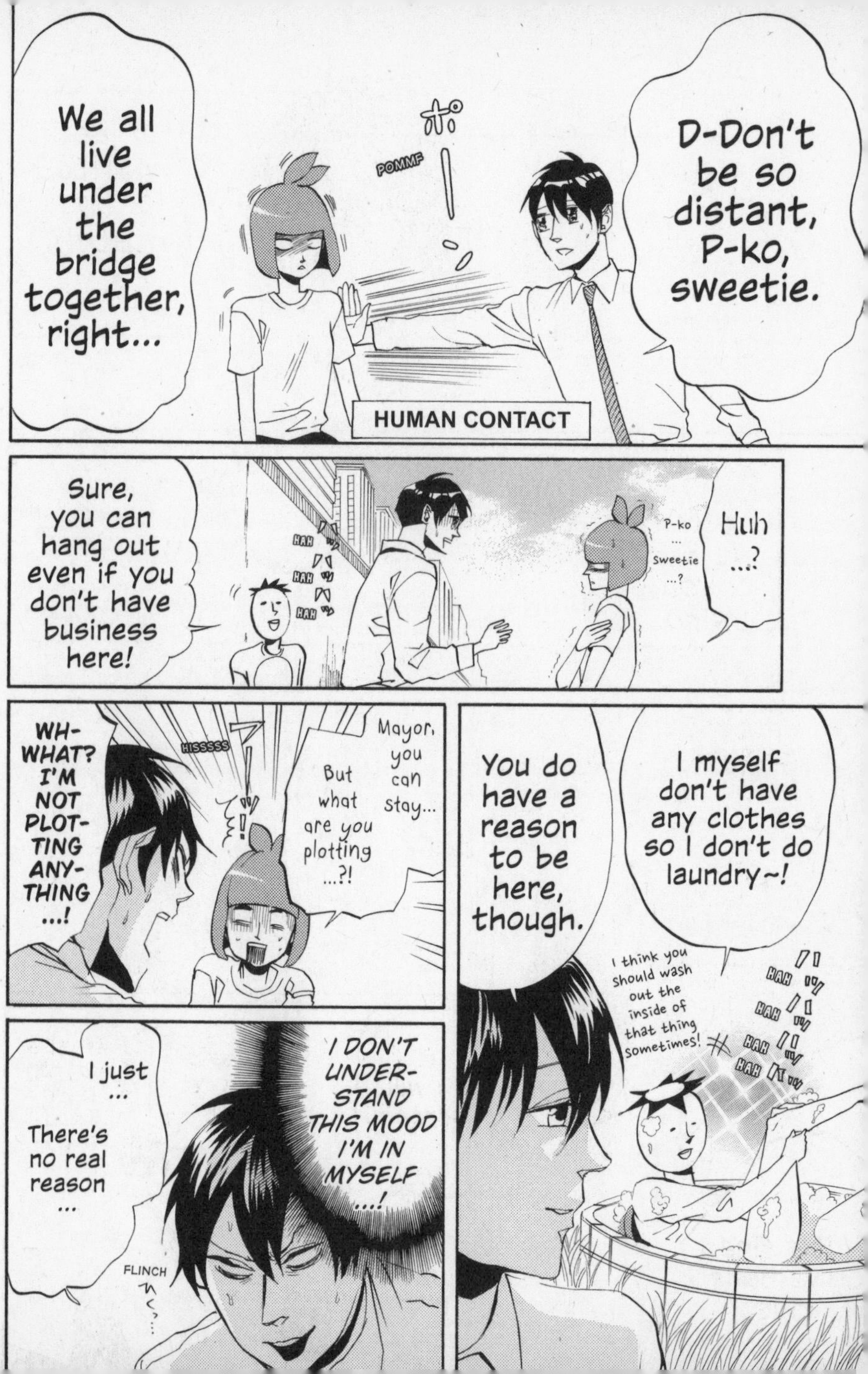
D-Don't be so distant, P-ko, sweetie.
POMMF
We all live under the bridge together, right...
HUMAN CONTACT
Huh ...?
P-ko ... sweetie ...?
HAH HAH HAH
Sure, you can hang out even if you don't have business here!
I myself don't have any clothes so I don't do laundry~!
You do have a reason to be here, though.
I think you should wash out the inside of that thing sometimes!
HAH HAH HAH HAH
Mayor, you can stay...
But what are you plotting ...?!
HISSSSS
WH-WHAT? I'M NOT PLOTTING ANYTHING ...!
I DON'T UNDERSTAND THIS MOOD I'M IN MYSELF ...!
I just ...
There's no real reason ...
FLINCH

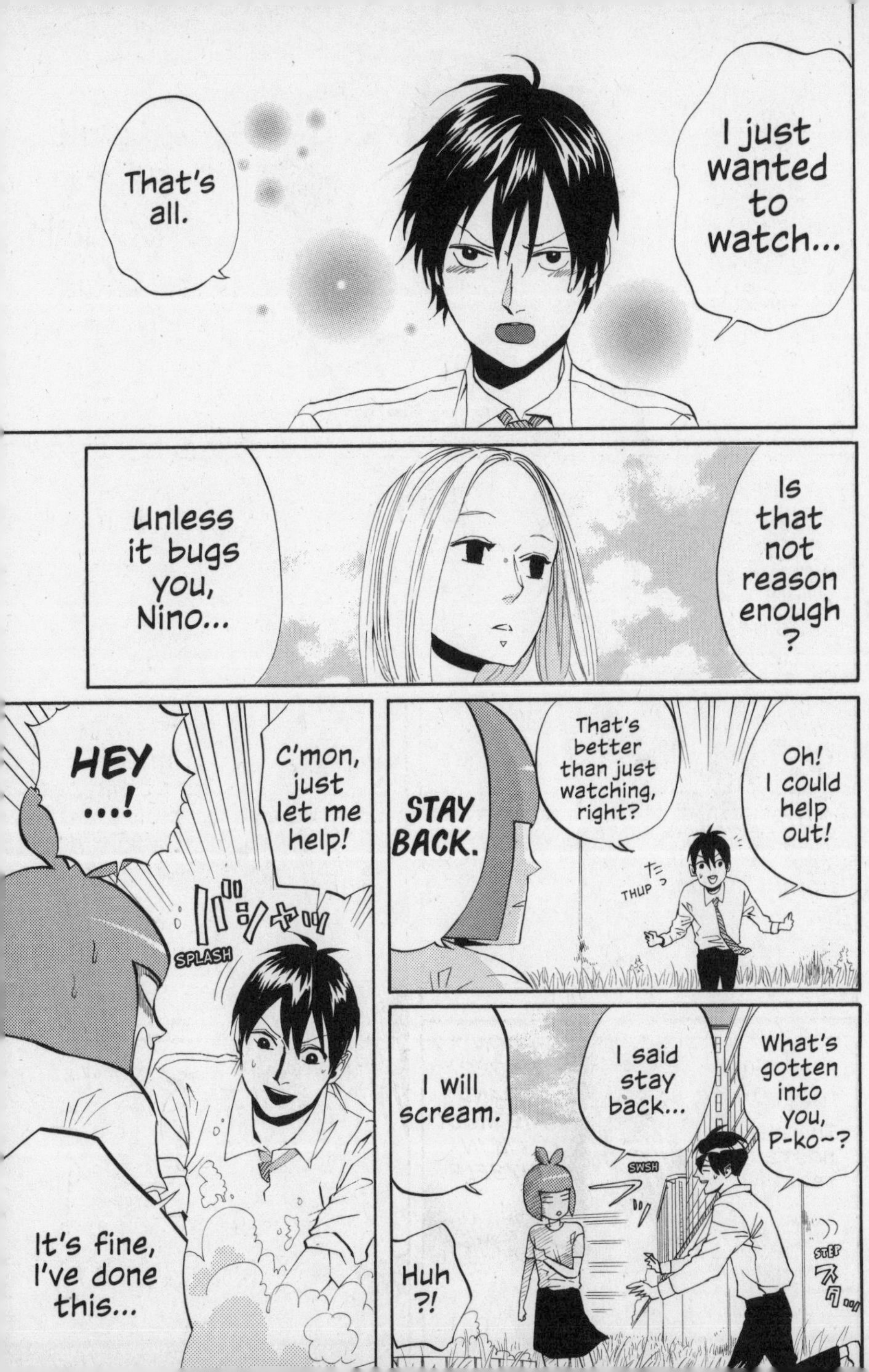
I just wanted to watch...
That's all.
Is that not reason enough?
Unless it bugs you, Nino...
Oh! I could help out!
THUP
That's better than just watching, right?
STAY BACK.
What's gotten into you, P-ko~?
STEP
SWSH
I said stay back...
I will scream.
Huh ?!
C'mon, just let me help!
HEY ...!
SPLASH
It's fine, I've done this...

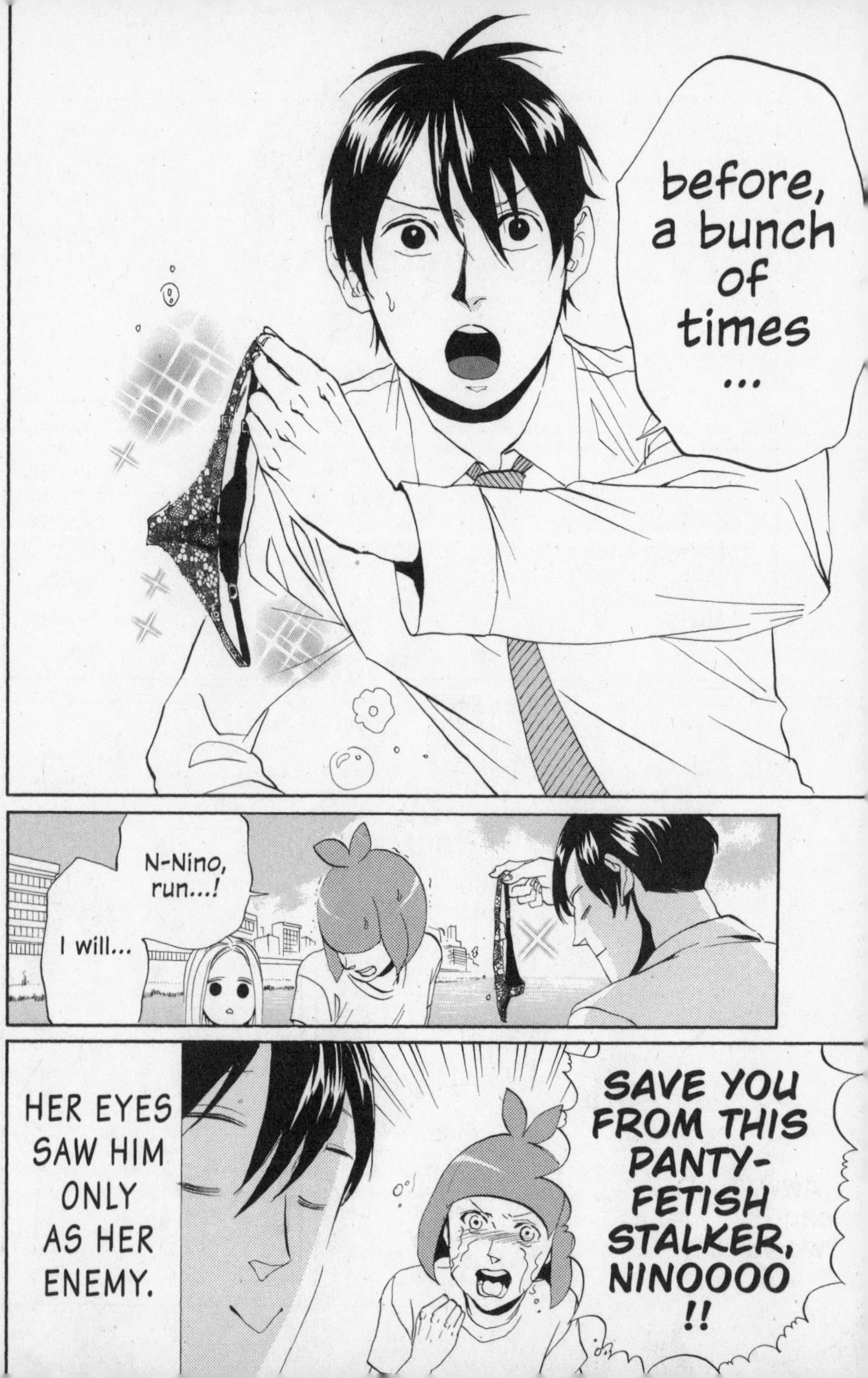
before, a bunch of times ...
N-Nino, run...!
I will...
SAVE YOU FROM THIS PANTY-FETISH STALKER, NINOOOO !!
HER EYES SAW HIM ONLY AS HER ENEMY.

Chapter 141: Dyed Goods

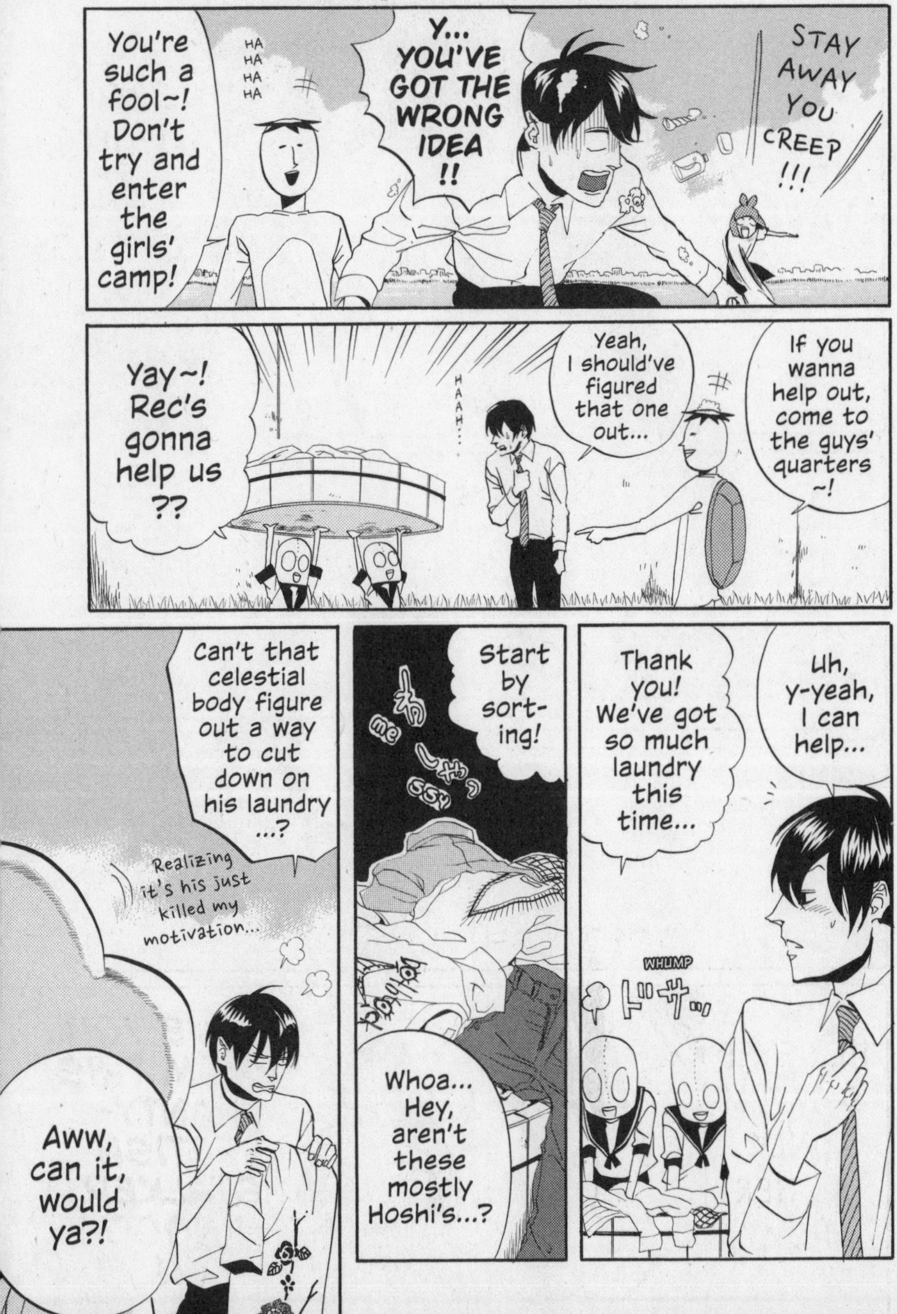

STAY AWAY YOU CREEP!!!
Y... YOU'VE GOT THE WRONG IDEA!!
HA HA HA HA
You're such a fool~! Don't try and enter the girls' camp!
If you wanna help out, come to the guys' quarters~!
Yeah, I should've figured that one out...
HAAH...
Yay~! Rec's gonna help us??
Uh, y-yeah, I can help...
Thank you! We've got so much laundry this time...
WHUMP
Start by sorting!
Whoa... Hey, aren't these mostly Hoshi's...?
Can't that celestial body figure out a way to cut down on his laundry...?
Realizing it's his just killed my motivation...
Aww, can it, would ya?!

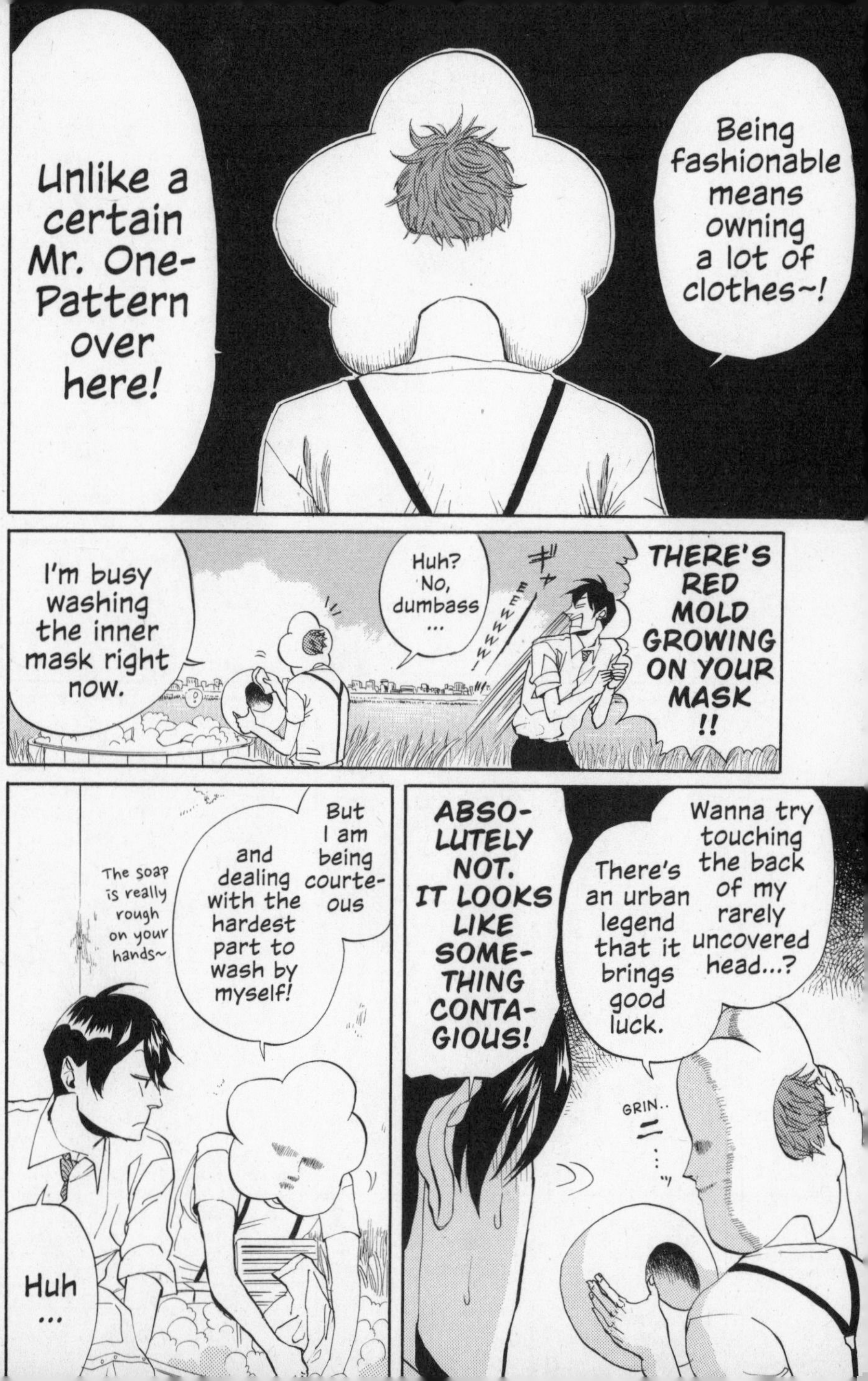
Being fashionable means owning a lot of clothes~!
Unlike a certain Mr. One-Pattern over here!
THERE'S RED MOLD GROWING ON YOUR MASK !!
ギャ
EEWWWW
Huh? No, dumbass ...
I'm busy washing the inner mask right now.
Wanna try touching the back of my rarely uncovered head...?
There's an urban legend that it brings good luck.
GRIN..
ABSOLUTELY NOT. IT LOOKS LIKE SOMETHING CONTAGIOUS!
But I am being courteous
and dealing with the hardest part to wash by myself!
The soap is really rough on your hands~
Huh ...

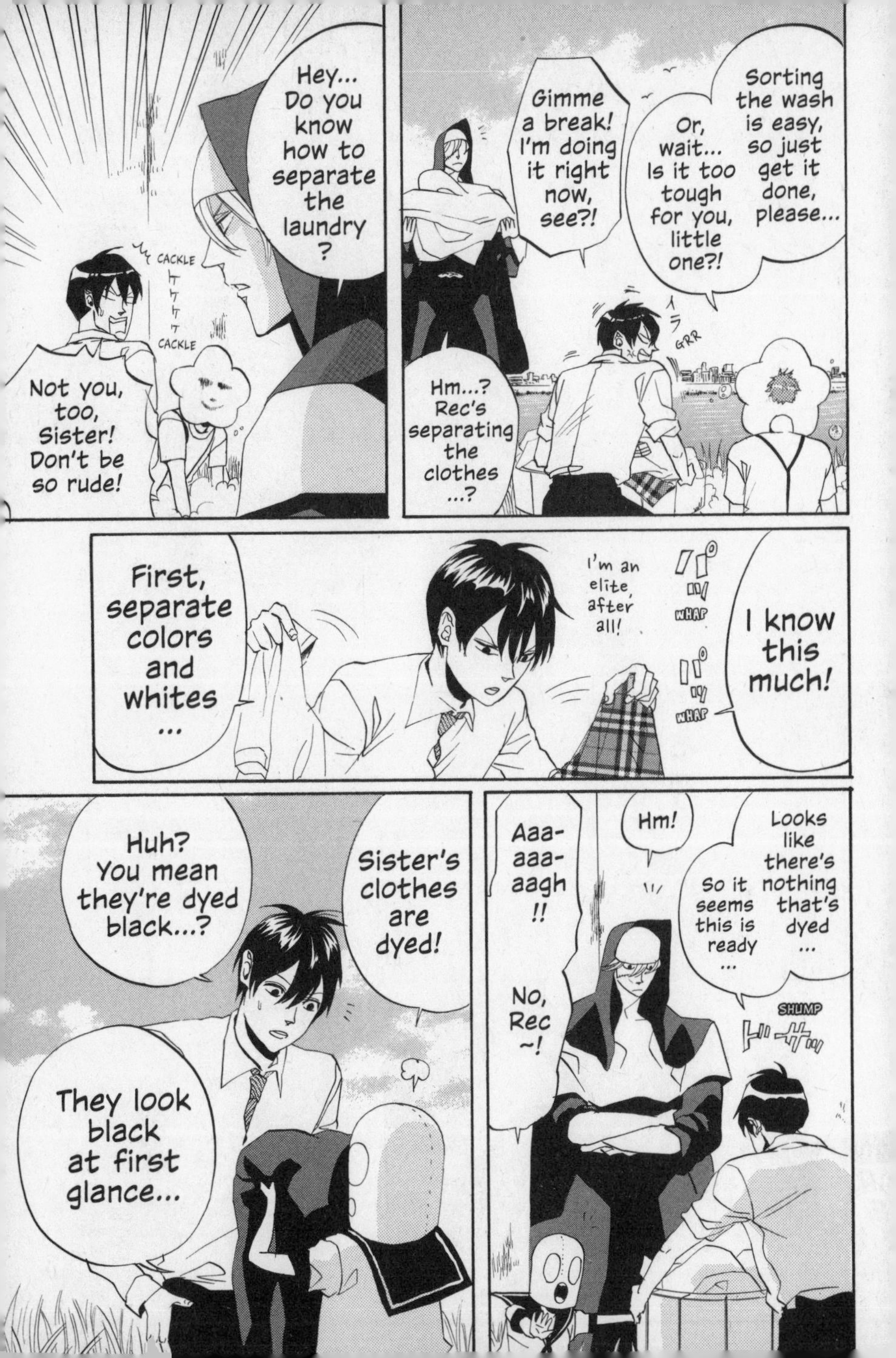
Sorting the wash is easy, so just get it done, please...
Or, wait... Is it too tough for you, little one?!
Gimme a break! I'm doing it right now, see?!
GRR
Hm...? Rec's separating the clothes ...?
Hey... Do you know how to separate the laundry ?
CACKLE
CACKLE
Not you, too, Sister! Don't be so rude!
I know this much!
WHAP
WHAP
I'm an elite, after all!
First, separate colors and whites ...
Looks like there's nothing that's dyed ...
So it seems this is ready ...
Hm!
SHUMP
Aaa-aaa-aagh !!
No, Rec ~!
Sister's clothes are dyed!
Huh? You mean they're dyed black...?
They look black at first glance...

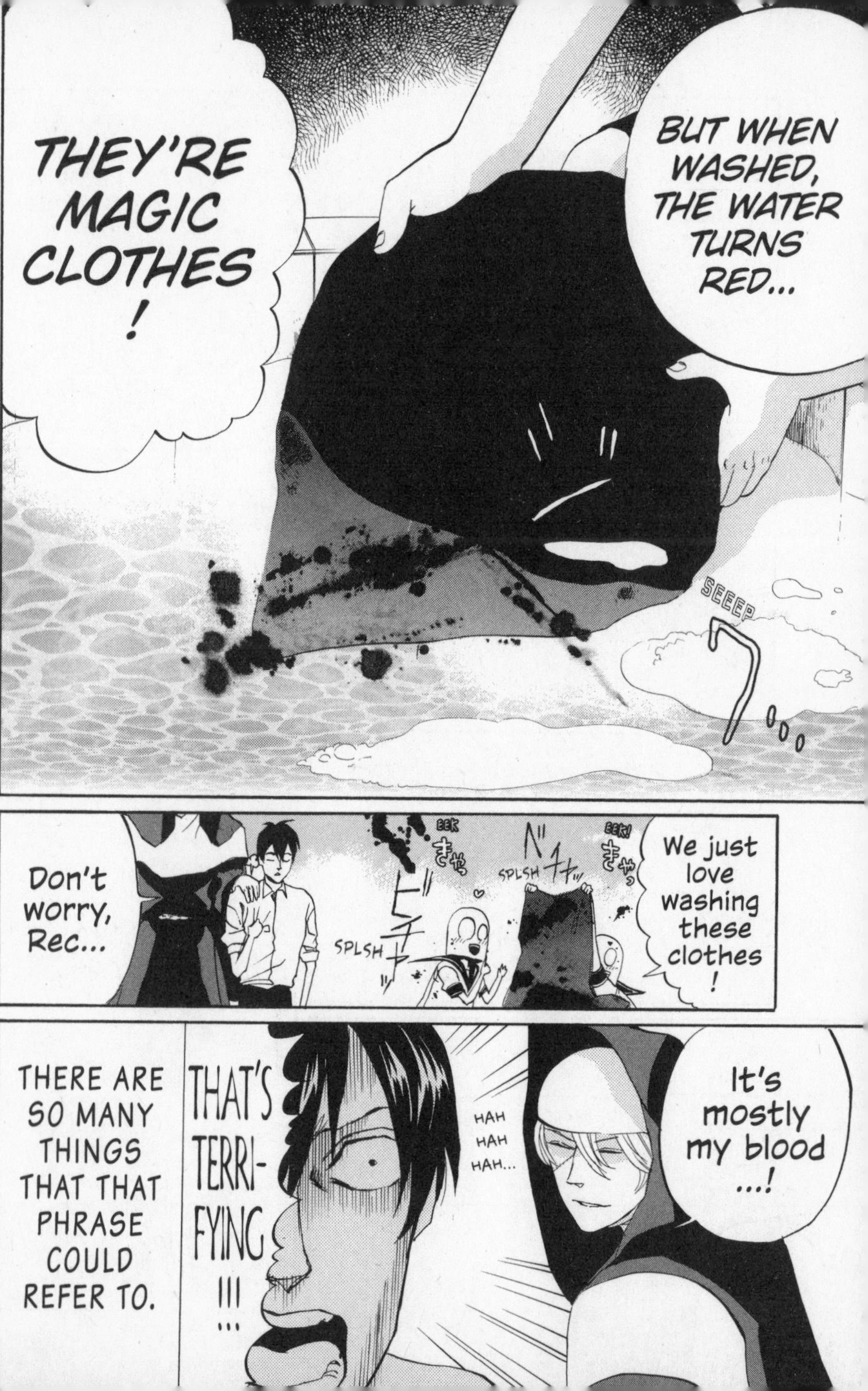
BUT WHEN WASHED, THE WATER TURNS RED...
THEY'RE MAGIC CLOTHES!
SEEEP
We just love washing these clothes!
EEK!
SPLSH
EEK
SPLSH
Don't worry, Rec...
It's mostly my blood...!
HAH HAH HAH...
THAT'S TERRIFYING!!!...
THERE ARE SO MANY THINGS THAT THAT PHRASE COULD REFER TO.

Chapter 142: Big Family

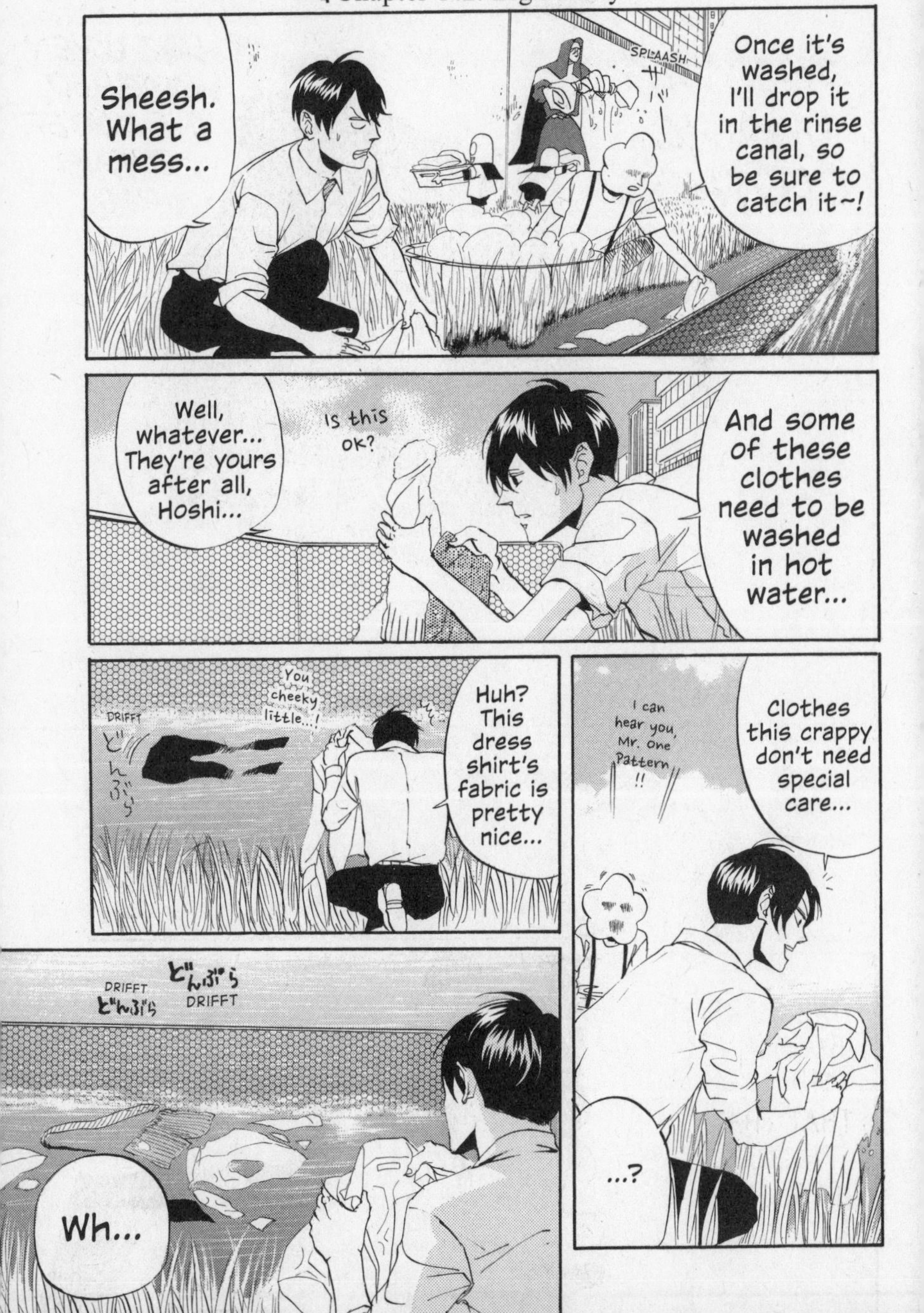
Once it's washed, I'll drop it in the rinse canal, so be sure to catch it~!
SPLAASH
Sheesh. What a mess...
And some of these clothes need to be washed in hot water...
Is this ok?
Well, whatever... They're yours after all, Hoshi...
Clothes this crappy don't need special care...
I can hear you, Mr. One Pattern!!
...?
Huh? This dress shirt's fabric is pretty nice...
You cheeky little...!
DRIFFT
どんぶら
どんぶら
DRIFFT
DRIFFT
どんぶら
Wh...

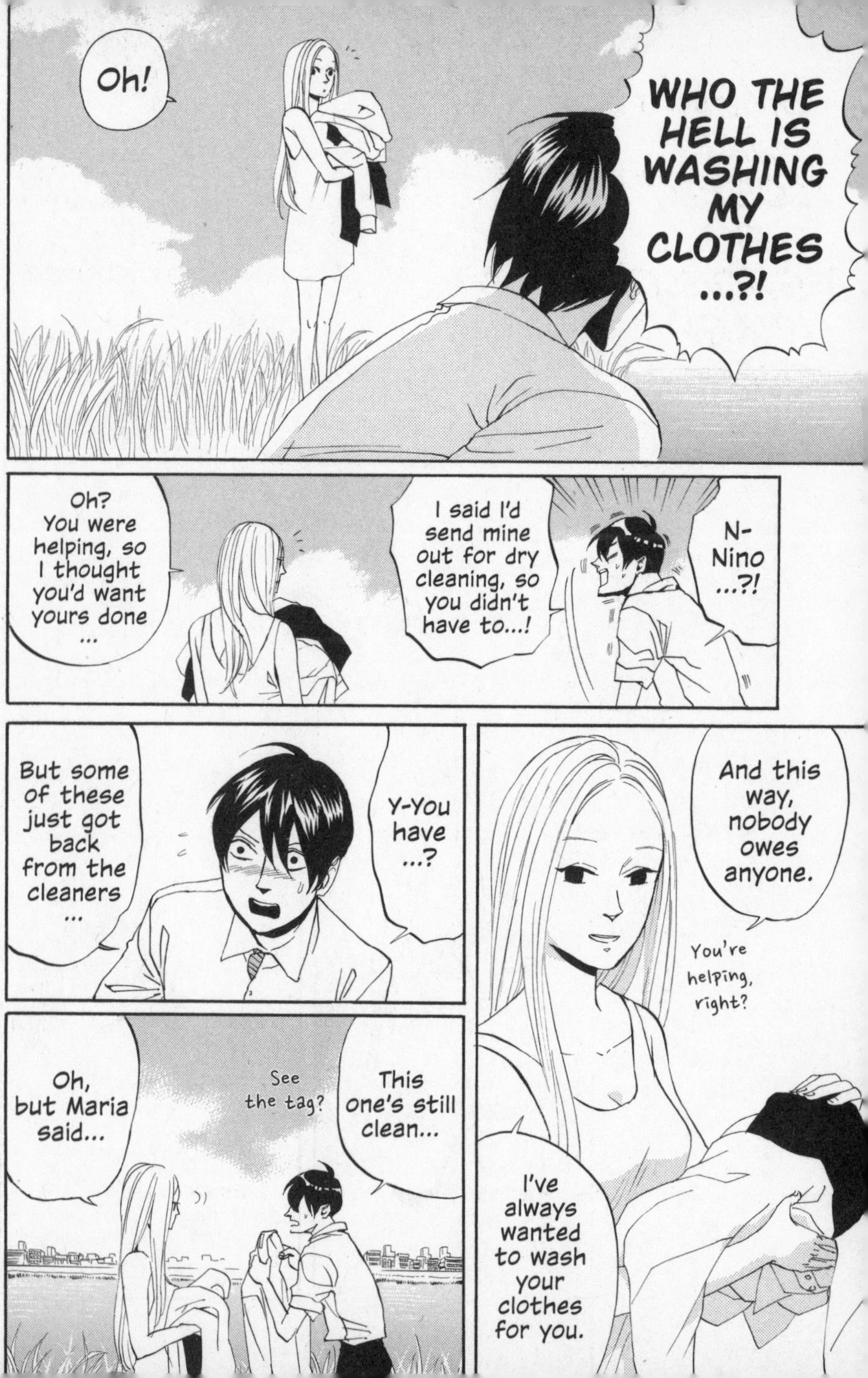
WHO THE HELL IS WASHING MY CLOTHES ...?!
Oh!
N-Nino ...?!
I said I'd send mine out for dry cleaning, so you didn't have to...!
Oh? You were helping, so I thought you'd want yours done ...
And this way, nobody owes anyone.
You're helping, right?
I've always wanted to wash your clothes for you.
Y-You have ...?
But some of these just got back from the cleaners ...
This one's still clean...
See the tag?
Oh, but Maria said...

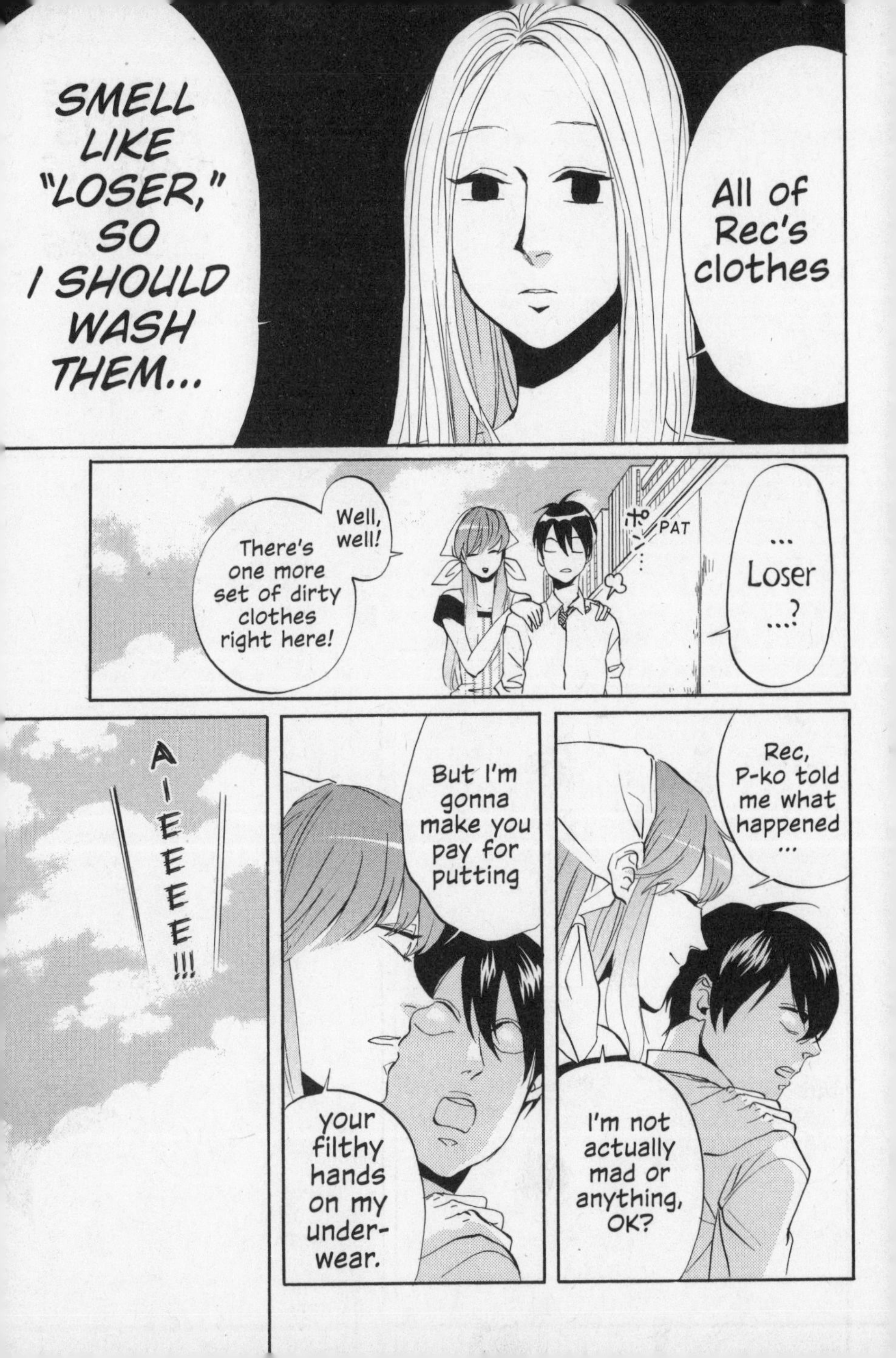
All of Rec's clothes
SMELL LIKE "LOSER," SO I SHOULD WASH THEM...
... Loser ...?
ポン PAT
Well, well! There's one more set of dirty clothes right here!
Rec, P-ko told me what happened ...
I'm not actually mad or anything, OK?
But I'm gonna make you pay for putting
your filthy hands on my under-wear.
AIEEEEE!!!

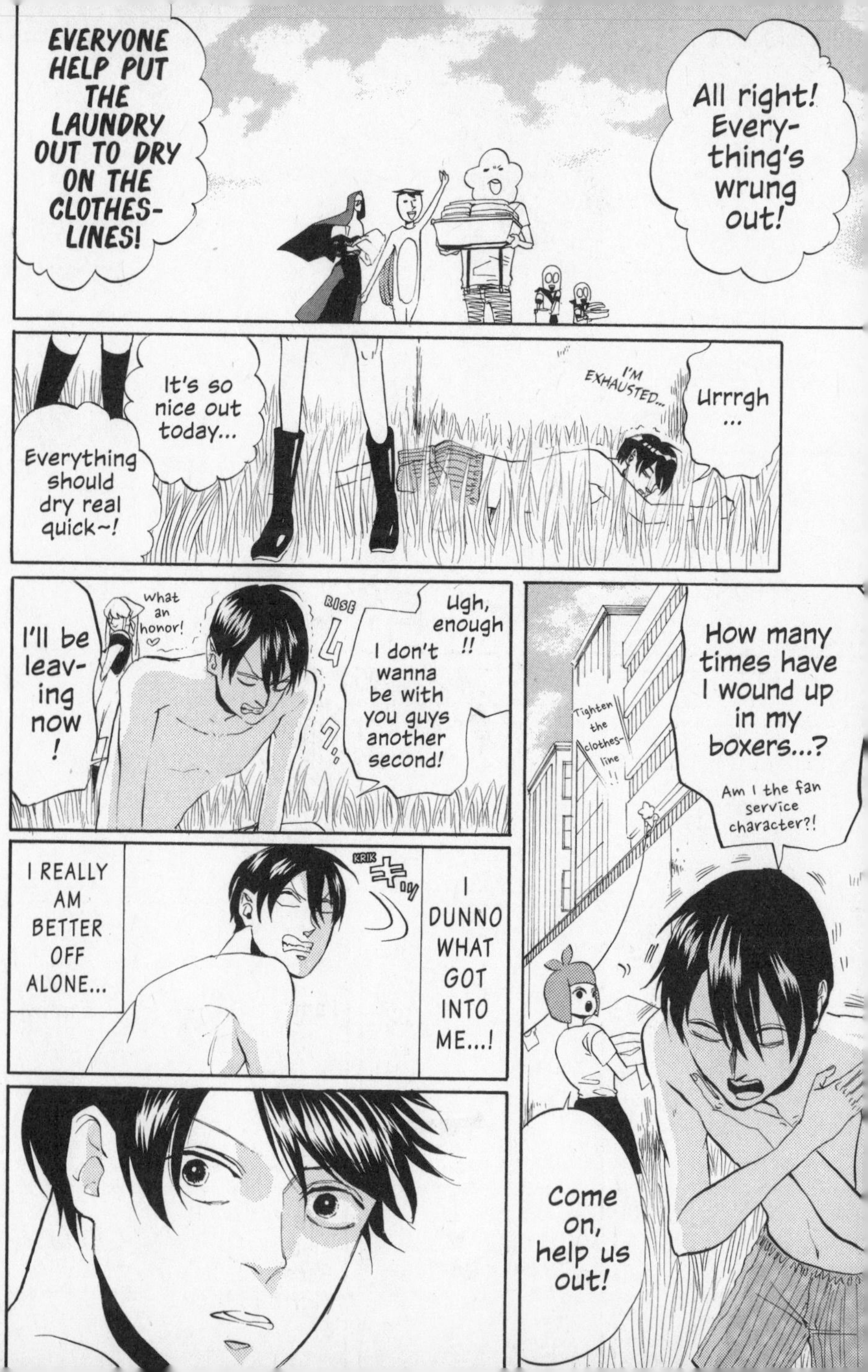
All right! Everything's wrung out!
EVERYONE HELP PUT THE LAUNDRY OUT TO DRY ON THE CLOTHES-LINES!
Urrrgh ...
I'M EXHAUSTED...
It's so nice out today...
Everything should dry real quick~!
How many times have I wound up in my boxers...?
Am I the fan service character?!
Tighten the clothes-line !!
Come on, help us out!
Ugh, enough !!
I don't wanna be with you guys another second!
RISE
I'll be leaving now !
what an honor! ♡
KRIK
I DUNNO WHAT GOT INTO ME...!
I REALLY AM BETTER OFF ALONE...

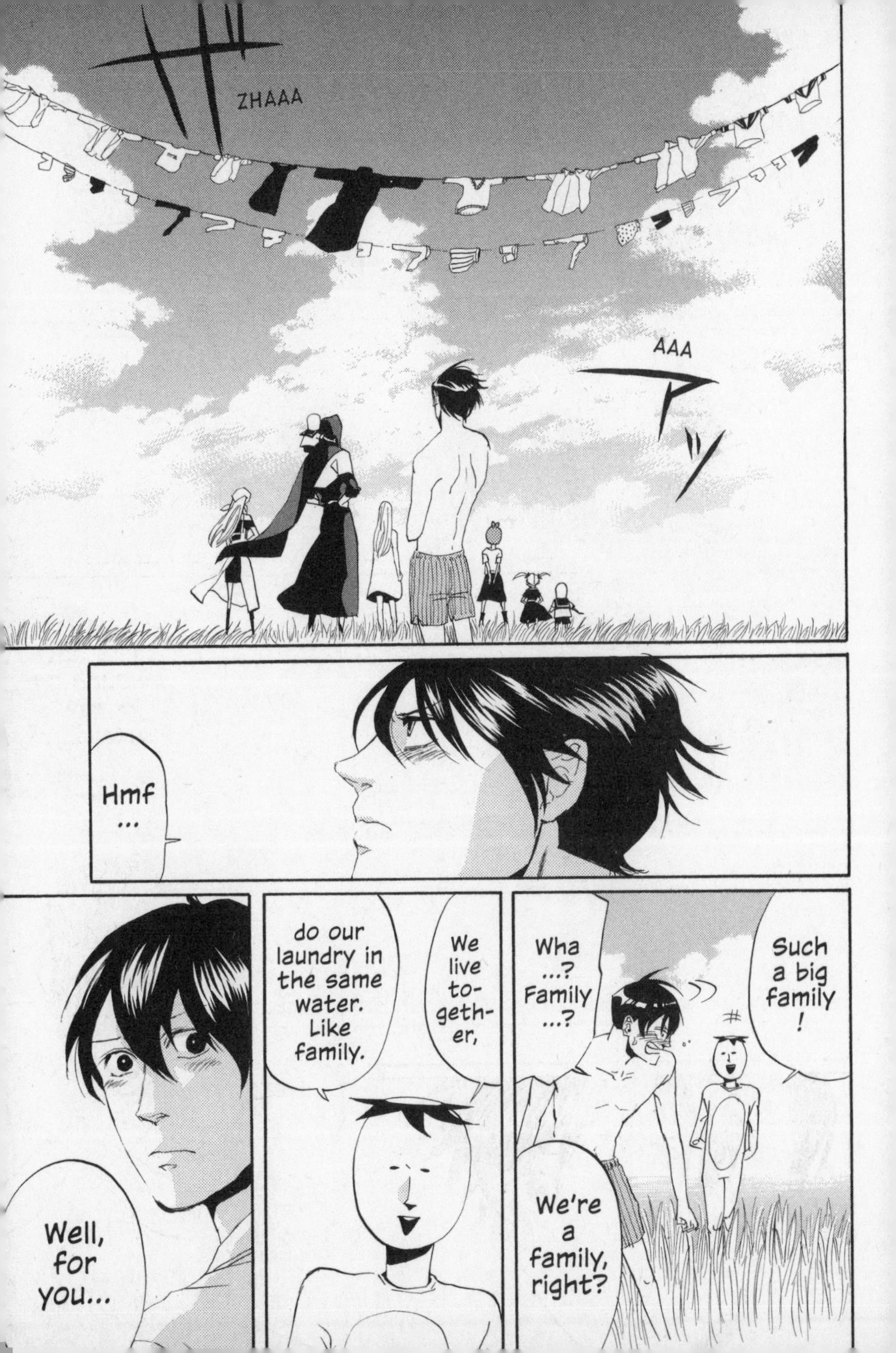
ZHAAA
AAA
Hmf ...
Such a big family!
Wha ...? Family ...?
We're a family, right?
We live to-geth-er,
do our laundry in the same water. Like family.
Well, for you...

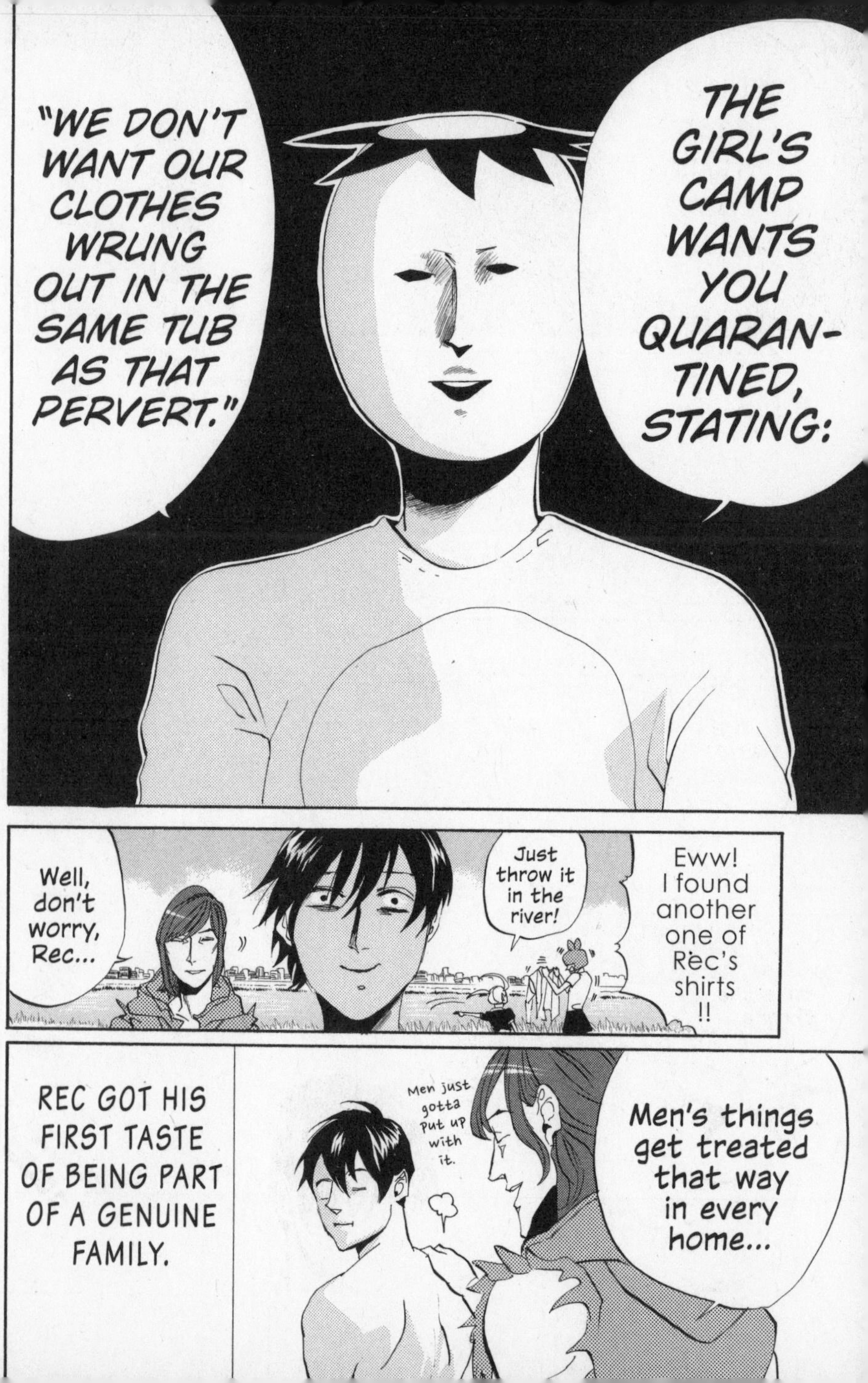
THE GIRL'S CAMP WANTS YOU QUARANTINED, STATING:
"WE DON'T WANT OUR CLOTHES WRUNG OUT IN THE SAME TUB AS THAT PERVERT."
Eww! I found another one of Rec's shirts !!
Just throw it in the river!
Well, don't worry, Rec...
Men's things get treated that way in every home...
Men just gotta put up with it.
REC GOT HIS FIRST TASTE OF BEING PART OF A GENUINE FAMILY.

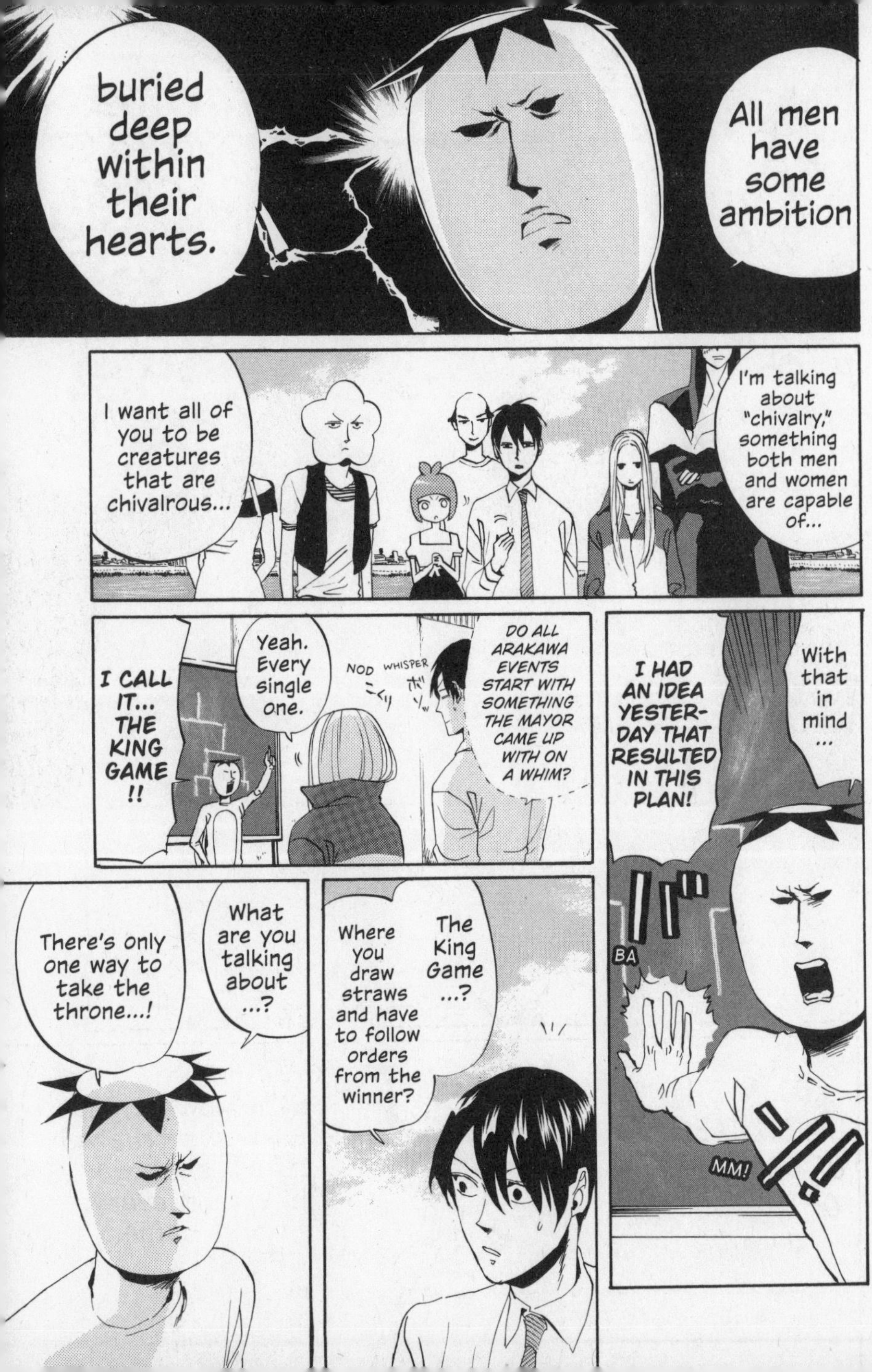
All men have some ambition
buried deep within their hearts.
I'm talking about "chivalry," something both men and women are capable of...
I want all of you to be creatures that are chivalrous...!
With that in mind...
I HAD AN IDEA YESTERDAY THAT RESULTED IN THIS PLAN!
BA
MM!
DO ALL ARAKAWA EVENTS START WITH SOMETHING THE MAYOR CAME UP WITH ON A WHIM?
WHISPER
NOD
Yeah. Every single one.
I CALL IT... THE KING GAME !!
The King Game ...?
Where you draw straws and have to follow orders from the winner?
What are you talking about ...?
There's only one way to take the throne...!

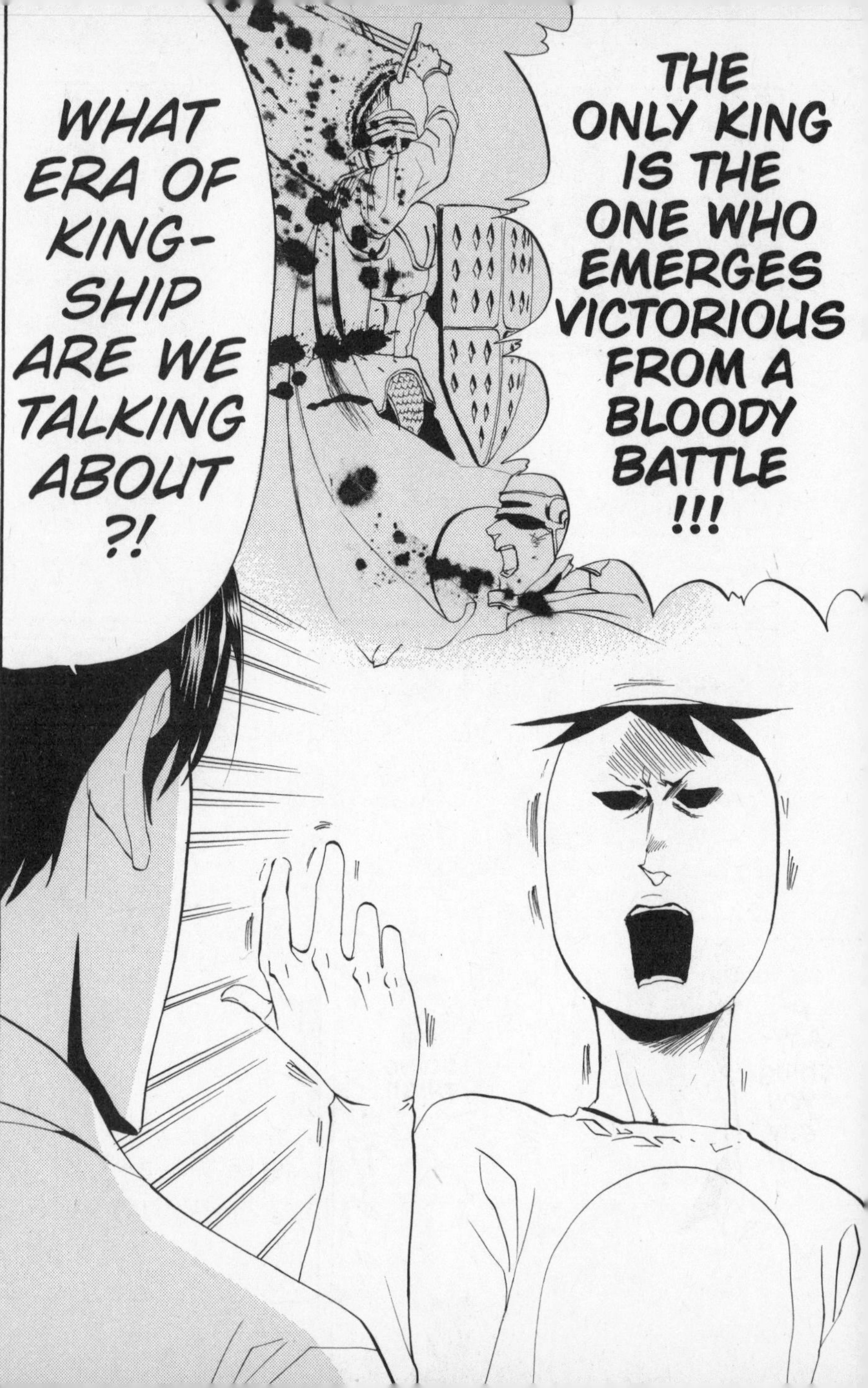
THE ONLY KING IS THE ONE WHO EMERGES VICTORIOUS FROM A BLOODY BATTLE !!!
WHAT ERA OF KING-SHIP ARE WE TALKING ABOUT ?!

Chapter 143: The King's Decree

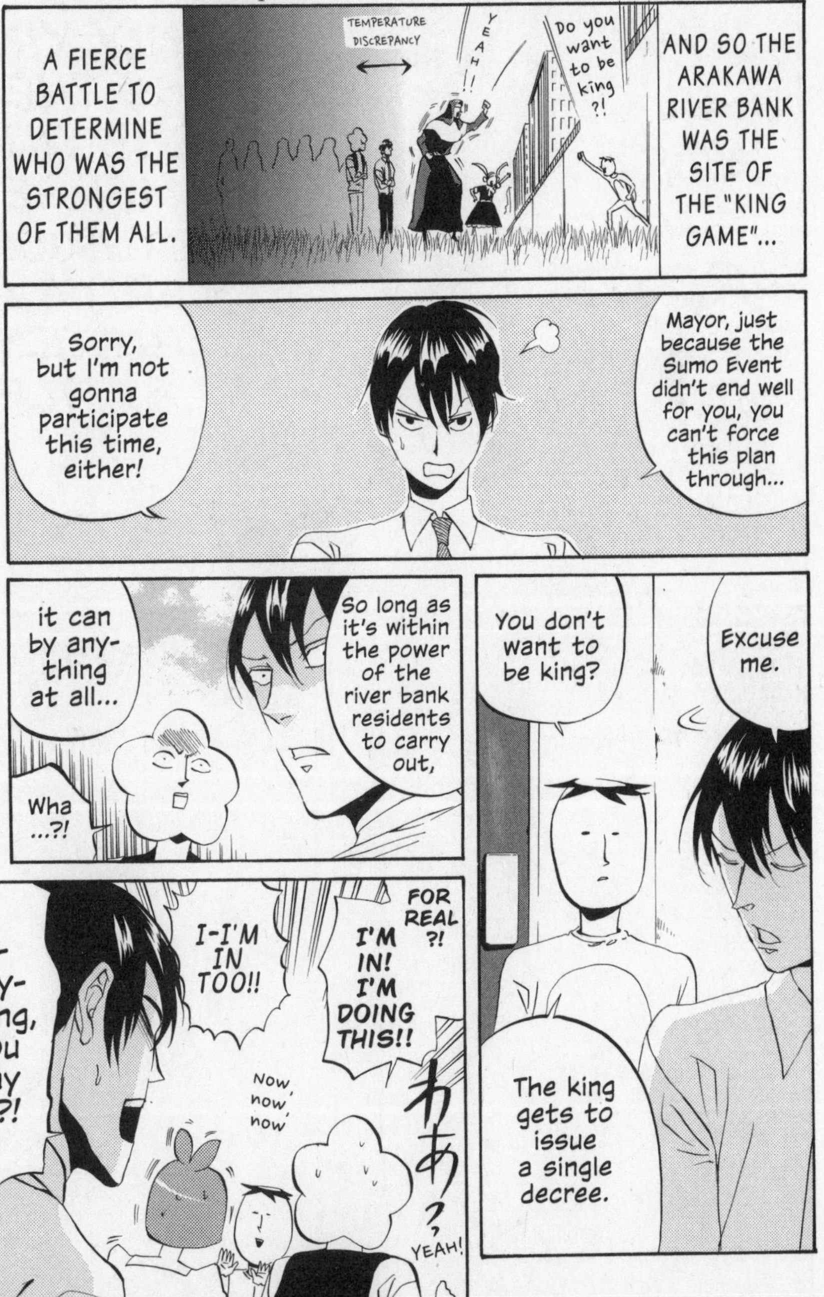
AND SO THE ARAKAWA RIVER BANK WAS THE SITE OF THE "KING GAME"...
Do you want to be king?!
YEAH!!
TEMPERATURE DISCREPANCY
A FIERCE BATTLE TO DETERMINE WHO WAS THE STRONGEST OF THEM ALL.
Mayor, just because the Sumo Event didn't end well for you, you can't force this plan through...
Sorry, but I'm not gonna participate this time, either!
Excuse me.
You don't want to be king?
The king gets to issue a single decree.
So long as it's within the power of the river bank residents to carry out,
it can by anything at all...
Wha...?!
FOR REAL?!
I'M IN! I'M DOING THIS!!
I-I'M IN TOO!!
A- Any-thing, you say...?!
Now, now, now
わあ
YEAH!

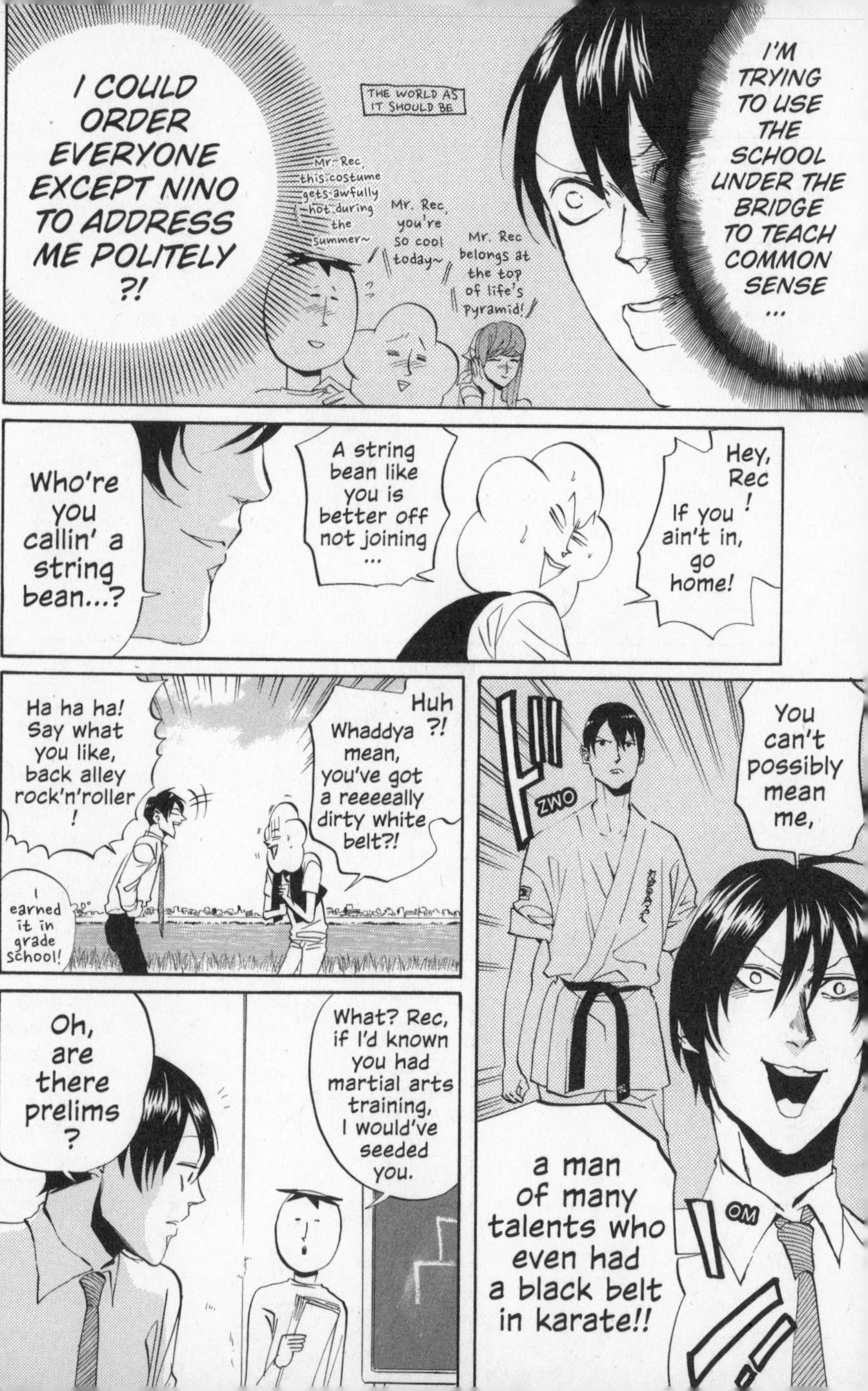
I'M TRYING TO USE THE SCHOOL UNDER THE BRIDGE TO TEACH COMMON SENSE ...
THE WORLD AS IT SHOULD BE
I COULD ORDER EVERYONE EXCEPT NINO TO ADDRESS ME POLITELY ?!
Mr. Rec belongs at the top of life's pyramid!
Mr. Rec, you're so cool today~
Mr. Rec, this costume gets awfully hot during the summer~
Hey, Rec! If you ain't in, go home!
A string bean like you is better off not joining ...
Who're you callin' a string bean...?
You can't possibly mean me,
ZWO
OM
a man of many talents who even had a black belt in karate!!
Huh?! Whaddya mean, you've got a reeeeally dirty white belt?!
Ha ha ha! Say what you like, back alley rock'n'roller!
I earned it in grade school!
What? Rec, if I'd known you had martial arts training, I would've seeded you.
Oh, are there prelims?

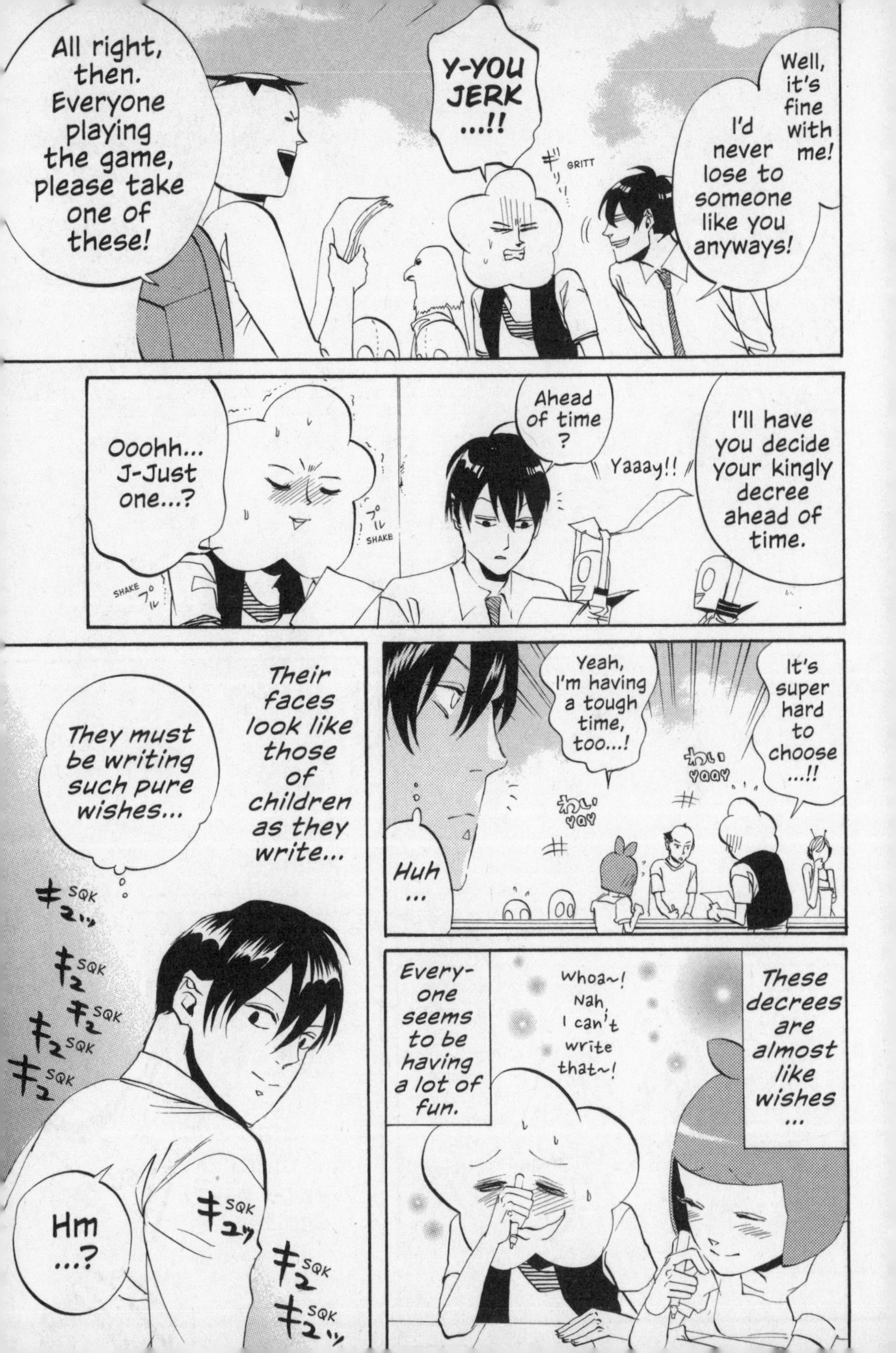

Well, it's fine with me! I'd never lose to someone like you anyways!
GRITT
Y-YOU JERK ...!!
All right, then. Everyone playing the game, please take one of these!
I'll have you decide your kingly decree ahead of time.
Yaaay!!
Ahead of time?
SHAKE
Ooohh... J-Just one...?
SHAKE
It's super hard to choose ...!!
YAAY
Yeah, I'm having a tough time, too...!
YAY
Huh ...
These decrees are almost like wishes ...
Whoa~! Nah, I can't write that~!
Every-one seems to be having a lot of fun.
Their faces look like those of children as they write...
They must be writing such pure wishes...
SQK
SQK
SQK
SQK
SQK
Hm ...?
SQK
SQK
SQK

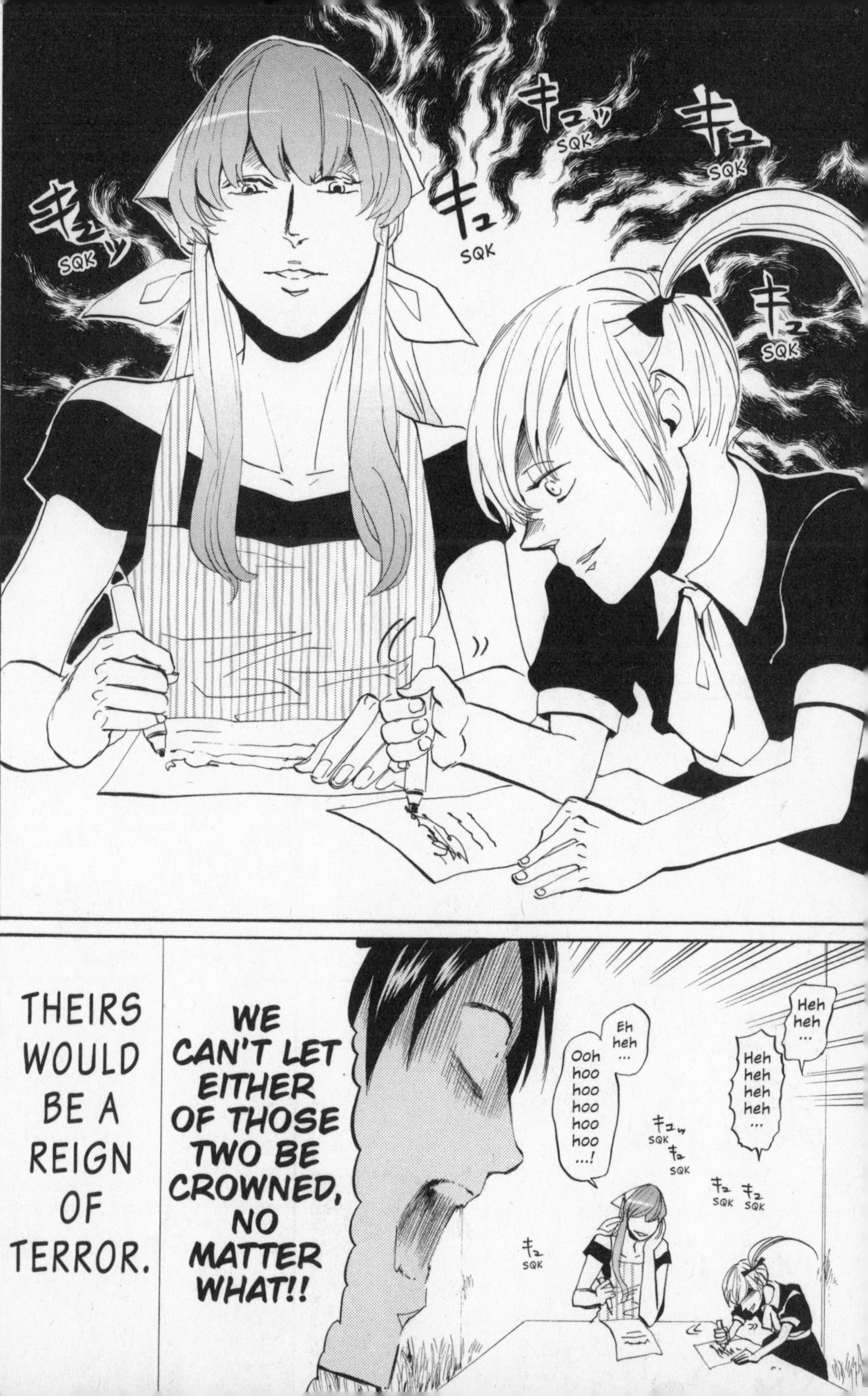
キュッ
SQK
キュッ
SQK
キュ
SQK
キュ
SQK
キュ
SQK
Heh heh ...
Heh heh heh heh ...
Eh heh ...
Ooh hoo hoo hoo hoo hoo ...!
キュッ
SQK
キュ
SQK
キュ
SQK
キュ
SQK
キュ
SQK
WE CAN'T LET EITHER OF THOSE TWO BE CROWNED, NO MATTER WHAT!!
THEIRS WOULD BE A REIGN OF TERROR.

Chapter 144: Prelims Begin

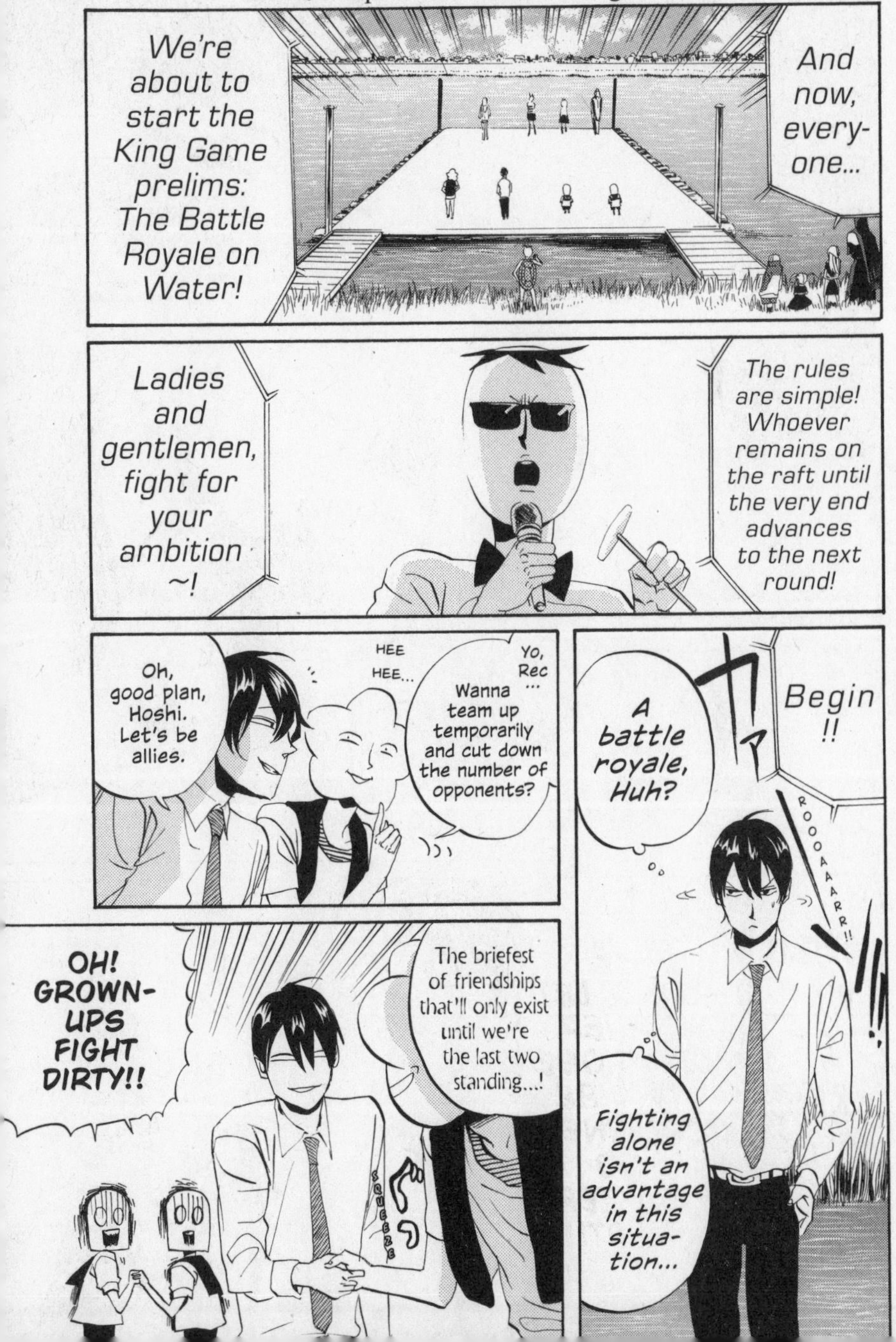

And now, every-one...
We're about to start the King Game prelims: The Battle Royale on Water!
The rules are simple! Whoever remains on the raft until the very end advances to the next round!
Ladies and gentlemen, fight for your ambition ~!
Begin !!
A battle royale, Huh?
ROOOAAARR!!
Fighting alone isn't an advantage in this situa-tion...
Yo, Rec... Wanna team up temporarily and cut down the number of opponents?
HEE HEE...
Oh, good plan, Hoshi. Let's be allies.
The briefest of friendships that'll only exist until we're the last two standing...!
OH! GROWN-UPS FIGHT DIRTY!!
SQUEEZE

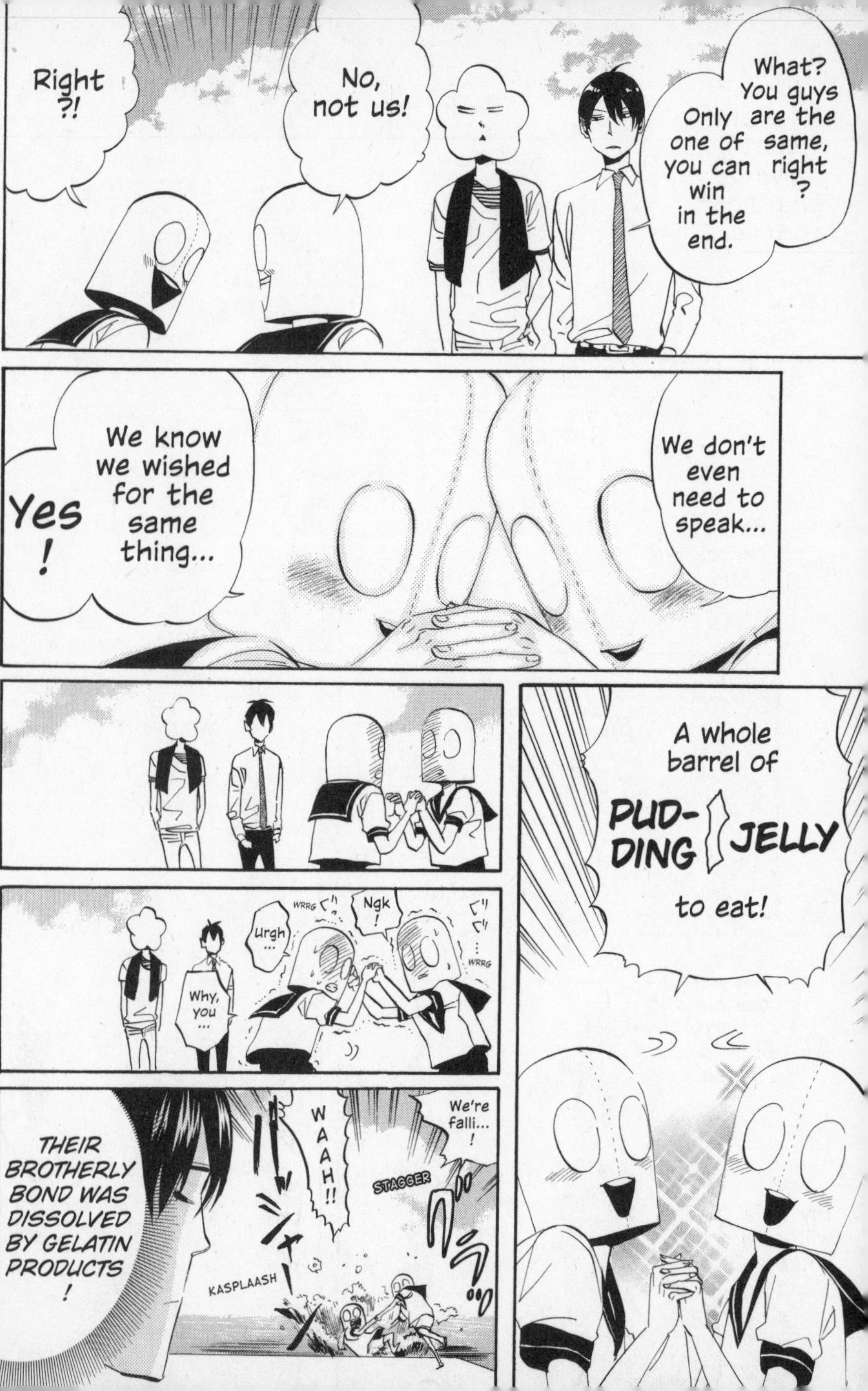
What? You guys are the same, right?
Only one of you can win in the end.
No, not us!
Right?!
We don't even need to speak...
We know we wished for the same thing...
Yes!
A whole barrel of PUDDING JELLY to eat!
Ngk!
WRRG
WRRG
Urgh...
Why, you...
We're falli...!
WAAAH!!
STAGGER
KASPLAASH
THEIR BROTHERLY BOND WAS DISSOLVED BY GELATIN PRODUCTS!

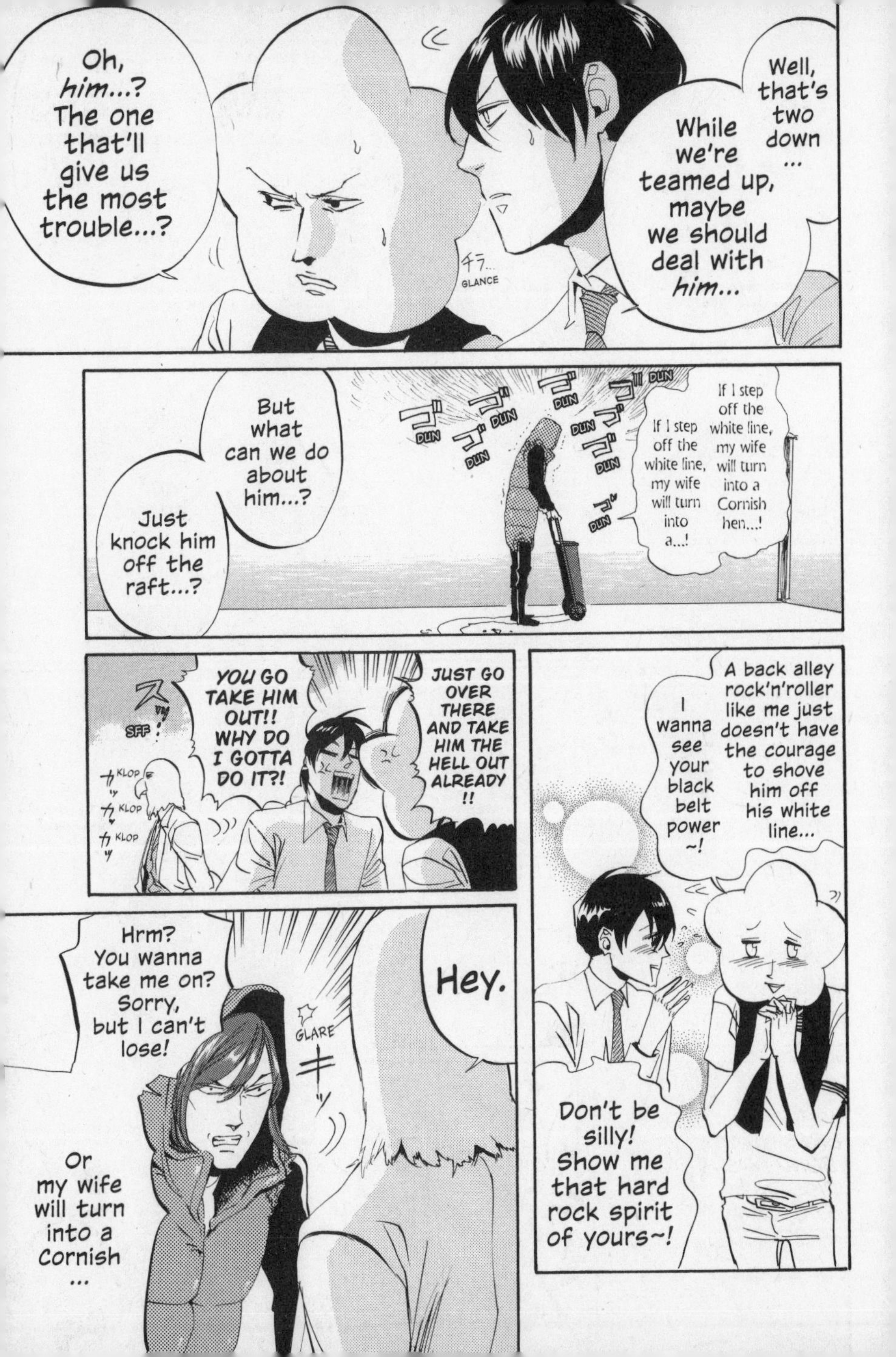

Well, that's two down ...
While we're teamed up, maybe we should deal with *him*...
チラ... GLANCE
Oh, *him*...? The one that'll give us the most trouble...?
If I step off the white line, my wife will turn into a Cornish hen...!
If I step off the white line, my wife will turn into a...!
DUN DUN DUN DUN DUN DUN DUN DUN
But what can we do about him...?
Just knock him off the raft...?
A back alley rock'n'roller like me just doesn't have the courage to shove him off his white line...
I wanna see your black belt power ~!
Don't be silly! Show me that hard rock spirit of yours~!
JUST GO OVER THERE AND TAKE HIM THE HELL OUT ALREADY !!
YOU GO TAKE HIM OUT!! WHY DO I GOTTA DO IT?!
SFF
KLOP
KLOP
KLOP
Hey.
GLARE
Hrm? You wanna take me on? Sorry, but I can't lose!
Or my wife will turn into a Cornish ...

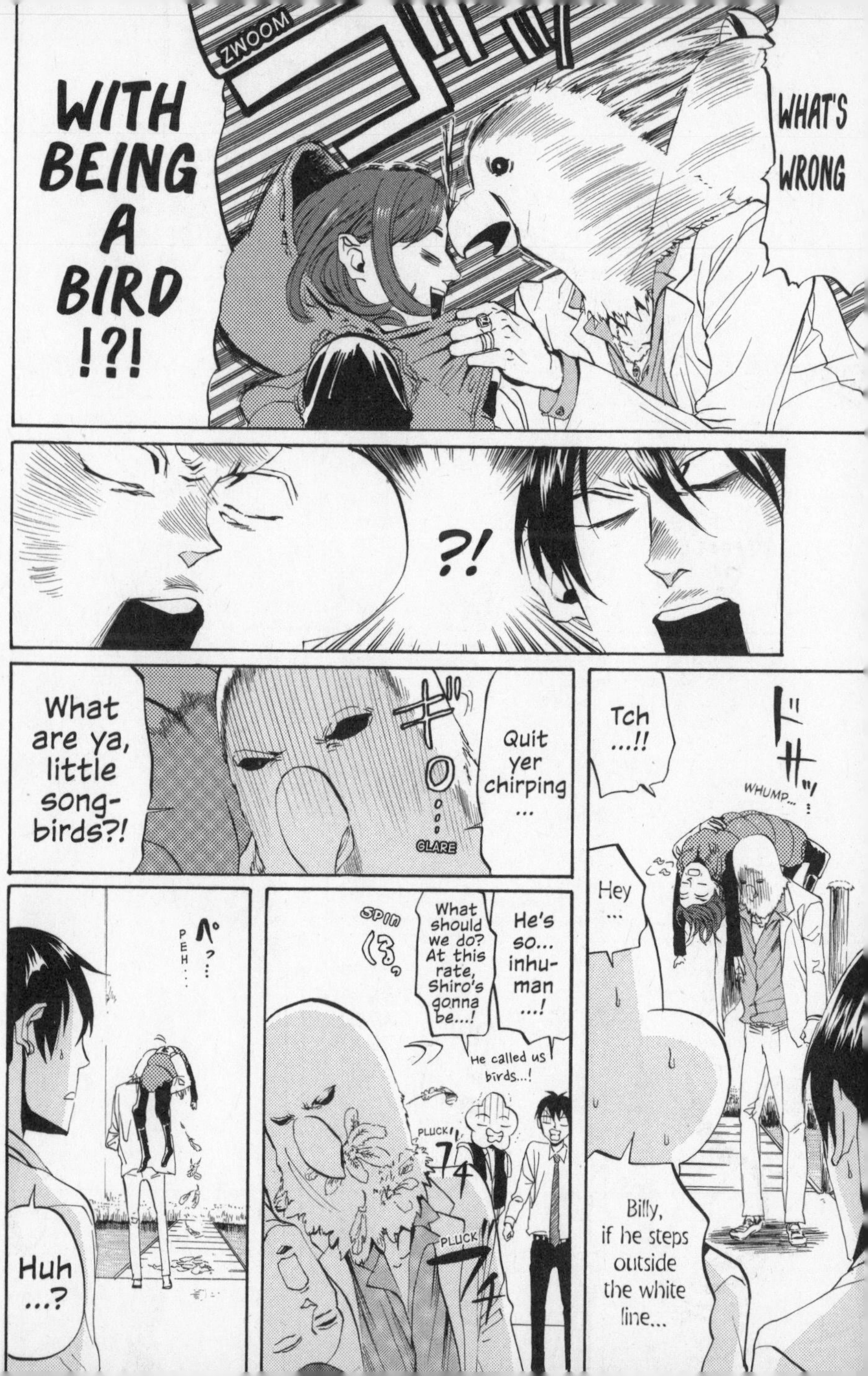
ZWOOM
WHAT'S WRONG
WITH BEING A BIRD !?!
?!
Tch ...!!
WHUMP...
Hey ...
Billy, if he steps outside the white line...
Quit yer chirping ...
GLARE
What are ya, little song-birds?!
He's so... inhuman ...!
What should we do? At this rate, Shiro's gonna be...!
SPIN
He called us birds...!
PLUCK
PLUCK
PEH...
Huh ...?

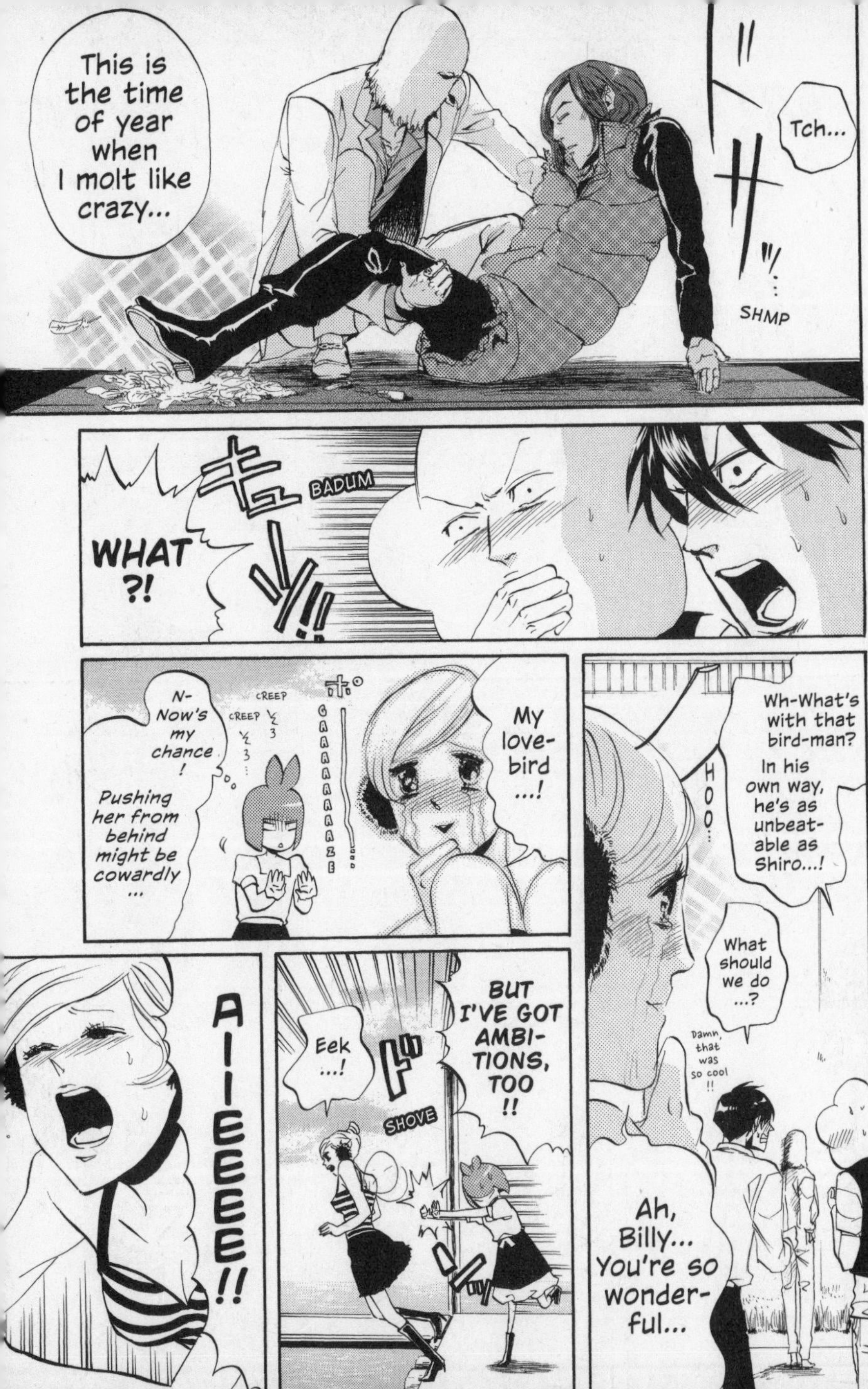
Tch...
SHMP
This is the time of year when I molt like crazy...
BADUM
WHAT?!
Wh-What's with that bird-man?
HOO...
In his own way, he's as unbeatable as Shiro...!
What should we do ...?
Damn, that was so cool !!
Ah, Billy... You're so wonderful...
My love-bird ...!
GAAAAAAAAAAZE
CREEP
CREEP
N-Now's my chance!
Pushing her from behind might be cowardly ...
BUT I'VE GOT AMBITIONS, TOO !!
Eek ...!
SHOVE
AIIEEEE!!

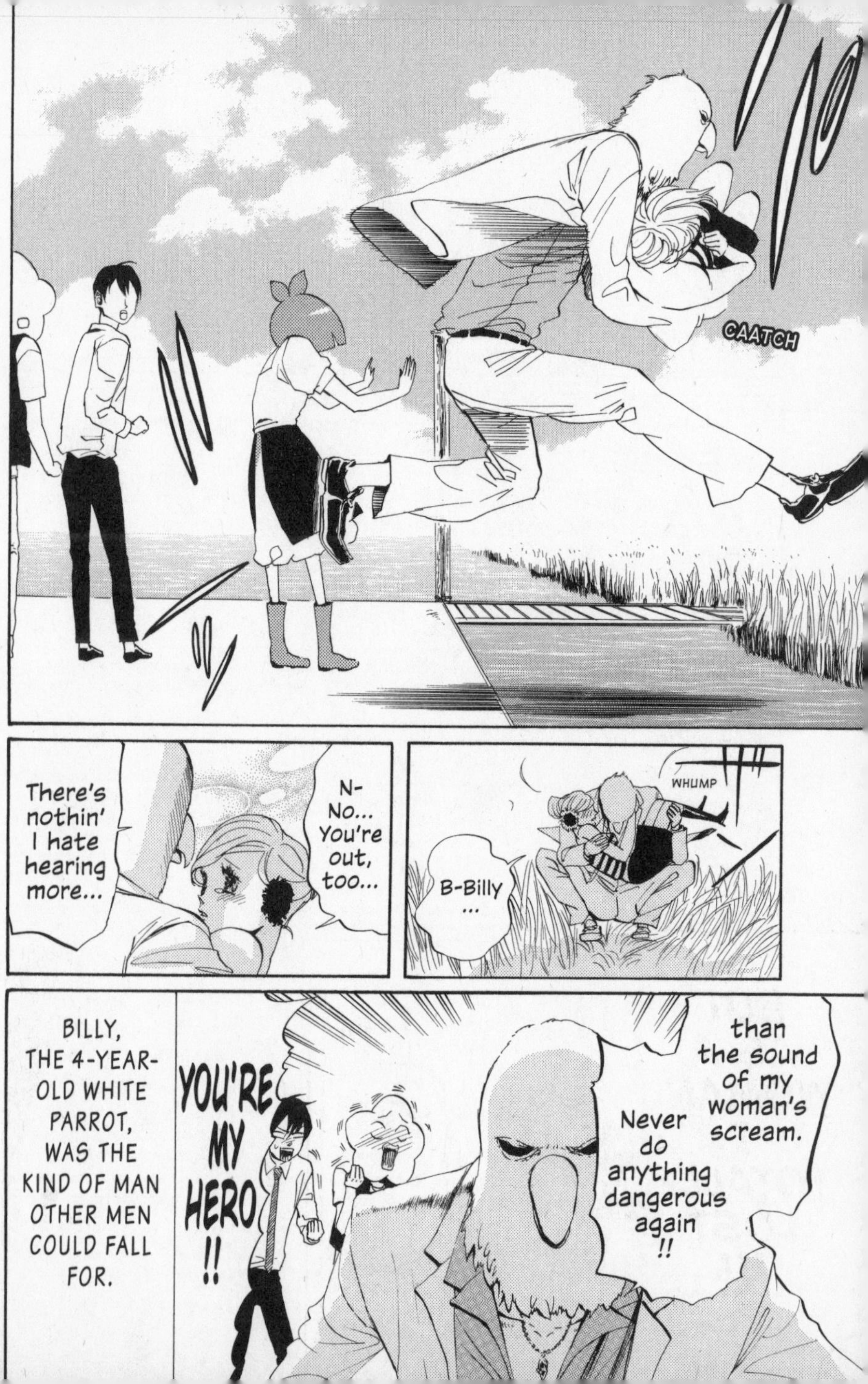
CAATCH
WHUMP
B-Billy ...
N- No... You're out, too...
There's nothin' I hate hearing more...
than the sound of my woman's scream.
Never do anything dangerous again !!
YOU'RE MY HERO !!
BILLY, THE 4-YEAR-OLD WHITE PARROT, WAS THE KIND OF MAN OTHER MEN COULD FALL FOR.

Chapter 145: Doorway to the Strongest

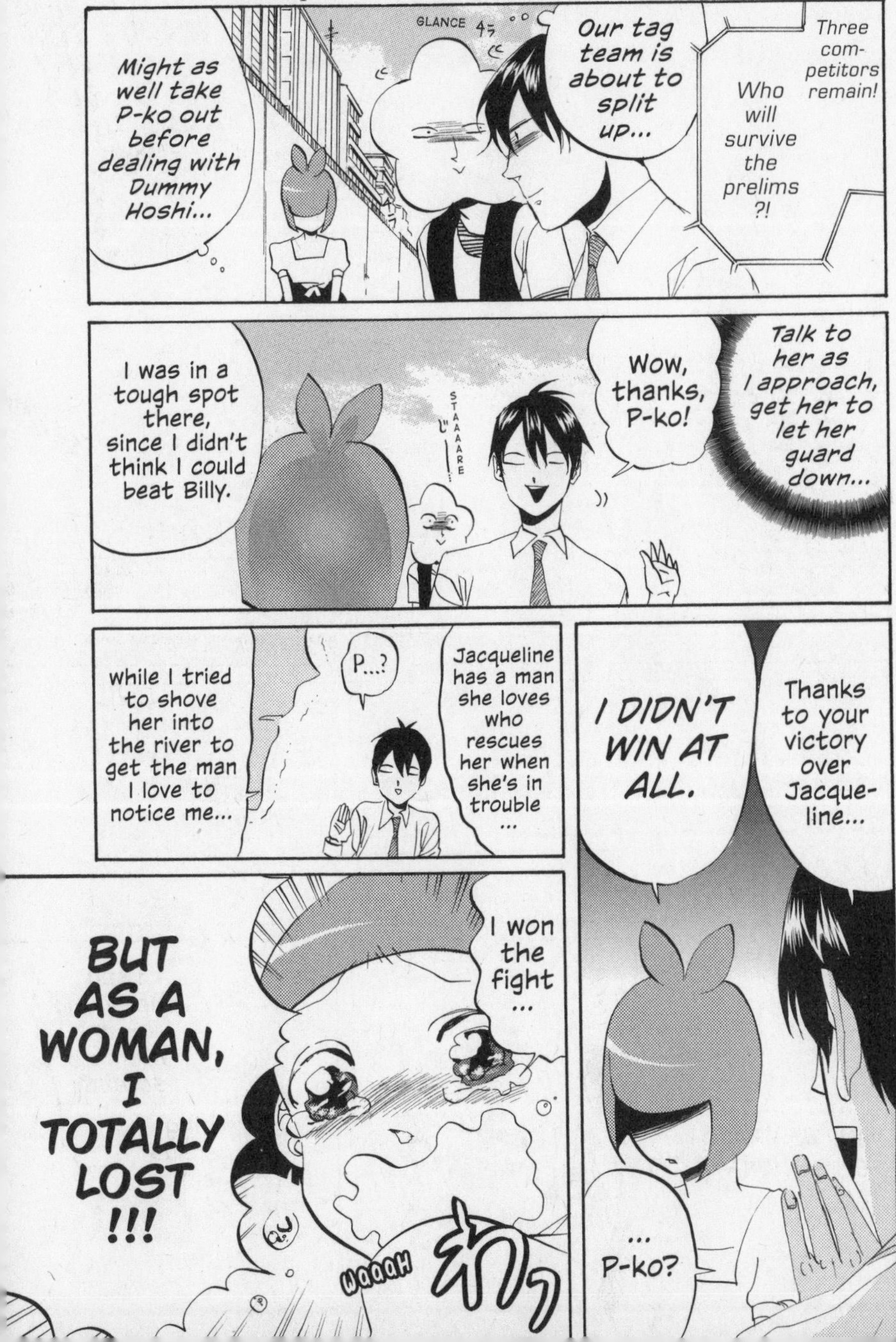

Three competitors remain! Who will survive the prelims?!
Our tag team is about to split up...
GLANCE
Might as well take P-ko out before dealing with Dummy Hoshi...
Talk to her as I approach, get her to let her guard down...
Wow, thanks, P-ko!
STAAAAARE
I was in a tough spot there, since I didn't think I could beat Billy.
Thanks to your victory over Jacqueline...
I DIDN'T WIN AT ALL.
... P-ko?
Jacqueline has a man she loves who rescues her when she's in trouble...
P...?
while I tried to shove her into the river to get the man I love to notice me...
I won the fight...
BUT AS A WOMAN, I TOTALLY LOST!!!
WAAAH

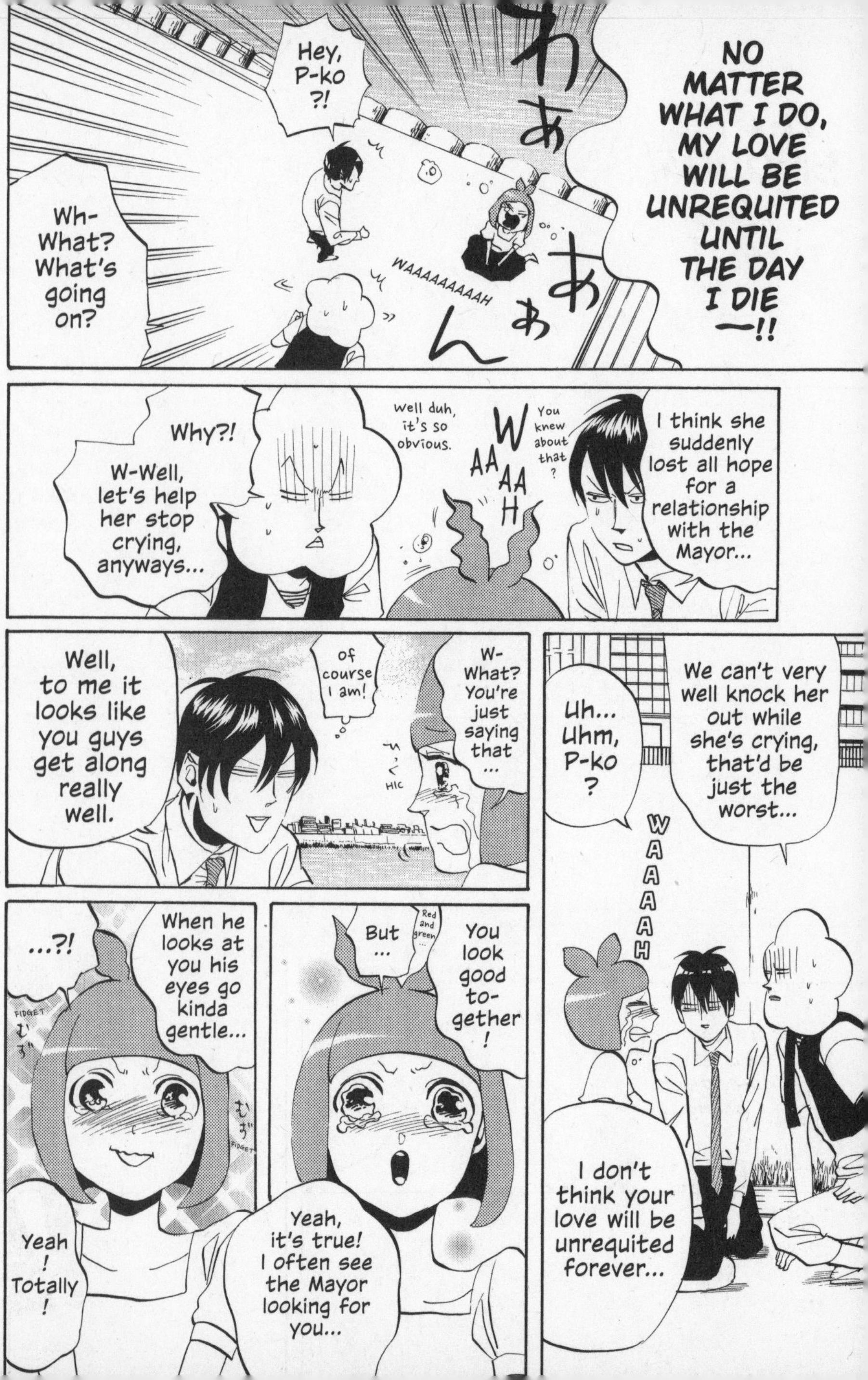

NO MATTER WHAT I DO, MY LOVE WILL BE UNREQUITED UNTIL THE DAY I DIE—!!
わぁあぁあん
Hey, P-ko?!
WAAAAAAAAAH
Wh- What? What's going on?
I think she suddenly lost all hope for a relationship with the Mayor...
You knew about that?
WAAAAH
Well duh, it's so obvious.
Why?!
W-Well, let's help her stop crying, anyways...
We can't very well knock her out while she's crying, that'd be just the worst...
Uh... Uhm, P-ko?
WAAAAAH
I don't think your love will be unrequited forever...
W- What? You're just saying that...
of course I am!
HIC
Well, to me it looks like you guys get along really well.
You look good together!
Red and green...
But...
Yeah, it's true! I often see the Mayor looking for you...
When he looks at you his eyes go kinda gentle...
...?!
FIDGET
FIDGET
Yeah! Totally!

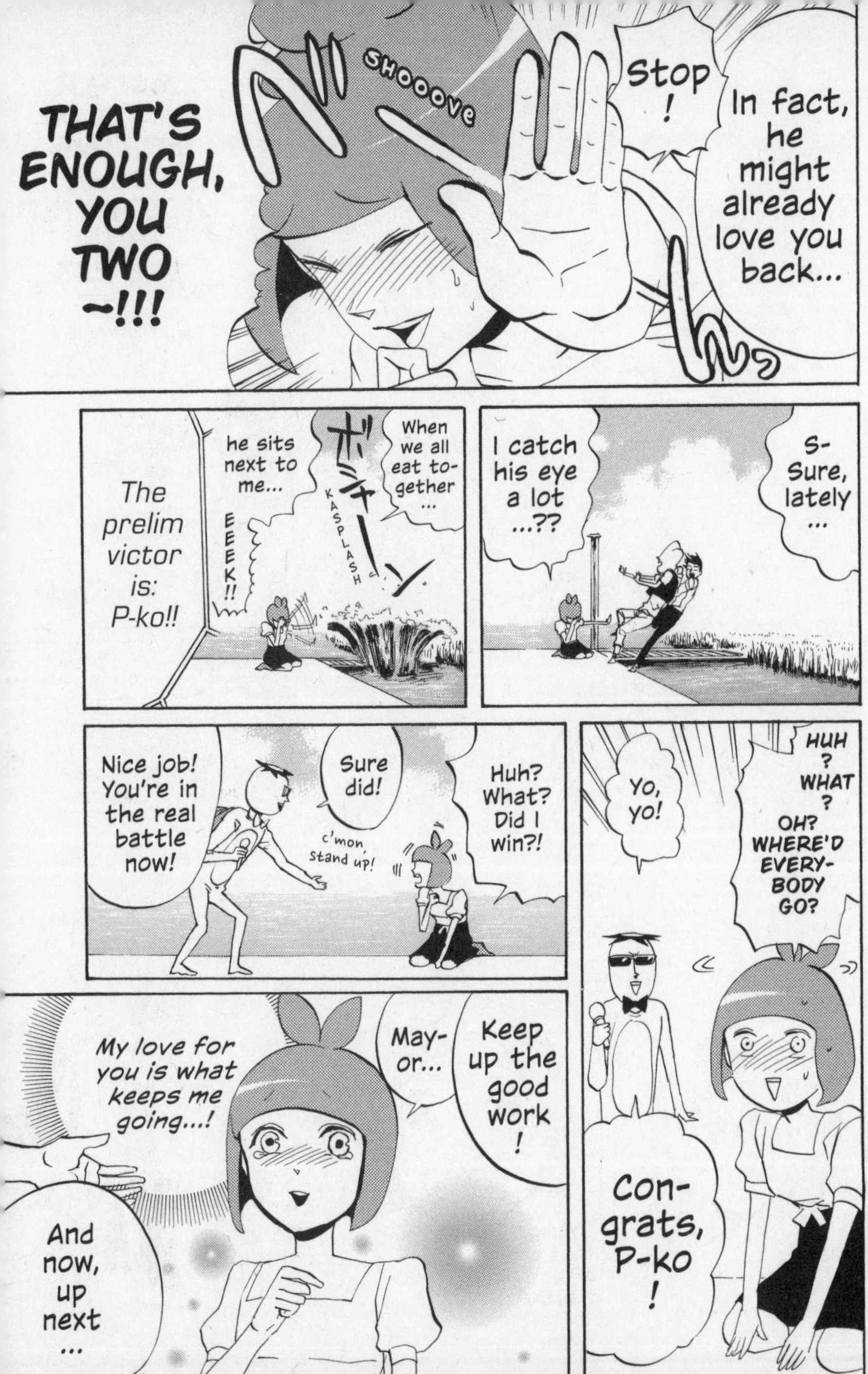
In fact, he might already love you back...
Stop!
SHOOOVE
THAT'S ENOUGH, YOU TWO~!!!
S-Sure, lately...
I catch his eye a lot...??
When we all eat together...
KASPLASH
he sits next to me...
EEEEK!!
The prelim victor is: P-ko!!
HUH? WHAT? OH? WHERE'D EVERYBODY GO?
Yo, yo!
Congrats, P-ko!
Huh? What? Did I win?!
Sure did!
c'mon, stand up!
Nice job! You're in the real battle now!
Keep up the good work!
Mayor...
My love for you is what keeps me going...!
And now, up next...

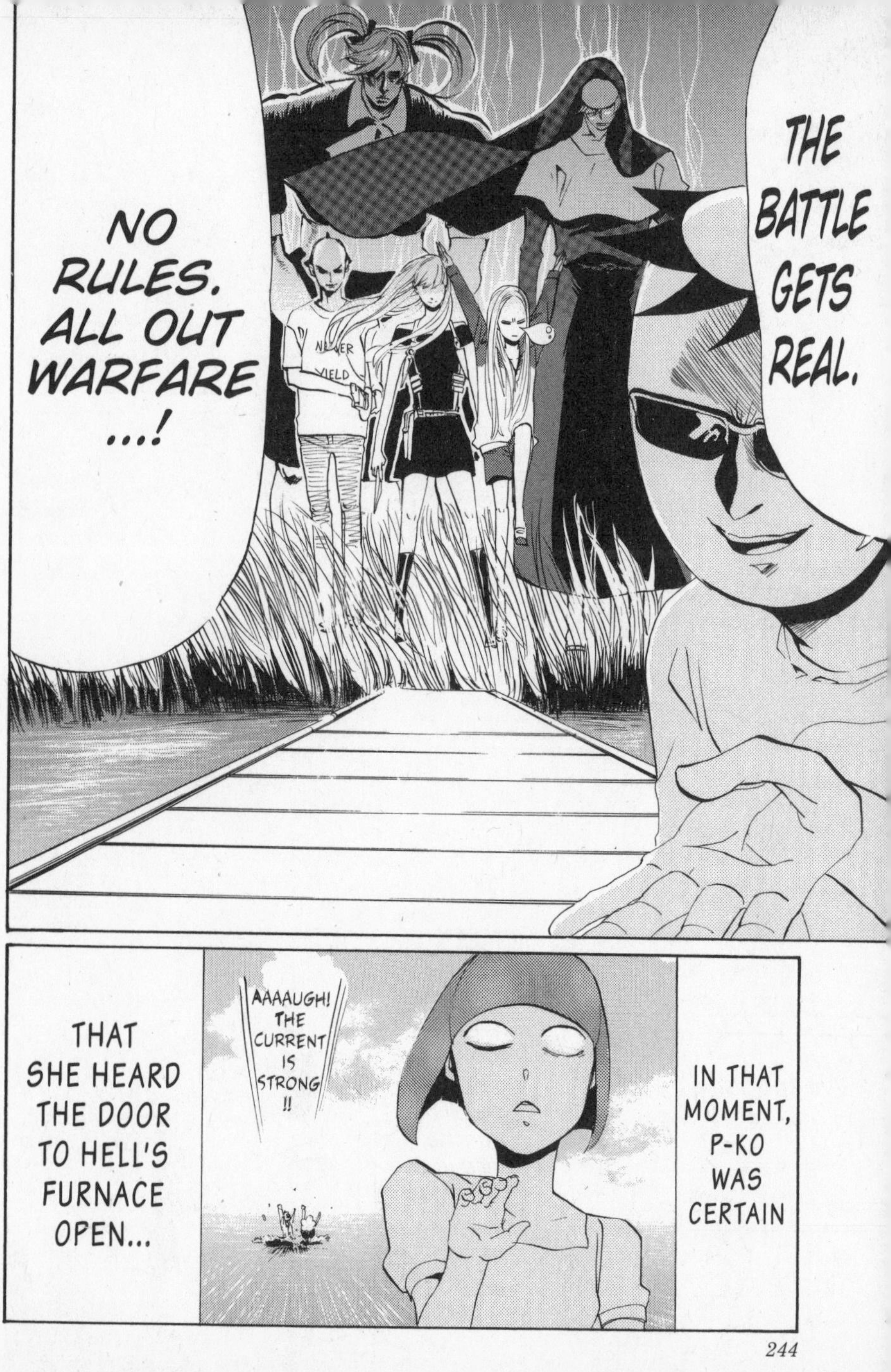
THE BATTLE GETS REAL.
NO RULES. ALL OUT WARFARE ...!
IN THAT MOMENT, P-KO WAS CERTAIN
AAAAUGH! THE CURRENT IS STRONG!!
THAT SHE HEARD THE DOOR TO HELL'S FURNACE OPEN...

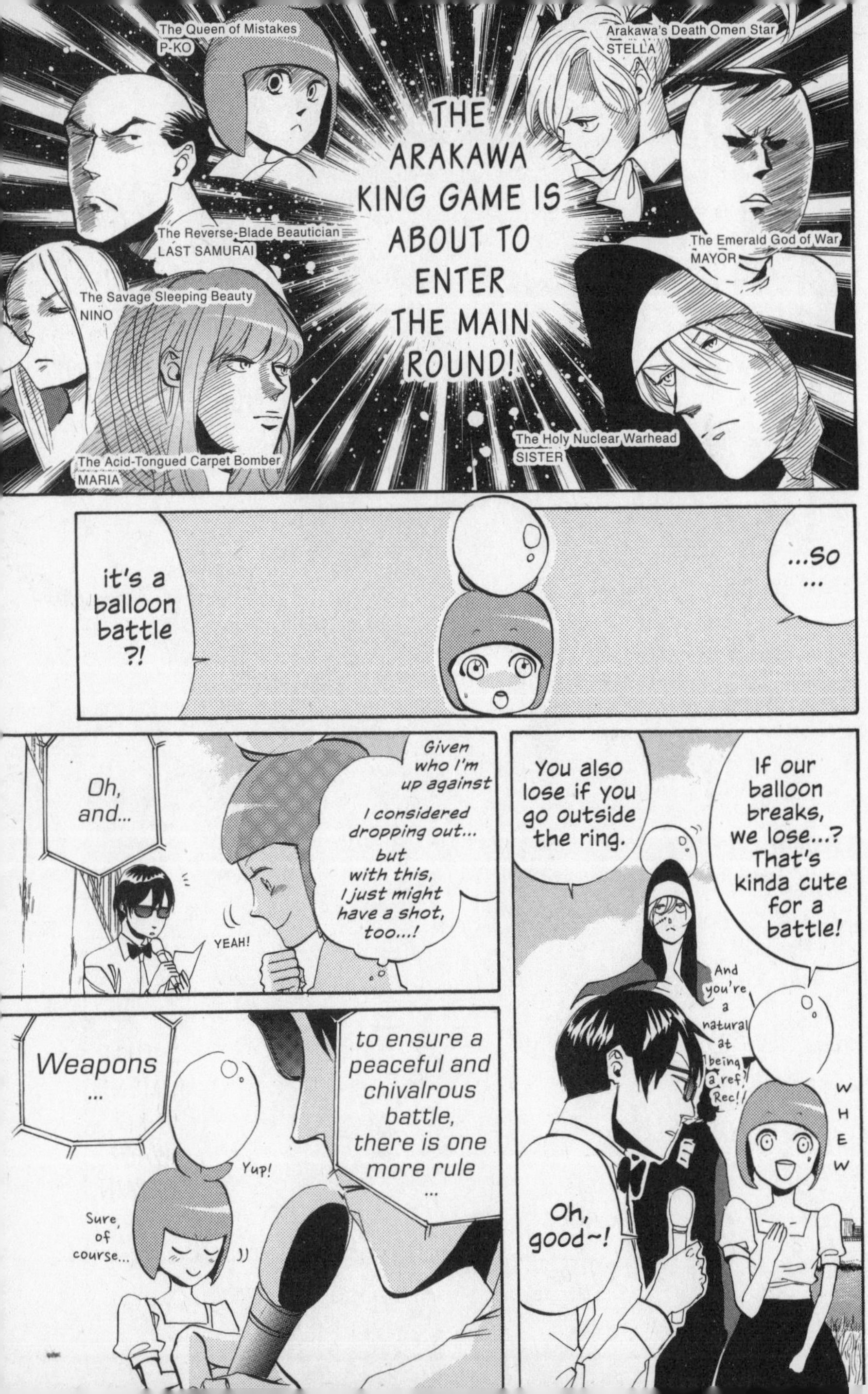
Arakawa's Death Omen Star
STELLA
The Emerald God of War
MAYOR
The Holy Nuclear Warhead
SISTER
THE ARAKAWA KING GAME IS ABOUT TO ENTER THE MAIN ROUND!
The Queen of Mistakes
P-KO
The Reverse-Blade Beautician
LAST SAMURAI
The Savage Sleeping Beauty
NINO
The Acid-Tongued Carpet Bomber
MARIA
...So ...
it's a balloon battle ?!
If our balloon breaks, we lose...? That's kinda cute for a battle!
You also lose if you go outside the ring.
And you're a natural at being a ref, Rec!
WHEW
Oh, good~!
Given who I'm up against
I considered dropping out... but with this, I just might have a shot, too...!
YEAH!
Oh, and...
to ensure a peaceful and chivalrous battle, there is one more rule ...
Yup!
Weapons ...
Sure, of course...

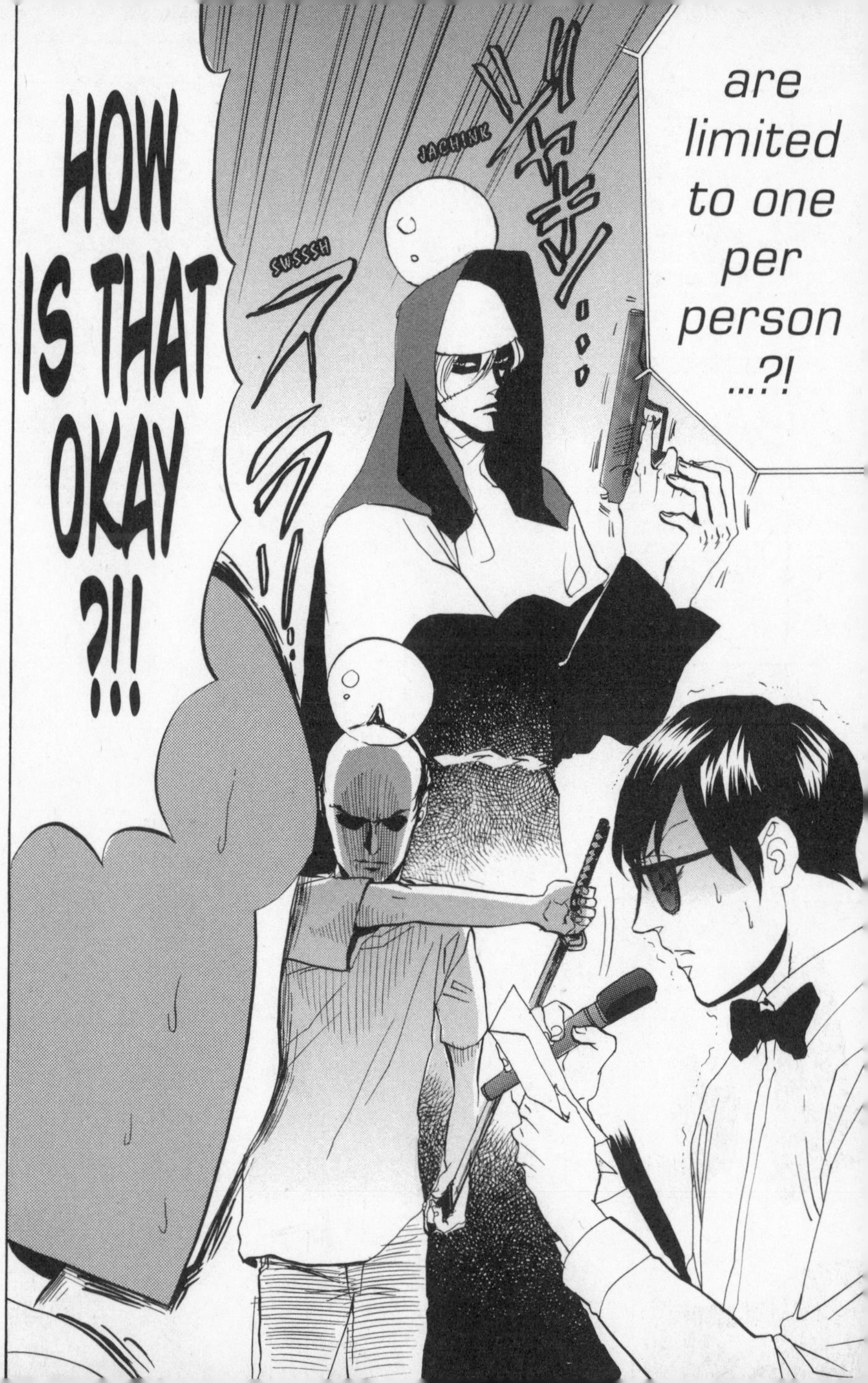
are limited to one per person ...?!
JACHINK
SWSSSH
HOW IS THAT OKAY ?!!

Chapter 146: Bloody Battle Begins

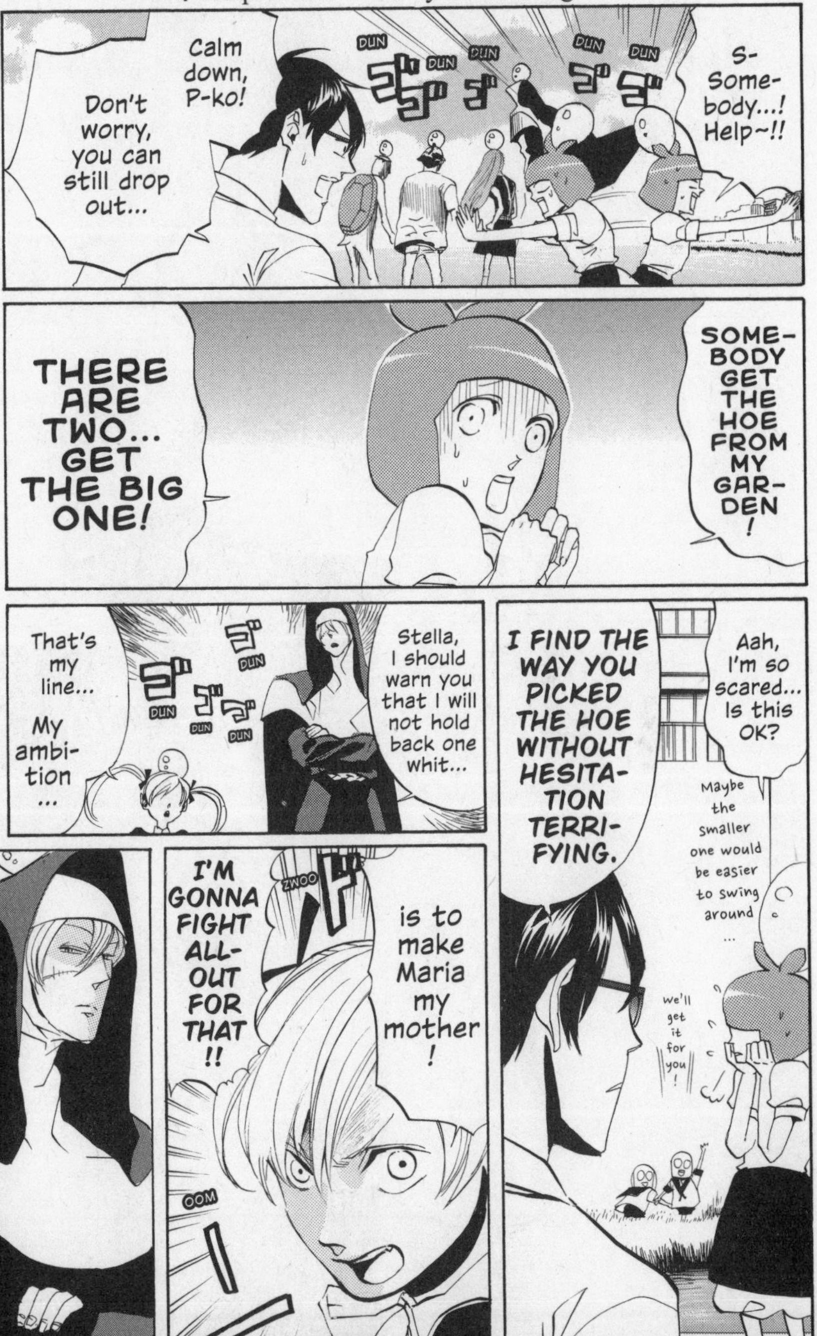
S- Some-body...! Help~!!
DUN DUN DUN DUN DUN
Calm down, P-ko!
Don't worry, you can still drop out...
SOME-BODY GET THE HOE FROM MY GAR-DEN!
THERE ARE TWO... GET THE BIG ONE!
Aah, I'm so scared... Is this OK?
I FIND THE WAY YOU PICKED THE HOE WITHOUT HESITA-TION TERRI-FYING.
Maybe the smaller one would be easier to swing around...
we'll get it for you!
Stella, I should warn you that I will not hold back one whit...
DUN DUN DUN DUN
That's my line...
My ambi-tion...
is to make Maria my mother!
ZWOO
I'M GONNA FIGHT ALL-OUT FOR THAT!!
OOM

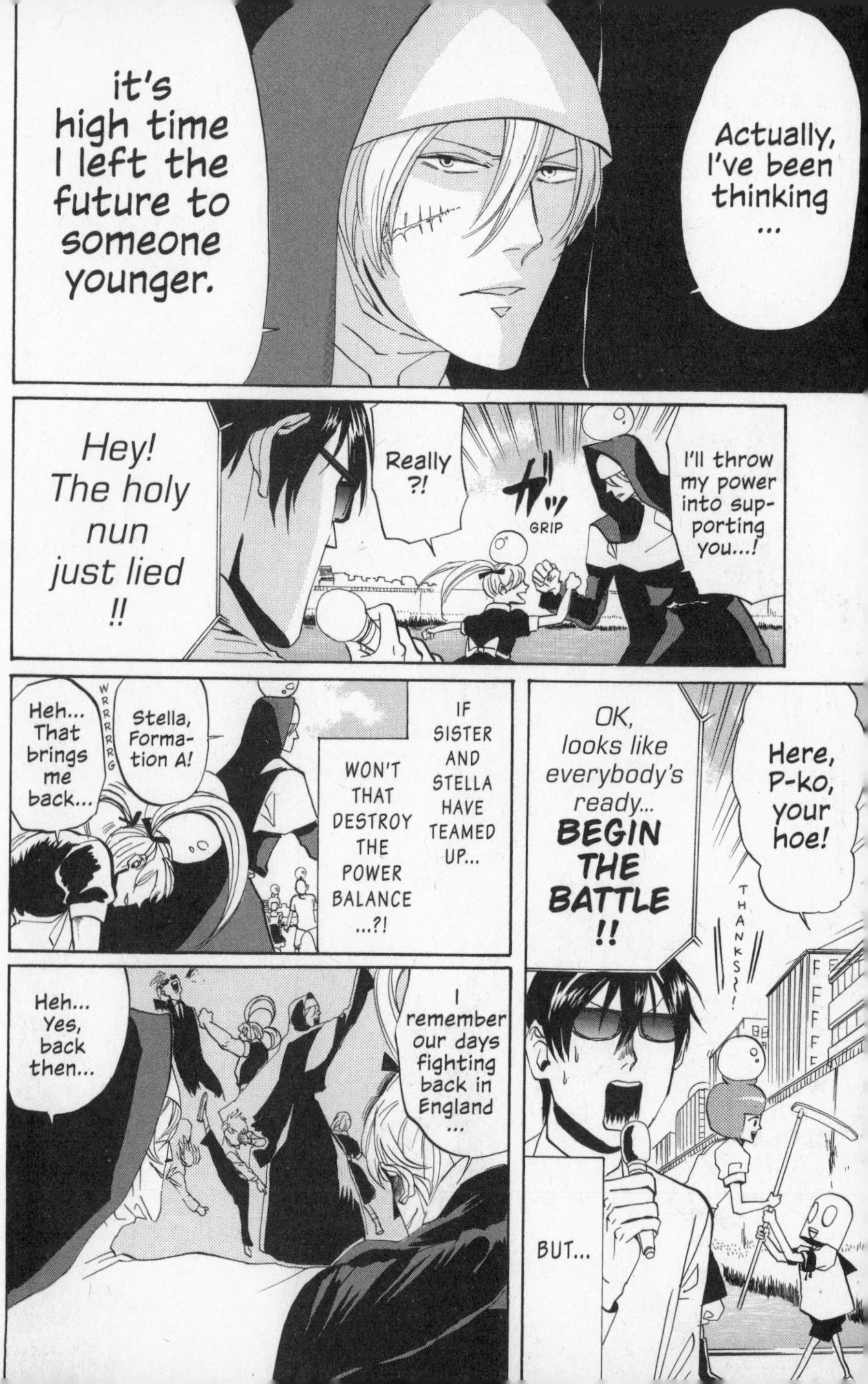

Actually, I've been thinking ...
it's high time I left the future to someone younger.
I'll throw my power into sup-porting you...!
GRIP
Really ?!
Hey! The holy nun just lied !!
Here, P-ko, your hoe!
OK, looks like everybody's ready... BEGIN THE BATTLE !!
THANKS~!
BUT...
IF SISTER AND STELLA HAVE TEAMED UP...
WON'T THAT DESTROY THE POWER BALANCE ...?!
Stella, Forma-tion A!
WRRRRRG
Heh... That brings me back...
I remember our days fighting back in England ...
Heh... Yes, back then...

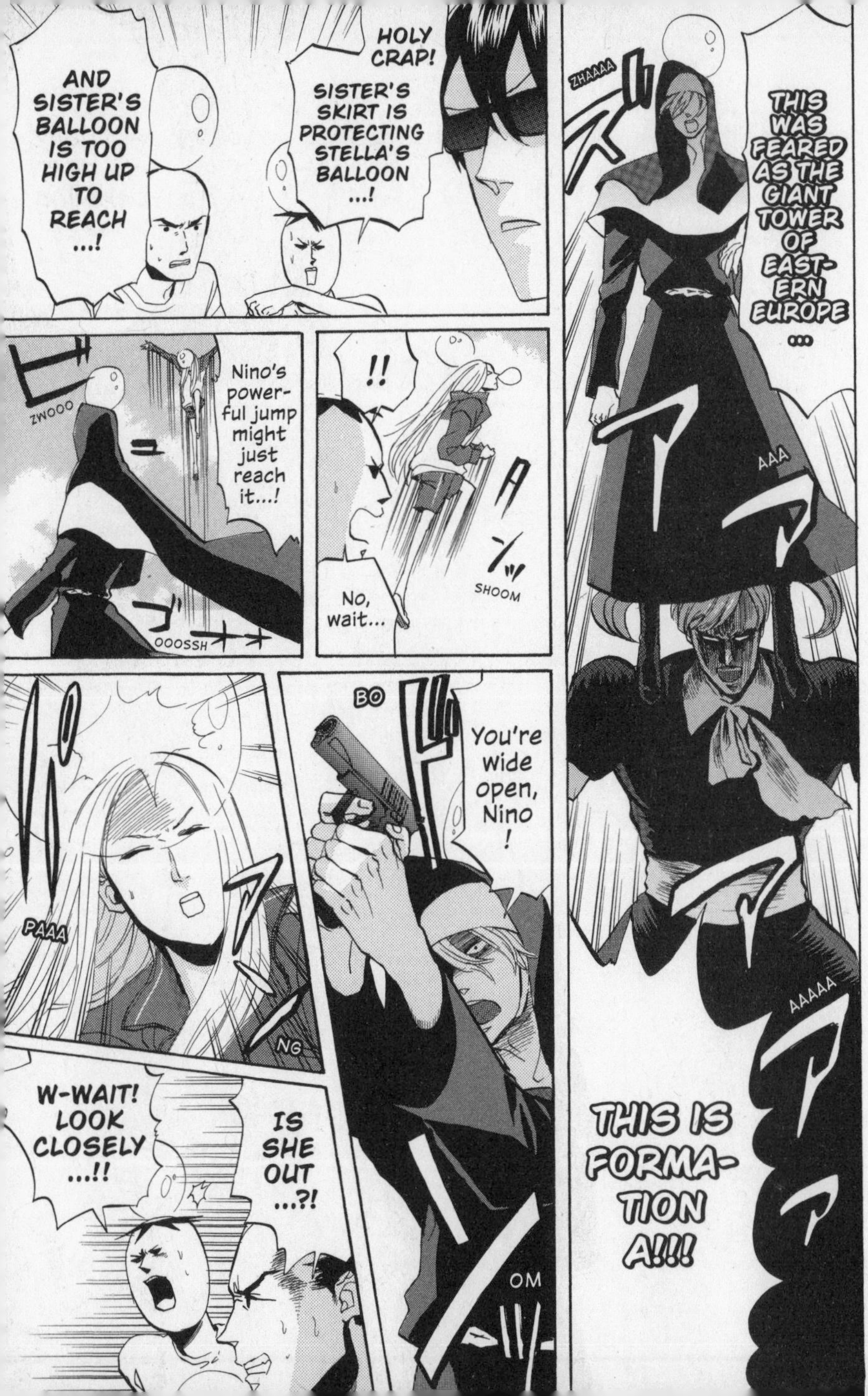
ZHAAAA
THIS WAS FEARED AS THE GIANT TOWER OF EAST-ERN EUROPE ...
AAA
AAAAA
THIS IS FORMA-TION A!!!
HOLY CRAP!
SISTER'S SKIRT IS PROTECTING STELLA'S BALLOON ...!
AND SISTER'S BALLOON IS TOO HIGH UP TO REACH ...!
!!
SHOOM
No, wait...
Nino's power-ful jump might just reach it...!
ZWOOO
OOOSSH
BO
You're wide open, Nino !
OM
PAAA
NG
W-WAIT! LOOK CLOSELY ...!!
IS SHE OUT ...?!

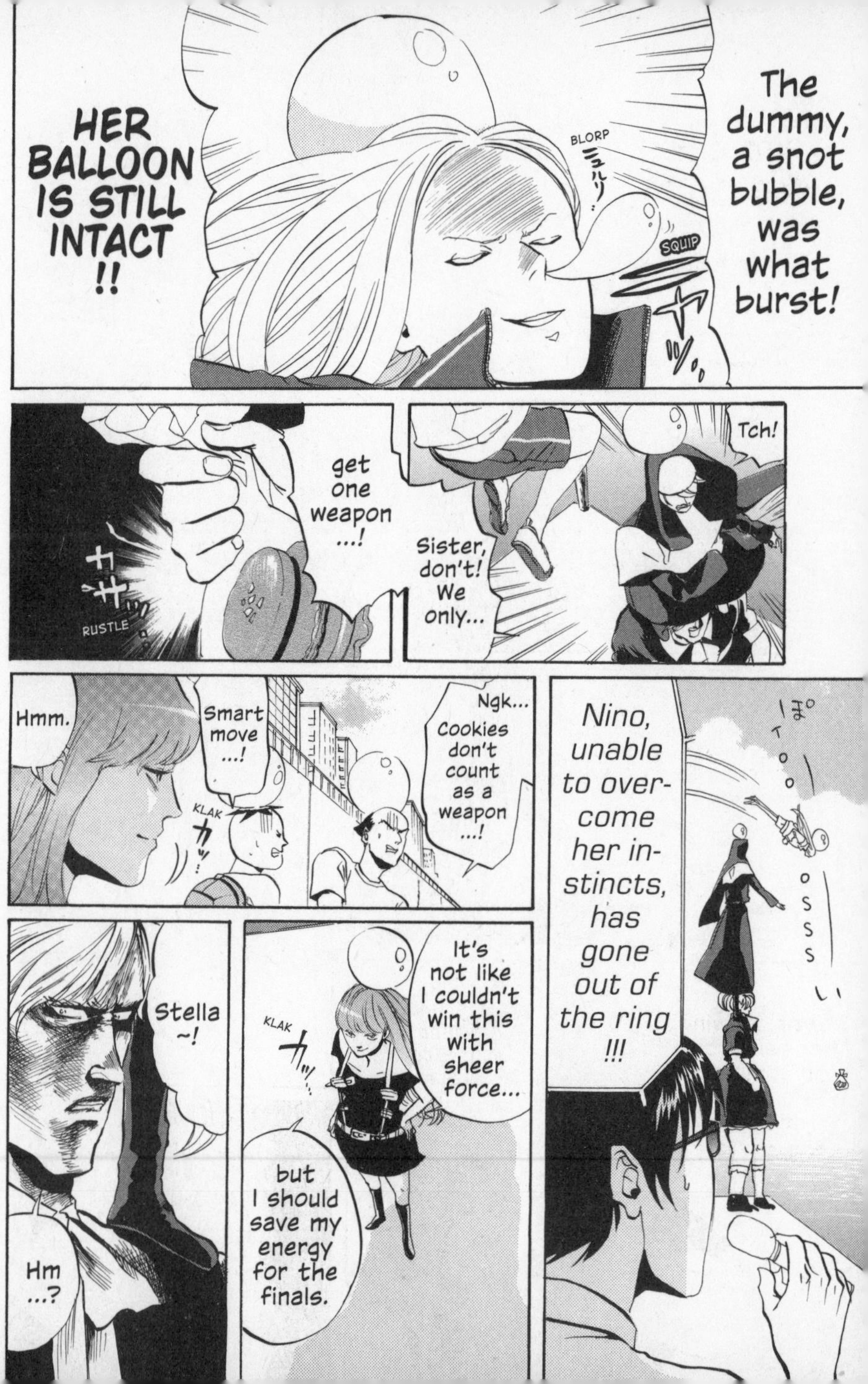

The dummy, a snot bubble, was what burst!
BLORP
SQUIP
HER BALLOON IS STILL INTACT !!
Tch!
Sister, don't! We only...
get one weapon ...!
RUSTLE
Nino, unable to over-come her in-stincts, has gone out of the ring !!!
Ngk... Cookies don't count as a weapon ...!
Smart move ...!
KLAK
Hmm.
It's not like I couldn't win this with sheer force...
KLAK
but I should save my energy for the finals.
Stella ~!
Hm ...?

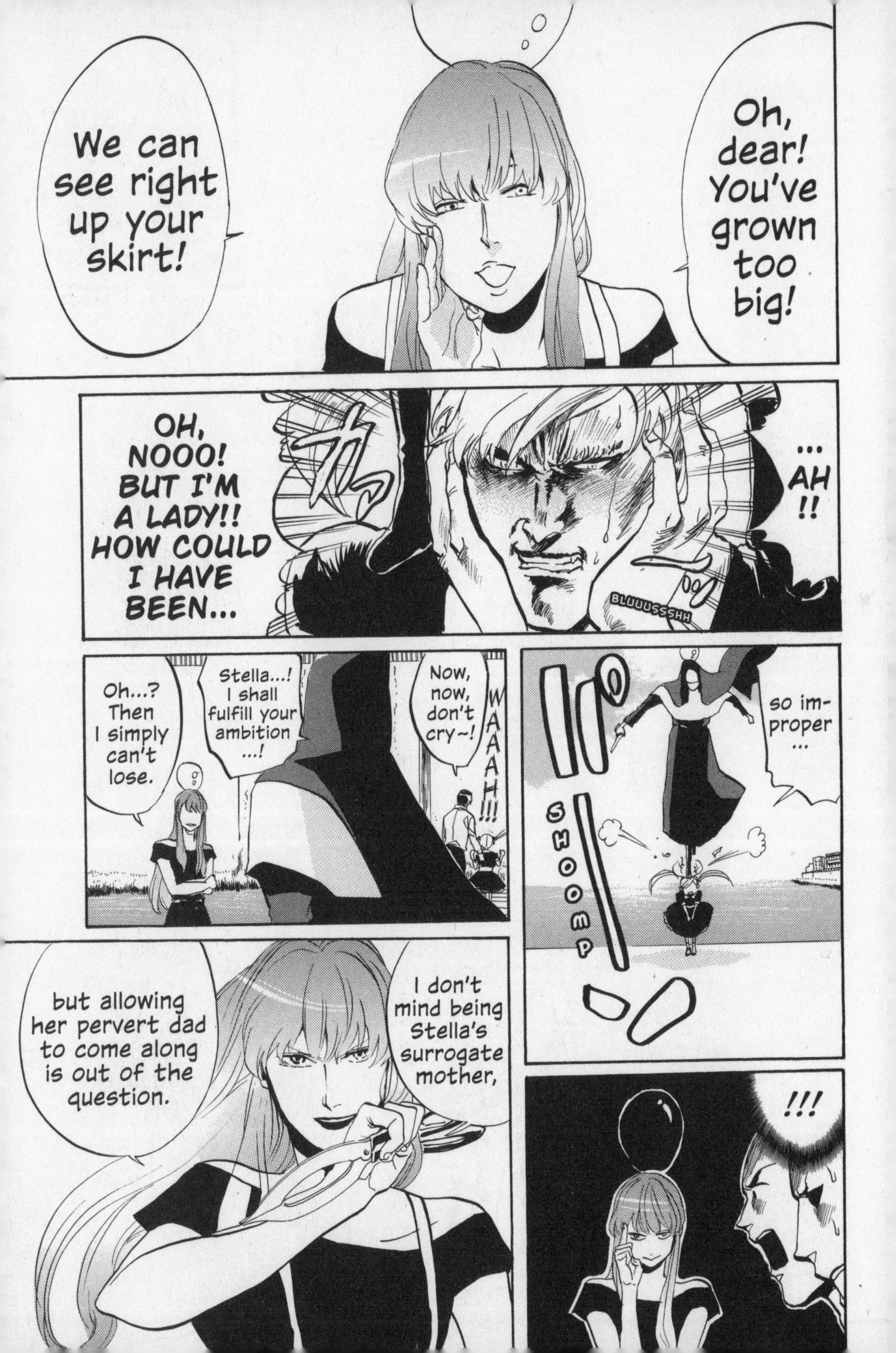
Oh, dear! You've grown too big!
We can see right up your skirt!
...AH!!
BLUUUSSSHH
OH, NOOO! BUT I'M A LADY!! HOW COULD I HAVE BEEN...
so im-proper...
SHOOOMP
WAAAAH!!!
Now, now, don't cry~!
Stella...! I shall fulfill your ambition...!
Oh...? Then I simply can't lose.
I don't mind being Stella's surrogate mother,
but allowing her pervert dad to come along is out of the question.
!!!

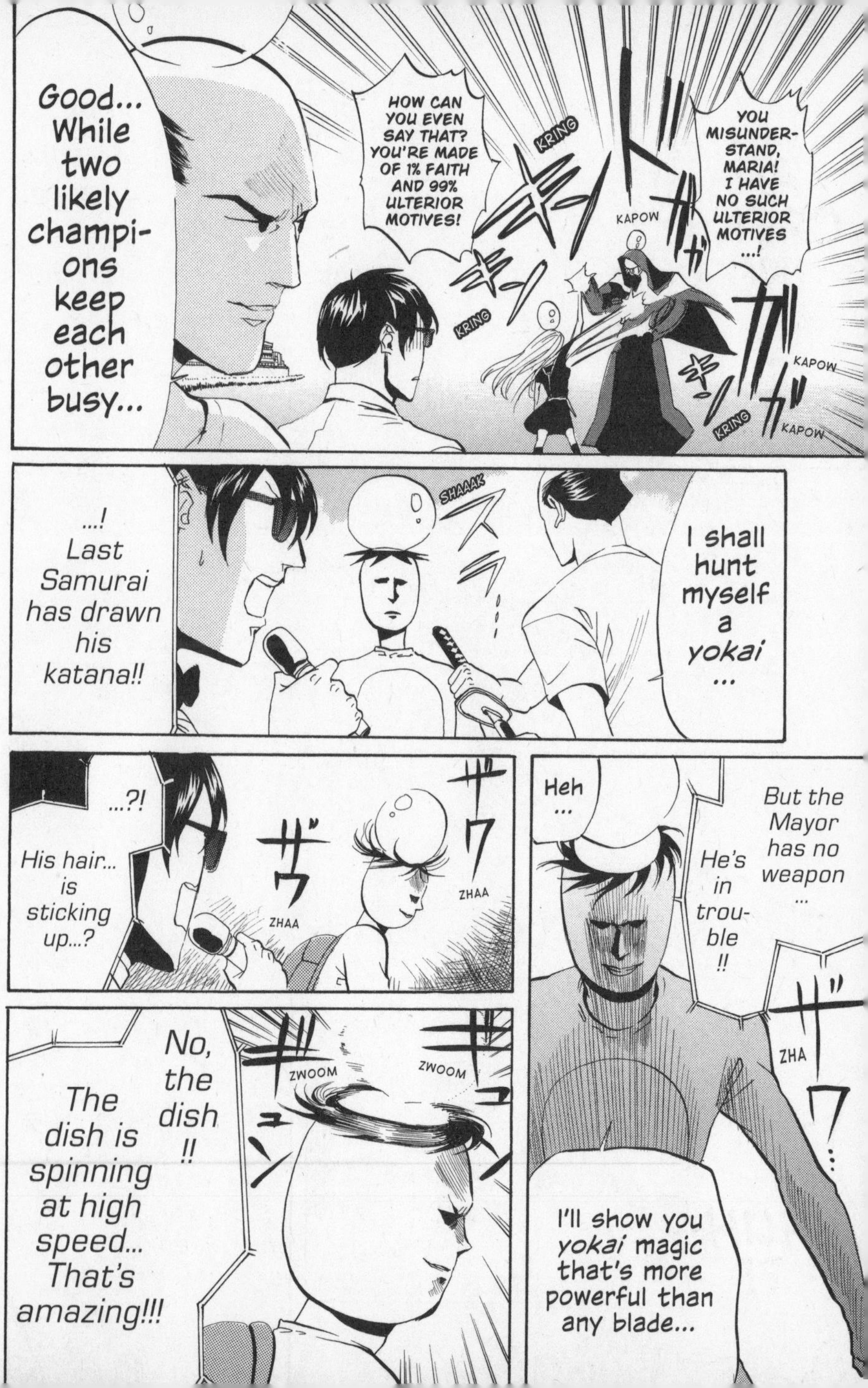
Good... While two likely champi-ons keep each other busy...
HOW CAN YOU EVEN SAY THAT? YOU'RE MADE OF 1% FAITH AND 99% ULTERIOR MOTIVES!
KRING
KRING
KAPOW
YOU MISUNDER-STAND, MARIA! I HAVE NO SUCH ULTERIOR MOTIVES ...!
KAPOW
KRING
KAPOW
I shall hunt myself a *yokai* ...
SHAAAK
...! Last Samurai has drawn his katana!!
But the Mayor has no weapon ...
He's in trou-ble !!
Heh ...
ZHA
I'll show you *yokai* magic that's more powerful than any blade...
ZHAA
ZHAA
...?! His hair... is sticking up...?
ZWOOM
ZWOOM
No, the dish !!
The dish is spinning at high speed... That's amazing!!!

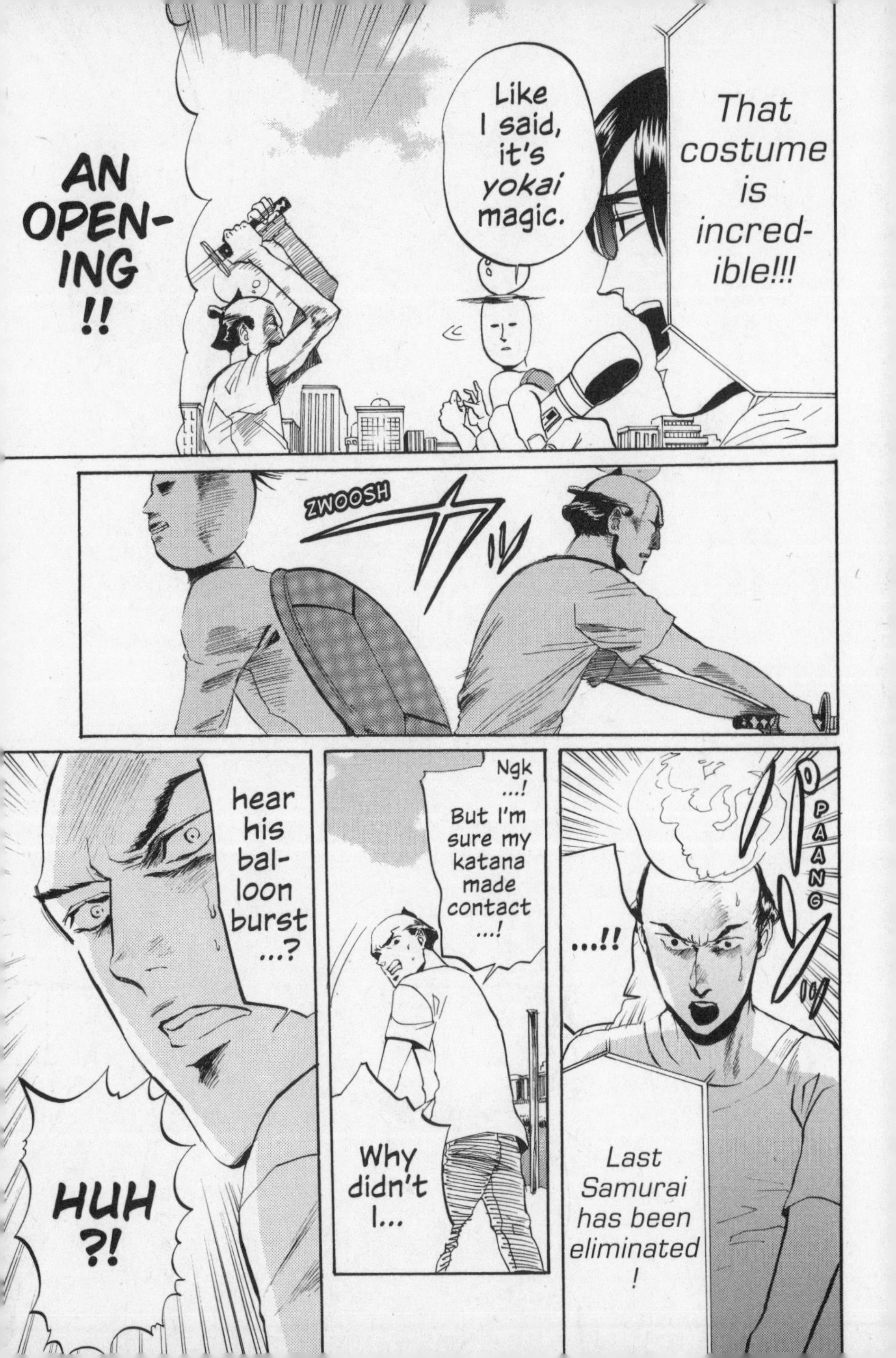
That costume is incred-ible!!!
Like I said, it's yokai magic.
AN OPEN-ING!!
ZWOOSH
PAANG
...!!
Last Samurai has been eliminated!
Ngk ...! But I'm sure my katana made contact ...!
Why didn't I...
hear his bal-loon burst ...?
HUH ?!

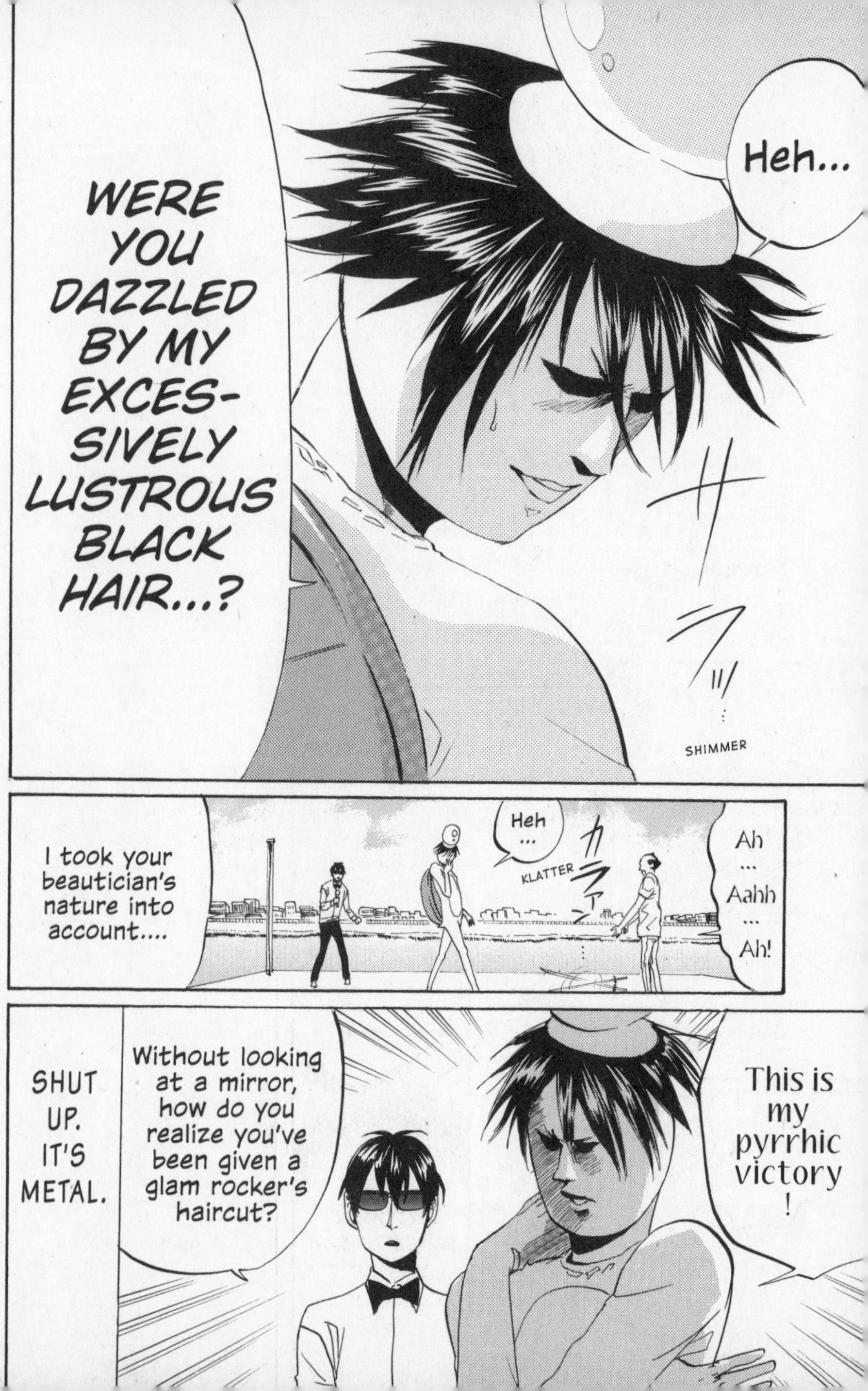

Heh...
WERE YOU DAZZLED BY MY EXCES-SIVELY LUSTROUS BLACK HAIR...?
SHIMMER
Ah ... Aahh ... Ah!
Heh ...
KLATTER
I took your beautician's nature into account....
This is my pyrrhic victory!
Without looking at a mirror, how do you realize you've been given a glam rocker's haircut?
SHUT UP. IT'S METAL.

Chapter 147: The Fateful Showdown

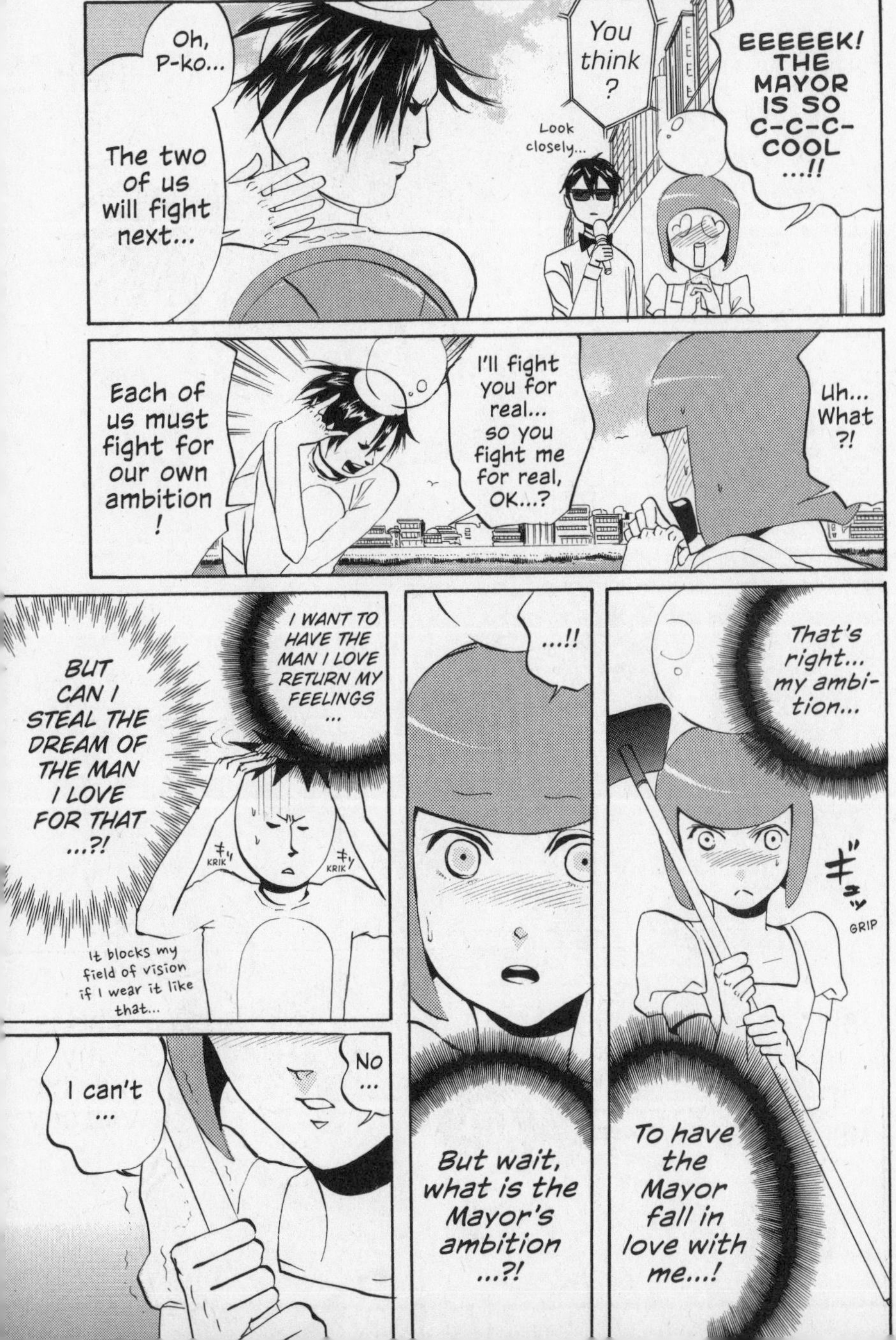
EEEEEK! THE MAYOR IS SO C-C-C-COOL ...!!
You think ?
Look closely...
Oh, P-ko...
The two of us will fight next...
Uh... What ?!
I'll fight you for real... so you fight me for real, OK...?
Each of us must fight for our own ambition !
That's right... my ambi-tion...
GRIP
To have the Mayor fall in love with me...!
...!!
But wait, what is the Mayor's ambition ...?!
I WANT TO HAVE THE MAN I LOVE RETURN MY FEELINGS ...
BUT CAN I STEAL THE DREAM OF THE MAN I LOVE FOR THAT ...?!
KRIK
KRIK
It blocks my field of vision if I wear it like that...
No ...
I can't ...

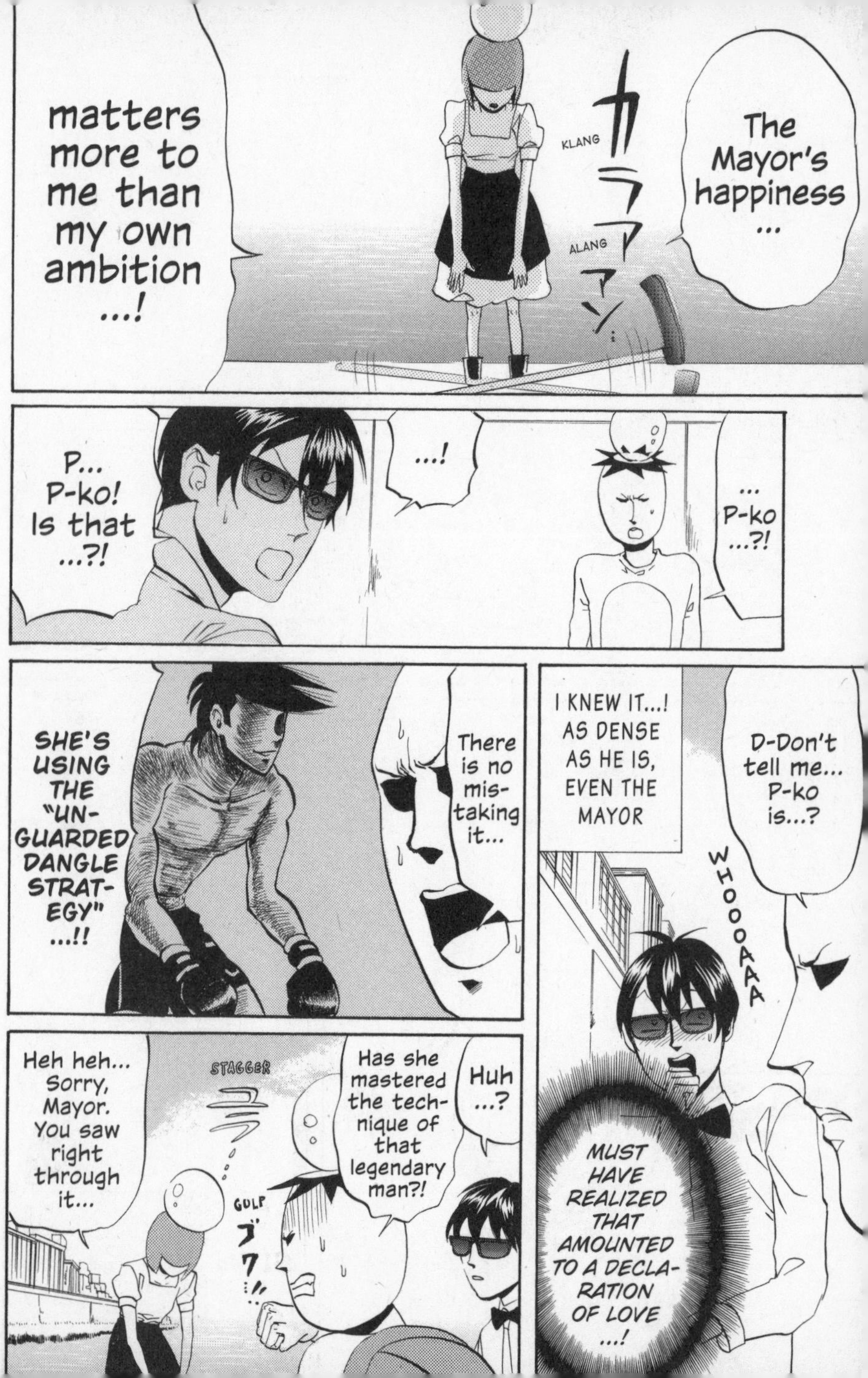
The Mayor's happiness ...
KLANG
ALANG
matters more to me than my own ambition ...!
... P-ko ...?!
...!
P... P-ko! Is that ...?!
D-Don't tell me... P-ko is...?
I KNEW IT...! AS DENSE AS HE IS, EVEN THE MAYOR
WHOOOAAA
MUST HAVE REALIZED THAT AMOUNTED TO A DECLARATION OF LOVE ...!
There is no mistaking it...
SHE'S USING THE "UNGUARDED DANGLE STRATEGY" ...!!
Huh ...?
Has she mastered the technique of that legendary man?!
GULP
STAGGER
Heh heh... Sorry, Mayor. You saw right through it...

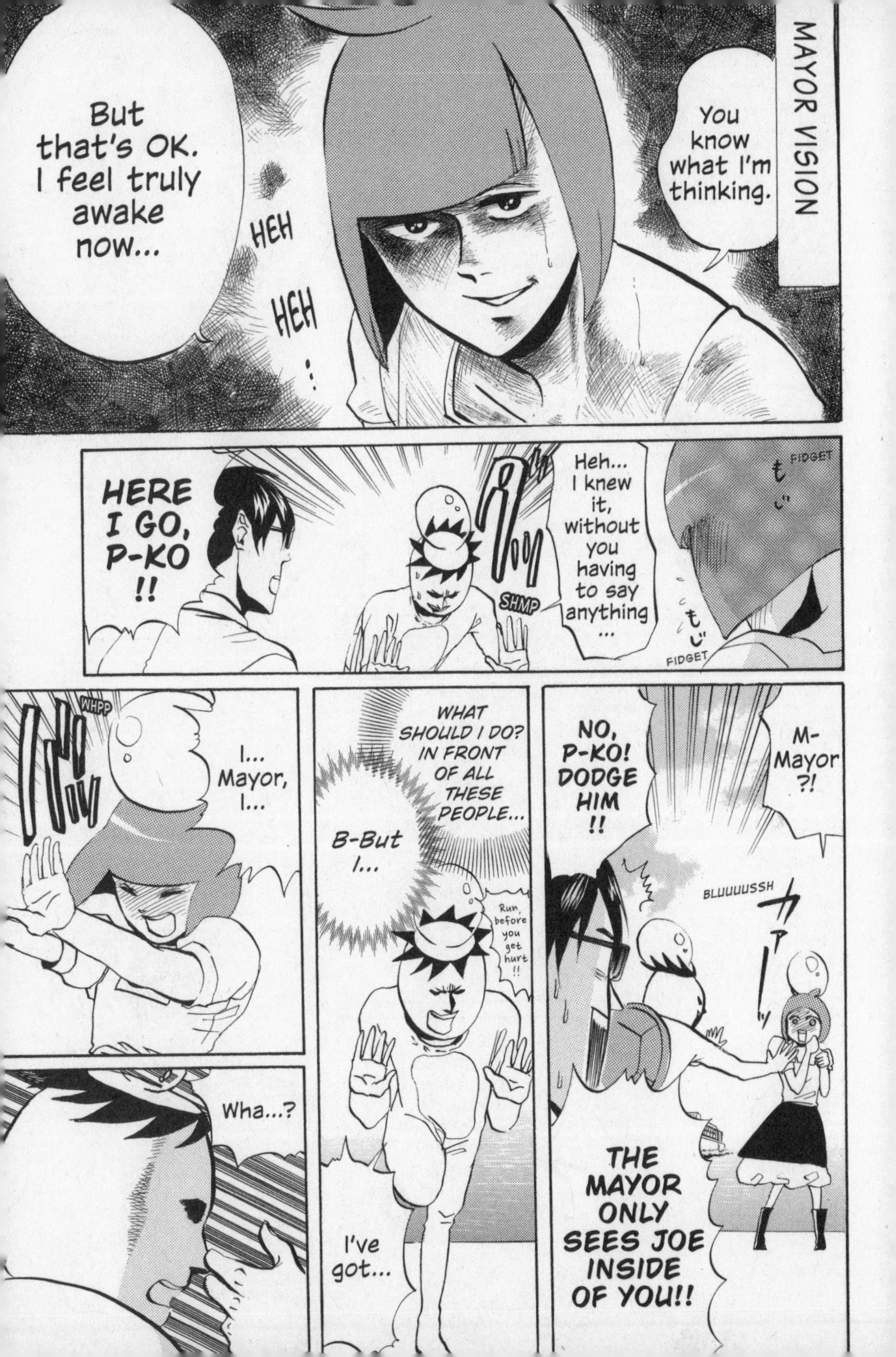
MAYOR VISION
You know what I'm thinking.
But that's OK. I feel truly awake now...
HEH
HEH
...
FIDGET
Heh... I knew it, without you having to say anything ...
FIDGET
SHMP
HERE I GO, P-KO!!
M-Mayor?!
NO, P-KO! DODGE HIM!!
BLUUUUSSH
THE MAYOR ONLY SEES JOE INSIDE OF YOU!!
WHAT SHOULD I DO? IN FRONT OF ALL THESE PEOPLE...
B-But I...
Run, before you get hurt!!
I've got...
WHPP
I... Mayor, I...
Wha...?

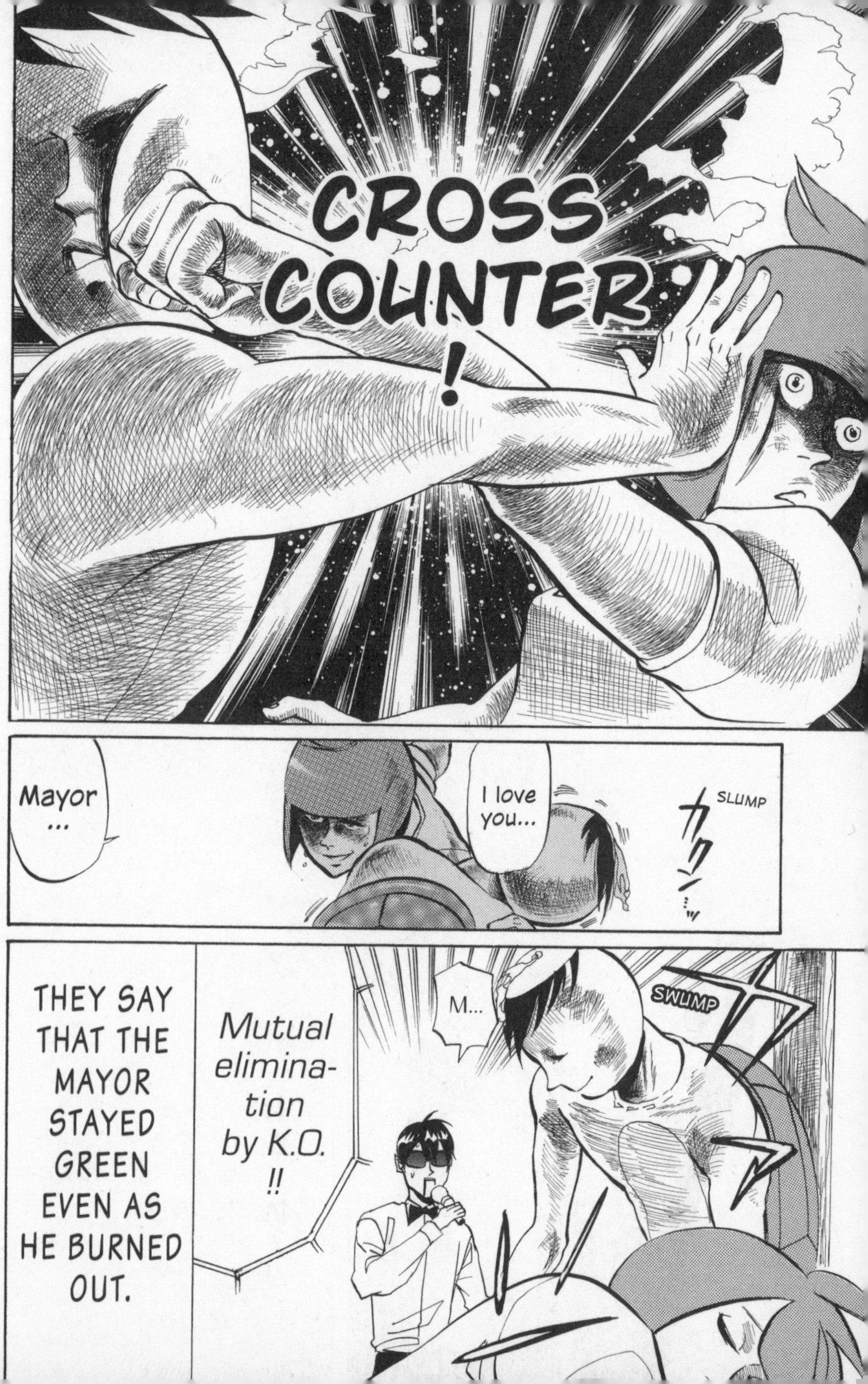
CROSS COUNTER !
SLUMP
カクン…
I love you...
Mayor ...
SWUMP
M...
Mutual elimina-tion by K.O. !!
THEY SAY THAT THE MAYOR STAYED GREEN EVEN AS HE BURNED OUT.

Chapter 148: Final Battle Participants Determined

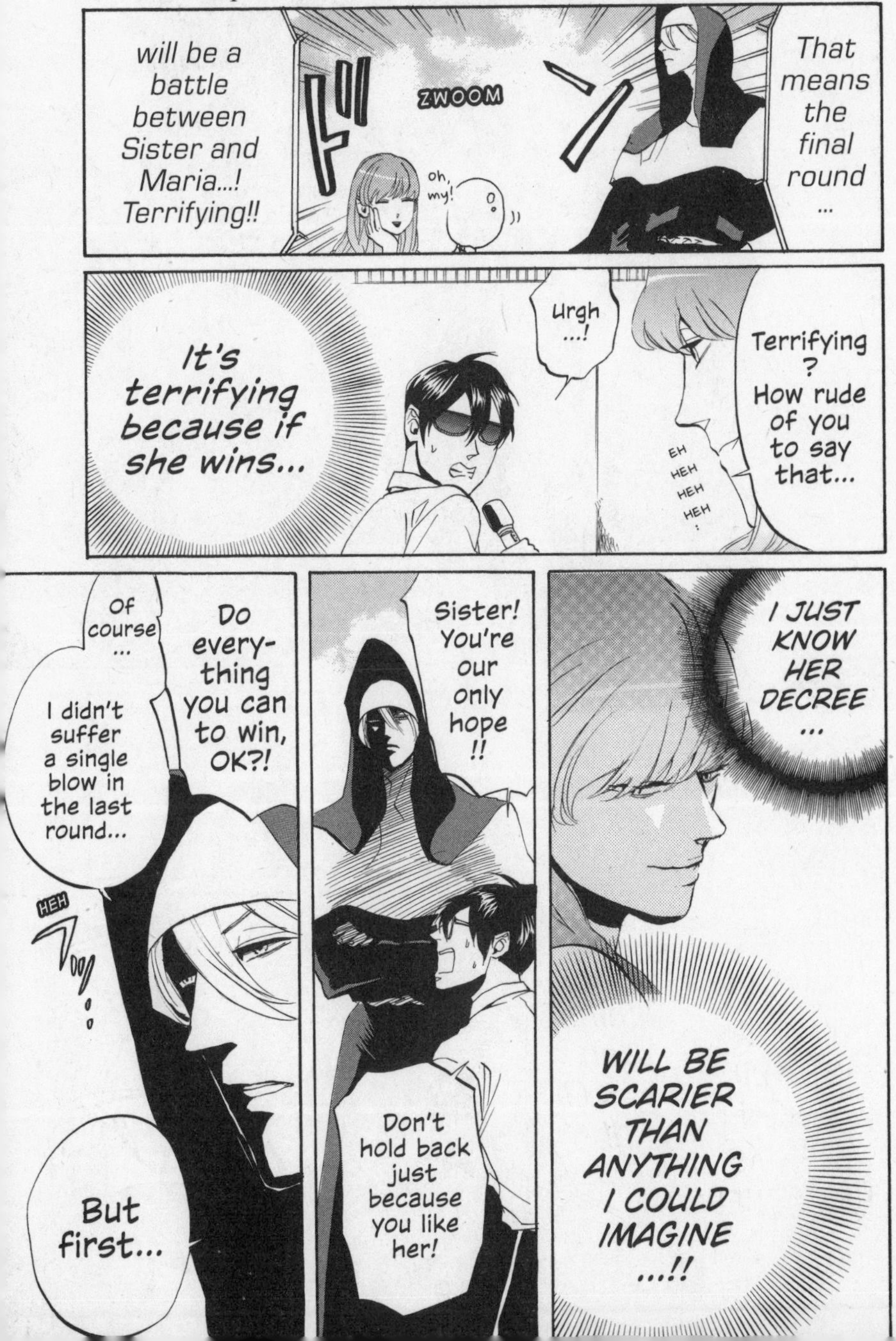
That means the final round ...
ZWOOM
oh, my!
will be a battle between Sister and Maria...! Terrifying!!
Terrifying? How rude of you to say that...
EH HEH HEH HEH
Urgh ...!
It's terrifying because if she wins...
I JUST KNOW HER DECREE ...
WILL BE SCARIER THAN ANYTHING I COULD IMAGINE ...!!
Sister! You're our only hope!!
Don't hold back just because you like her!
Do every-thing you can to win, OK?!
Of course ...
I didn't suffer a single blow in the last round...
HEH
But first...

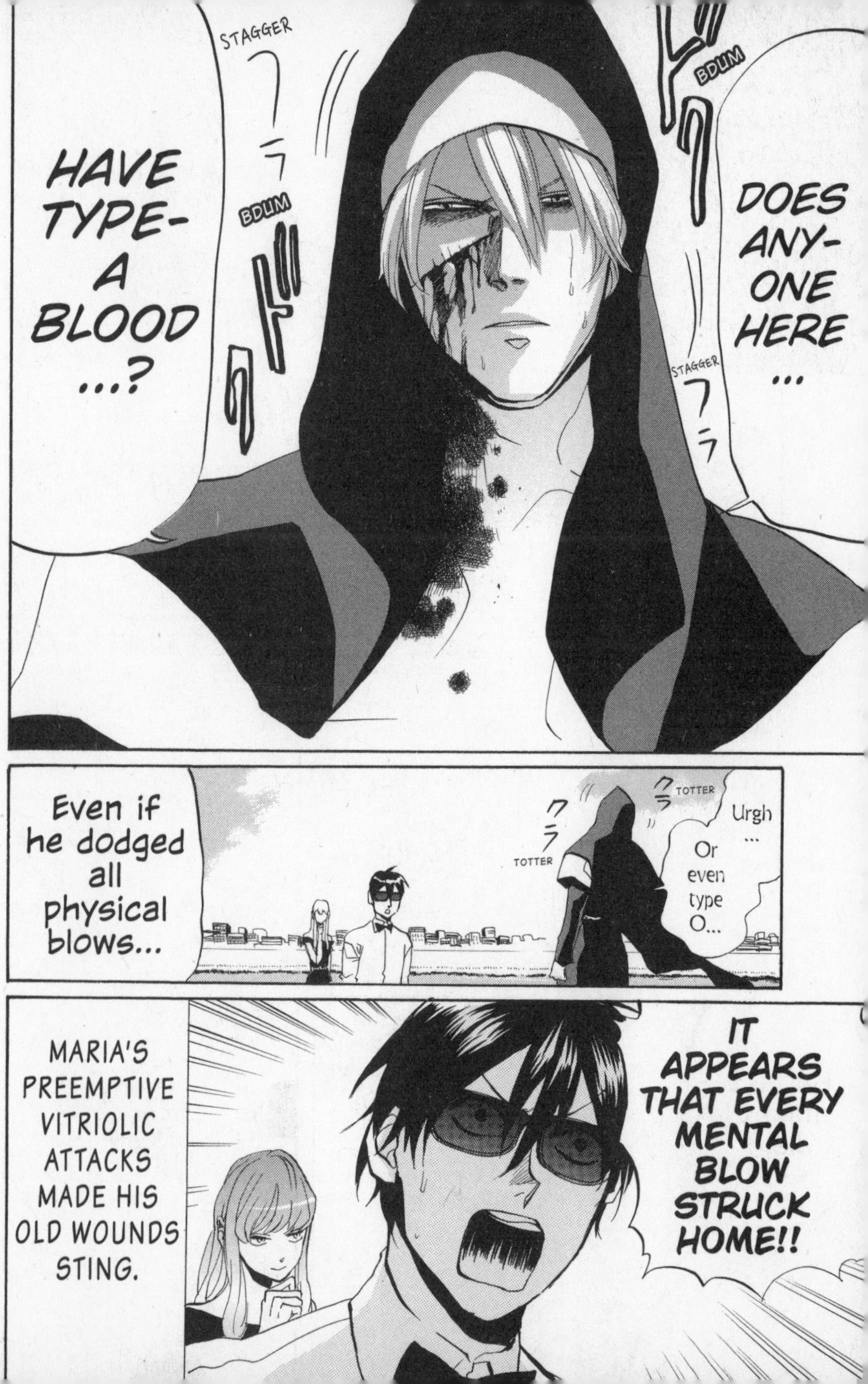
BDUM
STAGGER
DOES ANYONE HERE...
STAGGER
BDUM
HAVE TYPE-A BLOOD...?
TOTTER
Urgh...
Or even type O...
TOTTER
Even if he dodged all physical blows...
IT APPEARS THAT EVERY MENTAL BLOW STRUCK HOME!!
MARIA'S PREEMPTIVE VITRIOLIC ATTACKS MADE HIS OLD WOUNDS STING.

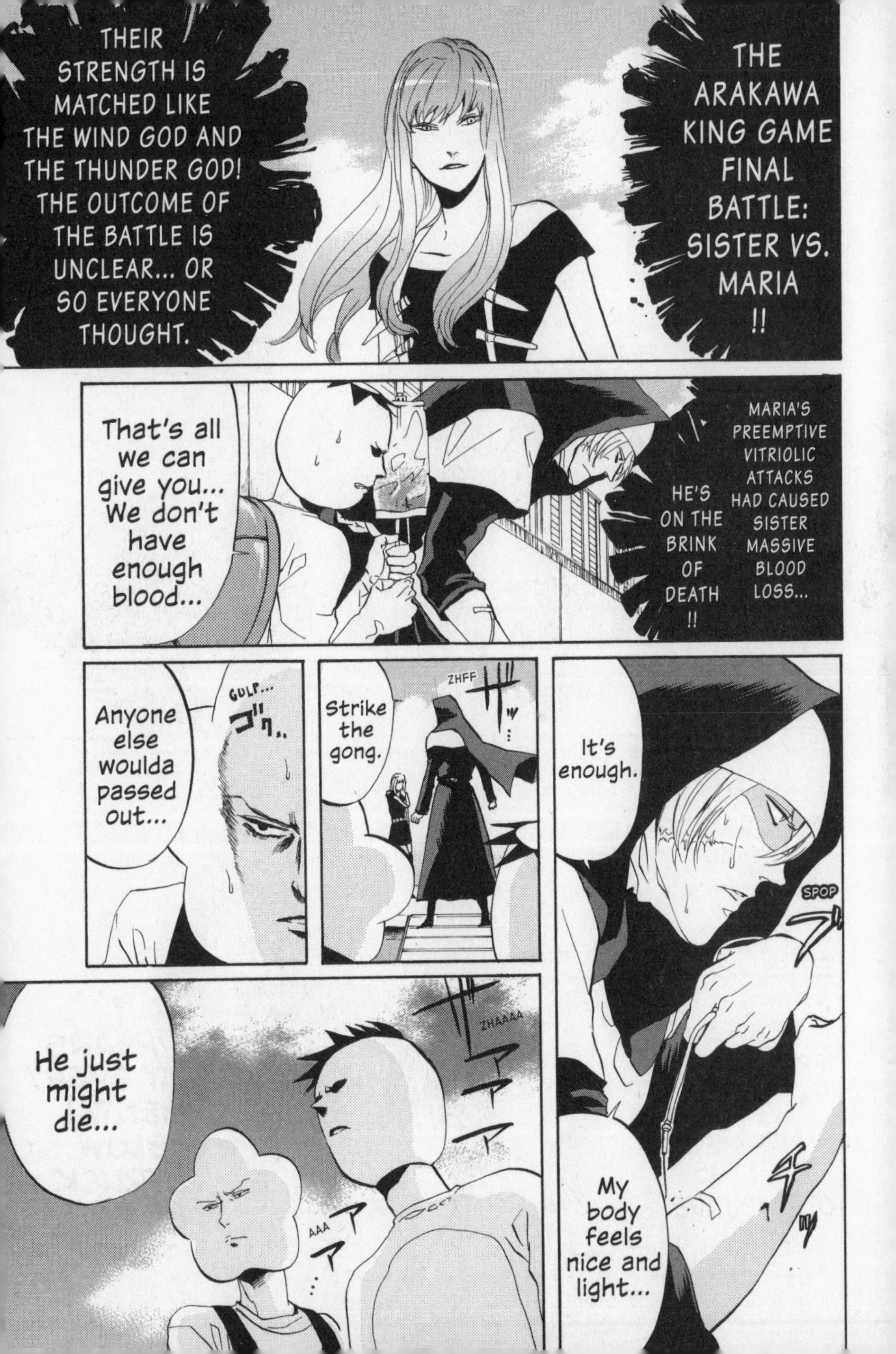

THE ARAKAWA KING GAME FINAL BATTLE: SISTER VS. MARIA !!
THEIR STRENGTH IS MATCHED LIKE THE WIND GOD AND THE THUNDER GOD! THE OUTCOME OF THE BATTLE IS UNCLEAR... OR SO EVERYONE THOUGHT.
MARIA'S PREEMPTIVE VITRIOLIC ATTACKS HAD CAUSED SISTER MASSIVE BLOOD LOSS...
HE'S ON THE BRINK OF DEATH !!
That's all we can give you... We don't have enough blood...
It's enough.
SPOP
My body feels nice and light...
ZHFF
Strike the gong.
GULP...
Anyone else woulda passed out...
ZHAAAA
He just might die...
AAA

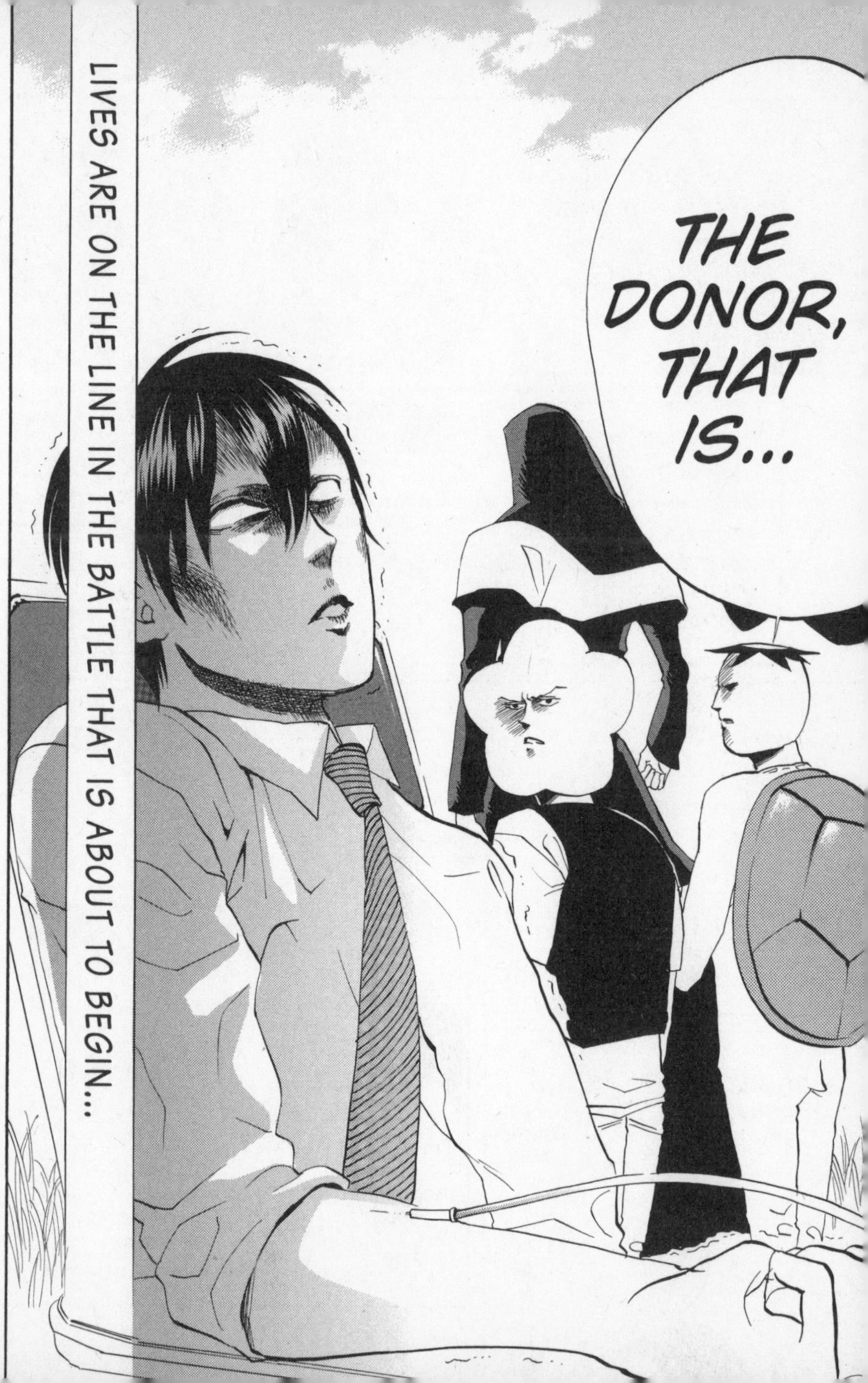
THE DONOR, THAT IS...
LIVES ARE ON THE LINE IN THE BATTLE THAT IS ABOUT TO BEGIN...

Chapter 149: The Destined Confrontation

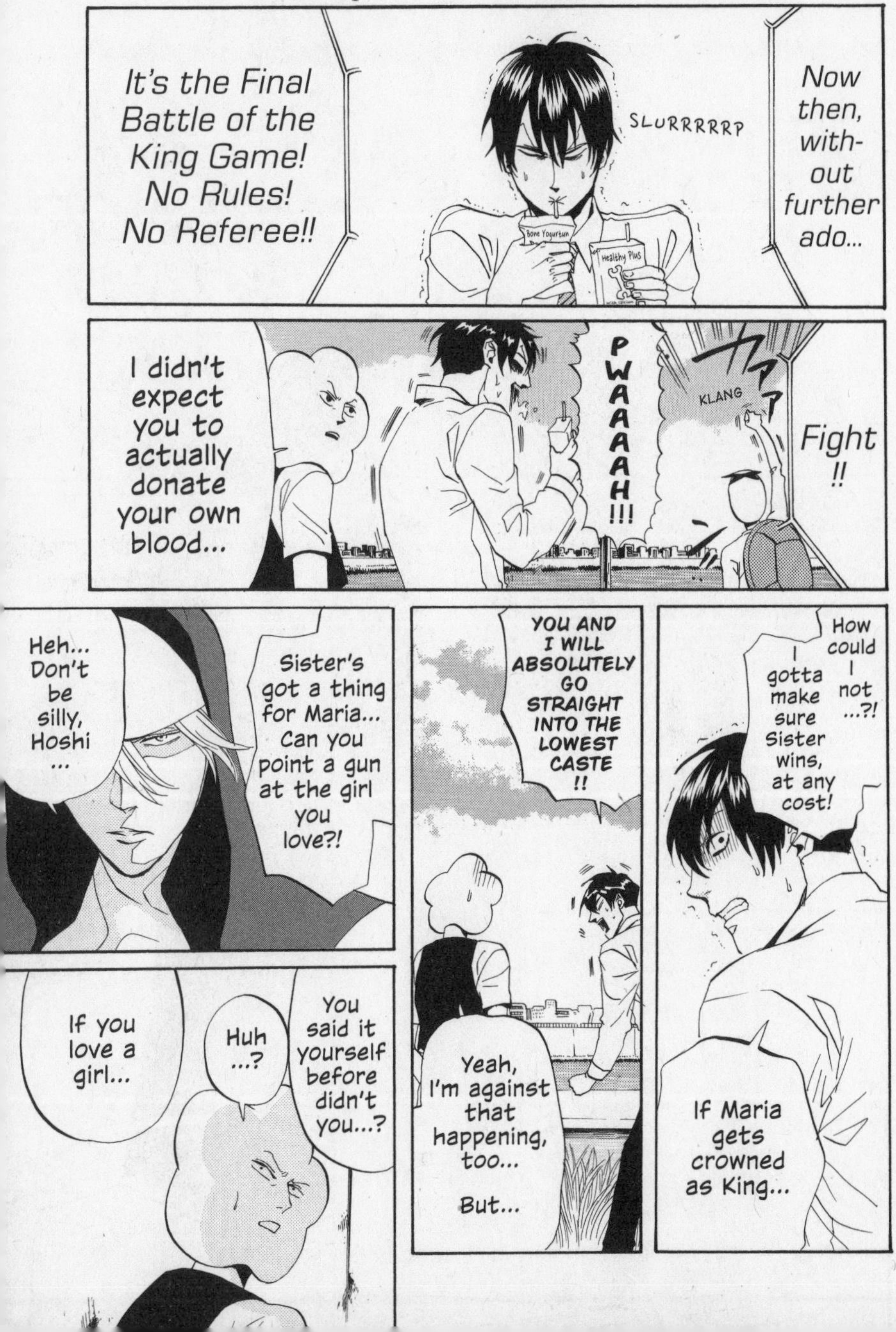
Now then, without further ado...
SLURRRRP
Healthy Plus
Bone Yogurtun
It's the Final Battle of the King Game! No Rules! No Referee!!
Fight!!
KLANG
PWAAAAAH!!!
I didn't expect you to actually donate your own blood...
How could I not...?!
I gotta make sure Sister wins, at any cost!
If Maria gets crowned as King...
YOU AND I WILL ABSOLUTELY GO STRAIGHT INTO THE LOWEST CASTE!!
Yeah, I'm against that happening, too...
But...
Sister's got a thing for Maria... Can you point a gun at the girl you love?!
Heh... Don't be silly, Hoshi...
You said it yourself before didn't you...?
Huh...?
If you love a girl...

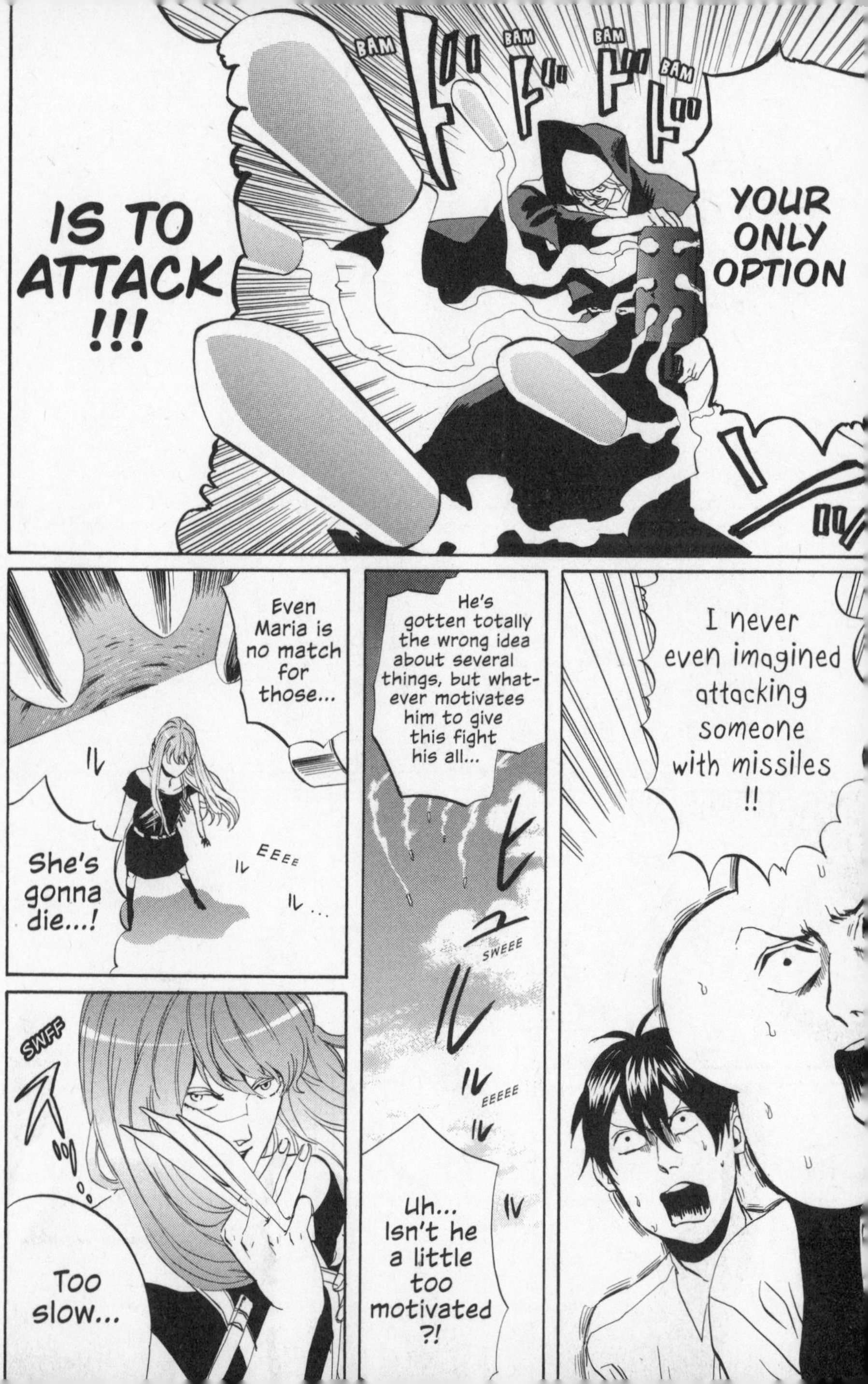
BAM
BAM
BAM
BAM
YOUR ONLY OPTION
IS TO ATTACK !!!
I never even imagined attacking someone with missiles !!
He's gotten totally the wrong idea about several things, but whatever motivates him to give this fight his all...
SWEEE
EEEEE
Uh... Isn't he a little too motivated ?!
Even Maria is no match for those...
EEEE
She's gonna die...!
SWFF
Too slow...

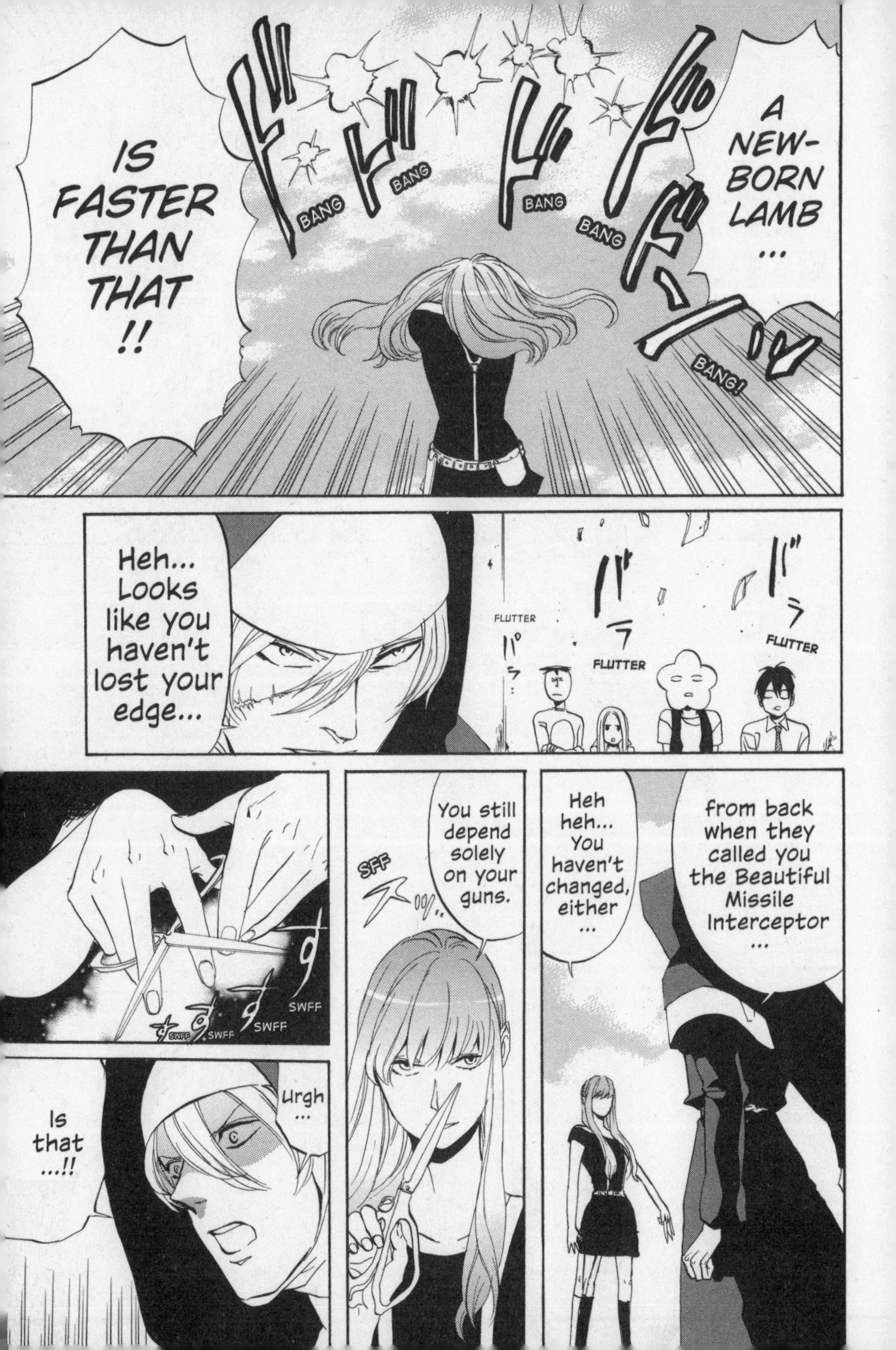
A NEW-BORN LAMB ...
BANG
BANG
BANG
BANG
BANG!
IS FASTER THAN THAT !!
FLUTTER
FLUTTER
FLUTTER
Heh... Looks like you haven't lost your edge...
Heh heh... You haven't changed, either ...
from back when they called you the Beautiful Missile Interceptor ...
You still depend solely on your guns.
SFF
SWFF
SWFF
SWFF
SWFF
Urgh ...
Is that ...!!

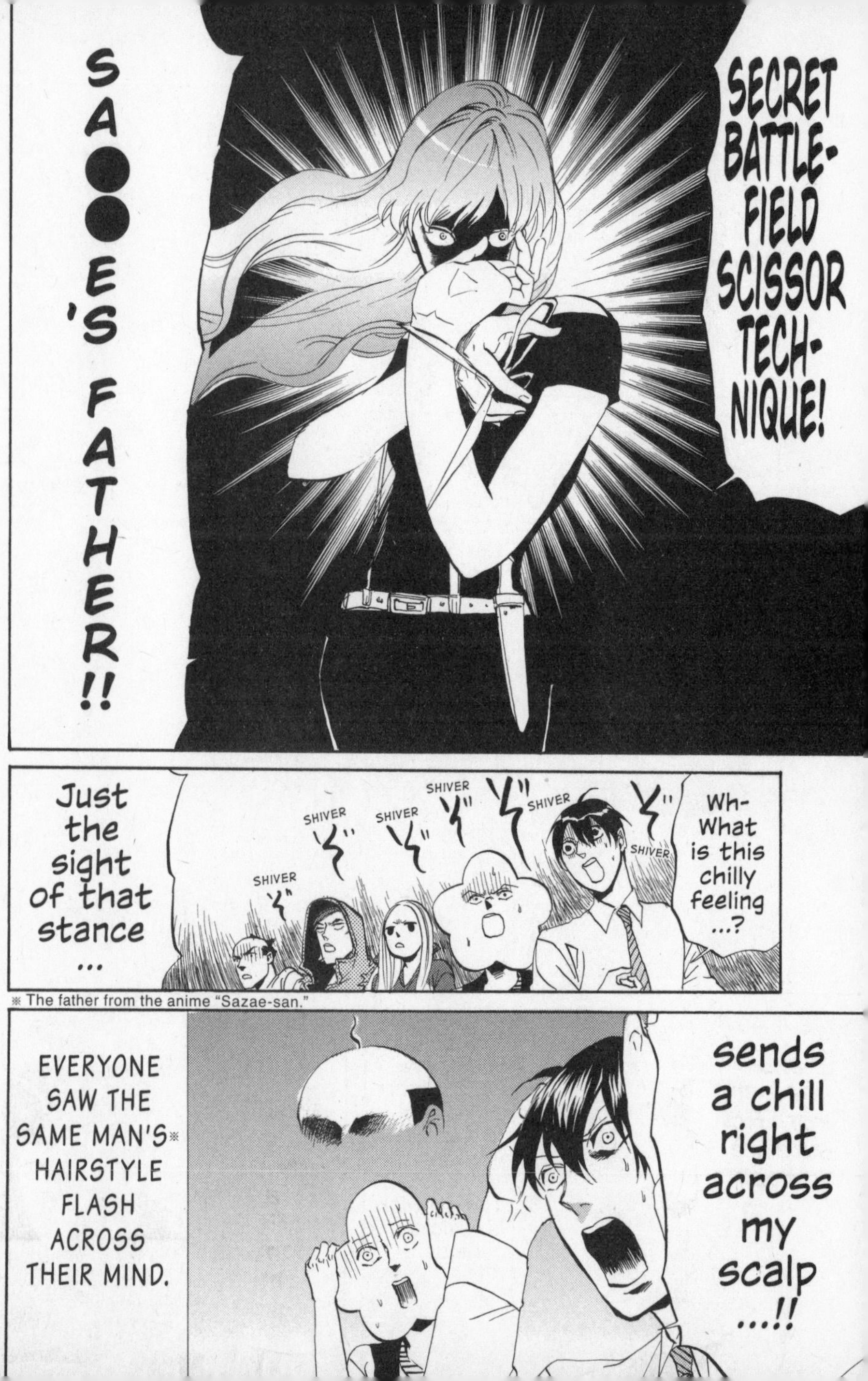
SECRET BATTLE-FIELD SCISSOR TECH-NIQUE!
SA●●E'S FATHER!!
Wh- What is this chilly feeling ...?
SHIVER
SHIVER
SHIVER
SHIVER
SHIVER
SHIVER
Just the sight of that stance ...
sends a chill right across my scalp ...!!
EVERYONE SAW THE SAME MAN'S※ HAIRSTYLE FLASH ACROSS THEIR MIND.
※ The father from the anime "Sazae-san."

Chapter 150: The Voice of God

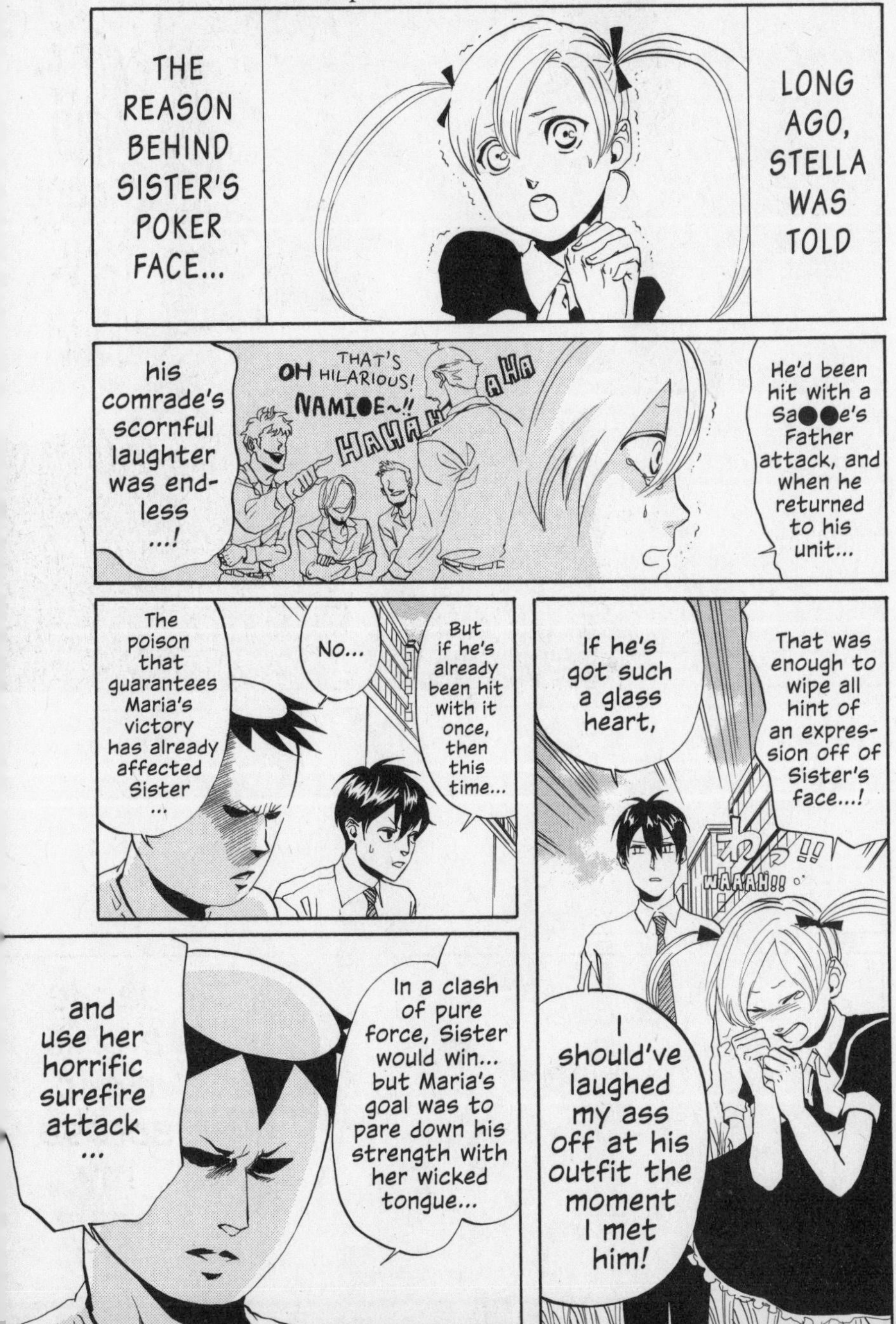
LONG AGO, STELLA WAS TOLD
THE REASON BEHIND SISTER'S POKER FACE...
He'd been hit with a Sa●●e's Father attack, and when he returned to his unit...
AHA
HAHAH
NAMI●E~!!
OH THAT'S HILARIOUS!
his comrade's scornful laughter was endless...!
That was enough to wipe all hint of an expression off of Sister's face...!
If he's got such a glass heart,
WAAAH!!
I should've laughed my ass off at his outfit the moment I met him!
But if he's already been hit with it once, then this time...
No...
The poison that guarantees Maria's victory has already affected Sister ...
In a clash of pure force, Sister would win... but Maria's goal was to pare down his strength with her wicked tongue...
and use her horrific surefire attack ...

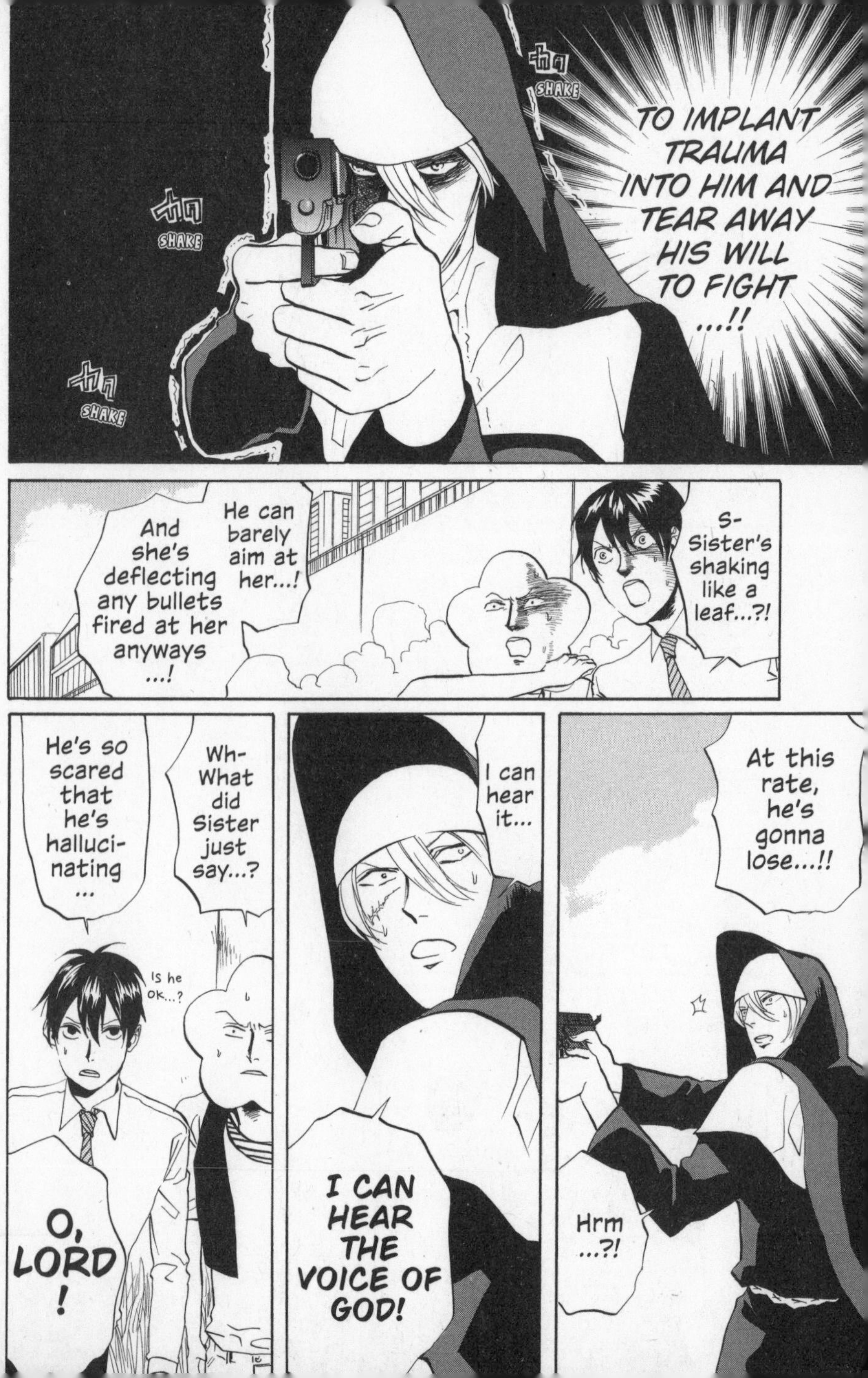
SHAKE
TO IMPLANT TRAUMA INTO HIM AND TEAR AWAY HIS WILL TO FIGHT ...!!
SHAKE
SHAKE
S- Sister's shaking like a leaf...?!
He can barely aim at her...!
And she's deflecting any bullets fired at her anyways ...!
At this rate, he's gonna lose...!!
Hrm ...?!
I can hear it...
I CAN HEAR THE VOICE OF GOD!
Wh- What did Sister just say...?
He's so scared that he's halluci-nating ...
Is he OK...?
O, LORD !

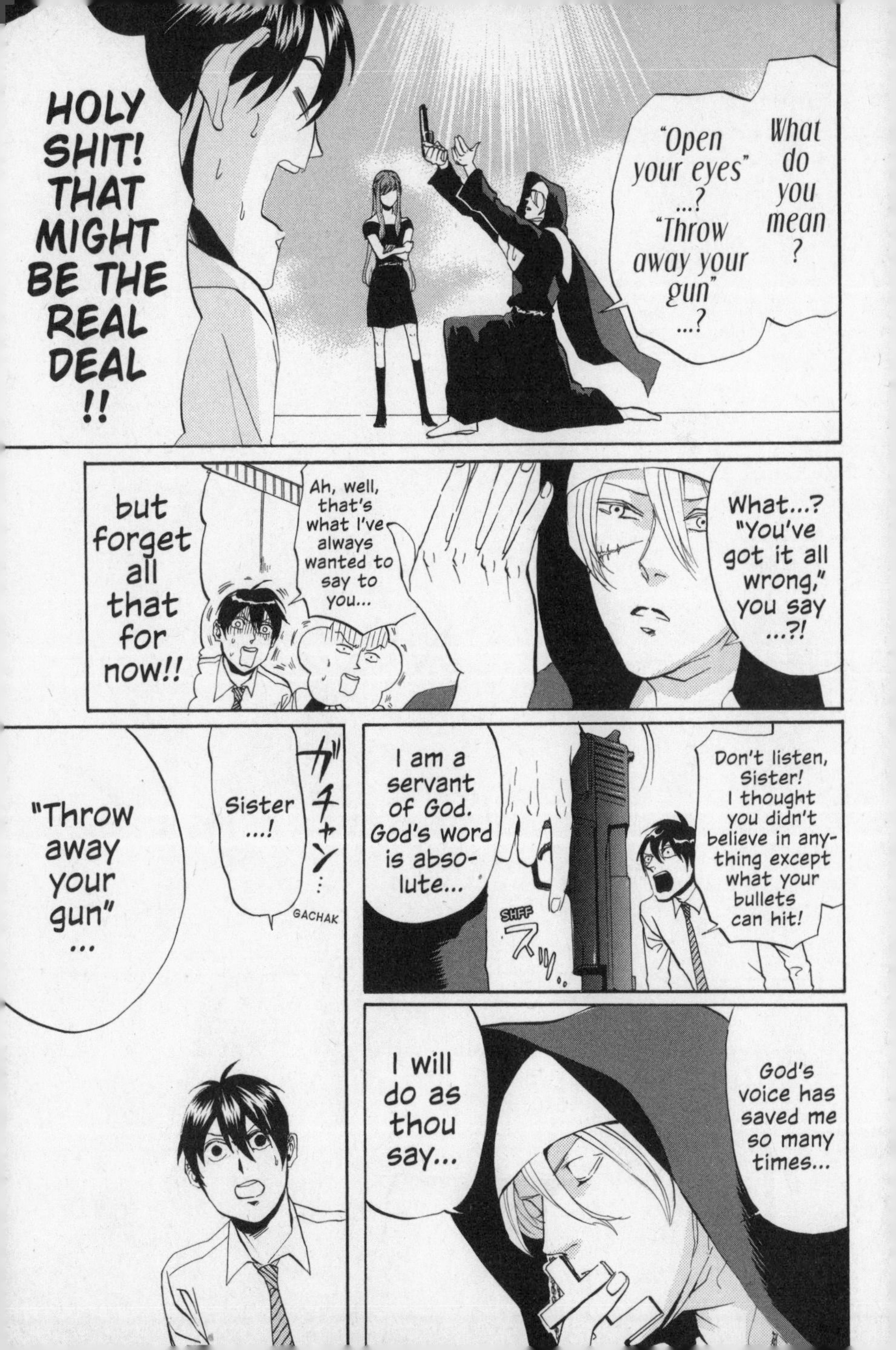
What do you mean?
"Open your eyes"...? "Throw away your gun"...?
HOLY SHIT! THAT MIGHT BE THE REAL DEAL!!
What...? "You've got it all wrong," you say...?!
Ah, well, that's what I've always wanted to say to you...
but forget all that for now!!
Don't listen, Sister! I thought you didn't believe in any-thing except what your bullets can hit!
SHFF
I am a servant of God. God's word is abso-lute...
God's voice has saved me so many times...
I will do as thou say...
GACHAK
Sister...!
"Throw away your gun"...

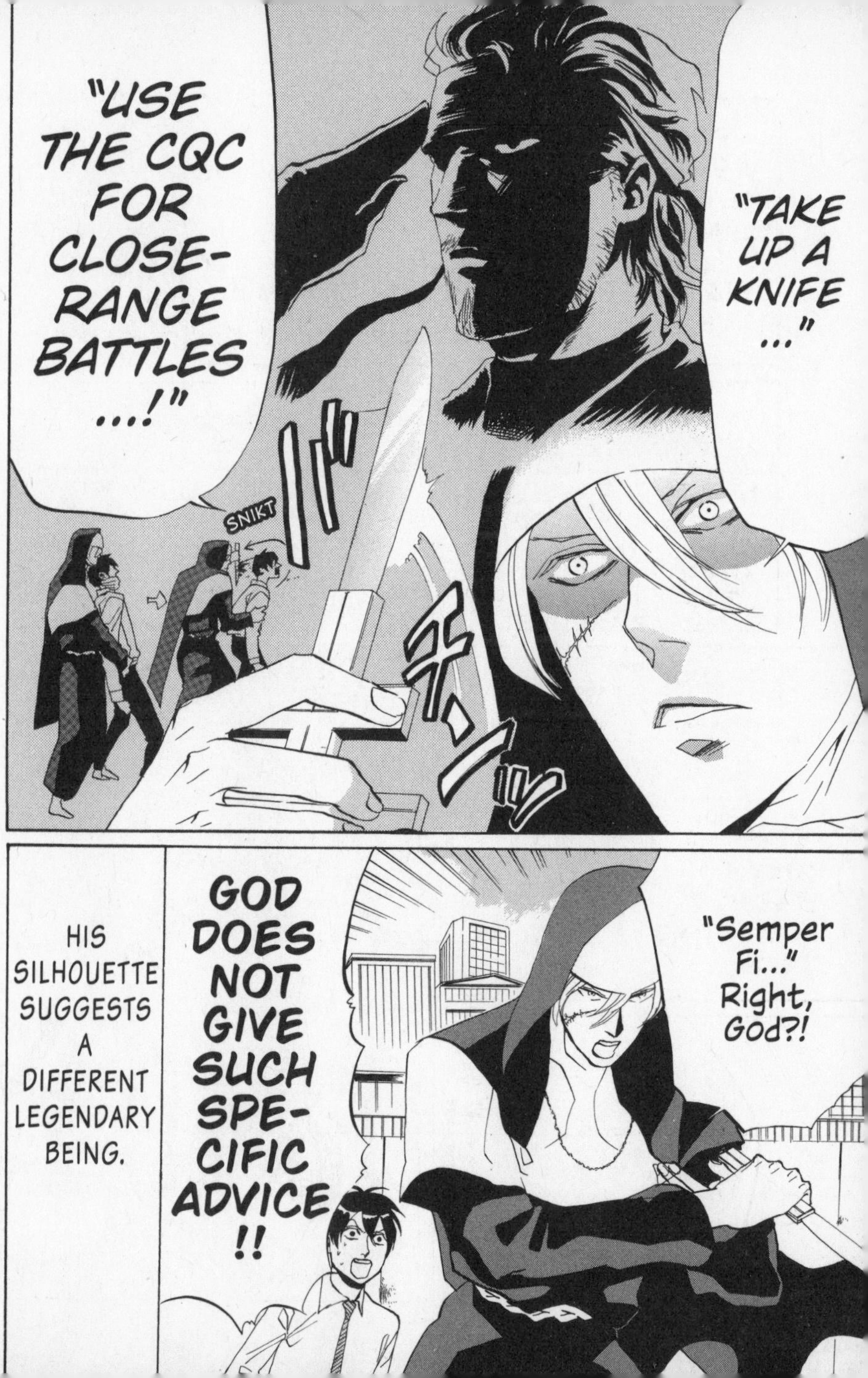
"TAKE UP A KNIFE ..."
"USE THE CQC FOR CLOSE-RANGE BATTLES ...!"
SNIKT
"Semper Fi..." Right, God?!
GOD DOES NOT GIVE SUCH SPE-CIFIC ADVICE !!
HIS SILHOUETTE SUGGESTS A DIFFERENT LEGENDARY BEING.

☞ Chapter 151: Lethal Weapon

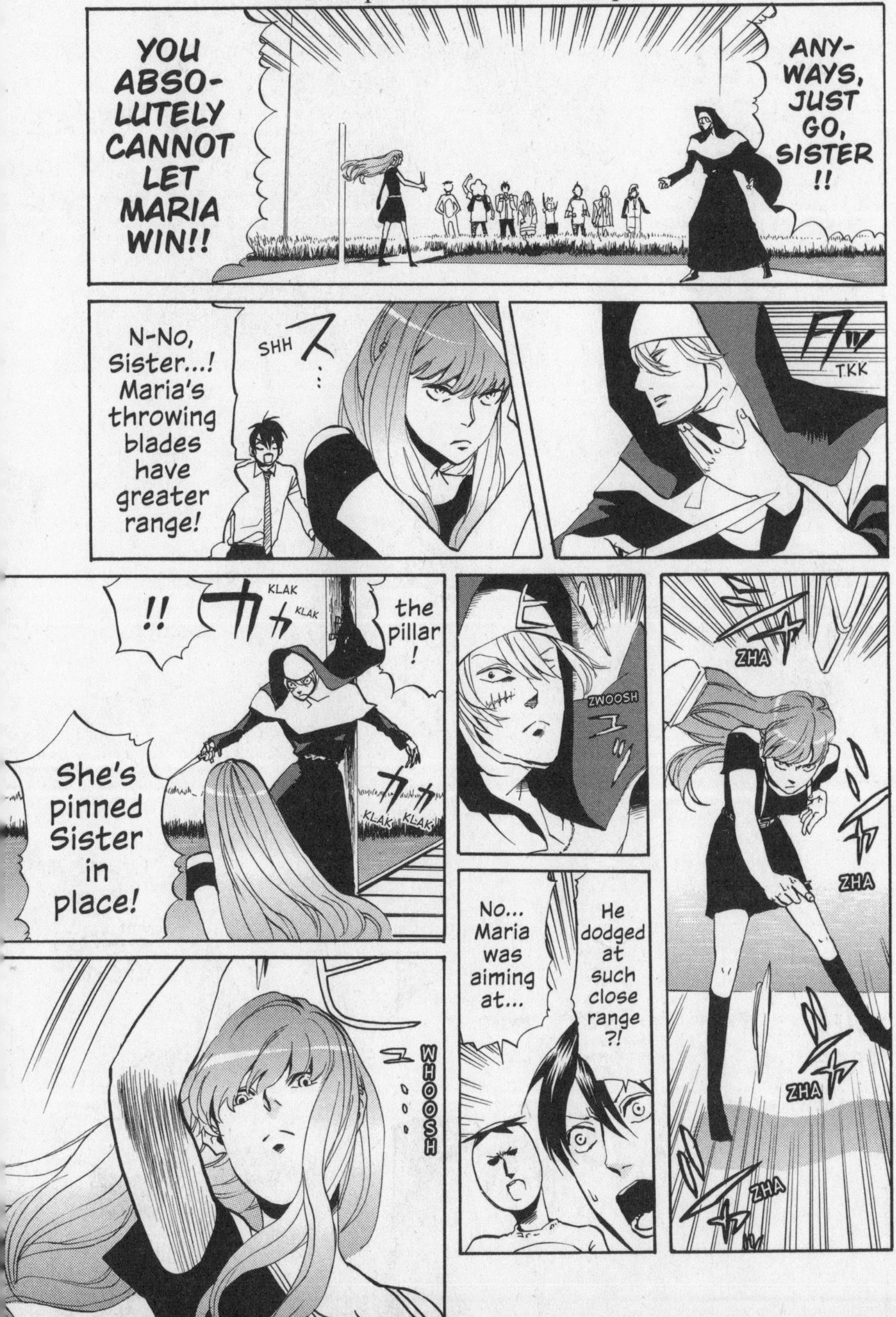
ANY-WAYS, JUST GO, SISTER!!
YOU ABSOLUTELY CANNOT LET MARIA WIN!!
T.KK
SHH
N-No, Sister...! Maria's throwing blades have greater range!
ZHA
ZHA
ZHA
ZHA
ZWOOSH
He dodged at such close range?!
No... Maria was aiming at...
the pillar!
KLAK KLAK
!!
KLAK KLAK
She's pinned Sister in place!
WHOOSH...

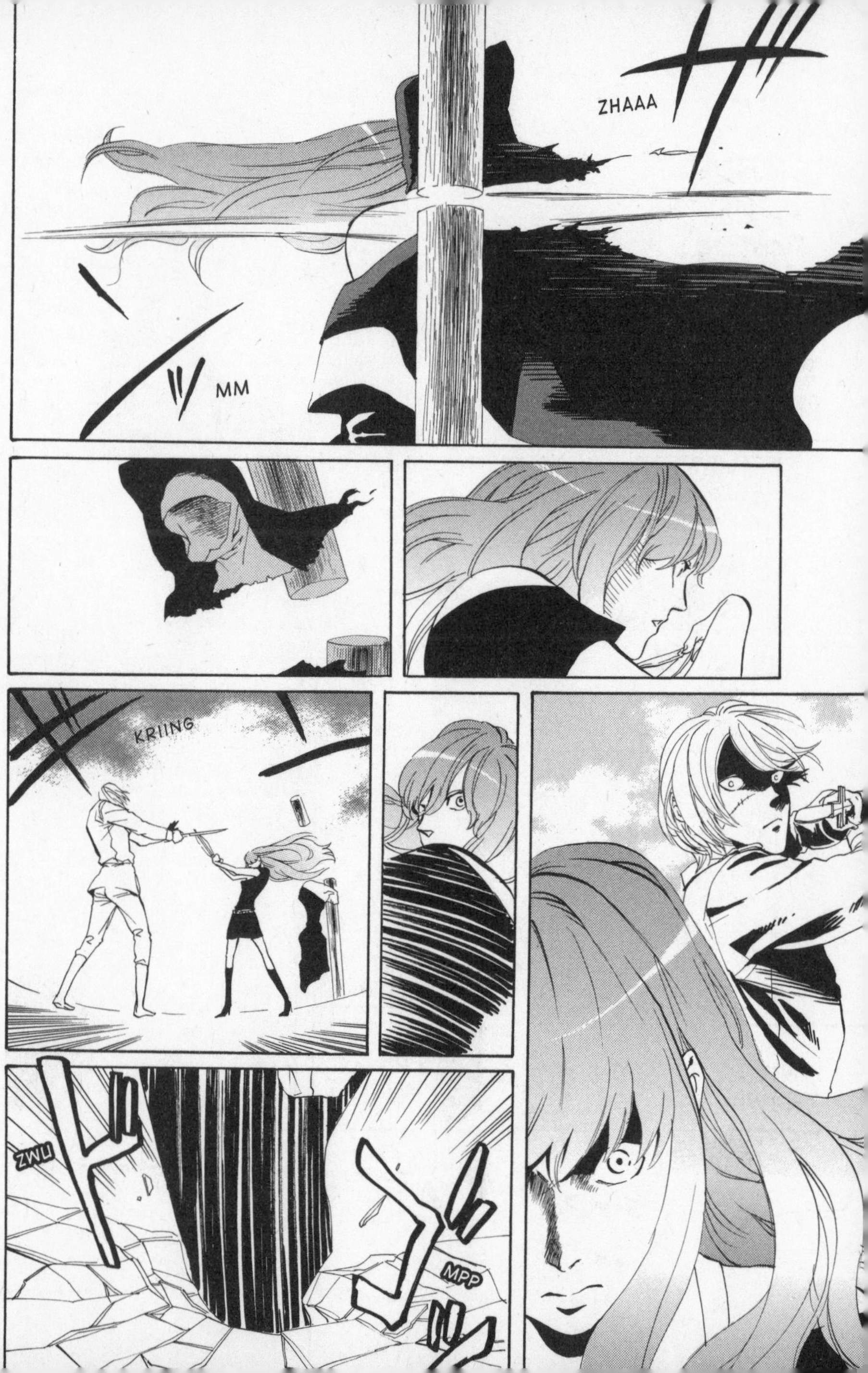
ZHAAA
MM
KRIING
ZWU
MPP

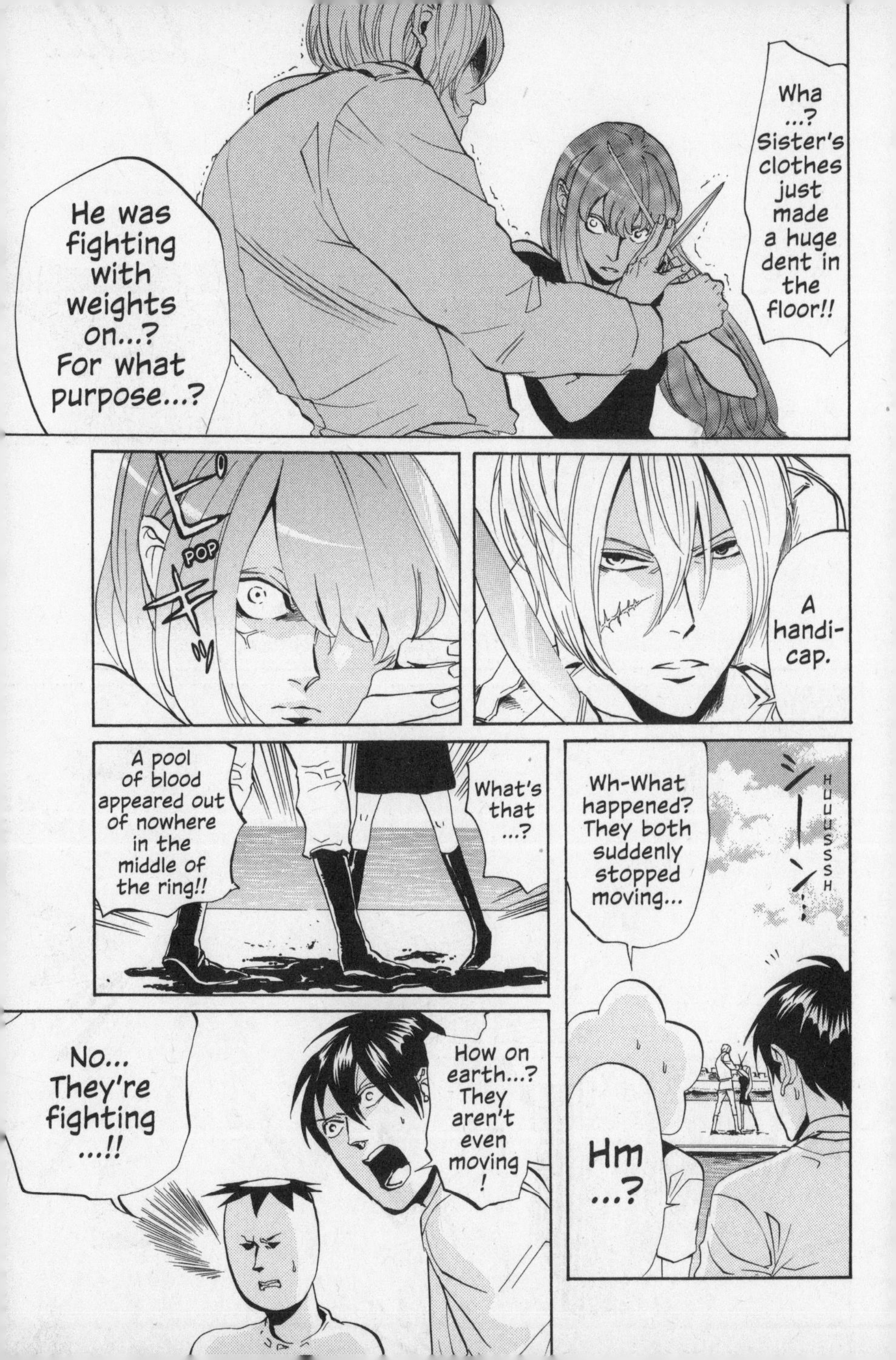
Wha...? Sister's clothes just made a huge dent in the floor!!
He was fighting with weights on...? For what purpose...?
A handi-cap.
POP
HUUUSSH
Wh-What happened? They both suddenly stopped moving...
Hm...?
What's that...?
A pool of blood appeared out of nowhere in the middle of the ring!!
How on earth...? They aren't even moving!
No... They're fighting...!!

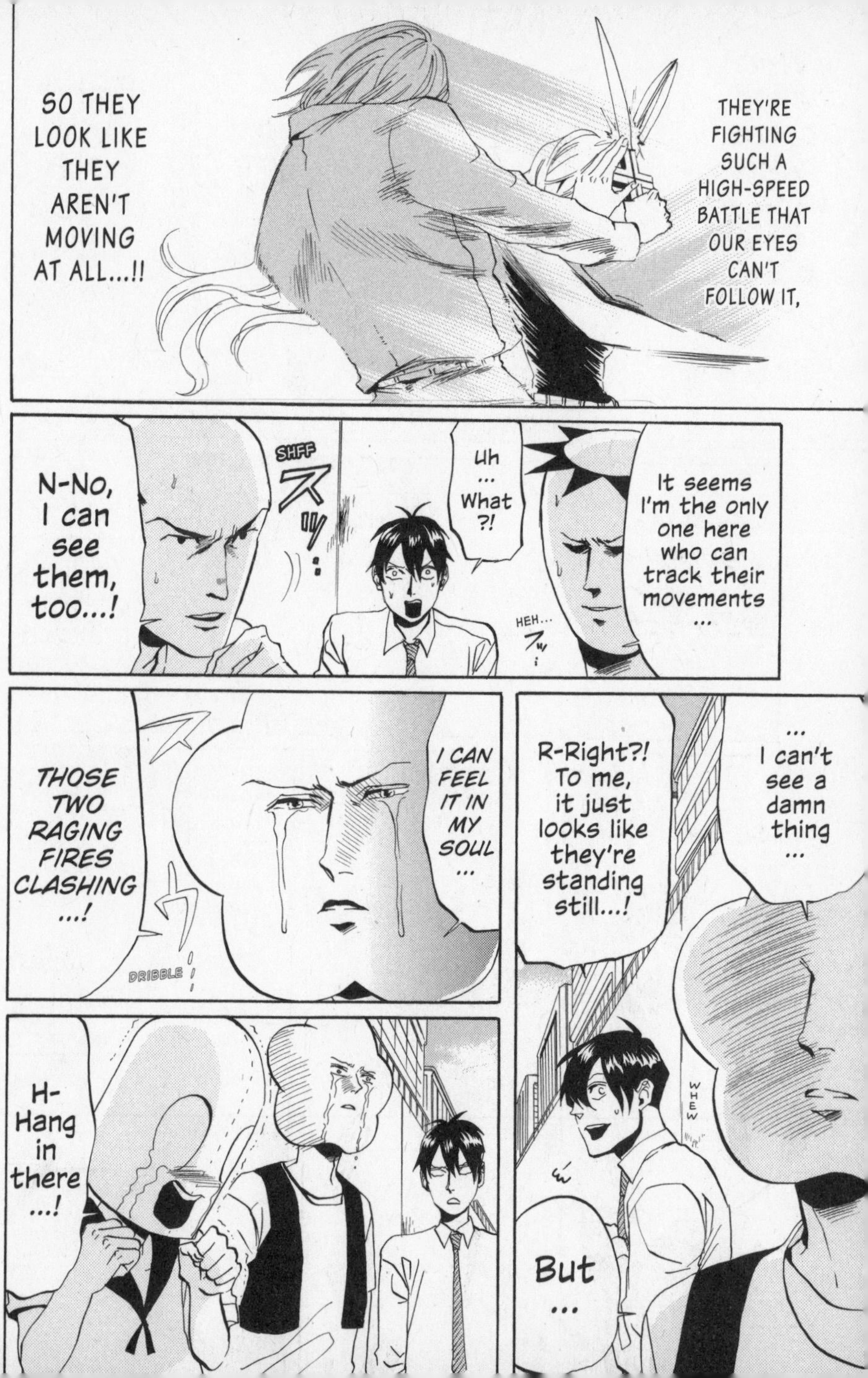
THEY'RE FIGHTING SUCH A HIGH-SPEED BATTLE THAT OUR EYES CAN'T FOLLOW IT,
SO THEY LOOK LIKE THEY AREN'T MOVING AT ALL...!!
It seems I'm the only one here who can track their movements ...
HEH...
Uh ... What ?!
SHFF
N-No, I can see them, too...!
... I can't see a damn thing ...
R-Right?! To me, it just looks like they're standing still...!
I CAN FEEL IT IN MY SOUL ...
THOSE TWO RAGING FIRES CLASHING ...!
DRIBBLE
WHEW
But ...
H-Hang in there ...!

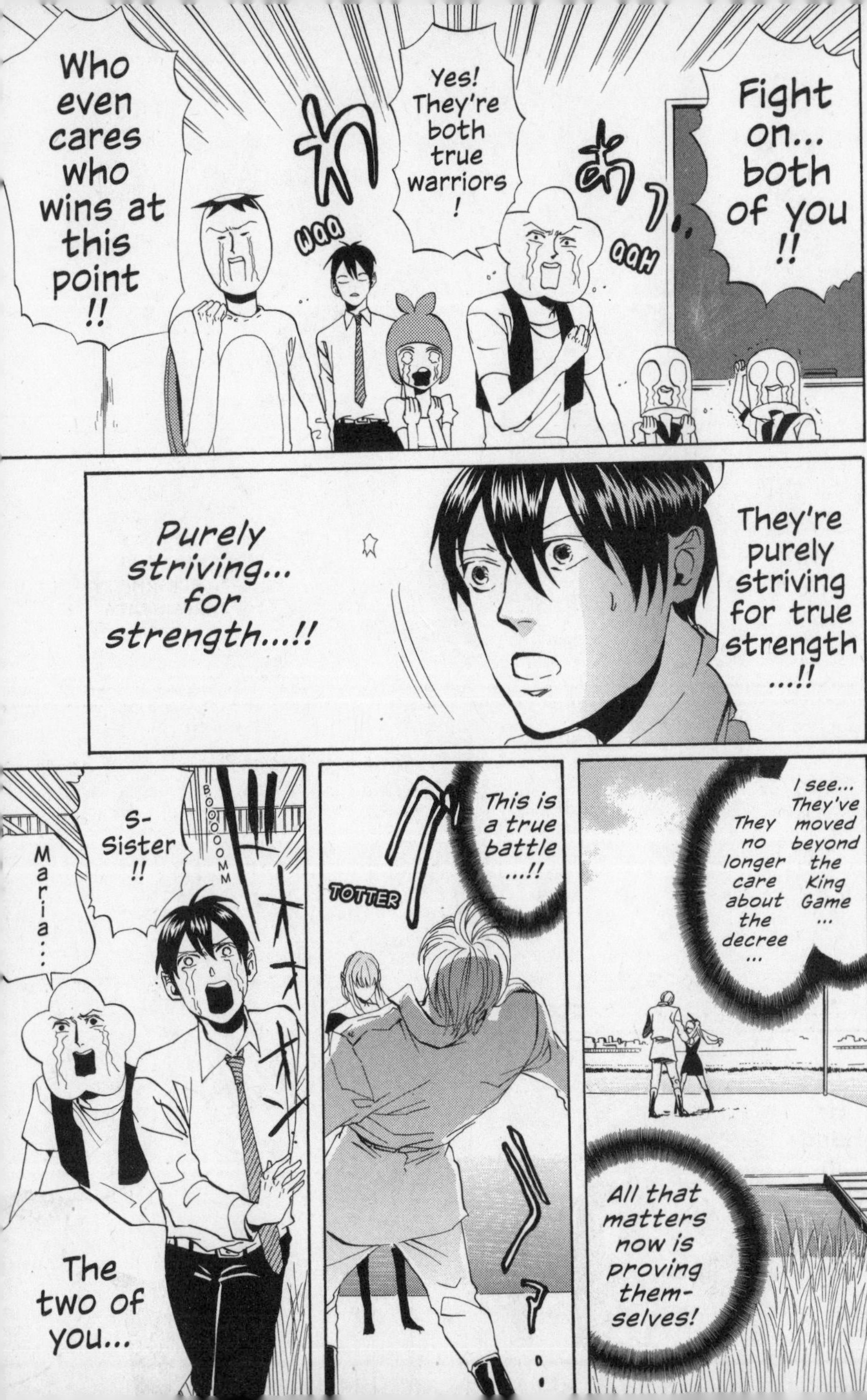
Fight on... both of you!!
あっ
AAH
Yes! They're both true warriors!
わ
WAA
Who even cares who wins at this point!!
They're purely striving for true strength...!!
Purely striving... for strength...!!
I see... They've moved beyond the King Game...
They no longer care about the decree...
All that matters now is proving themselves!
This is a true battle...!!
TOTTER
S-Sister!!
BOOOOOMM
Maria...
The two of you...

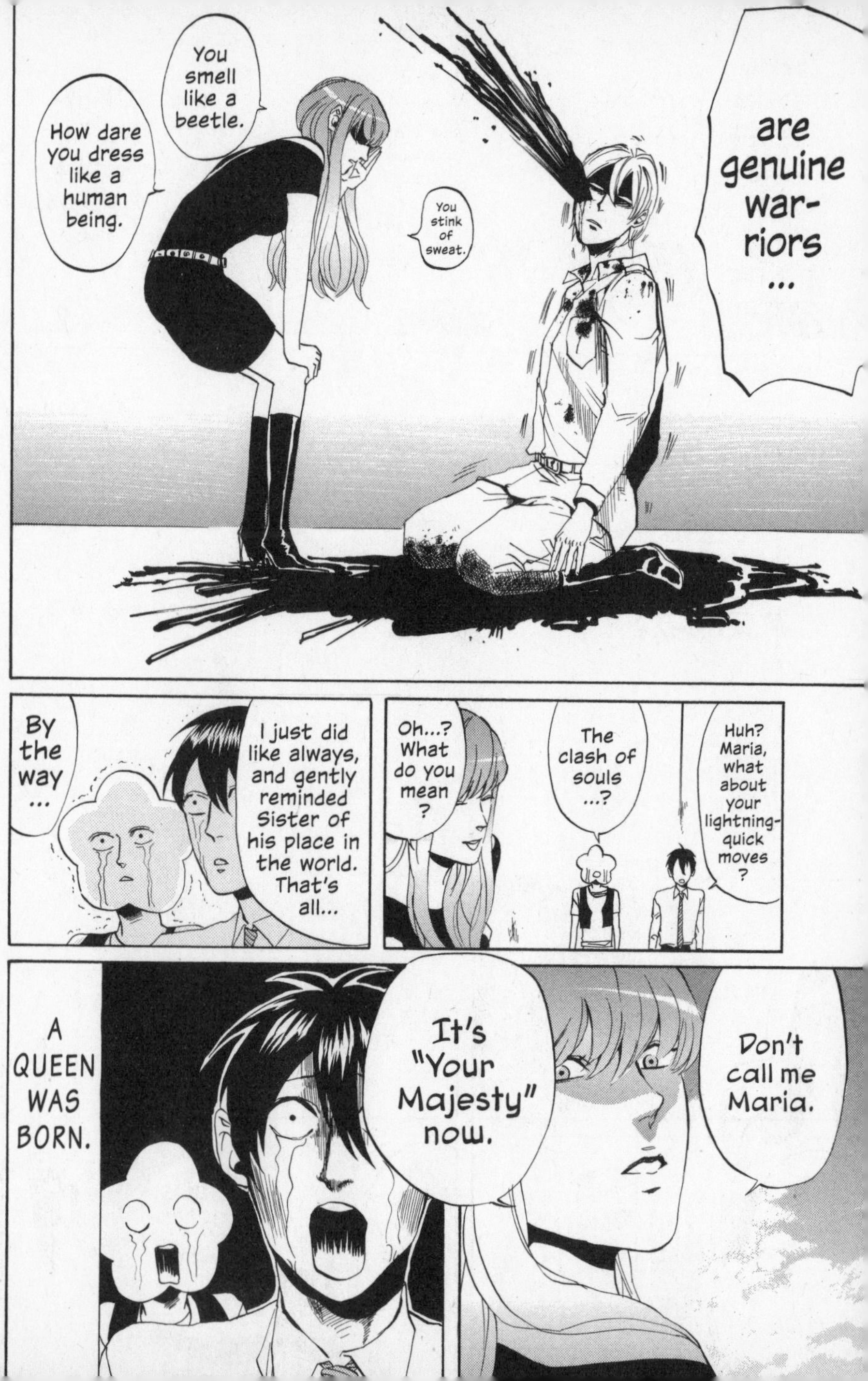
are genuine war- riors ...
You stink of sweat.
You smell like a beetle.
How dare you dress like a human being.
Huh? Maria, what about your lightning-quick moves?
The clash of souls ...?
Oh...? What do you mean?
I just did like always, and gently reminded Sister of his place in the world. That's all...
By the way ...
Don't call me Maria.
It's "Your Majesty" now.
A QUEEN WAS BORN.

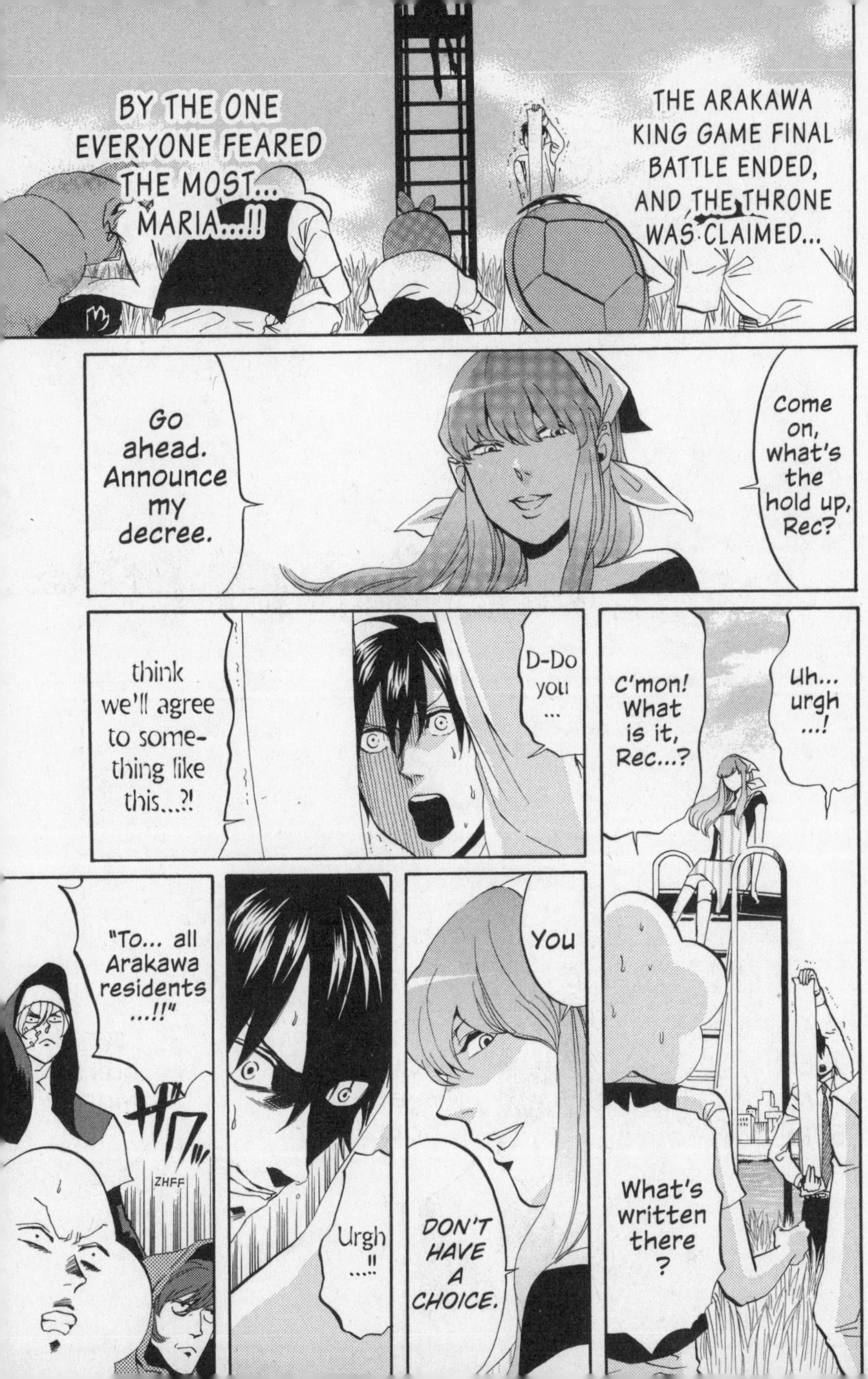
THE ARAKAWA KING GAME FINAL BATTLE ENDED, AND THE THRONE WAS CLAIMED...
BY THE ONE EVERYONE FEARED THE MOST... MARIA...!!
Come on, what's the hold up, Rec?
Go ahead. Announce my decree.
Uh... urgh ...!
C'mon! What is it, Rec...?
What's written there?
D-Do you ...
think we'll agree to some-thing like this...?!
You
DON'T HAVE A CHOICE.
Urgh ...!!
ZHFF
"To... all Arakawa residents ...!!"

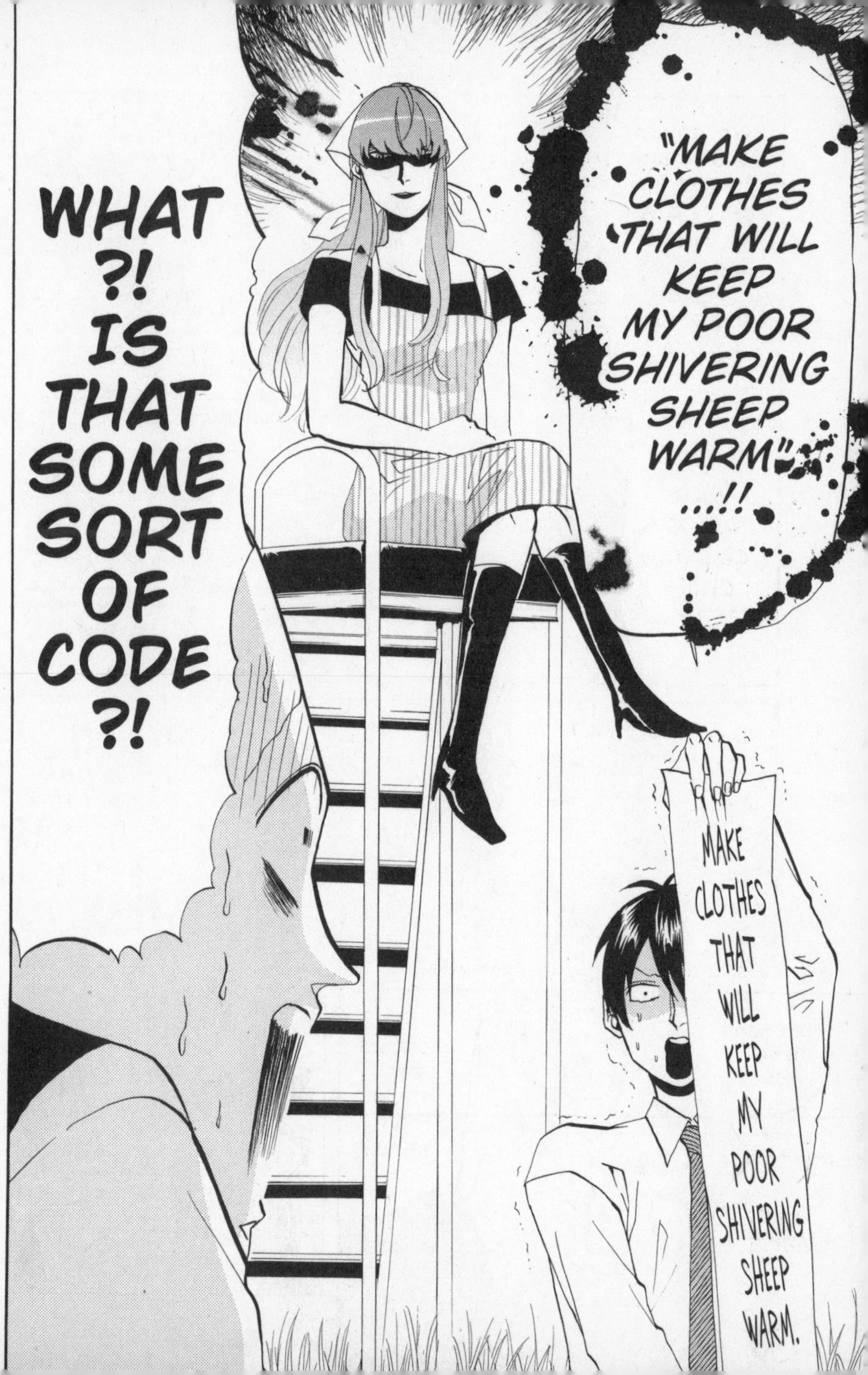

"MAKE CLOTHES THAT WILL KEEP MY POOR SHIVERING SHEEP WARM"...!!
MAKE CLOTHES THAT WILL KEEP MY POOR SHIVERING SHEEP WARM.
WHAT?! IS THAT SOME SORT OF CODE?!

Chapter 152: Maria's Wish

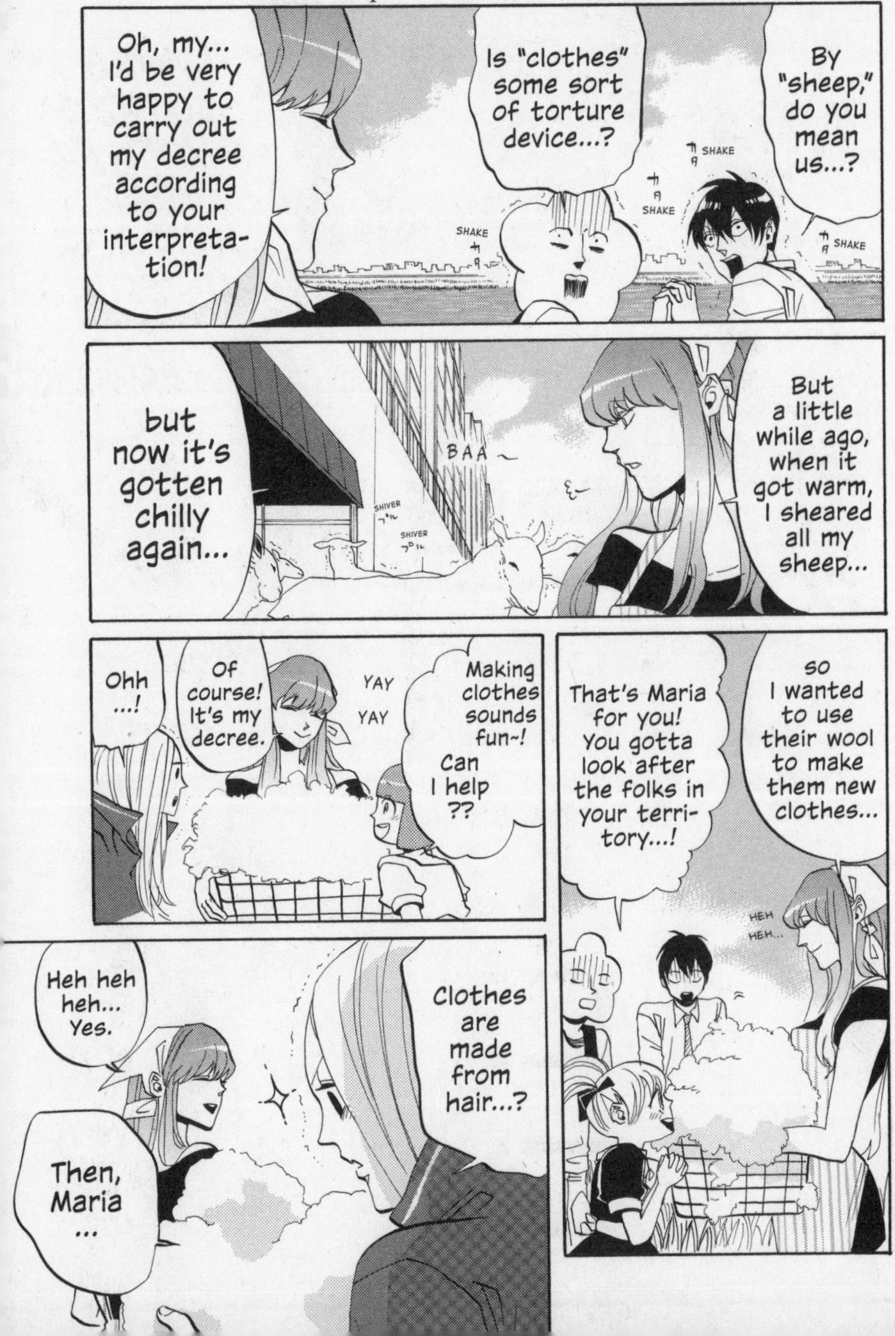

By "sheep," do you mean us...?
SHAKE
SHAKE
SHAKE
Is "clothes" some sort of torture device...?
SHAKE
Oh, my... I'd be very happy to carry out my decree according to your interpretation!
But a little while ago, when it got warm, I sheared all my sheep...
BAA~
SHIVER
SHIVER
but now it's gotten chilly again...
so I wanted to use their wool to make them new clothes...
HEH HEH...
That's Maria for you! You gotta look after the folks in your territory...!
Making clothes sounds fun~! Can I help??
YAY
YAY
Of course! It's my decree.
Ohh...!
Clothes are made from hair...?
Heh heh heh... Yes.
Then, Maria...

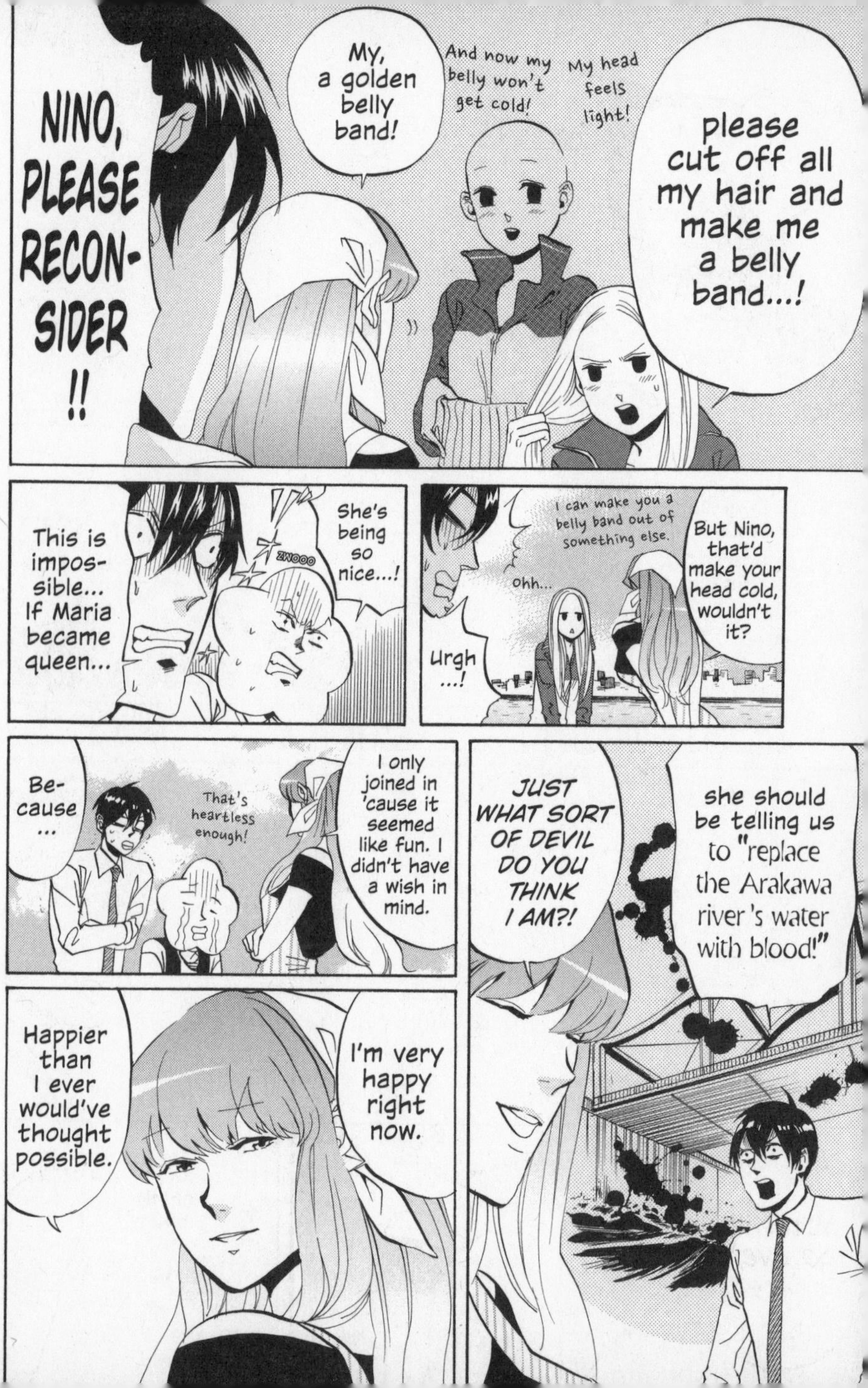
please cut off all my hair and make me a belly band...!
My head feels light!
And now my belly won't get cold!
My, a golden belly band!
NINO, PLEASE RECON-SIDER!!
But Nino, that'd make your head cold, wouldn't it?
I can make you a belly band out of something else.
ohh...
Urgh...!
She's being so nice...!
ZWOOO
This is impos-sible... If Maria became queen...
she should be telling us to "replace the Arakawa river's water with blood!"
JUST WHAT SORT OF DEVIL DO YOU THINK I AM?!
I only joined in 'cause it seemed like fun. I didn't have a wish in mind.
That's heartless enough!
Be-cause...
I'm very happy right now.
Happier than I ever would've thought possible.

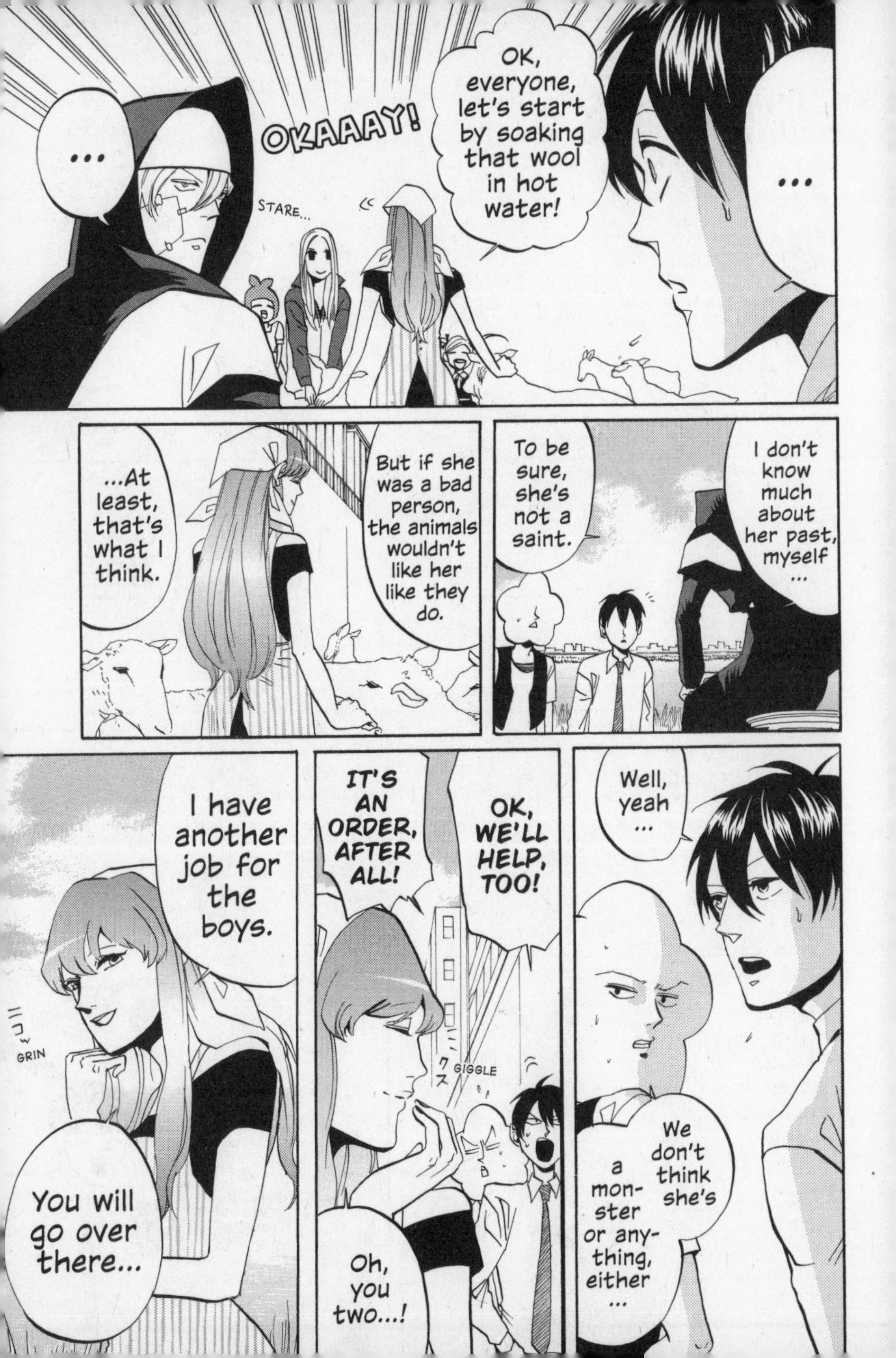
...
OK, everyone, let's start by soaking that wool in hot water!
OKAAAY!
STARE...
...
I don't know much about her past, myself ...
To be sure, she's not a saint.
But if she was a bad person, the animals wouldn't like her like they do.
...At least, that's what I think.
Well, yeah ...
We don't think she's a monster or anything, either ...
OK, WE'LL HELP, TOO!
IT'S AN ORDER, AFTER ALL!
GIGGLE
Oh, you two...!
I have another job for the boys.
GRIN
You will go over there...

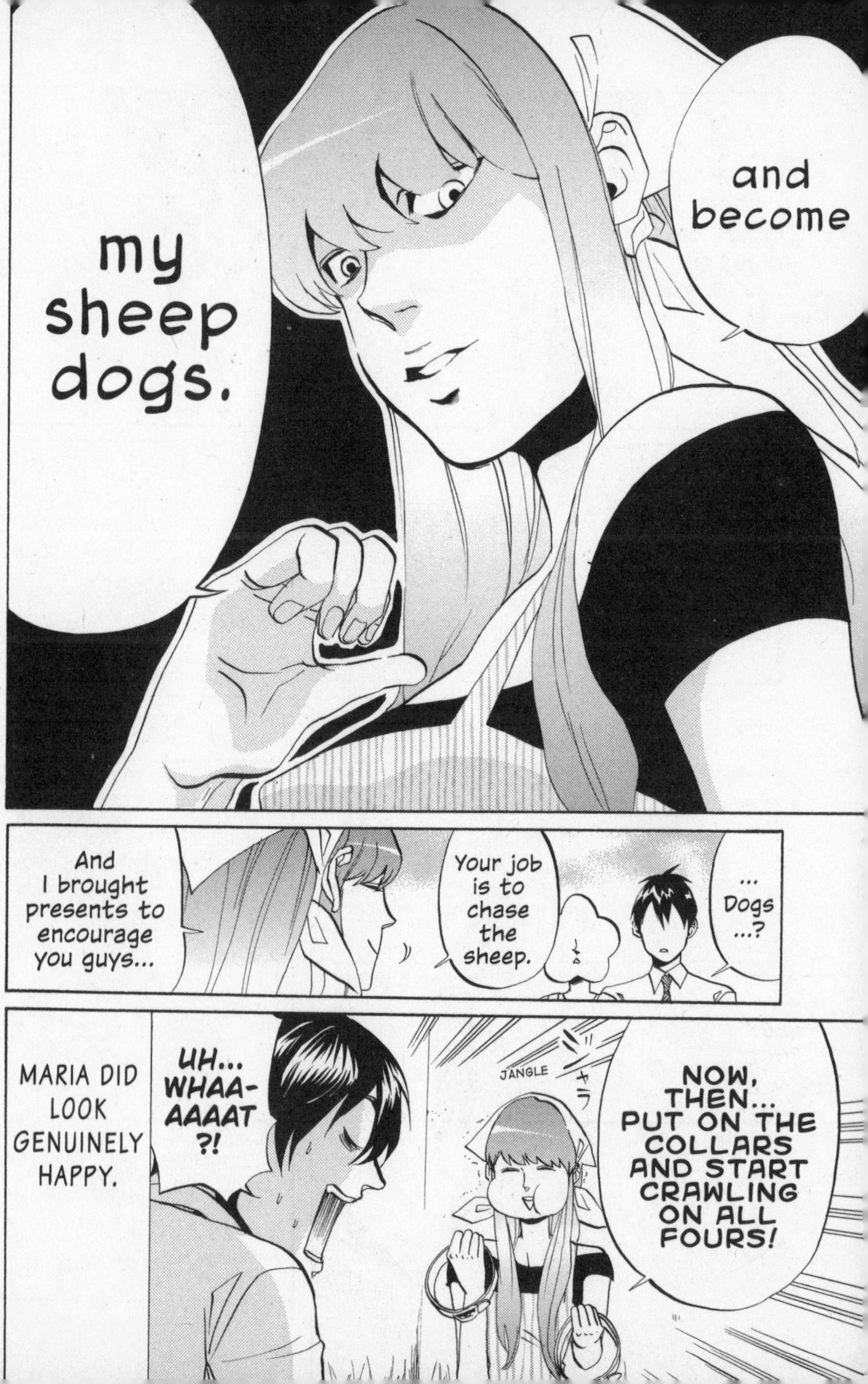
and become
my sheep dogs.
... Dogs ...?
Your job is to chase the sheep.
And I brought presents to encourage you guys...
NOW, THEN... PUT ON THE COLLARS AND START CRAWLING ON ALL FOURS!
JANGLE
UH... WHAA-AAAAT?!
MARIA DID LOOK GENUINELY HAPPY.

Chapter 153: A Dog's Life

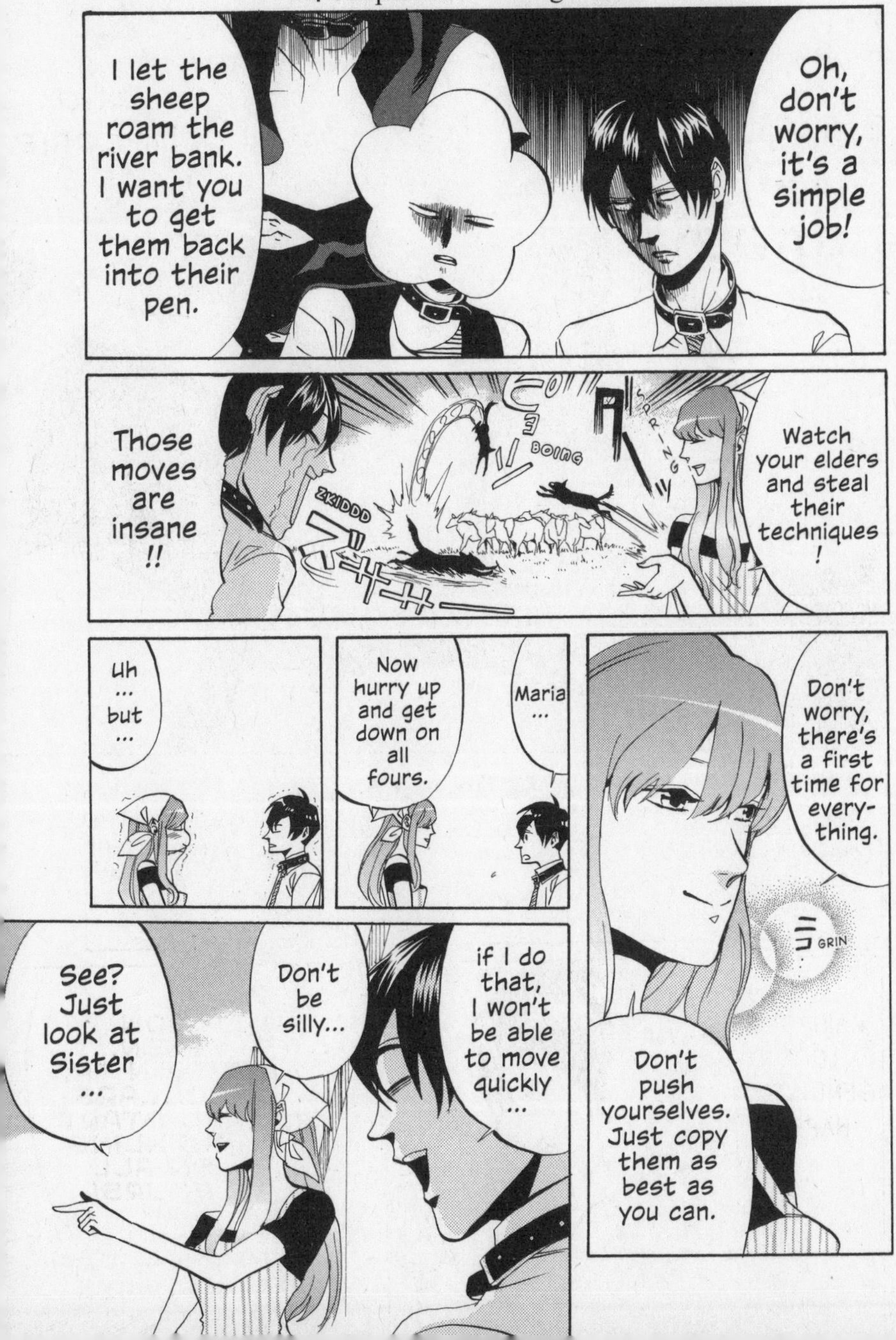

Oh, don't worry, it's a simple job!
I let the sheep roam the river bank. I want you to get them back into their pen.
Watch your elders and steal their techniques!
SPRING
BOING
ZKIDDD
Those moves are insane!!
Don't worry, there's a first time for every-thing.
GRIN
Don't push yourselves. Just copy them as best as you can.
Maria ...
Now hurry up and get down on all fours.
Uh ... but ...
if I do that, I won't be able to move quickly ...
Don't be silly...
See? Just look at Sister ...

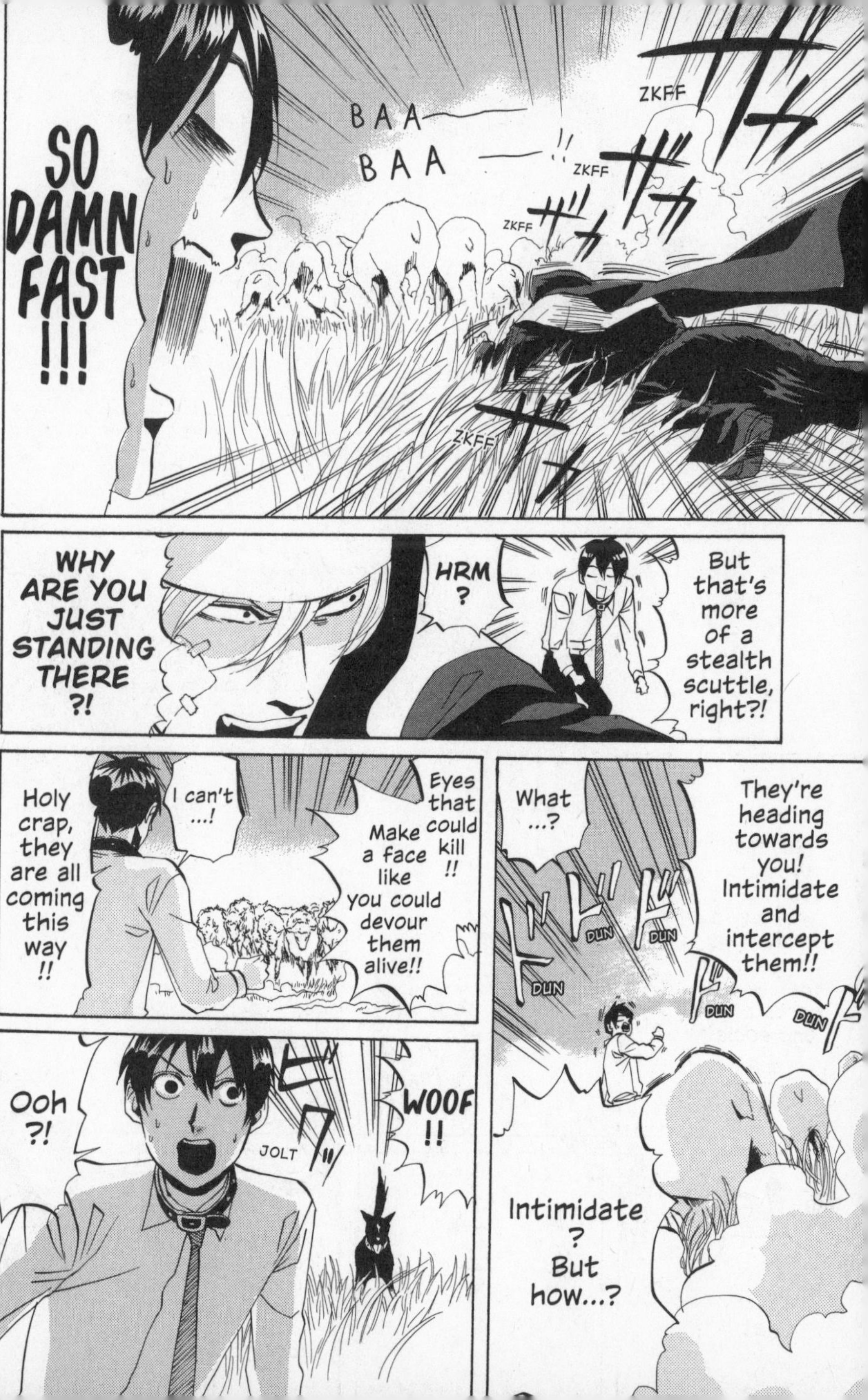
ZKFF
ZKFF
ZKFF
BAA BAA
!!
SO DAMN FAST!!!
ZKFF
But that's more of a stealth scuttle, right?!
HRM?
WHY ARE YOU JUST STANDING THERE?!
They're heading towards you! Intimidate and intercept them!!
What...?
DUN
DUN
DUN
DUN
DUN
Intimidate? But how...?
Eyes that could kill!!
Make a face like you could devour them alive!!
I can't...!
Holy crap, they are all coming this way!!
WOOF!!
JOLT
Ooh?!

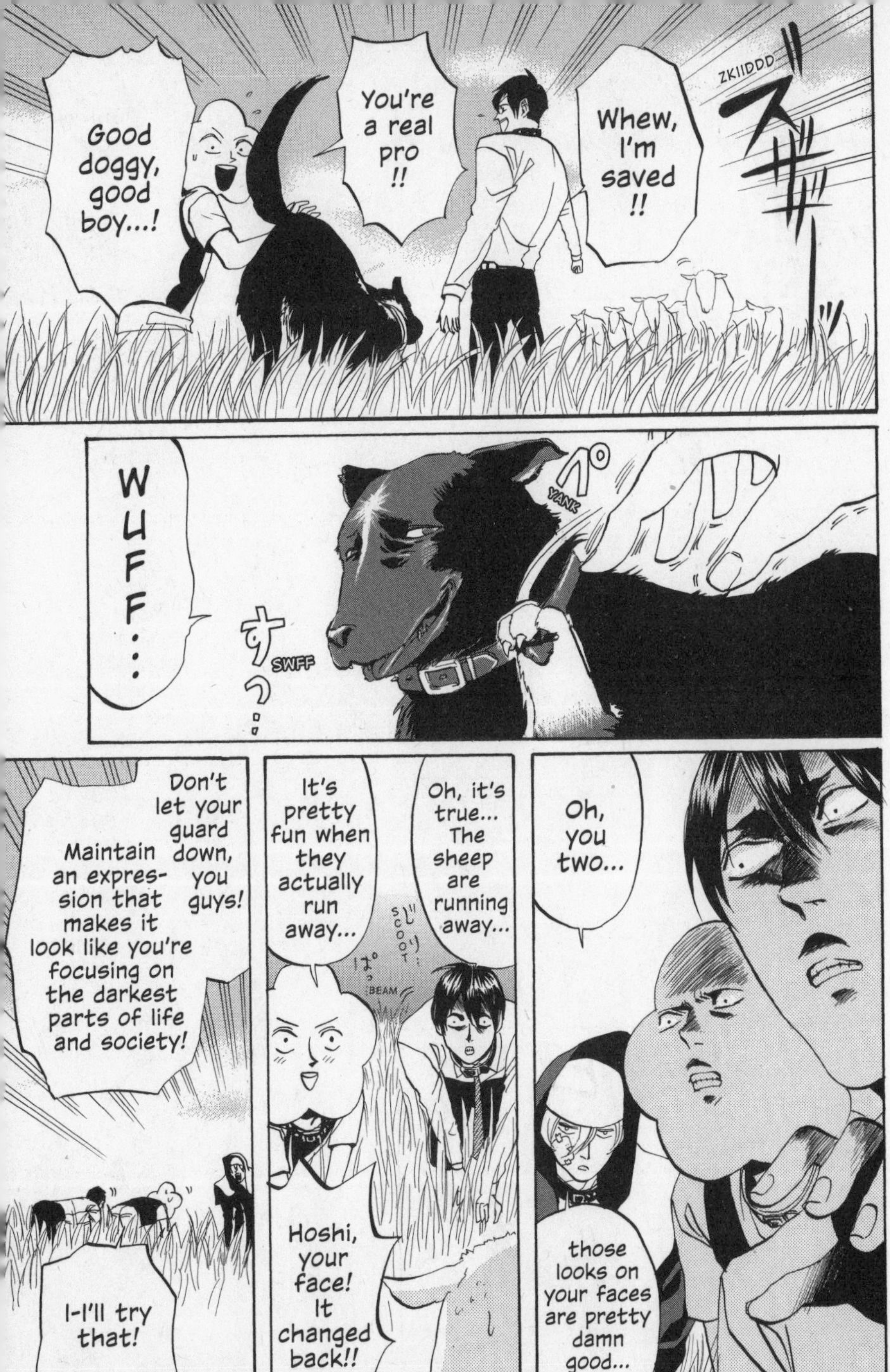

ズザザーッ
ZKIIDDD
Whew, I'm saved!!
You're a real pro!!
Good doggy, good boy...!
ぺ
YANK
すっ
SWFF
WUFF...
Oh, you two...
those looks on your faces are pretty damn good...
Oh, it's true... The sheep are running away...
It's pretty fun when they actually run away...
SCOOT
BEAM
Hoshi, your face! It changed back!!
Don't let your guard down, you guys!
Maintain an expression that makes it look like you're focusing on the darkest parts of life and society!
I-I'll try that!

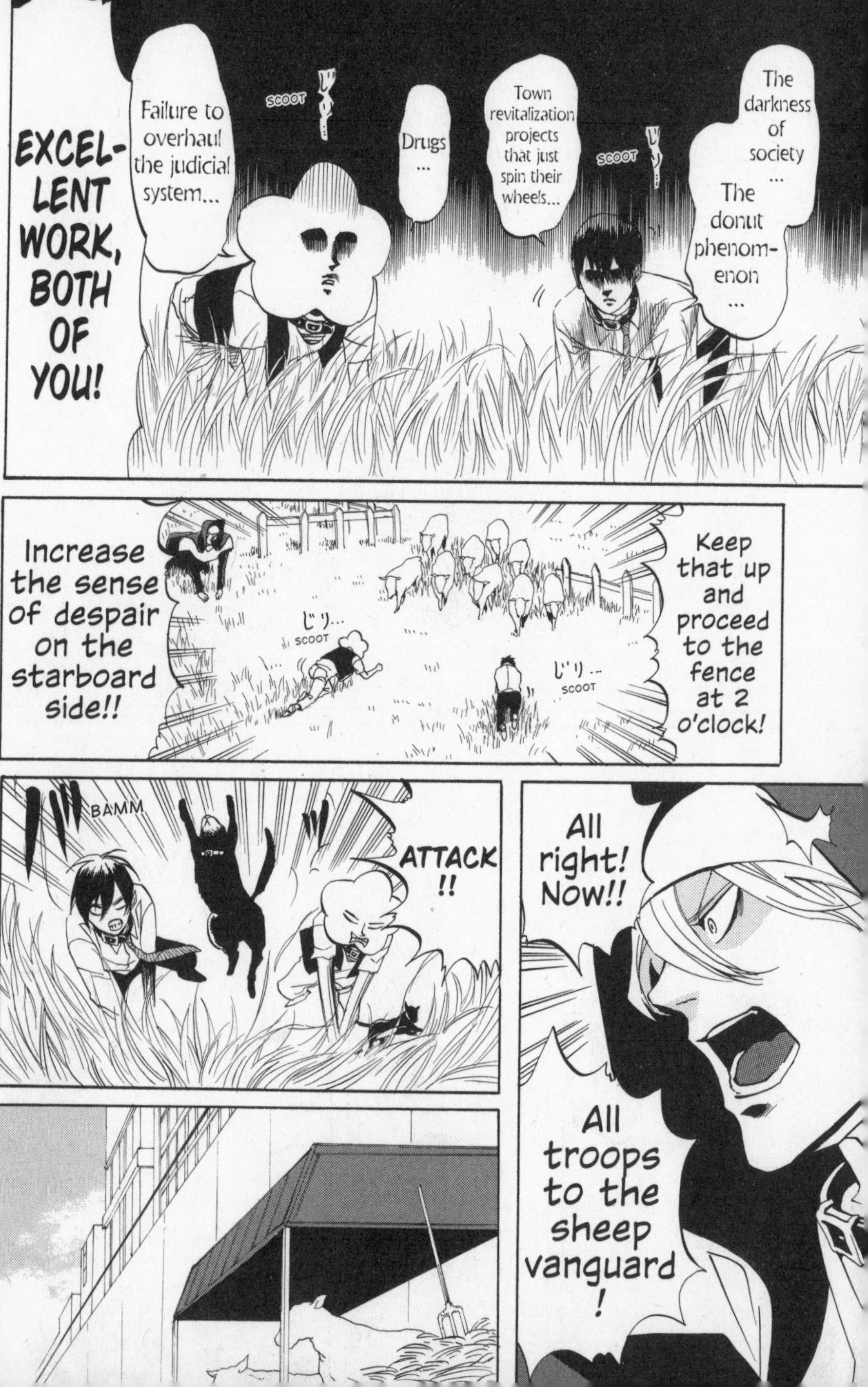
The darkness of society... The donut phenomenon...
SCOOT
Town revitalization projects that just spin their wheels...
Drugs...
SCOOT
Failure to overhaul the judicial system...
EXCELLENT WORK, BOTH OF YOU!
Keep that up and proceed to the fence at 2 o'clock!
じり… SCOOT
じり… SCOOT
Increase the sense of despair on the starboard side!!
All right! NOW!!
All troops to the sheep vanguard!
ATTACK!!
BAMM

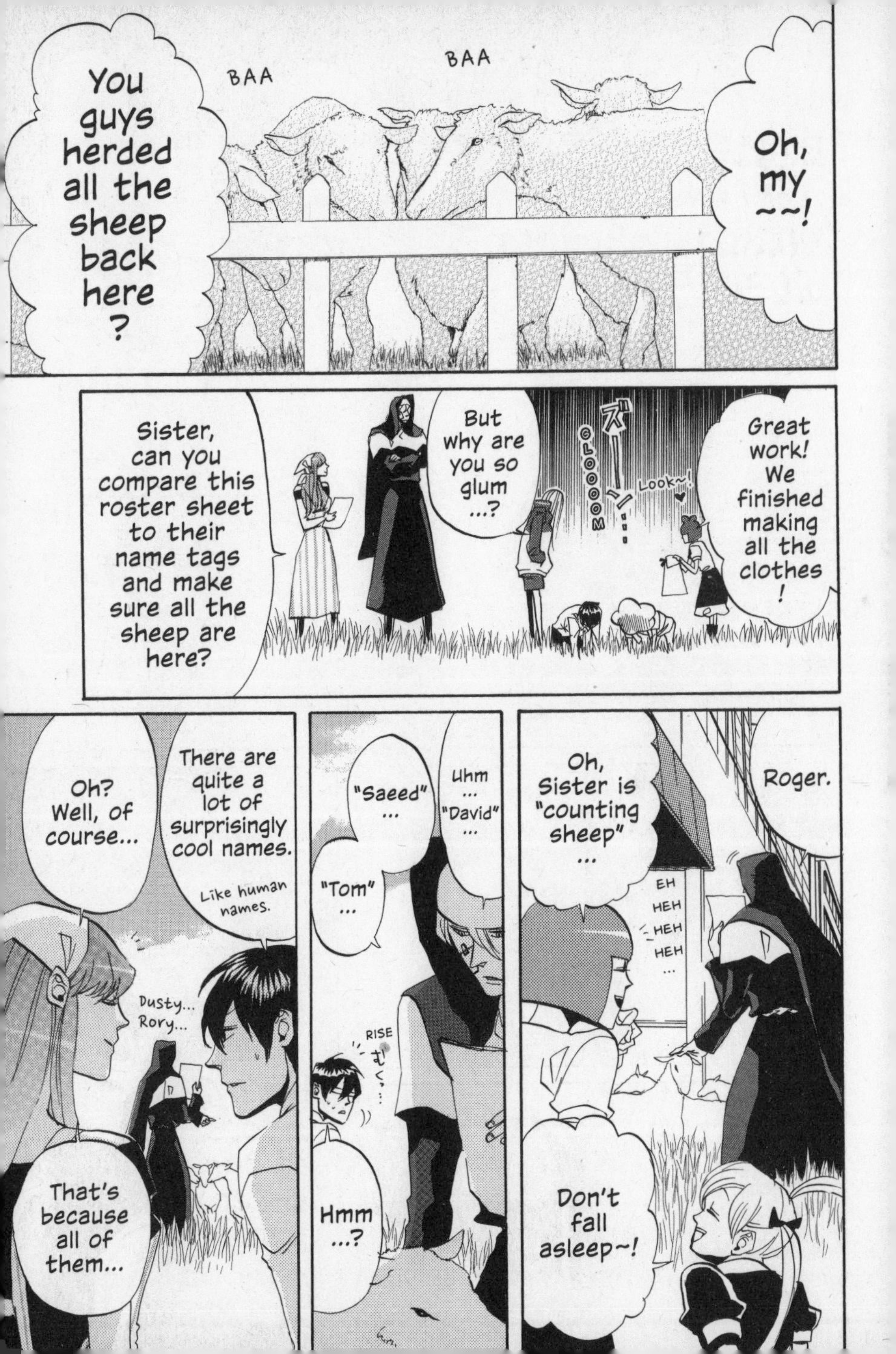
Oh, my ~~!
BAA
BAA
You guys herded all the sheep back here?
Great work! We finished making all the clothes!
Look~!
GLOOOOOM
But why are you so glum ...?
Sister, can you compare this roster sheet to their name tags and make sure all the sheep are here?
Roger.
Oh, Sister is "counting sheep" ...
EH HEH HEH HEH ...
Don't fall asleep~!
Uhm ... "David" ...
"Saeed" ...
"Tom" ...
RISE
Hmm ...?
There are quite a lot of surprisingly cool names.
Like human names.
Oh? Well, of course...
Dusty... Rory...
That's because all of them...

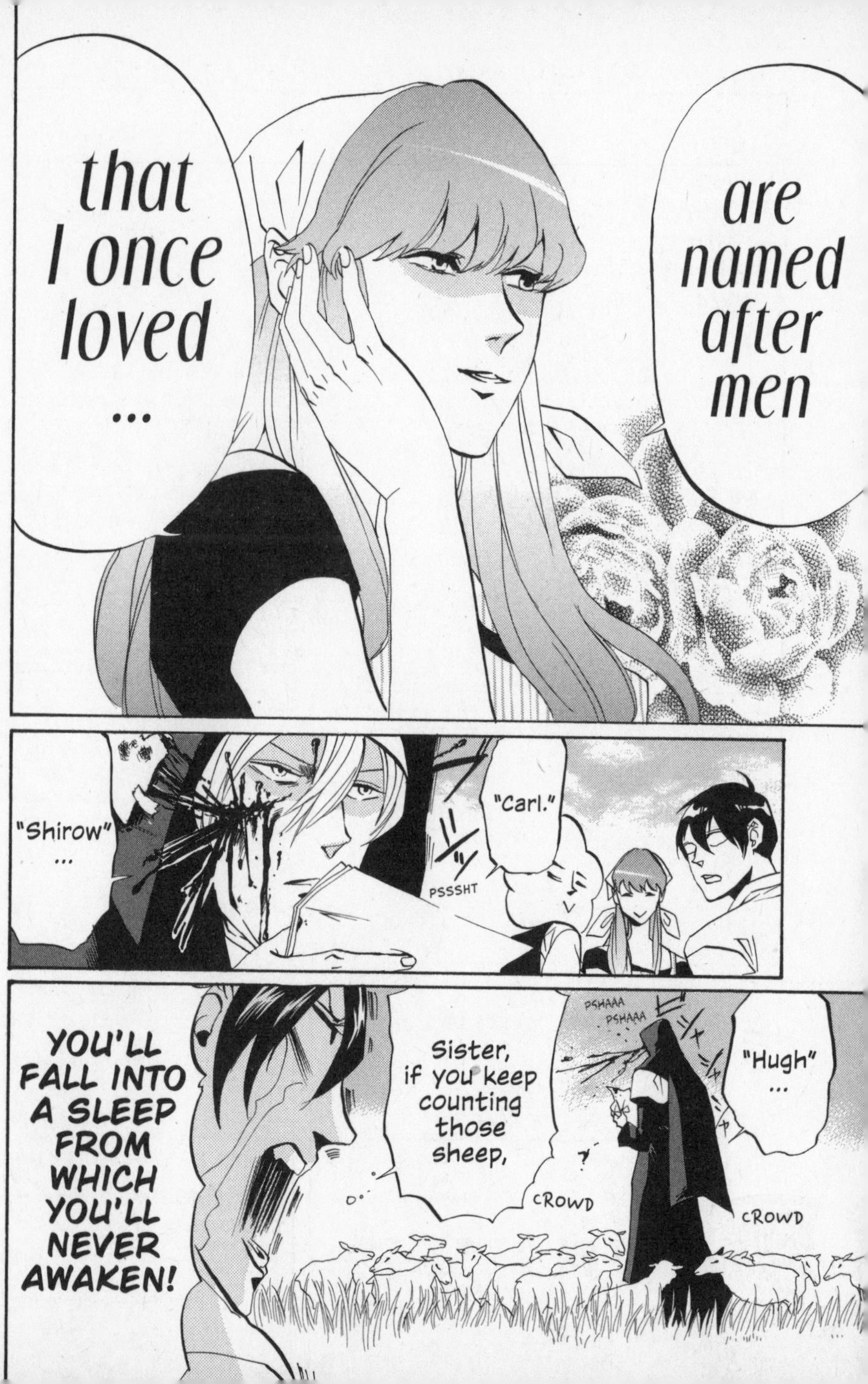
are named after men
that I once loved ...
"Carl."
PSSSHT
"Shirow" ...
"Hugh" ...
PSHAAA PSHAAA
CROWD
Sister, if you keep counting those sheep,
CROWD
YOU'LL FALL INTO A SLEEP FROM WHICH YOU'LL NEVER AWAKEN!

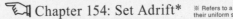

Chapter 154: Set Adrift*

※ Refers to a custom where graduates set their uniform scarves drifting down a river

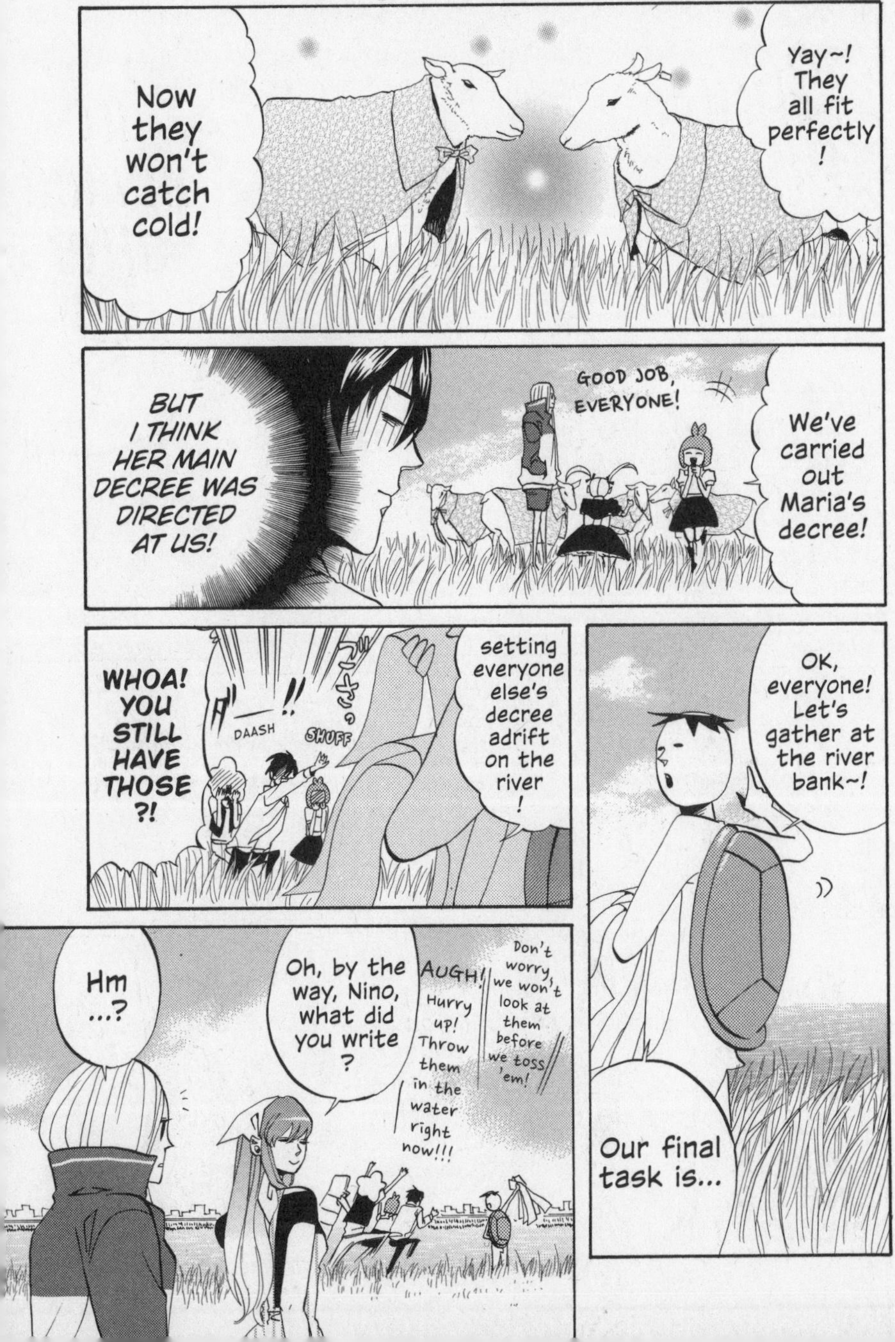

Yay~! They all fit perfectly!
Now they won't catch cold!
We've carried out Maria's decree!
GOOD JOB, EVERYONE!
BUT I THINK HER MAIN DECREE WAS DIRECTED AT US!
OK, everyone! Let's gather at the river bank~!
Our final task is...
setting everyone else's decree adrift on the river!
SHUFF
DAASH
WHOA! YOU STILL HAVE THOSE?!
Don't worry, we won't look at them before we toss 'em!
AUGH! Hurry up! Throw them in the water right now!!!
Oh, by the way, Nino, what did you write?
Hm...?

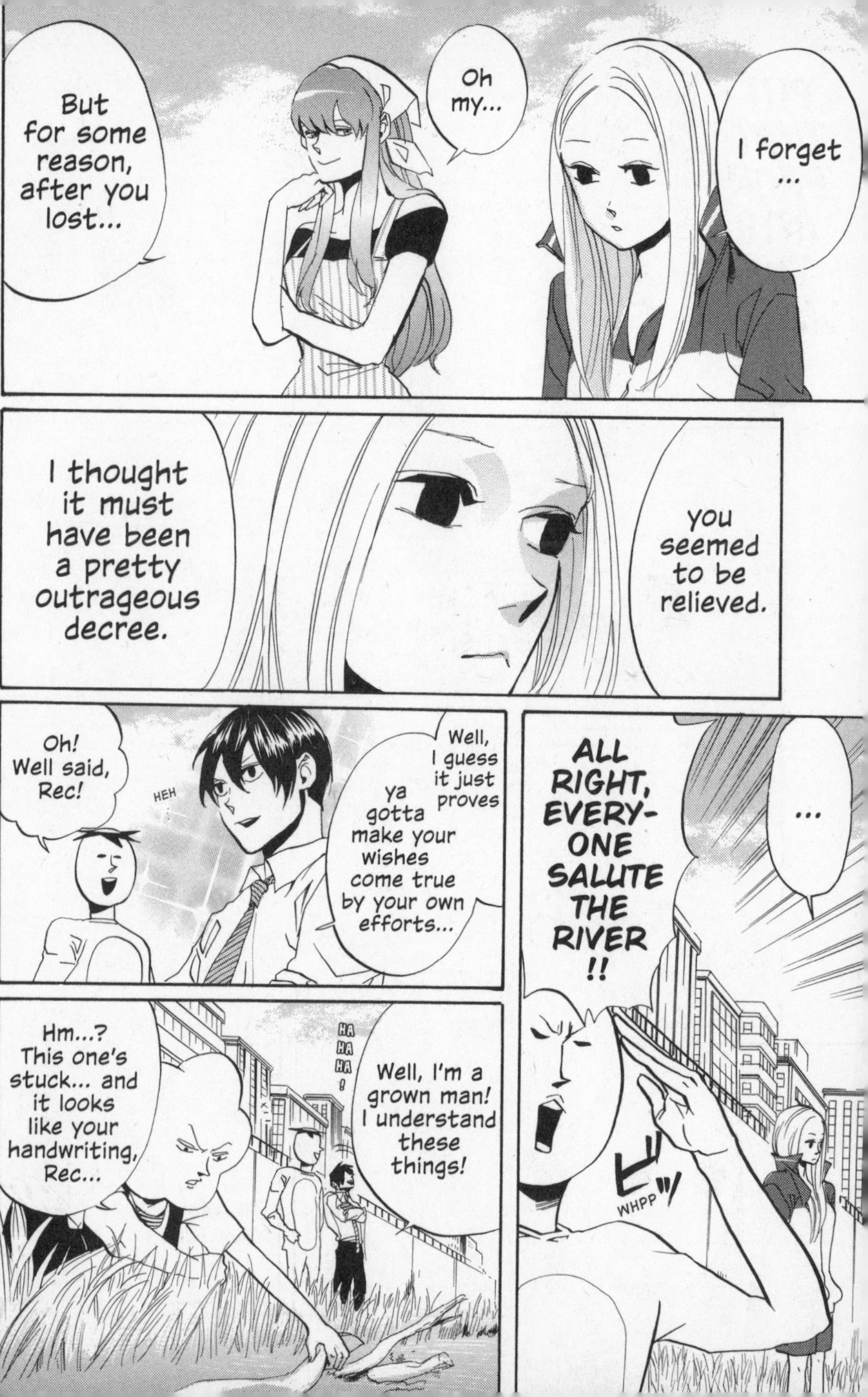
I forget ...
Oh my...
But for some reason, after you lost...
you seemed to be relieved.
I thought it must have been a pretty outrageous decree.
...
ALL RIGHT, EVERY-ONE SALUTE THE RIVER !!
WHPP
Well, I guess it just proves ya gotta make your wishes come true by your own efforts...
HEH
Oh! Well said, Rec!
Well, I'm a grown man! I understand these things!
HA HA HA!
Hm...? This one's stuck... and it looks like your handwriting, Rec...

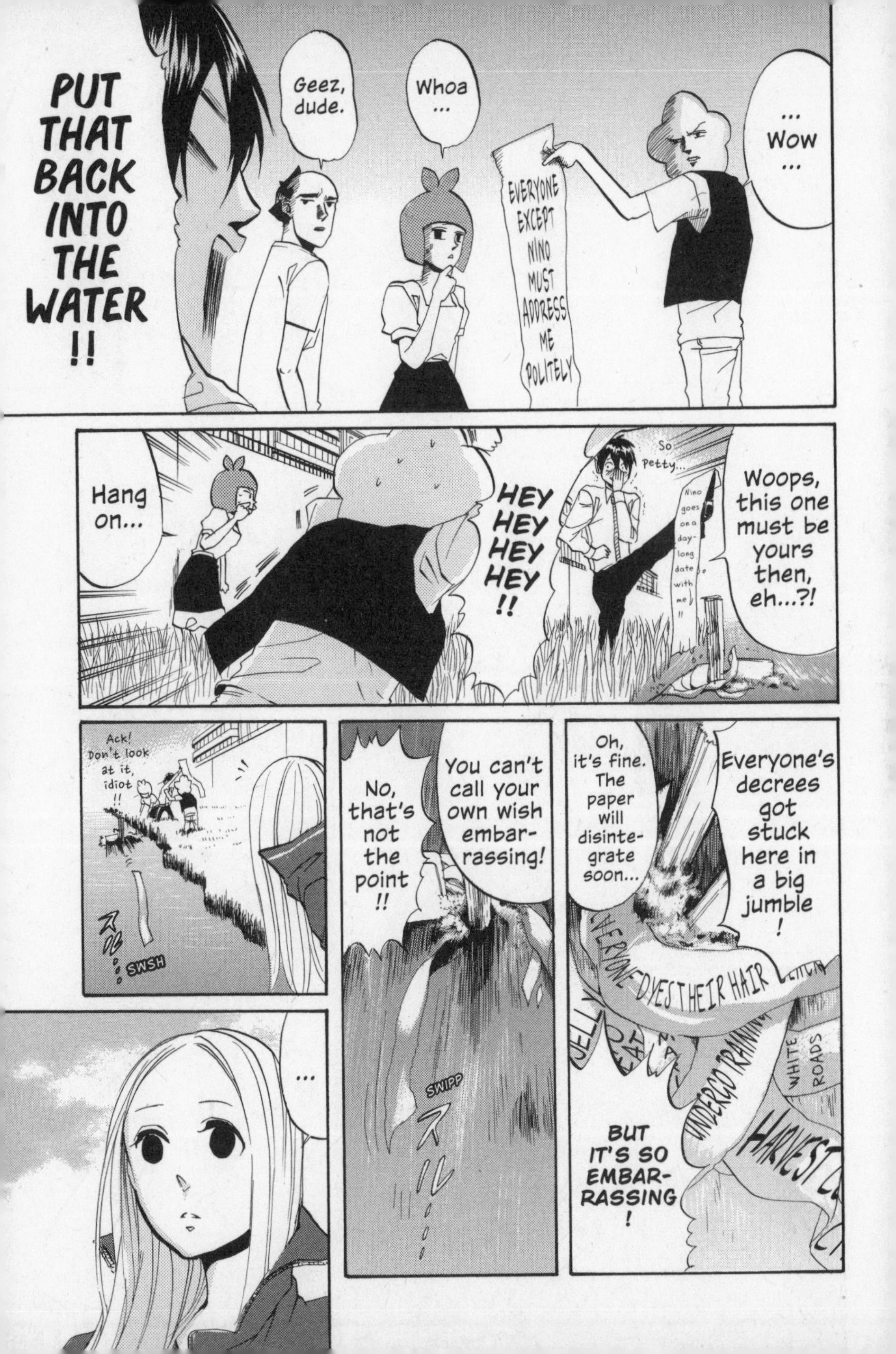
... Wow ...
EVERYONE EXCEPT NINO MUST ADDRESS ME POLITELY
Whoa ...
Geez, dude.
PUT THAT BACK INTO THE WATER !!
Woops, this one must be yours then, eh...?!
Nino goes on a day-long date with me !!
So petty...
HEY HEY HEY HEY !!
Hang on...
Everyone's decrees got stuck here in a big jumble !
Oh, it's fine. The paper will disintegrate soon...
EVERYONE DYES THEIR HAIR
UNDERGO TRAINING
WHITE ROADS
BUT IT'S SO EMBARRASSING !
You can't call your own wish embarrassing!
No, that's not the point !!
SWIPP
Ack! Don't look at it, idiot !!
SWSH
...

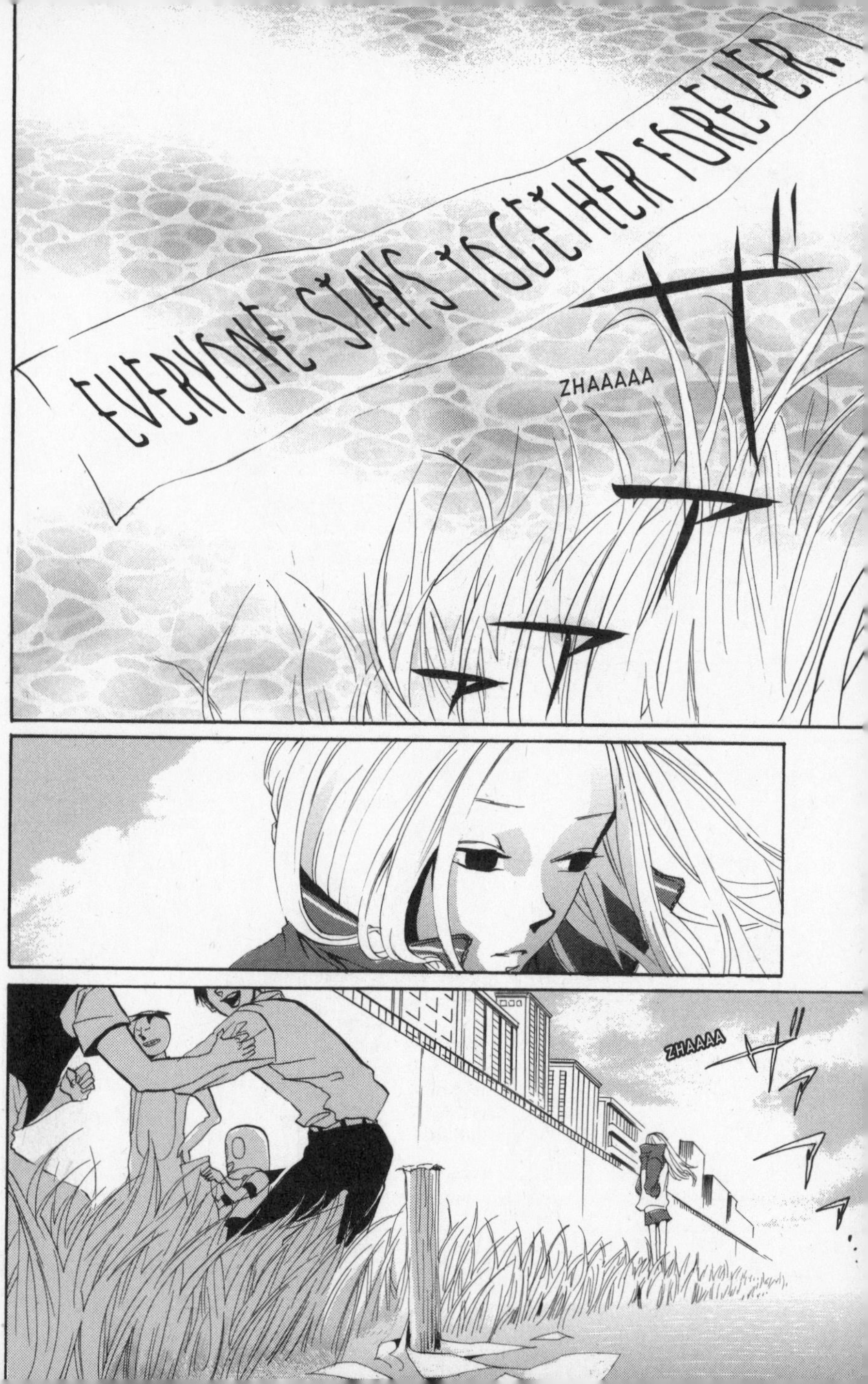
EVERYONE STAYS TOGETHER FOREVER.
ZHAAAAA
ZHAAAA

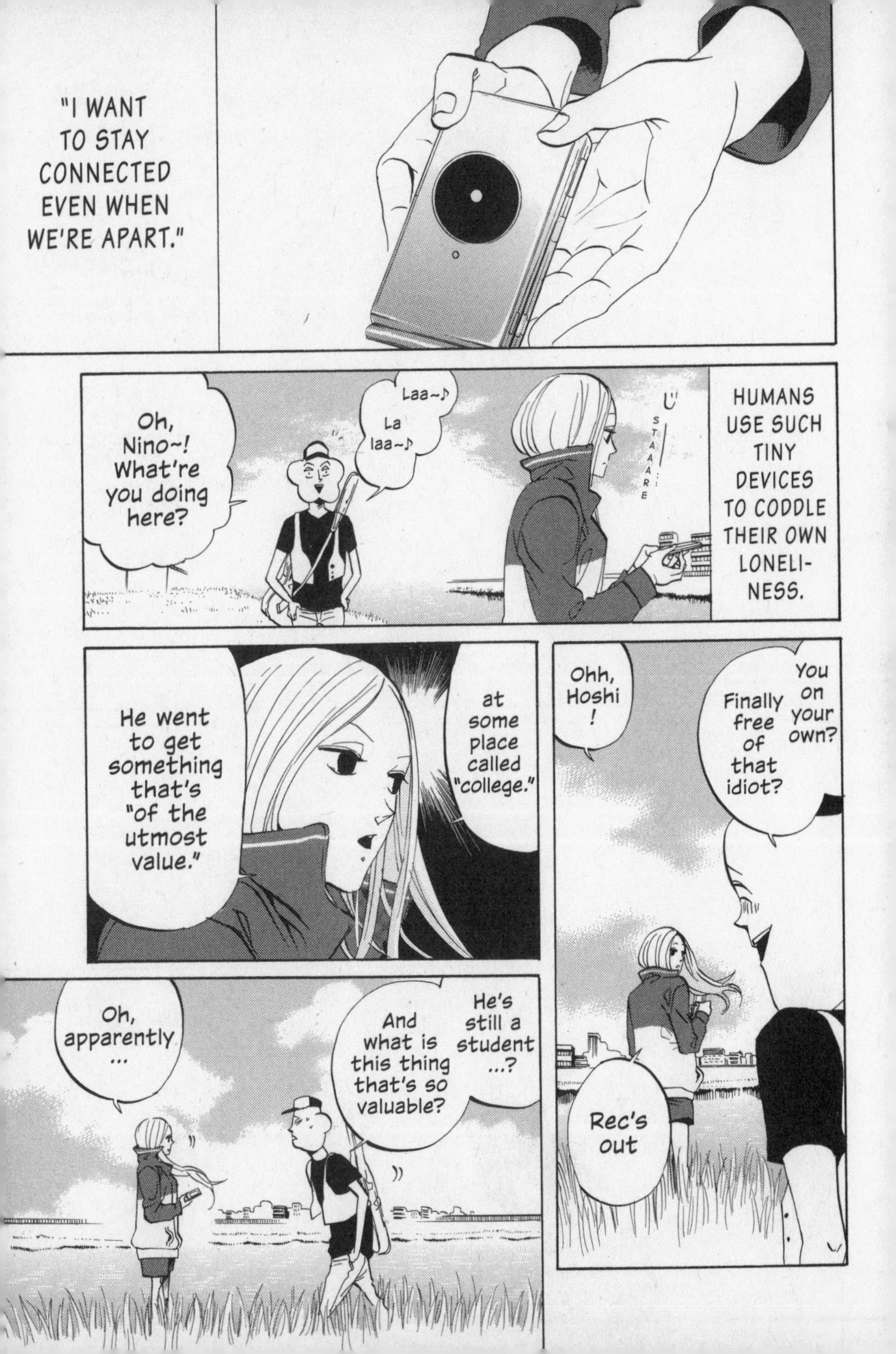
"I WANT TO STAY CONNECTED EVEN WHEN WE'RE APART."
HUMANS USE SUCH TINY DEVICES TO CODDLE THEIR OWN LONELI-NESS.
STAAARE
Laa~♪ La laa~♪
Oh, Nino~! What're you doing here?
You on your own?
Finally free of that idiot?
Ohh, Hoshi!
Rec's out
at some place called "college."
He went to get something that's "of the utmost value."
He's still a student ...?
And what is this thing that's so valuable?
Oh, apparently ...

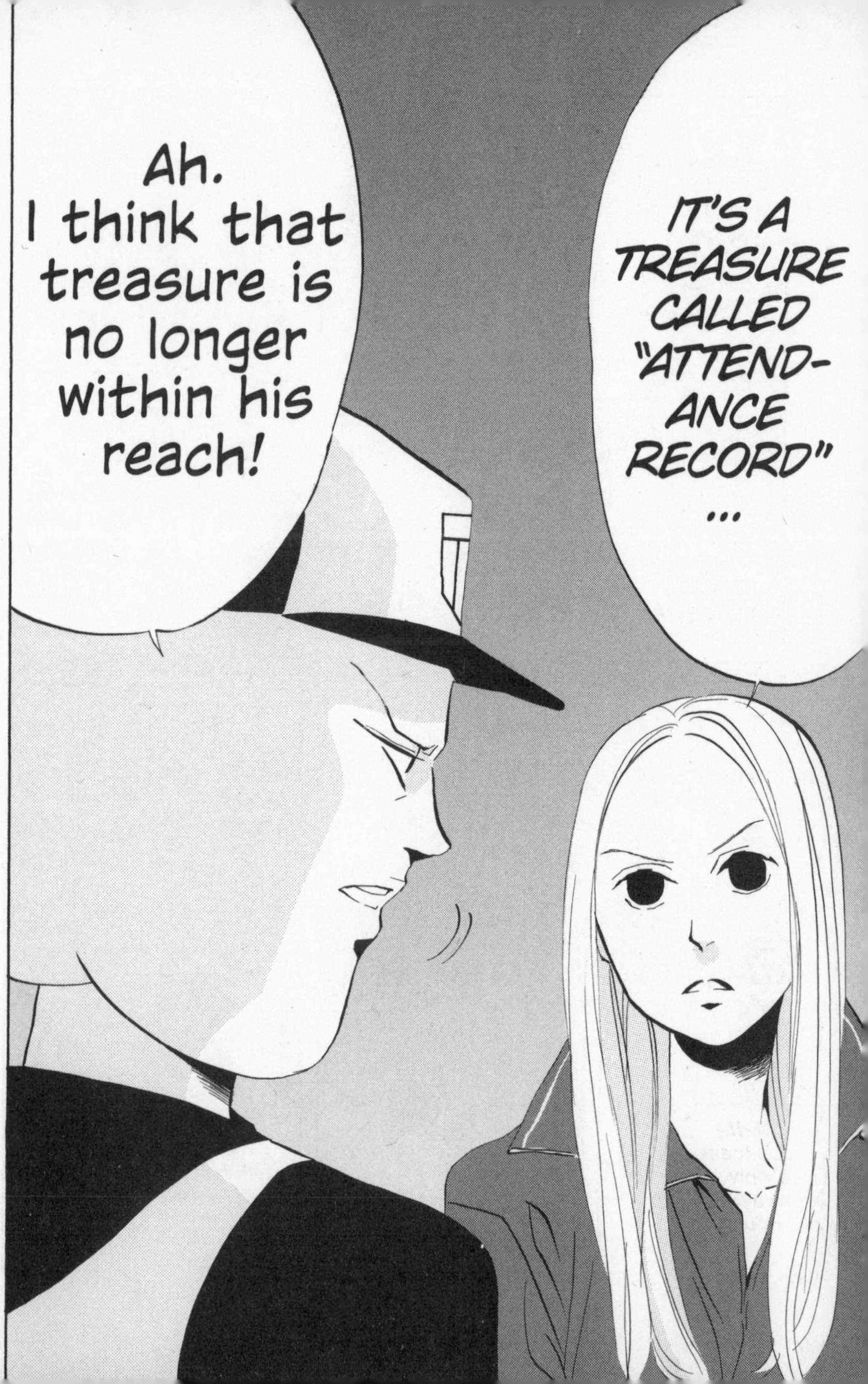
IT'S A TREASURE CALLED "ATTEND-ANCE RECORD" ...
Ah. I think that treasure is no longer within his reach!

☞ Chapter 155: Love Call & Love Text

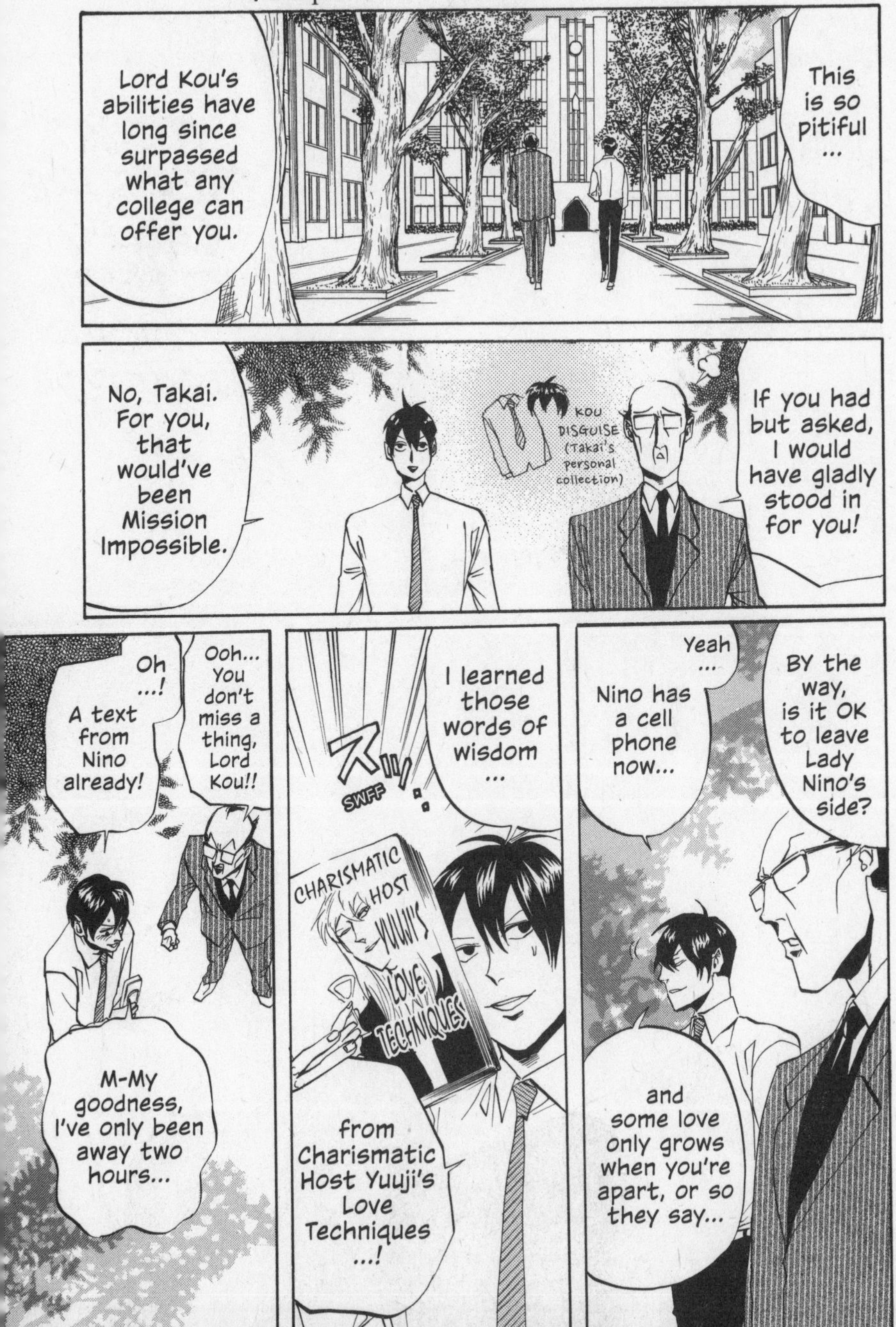
This is so pitiful ...
Lord Kou's abilities have long since surpassed what any college can offer you.
If you had but asked, I would have gladly stood in for you!
KOU DISGUISE (Takai's personal collection)
No, Takai. For you, that would've been Mission Impossible.
BY the way, is it OK to leave Lady Nino's side?
Yeah ...
Nino has a cell phone now...
and some love only grows when you're apart, or so they say...
I learned those words of wisdom ...
SWFF
CHARISMATIC HOST YUUJI'S LOVE TECHNIQUES
from Charismatic Host Yuuji's Love Techniques ...!
Ooh... You don't miss a thing, Lord Kou!!
Oh ...! A text from Nino already!
M-My goodness, I've only been away two hours...

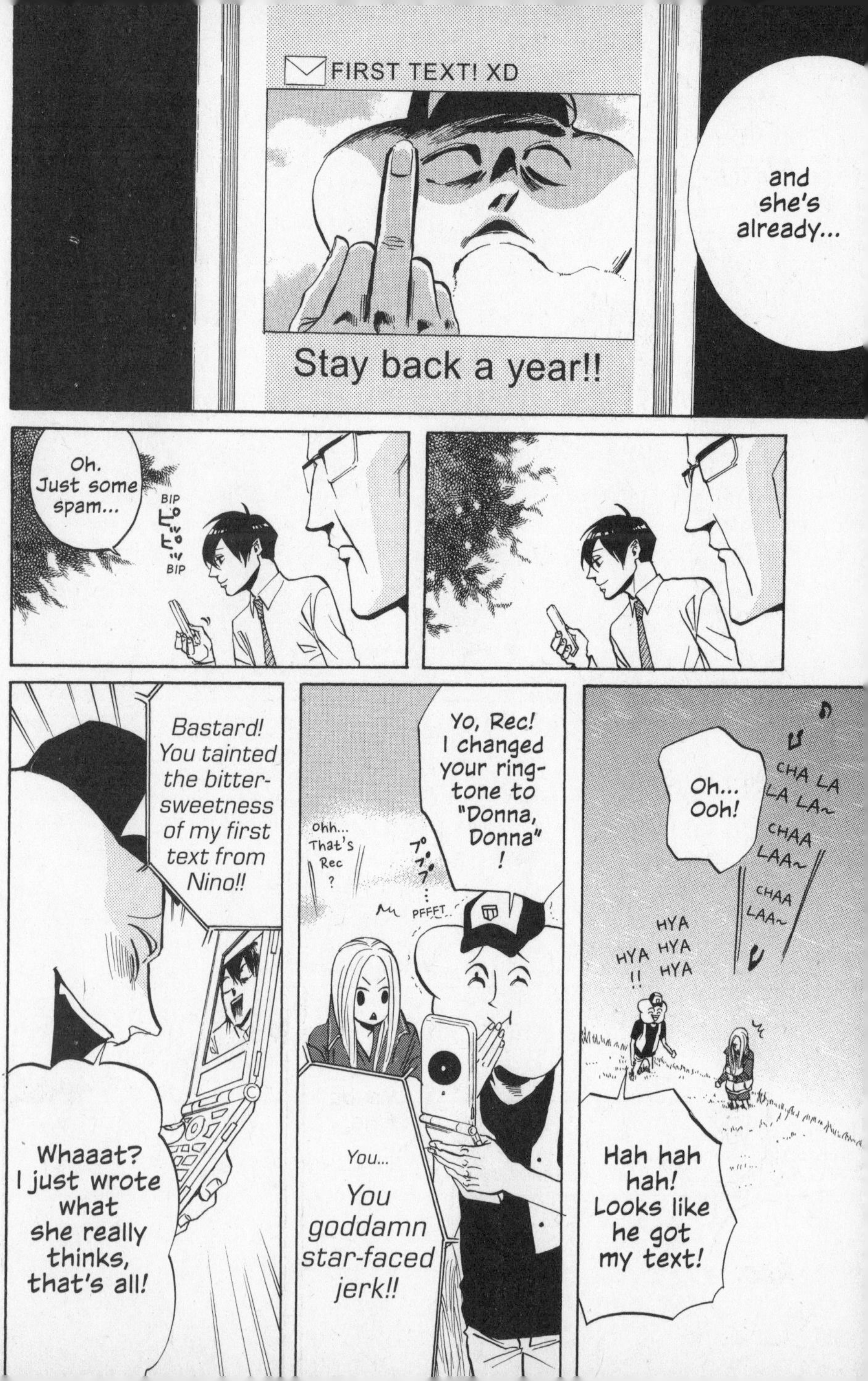
and she's already...
FIRST TEXT! XD
Stay back a year!!
Oh. Just some spam...
BIP
BIP
Oh... Ooh!
CHA LA LA LA~
CHAA LAA~
CHAA LAA~
HYA HYA HYA
HYA !!
Hah hah hah! Looks like he got my text!
Yo, Rec! I changed your ringtone to "Donna, Donna"!
Ohh... That's Rec?
PFFFT
You...
You goddamn star-faced jerk!!
Bastard! You tainted the bitter-sweetness of my first text from Nino!!
Whaaat? I just wrote what she really thinks, that's all!

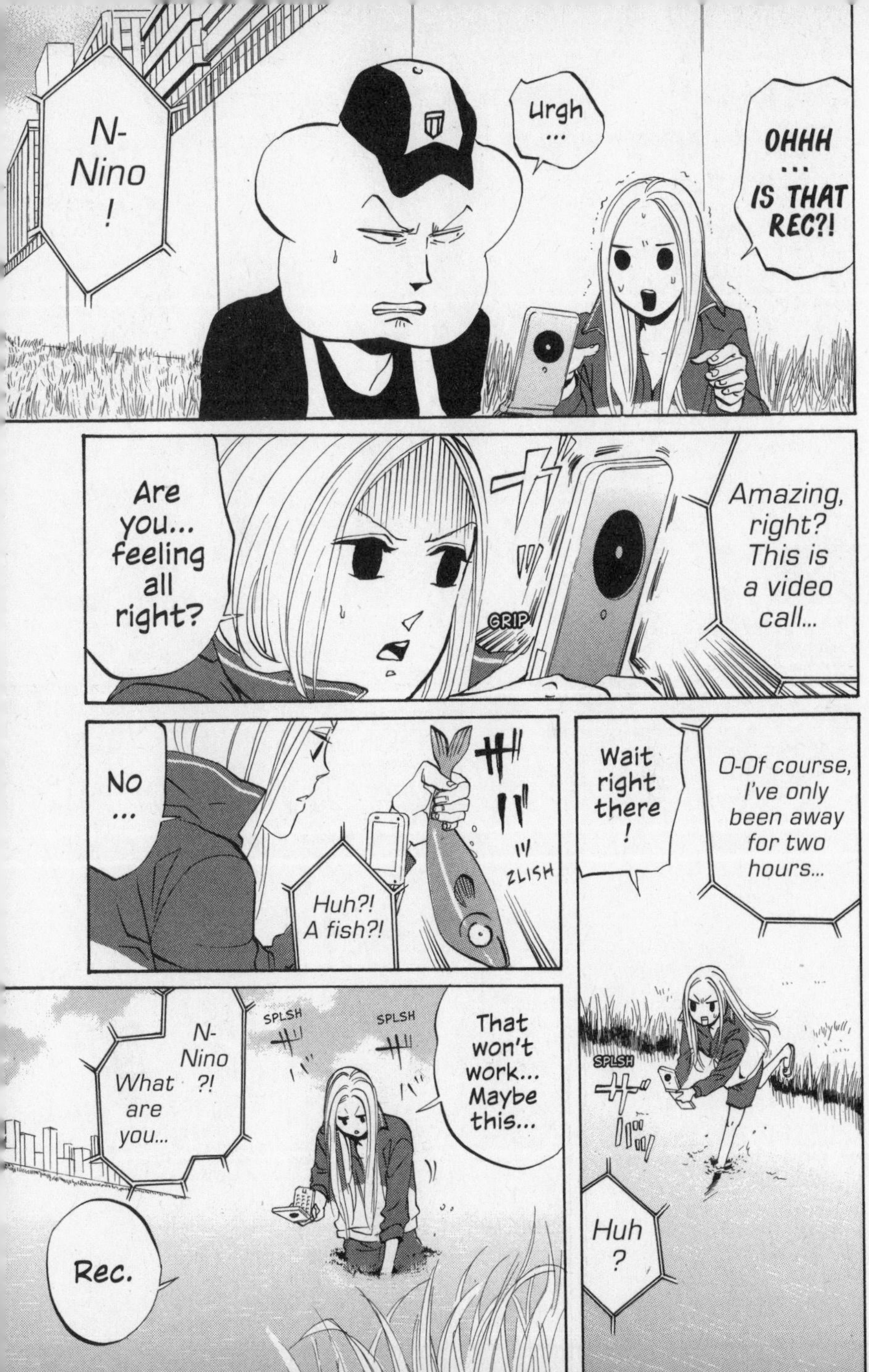
OHHH ... IS THAT REC?!
Urgh ...
N-Nino!
Amazing, right? This is a video call...
GRIP
Are you... feeling all right?
O-Of course, I've only been away for two hours...
Wait right there!
ZLISH
No ...
Huh?! A fish?!
SPLSH
Huh ?
That won't work... Maybe this...
SPLSH
SPLSH
N-Nino ?!
What are you...
Rec.

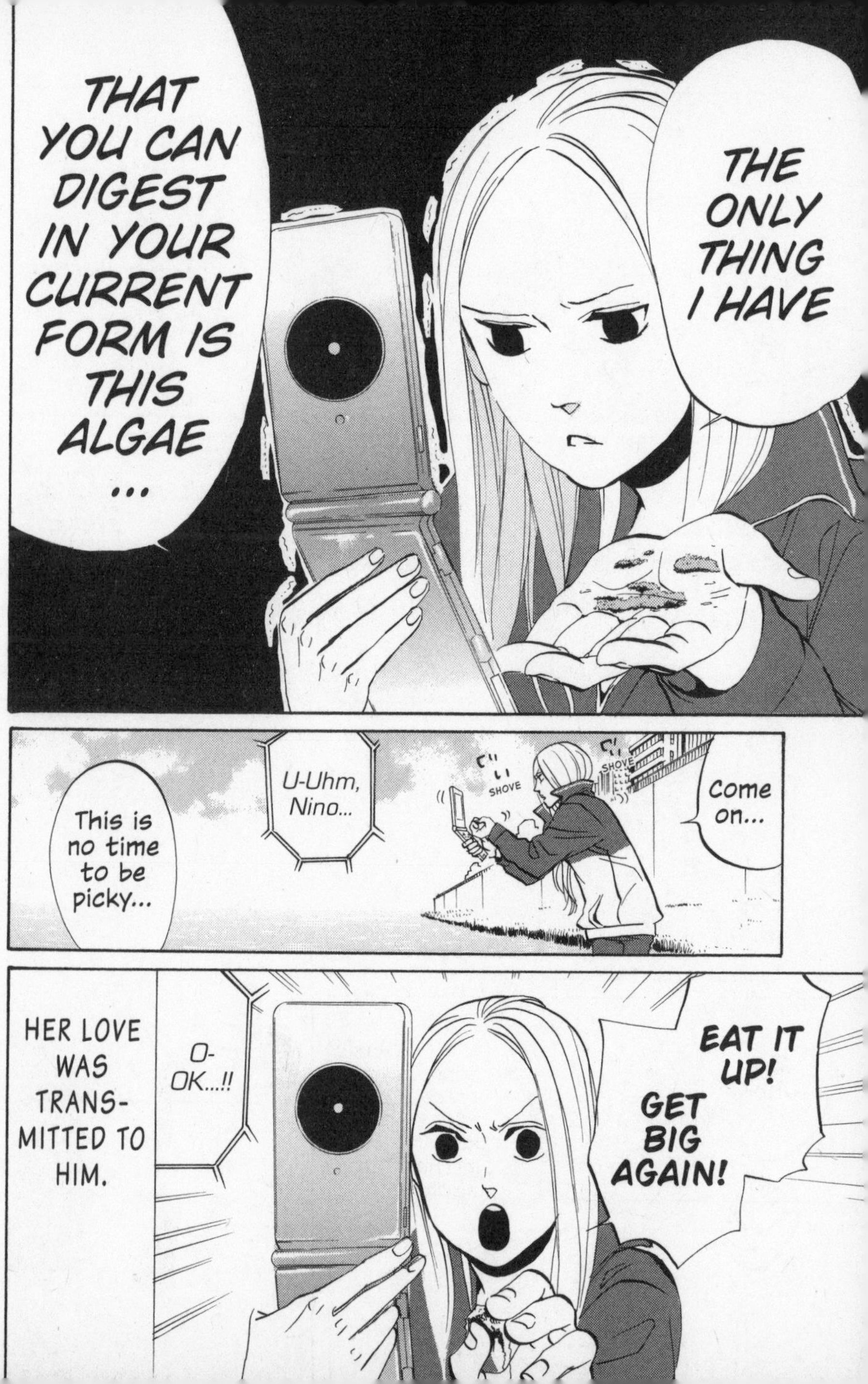
THE ONLY THING I HAVE
THAT YOU CAN DIGEST IN YOUR CURRENT FORM IS THIS ALGAE ...
Come on...
SHOVE
SHOVE
U-Uhm, Nino...
This is no time to be picky...
EAT IT UP!
GET BIG AGAIN!
O-OK...!!
HER LOVE WAS TRANS-MITTED TO HIM.

Chapter 156: Love Tactics

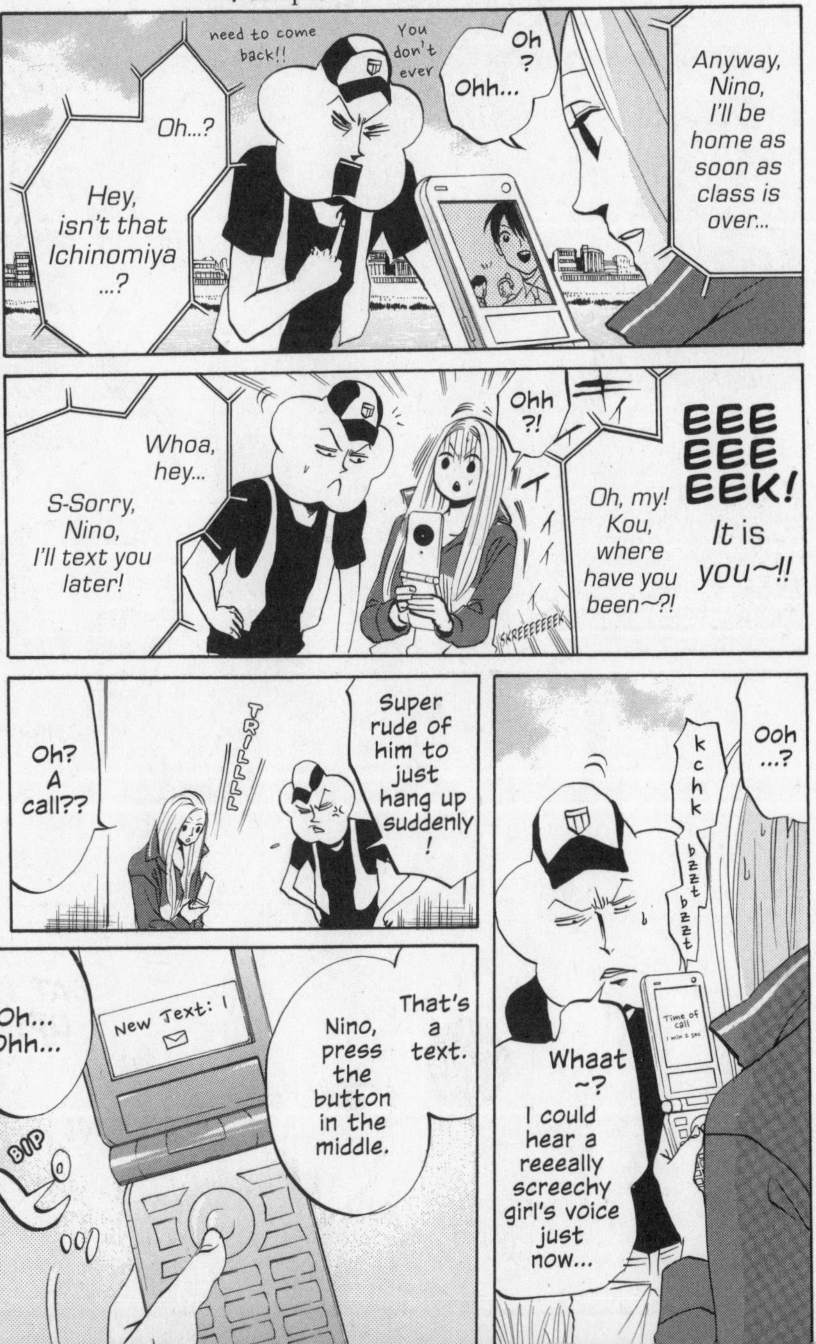

Anyway, Nino, I'll be home as soon as class is over...
Oh? Ohh...
You don't ever need to come back!!
Oh...?
Hey, isn't that Ichinomiya ...?
EEEEEEEEEK!
It is you~!!
Oh, my! Kou, where have you been~?!
SKREEEEEEEK
Ohh ?!
Whoa, hey...
S-Sorry, Nino, I'll text you later!
Ooh ...?
kchk
bzzt bzzt
Whaat ~?
I could hear a reeeally screechy girl's voice just now...
Time of call
Super rude of him to just hang up suddenly !
TRILLLL
Oh? A call??
That's a text.
Nino, press the button in the middle.
New Text: 1
Oh... Ohh...
BIP

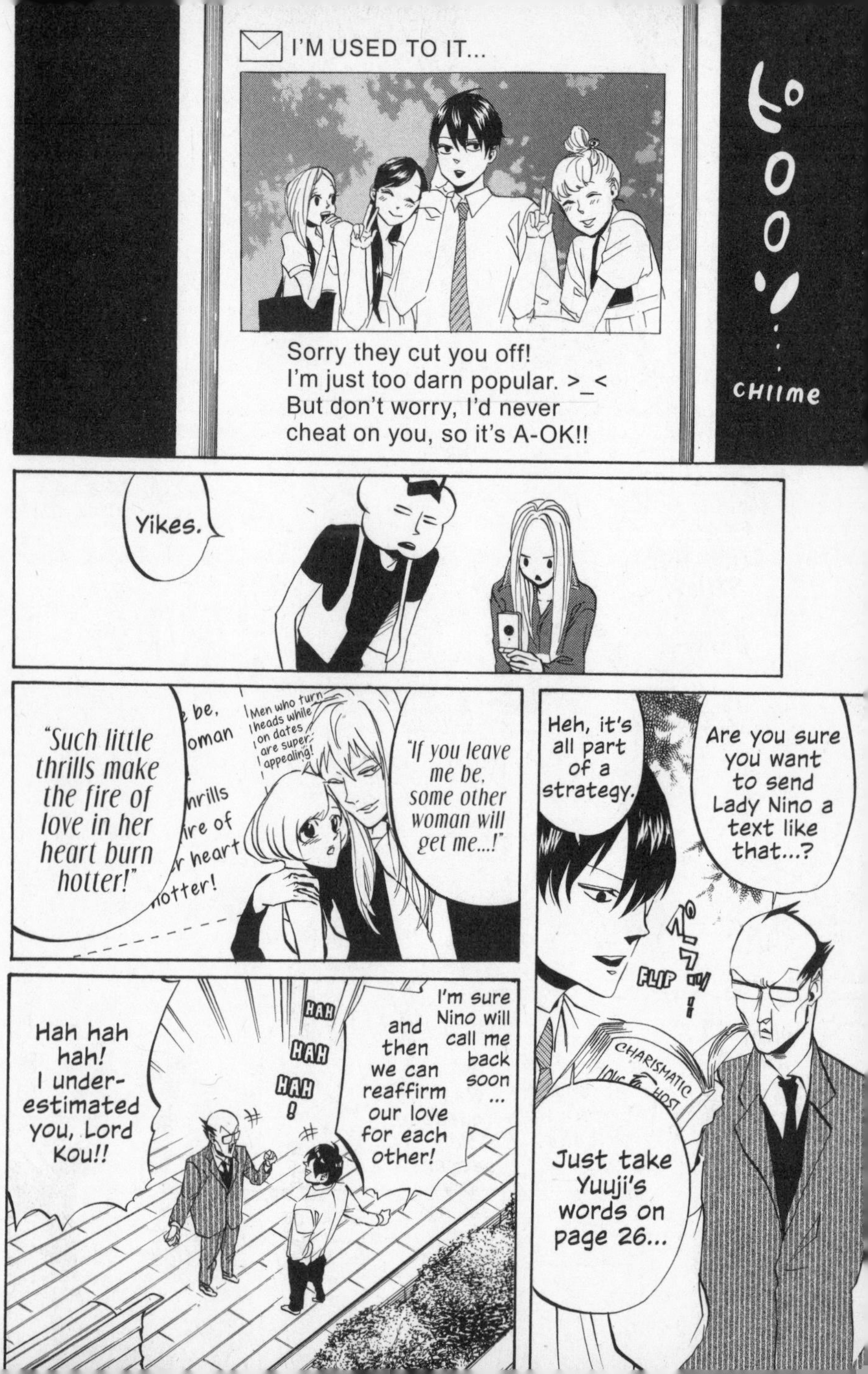
CHIIME
I'M USED TO IT...
Sorry they cut you off!
I'm just too darn popular. >_<
But don't worry, I'd never cheat on you, so it's A-OK!!
Yikes.
Are you sure you want to send Lady Nino a text like that...?
Heh, it's all part of a strategy.
FLIP
Just take Yuuji's words on page 26...
"If you leave me be, some other woman will get me...!"
Men who turn heads while on dates are super-appealing!
"Such little thrills make the fire of love in her heart burn hotter!"
I'm sure Nino will call me back soon...
and then we can reaffirm our love for each other!
HAH HAH HAH!
Hah hah hah! I under-estimated you, Lord Kou!!

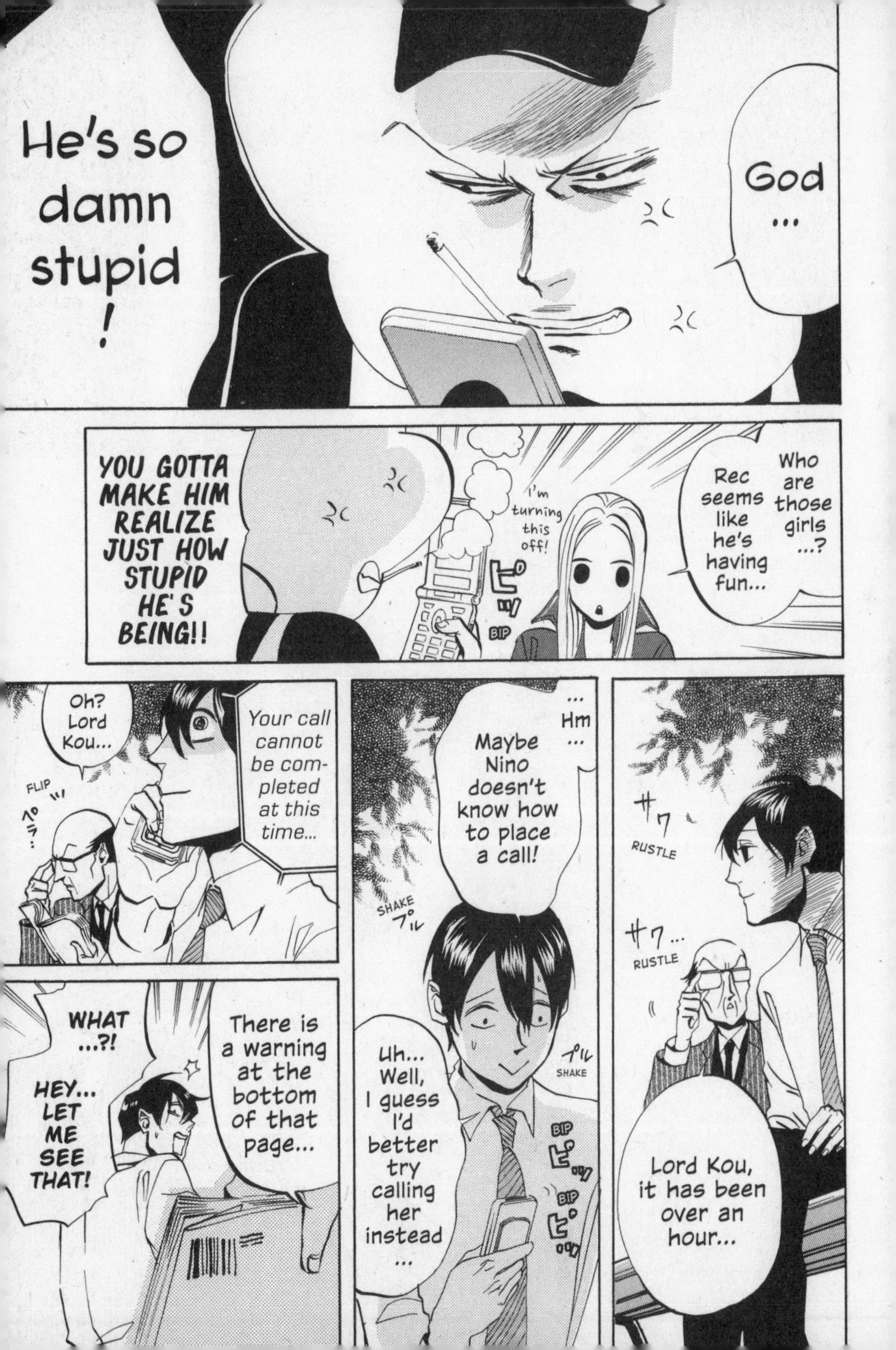
God ...
He's so damn stupid !
Who are those girls ...?
Rec seems like he's having fun...
I'm turning this off!
BIP
YOU GOTTA MAKE HIM REALIZE JUST HOW STUPID HE'S BEING!!
RUSTLE
RUSTLE
Lord Kou, it has been over an hour...
... Hm ...
Maybe Nino doesn't know how to place a call!
SHAKE
SHAKE
Uh... Well, I guess I'd better try calling her instead ...
BIP
BIP
Your call cannot be completed at this time...
Oh? Lord Kou...
FLIP
There is a warning at the bottom of that page...
WHAT ...?!
HEY... LET ME SEE THAT!

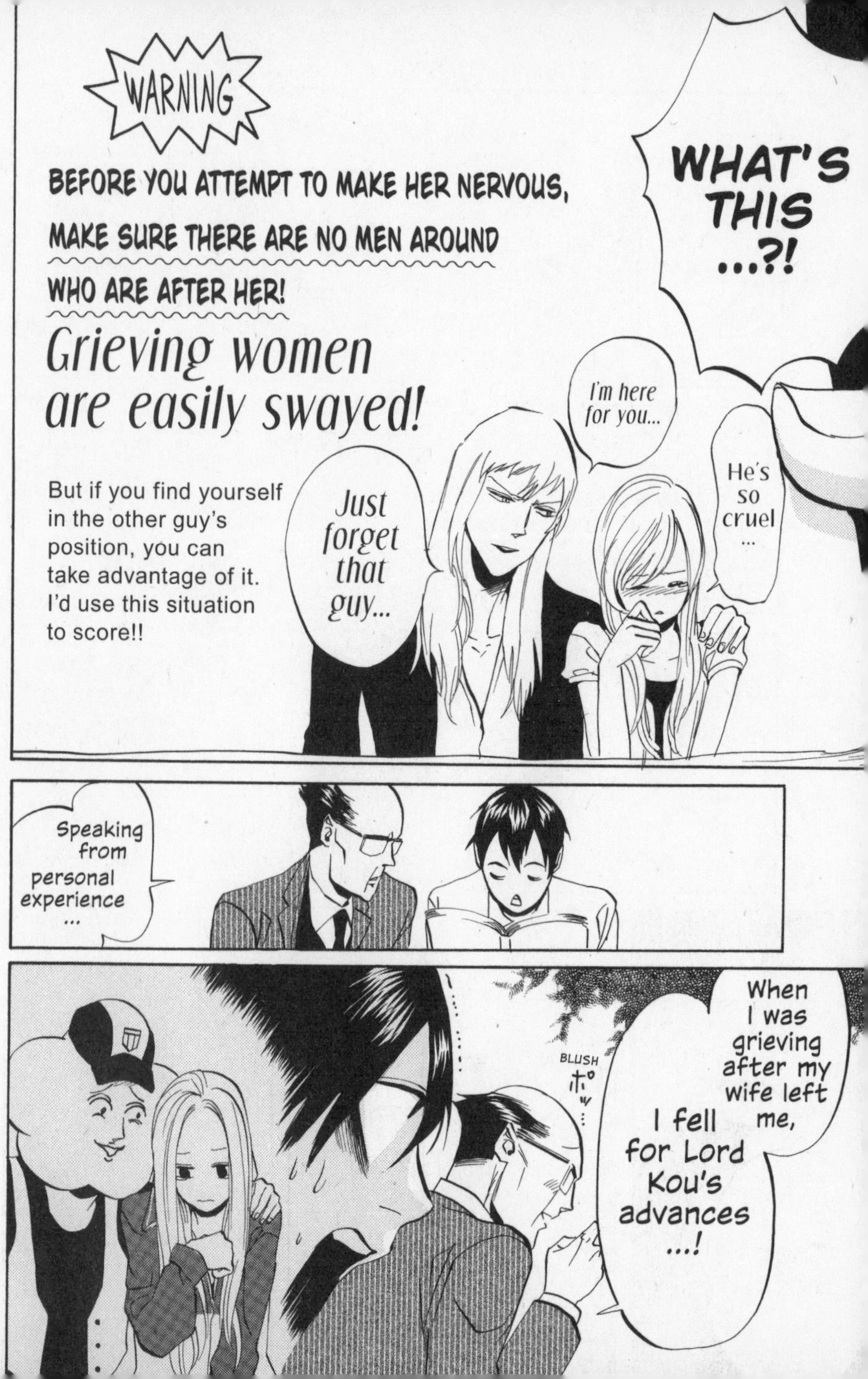
WHAT'S THIS ...?!
WARNING
BEFORE YOU ATTEMPT TO MAKE HER NERVOUS, MAKE SURE THERE ARE NO MEN AROUND WHO ARE AFTER HER!
Grieving women are easily swayed!
I'm here for you...
He's so cruel ...
Just forget that guy...
But if you find yourself in the other guy's position, you can take advantage of it. I'd use this situation to score!!
Speaking from personal experience ...
When I was grieving after my wife left me,
I fell for Lord Kou's advances ...!
BLUSH
...

Chapter 157: Yuuji Tricked Me

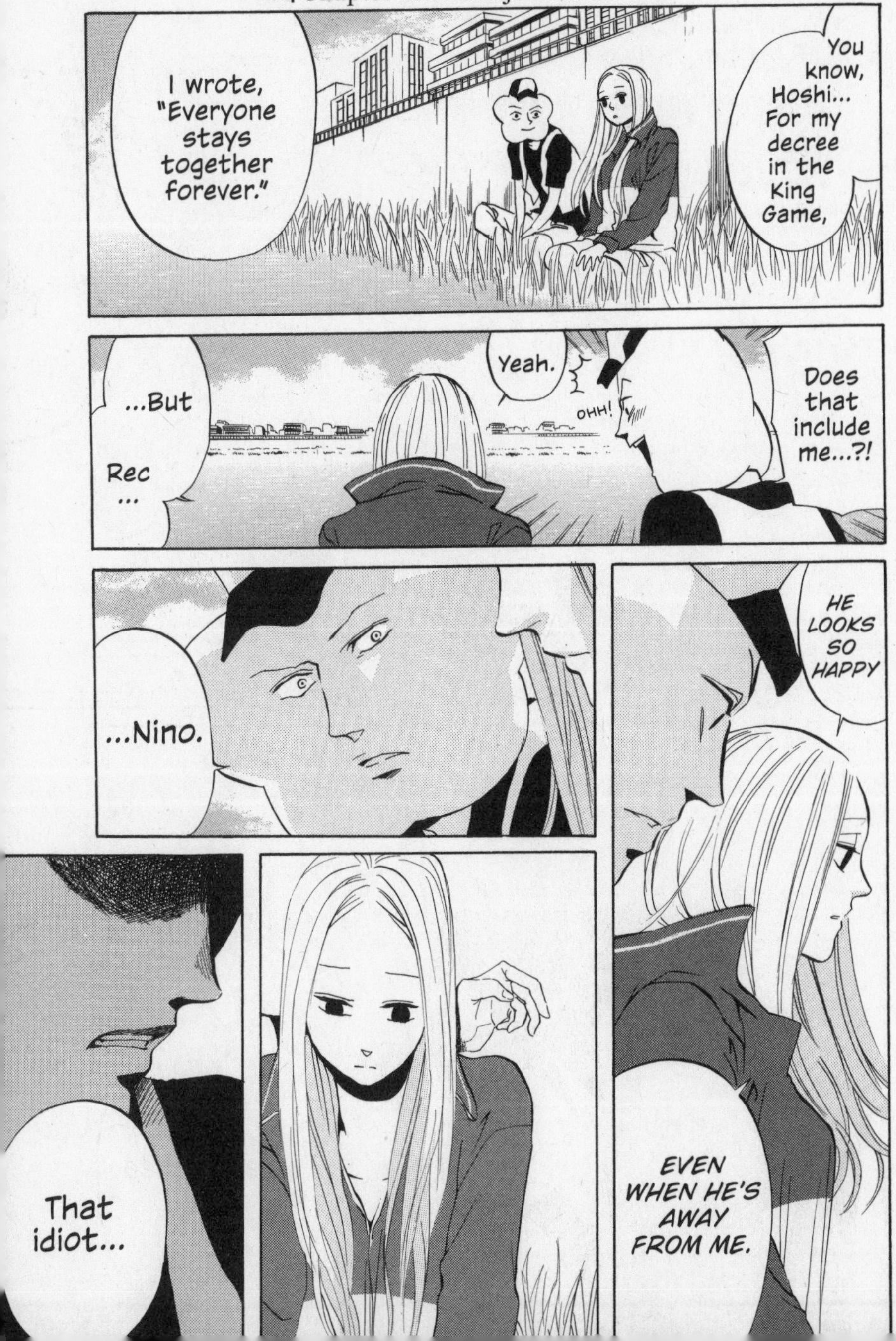
You know, Hoshi... For my decree in the King Game,
I wrote, "Everyone stays together forever."
Does that include me...?!
OHH!
Yeah.
...But Rec...
HE LOOKS SO HAPPY
EVEN WHEN HE'S AWAY FROM ME.
...Nino.
That idiot...

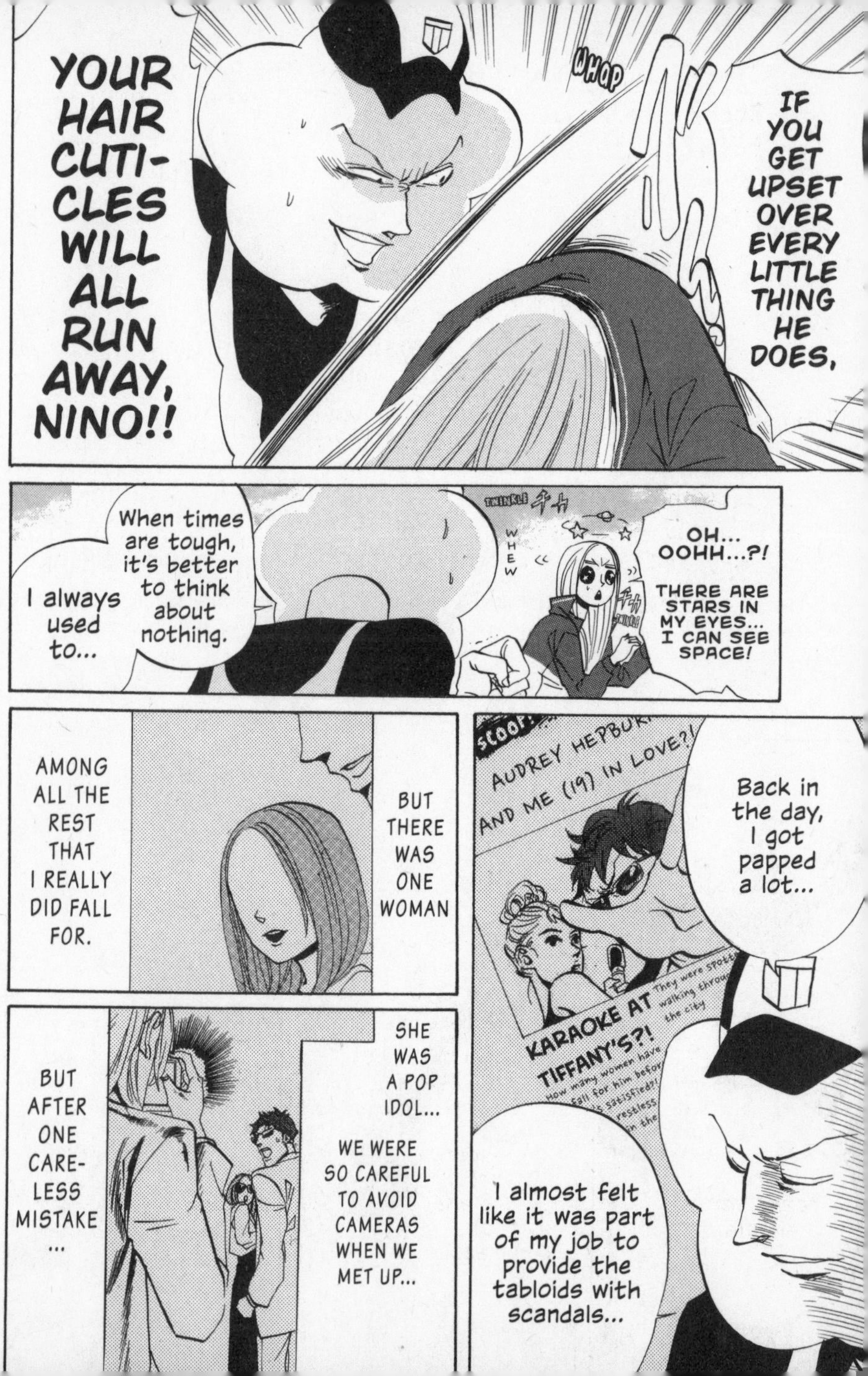
WHAP
IF YOU GET UPSET OVER EVERY LITTLE THING HE DOES,
YOUR HAIR CUTI-CLES WILL ALL RUN AWAY, NINO!!
TWINKLE
WHEW
OH... OOHH...?!
THERE ARE STARS IN MY EYES... I CAN SEE SPACE!
TWINKLE
When times are tough, it's better to think about nothing.
I always used to...
SCOOP!
AND ME (19) IN LOVE?!
KARAOKE AT TIFFANY'S?!
Back in the day, I got papped a lot...
I almost felt like it was part of my job to provide the tabloids with scandals...
BUT THERE WAS ONE WOMAN
AMONG ALL THE REST THAT I REALLY DID FALL FOR.
SHE WAS A POP IDOL...
WE WERE SO CAREFUL TO AVOID CAMERAS WHEN WE MET UP...
BUT AFTER ONE CARE-LESS MISTAKE ...

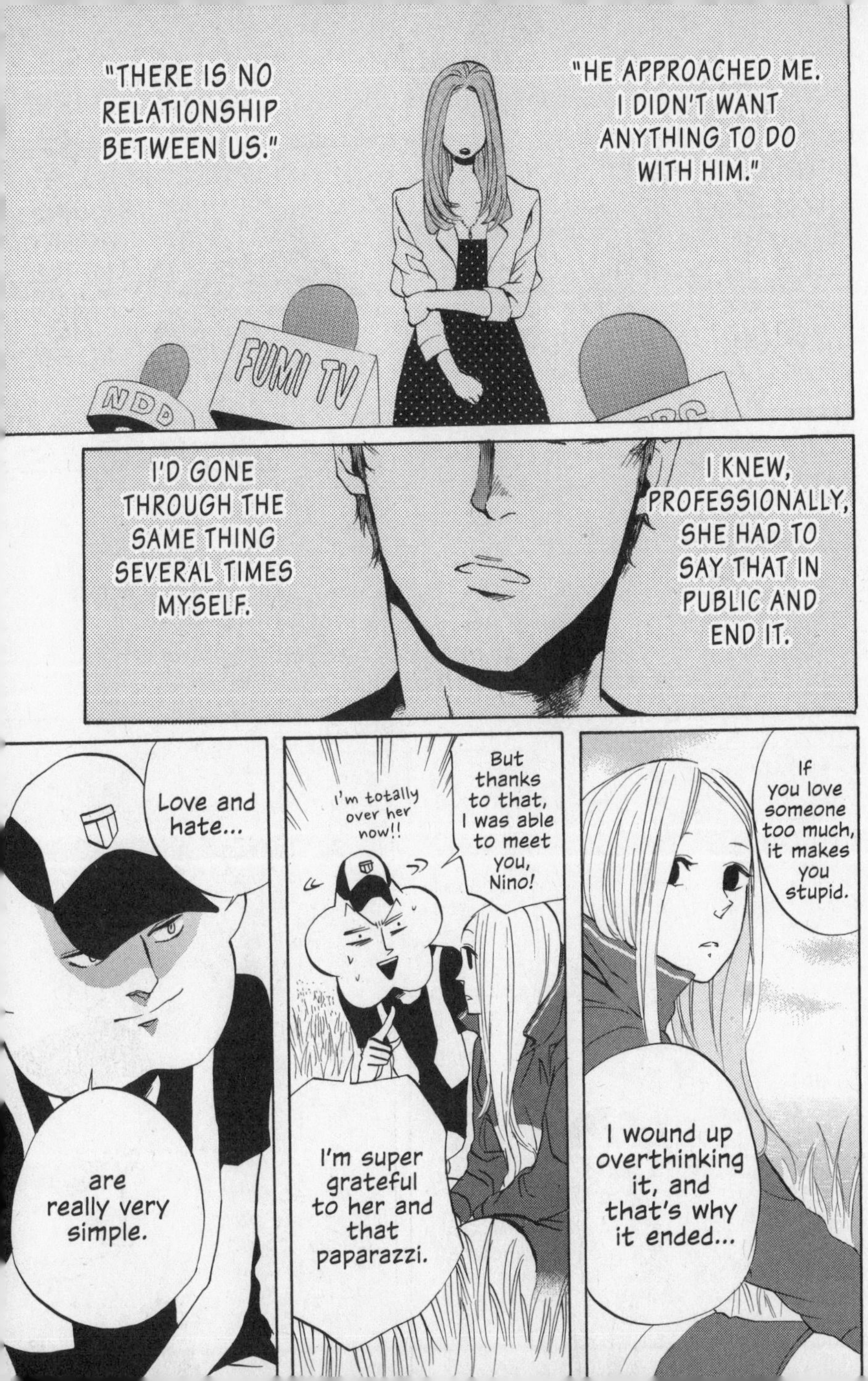
"HE APPROACHED ME. I DIDN'T WANT ANYTHING TO DO WITH HIM."
"THERE IS NO RELATIONSHIP BETWEEN US."
FUMI TV
NDD
I KNEW, PROFESSIONALLY, SHE HAD TO SAY THAT IN PUBLIC AND END IT.
I'D GONE THROUGH THE SAME THING SEVERAL TIMES MYSELF.
If you love someone too much, it makes you stupid.
I wound up overthinking it, and that's why it ended...
But thanks to that, I was able to meet you, Nino!
I'm totally over her now!!
I'm super grateful to her and that paparazzi.
Love and hate...
are really very simple.

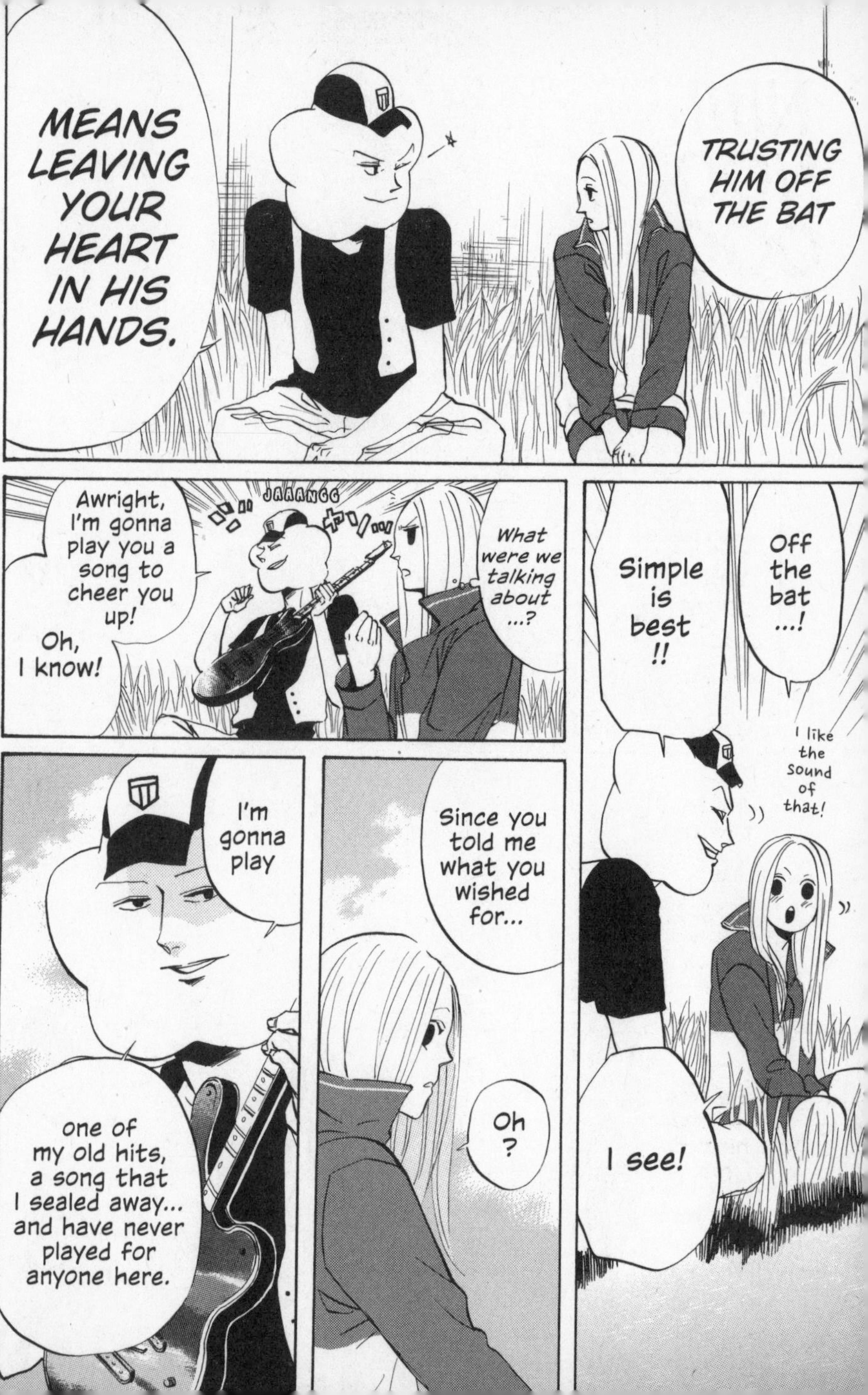
TRUSTING HIM OFF THE BAT
MEANS LEAVING YOUR HEART IN HIS HANDS.
Off the bat ...!
Simple is best !!
I like the sound of that!
I see!
What were we talking about ...?
JAAAANGG
Awright, I'm gonna play you a song to cheer you up!
Oh, I know!
Since you told me what you wished for...
Oh ?
I'm gonna play
one of my old hits, a song that I sealed away... and have never played for anyone here.

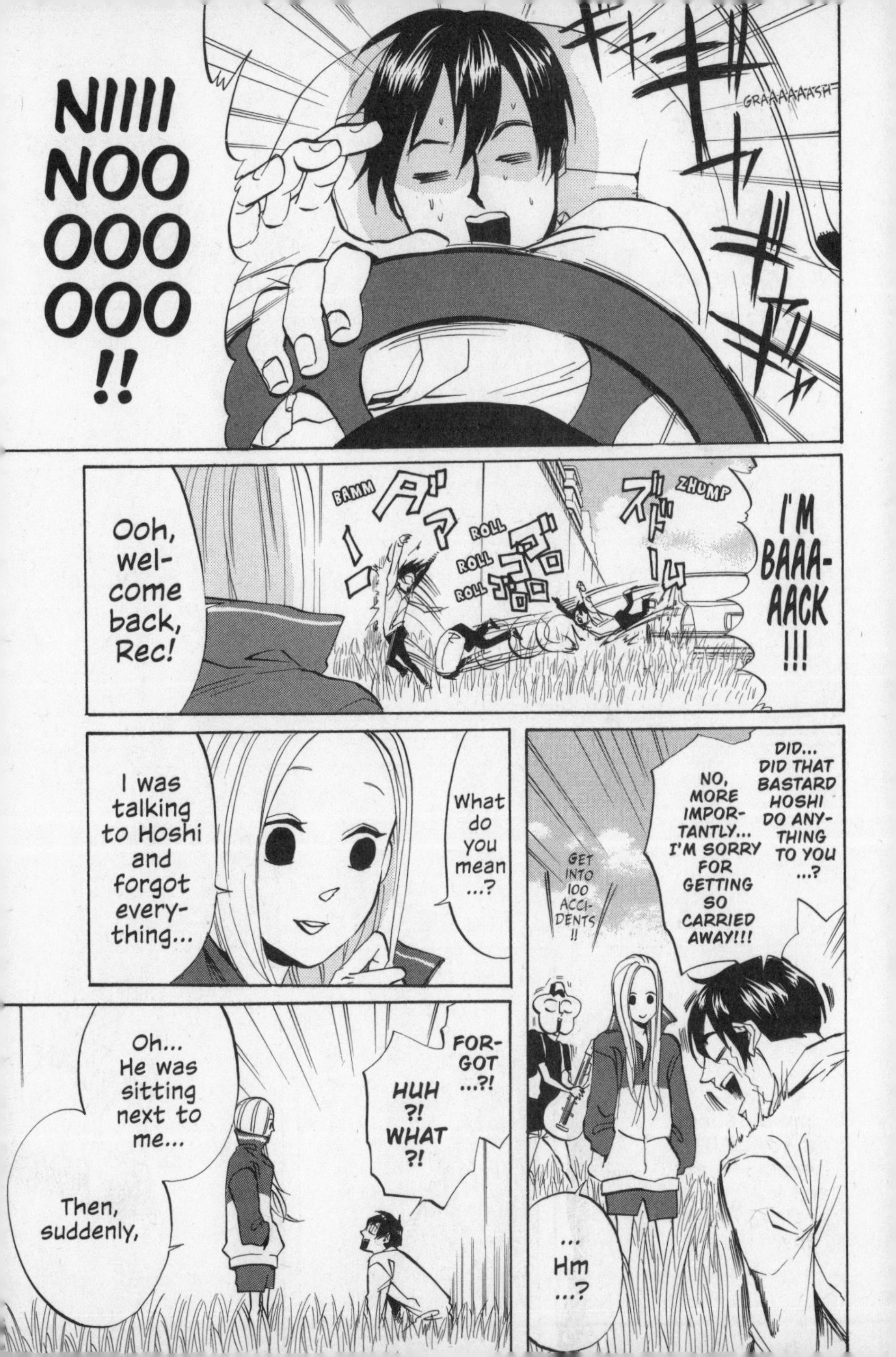
GRAAAAAASH
NIIII NOOOOOOOOO!!
I'M BAAAACK!!!
ZHUMP
ROLL ROLL ROLL
BAMM
Ooh, wel-come back, Rec!
DID... DID THAT BASTARD HOSHI DO ANY-THING TO YOU ...?
NO, MORE IMPOR-TANTLY... I'M SORRY FOR GETTING SO CARRIED AWAY!!!
GET INTO 100 ACCI-DENTS !!
... Hm ...?
What do you mean ...?
I was talking to Hoshi and forgot every-thing...
FOR-GOT ...?!
HUH ?! WHAT ?!
Oh... He was sitting next to me...
Then, suddenly,

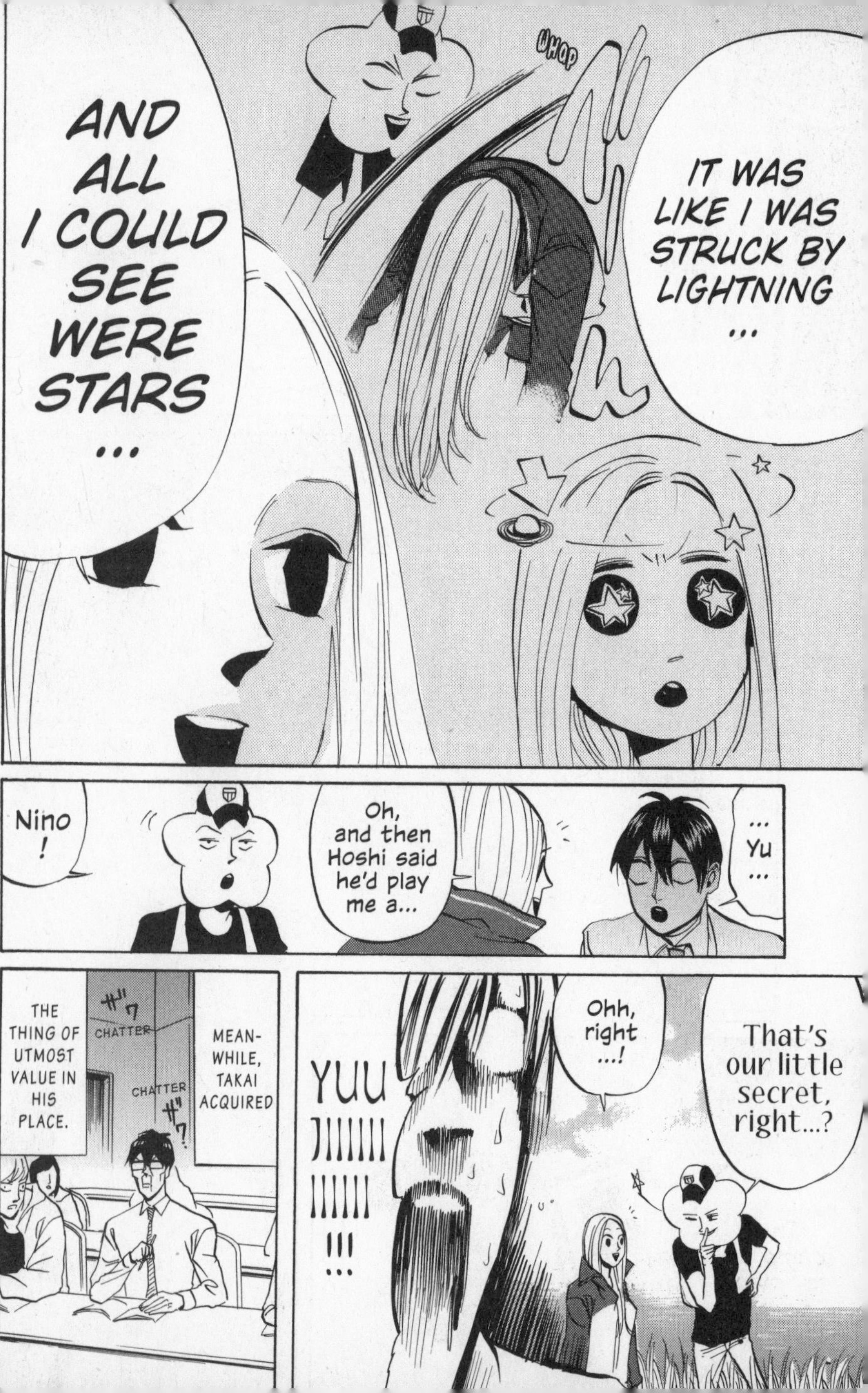
WHAP
IT WAS LIKE I WAS STRUCK BY LIGHTNING ...
AND ALL I COULD SEE WERE STARS ...
... Yu ...
Oh, and then Hoshi said he'd play me a...
Nino !
That's our little secret, right...?
Ohh, right ...!
YUU !!!!!!!!!!!!!! ...
MEAN-WHILE, TAKAI ACQUIRED
THE THING OF UTMOST VALUE IN HIS PLACE.
ザワ CHATTER
CHATTER ザワ

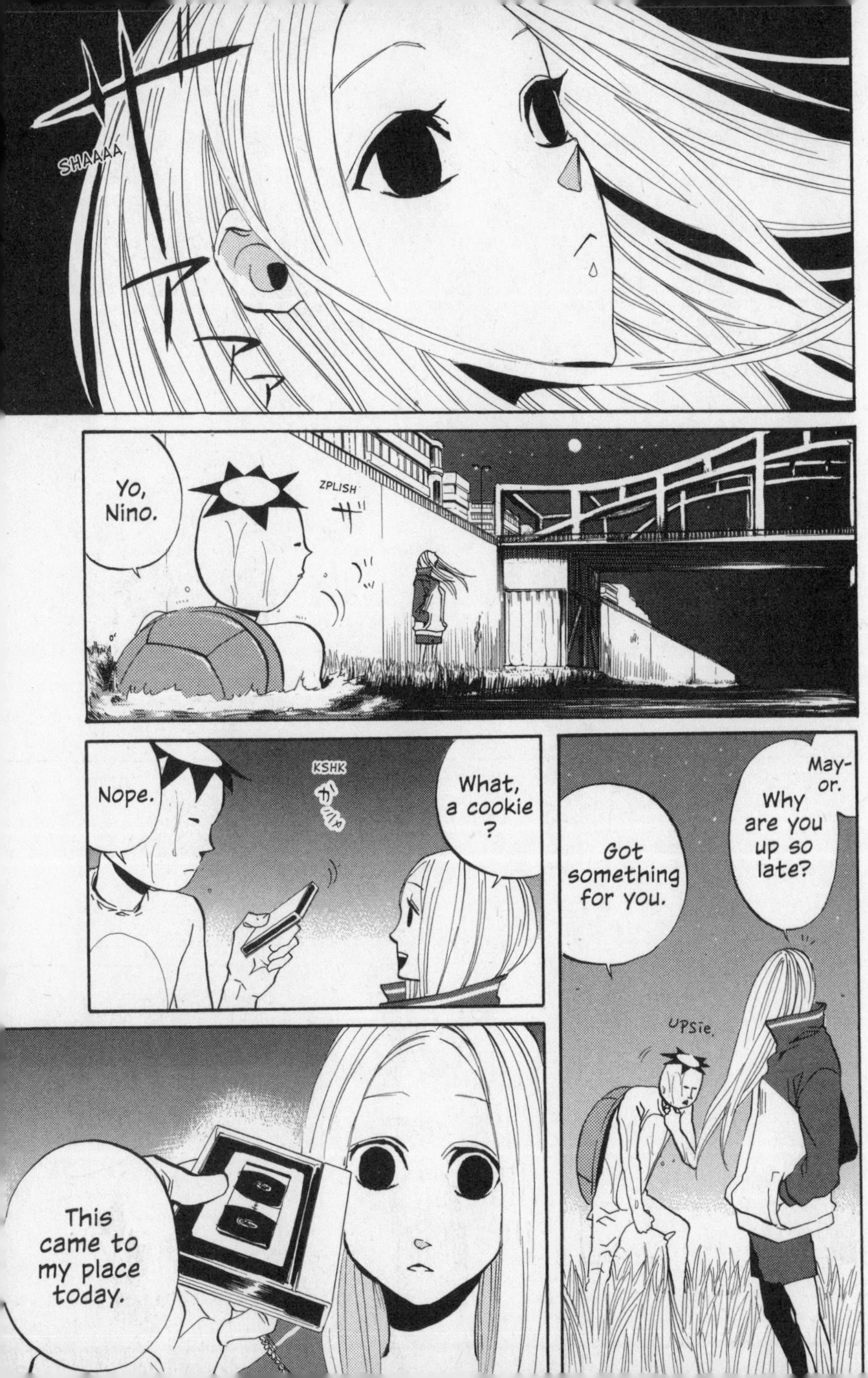
SHAAAA
ZPLISH
Yo, Nino.
May-or. Why are you up so late?
Got something for you.
UPSie.
What, a cookie?
KSHK
Nope.
This came to my place today.

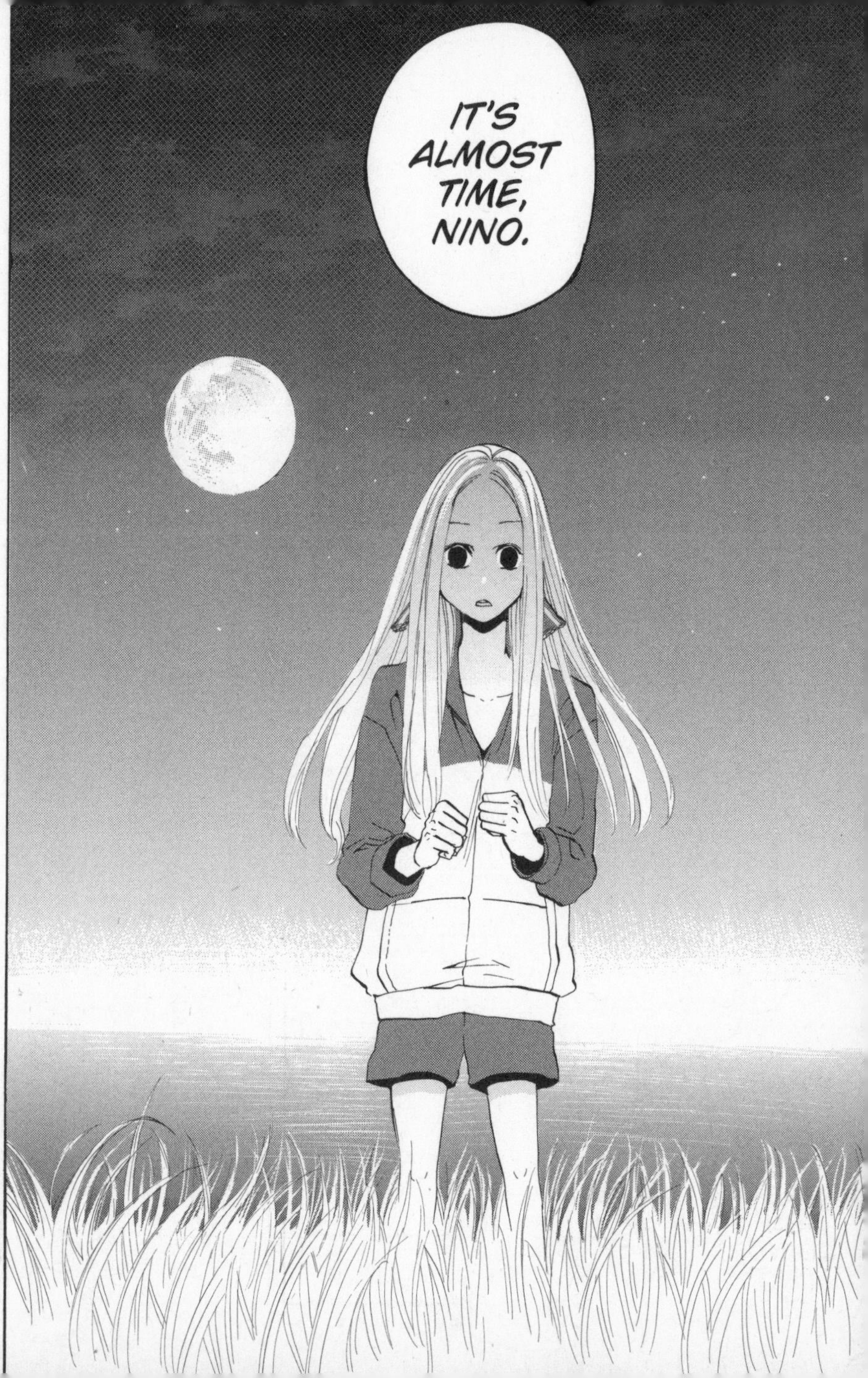
IT'S ALMOST TIME, NINO.

Chapter 158: Code Deciphered

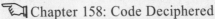

Uh... so with that in mind, about our subsequent operating procedures,
if you examine this graph, you'll see that...
the key to increasing profits at our Hong Kong branch is ...
THP
THP
utilizing the production line for wearing shoes or slippers indoors...
THP
SHMP
and depending on a successful landing on the carpet ...
increasing sales in the Venusian sector...
KLNK
will result in domestic Japanese tables ...
WRRRRRG
steadily rising...
BA
AM
WHAT IN GOD'S NAME ARE YOU DOING, NINO ?!

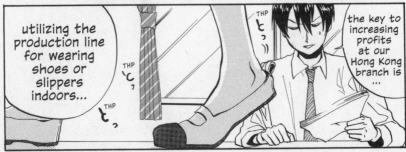

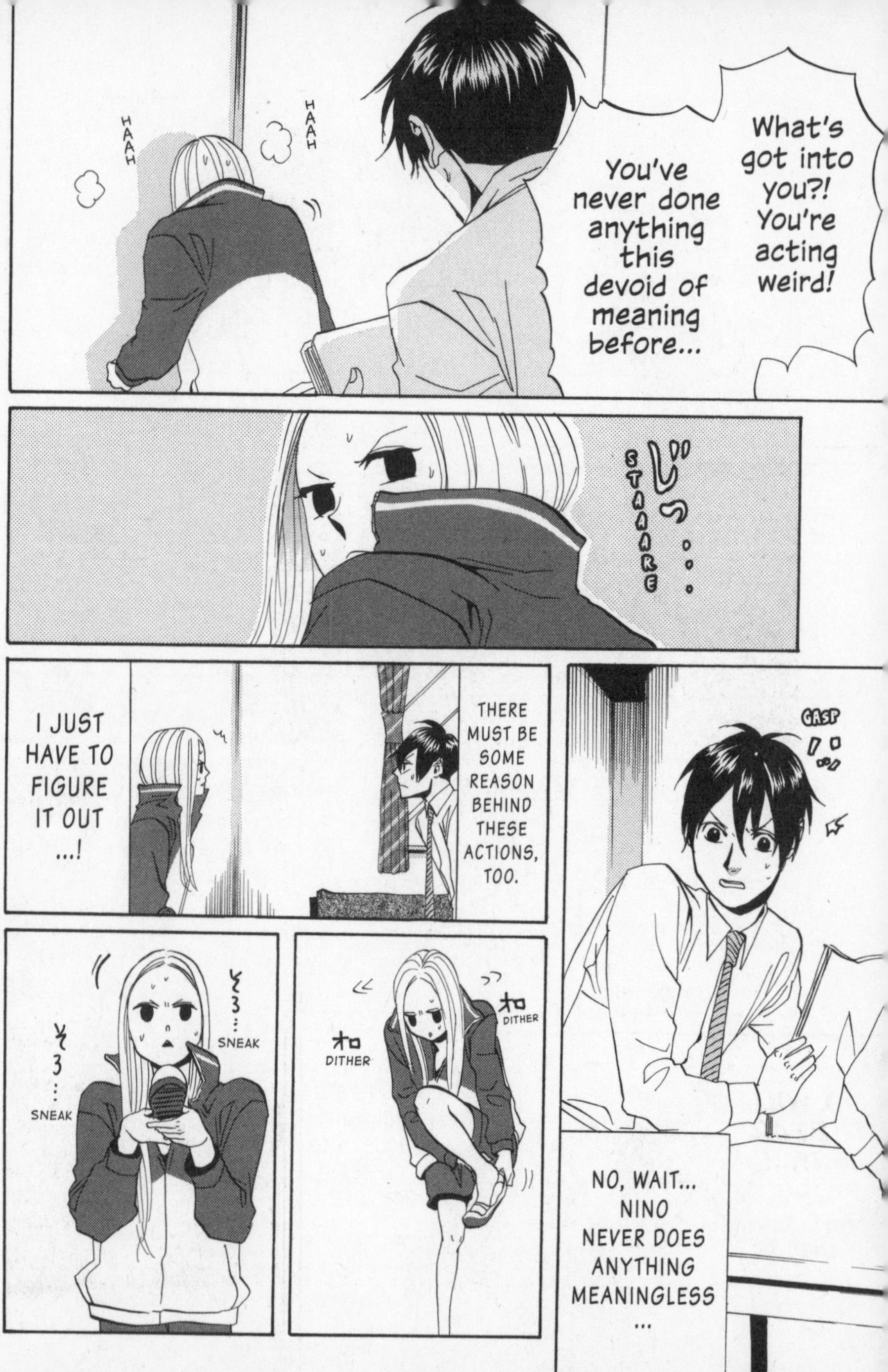
What's got into you?! You're acting weird!
You've never done anything this devoid of meaning before...
HAAAH
HAAAH
じっ...
STAAARE
GASP
NO, WAIT... NINO NEVER DOES ANYTHING MEANINGLESS ...
THERE MUST BE SOME REASON BEHIND THESE ACTIONS, TOO.
I JUST HAVE TO FIGURE IT OUT ...!
オロ
DITHER
オロ
DITHER
そろ...
SNEAK
そろ...
SNEAK

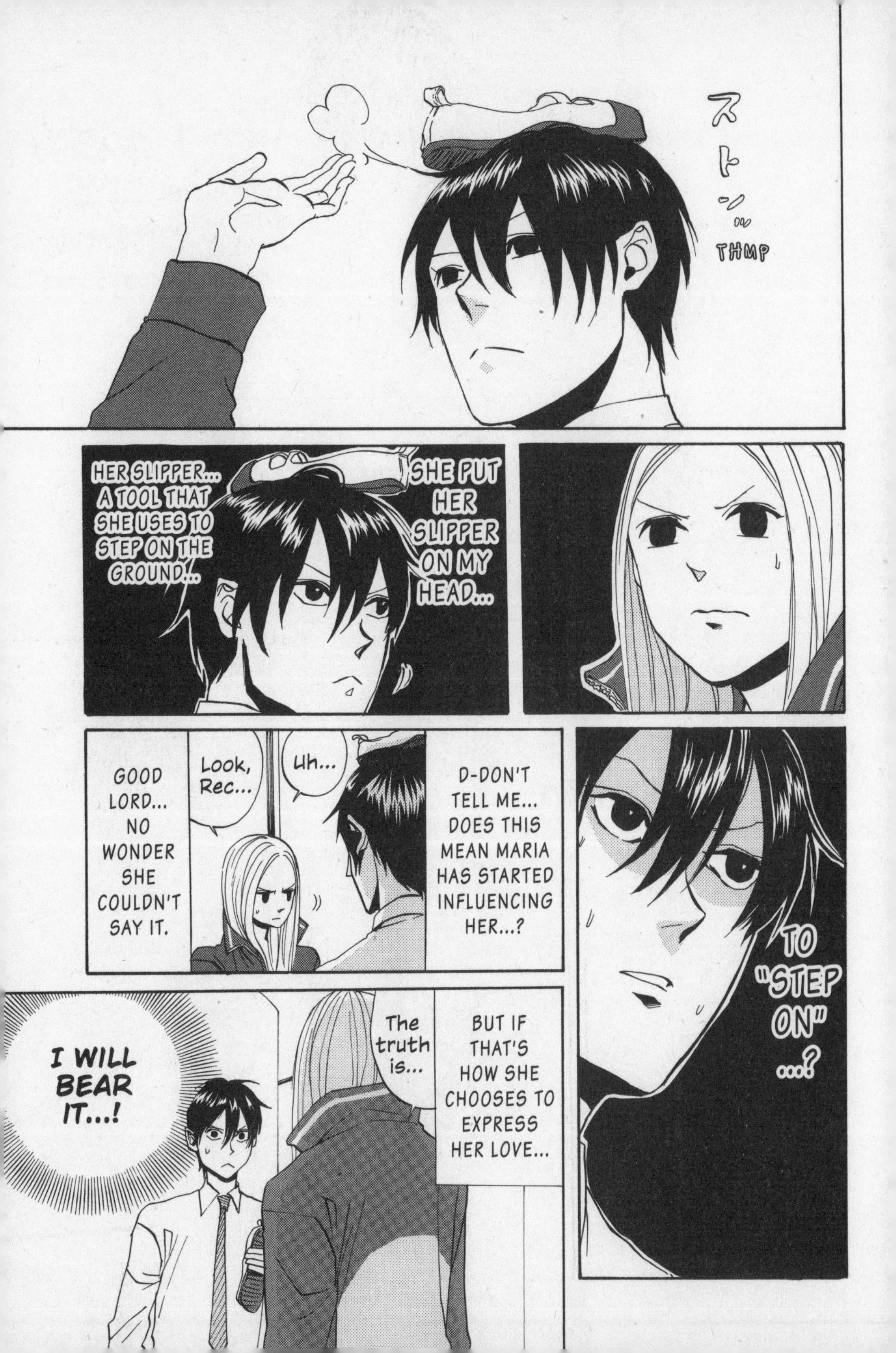
ストン
THMP
SHE PUT HER SLIPPER ON MY HEAD...
HER SLIPPER... A TOOL THAT SHE USES TO STEP ON THE GROUND...
TO "STEP ON" ...?
D-DON'T TELL ME... DOES THIS MEAN MARIA HAS STARTED INFLUENCING HER...?
Uh...
Look, Rec...
GOOD LORD... NO WONDER SHE COULDN'T SAY IT.
BUT IF THAT'S HOW SHE CHOOSES TO EXPRESS HER LOVE...
The truth is...
I WILL BEAR IT...!

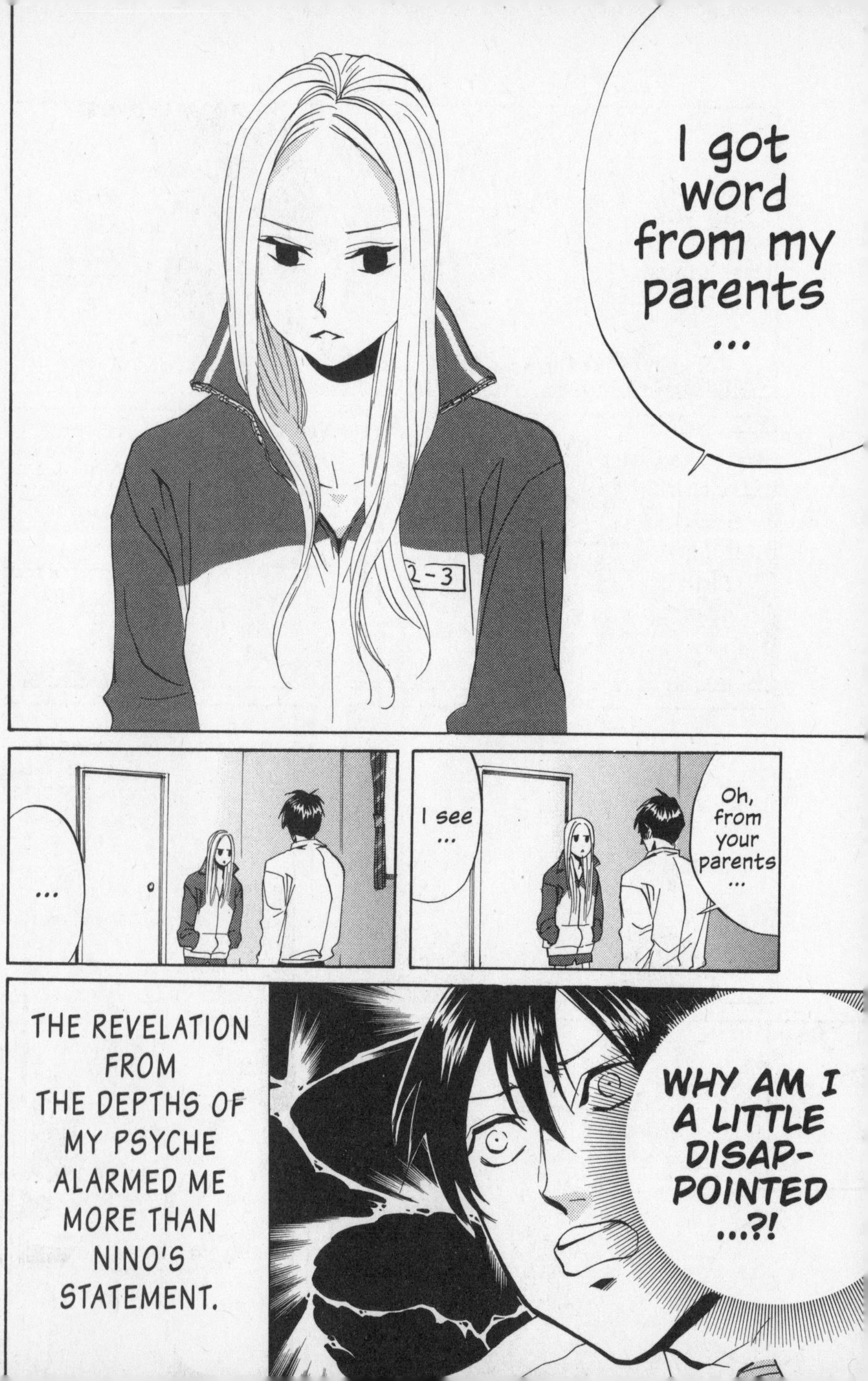
I got word from my parents ...
Oh, from your parents ...
I see ...
...
WHY AM I A LITTLE DISAP- POINTED ...?!
THE REVELATION FROM THE DEPTHS OF MY PSYCHE ALARMED ME MORE THAN NINO'S STATEMENT.

Chapter 159: Everything, Suddenly...

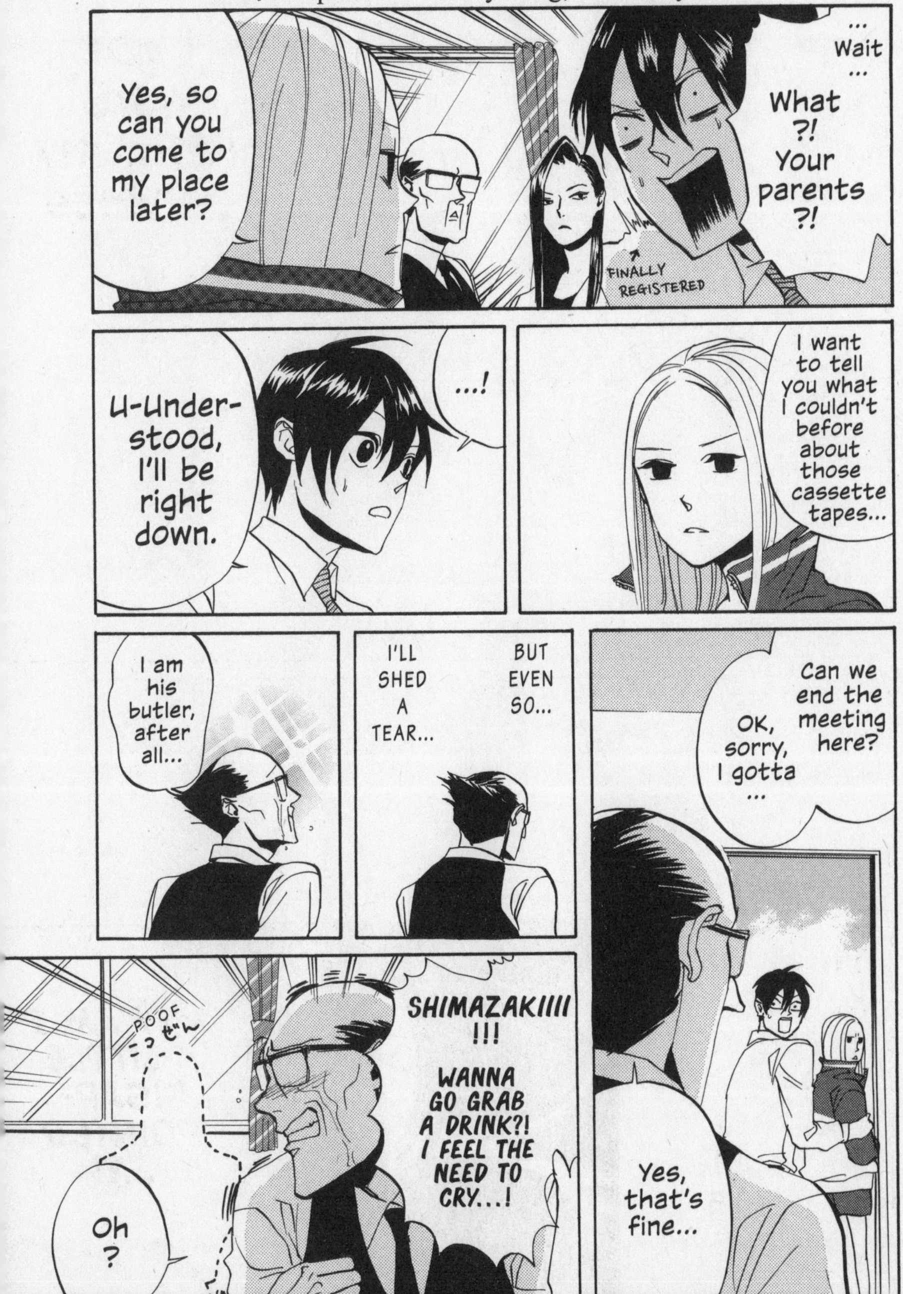
... Wait ...
What?! Your parents?!
Yes, so can you come to my place later?
FINALLY REGISTERED
I want to tell you what I couldn't before about those cassette tapes...
...!
U-Understood, I'll be right down.
Can we end the meeting here?
OK, sorry, I gotta ...
Yes, that's fine...
BUT EVEN SO...
I'LL SHED A TEAR...
I am his butler, after all...
SHIMAZAKIIII!!!
WANNA GO GRAB A DRINK?! I FEEL THE NEED TO CRY...!
POOF こっぜん
Oh?

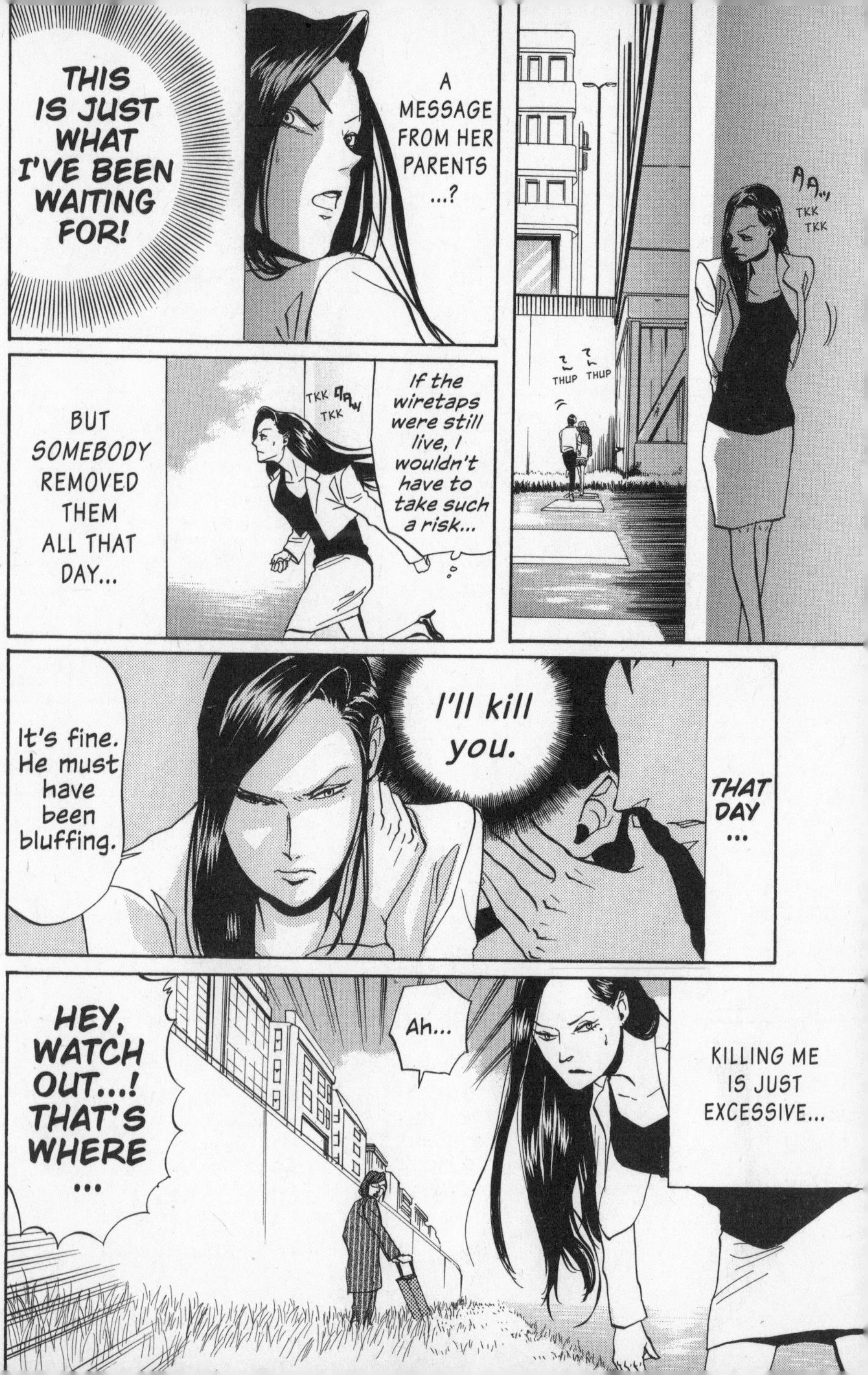
TKK
TKK
THUP THUP
A MESSAGE FROM HER PARENTS ...?
THIS IS JUST WHAT I'VE BEEN WAITING FOR!
If the wiretaps were still live, I wouldn't have to take such a risk...
TKK TKK
BUT SOMEBODY REMOVED THEM ALL THAT DAY...
THAT DAY ...
I'll kill you.
It's fine. He must have been bluffing.
KILLING ME IS JUST EXCESSIVE...
Ah...
HEY, WATCH OUT...! THAT'S WHERE ...

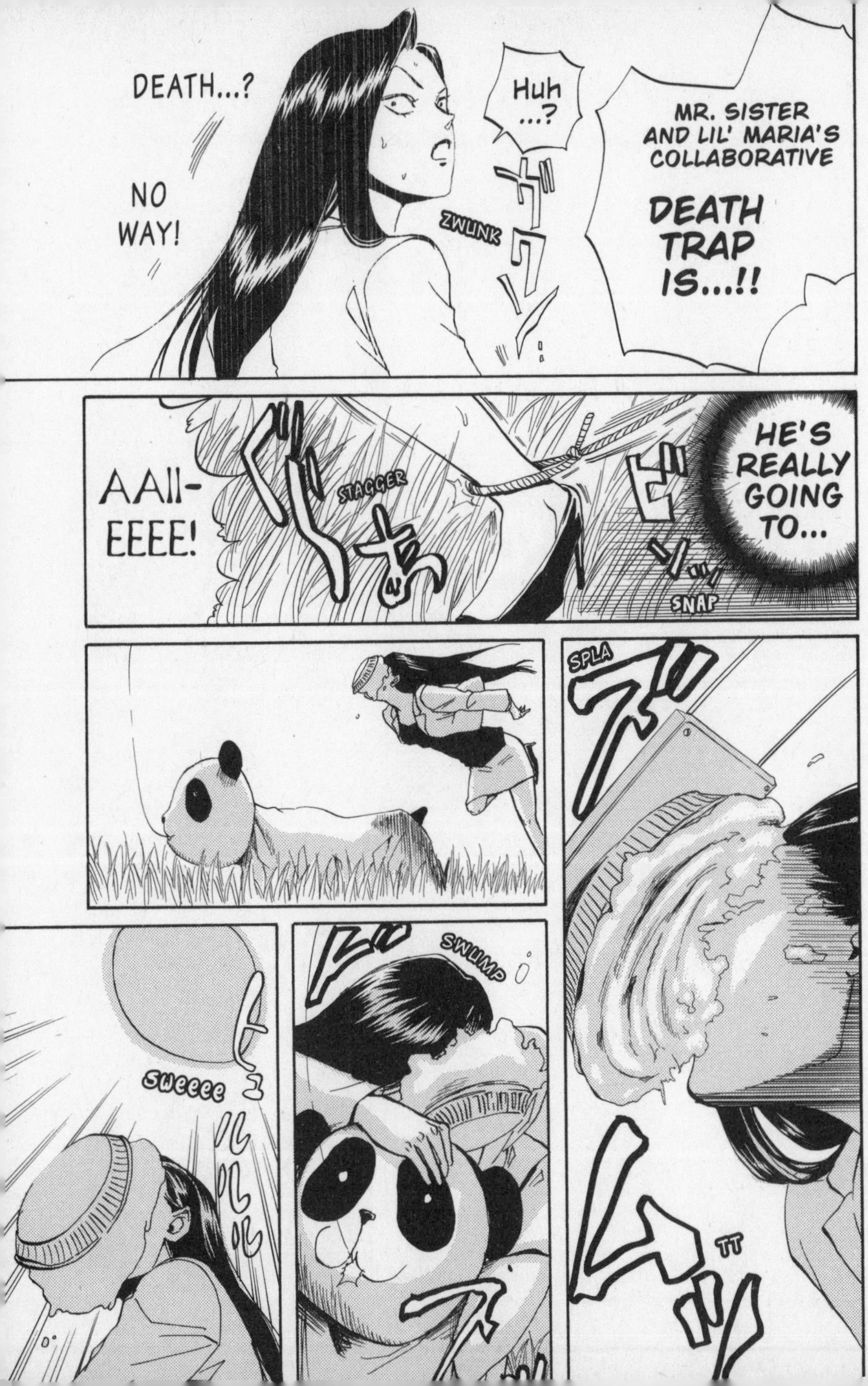
MR. SISTER AND LIL' MARIA'S COLLABORATIVE
DEATH TRAP IS...!!
Huh ...?
ZWUNK
DEATH...?
NO WAY!
HE'S REALLY GOING TO...
SNAP
STAGGER
AAII-EEEE!
SPLA
TT
SWUMP
sweeee

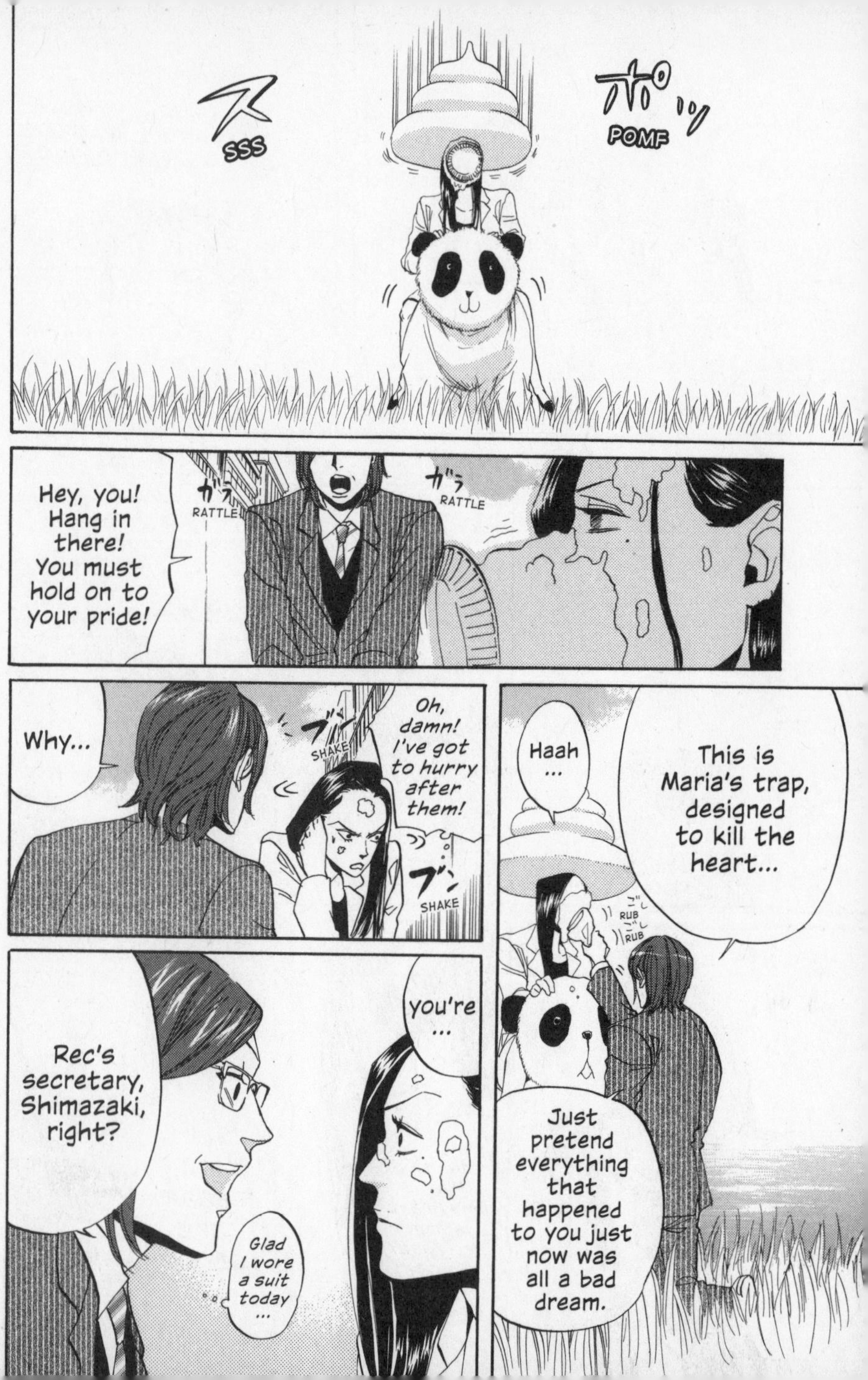

ポッ
POMF
ス
SSS
ガラ
RATTLE
ガラ
RATTLE!
Hey, you! Hang in there! You must hold on to your pride!
This is Maria's trap, designed to kill the heart...
Haah ...
ゴシ
RUB
ゴシ
RUB
Just pretend everything that happened to you just now was all a bad dream.
Oh, damn! I've got to hurry after them!
SHAKE
Why...
SHAKE
you're ...
Rec's secretary, Shimazaki, right?
Glad I wore a suit today ...

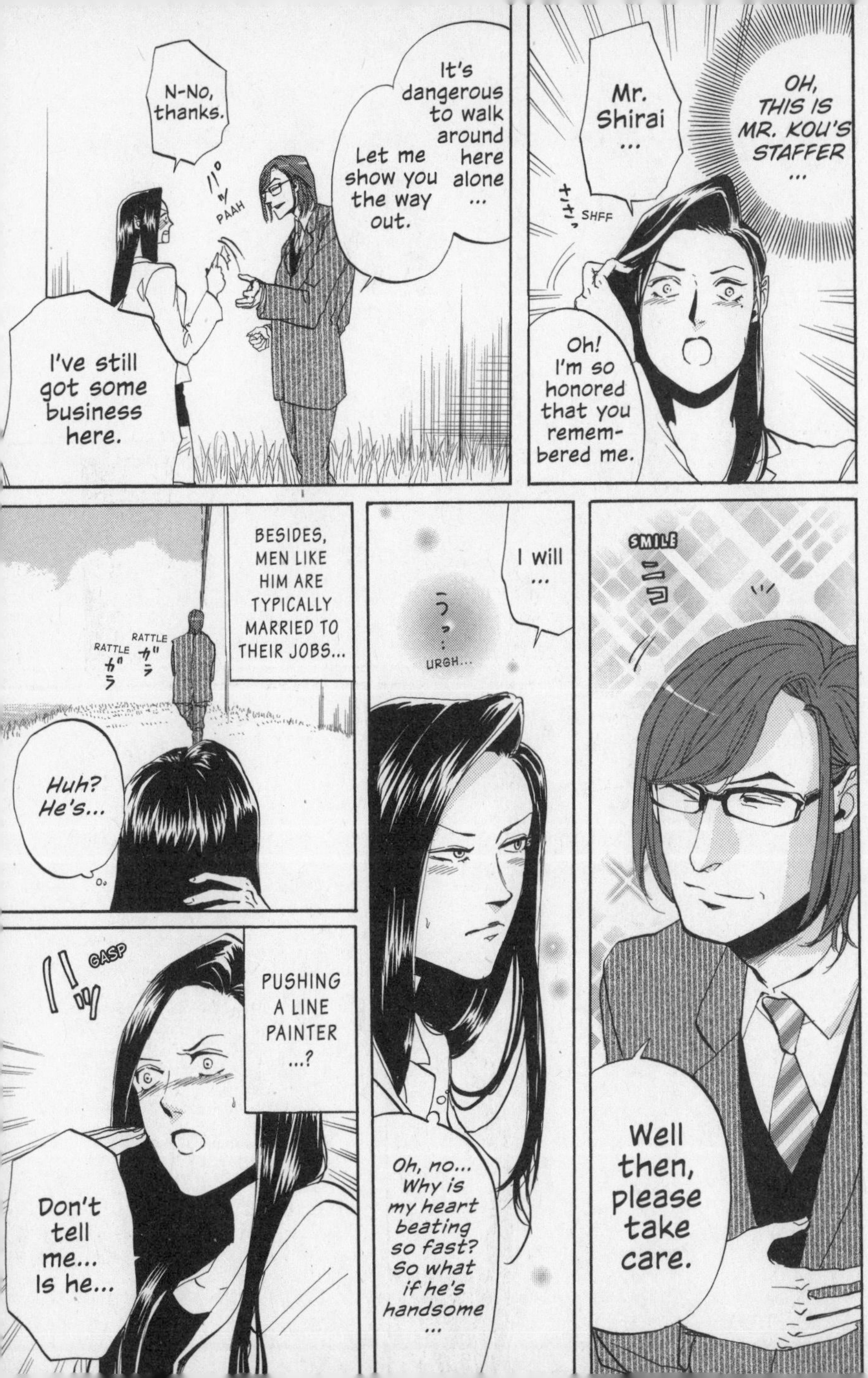
OH, THIS IS MR. KOU'S STAFFER ...
Mr. Shirai ...
ささっ SHFF
Oh! I'm so honored that you remembered me.
It's dangerous to walk around here alone ...
Let me show you the way out.
N-No, thanks.
パッ PAAH
I've still got some business here.
ニコ SMILE
Well then, please take care.
I will ...
うっ… URGH...
Oh, no... Why is my heart beating so fast? So what if he's handsome ...
BESIDES, MEN LIKE HIM ARE TYPICALLY MARRIED TO THEIR JOBS...
ガラ RATTLE
ガラ RATTLE
Huh? He's...
ハッ GASP
PUSHING A LINE PAINTER ...?
Don't tell me... Is he...

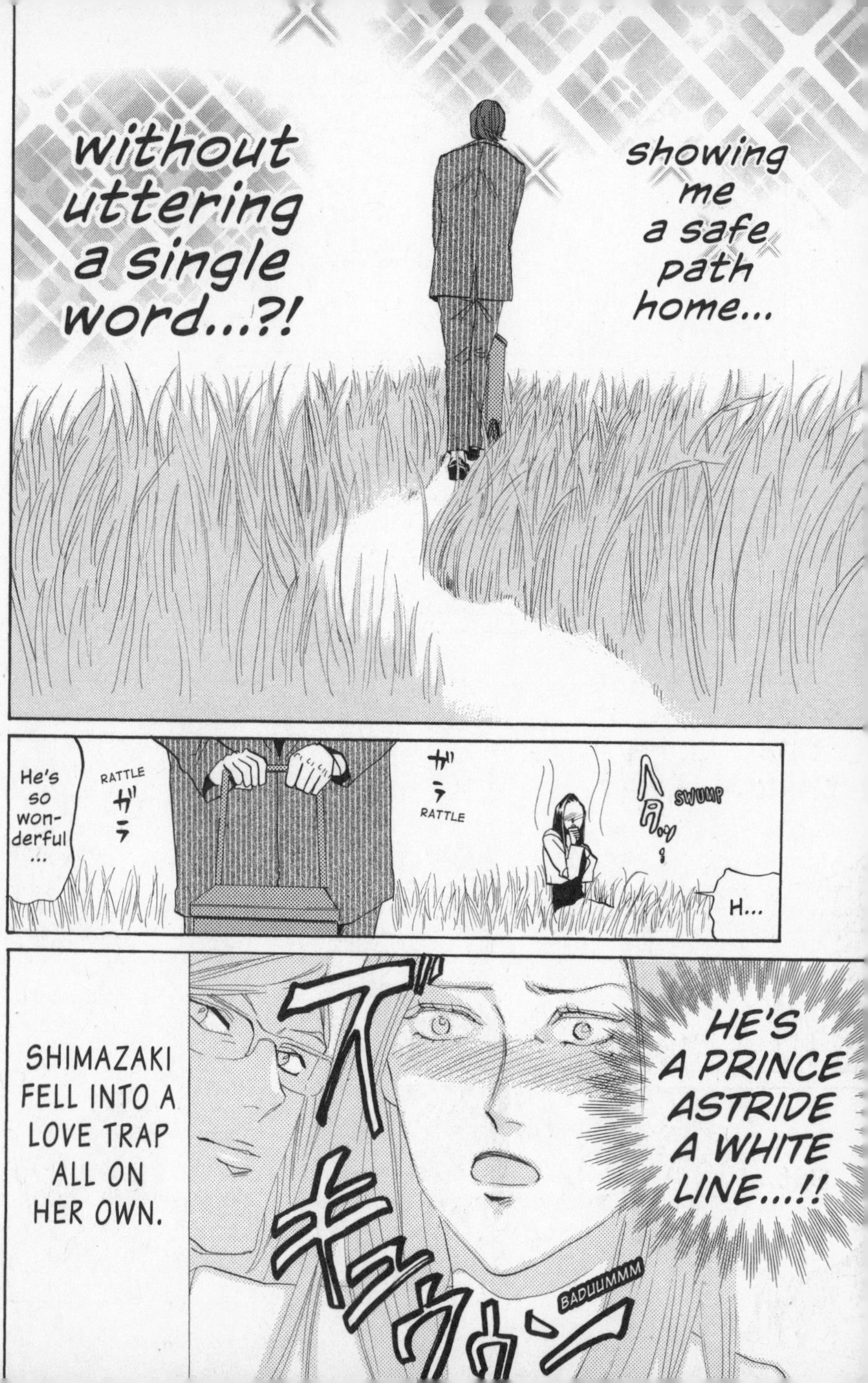
showing me a safe path home...
without uttering a single word...?!
H...
SWUMP
RATTLE
RATTLE
He's so won-derful...
HE'S A PRINCE ASTRIDE A WHITE LINE...!!
BADUUMMM
SHIMAZAKI FELL INTO A LOVE TRAP ALL ON HER OWN.

Chapter 160: Confession

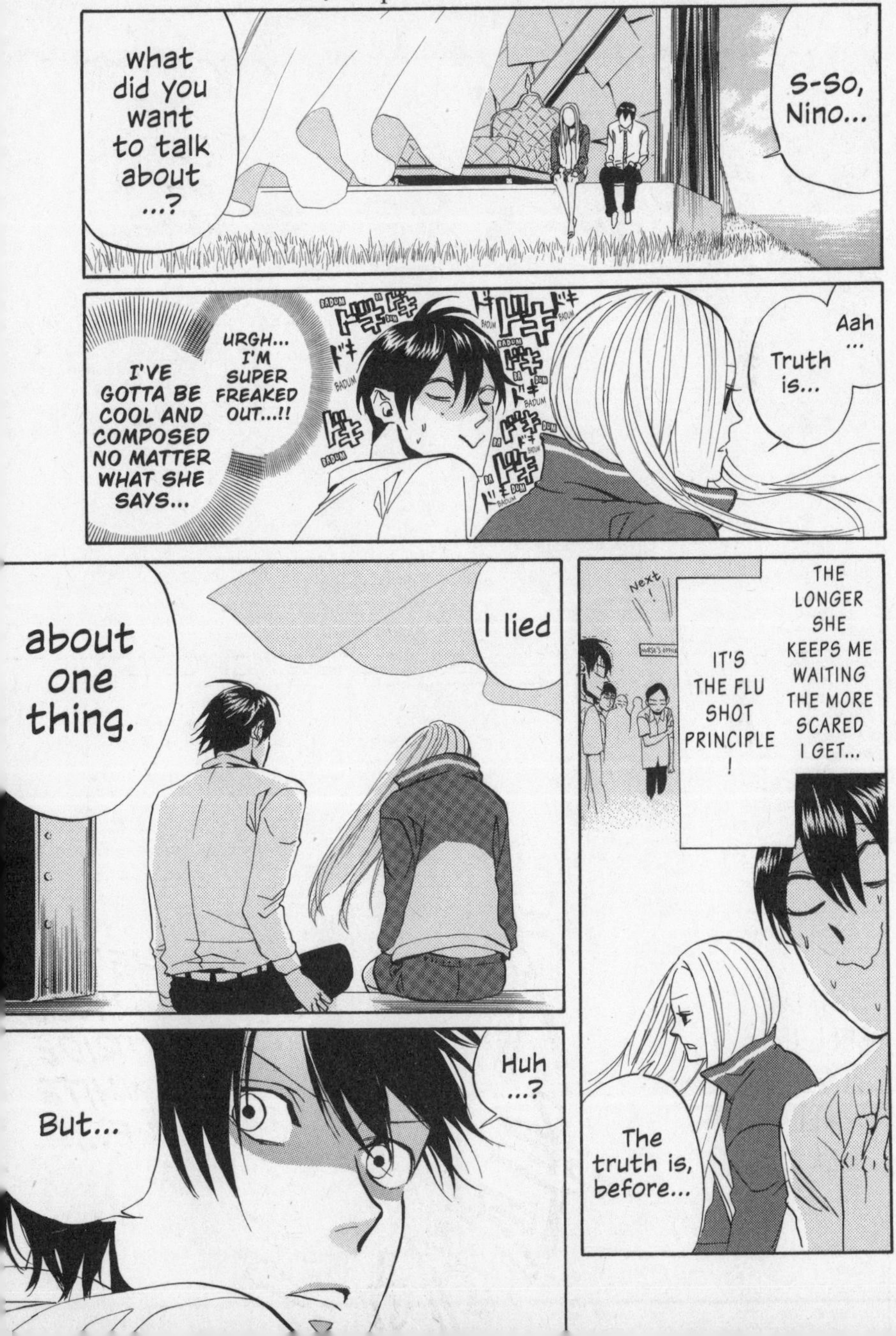
S-So, Nino...
what did you want to talk about ...?
Aah ... Truth is...
BADUM ドキ
URGH... I'M SUPER FREAKED OUT...!!
I'VE GOTTA BE COOL AND COMPOSED NO MATTER WHAT SHE SAYS...
THE LONGER SHE KEEPS ME WAITING THE MORE SCARED I GET...
IT'S THE FLU SHOT PRINCIPLE !
Next !
The truth is, before...
I lied
about one thing.
Huh ...?
But...

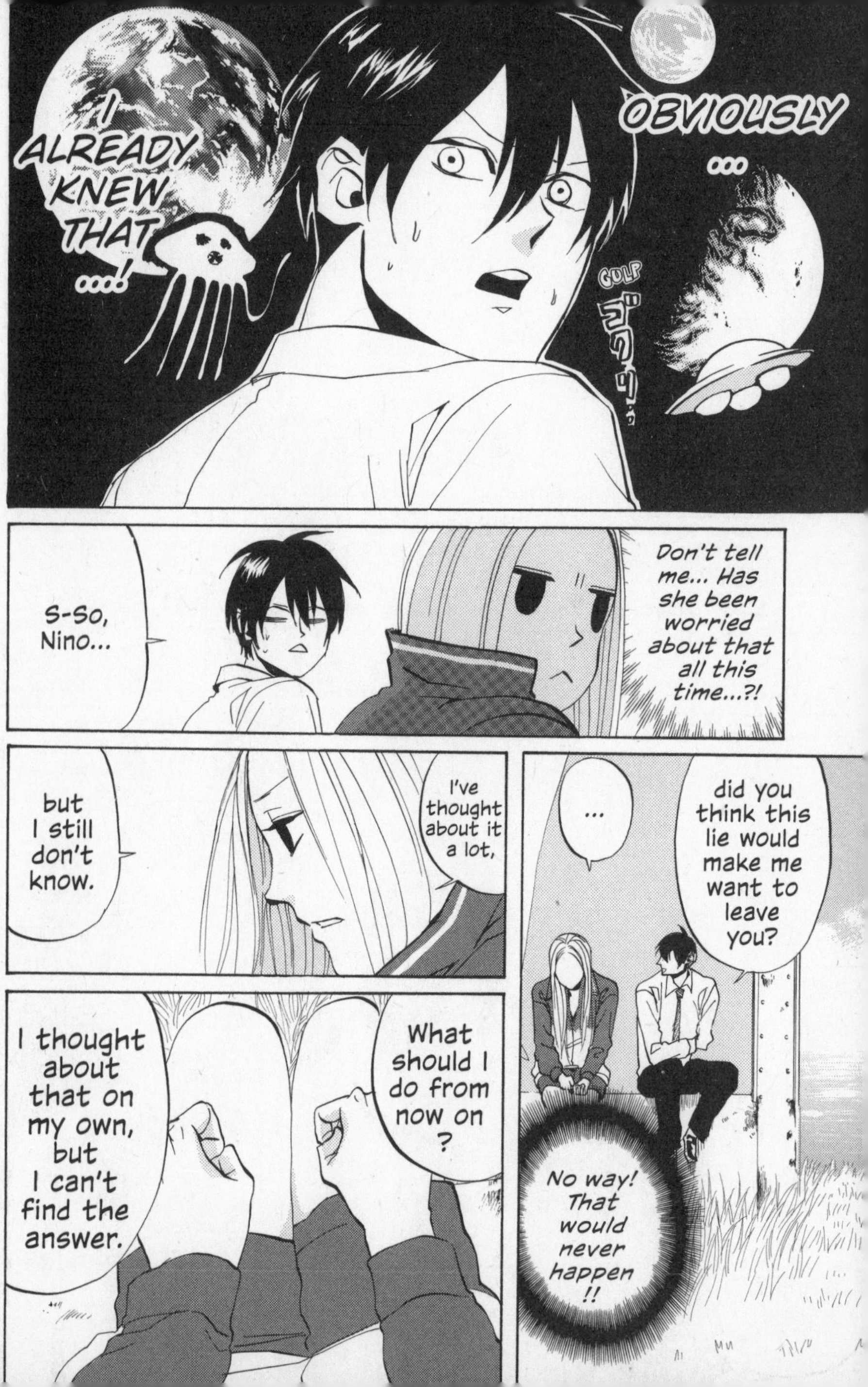
OBVIOUSLY ...
GULP
I ALREADY KNEW THAT ...!
Don't tell me... Has she been worried about that all this time...?!
S-So, Nino...
did you think this lie would make me want to leave you?
...
No way! That would never happen!!
I've thought about it a lot,
but I still don't know.
What should I do from now on?
I thought about that on my own, but I can't find the answer.

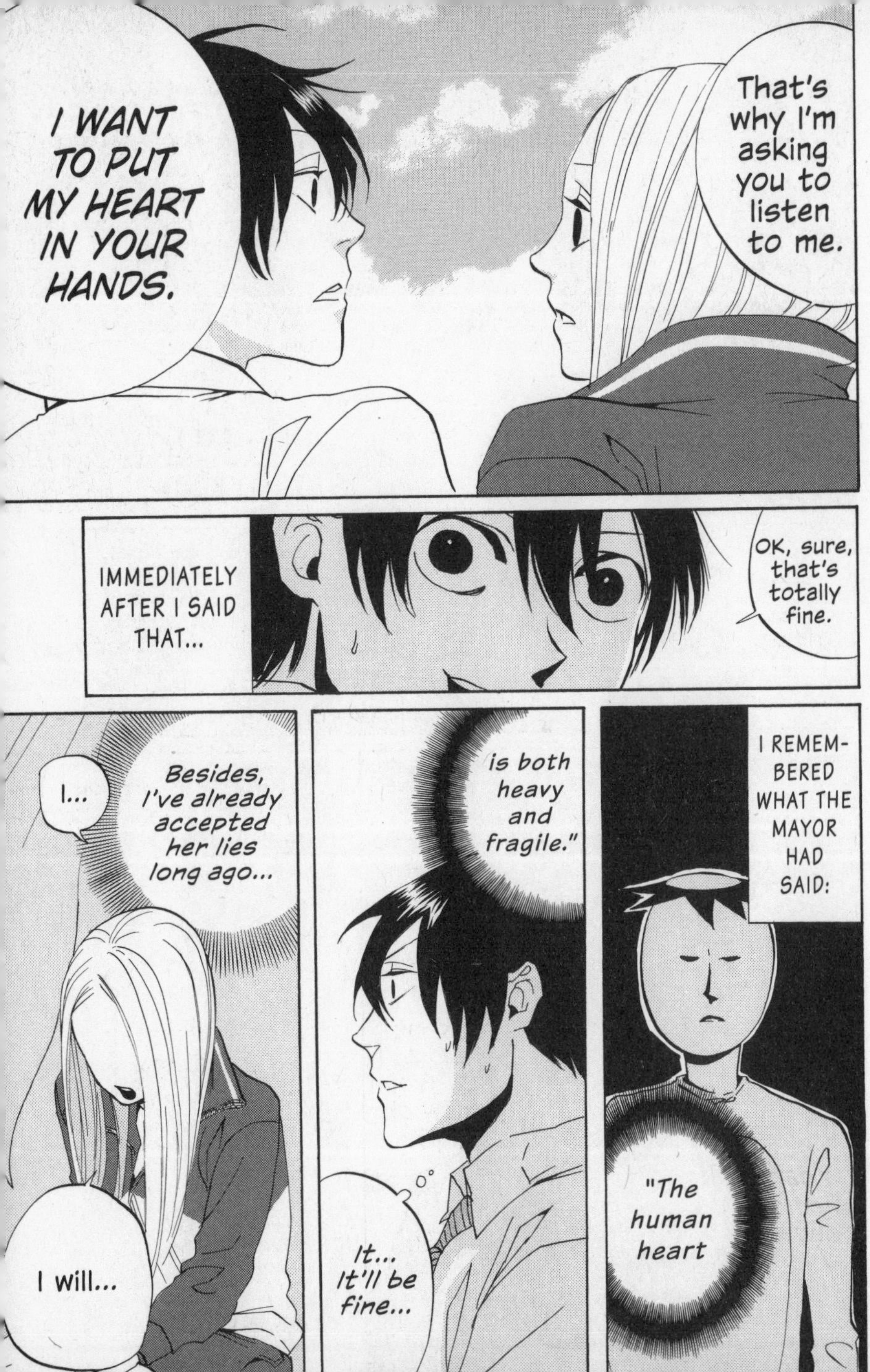

That's why I'm asking you to listen to me.
I WANT TO PUT MY HEART IN YOUR HANDS.
OK, sure, that's totally fine.
IMMEDIATELY AFTER I SAID THAT...
I REMEMBERED WHAT THE MAYOR HAD SAID:
"The human heart
is both heavy and fragile."
It... It'll be fine...
Besides, I've already accepted her lies long ago...
I...
I will...

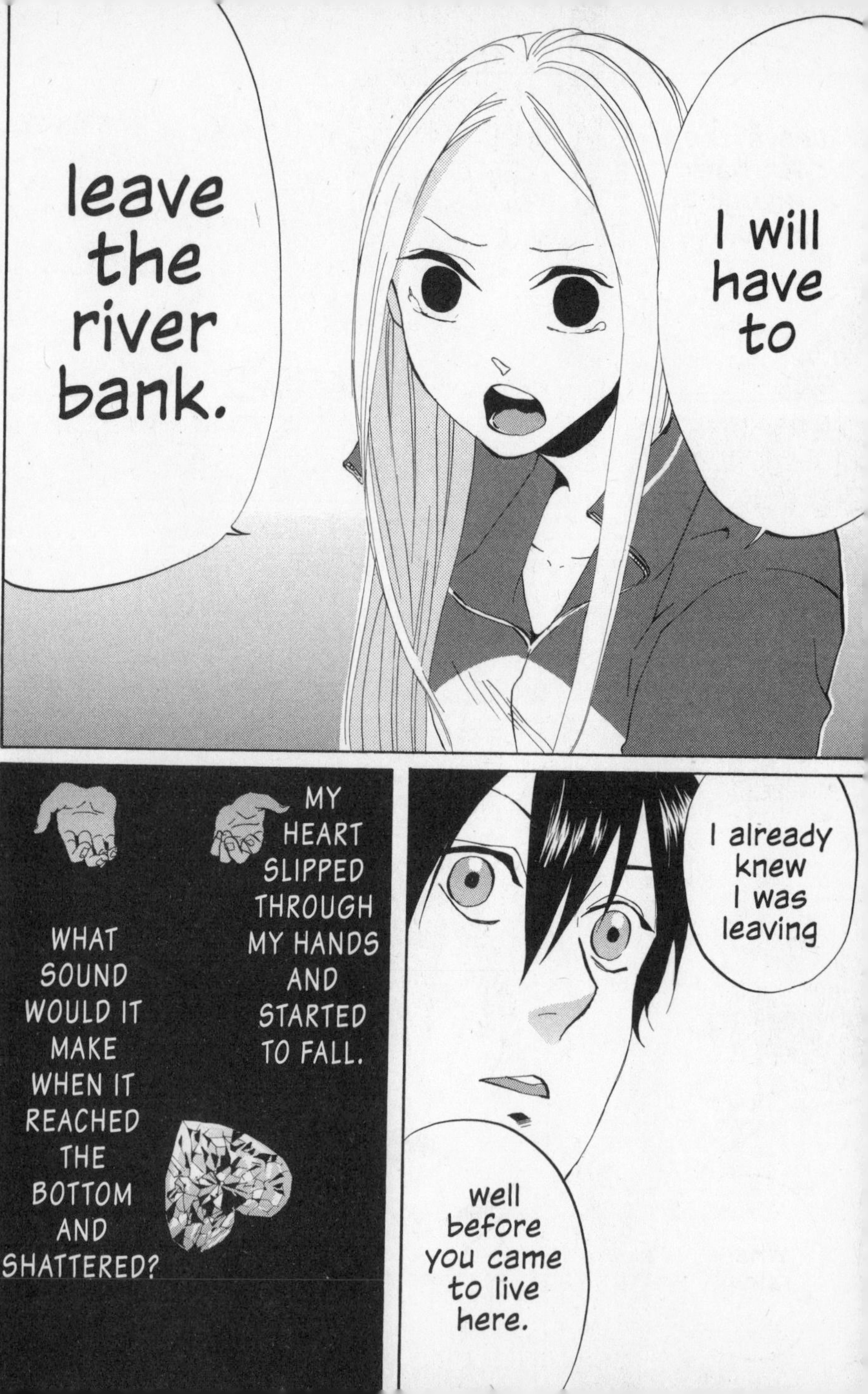
I will have to
leave the river bank.
I already knew I was leaving
well before you came to live here.
MY HEART SLIPPED THROUGH MY HANDS AND STARTED TO FALL.
WHAT SOUND WOULD IT MAKE WHEN IT REACHED THE BOTTOM AND SHATTERED?

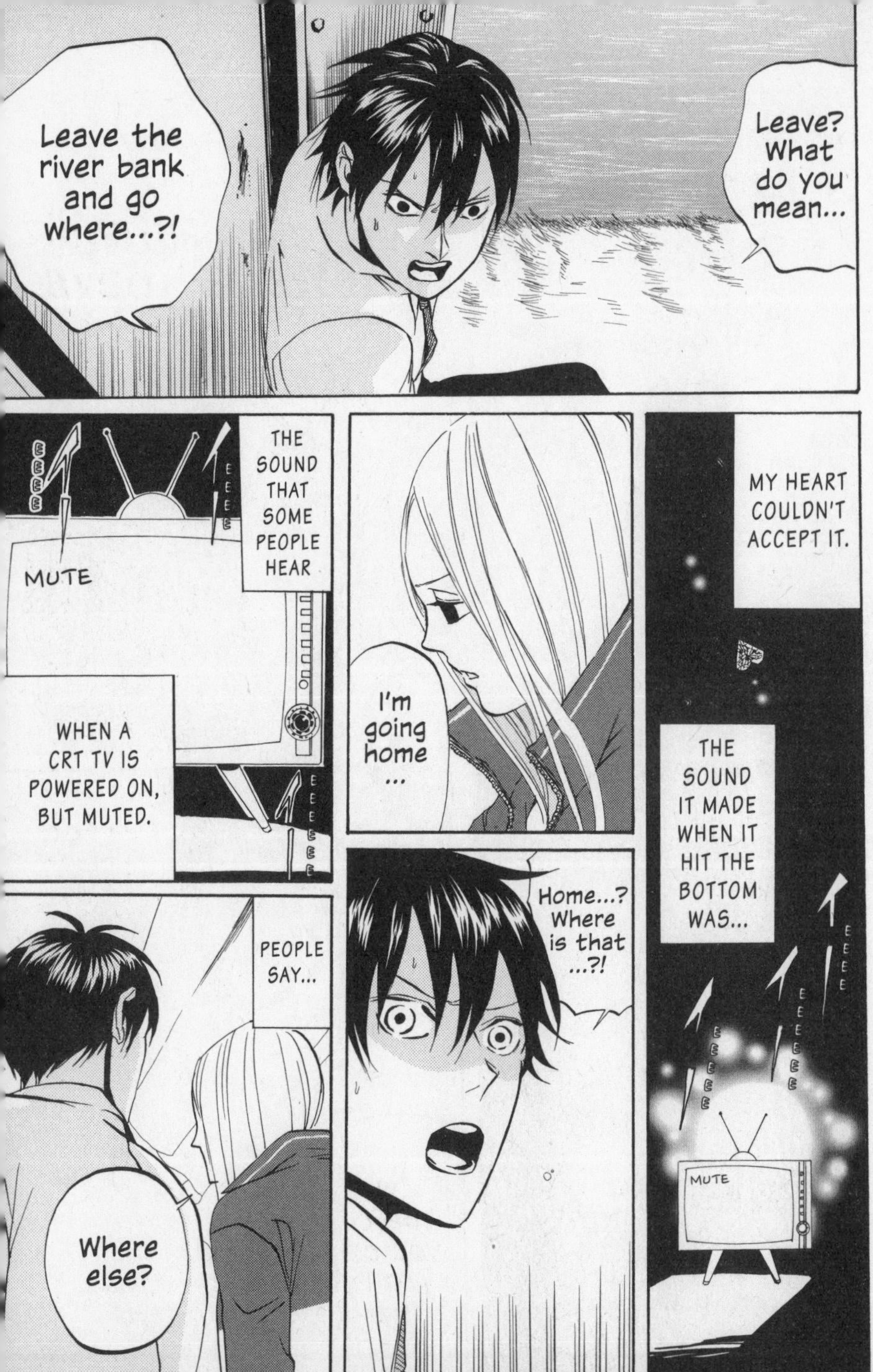

Leave? What do you mean...
Leave the river bank and go where...?!
MY HEART COULDN'T ACCEPT IT.
THE SOUND IT MADE WHEN IT HIT THE BOTTOM WAS...
EEEE
EEEEE
EEEEE
MUTE
I'm going home...
THE SOUND THAT SOME PEOPLE HEAR
EEEE
EEEE
MUTE
WHEN A CRT TV IS POWERED ON, BUT MUTED.
EEEEEEE
Home...? Where is that...?!
PEOPLE SAY...
Where else?

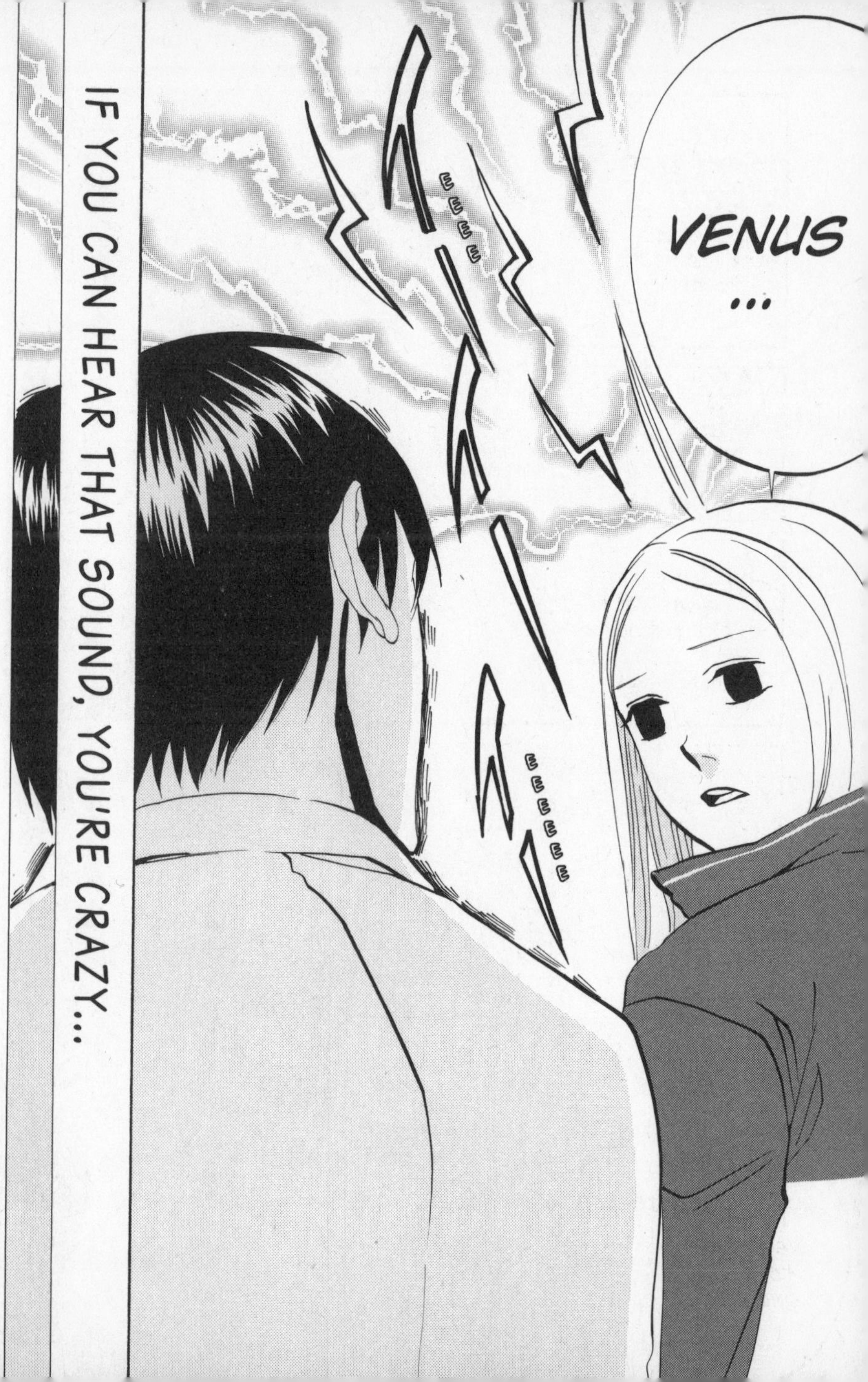
VENUS ...
EEEE
EEEEEE
IF YOU CAN HEAR THAT SOUND, YOU'RE CRAZY...

Chapter 161: Decision

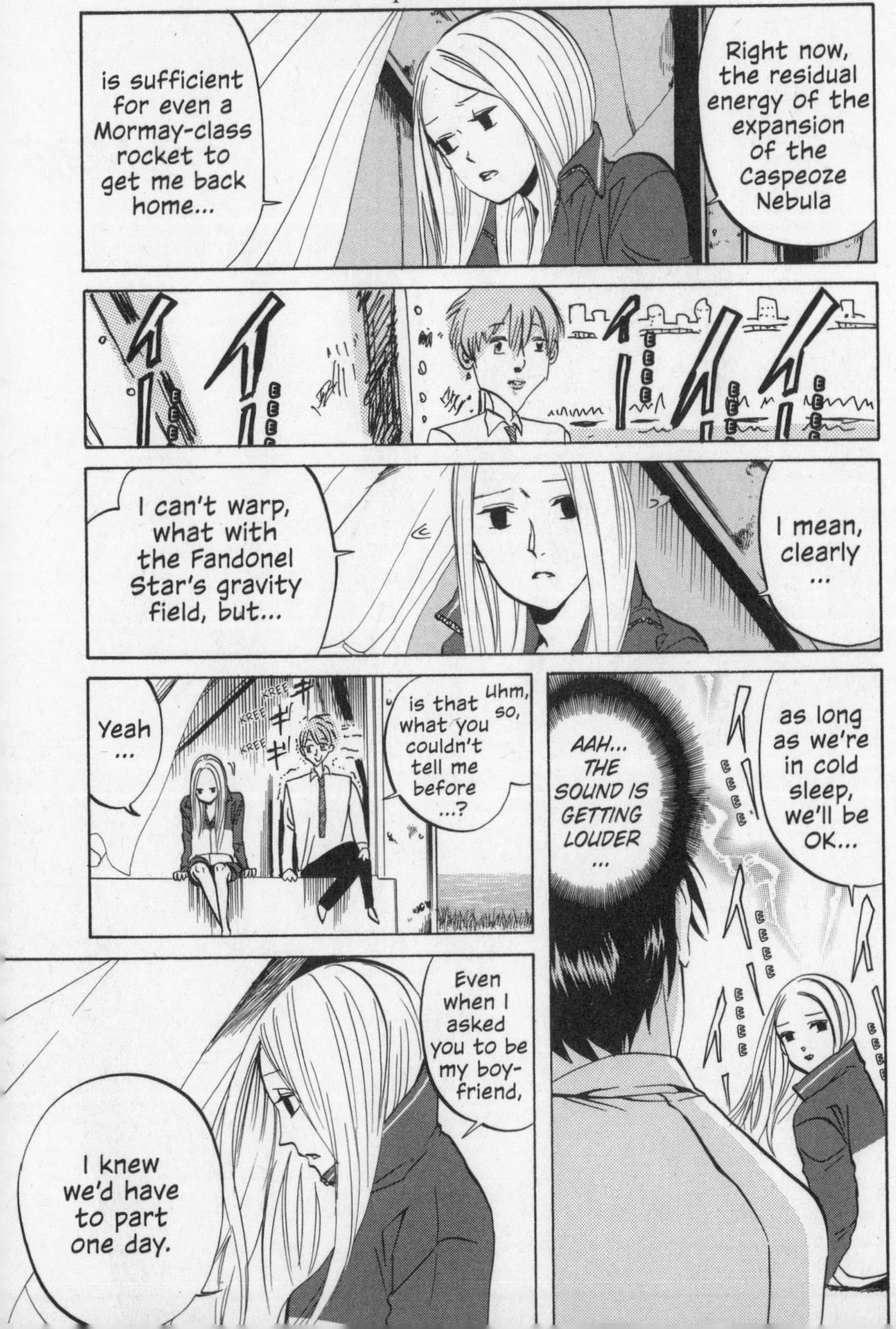
Right now, the residual energy of the expansion of the Caspeoze Nebula
is sufficient for even a Mormay-class rocket to get me back home...
I mean, clearly ...
I can't warp, what with the Fandonel Star's gravity field, but...
as long as we're in cold sleep, we'll be OK...
AAH... THE SOUND IS GETTING LOUDER ...
Uhm, so,
is that what you couldn't tell me before ...?
Yeah ...
Even when I asked you to be my boy-friend,
I knew we'd have to part one day.

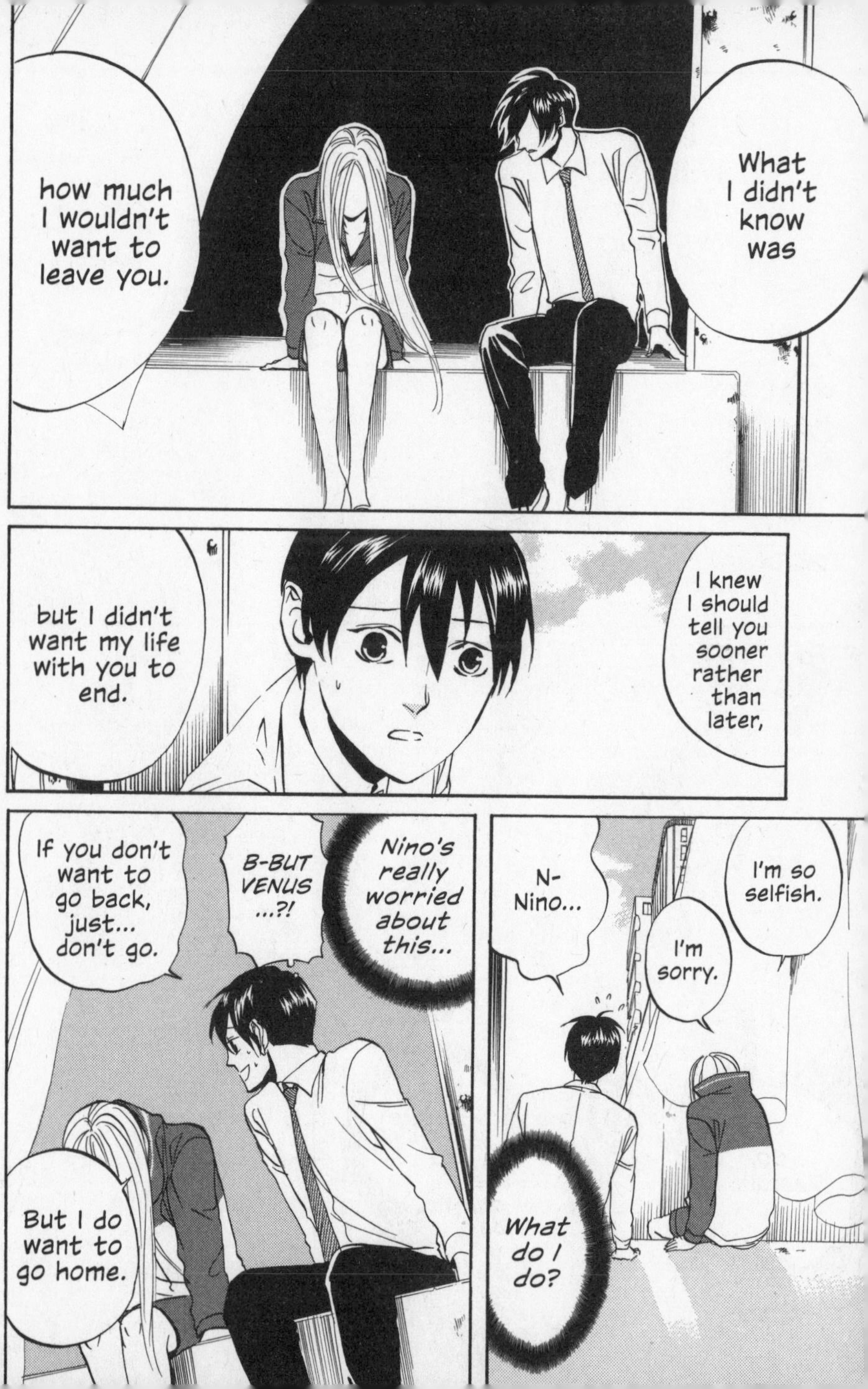

What I didn't know was
how much I wouldn't want to leave you.
I knew I should tell you sooner rather than later,
but I didn't want my life with you to end.
I'm so selfish.
I'm sorry.
N- Nino...
What do I do?
Nino's really worried about this...
B-BUT VENUS ...?!
If you don't want to go back, just... don't go.
But I do want to go home.

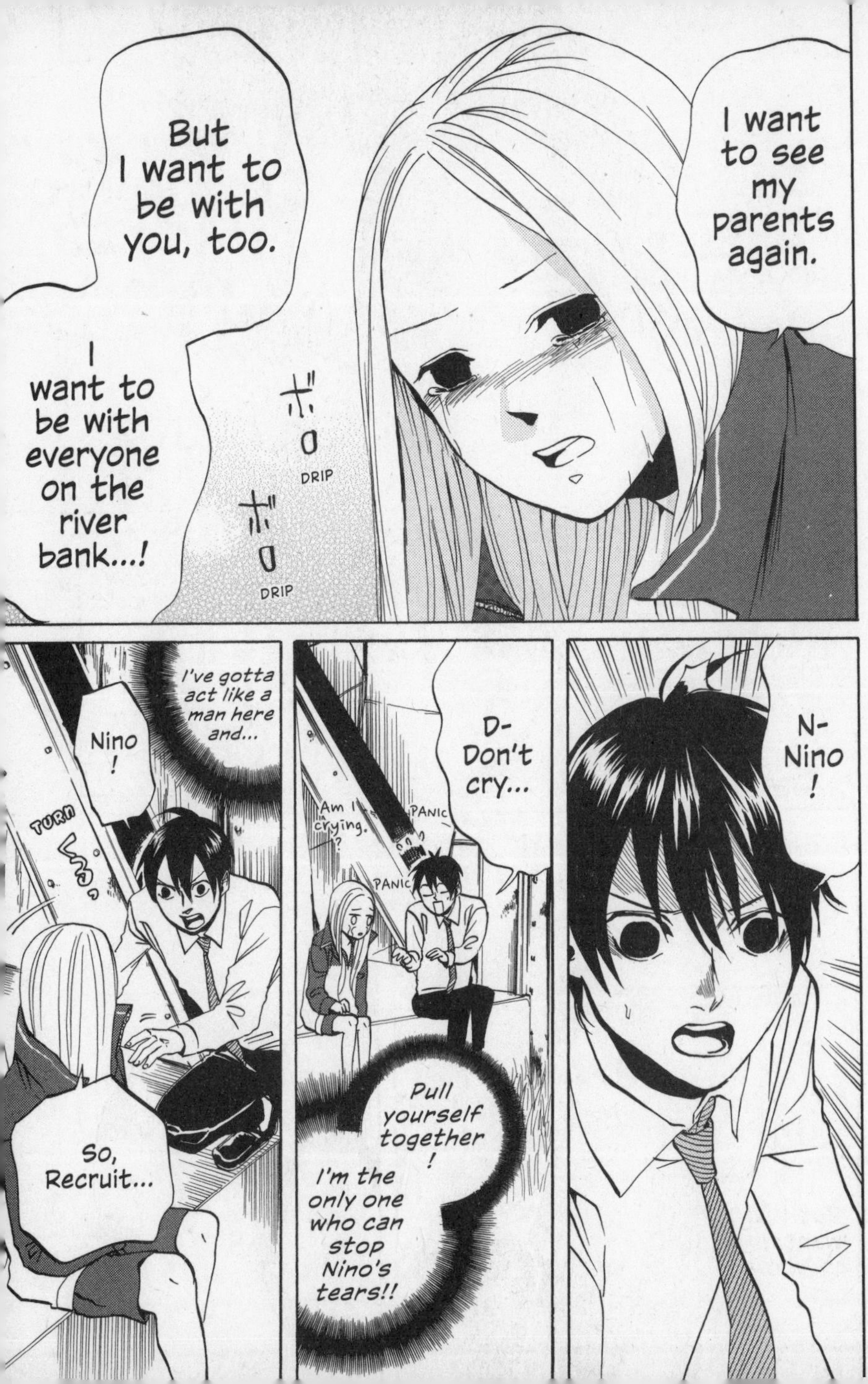
I want to see my parents again.
But I want to be with you, too.
I want to be with everyone on the river bank...!
DRIP
DRIP
N-Nino!
D-Don't cry...
PANIC
Am I crying?
PANIC
Pull yourself together!
I'm the only one who can stop Nino's tears!!
I've gotta act like a man here and...
Nino!
TURN
So, Recruit...

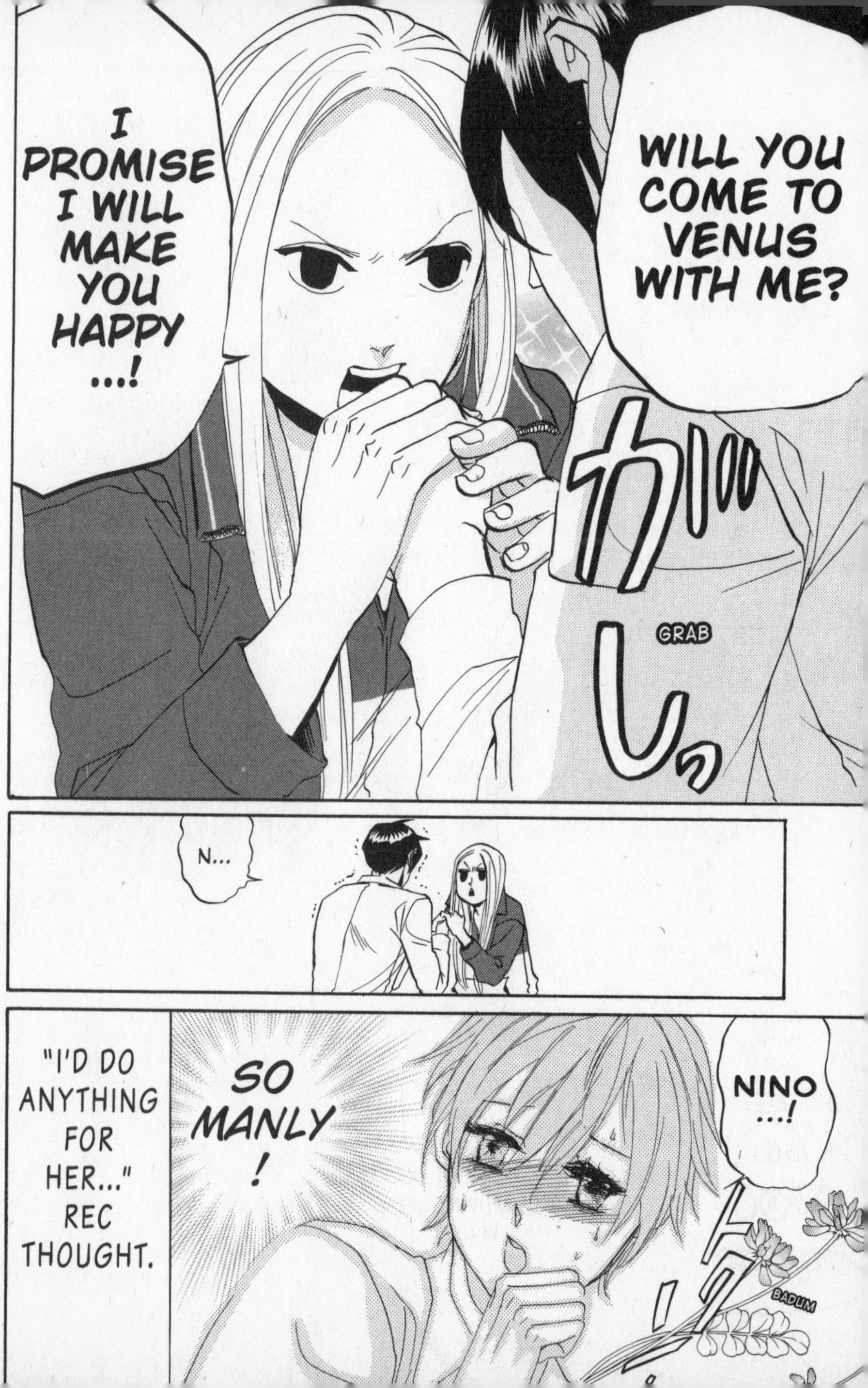
WILL YOU COME TO VENUS WITH ME?
I PROMISE I WILL MAKE YOU HAPPY ...!
わしっ
GRAB
N...
NINO ...!
BADUM
SO MANLY !
"I'D DO ANYTHING FOR HER..." REC THOUGHT.

Chapter 162: Dreaming of Life on Venus

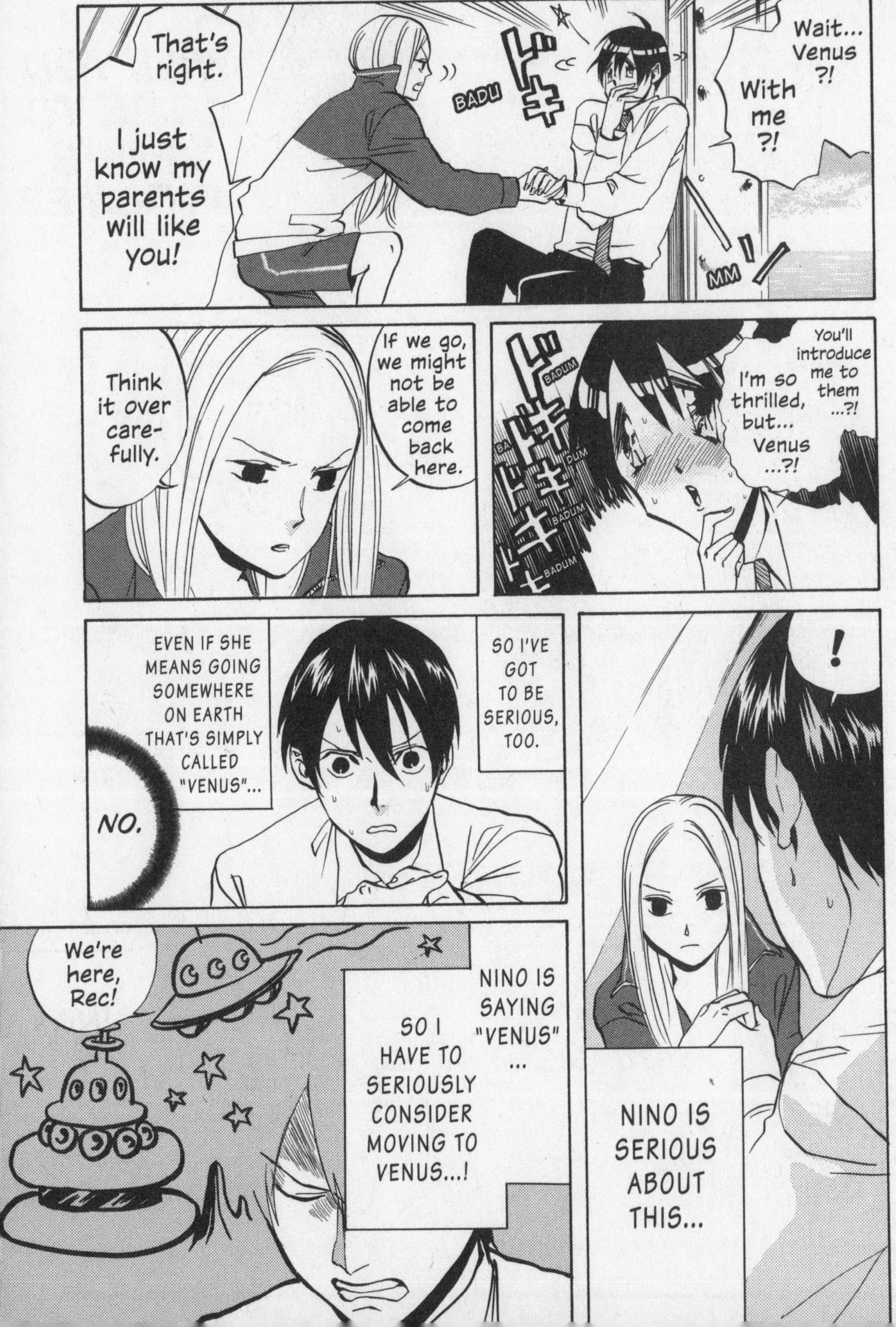

Wait... Venus ?!
With me ?!
BADU
That's right.
I just know my parents will like you!
MM
You'll introduce me to them ...?!
I'm so thrilled, but... Venus ...?!
BADUM
BA DUM
BADUM
BADUM
If we go, we might not be able to come back here.
Think it over carefully.
!
NINO IS SERIOUS ABOUT THIS...
SO I'VE GOT TO BE SERIOUS, TOO.
EVEN IF SHE MEANS GOING SOMEWHERE ON EARTH THAT'S SIMPLY CALLED "VENUS"...
NO.
NINO IS SAYING "VENUS" ...
SO I HAVE TO SERIOUSLY CONSIDER MOVING TO VENUS...!
We're here, Rec!

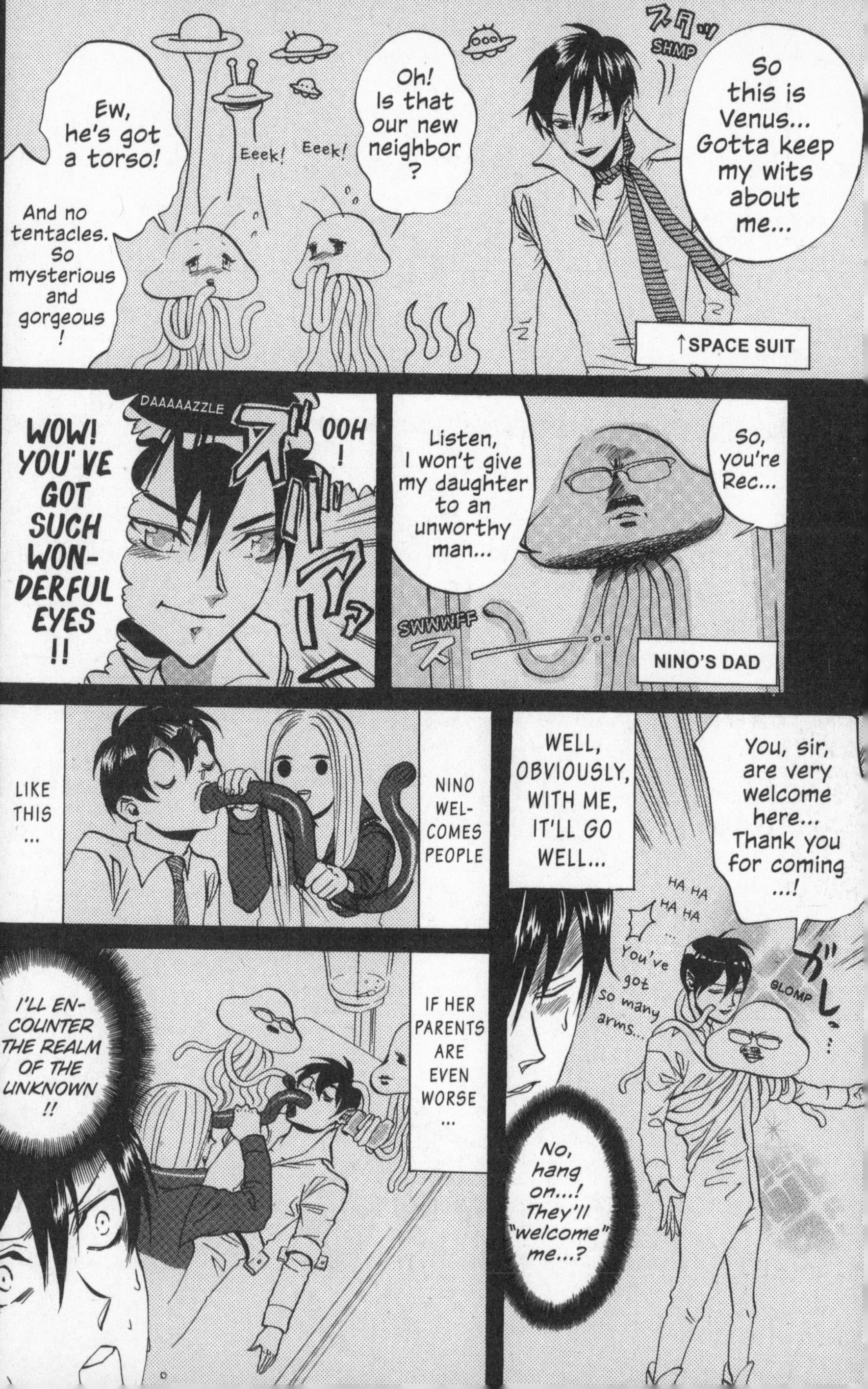
SHMP
So this is Venus... Gotta keep my wits about me...
↑SPACE SUIT
Oh! Is that our new neighbor?
Eeek!
Eeek!
Ew, he's got a torso!
And no tentacles. So mysterious and gorgeous!
So, you're Rec...
Listen, I won't give my daughter to an unworthy man...
SWWWFF
NINO'S DAD
OOH!
DAAAAAZZLE
WOW! YOU'VE GOT SUCH WON-DERFUL EYES!!
You, sir, are very welcome here... Thank you for coming...!
WELL, OBVIOUSLY, WITH ME, IT'LL GO WELL...
HA HA HA HA... You've got so many arms...
GLOMP
No, hang on...! They'll "welcome" me...?
NINO WEL-COMES PEOPLE
LIKE THIS...
IF HER PARENTS ARE EVEN WORSE...
I'LL EN-COUNTER THE REALM OF THE UNKNOWN!!

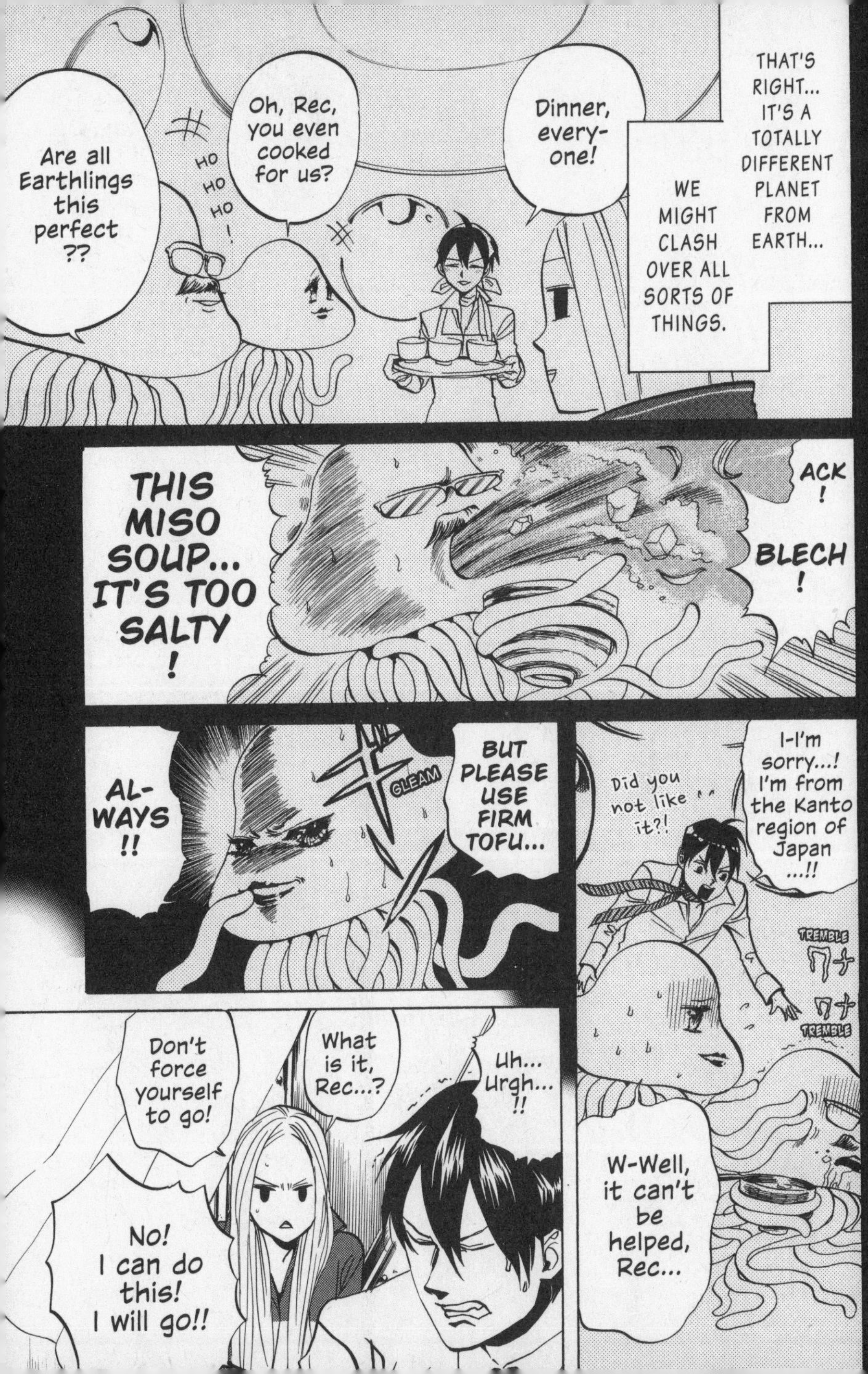
THAT'S RIGHT... IT'S A TOTALLY DIFFERENT PLANET FROM EARTH...
WE MIGHT CLASH OVER ALL SORTS OF THINGS.
Dinner, everyone!
Oh, Rec, you even cooked for us?
HO HO HO!
Are all Earthlings this perfect??
ACK!
BLECH!
THIS MISO SOUP... IT'S TOO SALTY!
I-I'm sorry...! I'm from the Kanto region of Japan ...!!
Did you not like it?!
TREMBLE
TREMBLE
W-Well, it can't be helped, Rec...
BUT PLEASE USE FIRM TOFU...
GLEAM
ALWAYS!!
Uh... Urgh... !!
What is it, Rec...?
Don't force yourself to go!
No! I can do this! I will go!!

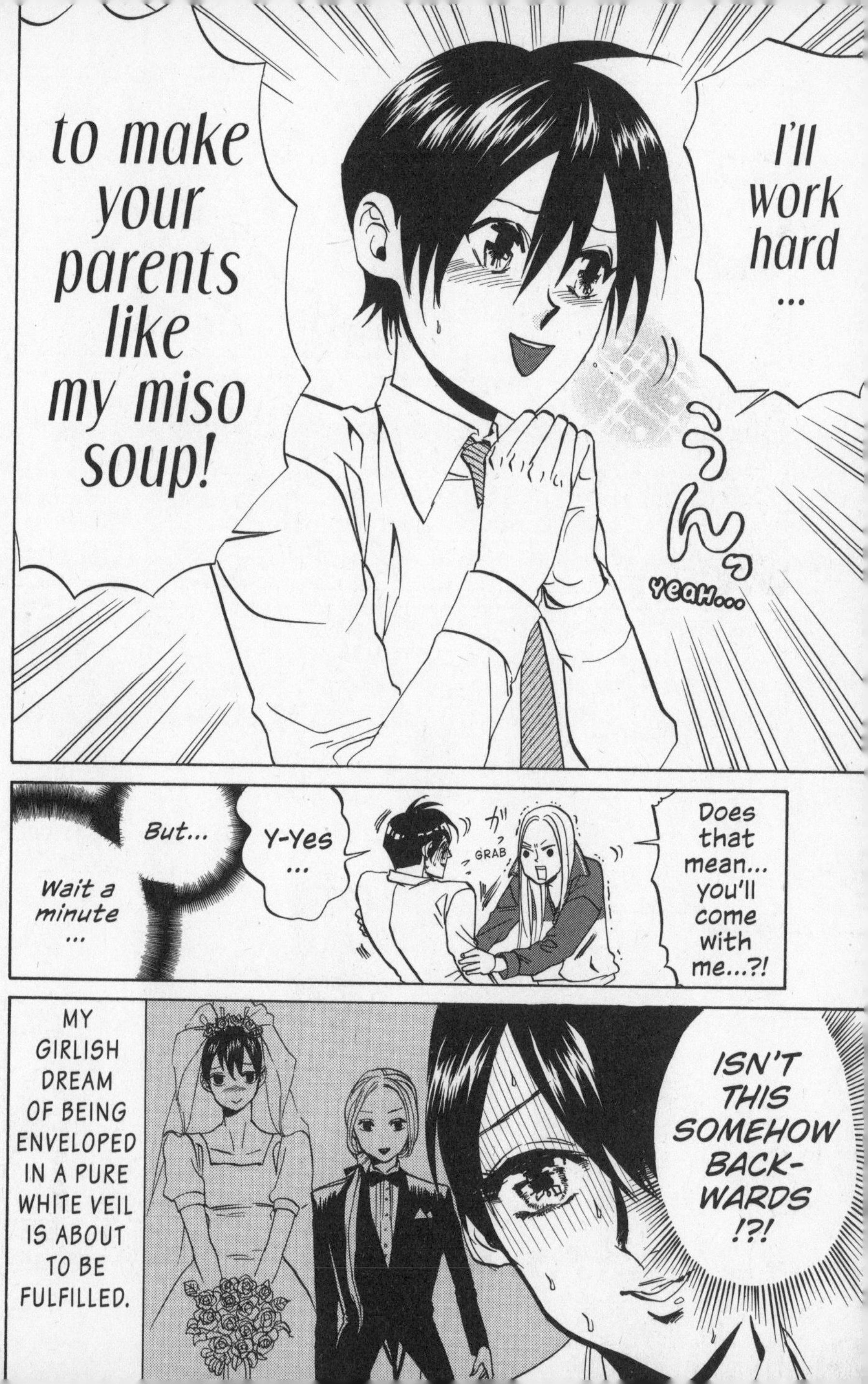

I'll work hard ...
to make your parents like my miso soup!
うん
YEAH...
Does that mean... you'll come with me...?!
ガ
GRAB
Y-Yes ...
But...
Wait a minute ...
ISN'T THIS SOMEHOW BACK-WARDS !?!
MY GIRLISH DREAM OF BEING ENVELOPED IN A PURE WHITE VEIL IS ABOUT TO BE FULFILLED.

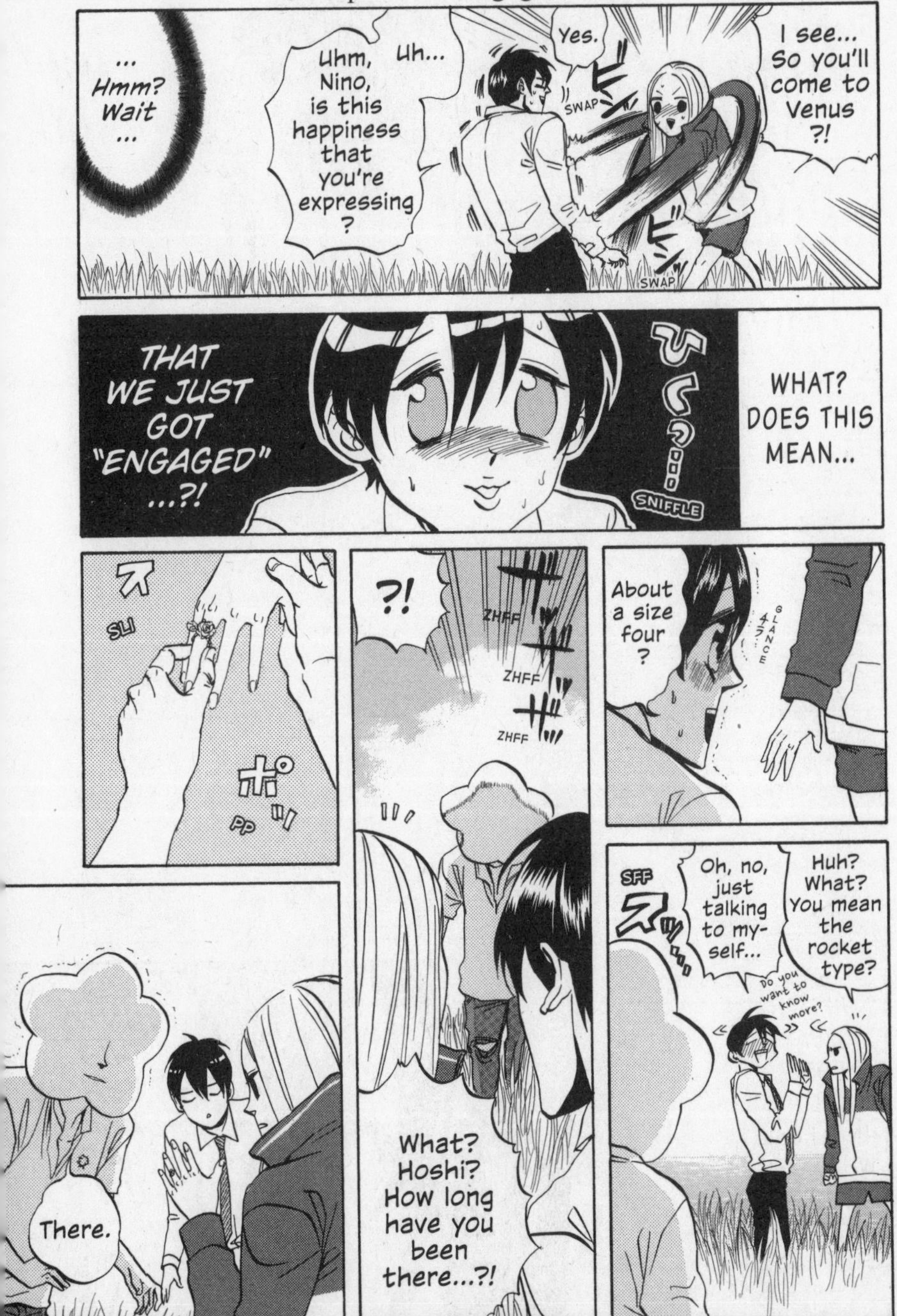
I see... So you'll come to Venus?!
Yes.
SWAP
Uh...
Uhm, Nino, is this happiness that you're expressing?
... Hmm? Wait ...
SWAP
WHAT? DOES THIS MEAN...
SNIFFLE
THAT WE JUST GOT "ENGAGED" ...?!
About a size four?
GLANCE
Huh? What? You mean the rocket type?
Oh, no, just talking to myself...
Do you want to know more?
SFF
?!
ZHFF
ZHFF
ZHFF
What? Hoshi? How long have you been there...?!
SLI
PP
There.

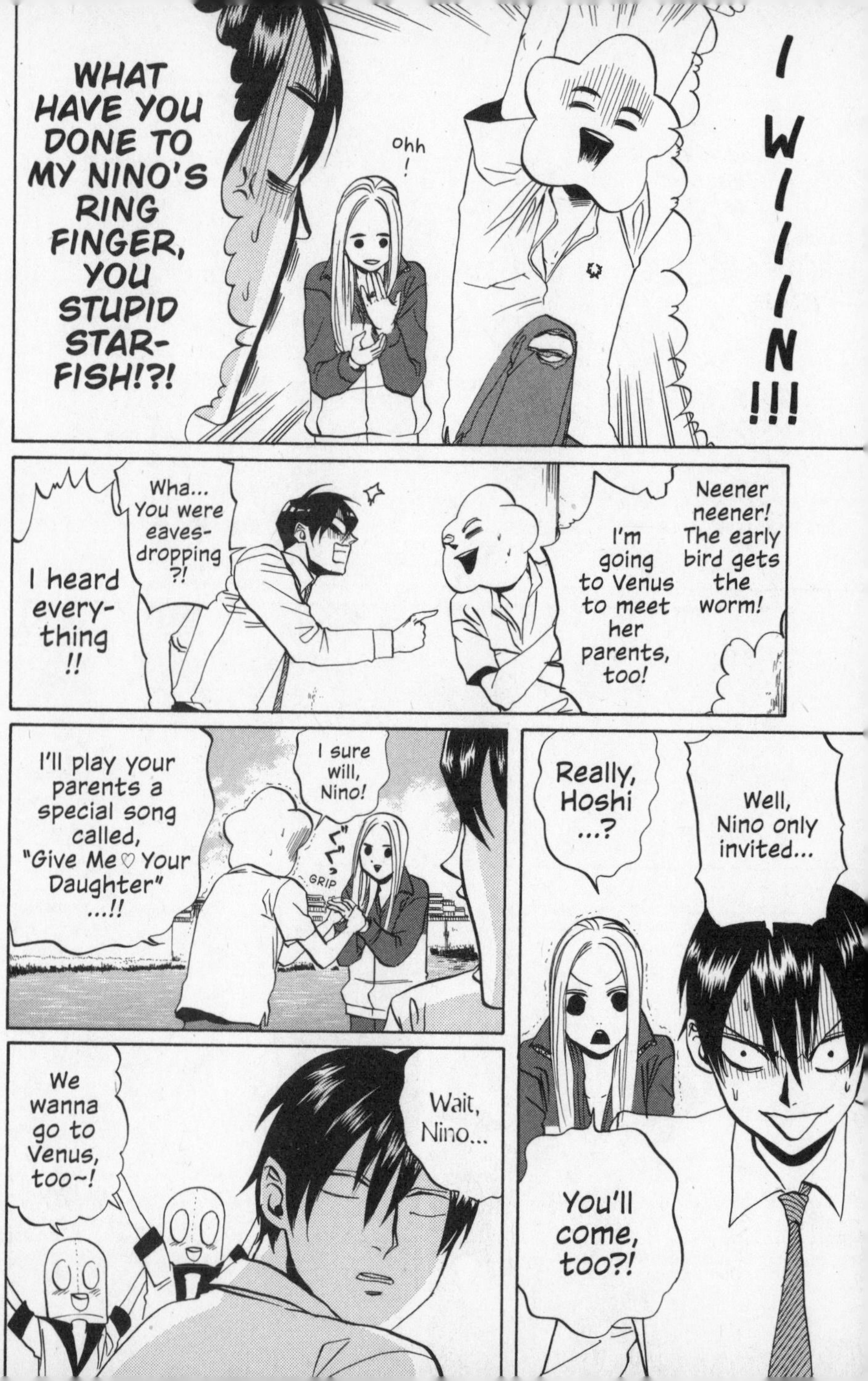
I WIIIIN!!!
Ohh!
WHAT HAVE YOU DONE TO MY NINO'S RING FINGER, YOU STUPID STARFISH!?!
Neener neener! The early bird gets the worm!
I'm going to Venus to meet her parents, too!
Wha... You were eaves-dropping?!
I heard every-thing!!
Well, Nino only invited...
Really, Hoshi ...?
You'll come, too?!
I sure will, Nino!
GRIP
I'll play your parents a special song called, "Give Me ♡ Your Daughter" ...!!
Wait, Nino...
We wanna go to Venus, too~!

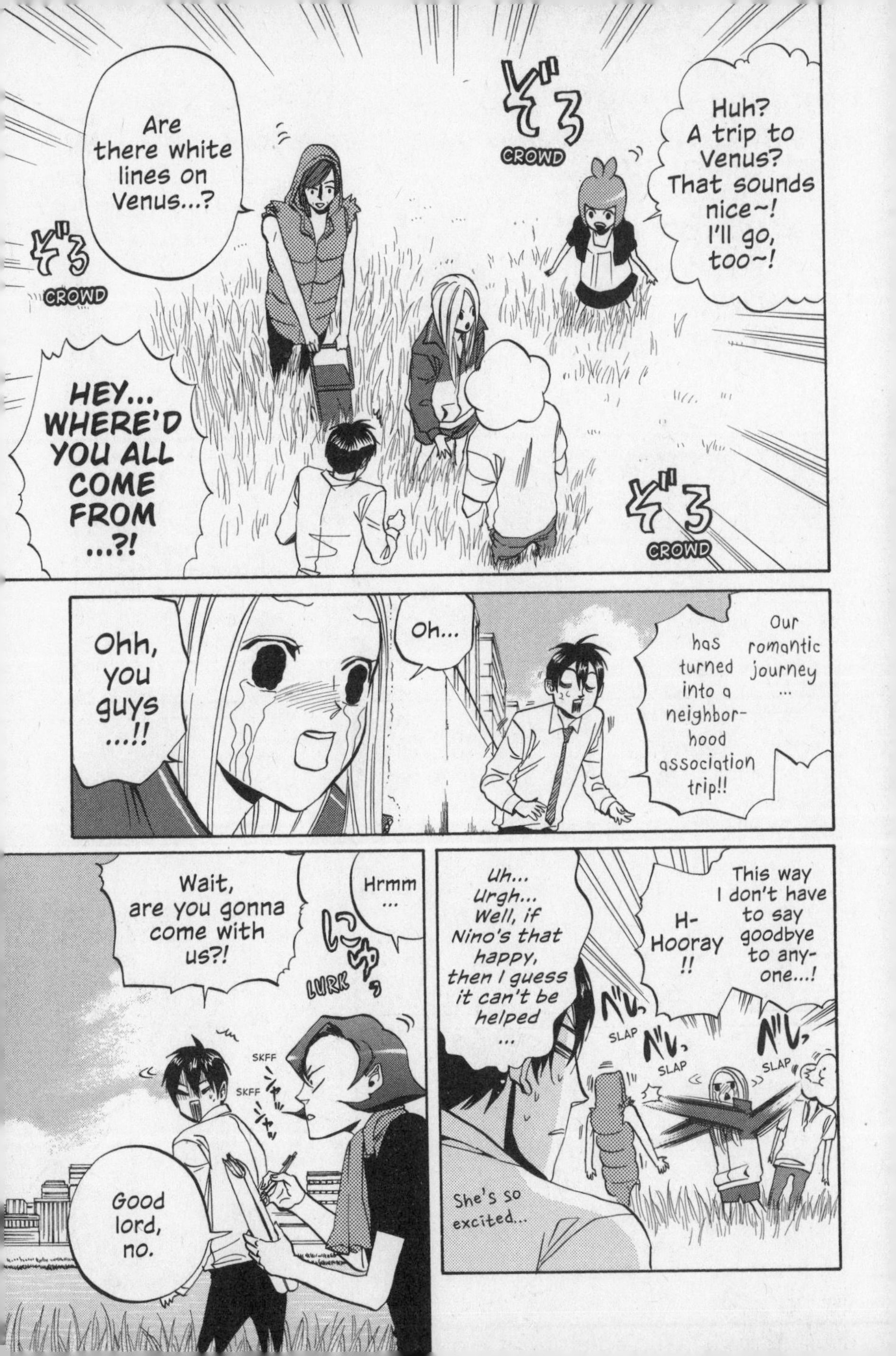
Huh? A trip to Venus? That sounds nice~! I'll go, too~!
CROWD
Are there white lines on Venus...?
CROWD
HEY... WHERE'D YOU ALL COME FROM ...?!
CROWD
Our romantic journey ... has turned into a neighbor-hood association trip!!
Oh...
Ohh, you guys ...!!
This way I don't have to say goodbye to any-one...!
H-Hooray !!
SLAP
SLAP
SLAP
Uh... Urgh... Well, if Nino's that happy, then I guess it can't be helped ...
She's so excited...
Hrmm ...
Wait, are you gonna come with us?!
LURK
SKFF
SKFF
Good lord, no.

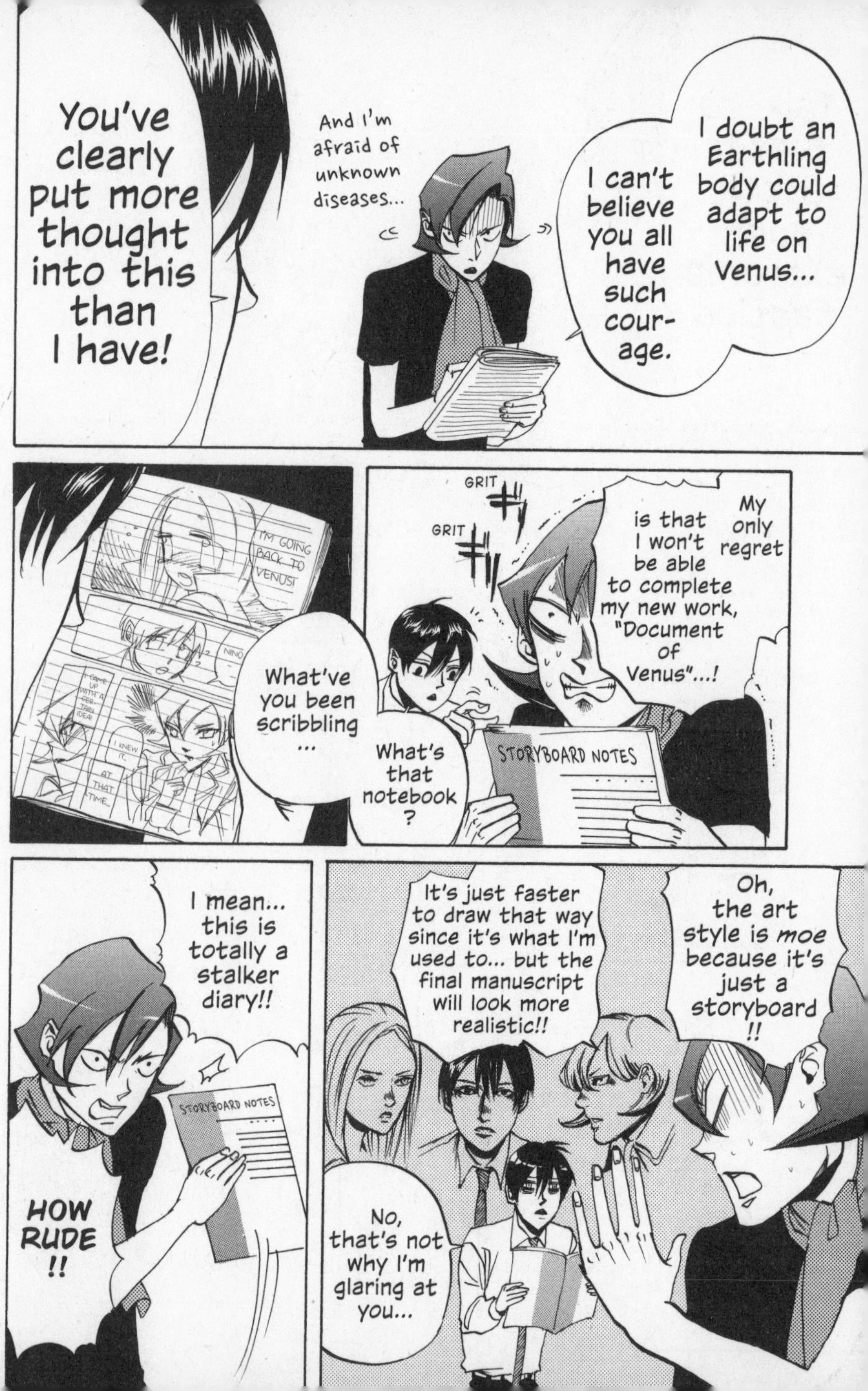
I doubt an Earthling body could adapt to life on Venus...
I can't believe you all have such cour-age.
And I'm afraid of unknown diseases...
You've clearly put more thought into this than I have!
My only regret
is that I won't be able to complete my new work, "Document of Venus"...!
GRIT
GRIT
What's that notebook?
What've you been scribbling...
STORYBOARD NOTES
I'M GOING BACK TO VENUS!
NINO
I CAME UP WITH A CER-TAIN IDEA!
I KNEW IT.
AT THAT TIME.
Oh, the art style is *moe* because it's just a storyboard!!
It's just faster to draw that way since it's what I'm used to... but the final manuscript will look more realistic!!
No, that's not why I'm glaring at you...
I mean... this is totally a stalker diary!!
STORYBOARD NOTES
HOW RUDE!!

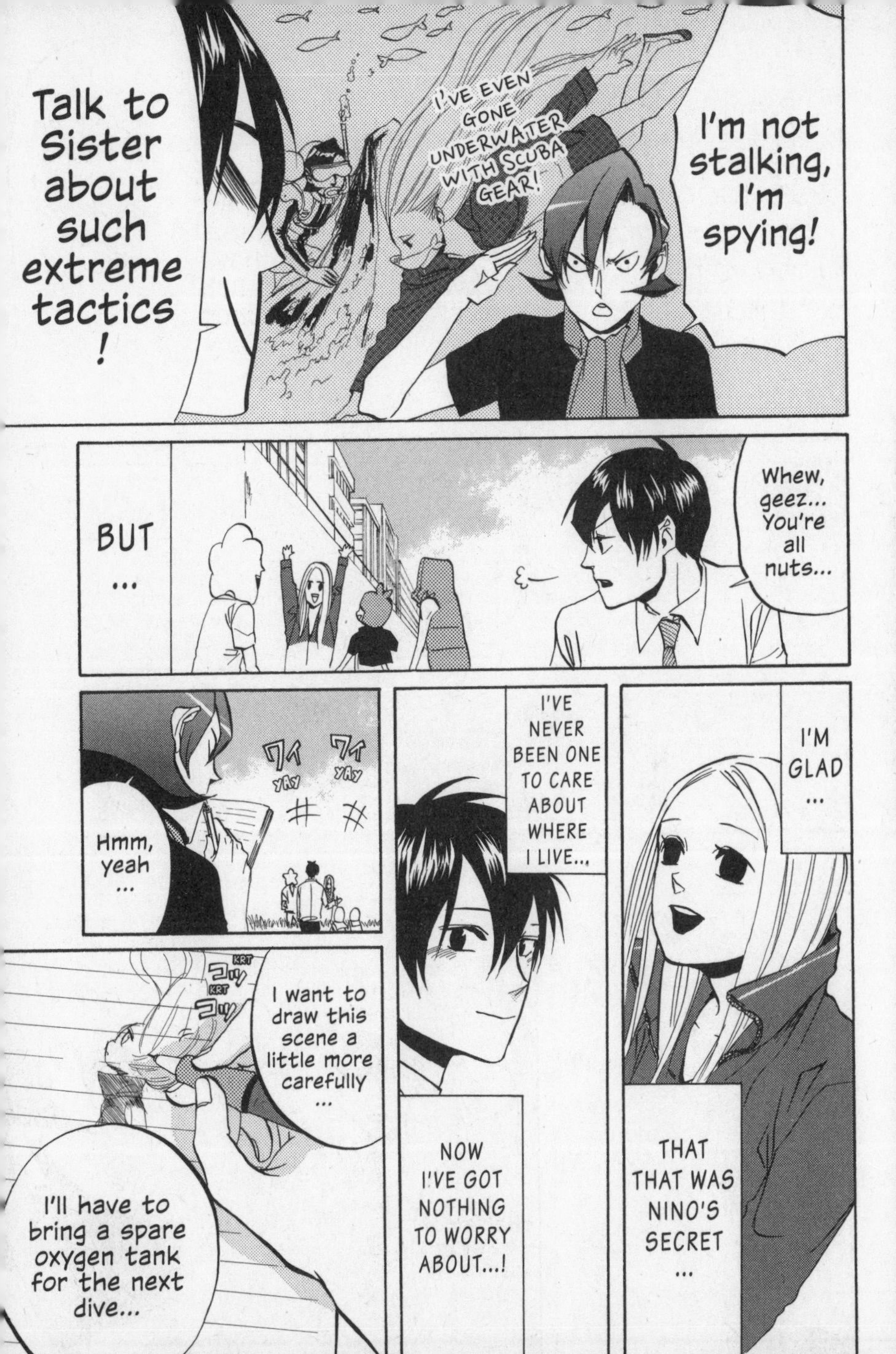

I'm not stalking, I'm spying!
I'VE EVEN GONE UNDERWATER WITH SCUBA GEAR!
Talk to Sister about such extreme tactics!
Whew, geez... You're all nuts...
BUT ...
I'M GLAD ...
THAT THAT WAS NINO'S SECRET ...
I'VE NEVER BEEN ONE TO CARE ABOUT WHERE I LIVE...
NOW I'VE GOT NOTHING TO WORRY ABOUT...!
ワイ YAY
ワイ YAY
Hmm, yeah ...
コツ KRT
コツ KRT
I want to draw this scene a little more carefully ...
I'll have to bring a spare oxygen tank for the next dive...

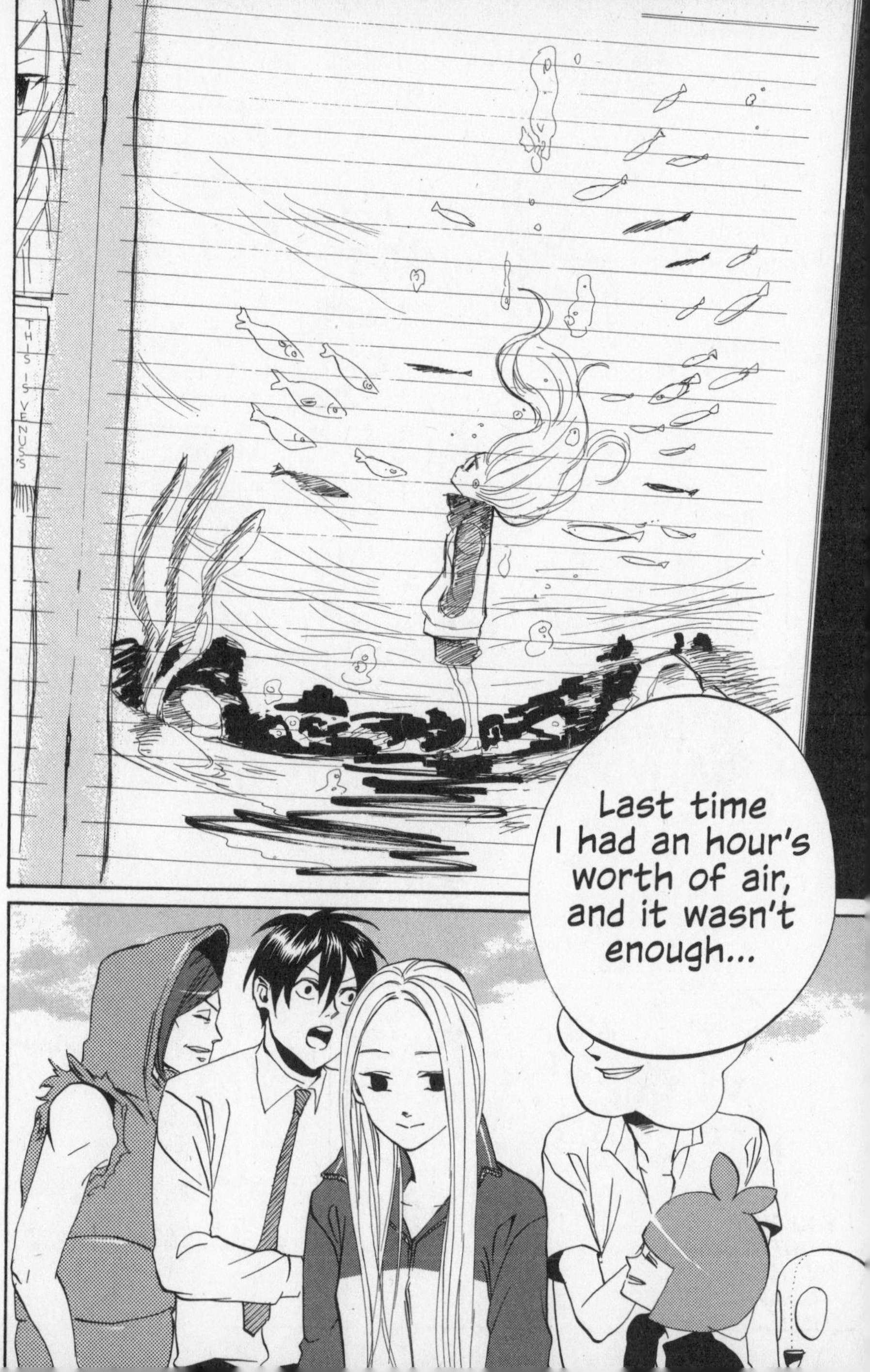
THIS IS VENUS'S
Last time I had an hour's worth of air, and it wasn't enough...

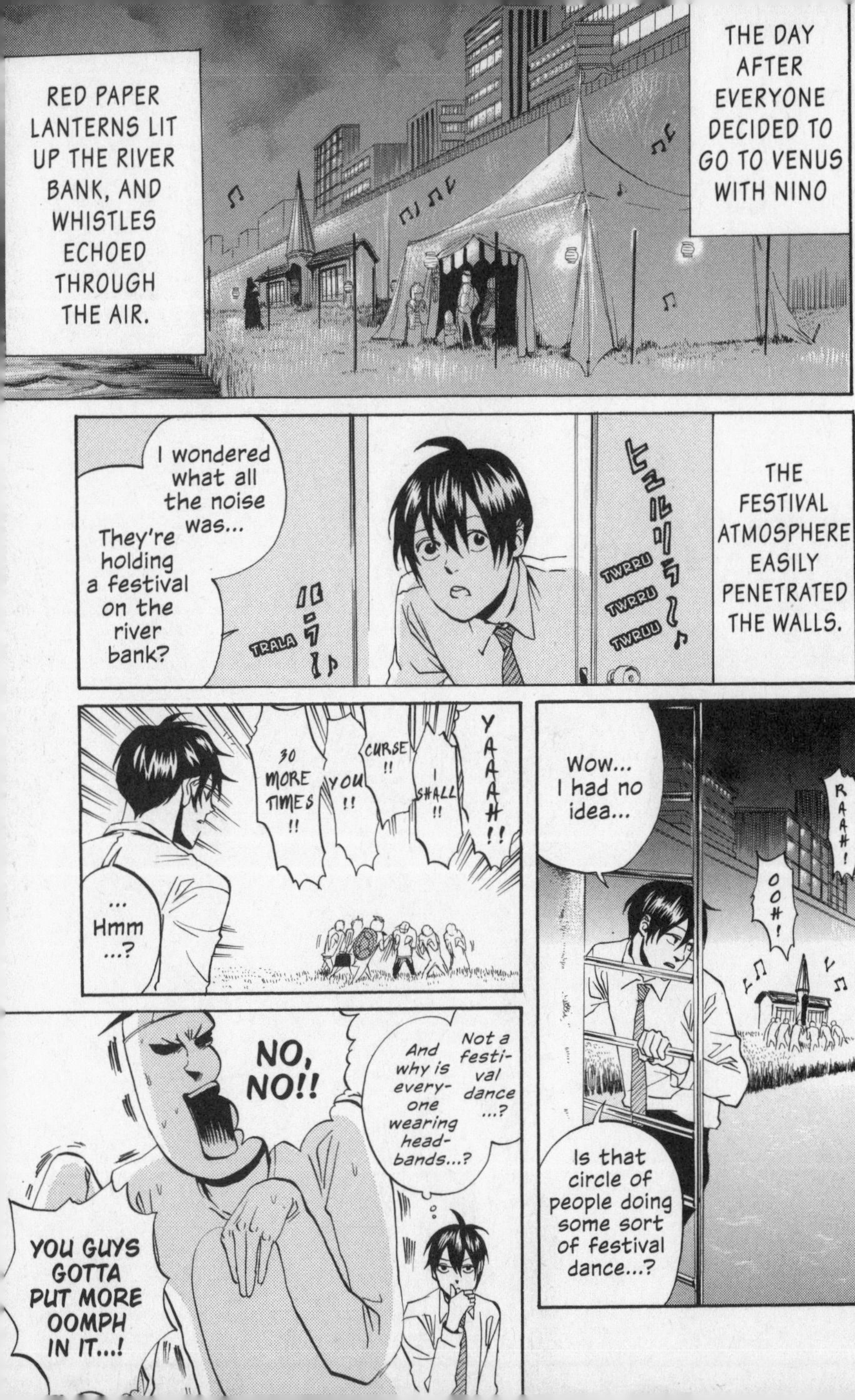

THE DAY AFTER EVERYONE DECIDED TO GO TO VENUS WITH NINO
RED PAPER LANTERNS LIT UP THE RIVER BANK, AND WHISTLES ECHOED THROUGH THE AIR.
THE FESTIVAL ATMOSPHERE EASILY PENETRATED THE WALLS.
TWRRU TWRRU TWRUU
I wondered what all the noise was...
They're holding a festival on the river bank?
TRALA
Wow... I had no idea...
RAAH!
OOH!
Is that circle of people doing some sort of festival dance...?
YAAAAH!!
I SHALL!!
CURSE!!
YOU!!
30 MORE TIMES!!
... Hmm ...?
Not a festi-val dance ...?
And why is every-one wearing head-bands...?
NO, NO!!
YOU GUYS GOTTA PUT MORE OOMPH IN IT...!

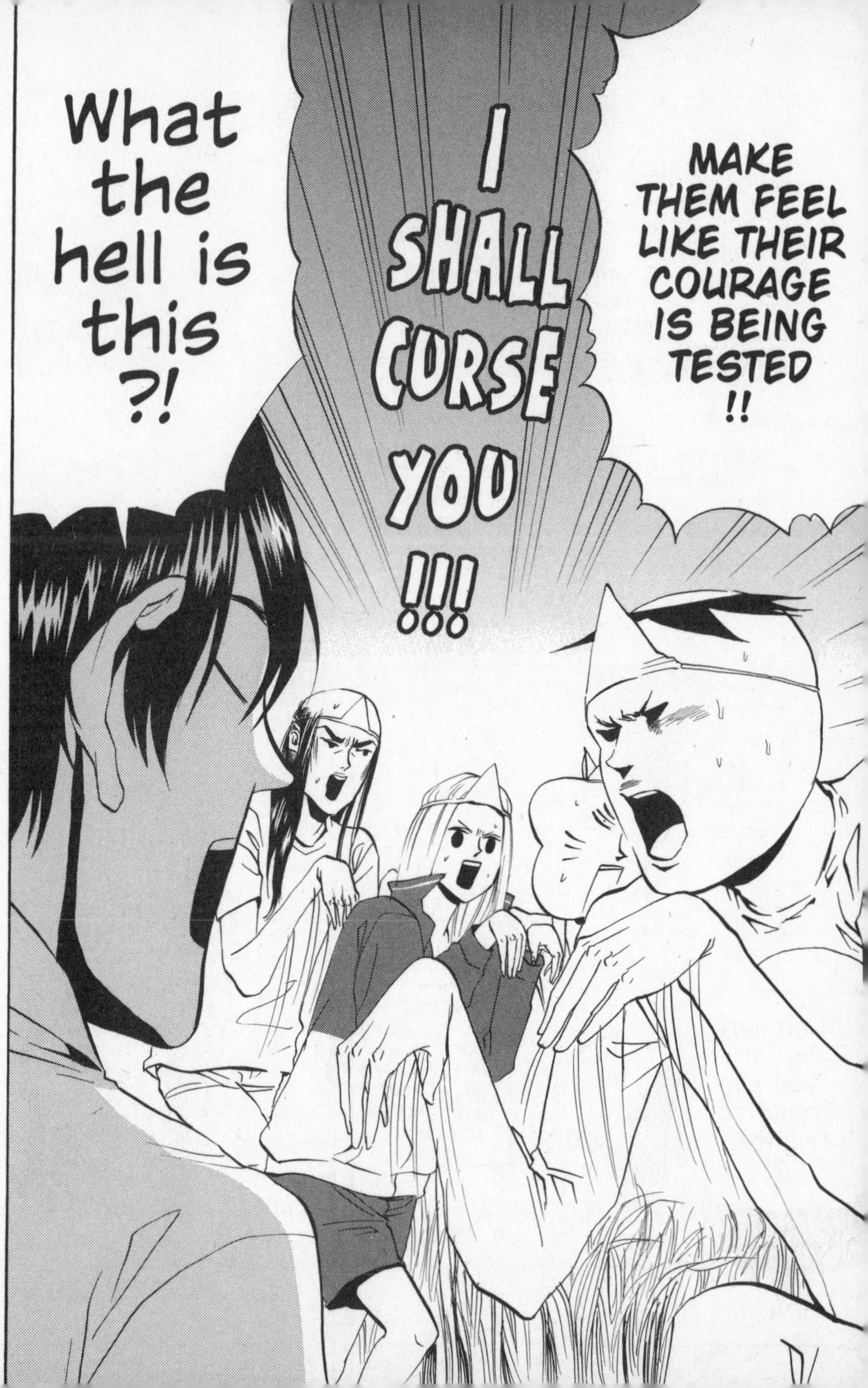
MAKE THEM FEEL LIKE THEIR COURAGE IS BEING TESTED!!
I SHALL CURSE YOU!!!
What the hell is this?!

Chapter 164: River Bank of Fear

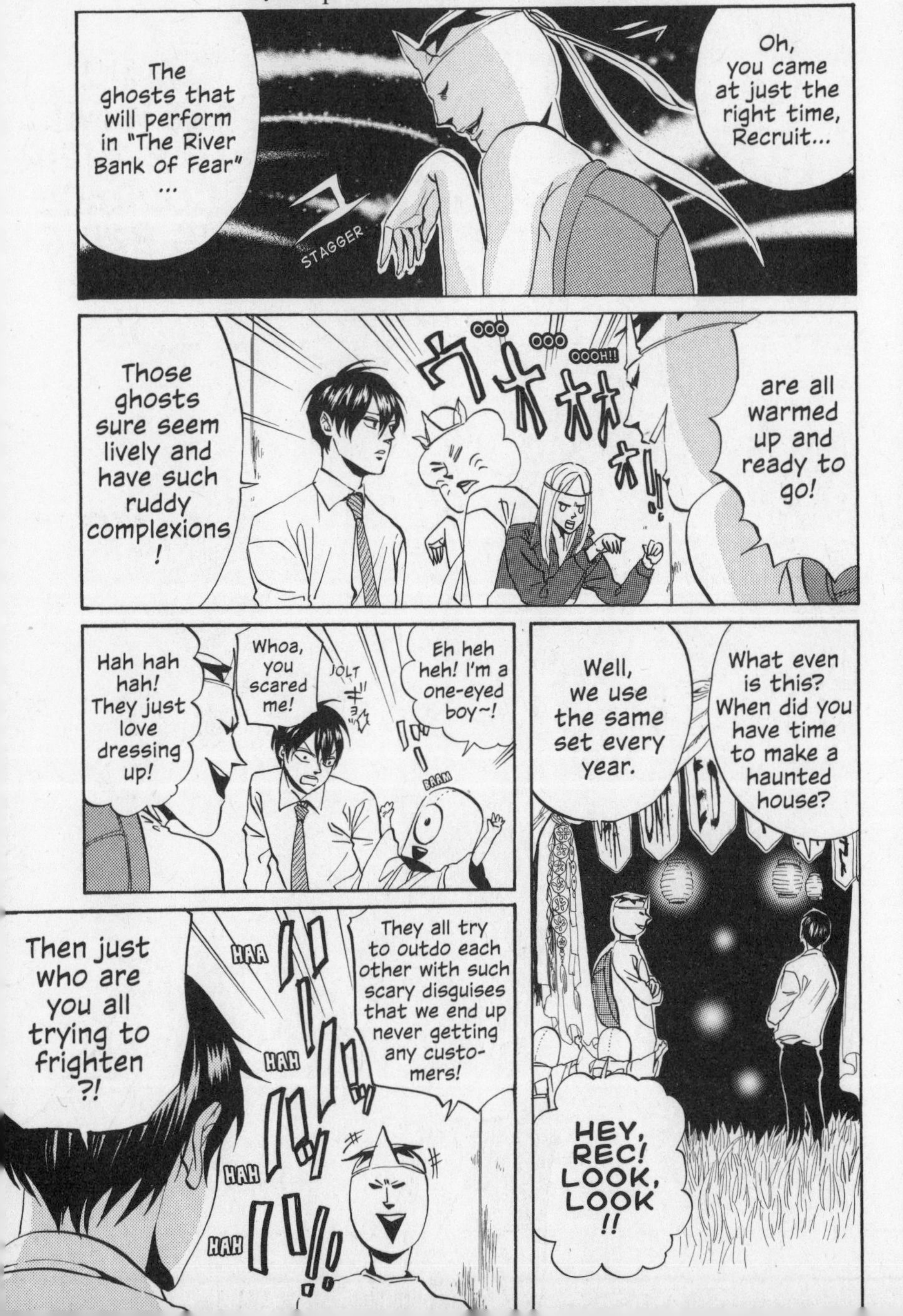
Oh, you came at just the right time, Recruit...
The ghosts that will perform in "The River Bank of Fear" ...
STAGGER
OOO OOO OOOH!!
are all warmed up and ready to go!
Those ghosts sure seem lively and have such ruddy complexions!
What even is this? When did you have time to make a haunted house?
Well, we use the same set every year.
HEY, REC! LOOK, LOOK!!
Eh heh heh! I'm a one-eyed boy~!
BAAM
JOLT
Whoa, you scared me!
Hah hah hah! They just love dressing up!
They all try to outdo each other with such scary disguises that we end up never getting any customers!
HAA
HAH
HAH
HAH
Then just who are you all trying to frighten?!

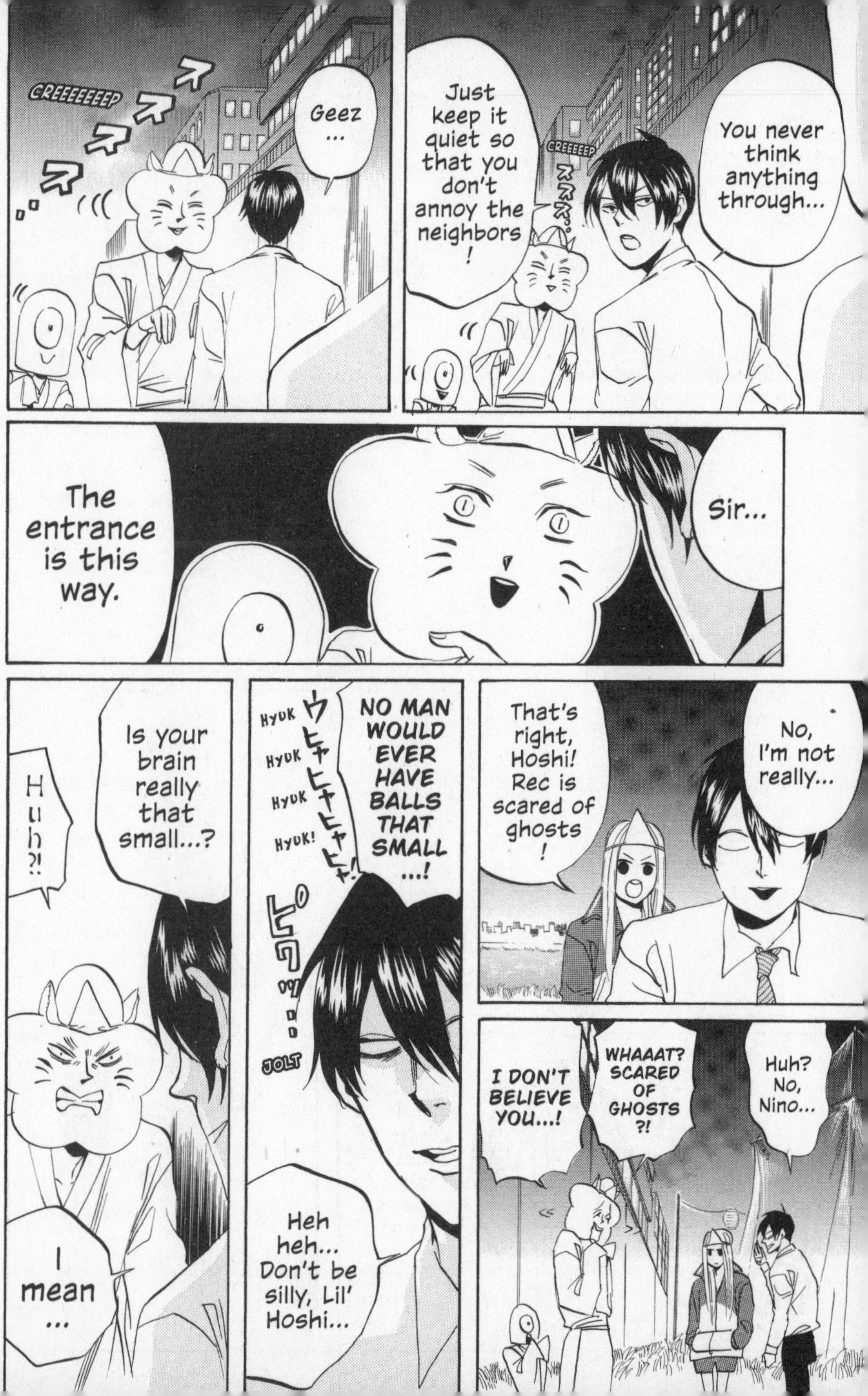
You never think anything through...
Just keep it quiet so that you don't annoy the neighbors!
CREEEEEP
Geez...
CREEEEEEEP
Sir...
The entrance is this way.
No, I'm not really...
That's right, Hoshi! Rec is scared of ghosts!
Huh? No, Nino...
WHAAAT? SCARED OF GHOSTS?!
I DON'T BELIEVE YOU...!
NO MAN WOULD EVER HAVE BALLS THAT SMALL...!
HYUK HYUK HYUK HYUK!
JOLT
Heh heh... Don't be silly, Lil' Hoshi...
Is your brain really that small...?
Huh?!
I mean...

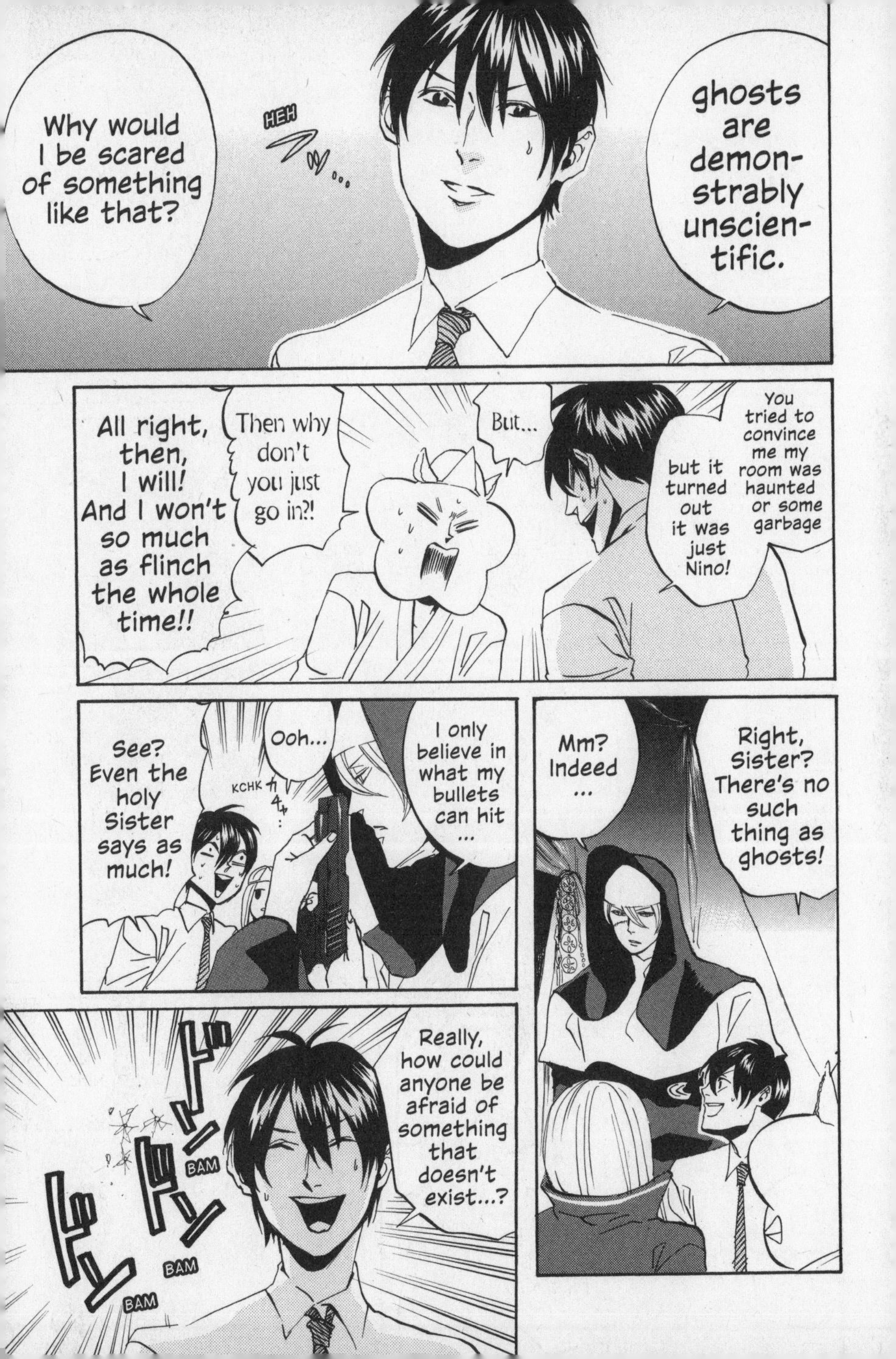
ghosts are demonstrably unscientific.
HEH
Why would I be scared of something like that?
You tried to convince me my room was haunted or some garbage
but it turned out it was just Nino!
But...
Then why don't you just go in?!
All right, then, I will! And I won't so much as flinch the whole time!!
Right, Sister? There's no such thing as ghosts!
Mm? Indeed ...
I only believe in what my bullets can hit ...
KCHK
Ooh...
See? Even the holy Sister says as much!
Really, how could anyone be afraid of something that doesn't exist...?
BAM
BAM
BAM

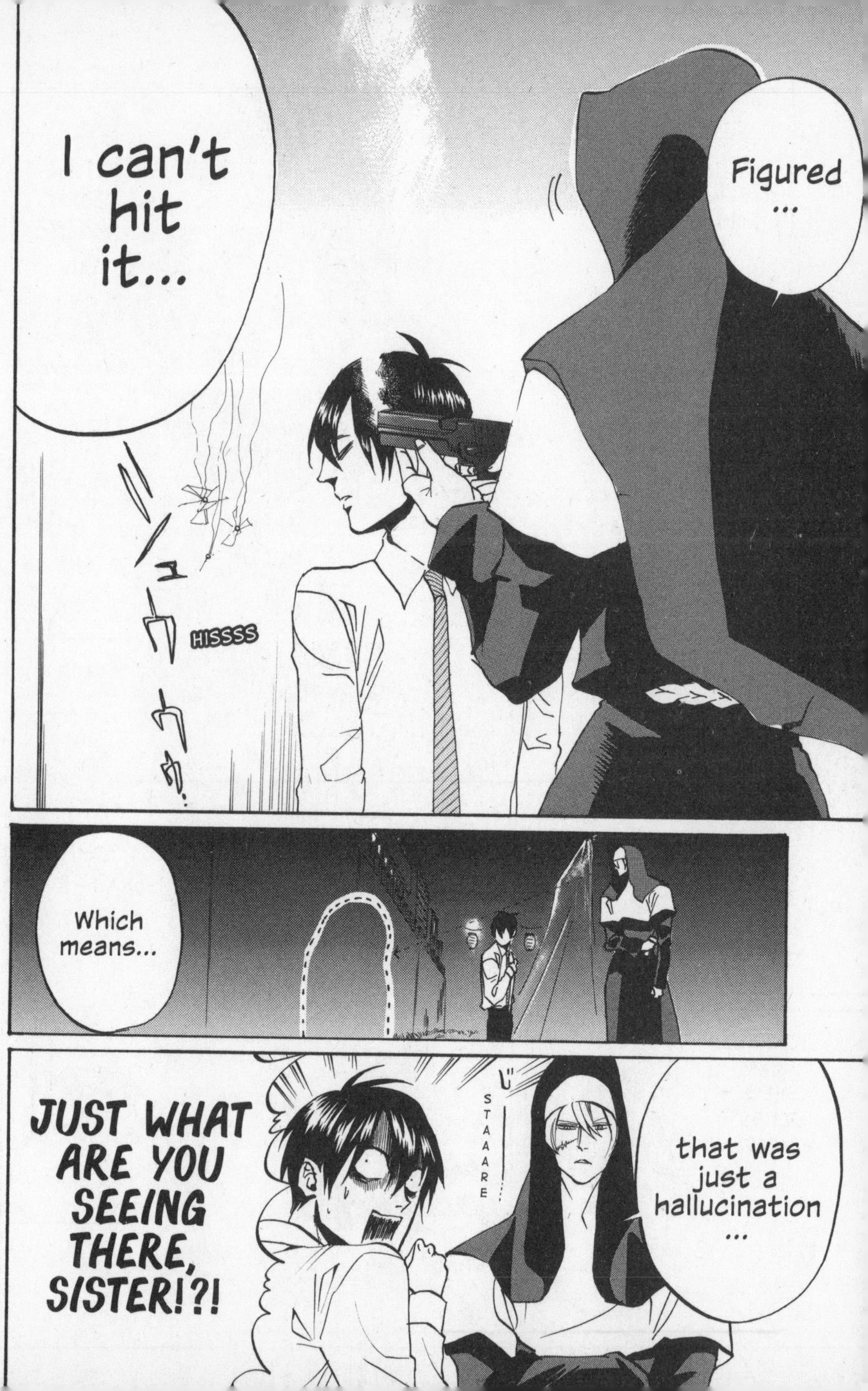
Figured ...
I can't hit it...
HISSSS
Which means...
that was just a hallucination ...
STAAARE
JUST WHAT ARE YOU SEEING THERE, SISTER!?!

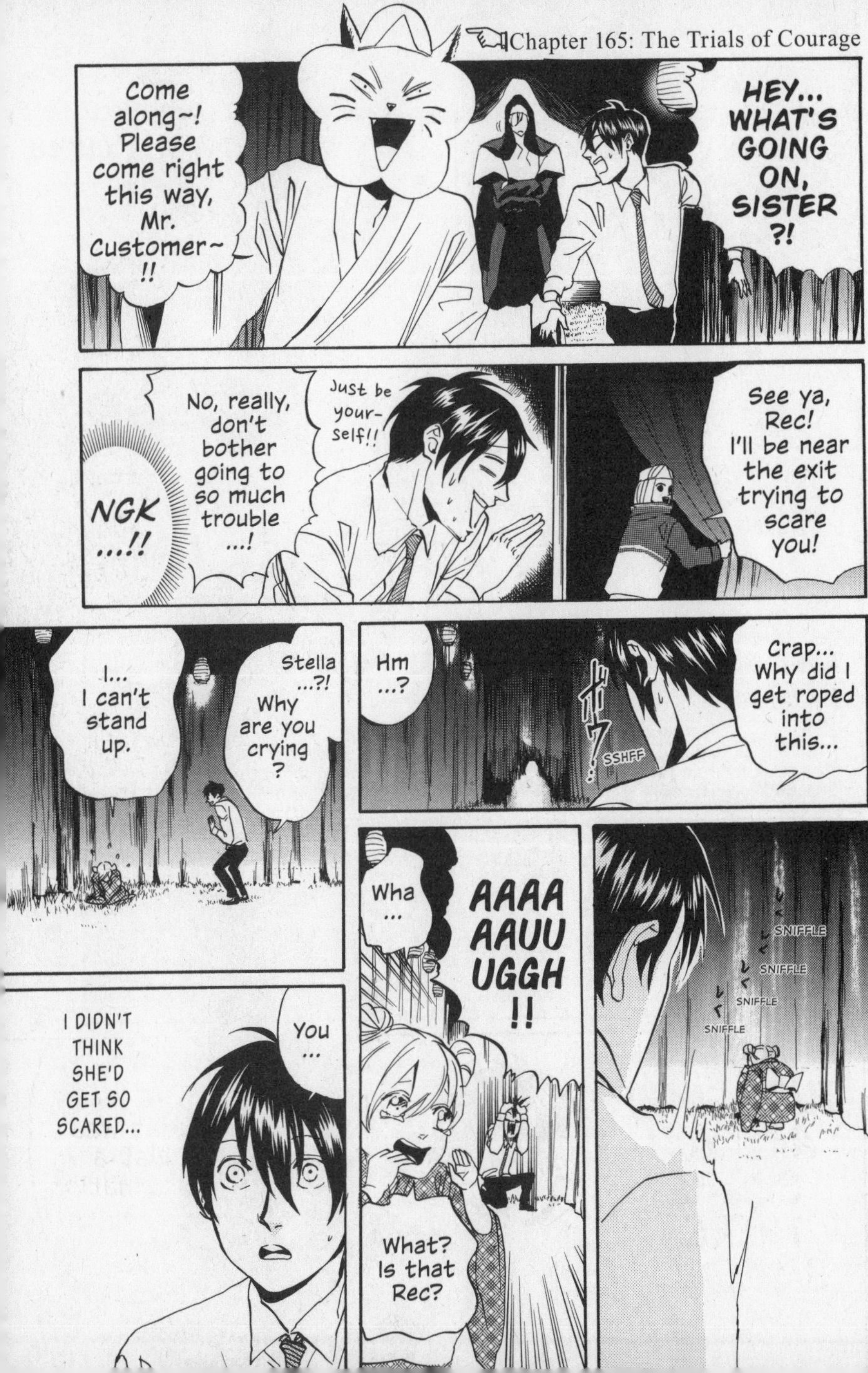
HEY... WHAT'S GOING ON, SISTER?!
Come along~! Please come right this way, Mr. Customer~!!
See ya, Rec! I'll be near the exit trying to scare you!
Just be your-self!!
No, really, don't bother going to so much trouble...!
NGK...!!
Crap... Why did I get roped into this...
SSHFF
Hm...?
SNIFFLE
SNIFFLE
SNIFFLE
SNIFFLE
Wha...
AAAAAAUUUGGH!!
What? Is that Rec?
Stella...?! Why are you crying?
I... I can't stand up.
You...
I DIDN'T THINK SHE'D GET SO SCARED...

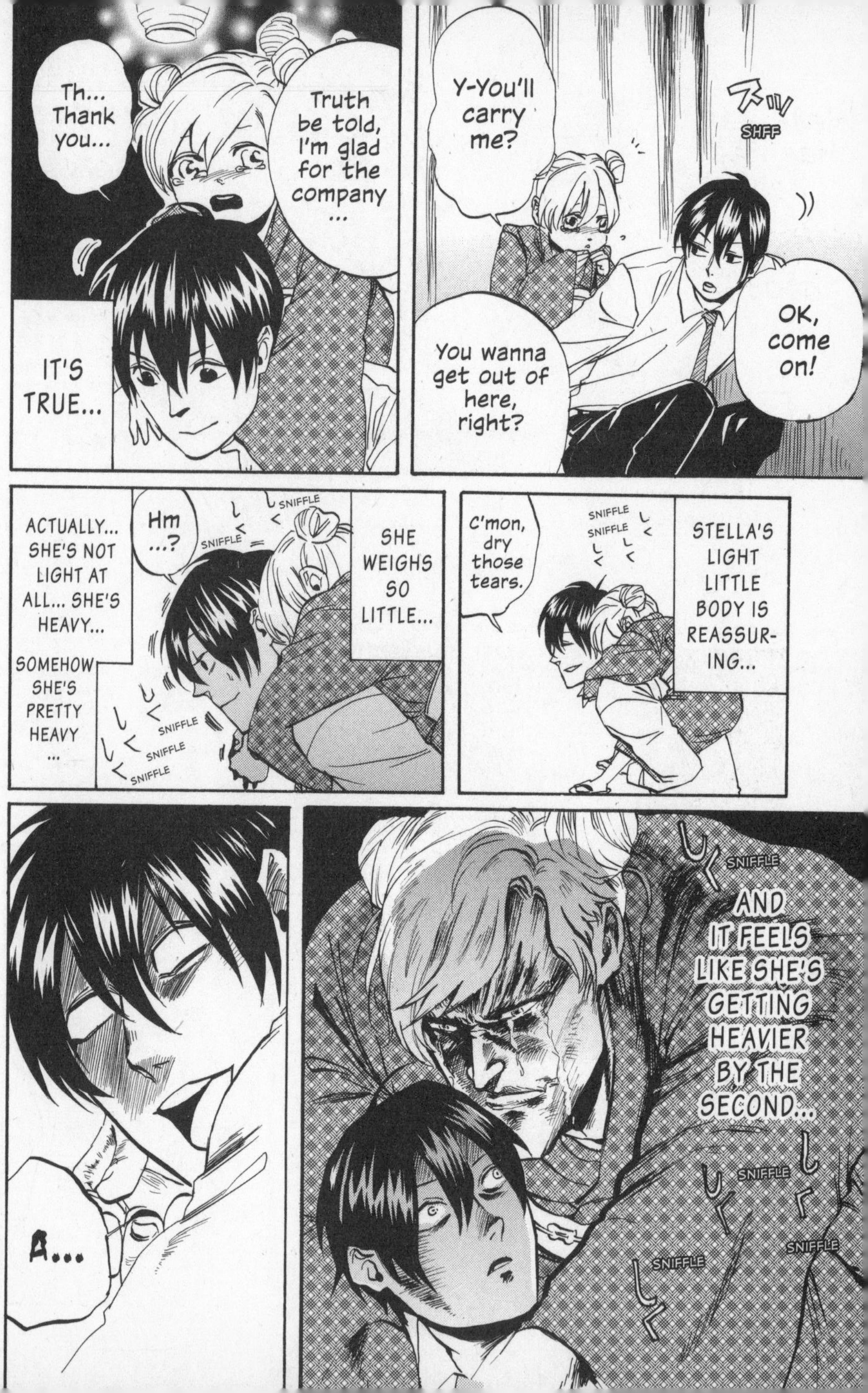
SHFF
Y-You'll carry me?
OK, come on!
You wanna get out of here, right?
Truth be told, I'm glad for the company...
Th... Thank you...
IT'S TRUE...
STELLA'S LIGHT LITTLE BODY IS REASSURING...
SNIFFLE
SNIFFLE
C'mon, dry those tears.
SHE WEIGHS SO LITTLE...
SNIFFLE
SNIFFLE
Hm...?
ACTUALLY... SHE'S NOT LIGHT AT ALL... SHE'S HEAVY...
SOMEHOW SHE'S PRETTY HEAVY...
SNIFFLE
SNIFFLE
SNIFFLE
SNIFFLE
AND IT FEELS LIKE SHE'S GETTING HEAVIER BY THE SECOND...
SNIFFLE
SNIFFLE
SNIFFLE
A...

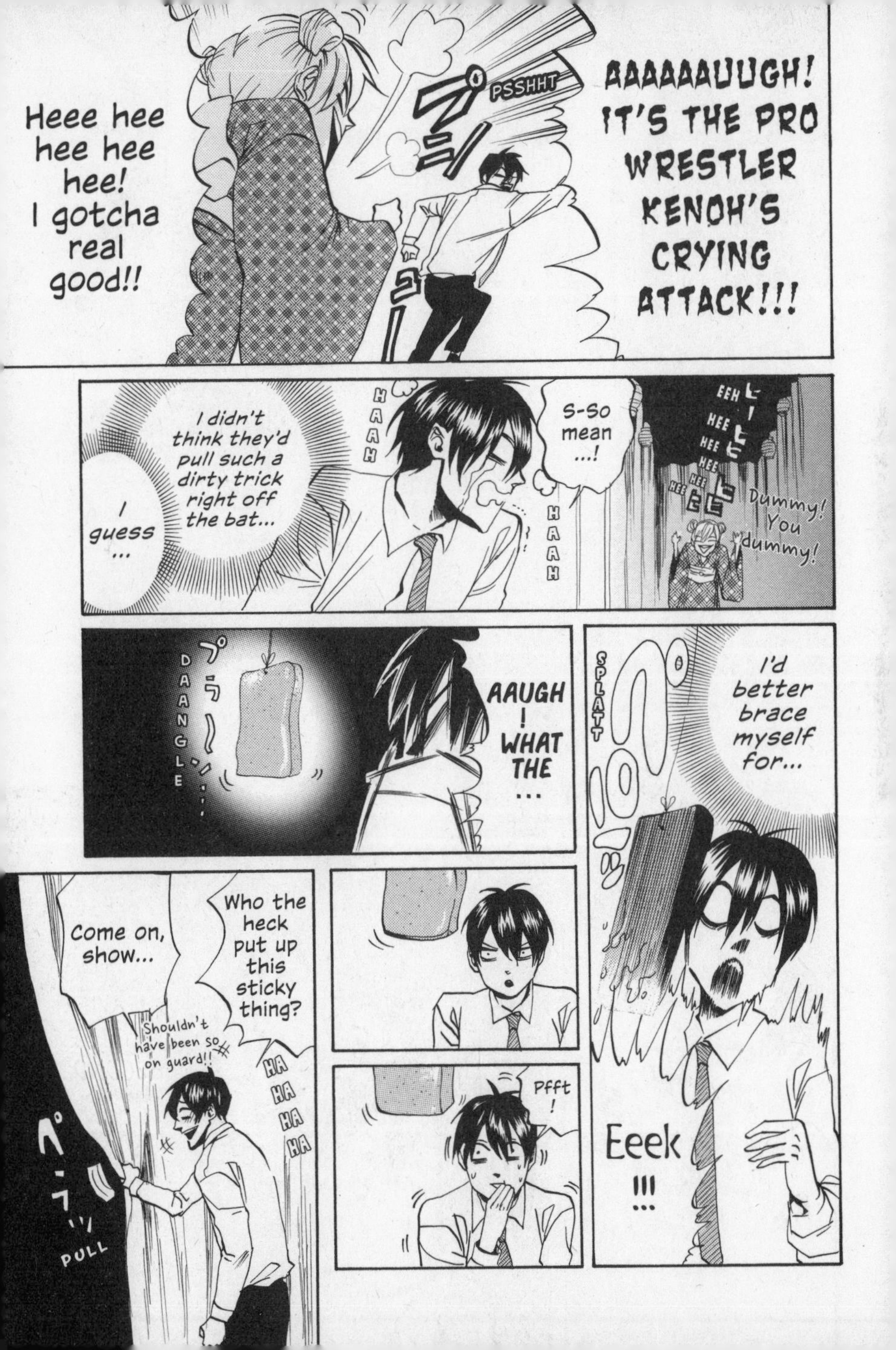
AAAAAAUUGH! IT'S THE PRO WRESTLER KENOH'S CRYING ATTACK!!!
PSSHHT
Heee hee hee hee hee! I gotcha real good!!
EEH HEE HEE HEE HEE HEE
Dummy! You dummy!
S-So mean ...!
HAAAH
HAAAH
I didn't think they'd pull such a dirty trick right off the bat...
I guess ...
I'd better brace myself for...
SPLATT
Eeek !!! ...
AAUGH! WHAT THE ...
DAAANGLE
Pfft!
Who the heck put up this sticky thing?
Come on, show...
Shouldn't have been so on guard!!
HA HA HA HA
PULL

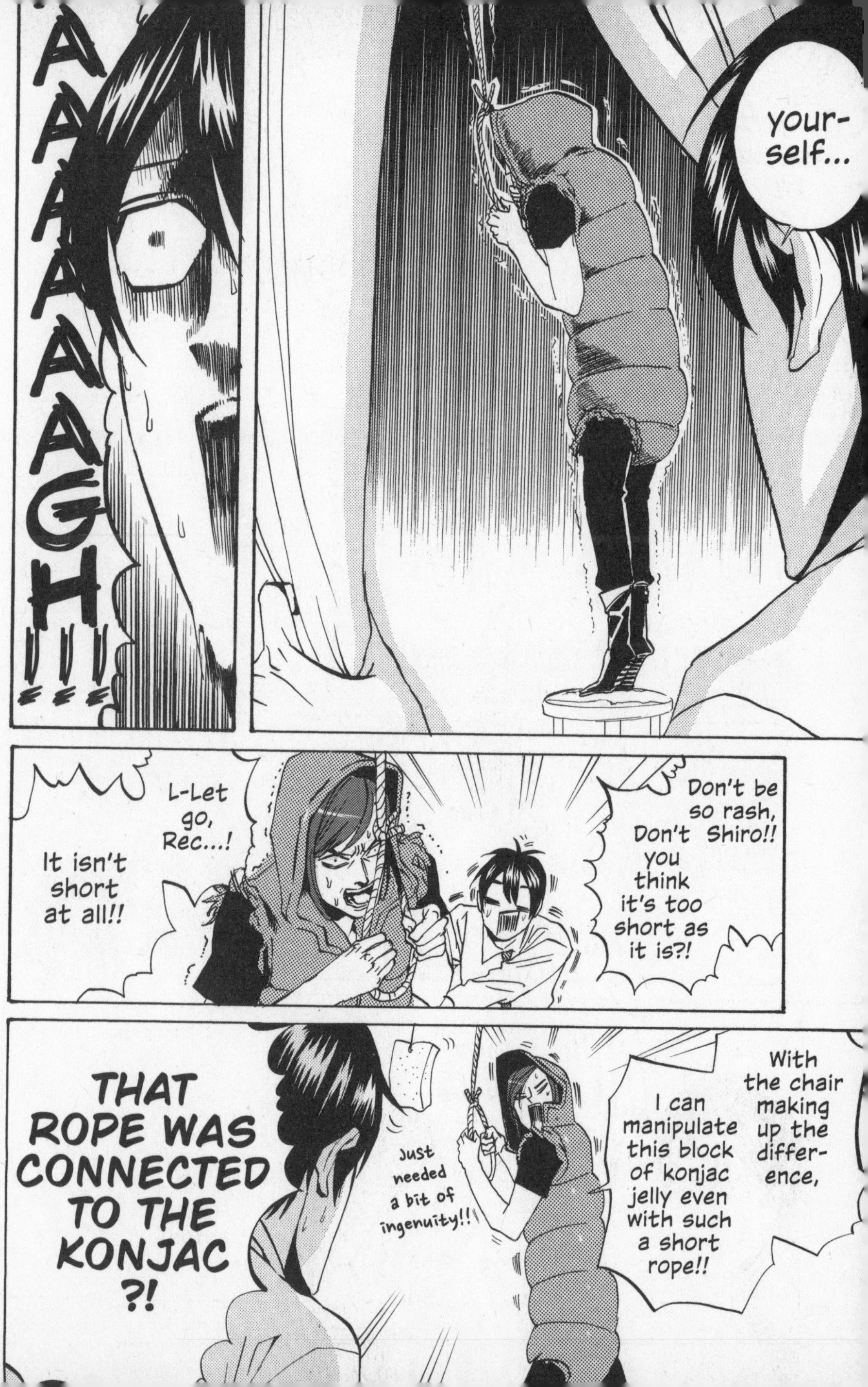
your-self...
AAAAAAAAGH!!!
Don't be so rash, Shiro!!
Don't you think it's too short as it is?!
L-Let go, Rec...!
It isn't short at all!!
With the chair making up the differ-ence,
I can manipulate this block of konjac jelly even with such a short rope!!
Just needed a bit of ingenuity!!
THAT ROPE WAS CONNECTED TO THE KONJAC ?!

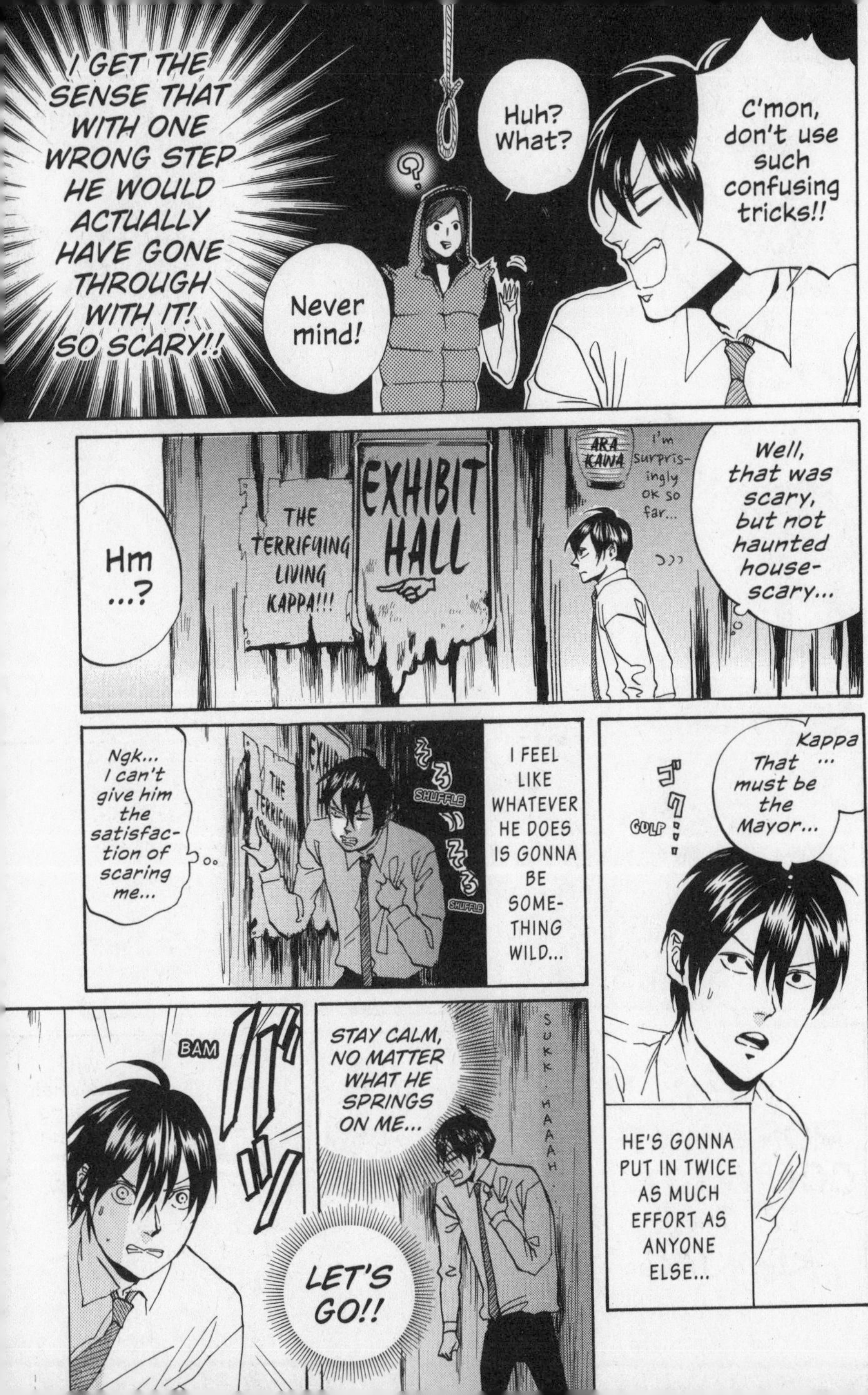
C'mon, don't use such confusing tricks!!
Huh? What?
I GET THE SENSE THAT WITH ONE WRONG STEP HE WOULD ACTUALLY HAVE GONE THROUGH WITH IT! SO SCARY!!
Never mind!
Well, that was scary, but not haunted house-scary...
I'm surprisingly ok so far...
ARA KAWA
EXHIBIT HALL
THE TERRIFYING LIVING KAPPA!!!
Hm ...?
Kappa ... That must be the Mayor...
GULP
HE'S GONNA PUT IN TWICE AS MUCH EFFORT AS ANYONE ELSE...
I FEEL LIKE WHATEVER HE DOES IS GONNA BE SOMETHING WILD...
SHUFFLE
SHUFFLE
Ngk... I can't give him the satisfaction of scaring me...
STAY CALM, NO MATTER WHAT HE SPRINGS ON ME...
SUKK... HAAAH...
LET'S GO!!
BAM

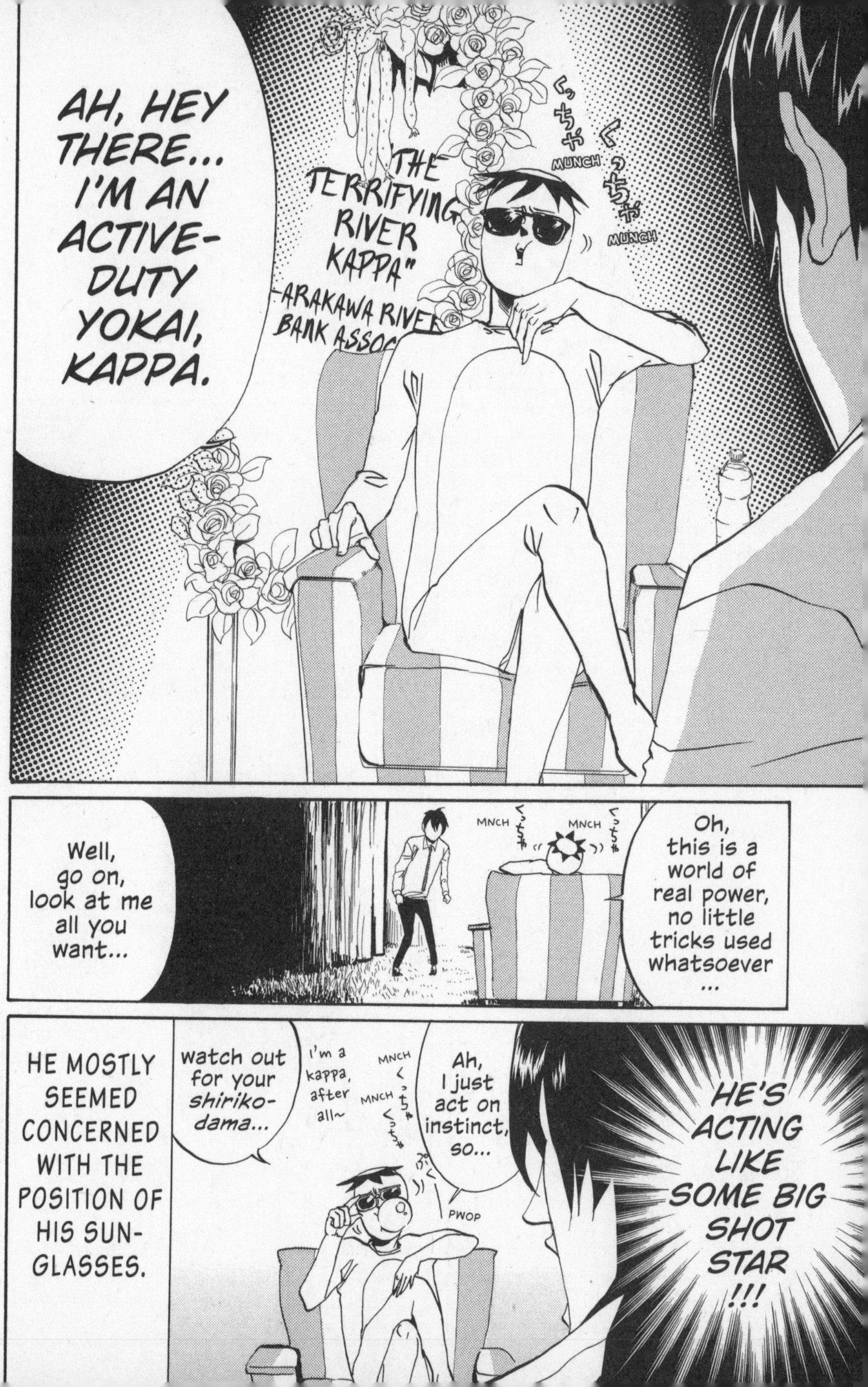
MUNCH
MUNCH
"THE TERRIFYING RIVER KAPPA"
-ARAKAWA RIVER BANK ASSOC
AH, HEY THERE... I'M AN ACTIVE-DUTY YOKAI, KAPPA.
Oh, this is a world of real power, no little tricks used whatsoever ...
MNCH
MNCH
Well, go on, look at me all you want...
HE'S ACTING LIKE SOME BIG SHOT STAR !!!
PWOP
Ah, I just act on instinct, so...
MNCH
MNCH
I'm a kappa, after all~
watch out for your shiriko-dama...
HE MOSTLY SEEMED CONCERNED WITH THE POSITION OF HIS SUN-GLASSES.

Chapter 166: The Greatest Fear

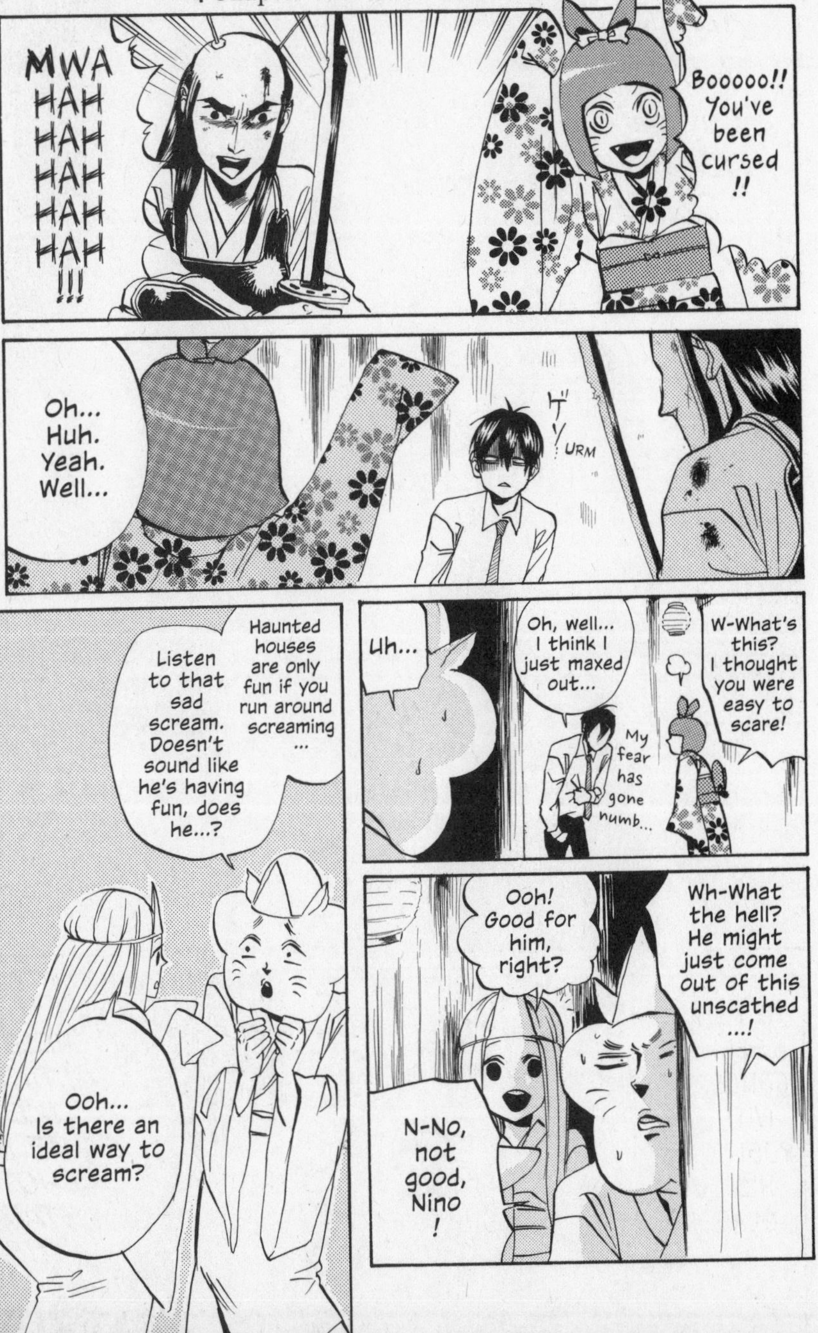
Booooo!! You've been cursed!!
MWA HAH HAH HAH HAH HAH HAH!!!
URM
Oh... Huh. Yeah. Well...
W-What's this? I thought you were easy to scare!
Oh, well... I think I just maxed out...
My fear has gone numb...
Uh...
Wh-What the hell? He might just come out of this unscathed...!
Ooh! Good for him, right?
N-No, not good, Nino!
Haunted houses are only fun if you run around screaming...
Listen to that sad scream. Doesn't sound like he's having fun, does he...?
Ooh... Is there an ideal way to scream?

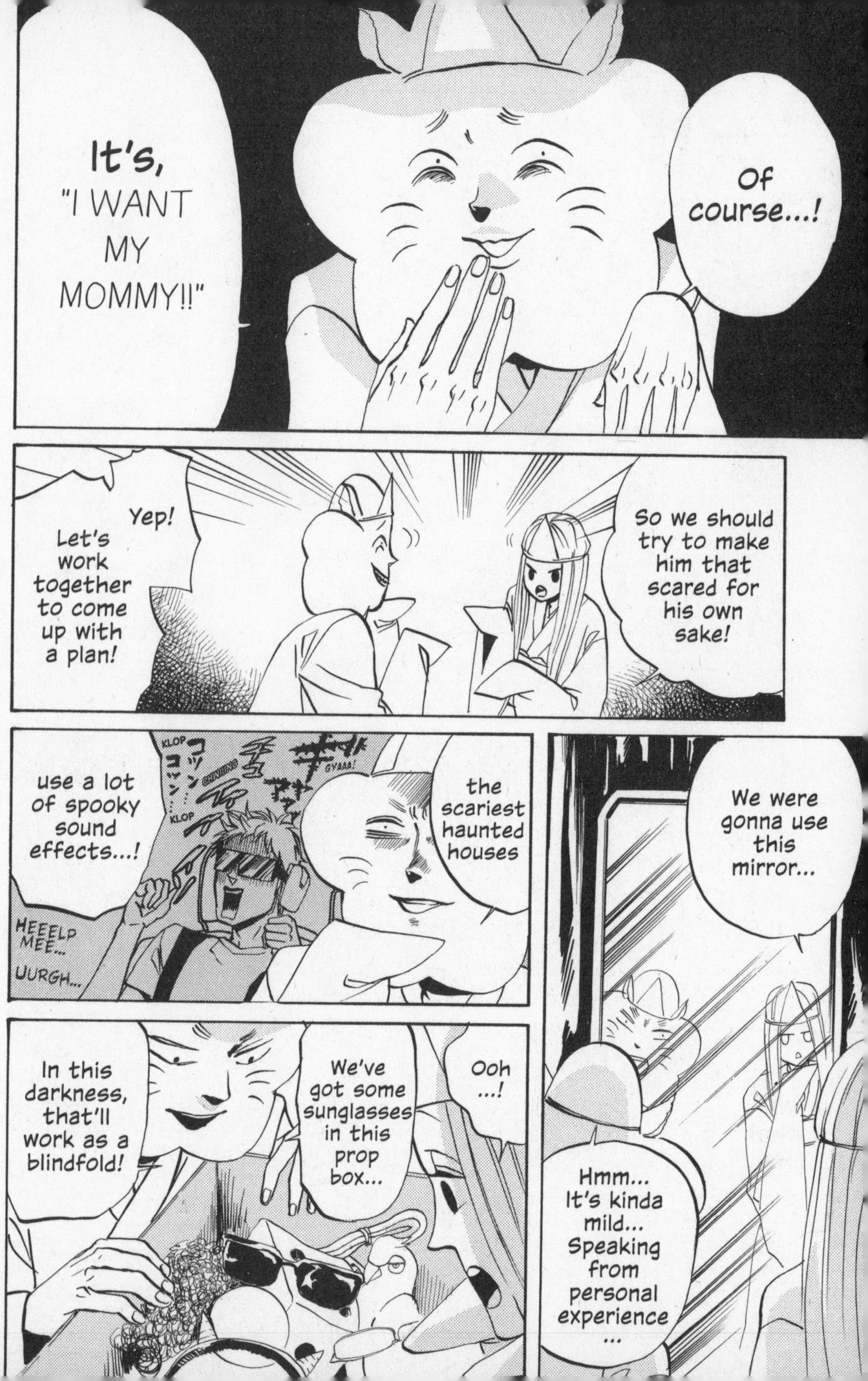

Of course...!
It's, "I WANT MY MOMMY!!"
So we should try to make him that scared for his own sake!
Yep! Let's work together to come up with a plan!
We were gonna use this mirror...
Hmm... It's kinda mild... Speaking from personal experience ...
the scariest haunted houses
GYAAA!
CHWIIING
コツン KLOP
コツン KLOP
use a lot of spooky sound effects...!
HEEELP MEE...
UURGH...
Ooh ...!
We've got some sunglasses in this prop box...
In this darkness, that'll work as a blindfold!

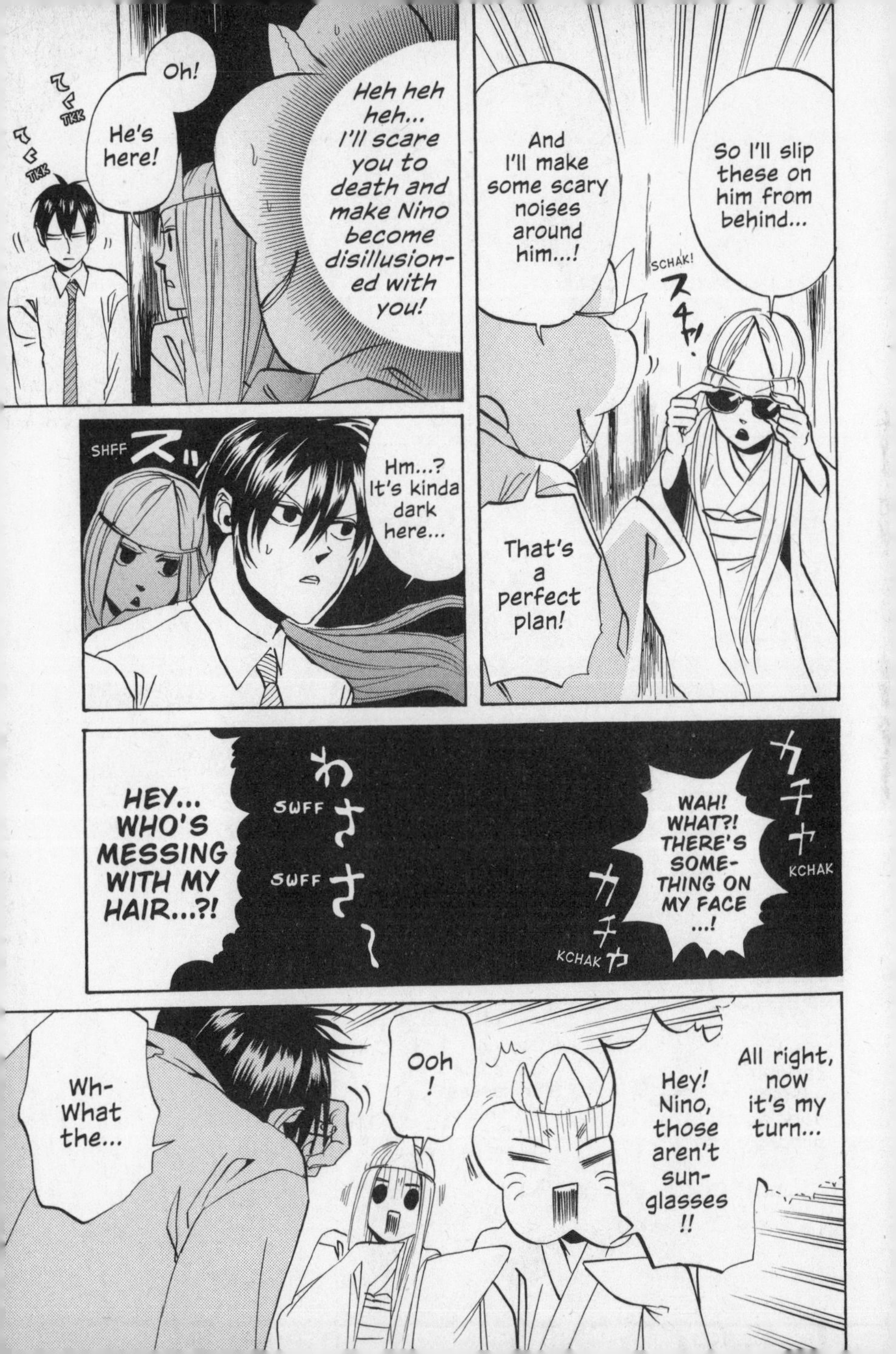

So I'll slip these on him from behind...
SCHAK!
And I'll make some scary noises around him...!
That's a perfect plan!
Heh heh heh... I'll scare you to death and make Nino become disillusioned with you!
Oh!
He's here!
TKK
TKK
SHFF
Hm...? It's kinda dark here...
KCHAK
WAH! WHAT?! THERE'S SOMETHING ON MY FACE ...!
KCHAK
SWFF
SWFF
HEY... WHO'S MESSING WITH MY HAIR...?!
All right, now it's my turn...
Hey! Nino, those aren't sunglasses !!
Ooh !
Wh- What the...

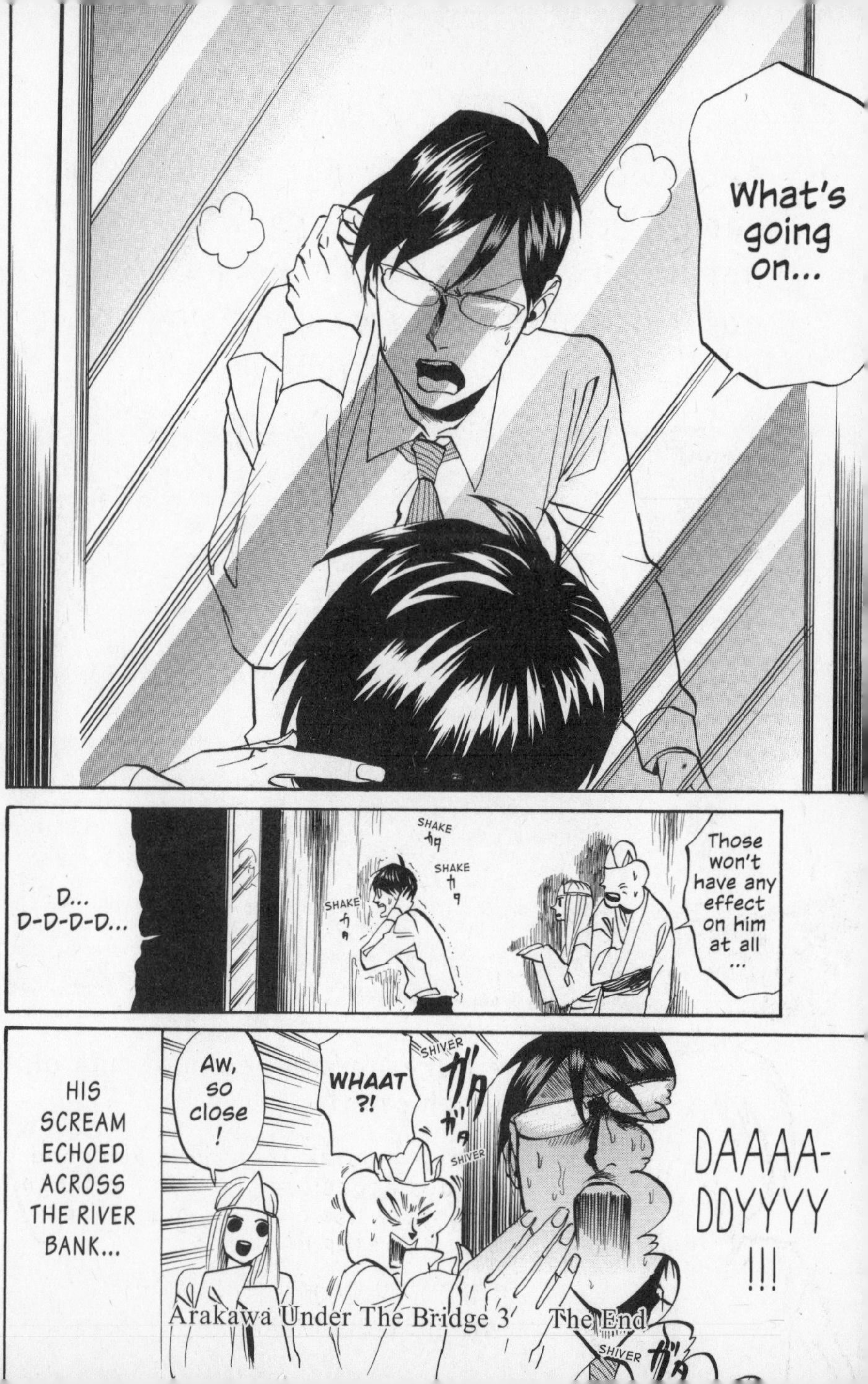
What's going on...
Those won't have any effect on him at all ...
SHAKE
SHAKE
SHAKE
D... D-D-D-D...
DAAAA-DDYYYY !!!
SHIVER
SHIVER
SHIVER
WHAAT ?!
Aw, so close !
HIS SCREAM ECHOED ACROSS THE RIVER BANK...
Arakawa Under The Bridge 3 The End

AFTERWORD

Arakawa Under the Bridge 3! I say the same stuff every time, I know, but I'm happy, so I'll say that I'm happy! I only got this far because of your support, dear reader, so thank you!

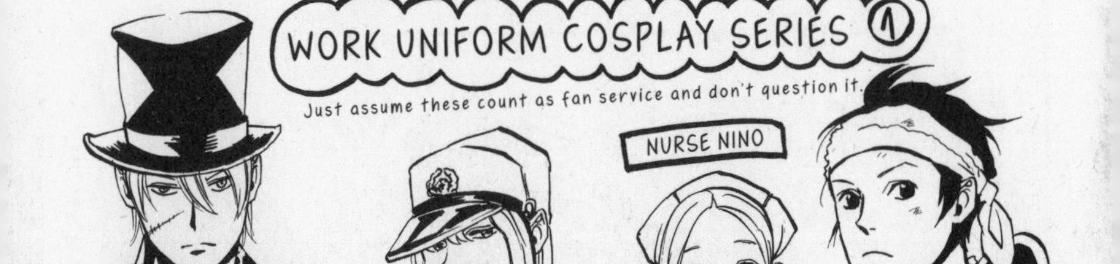
WORK UNIFORM COSPLAY SERIES ①
Just assume these count as fan service and don't question it.
NURSE NINO
PLASTERER REC
POLICEWOMAN MARIA
DOORMAN SISTER

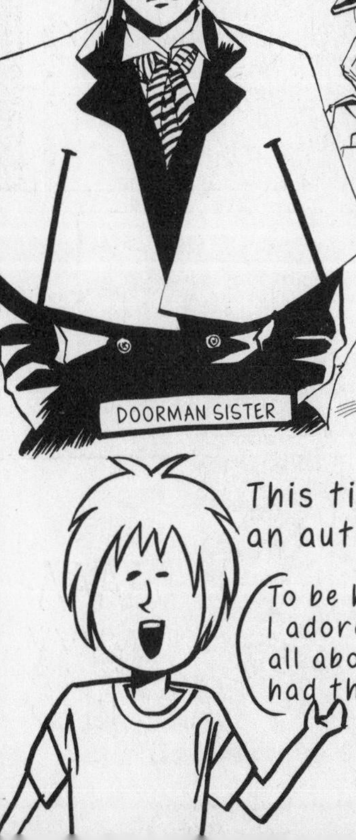

This time I drew a manga reporting on an autograph event.

To be honest, my sister just had a baby and I adore her and I considered making a manga all about my niece like a doting auntie, but had the sense to stop myself.

I hope you enjoy this bonus, even just a little!

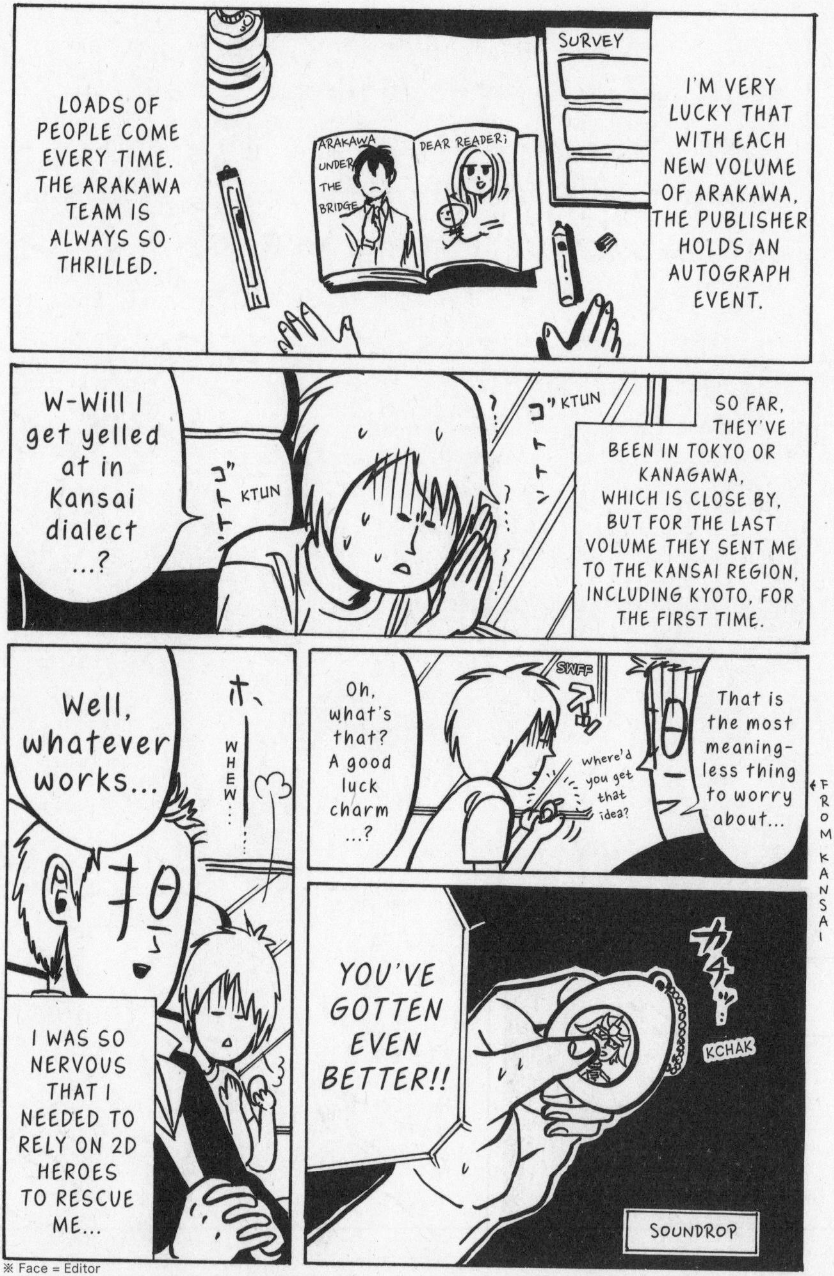

I'M VERY LUCKY THAT WITH EACH NEW VOLUME OF ARAKAWA, THE PUBLISHER HOLDS AN AUTOGRAPH EVENT.
SURVEY
ARAKAWA UNDER THE BRIDGE
DEAR READER;
LOADS OF PEOPLE COME EVERY TIME. THE ARAKAWA TEAM IS ALWAYS SO THRILLED.
SO FAR, THEY'VE BEEN IN TOKYO OR KANAGAWA, WHICH IS CLOSE BY, BUT FOR THE LAST VOLUME THEY SENT ME TO THE KANSAI REGION, INCLUDING KYOTO, FOR THE FIRST TIME.
KTUN
KTUN
W-Will I get yelled at in Kansai dialect ...?
That is the most meaning-less thing to worry about...
FROM KANSAI
Where'd you get that idea?
SWFF
Oh, what's that? A good luck charm ...?
KCHAK
YOU'VE GOTTEN EVEN BETTER!!
SOUNDROP
Well, whatever works...
WHEW...
I WAS SO NERVOUS THAT I NEEDED TO RELY ON 2D HEROES TO RESCUE ME...

※ Face = Editor

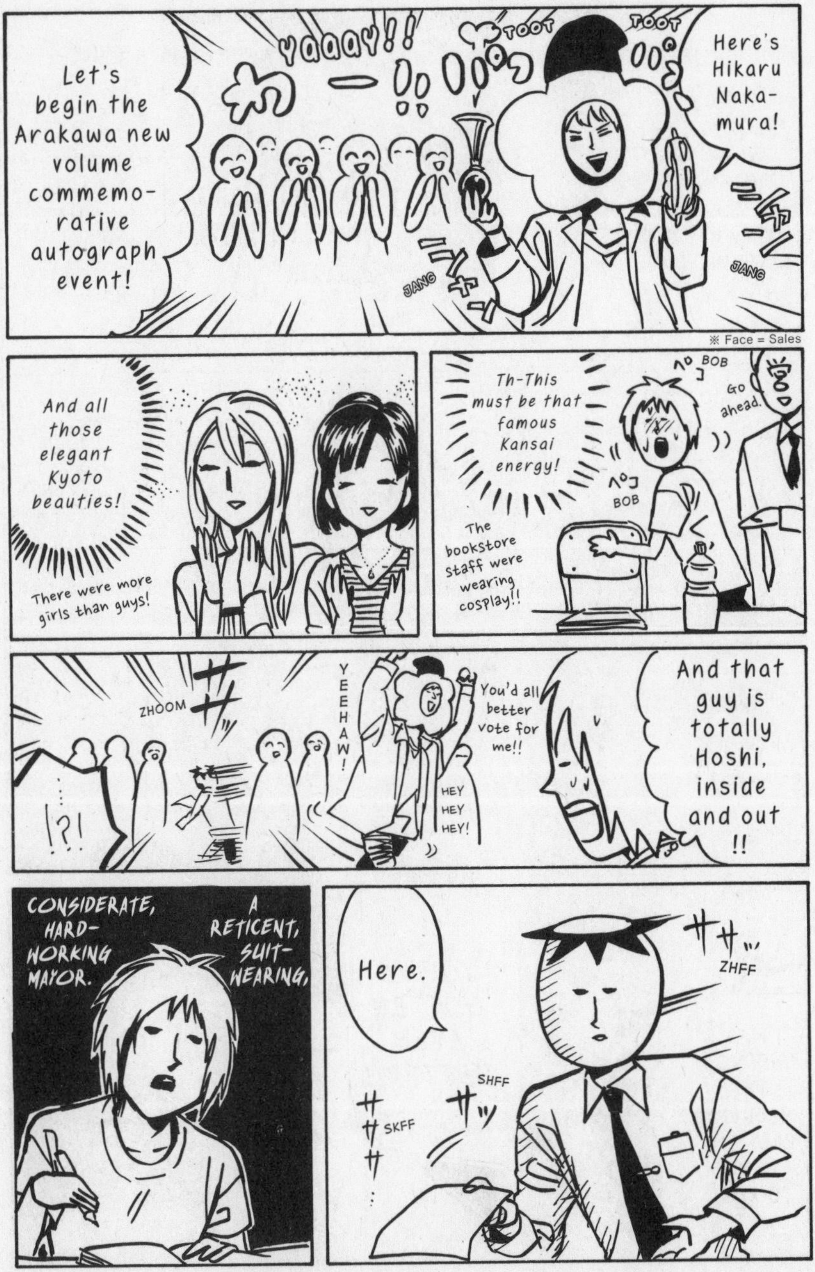
Here's Hikaru Naka-mura!
TOOT
TOOT
YAAAY!!
JANG
JANG
Let's begin the Arakawa new volume commemo-rative autograph event!
※ Face = Sales
BOB
Go ahead.
Th-This must be that famous Kansai energy!
BOB
The bookstore staff were wearing cosplay!!
And all those elegant Kyoto beauties!
There were more girls than guys!
And that guy is totally Hoshi, inside and out!!
You'd all better vote for me!!
YEEHAW!
HEY HEY HEY!
ZHOOM
...!?!
Here.
ZHFF
SHFF
SKFF
A RETICENT, SUIT-WEARING,
CONSIDERATE, HARD-WORKING MAYOR.

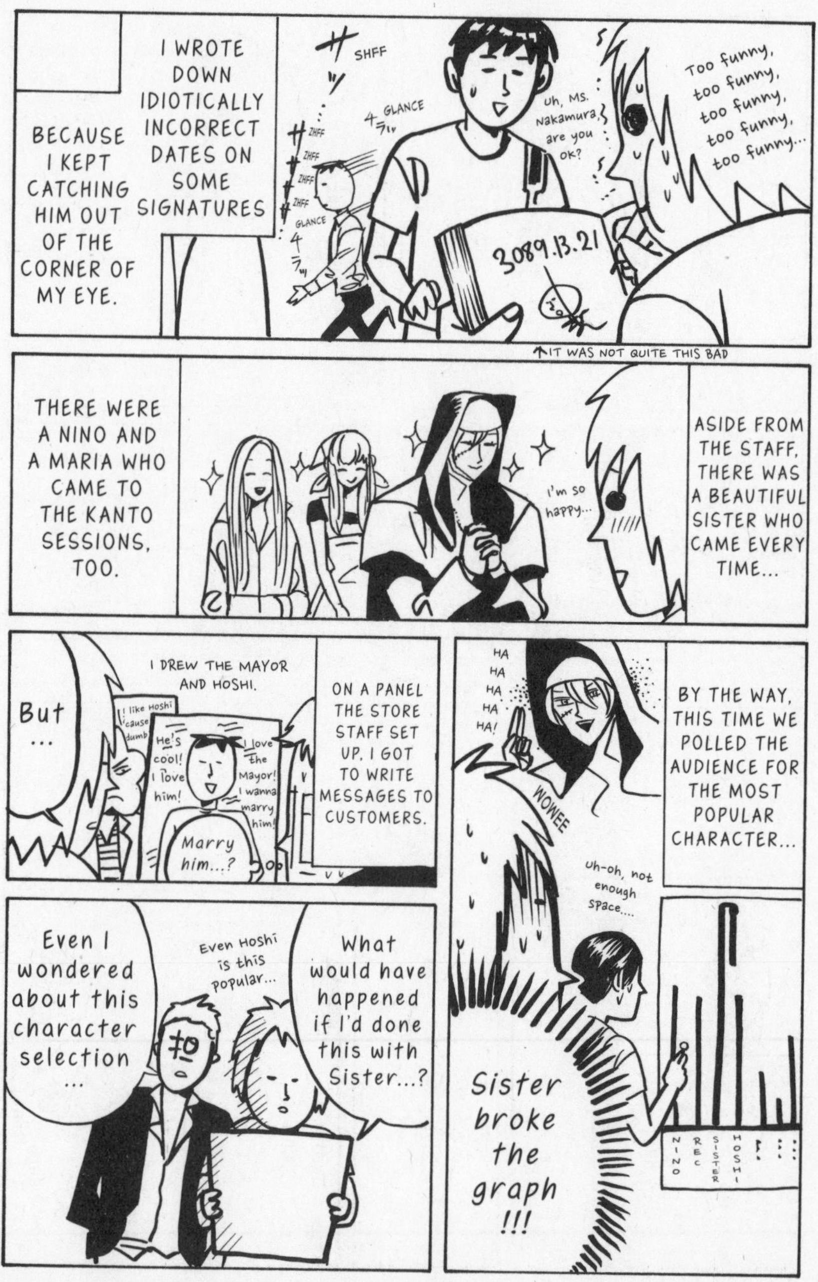
Too funny, too funny, too funny, too funny, too funny...
Uh, Ms. Nakamura, are you ok?
SHFF
GLANCE
ZHFF
ZHFF
ZHFF
ZHFF
GLANCE
3089.13.21
I WROTE DOWN IDIOTICALLY INCORRECT DATES ON SOME SIGNATURES
BECAUSE I KEPT CATCHING HIM OUT OF THE CORNER OF MY EYE.
↑IT WAS NOT QUITE THIS BAD
ASIDE FROM THE STAFF, THERE WAS A BEAUTIFUL SISTER WHO CAME EVERY TIME...
I'm so happy...
THERE WERE A NINO AND A MARIA WHO CAME TO THE KANTO SESSIONS, TOO.
BY THE WAY, THIS TIME WE POLLED THE AUDIENCE FOR THE MOST POPULAR CHARACTER...
HA HA HA HA HA!
WOWEE
ON A PANEL THE STORE STAFF SET UP, I GOT TO WRITE MESSAGES TO CUSTOMERS.
I DREW THE MAYOR AND HOSHI.
I love the Mayor! I wanna marry him!
He's cool! I love him!
I like Hoshi cause dumb
Marry him...?
But...
Uh-oh, not enough space....
NINO
REC
SISTER
HOSHI
Sister broke the graph!!!
What would have happened if I'd done this with Sister...?
Even Hoshi is this popular...
Even I wondered about this character selection...

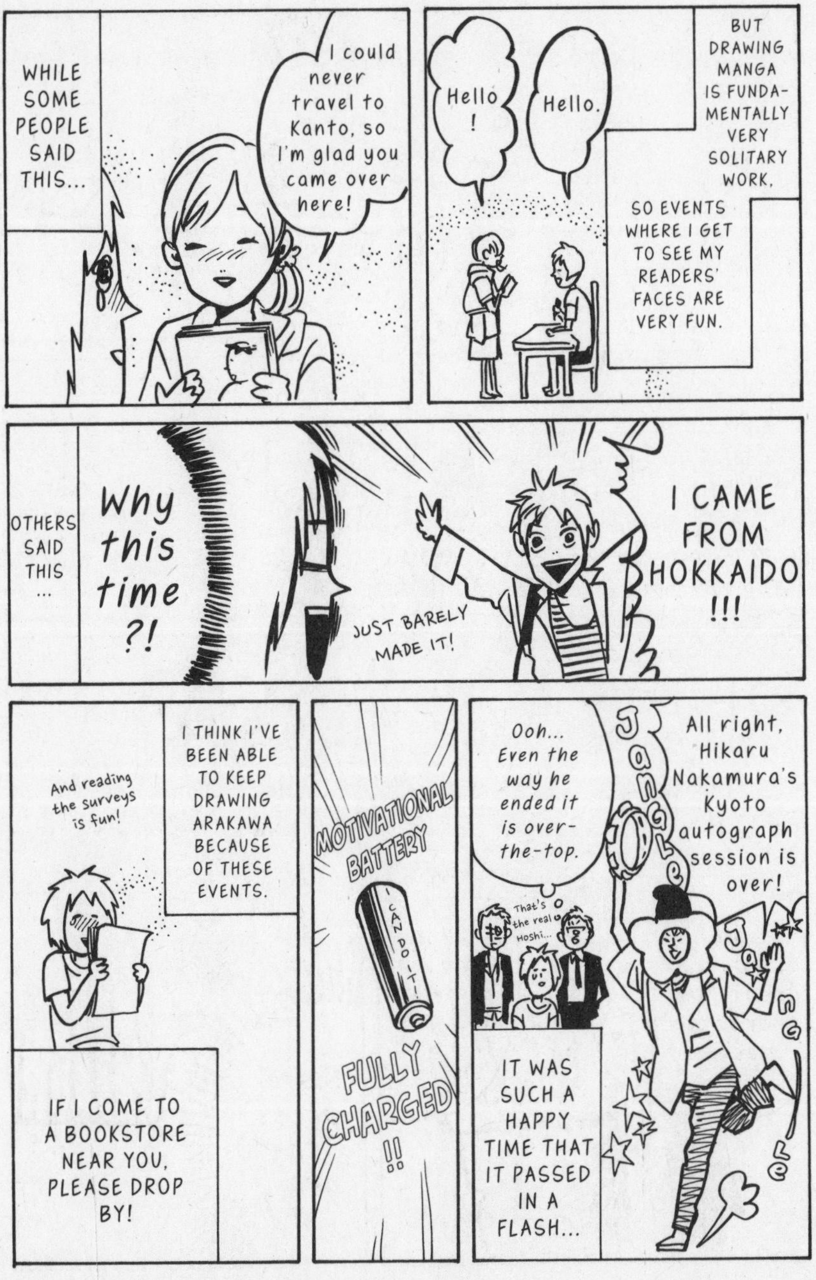
BUT DRAWING MANGA IS FUNDAMENTALLY VERY SOLITARY WORK,
Hello.
Hello!
SO EVENTS WHERE I GET TO SEE MY READERS' FACES ARE VERY FUN.
I could never travel to Kanto, so I'm glad you came over here!
WHILE SOME PEOPLE SAID THIS...
I CAME FROM HOKKAIDO!!!
JUST BARELY MADE IT!
Why this time?!
OTHERS SAID THIS...
All right, Hikaru Nakamura's Kyoto autograph session is over!
Jangle
Ooh... Even the way he ended it is over-the-top.
That's the real Hoshi...
Jangle
IT WAS SUCH A HAPPY TIME THAT IT PASSED IN A FLASH...
MOTIVATIONAL BATTERY
I CAN DO IT!
FULLY CHARGED!!
I THINK I'VE BEEN ABLE TO KEEP DRAWING ARAKAWA BECAUSE OF THESE EVENTS.
And reading the surveys is fun!
IF I COME TO A BOOKSTORE NEAR YOU, PLEASE DROP BY!

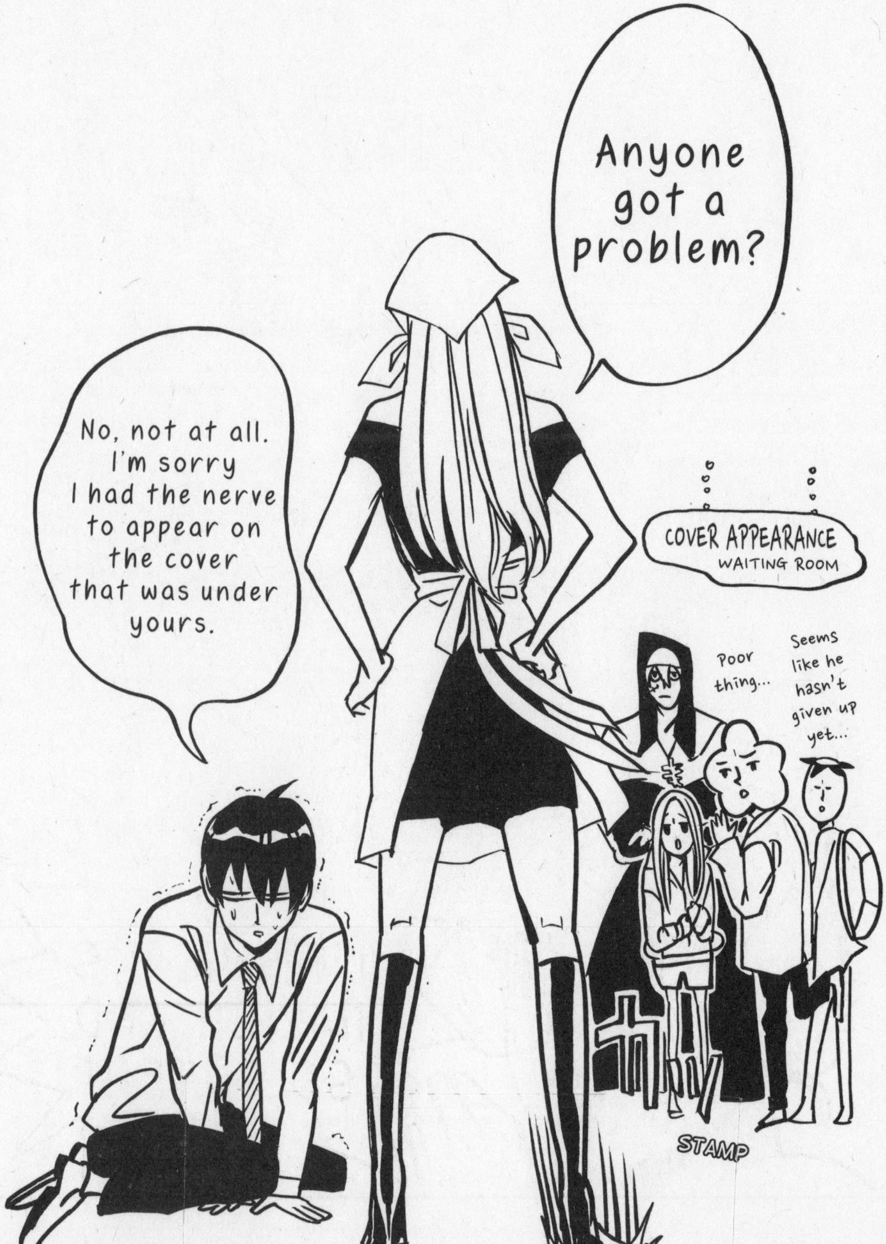
Anyone got a problem?
No, not at all. I'm sorry I had the nerve to appear on the cover that was under yours.
COVER APPEARANCE
WAITING ROOM
Seems like he hasn't given up yet...
Poor thing...
STAMP

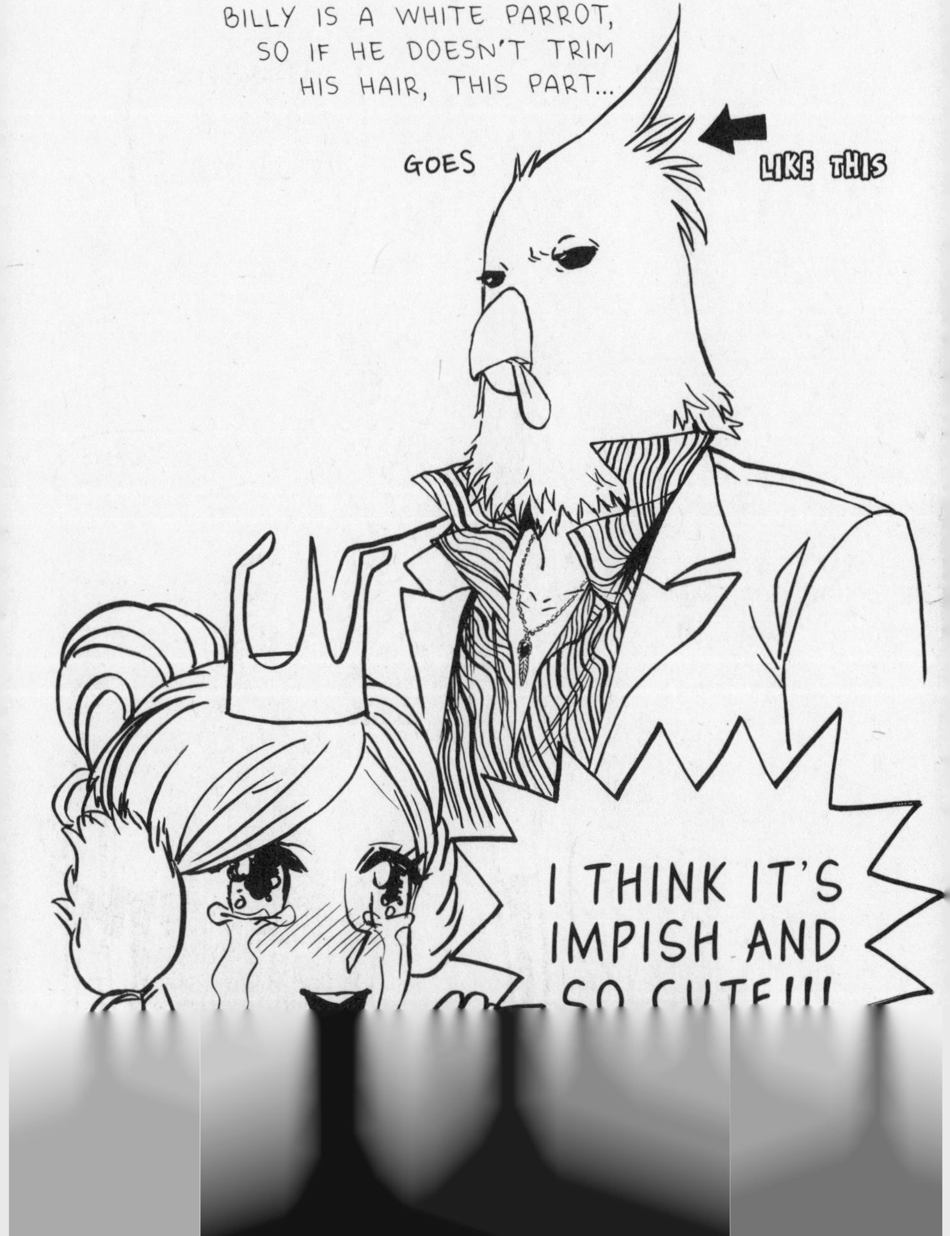
BILLY IS A WHITE PARROT, SO IF HE DOESN'T TRIM HIS HAIR, THIS PART...
GOES
LIKE THIS
I THINK IT'S IMPISH AND SO CUTE!!!

AUG 19 1

ARAKAWA UNDER THE BRIDGE 3
Hikaru Nakamura

Translation: Andrew Cunningham
Production: Risa Cho
          Tomoe Tsutsumi

ARAKAWA UNDER THE BRIDGE Vol. 5 & 6
© 2007 Hikaru Nakamura / SQUARE ENIX CO., LTD.
First Published in Japan in 2007 by SQUARE ENIX CO., LTD.
Translation rights arranged with SQUARE ENIX CO., LTD. and Vertical, Inc.
through Tuttle-Mori Agency, Inc. Translation © 2018 by SQUARE ENIX CO., LTD.

Translation provided by Vertical Comics, 2018
Published by Vertical, Inc., New York

Originally published in Japanese as *Arakawa Andaa Za Burijji 5 & 6*
by SQUARE ENIX Co., Ltd., 2007
Arakawa Andaa Za Burijji first serialized in *Young Gangan*, SQUARE ENIX Co.,
Ltd., 2004-2015

This is a work of fiction.

ISBN: 978-1-945054-43-3

Manufactured in Canada

First Edition

Vertical, Inc.
451 Park Avenue South
7th Floor
New York, NY 100
www.vertical-con

Vertical books are   ervices.

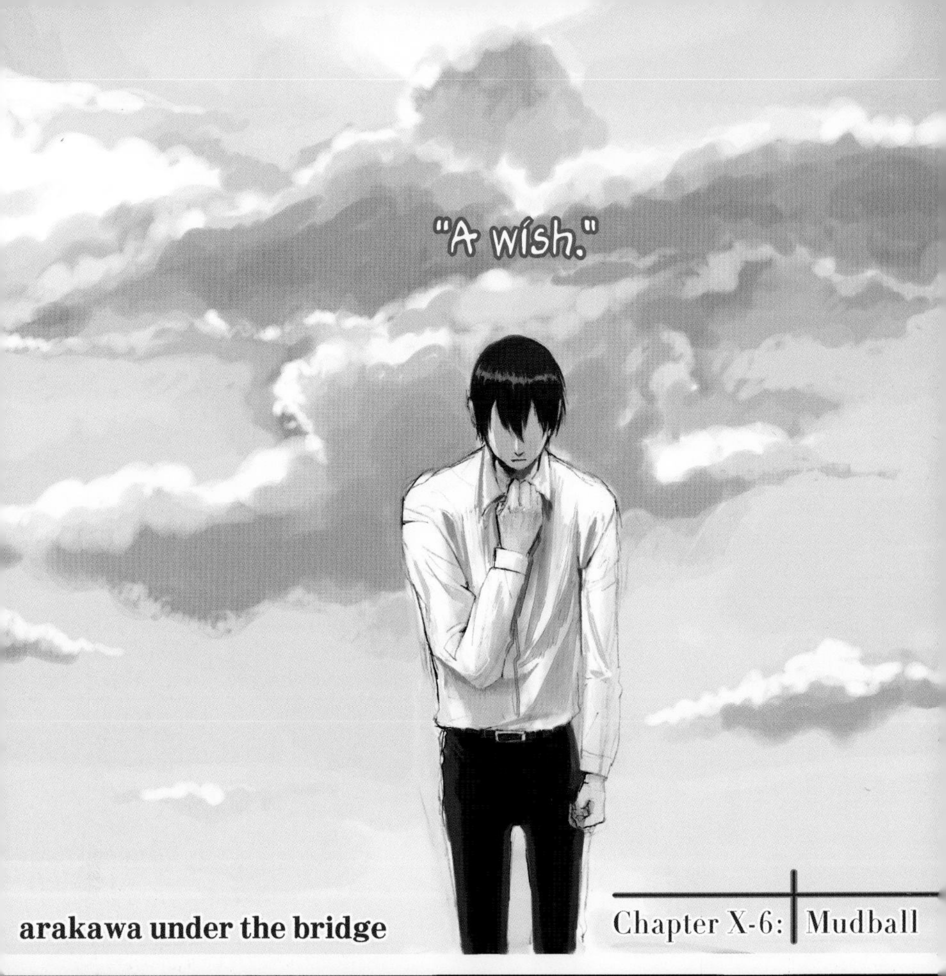
"A wish."
arakawa under the bridge
Chapter X-6: Mudball

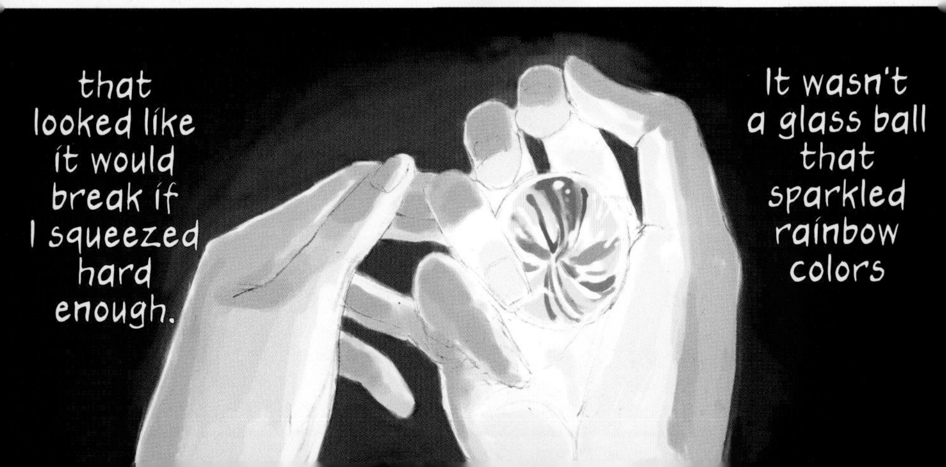
It wasn't a glass ball that sparkled rainbow colors
that looked like it would break if I squeezed hard enough.

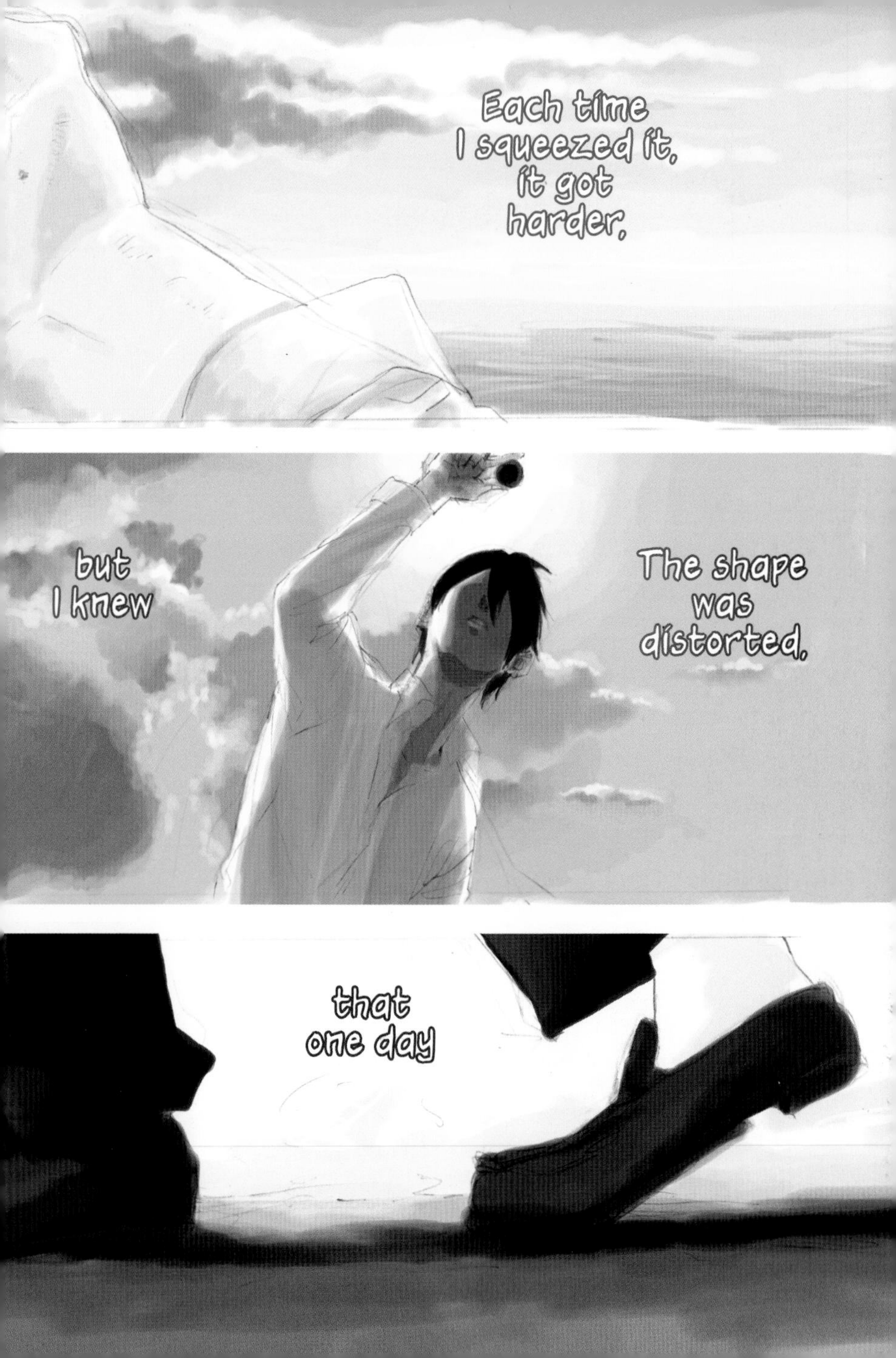
Each time I squeezed it, it got harder,
The shape was distorted,
but I knew
that one day

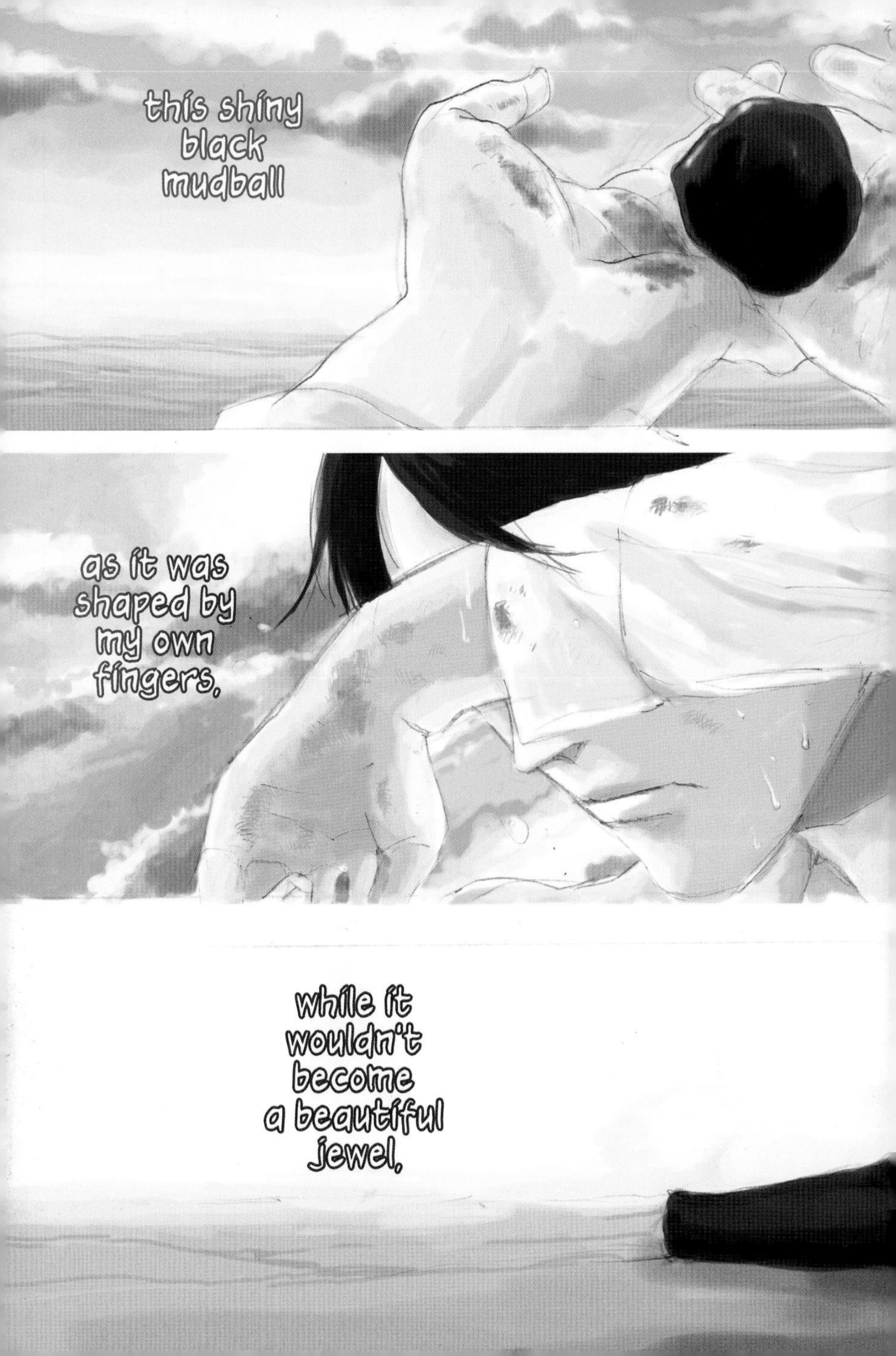
this shiny black mudball
as it was shaped by my own fingers,
while it wouldn't become a beautiful jewel,

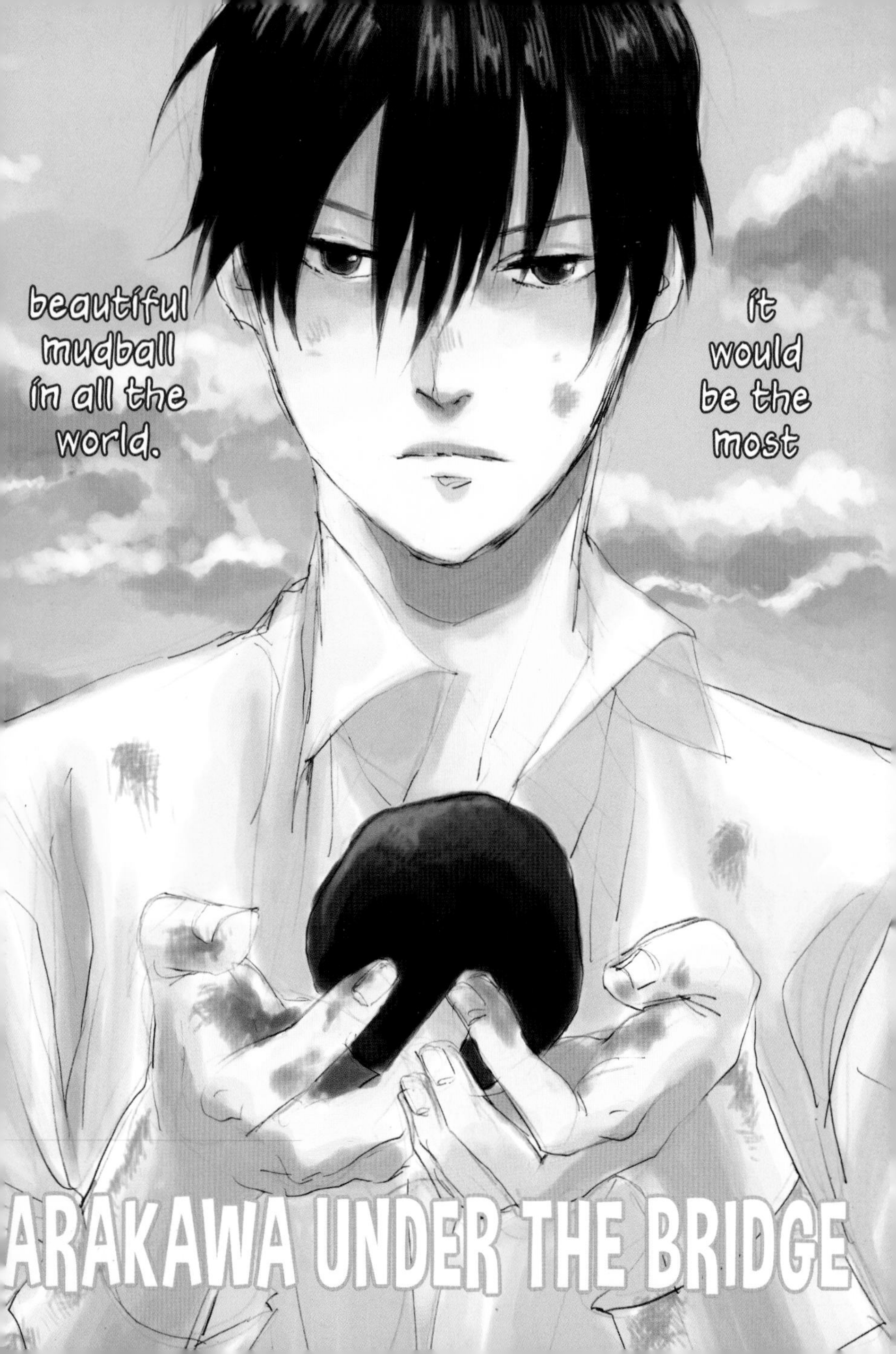
it would be the most
beautiful mudball in all the world.
ARAKAWA UNDER THE BRIDGE